# THE REMARKABLE MADAME PANDIT

# THE REMARKABLE MADAME PANDIT

Champion of India, Citizen of the World

MANU BHAGAVAN

Columbia University Press
*New York*

Columbia University Press
*Publishers Since 1893*
New York   Chichester, West Sussex

Copyright © Manu Bhagavan 2025
First published in India by Penguin Random House India

All rights reserved

Cataloging-in-Publication Data is available from the Library of Congress.
ISBN 978-0-231-22246-4 (hardback)
ISBN 978-0-231-22247-1 (trade paperback)
ISBN 978-0-231-56424-3 (ebook)
LCCN 2025020051

Cover design: Chang Jae Lee
Cover image: Vijaya Lakshmi Pandit of India, the only woman to head a delegation to the United Nations General Assembly, at the rostrum during the 37th meeting, 25 October 1946. UN Photo, UN7741718

GPSR Authorized Representative: Easy Access System Europe, Mustamäe tee 50, 10621 Tallinn, Estonia, gpsr.requests@easproject.com

*Dedicated to some remarkable women*

| | | |
|---|---|---|
| R.S. Chinmayamma | Kamalamma | Leela S. Bhagavan |
| Carolyn 'John' Beacham | Sophie Anoff | Shila Ramaiah |
| Joyce Raddatz | Mridula Kini | Nirmala Ramamurthy |
| Jane Umstead | Sarah Weddington | Beatrice Alexander |
| Eleanor Zelliot | Gail Minault | Barbara Welter |

# Contents

| | |
|---|---:|
| *Preface* | ix |
| *Chronology* | xix |
| *Glossary* | xxv |
| 1. Little Woman | 1 |
| 2. The Portrait of a Lady | 27 |
| 3. Knowing Why the Caged Bird Sings | 51 |
| 4. The Awakening | 72 |
| 5. The West with the Night | 103 |
| 6. The Time in Between | 119 |
| 7. The Night Watch | 145 |
| 8. The Good Earth | 170 |
| 9. Americanah | 209 |
| 10. White Teeth | 253 |
| 11. Love of Worker Bees | 277 |
| 12. Raw Silk | 308 |
| 13. Milk and Honey | 340 |
| 14. Brick Lane | 365 |
| 15. Home Fire | 394 |
| Coda: Fireflies in the Mist | 428 |
| *Notes* | 433 |
| *Archives Consulted* | 521 |
| *Acknowledgements* | 523 |
| *Index* | 527 |

# Preface

Vijaya Lakshmi Pandit was born in 1900 and lived a long, full life until her death in 1990. Her story is therefore intricately intertwined with that of her country, and through it, we also tell the story of India and the world in the twentieth century. She was born into an aristocratic family and grew up in Downton Abbeyesque surroundings, her 'upstairs-downstairs' run home in the city of Allahabad called Anand Bhawan, the Abode of Happiness. Sarup Nehru, her name given at birth, was the daughter of a powerful, gregarious, and extremely wealthy lawyer named Motilal, the second of three children.[1] She was closest to her elder brother, Jawaharlal. Nan, as she was commonly known, was a precocious child who was schooled by private tutors, only up to an intermediate level. But her real education stemmed from her love of reading, facilitated by Anand Bhawan's magnificent library, and through her intellectually stimulating environment. Luminaries of all kinds filtered in and out of the house, and she began travelling the globe from the age of five.

The family grew close to Mohandas Gandhi soon after his return to India from South Africa in 1914, and through the bond they developed, grew ever more involved in politics. While Nan found such matters interesting, the early years of her life were devoted to family affairs and romance. This caused a fair amount of heartburn, and she was steered towards more traditional choices by her relatives.

She married at the age of twenty and changed her name to Vijaya Lakshmi Pandit, taking her husband Ranjit's patronym as her own. The association with Gandhi dramatically altered her family's lifestyle—jewels, silks, delicately woven tapestries and the finest china, gave way to rough handwoven clothes and social upliftment work, especially for those from marginalized caste communities. By 1930, she entered prison for the first of three times, and through that fiery experience emerged tempered and steely, ready to do battle.

A truly extraordinary, indeed cinematic life followed as she became one of the most celebrated women of the twentieth century with her rise as one of the world's most recognized and respected diplomats. Several moments of her life really stand out. When she was still but a child, she and the rest of her family were accorded a special honour by King George and Queen Mary. Later, when she was touring Europe for the first time, she was picked up by the police for the attempted assassination of Mussolini. Back in India, as tensions mounted, she faced down angry, violent mobs, forcing them to disperse merely with the force of her personality and the power of her words. She also battled famine and disease to the point of personal collapse. In the late 1930s, she not only found herself in Czechoslovakia during the Sudeten Crisis but also squarely in the middle of things, with Lord Runciman staying right next to her. Shortly thereafter, she stood outside 10 Downing Street as Chamberlain declared peace for our time.

She served as a key, intellectual founding force of the United Nations (UN) and later was instrumental in resolving the Korean War. She became so beloved and so famous that ordinary folks like taxi drivers in the United States sang her praises. Even the incorrigible Winston Churchill was won over in the end.

She worked with the likes of Bertrand Russell and Robert Oppenheimer to prevent a nuclear disaster. Towards the end of her international career, she told US President John F. Kennedy not to go to Dallas.

And then, she resisted, fought against and helped defeat her niece, Prime Minister Indira Gandhi, to end the authoritarian Emergency in India and restore democracy.

Eloquent. Glamorous. Brilliant. 'The most remarkable woman' that Eleanor Roosevelt ever met.[2]

She was the first woman cabinet minister in India, and also the first woman of that rank in the British Empire to wield substantial power in matters of self-government and public health. She was elected the president of the All India Women's Conference (AIWC), where she tried to push its agendas from elite concerns to more people-oriented ones. And from there, she held a host of breakthrough positions that included: member of the Constituent Assembly of India, India's first ambassador to the UN, and to Moscow, and the first woman ambassador to the United States, with additional appointments to Mexico, Ireland and Spain. She also became the first woman president of the UN General Assembly, a member of the Indian Parliament, the high commissioner to the United Kingdom, the governor of Maharashtra and a representative to the UN Human Rights Commission.

An extraordinary life. But this synopsis should not give the impression of hagiography. While her career was remarkable, she faced many challenges, had many ups and downs, and did not always make the right decisions—as befitting for someone charting a new course. She battled depression and fatigue and suffered several breakdowns, sometimes publicly, sometimes privately. She was loving but had a sometimes-rocky relationship with members of her own family, particularly with her sister Betty and her sister-in-law Kamala. And while she was lauded for her prowess in the West, she was nonetheless eventually iced out as her brother's closest counsel and confidant on international matters by her long-standing rival and nemesis, V.K. Krishna Menon.

This book attempts to present Vijaya Lakshmi Pandit in all her complexity, balancing a focus on her professional struggles and achievements with concern for her personal trials and triumphs. It is in the fullness of this picture, where we can see her affection, courage, and talent sharpened by ambition and temper, that we can better understand what it was for this pioneering woman of substance to sometimes be dismissed for being all wit and charm. We can see more clearly what it meant for someone who had lost access to all her wealth when she was widowed to be criticized for her expensive tastes. And through such insights, we can better appreciate her contributions not only to India and its foreign policy, but also to the making of the post-war world order itself.

~

What can we say about Vijaya Lakshmi Pandit's contributions to international thought? There are two important points we need to keep in mind before proceeding. First, as India's leading voice in the global arena for at least a decade, she wielded considerable influence with plenty of latitude to act according to her judgement. Even so, she held official positions and was an emissary of her government, and thus whatever she said or did had to broadly fit into their policies, and she had to follow the parameters set by the foreign minister and prime minister, both, in this case, being the same person, her brother Jawaharlal Nehru. So, whatever positions she embraced and advocated, with one major exception (which I'll return to at the end of this preface), must be seen as part of the overall foreign policy framework of India. Second, Pandit was a prolific writer, but her book-length works were experiential—they covered the events during her ministership, her days in prison during the 1940s, and the broad sweep of her life. She did not write treatises on foreign policy, international relations, or philosophy. But she did write many letters and speeches, enough to fill volumes, and therein in various ways, large and small, explicated a meaningful and coherent world view, independently evolved, eclectic and cosmopolitan. This even, at times, put her at odds with Gandhi and Nehru, though this must be seen in dialogical rather than oppositional terms. These two points, taken together, are worth contemplating when we seek to reconstruct a history of international thought for India or anywhere else. That is, much as we can now see that women's historic unpaid labour in the home was nonetheless work that contributed to the financial well-being of the family, letters, conversations and the like must be seen as critical contributions to the larger narrative. Jawaharlal Nehru is often credited with shaping independent India's ideas, and for providing the most detailed understanding of international affairs in his country, often in deeply insightful, lengthy books. While this remains true, I think Vijaya Lakshmi Pandit's contributions, and indeed those of many other women, have neither been properly acknowledged, nor fully explored, on account of gender, and in part derivative of that, the manner and fora in which relevant ideas were expressed.

Returning to my first point, the basic objectives of India's official foreign policy were laid out by Jawaharlal Nehru in September 1946, just as he was taking over the interim government in anticipation of the Transfer of Power. These were '1. Full participation in international conferences . . . 2. Close contacts with other nations and co-operation with them in the furtherance of world peace. 3. Non-alignment with power groups. 4. Belief in the indivisibility of peace and freedom. 5. Special concern for emancipation of colonial and dependent countries. 6. Opposition to racialism. 7. Claim for equality and honorable treatment for the people of India anywhere in the world. [and] 8. Belief in the ultimate evolution of "One World" based on close cooperation and absence of exploitation.'[3]

Nehru believed in progressive internationalism, a holistic outlook he developed from 1919 in measure through exchanges with Gandhi, but in the context of a larger domestic and international literary sphere that included Rabindranath Tagore, Sarojini Naidu, Muhammad Iqbal and Wendell Willkie, as well as a range of Fabian socialists such as George Bernard Shaw, Bertrand Russell, and Sidney and Beatrice Webb, all of whom—at least through their writing—influenced his sister as well.

I have previously explained in my book, *The Peacemakers*, that the quest for One World was post-colonial India's strategic objective and the guiding star for its actions. Its famed policy of non-alignment, wherein it refused to subscribe to either Cold War bloc, was a plank in its larger foreign policy platform, not the platform itself. One World was a euphemism for world government, a supranational body that would help govern internationally connected, independent, autonomous states—a United Federation of the Planet if you will. While this was an airy goal, the frosty haze of the Cold War governed ground realities, and so the country was more immediately concerned with the prevention of nuclear annihilation. Vijaya Lakshmi Pandit's actions in the post-war world all follow this agenda, to which she subscribed, even long after her brother had given up.

~

One World was a concept that was to be built on certain key principles and values, basic rights and duties. Vijaya Lakshmi Pandit had a notion of rights that included the civil and political as well as the economic and social, a totalizing conception that would serve as the basis of India's external views, which in turn shaped the official United Nations organs it helped craft. She ultimately came to play a foundational role in the conceptualization and implementation of human rights. The rest of her vision for the world included global interdependence and collective security while nonetheless foregrounding anti-imperialism and anti-racism. It is also worth noting that while she spoke individually and of individualism, she also worked collaboratively with other women in the AIWC, fashioning collective responses. We can thus see illustrated in her life and actions the core values and principles of the One World concept and the other parameters of Indian foreign policy, well before her brother, or former US presidential candidate Wendell Willkie (over 1942–43), formalized them.

Vijaya Lakshmi Pandit travelled to New York in the latter half of 1946 to serve as the head of India's delegation to the new United Nations. This was her second trip stateside. On her first, she had led the counter-delegation to the United Nations Organization Conference in San Francisco, working with W.E.B. Du Bois and the National Association for the Advancement of Colored People (NAACP), a US-based civil rights organization. On that trip in 1945, she had articulated a vision for what the UN should be. In 1946, she turned that vision into reality, by duelling with South Africa's Jan Smuts about racially discriminatory laws. She outmanoeuvred him and won a super-majority vote in the UN in her favour. The result of this vote was of enduring consequence, for it established the precedent that state sovereignty was not, and could not be, impregnable. No state could hide behind the principle of state sovereignty to violate principles of human dignity and equality. And thus, it was this moment that established the precedent for international human rights norms and laws, as UN Assistant Secretary-General Henri Laugier noted when he opened the Human Rights Commission several weeks later.

We can see from this preliminary sketch that Vijaya Lakshmi Pandit made critical contributions to the post-war order in theory and practice. She not only helped develop India's core foreign policy objectives, in conjunction with other women, but she also helped establish one of the key principles of the international in the modern world, that the international community has a role to play in ensuring the basic protection of people everywhere.

Following India's independence, Vijaya Lakshmi Pandit became an official representative of her government, and her speeches and actions were intertwined with state policy, save for one exception. This was when she served as the president of the UN General Assembly. Then she specifically distanced herself from her country and her government, saying that her new role was different. Now she had to represent all people. This was a chance for her to be her true self, as she described it in her own words, 'a citizen of the world'.[4]

~

Seated on a dais, two figures lean into one another. At camera right sits Mahatma Gandhi, bespectacled, spartan in his loincloth, holding some sheaves of paper. On the left is his protégé and formal successor, Jawaharlal Nehru. Debonair in his starched white shirt and cap and homespun coarse-cotton vest with mandarin collar, he holds a pair of half-folded glasses. The faces of both men are relaxed as they share an intimate moment, a private quip, their heads ever so tilted towards one another. They laugh.

This picture was captured by renowned Associated Press (AP) photographer Max Desfor at the All-India Congress Committee meeting in Bombay on 6 July 1946. This multi-layered image spoke so much about these two men—their charisma, their shared chemistry, their close bond, their mutual admiration, their different personal choices. And it also captured the idea of the new India about to be made free from a long period of colonial rule. It caught people's imagination and became a defining photograph.

So, I was stunned a few years ago to find the original, framed so differently. In this, the camera takes a much wider angle. The 'V' between the two tilting heads is now not the centre of the image at all, but rather off to the top right. Nehru sits in the middle of the image and to his left is Vijaya Lakshmi Pandit. Radiant in an all-white, homespun sari with a sleeveless blouse, she glances off to the side with a knowing smirk on her face. There were three who were part of that moment. But she was sliced right out of it, erased from the public memory of that moment, and thus from the history of it altogether.

I have reflected on this photograph and its reproduction over several years, using the original for the cover of my previous book, *The Peacemakers*. All three of the figures were important to my narrative, but it was Nehru who was at the centre of it. The photo captured this perfectly.

When Max Desfor passed away at 104 in 2019, the AP featured the original photograph, the one that included Madame Pandit, as she was widely known, in the obituary carried by newspapers all over the world. The true story was now there for all to see.

But Vijaya Lakshmi Pandit's previous excision was not accidental. It was, rather, a purposeful act of exclusion, a knowing omission that purged her from the narrative, and part of a much more systemic deletion of women from the realms of achievement and action. As I looked into this a bit more, I soon discovered that Madame Pandit and her life seemed to hold many secrets. The story is quite a bit different than what is known.

There's another version of that Desfor photograph, taken by someone else, that I have only once had a glimpse of. In this version, Nehru is slanted more towards his sister. She is leaning in. Her face is wide and bright, and she is looking directly at her brother and the Mahatma. Her mouth is open in a toothy grin. There's a new possibility. She isn't simply amusedly listening in. She's telling the joke.[5]

~

Vijaya Lakshmi Pandit's extensive collection of papers is housed at the Nehru Memorial Museum and Library in Teen Murti, Delhi (now called the Prime Ministers' Museum and Library). Unlike those belonging to many others, her records have been kept open and accessible, a reflection, I think, of her commitment to transparency and open judgement. Indeed, these materials have been used by many scholars over the years to glean glimpses into a range of matters, often serving as an important source. Not everything in this collection is flattering, but nor is every detail revealed there either.

Every archive, however comprehensive, is at the same time incomplete, a partial view, sometimes purposefully obscured, through which what is seen is as important as that which is not.[6] In Vijaya Lakshmi Pandit's case, this in part was because of the many politically sensitive matters in which she was involved. But, in addition, she wanted a few things about her life to remain private as well, at least in that space, and so some of the absences may reflect deliberate choices.

To properly situate her in her life and times and to see her not only in the manner she saw herself but as others did, I have supplemented her papers with those from many of her contemporaries. These include, aside from correspondence, all kinds of informal and formal—some confidential—assessments of her. For instance, I have utilized secret records from the US Central Intelligence Agency and the Federal Bureau of Investigations. Similarly, I have mined archives from India, the UK, and around the world, over forty, for all bits of information. I have further interviewed many of her living associates or their descendants, many of whom appeared eager to share their particular piece of history with me.

There were tens of thousands of documents that resulted from this sweep, which I then sifted to find coherent threads, and which I tied in with published material of all kinds. What follows is interwoven narrative history. I try to explain and analyse events through the story itself. Where I have felt additional context or discussion was warranted, I have done so in my extensive notes.

Overall, I have tried to offer insight on a wide range of topics—India's foreign relations, Cold War dynamics, human rights, US civil rights, international gender norms, food security and more—while not losing sight of the person at the heart of the study. While I have therefore managed to excavate and explore many things, I have, out of necessity, had to limit myself on these issues to how they were directly relevant to the life story at hand. Some aspects thus await further investigation.

This is as it should be. For this book, in telling the tale of a path-breaking, globe-trotting woman, whose colourful, eventful life bridged colonial and post-colonial realities even as she took a battering ram to every barricade and barred entrance she encountered, I hope will itself open new doors of inquiry through which others will soon walk.[7]

# Chronology

| | |
|---|---|
| 1900 | Born Sarup Kumari Nehru on 18 August in Allahabad, United Provinces, to Motilal and Swarup Rani Nehru. |
| 1905 | Fifth birthday party in Bad Ems, Germany. |
| 1907 | Birth of Sarup's younger sister Krishna, known as Betty. |
| 1911 | Delhi Durbar; receives special attention from Queen Mary. |
| 1912 | Elder brother Jawaharlal returns home from Trinity College, Cambridge. |
| 1914–15 | Kamala Kaul enters Jawaharlal's life. Allen Dulles meets and spends time with her in Allahabad. |
| 1916 | Jawaharlal and Kamala married. Family trip to Kashmir where Sarup, aka Nan, has a notable brush with a cobra. |
| 1919 | Elopement with Syud Hossain. Marriage is annulled. Nan stays with Mahatma Gandhi at his Sabarmati Ashram in Ahmedabad, Gujarat. |
| 1920 | Childhood engagement to Rameshwari Nehru's brother is called off. Nan meets and is engaged to Ranjit Pandit. |
| 1921 | Marriage to Ranjit Pandit. Nan is rechristened Vijaya Lakshmi Pandit. Both join Gandhi's upliftment work several months later. |
| 1923 | Birth and death of the Pandits' first child, Vatsala. |
| 1924 | Birth of Chandralekha Pandit. |
| 1925 | Sarojini Naidu elected first Indian woman president of the Indian National Congress. |

| | |
|---|---|
| 1926 | Ranjit and VLP honeymoon in Europe and are detained for the attempted assassination of Benito Mussolini. |
| 1927 | Nayantara Pandit is born. |
| 1929 | Rita Pandit is born. |
| 1930 | Massacre at the Qissa Khwani Bazaar. Ranjit and Sardar Patel investigate. Ranjit is arrested. Motilal Nehru falls ill. |
| 1931 | Motilal Nehru, family patriarch, dies. |
| 1932 | VLP is arrested for activities related to 26 January, India's 'Independence Day'. |
| 1933 | VLP is released from prison. Ranjit releases his translation of the *Rajatarangini*. |
| 1934 | Betty marries Raja Hutheesing. Kamala Nehru begins to decline. VLP starts to oversee the Nehru/Pandit family. |
| 1935 | The Pandits acquire Khali estate, in Almora, in the Kumaon Hills, several hours from Dehra Dun.<br>Margaret Sanger visits India and works with VLP.<br>VLP is elected to the Allahabad Municipal Board. |
| 1936 | Kamala Nehru dies.<br>VLP's elder children enroll in Woodstock, an American missionary school in Mussoorie. |
| 1937 | VLP is elected to the United Provinces Legislature. She is named the first woman cabinet minister in the country that summer. |
| 1938 | Death of Swarup Rani and her sister, known as Bibima.<br>VLP battles a cholera outbreak at the Kumbh Mela in Haridwar.<br>VLP has near nervous breakdown from stress and travels to Europe for recovery.<br>August: VLP is in Czechoslovakia during the Sudeten Crisis.<br>September: VLP is in London outside 10 Downing Street as PM Chamberlain declares 'peace for our time'.<br>October: VLP speaks out against appeasement and makes headlines the day before Winston Churchill delivers his famous remarks on the same subject.<br>December: Back in India, VLP creates a mobile hospital program. |
| 1939 | Speaks out against rising Hindu/Muslim tension. |

| | |
|---|---|
| 1940 | Releases a book, *So I Became a Minister*. |
| | VLP is arrested again and serves several months in prison. |
| 1941 | Elected president of the All India Women's Conference. |
| 1942 | China's Chiangs visit India. |
| | Jawaharlal's daughter, Indira, marries Feroze Gandhi. |
| | Cripps Mission. |
| | Quit India campaign. |
| | Wendell Willkie One World tour. |
| | VLP is arrested for the third time. |
| 1943 | VLP's elder children head to the United States to study at Wellesley College. |
| | VLP begins work to fight the Bengal famine. |
| 1944 | Ranjit Pandit dies. VLP loses all of her wealth to Ranjit's brother, Pratap. |
| | December: VLP goes to the United States for a tour, and to be with her children. |
| 1945 | Becomes popularly known as 'Madame Pandit'. |
| | Radio debate broadcast in the United States propels her to national fame. |
| | Leads counterdelegation to the San Francisco Conference establishing the United Nations Organization. |
| 1946 | Elected to India's Constituent Assembly. |
| | Leads India's delegation to the new United Nations and becomes the first woman to lead a delegation. |
| | Walter White of the NAACP names her one of the two 'greatest women in the world'. |
| | Spearheads debate with South Africa over its laws and wins, setting a foundational precedent for modern human rights. |
| 1947 | The Asian Relations Conference is held in Delhi, born out of conversations with her colleagues during the San Francisco Conference. |
| | August: VLP named India's first ambassador to the Soviet Union. |
| 1948 | Mahatma Gandhi assassinated on 30 January. |
| 1949–51 | Serves as India's ambassador to the United States. She becomes a household name in the country and achieves celebrity status. |

| | |
|---|---|
| 1952 | Elected to the Indian Parliament in the independent country's first elections.<br>Leads a delegation to China. |
| 1953 | Elected the first woman president of the United Nations General Assembly.<br>Receives honorary degree from the United Kingdom's Queen Mother, chancellor of the University of London.<br>VLP and Indian team work to bring an end to the Korean War.<br>Oversees US President Eisenhower's 'Atoms for Peace' speech at the United Nations.<br>Named third 'Most Admired Woman' in the world by Gallup.<br>Popularly known as the 'First Lady of the World' and 'UN President'. |
| 1954–61 | Serves as high commissioner to the United Kingdom and ambassador to Ireland.<br>Tensions with Krishna Menon.<br>Helps resolve crises in the Suez and Hungary.<br>Marlon Brando names her the woman he 'particularly admired' in the world. |
| 1961–63 | Serves as governor of Maharashtra.<br>While serving as leader of India's UN delegation, tells JFK not to go to Dallas. |
| 1964 | Jawaharlal Nehru dies. VLP is elected to his old seat in Parliament.<br>Receives honorary degree from Oxford University. |
| 1965 | Calls members of the Indian government 'prisoners of indecision'.<br>Relationship with niece Indira Gandhi begins to fray.<br>War with Pakistan. VLP meets with Charles de Gaulle as part of diplomatic blitz. |
| 1967 | Betty dies. |
| 1968 | Retires from public life. |
| 1975 | Indira Gandhi declares an Emergency in India and suspends democracy.<br>VLP is placed under surveillance and has her communications censored. |

| | |
|---|---|
| 1976 | Nayantara Sahgal breaks silence over the Emergency by speaking to the press in the United States. VLP quickly follows suit from within India, sparking international criticism of Indira Gandhi. |
| 1977 | The Emergency ends and new elections are called. VLP comes out of retirement to campaign against her niece. The Opposition sweeps to victory. |
| 1990 | Vijaya Lakshmi Pandit dies. |

# Glossary

### The Family

CHANDRALEKHA (PANDIT) MEHTA   Eldest daughter of VLP.

INDIRA (NEHRU) GANDHI   VLP's niece. Daughter of Jawaharlal and Kamala Nehru. Prime Minister of India (1966–1977, 1980–1984).

JAWAHARLAL NEHRU   VLP's elder brother. Mahatma Gandhi's close friend, associate, and political heir. India's first prime minister (1946–1964).

KAMALA NEHRU   VLP's sister-in-law. Married to Jawaharlal Nehru. Mother of Indira Gandhi.

KRISHNA HUTHEESING (AKA BETTY)   VLP's younger sister.

MOTILAL NEHRU   Father of VLP. Married to Swarup Rani. Nehru family patriarch.

NANDLAL (NEHRU)   Uncle of VLP.

NAYANTARA (PANDIT) SAHGAL   VLP's middle daughter. One of independent India's most celebrated writers.

RAJA HUTHEESING   VLP's brother-in-law. Husband of Betty.

RAJVATI (AKA BIBIMA)   VLP's maternal aunt.

RAMESHWARI NEHRU   VLP's cousin by marriage. Activist and founding member of the All India Women's Conference.

RANJIT PANDIT   Husband of VLP.

RITA (PANDIT) DAR   Youngest daughter of VLP.

SWARUP RANI   Mother of VLP.

UMA NEHRU   VLP's cousin by marriage. Fiery activist.

VIJAYA LAKSHMI PANDIT (NÉE SARUP KUMARI NEHRU, AKA NAN)   Freedom fighter, pioneer, and celebrated diplomat and politician.

## Supporting Characters (Select)

AGA KHAN  Imam (leader) of Ismaili Muslims and one of the richest men in the world.

ANNIE BESANT  Indian home rule champion and the first woman president of the Indian National Congress.

ANUP SINGH  Leader of the US-based National Committee for India's Freedom.

ASAF ALI  Indian freedom fighter, husband to Aruna, and India's first ambassador to the United States.

ARUNA ASAF ALI  Prominent anticolonial activist and member of the All India Women's Conference.

B. R. AMBEDKAR  Dalit champion, credited with spearheading the drafting of India's constitution.

B. SHIVA RAO  Indian journalist with expertise on India's constitution.

CHARLES FAHY  Renowned lawyer who served as solicitor-general of the United States, 1941–45.

CLARE BOOTH LUCE  Pioneering Republican US Representative from Connecticut.

DOROTHY NORMAN  Acclaimed American writer and photographer.

G. D. BIRLA  Leading Indian industrialist and one of the country's richest men.

GIRJA SHANKAR BAJPAI  British India's agent-general (similar to ambassador) to the United States (1941–47). Secretary-general of independent India's Ministry of External Affairs (1947–52).

GOVIND BALLABH PANT  Premier of the United Provinces Congress government (1936–39, 1946–50); home minister (1955–61).

GRACE LANKESTER  Member of the Women's International League for Peace and Freedom.

HARTLEY SHAWCROSS  Renowned British lawyer and lead prosecutor of the Nuremberg Trials.

HENRY LUCE  Publisher of *Time* and *Life* magazines and husband of Clare Booth Luce.

ISAMU NOGUCHI  Japanese American sculptor and designer.

J. J. SINGH  Founder and president of the India League of America.

K. P. S. MENON  One of India's leading diplomats. First foreign secretary (1948–52).

K. Shridharani (aka Shrid)  Journalist and activist associated with the US National Committee for India's Freedom.
Kamaladevi Chattopadhyay  Pioneering Indian freedom fighter and founding member of the All India Women's Conference.
Khan Abdul Gaffar Khan (aka Frontier Gandhi)  Pathan leader of the Kudai Kitmatgar, a regional nonviolence movement aligned with Mahatma Gandhi's broader efforts.
Lal Bahadur Shastri  Indian politician and prime minister (1964–66).
Louis Mountbatten  Last British viceroy to India. Husband of Edwina.
Margaret Cousins  Prominent Irish Indian activist and founder of the All India Women's Conference.
Maulana Azad  Indian politician and leading Muslim voice within the Indian National Congress.
Mohandas K. Gandhi (aka the Mahatma)  Leader of India's anticolonial movement and advocate of nonviolence.
Muhammad Ali Jinnah  Leader of the Muslim League and advocate of Pakistan.
Pearl Buck  Nobel Prize–winning author of the *The Good Earth*. Advocate for India and critical ally of VLP.
Padmaja Naidu  Daughter of Sarojini. One of VLP's closest friends.
Rabindranath Tagore  Indian writer and artist. First non-European awarded a Nobel Prize.
Rajendra Prasad  First president of India (1952–62).
Rajkumari Amrit Kaur  Activist and founding member of the All India Women's Conference.
Richard Walsh  Founder and editor, The John Day Company, publisher of Jawaharlal Nehru. Married to Pearl Buck.
Sardar Vallabhbhai Patel (aka the Iron Man of India)  Mahatma Gandhi's right-leaning lieutenant. Deputy prime minister and home minister of independent India (1947–50).
Sarojini Naidu (aka the Nightingale of India)  Celebrated poet, writer, and activist. First Indian woman president of the Indian National Congress.
Stafford Cripps  British Labour politician. Led the Cripps Mission and was part of the Cabinet Mission to India.

SUBHAS CHANDRA BOSE (AKA NETAJI)   Prominent Indian politician and popular national leader. Leader of the Indian National Army, embedded in Japanese Axis forces.
SYUD HOSSAIN   Journalist. Brief elopement with VLP before marriage annulled.
TEJ BAHADUR SAPRU   Leading Indian lawyer and politician.
V. K. KRISHNA MENON   Brilliant, left-leaning anticolonial activist and diplomat. VLP's bête noire.

Additional Terms

ALL INDIA WOMEN'S CONFERENCE   Leading women's advocacy organization in India.
AMRITSAR MASSACRE (AKA THE JALLIANWALA BAGH MASSACRE)   British forces led by General Reginald Dyer opened fire on an unarmed group of Indians gathered in an enclosed garden to celebrate a festival (and some to protest repressive laws) in Amritsar, Punjab, in April 1919. Estimates of those killed range from the hundreds to over a thousand.
ANAND BHAWAN   Stately manor home of the Nehrus.
ATLANTIC CHARTER   British and American statement of goals for World War II.
CASTE   Term used to describe the system of hereditary social structure in India.
CRIPPS MISSION   Failed effort led by Sir Stafford Cripps to resolve disputes in India between various parties and British government.
DECLARATION BY UNITED NATIONS   Statement formalizing the alliance supporting the Atlantic Charter against the Axis in World War II.
FOUR FREEDOMS   Derived from FDR's 1941 State of the Union speech, advocating freedom of speech and religion, and freedom from want and fear.
INDIAN NATIONAL CONGRESS (AKA THE CONGRESS)   Initially a forum for Indians to petition the government for change; blossomed into the leading anticolonial organization in the region.
KUDAI KITMATGAR   Nonviolent movement centered in the northwestern part of the subcontinent. Led by Khan Abdul Gaffar Khan.
LUCKNOW PACT   Agreement between the Indian National Congress and the Muslim League in 1916 to jointly advocate for expanded,

democratic self-governance in India, with Muslims allowed separate electorates (the ability to elect their own representatives).

MORLEY-MINTO REFORMS  British reforms in India in 1909 that granted limited representation in response to Indian agitation.

MONTAGU-CHELMSFORD REFORMS  Follow-up British reforms in India in 1919 that promised greater Indian participation in governance, but through the principle of dyarchy, withheld all real power.

MUSLIM LEAGUE (AKA THE ALL-INDIA MUSLIM LEAGUE)  An organization established in 1906 to advocate for Muslim interests. After Jinnah took over in 1934, the league grew devoted to the idea of Pakistan and developed greater mass appeal.

POONA (PUNE) PACT  Agreement between Dr. Ambedkar and Mahatma Gandhi guaranteeing Dalits reserved seats in joint electorates.

POORNA SWARAJ  1929 Congress resolution calling for the complete independence of India.

SIMON COMMISSION  British parliamentary mission to India to explore constitutional reforms that was widely condemned for not including any Indian voices.

SYKES-PICOT AGREEMENT  Secret agreement between Britain and France in 1916 to divide certain territories of the Ottoman Empire between them after World War I.

UNTOUCHABILITY  Discriminatory practices oppressing Dalits in India within the caste system.

VICEROY  Representative of the British Crown in India and head of the British Indian government.

# THE
REMARKABLE
MADAME PANDIT

CHAPTER ONE

# Little Woman

It was a beautiful May afternoon, the kind best spent outdoors. Nan Nehru was stretched out reading on the grass on her first visit to her family's ancestral home in Kashmir. The princely state was renowned for its serene beauty, little hamlets and villages tucked into majestic mountains. The Nehrus had come to Achabal, a town in the Kashmir Valley about 30–40 miles from the capital of Srinagar, to enjoy its legendary gardens, which had been designed by the Mughal Empress Nur Jahan in the seventeenth century. Streams and a natural spring complemented engineered waterfalls and fountains, providing a calm but striking backdrop that brought its flowers into colourful relief.

The family had camped out under the awning of boonyi trees, a subcontinental variant of sycamores. Nan lay a short distance from the family's pitched tents, on her stomach resting her head in her hands, overlooking a brook. Her father, family patriarch Motilal, sat on a chair nearby engrossed in a book. Out of the corner of his eye, something caught his attention. He looked up and gasped.

'Nan, don't stir,' he said guardedly under his breath. Hovering over his daughter was a giant king cobra, hood unfurled, coiled in striking position. The cobra swayed back and forth as if to some music only it could hear, too far for Motilal to reach. Suddenly, the snake darted.

It glided right under her arm and out into the brush. Nan screamed in fright and stood up. Her mother Swarup Rani came racing out of her tent when she heard the commotion but inexplicably started beaming when she learned what had happened. When Motilal looked at her puzzled, she declared the event a good omen, and a sign that her daughter was destined for great things.[1]

~

The Nehrus had migrated to Delhi from Kashmir in the early 1700s, over several generations growing into a prominent family.[2] Motilal was born to Pandit Gangadhar, the chief of police (*kotwal*) under Bahadur Shah Zafar, the last of the Mughal line. Gangadhar had whisked his family out of Delhi and escaped to Agra following the Rebellion of 1857, but he died soon thereafter. Motilal's eldest brother, Nandlal, took responsibility for the family while their mother grew into a fierce and sure-footed woman who was determined to carve out a life for herself whatever social convention might dictate. (Nan would later impishly recall that she may have picked up a trait or two from her grandmother.) The family excelled, as some siblings marked achievements through academics, while others did so through world travel. Motilal led a carefree life and was perpetually of buoyant spirit. He did well enough in school but his interest, in his younger days, lay primarily in sports, and in living life to its fullest. He eventually attended Allahabad University, though he missed a few requirements to secure his bachelor's degree. That, however, did not prevent him from pursuing higher studies. He took up law like his brother, topped his exams in 1883, and began to practice. He joined his brother's firm in 1886.

Nandlal had been married at age twelve in 1857, and by the time Motilal arrived, he had seven children—two daughters and five sons. Motilal too had been married when he was a teenager, but he lost his wife and their child to tragic circumstances. He married again before moving to Allahabad, to Swarup Rani, whose family also came from Kashmir. They were a striking couple—he dashing, and she beautiful. But Swarup Rani was very thin and delicate, and fell sick easily, causing never-ending concern in their household. They lost their first child soon after birth, adding to their heartache. And then, in 1887, just after moving back to Allahabad, Motilal's family reunion was also cut short when Nandlal died suddenly. At only twenty-five, and with no inherited property or title, Motilal found himself responsible for his large, extended family of nieces and nephews.³

~

Motilal took over the family's profitable law practice with gusto. He now directed his boundless energy, enthusiasm, and irrepressible joie-de-vivre, towards his work, and he skyrocketed to fame as a superstar lawyer. And with this success came new-found wealth. Motilal prioritized the security and comfort of his family. He showered them with affection, looked after everyone's studies, and made sure that all their basic needs were taken care of.

The family until then had lived in the crowded city centre of Allahabad, an area full of daily hubbub but decidedly cramped and unconducive to a gentle lifestyle. Motilal was particularly concerned about his home environment because he was worried about his wife's health. And so he took the momentous decision to buy a house, a big move not only because such a residence was an expensive status symbol generally, but especially because in India at that time, it was a luxury few Indians could afford. Motilal acquired a modest bungalow at 9, Elgin Road, in the 'Civil Lines' part of town. While Civil Lines was connected to the rest of the city, it represented a separate and starkly different reality. Suddenly narrow lanes opened up into broad avenues, there was greenery as far as the eye could see, and people numbered fewer and further between.

Civil Lines was in fact the designated home of Europeans and Anglo-Indians. It was designed to be expensive and exclusive, to keep most Indians out. It was therefore an achievement, and a statement, when Motilal moved in, his large extended family in tow.⁴

In 1889, Swarup Rani gave birth to another child, a son they named Jawaharlal, who immediately became the centre of attention and the subject of much doting. For the next few years, the boy enjoyed terrific freedom to live and play, but not at the expense of picking up life lessons along the way.

Motilal was gregarious and larger than life, famous for his booming laugh that would echo everywhere and a cheerful personality that could fill any room. But he was also a man of precision and high expectations, and a terrifying temper that he could unleash on anyone who fell short of his exacting standards. Jawaharlal grasped this early but learned it first-hand at six, in an episode the entire family would recall for decades after. Wandering about the house, the young boy came upon his father's things, took a fancy to a fountain pen found there and pocketed it. When Motilal discovered that the pen was missing, he ordered everyone in the house to look for it, creating a terrific commotion, until the thing was at last found in Jawaharlal's possession. Motilal beat his son black and blue to such a degree that the child required treatment for days afterwards.[5]

This incident was, of course, in keeping with the norms of the day, where all kinds of everyday violence, especially by men in the home, was sanctioned. Women, children and serving staff were all, always, subject to the moody whims of men both within and outside of home.

By all accounts, Motilal was rarely physical or aggressive, and his anger was usually fleeting, much like a fast summer storm, though this of course did not make his occasional outbursts any more excusable. Still, the very fact that the story of Jawaharlal and the fountain pen became part of the family lore revealed how genuinely unusual it was. The general tenor of Motilal's character was one of affection if also one of professionalism: his children and relatives universally remember him as supremely loving and generous.

The year after the pen incident, one of Motilal's other siblings, Bansidhar, decided to travel to Europe, and left his son Shridhar, of Jawaharlal's age, in his brother's care for several months. Motilal immediately enrolled both boys into the local convent school. Their stay lasted six months.[6]

Motilal had been earning about Rs 2000 a month for some time by then, not an inconsiderable sum, but was still on his way up, earning within the next several years over Rs 10,000 a month. Almost all the cases he handled involved disputes between wealthy land-holding elites (*zamindars*), arguing over property. There were spectacular sums involved, and cases could go on for years or longer.[7] Motilal was highly regarded, and always in demand, and so he grew very rich through his career. There would be nothing that was beyond the reach of his family. From that point onwards, Jawaharlal was to be tutored privately, the most elite and expensive option possible.[8]

Shridhar left Allahabad to rejoin his father, who returned from his international travels a thoroughly changed man. Bansidhar had

had many wild adventures while travelling through Europe, the UK and the United States. He had had the opportunity to meet and interview the 25th US President, William McKinley, for instance. When Bansidhar returned, his mind had expanded. He exhibited freedom and an exuberance that he had not shown before.

Motilal immediately determined that he too needed to travel abroad. This was not a decision made lightly since his community of Kashmiri Saraswat Brahmins did not condone foreign travel. Indeed, the community had previously split when another lawyer from Allahabad, Pandit Bishan Narayan Dhar, had gone abroad and, on his return, opted to conduct a purification ceremony so that he could rejoin society. His community, however, disagreed as to whether the ceremony was sufficient, and split: one side became known as the Bishan Sabha (the Community of Bishan) and the other the Dharm Sabha (the Community of Righteousness).

Motilal's trip changed him fundamentally, as it introduced him to all kinds of new ways of living. He found many things to admire in Europe. Motilal returned to India, much like his brother, more worldly, cosmopolitan, and determined to bring various elements from his travels into his daily routine.

As a first matter, he announced that he had no intention of performing any kind of purification ceremony, chalking up such things to superstition and discrimination. He was excommunicated, but this only made him dig in more. He relished every opportunity to ridicule his opponents and to mock the fear that lay at the core of their conservatism. His showy resistance fissured the community again, the new, third group calling themselves, unsurprisingly, the Moti Sabha (the Community of Moti [a double entendre meaning 'pearl' and Motilal]). More importantly, it basically broke the bar on foreign travel for young Kashmiris, who now began to move about more freely and casually.[9]

Motilal started to introduce himself as M. Nehru, adopting a surname in the manner common to Europeans he had met, and using his clan's shorthand moniker for this purpose. He loved the further distinction this brought him.

He had also brought many fine things back from his tour, and now he needed a proper place to put them. A few months later, in 1900, he found it, at 1 Church Road. He purchased the entire 10-

acre estate for Rs 20,000.[10] The mansion at the centre of his new property was enormous, with a long arcade of interlinked archways distinguishing its façade. 'In the middle of the building was a big, square open courtyard with shallow steps leading up to a deep veranda running all the way round and onto which opened the bedrooms. A tiered fountain [could be found] in the centre of the courtyard . . .'[11]

When Motilal purchased it, the house was somewhat run down, but had a history. It was the previous home of two distinguished judges of Allahabad, one of whom was the son of Sir Syed Ahmed Khan, the renowned social reformer of the nineteenth century, based out of Aligarh.[12] Motilal enthusiastically poured money into renovations, adding amenities of all kinds. By the time he was done with it, the entire estate came to rather resemble the fictional, English manor depicted in *Downton Abbey*.

Anand Bhawan (Abode of Joy), as the Nehru house came to be known, was the first in Allahabad to have electricity and running water as well as an indoor swimming pool. Motilal had gardens created, as well as an orchard, horse stables and a riding ring and tennis courts.[13] He hired a massive staff to help maintain and look after the place. On the inside, each room was tastefully decorated with ornate rugs and elegant furniture; the kitchen was stocked with the finest of chinas, and wines. The house was divided into Indian and Western halves, and each wing was designed accordingly, with staff and family etiquette following the pattern of whichever part of the house they were in.

Anand Bhawan was a sparkling jewel, but its acquisition was not the most momentous thing to happen to the Nehrus in 1900. That occurred on 18 August, when Swarup Rani gave birth to another child, a girl whom they named Sarup Kumari.[14]

~

The Nehru lifestyle was an exception, not the rule, in India at the turn of the century. The British Crown was sovereign. It was the interests of the little isles in the eastern Atlantic that drove policy. And those who lived well, almost always European, did so at the expense of destitute multitudes.

The British, who had been a minor presence in the subcontinent since the time of Akbar in the sixteenth century, expanded their operations over the first half of the seventeenth, competing with the French for strategic assets. When the brilliant Governor-general François Dupleix was recalled home to France by King Louis XV and Madame de Pompadour, his young British rival, Robert Clive, made a move to dominate the area, securing a major victory in the 1757 Battle of Plassey under the aegis of the English East India Company. Britain, based in the north-east, was now a serious force in the region, though it had to contend with several other powers, and remained officially under the nominal rule of the Mughal ruler based in Delhi.

With the defeat of Tipu Sultan and his southern stronghold of Mysore in 1799, the British assumed direct or indirect control over the majority of southern Asia, and the Mughal ruler was reduced to a token figurehead.[15] It would still be another half a century before the British assumed full authority.

But once they did, the British failed to come to terms with the glaring inconsistencies of their colonial enterprise, and within a few years of facing a rebellion in 1857, discontent was again on the rise. One particularly astute observer, Allan Octavian Hume, knew what was coming. He had witnessed the events of the mid-century and concluded correctly that the people were revolting against a government that had utterly failed them. Hume saw the cackling ghost of the well-known Anglicist, Thomas Babington Macaulay—who had infamously disparaged all non-Western learning and called for the creation of a mediating class of brown Englishmen—whispering in the ear of every colonial official, writing that 'a studied and invariable disregard, if not actually contempt for the opinions and feelings of our subjects, is at the present day the leading characteristic of our government in every branch of the administration'.[16] Hume himself took up the mantle of administrator for a while. Hoping to lead by example, he proved himself to be able, upright, honest and earnest. But it was hardly enough, and he later realized that there was so much unhappiness, the British could once again face violent resistance. While he sympathized with the local people, he did not wish to see this happen.

And so, in 1885, Hume helped to establish the Indian National Congress, a new organization where Indians could vent their grievances and frustrations and participate in very limited self-governance. It was a development that would change India's landscape, and the lives of the Nehrus, forever.

~

Big crowds had gathered and were cheering. Sarup intuitively knew that she had to take the time to greet each one of the guests, to personally shake hands with everyone, even though she was exhausted. It was her fifth birthday party after all.

The Nehrus were in the town of Bad Ems in imperial Germany, then helmed by Kaiser Wilhelm II. It was Motilal's third trip abroad, but the first for the rest of the family. Jawaharlal was now sixteen, and his father had decided it was time for him to attend a formal school. Nothing but the best would do.

Jawaharlal had been well trained, uniquely so, by then, tutored by Ferdinand Brooks for several years. Brooks, of Irish and French descent, had been introduced to the Nehrus by their mutual friend Annie Besant. Brooks and Besant both practised Theosophy, a quirky philosophical spiritualism that had been established by the mystics Colonel (Henry) Olcott and Madame (Helena) Blavatsky.[17] Brooks instilled in the young Jawaharlal a love of learning—of reading and the pursuit of science. He amassed an eclectic library and built a small laboratory in Anand Bhawan. The young boy, with no one his age to engage, whiled away his days poring over the fine details of his books, the very best of English literature, and conducting interesting experiments.

Motilal eventually decided that Jawaharlal was ready to attend school in London, though he was 'in the dark' about where to send him. He was under the impression that he was acting too late, and that all the best schools had no more openings. Still, the family made their way a quarter of the way across the world, in the hope that Motilal could still make something happen. Motilal turned to friends upon his arrival, and through them gained Jawaharlal the permission to sit for the entrance exam that September at Harrow, one of England's most prestigious schools.

Motilal had brought the rest of his family along in the hopes of attending to the health of Swarup Rani, then in late pregnancy. But

London had not been kind. Doctors recommended that they seek care in special European facilities. So, leaving Jawaharlal to study Latin in preparation for Harrow's test, the family came to Cologne, and from there journeyed to the spa town of Bad Homburg. Motilal and Swarup Rani immersed themselves in mineral baths, hoping the medicinal waters could relax and heal them, and were quite discouraged when they found no relief for their ailments. Adding to their disappointment, Motilal had had high hopes of joining the local tennis clubs, reputed for their superlative quality, but he quickly gave up the idea when he discovered that the men and women who played there did so with more grace, finesse and skill than he could ever muster. So, the family again packed up their things and travelled to Bad Ems in the Rhine Valley. It too was acclaimed for its spas, fed by mineral springs, and was a popular getaway for the rich, the royal and the renowned. Bad Ems was also strikingly beautiful, situated on either bank of the Lahn River, and nestled among surrounding hills of greenery. Motilal thought it all wonderful. He decided to throw Sarup, affectionately called Nanhi (Little One) by the family, a small party.[18] His precocious daughter had round cheeks, thick, dark curly hair and an intense gaze. She was already 'universally admired'.[19]

There was a children's school in front of the hotel where Motilal and his family were staying, and he invited all the students to attend the birthday celebration. The four hundred-odd who showed up had to be welcomed in smaller groups. They were all given a grand tea party on palatial hotel grounds. Some of the children brought Sarup small gifts like note paper, supplementing fancy earrings that Motilal had purchased from a local jeweller. The jeweller also sent flowers, as did other guests staying at the hotel, which supplied a lavish cake. Motilal crowed that it 'was the greatest birthday Nanni [sic] has ever had, or perhaps will have in the future'.[20] The incredible affair cost Motilal only £15, so he took a special pleasure in the fact that guests and gawkers alike concluded he had to be some kind of Indian Prince.

Sarup, for her part, was unruffled by the whole business. Her primary concern was her elder brother, now absent. To keep him informed, she decided to pen him a few letters. Motilal could not read a word, seeing only 'crooked lines and loops', and gently chided his daughter. She retorted, 'You do not know German, this is German.'[21]

Such quick wit, a perfect mix of sweet and sour, would refine in later years to become one of the signature elements of her personality.

Sarup was the only member of the family who seemed to benefit from the trip to Europe. Both Swarup Rani and Motilal seemed as tired and ill as when they arrived, so they were grateful when the time came for them to return to London in time for the Harrow exam. Jawaharlal gained admission and his father again busied himself settling his son in. But at the hour of departure, Motilal's efficient management and hard-nosed actions were revealed as mere cover for a much softer soul. In a final letter sent from Marseilles before boarding the ship home, he said, 'I never thought I loved you so much as when I had to part with you . . . But my sense of duty to you is as strong as it ever was, and as for the poor weak heart, it is in your keeping. I . . . say farewell, mine own darling boy, take care of yourself. In doing so, you will be taking care of your parents.'[22]

~

Four members of the family had left India for London and four made the return trip. In Jawaharlal's place was Lillian Hooper. She accompanied the Nehrus and took up residence at Anand Bhawan as a governess. Sarup promptly dubbed her 'Toopie'. But Toopie just as quickly turned the tables. She found the pet name Nanhi too cumbersome and shortened it to 'Nan', a name by which Sarup would forever after be known to close friends and family alike.[23]

Hooper was tasked with Nan's general oversight, and with her education, which was supplemented by a series of private tutors.[24] In some measure, this followed the model used for Jawaharlal. Motilal was sure the local schools were deficient in all sorts of ways, and private tutors were, and were seen as, the proper way to instruct elite youth. At the same time, Motilal was caught in a bit of a bind. He liked, admired and supported many strong-minded and forceful women, and he believed unequivocally that women were just as capable as men at virtually anything. At the same time, he simply gave no thought to his daughter's education. Of course, he had not planned out Jawaharlal's schooling either and had made decisions for his son often at the last possible moment, just as he had done with Harrow. Still, across classes in India, it was believed that the destiny of a girl was tied up in marriage, and it, and not a career, was the ultimate objective of most parents. Motilal and the highly traditional Swarup Rani were no exception; Nan was engaged when she was thirteen to a boy several years her elder, from a reputed family.[25] Whether Motilal intended only a limited education, or whether he merely gave the whole thing little thought and left it to fate, Hooper and the tutors would be the only formal teaching that his young daughter would ever receive.

Nan's curiosity was nonetheless piqued by her favourite instructor, Pandit Mahavir Prasad Malaviya, who shared with her his love of language and literature. Through him, she supplemented her reading of Dickens, Shakespeare and English poetry with Hindi masterpieces like Tulsidas's *Ramcharitmanas*. She also learned Sanskrit. She had a way with words in any language, and from her mid-teens began writing for Hindi magazines on a range of literary topics.[26]

Nan benefited from several things. She was insatiably curious and fiercely determined. She wanted to know everything, and yet by nature was unafraid to question the things she learned. In this, she was helped, above all, by her brother, who became her true guide in life. He was physically far away, returning to India for only three weeks over seven years, and yet she never felt closer to him. 'I'm sure my brother didn't realize he was my teacher. I didn't realize it myself until a good deal later,' she later recalled.[27]

Hooper and the tutors used books in Anand Bhawan's vast library to teach. These had been the very same books that Jawaharlal, eleven years Nan's senior, had read and re-read earlier, scribbling notes and questions throughout. While gibberish to anyone else, to Nan these marginalia were a secret code her brother had left just for her. She was on a hunt for treasure—wisdom—and had to be prepared to go wherever the messages hidden in scrawled cypher led her.[28]

Repeatedly, Hooper would follow the words on the page, while her young student grew bolder in her critical engagement. She queried British actions to put down the 1857 rebellion, wondering why they could not see their own barbarism. In another instance, she objected strongly to the infamous story of the Black Hole of Calcutta, when the Nawab of Bengal, in retaliation for a campaign of Robert Clive, ostensibly forced a hundred and forty-six English people into a small, cramped cell, where they died from suffocation and inhumane conditions. Nan found records indicating that the number was sixty-three and that the incident had actually been an accident. When Hooper replied that the Indian source her student had used might be biased, Nan flipped the point around and asked if the same could not be said of all the British authors she was reading.[29]

Jawaharlal was more than just a ghostly presence conjured by the strange spell-like markings he had drawn on page after page of dusty books, at least in the first year after he left home. Each member of the family would send him a letter regularly, and he in turn would write back. Motilal had gently nudged both son and daughter in this direction just before he had left London. He wrote to his son a few months later, in February 1906: 'The picture post-card, I posted as from you, came in good time and she [Nanhi] was well pleased with it. She now wants you to write her a letter.' The next month, he informed Jawaharlal of the 'rapid progress' his daughter was making in her studies: 'She can speak 170 English words correctly and can repeat multiplication tables up to 3.'[30] Jawaharlal soon started a regular home correspondence, sharing his ruminations on a wide range of subjects, from history and politics to literature. His father usually reacted strongly, and negatively, to his son's writings, which he felt were sometimes meant to personally irritate him, so critical was Jawaharlal of virtually all the things that Motilal liked and admired in the world. Nan often pondered over her brother's letters and went to learn more about the topics he was writing about. She also picked up important cues from the reactions Jawaharlal's letters provoked in their father, that it was possible and necessary to disagree and debate with even people you loved and admired, and that there was a way to do this without destroying any underlying relationships.

~

Two years after the Nehrus returned to India, on 2 November 1907, Swarup Rani gave birth to another child, a girl they named Krishna at Jawaharlal's behest. Swarup Rani and Motilal started calling their new little girl *beti* (affectionate for dear daughter), but Toopie Hooper heard the word as Betty, and so she became. Unlike Nan, Betty strongly disliked her nickname, and reverted to Krishna when she got older, though her immediate family members continued to use the Anglicized moniker given by the governess.³¹

Krishna was born nearly two years to the day of another sibling, born on 4 November 1905, but the baby Ratan Lal had only lived for a month. It was likely a difficult pregnancy that had caused Swarup Rani's ill health while on their European trip. Her health bounced up and down until Krishna was born. Afterwards, it declined further, her low points making her a near invalid, while her relatively normal days were few and far between.

To help care for their mother, Nan and Krishna's maternal aunt, Rajvati, moved into Anand Bhawan, and became a strong additional presence. Rajvati had been widowed at a very early age, and Nan always felt, with some bitterness, that societal restrictions placed on her aunt kept her from blossoming fully. Known to the children as Bibima, the loving Rajvati brought a strong sense of traditionalism and religiosity to the house, complementing that of her sister and Nandrani, the widow of Nandlal. Together, these women balanced out Motilal's Western orientation, and assured that the children would be as at home in India as in the rest of the world.

Nan, and to some extent her sister as well, absorbed the lesson immediately, maintaining throughout their lives an easy grace and charm that made them perfectly comfortable almost anywhere, and in almost any setting. For his part, Motilal conveyed his love of life, his absolute self-assurance that he belonged everywhere, in any circle, and his determination for success. Nothing was ever to serve as a barrier that could not be overcome, though this was an admonition later tempered by Jawaharlal's intuitive understanding that privilege opened many doors that would otherwise remain shut, and the family's drive had, therefore, to be spent in service of the less fortunate.

In these early years, nothing captured Motilal's prime directive more than the girls' mastery of horsemanship. The riding and maintenance of horses was considered a fine art, and a popular pastime of elites throughout Europe and its extended empires. Women rode horses, though Victorian impulses dictated that they had to ride side-saddle for fear of indecency. In India, where horse riding was primarily the prerogative of the princes, it was not unheard of for women to ride cross-saddle—the Rani of Jhansi, a heroine of the 1857 Rebellion, was but the most famous example—but it was still unusual. Motilal kept a stable of prized horses, and the girls learned from a coachman, Mohammed Hussain, a retired Indian Army officer employed with the family. In keeping with the widespread view, Hussain did not think girls should ride, yet he taught Nan and Betty anyway.[32]

Nan learnt her lessons, perhaps too well. Where Motilal wanted her to be unafraid to stand tall, she was sure that her head had to remain unbowed. One summer, the family was vacationing in the cool hills north of Delhi as they did for several months out of every year, in the resort town of Mussoorie. Nan made her way back home from a ride when she realized that it was quite late. The main road was known as the Mall, and horses were not allowed to go faster than a walk. In haste to get home, Nan put her horse into a canter, just short of a gallop, and rushed by evening strollers. The bright colours worn by pedestrians distracted the horse though, and it brushed the hat of a woman accompanying an elderly British colonel. The officer shouted, 'Keep your damned horse in order,' and hit Nan's steed with his walking stick. Nan whipped around and acerbically retorted, 'Keep your damned wife to the right side of the road.' Motilal was livid, and Nan lost her riding privileges for the rest of that season.[33]

~

Anand Bhawan was a hub of activity in Allahabad. As a preeminent lawyer known for generosity, and a flair for grand but not ostentatious display, Motilal kept rather august company, Indian and British alike. Among his closest friends were Sir Harcourt Butler, a fellow Harrovian (though many years Jawaharlal's senior of course), a member of the Indian Civil Service, and a member of the Viceroy's Council. Nan called him Uncle Harcourt. But just as frequent visitors, and ultimately far more influential on the household, were Gopal Krishna Gokhale and Sarojini Naidu. Butler was personally endearing. Gokhale and Naidu were inspirational.

Motilal had known Gokhale for quite some time, both instrumental in the development of the Indian National Congress. Three years after its founding, the Congress held its annual meeting in Allahabad, and Motilal attended as one of 1400 delegates. Hume had by then judged the Congress' initial campaigns a failure, not because its message was wrong, but because he had misjudged the British desire to be responsive.[34]

Motilal grew more involved. Soon, he served on the Subjects Committee, along with Gokhale and other rising stalwarts, Surendranath Banerjea and Pandit Madan Mohan Malaviya.[35]

Gokhale modelled himself after Mahadev Ranade, one of the original founding members of the Congress and a devoted champion of social reform. Their gentle demeanours masked steely determination to effect change, though with an ironclad commitment to work within existing systems, however flawed. The petition was their weapon of choice.

Just as the Congress was getting off the ground, however, many who were hungry for change were ready for a more radical course of action. Protests against British cotton tariffs broke out in 1896, and two British officials were assassinated.[36] Hume had foreseen all of this and had hoped his organization would funnel such discontent into productive but calm channels. When the new Viceroy, Lord Curzon, took charge in 1899, he immediately concluded that the government had in fact been too lax, too willing to accommodate pressures from the local population, and he immediately set out to undo previously made concessions. He reduced Indian representation in local administration, and, in his most aggressive move, partitioned the province of Bengal into Eastern and Western, and Hindu and Muslim, halves, declaring that 'one of our main objects is to split up and thereby weaken the opponents to our rule'.[37]

Curzon's actions had the opposite effect, uniting the opposition into the Swadeshi Movement. Activists adopted more aggressive tactics that included protests and the boycotting of some goods. They also set a new goal of *swaraj*, a somewhat vague term that meant self-control, but implied, possibly, actual independence. Broadly speaking, there were four types of nationalists working together, who were, at times, at odds with one another: the moderates, led by Gokhale and a few others; reformers who called on Indians to make changes and improvements from within, exemplified by the writer Rabindranath Tagore; the extremists, who demanded strong and visible resistance to British rule, headlined by Bal Gangadhar Tilak among others; and revolutionaries, who were ready to deploy violence in the name of freedom.[38]

Motilal was nonplussed by all of this. He sided with Gokhale and Malaviya, admitting to his son that his 'own views are even more moderate than those of the so-called Moderates'.[39] He hosted meetings in Anand Bhawan, and worried about the direction in which the country was heading. While he was all for Indian participation in the government, he opposed any kind of hardline or radical position. Motilal was pressed into accepting the presidency of a regional meeting and reluctantly accepted, fretting that agitated students, in particular, were on the other side of the political spectrum and would fight his positions. Jawaharlal, who had spent those past few years reading widely at Harrow, urged his father on: 'You may not agree with the ways of the new Extremist party, but I do not think that you are such a slow and steady person as you make yourself out to be.'[40]

Motilal's political activism also brought him into contact with Sarojini Naidu, who in her twenties had found an interest in politics when her home state of Bengal was cut in two by Curzon. A few years before, she had married a young doctor from South India, breaking several conventions along the way, all with her parents' approval. Blessed with a brash and witty personality, Mrs Naidu too filled any room she entered. She was approachable, friendly, and not to be trifled with. Nan was agog with admiration. Over the next decade, together with Annie Besant, Mrs Naidu grew to become Nan's idol and role model.[41] Over the same period, she also developed a fast friendship with Padmaja, Mrs Naidu's daughter, who was the same age as Nan. Their bond would last a lifetime.

~

Despite everything swirling around her, Nan's childhood was unhurried and idyllic, completely sheltered from the storms outside. She was, in every way, a child of exceptional privilege, not only because of her family's great wealth, but because the extraordinary was her ordinary, every day bringing encounters and engagement with the most exceptional people. Most importantly, she was completely cocooned in love by her doting father, mother and aunt, and on through her vast extended family. Holidays, like *Navroz* (the Kashmiri New Year), Holi and Diwali were all celebrated without inhibition, Anand Bhawan glittering like the fairy tale palace it in almost every sense truly was. In her later years, Nan recalled with a special fondness the incredible delicacies she dined on with frequency, a global cuisine served from the Western and Indian kitchens. She developed a taste for good food, and the skills to make it herself, important assets that would serve her well in later life.

Perhaps the most memorable event of her childhood took place in 1911, when Motilal took Swarup Rani, Nan and Betty to Delhi, to attend the coronation of King George V as Emperor at the Delhi Durbar. This was to be a lavish affair. The British came to see the native monarchs of India as indispensable collaborators, whose participation and support were necessary for the maintenance and stability of the Raj, as British Indian rule came to be known. They developed complex pageantry involving coats of arms and gun salutes to embellish Indian practices and incorporate them into a larger imperial whole. The result was a grand but garish mishmash of peculiar customs.

The Indian princes were ranked according to their prestige, wealth and power, with larger states recognized with more gun salutes. The coronation involved fancy parades and bejewelled royalty, a total spectacle. The highest nobility had to pay homage to King George and Queen Mary and follow strict protocol while doing so. Motilal, a non-royal representing a delegation from the United Provinces, was invited to present as well, which he considered a particular honour. The family travelled with the state delegation, which included the British lieutenant-governor, Leslie Porter, in an official train. The Porters took a special interest in the Nehrus, dining personally with them, and seeing that their every need was looked after.

Once they arrived in Delhi, the Nehrus received invitations to many important functions, and were even honoured with 'special bows from the King and the Queen'. Nan, moreover, 'received special attention from the Queen, who would certainly have spoken to her, had it not been for the stiff formality of the occasion'.[42]

At the main ceremony, Motilal was seated near Maharaja Sayaji Rao of Baroda, one of the most distinguished and honoured of all the princes, who had visited Anand Bhawan only months before. Motilal later recalled their conversation at the Durbar: 'He asked me what

I thought of the show and on my saying that it was the grandest tamasha [show, of a performative nature] I had seen, remarked that it would have been alright if we had not to act in it like animals in a circus.'[43]

Sayaji Rao had long bristled at British colonial control. He had carefully engineered a reputation as a progressive ruler over the previous decade, a reformer who could deliver better results than the British state. His rule undermined much of the imperial premise. The Maharaja particularly resented Lord Curzon and felt that India deserved much better. When Sayaji Rao's turn came at the great Durbar, he turned his back on George and Mary and created an international incident in the process. His actions were not that different from those of several other rulers, yet British officialdom was abuzz with that affront.

Sayaji Rao had apparently been miscounselled by a British advisor, and the entire event turned into more of an effort by the British to put the prince in his place.[44] Motilal, for his part, was aghast by the affair, in the aftermath writing to Jawaharlal that he thought the whole thing rather silly. He could not understand why the Gaekwad would go to the trouble to insult the king, only to apologize for his actions immediately thereafter. Jawaharlal agreed but also blamed the press for hyping the story.[45]

~

Jawaharlal had completed his studies at Harrow after two years and had subsequently gained admission to Trinity College, Cambridge. As in Harrow, Jawaharlal spent his days in rarified company, though now with much greater freedom than he had in boarding school. He read widely, and gained an appreciation of human suffering, and of the power of politics to ameliorate. He kept up his regular correspondence with home, engaging his father on all sorts of issues, and at times instructing him on what he could do better. Motilal alternated between bemusement and frustration at his son's audacity.

Eight months after the Delhi Durbar, Jawaharlal returned to India, and Anand Bhawan. He had been called to the bar in London just before his departure, so shortly after his arrival he took up a position as a barrister in the Allahabad High Court. Cousins who had also travelled for their studies returned home around the same time, and Anand Bhawan hummed with life, love and laughter, more vivacious than ever.[46]

Jawaharlal was always larger than life for Nan: a paragon of virtue, and blinding brilliance, to be admired and adored. She was very young when he went abroad, but he remained a fulsome presence in her life through his notes and his letters. While he was physically absent, Nan mentally summoned him as needed, developing a certain spiritual affinity with him over the years. She felt blessed, and made whole again, to have him physically by her side once more.

The siblings spent hours each day reading, immersing themselves in literature, religion, poetry and politics, and then spent hours more in discussion. They prompted each other to ponder a line from a Beddoes poem: 'If there were dreams to sell / what would you buy.' Their answers ranged from the personal and mundane to their hopes for their country. Under Jawaharlal's tutelage, Nan wrote essays on a range of topics and began to amass a rhetorical arsenal.[47]

When Nan was fourteen, she met and got to know Kamala Kaul, who had gotten engaged to Jawaharlal. Kamala was from Delhi but came to Allahabad, where she stayed with her aunt so that she might get accustomed to the Nehrus and their lifestyle. It was a difficult adjustment. Kamala was by nature demure and discreet. Anand Bhawan, conversely, was a bit like a railway station, with people hustling and bustling about in a great flurry of excitement. The lavish displays seemed vulgar. Still, she made the best of it, and planning for the wedding proceeded.

Motilal, for his part, remained blissfully, and perhaps wilfully, unaware of his future daughter-in-law's discomfort with the over-the-top display. He designed and oversaw the manufacture of dazzling bejewelled ornaments he planned to give her. Kamala and Jawaharlal had to have the finest of everything. The wedding was fixed for the first day of spring in February 1916. Motilal arranged for a special train to take guests and family members from Allahabad to Delhi, where the ceremony was to take place. It was one of the grandest parties ever thrown.[48]

That summer, the family visited Kashmir for the first time. Jawaharlal, always an adventurous spirit, decided to go trekking in the nearby mountains with his friends. They hoped to see the famous Amarnath Cave, a legendary Hindu pilgrimage site where Shiva and Parvati are said to have shared the great secrets of the universe. Shiva was said to manifest in the cave in the form of an ice *lingam*.

To get to the caves, the expedition, led by a guide, had to cross a mountain and several glaciers. En route, Jawaharlal fell through a large crack in the ice, and was saved only by the rope that connected him to his fellow hikers. Undaunted, the friends carried on, but eventually had to turn back without seeing the cave as they had hoped. Still the visit did not end without the witness of divine grace for the Nehrus. It was on this same trip that Nan had her encounter with the cobra.[49]

~

In April 1916, in the weeks before the Nehrus travelled to Kashmir, a small band of resisters revolted against British rule in Ireland. The Easter Rebellion, as it came to be known, was swiftly and brutally put down. What it was about this moment that she found fascinating she could not say, but in it, as opposed to the ongoing World War, Nan found a new kind of inspiration.[50]

The same month as the Irish Rebellion, Tilak launched the Home Rule League in Bombay, provincially focused, and now calling for autonomous self-rule in India. In September, Annie Besant decided to create another chapter to cover the rest of India, this one based in Madras.[51] Nan was enthralled and looked to sign up immediately. Too young, she opted to volunteer in her hometown office where she was given various clerical tasks. Still, she felt that she was a part of something much greater. It filled her with pride and purpose. Her brother, sensing this, later gifted her a pin emblazoned with the emerald and ruby-encrusted initials 'H.R'.[52]

In December, Nan travelled to Lucknow for her first meeting of the Indian National Congress. It was an eventful turning point. Muhammad Ali Jinnah, who had joined Besant in the creation of the Home Rule League, now formally brought the Muslim League into an alliance with the Congress through the Lucknow Pact. Nan noted his elegance but detected a touch of haughtiness too.

She was agog the entire event, watching her heroes, Besant and Naidu, in action. They were both mesmerizing with their oratorical prowess, and Nan set a new goal for herself: to speak and to command the stage like them.

She was much less impressed with another speaker, who seemed odd and out of place to her. Recently returned from South Africa, Mohandas K. Gandhi was someone she felt she just could not understand.[53]

Gokhale, who always doted on Nan during his frequent visits to Anand Bhawan, had been campaigning until he died in early 1915 against the treatment of Indian migrants in South Africa. The community had grown there over the years, starting as supportive labour for British colonial settlers. Over time, though, Indians expanded into many spheres of activity and sparked British resentment as a result. Official and unofficial forms of discrimination grew in intensity. Gandhi had achieved fame for his campaigns there, but it was Gokhale who made the issue relatable to Nan.[54]

~

Nan found inspiration closer to home as well. She had two cousins by marriage who had emerged as fiery political activists, Rameshwari and Uma Nehru. Rameshwari, whose brother was Nan's fiancé, had launched the Allahabad Women's Society (Prayag Mahila Samiti), drawing an astonishing seventy-five women to the first meeting. She subsequently helped to start *Stri Darpan* (The Women's Mirror), an influential Hindi magazine dedicated to women's issues.[55] Uma was perhaps the most radical and provocative of the Nehru women at that time, writing regularly for *Stri Darpan* and for another publication called *Maryada*, where she called out patriarchy for enslaving women. 'We will not accept it any longer!' she forthrightly declared.[56]

Throughout 1917, Uma and Rameshwari agitated and made waves, even securing the attention of the Viceroy, Lord Chelmsford. They used this connection to push for women's suffrage.[57] In the meantime, they used *Stri Darpan* to amplify the message of the Women's Indian Association, a new national institution established by Besant and fellow Theosophical Society members Dorothy Jinarajadasa and Margaret Cousins. Cousins was a feminist internationalist, and equally concerned with both the liberation of women and of India.[58]

Nan attended meetings in Allahabad on occasion. Though her role was limited to serving water and tending to babies, she felt as though she were participating in something larger.[59]

By the end of the year, just as she turned eighteen, she found another kind of excitement at home. Jawaharlal and Kamala welcomed their first and only child into the world, daughter Indira Priyadarshini Nehru.

~

Nan was growing into a stunningly beautiful young woman with black, wavy hair and a vivacious smile, backed by a keen mind, quick wit and big personality. She began to draw the notice of men. Most passed innocently enough.[60] But this changed in 1919 when she met someone unlike anyone she had encountered before. His name was Syud Hossain.

Nan had always been free to do as she pleased, raised with an ecumenical approach. She had been taught to mingle as equals with people of all religions, castes and communities. During her late teens, she drew further inspiration from the liberalizing, radicalizing voices of the Nehru women, as she watched her cousins upend long-held conventions about marriage and the place of women in the home.

Hossain was a handsome, sophisticated Muslim journalist who had moved back to India from London in 1916. He had been abroad for several years studying. Upon his return, he took up residence in Bombay, and joined the *Bombay Chronicle* as associate editor.

The *Chronicle* was a powerful and provocative publication. It had been established in 1910 by Sir Pherozeshah Mehta, one of the founding members of the Indian National Congress, and a former president of the organization. Like Motilal, Mehta's inclinations were towards moderation, seeking broadly to work within the existing colonial system to better the lot of native peoples in a variety of ways. In 1913, Mehta had hired Benjamin Guy Horniman, known as B.G., to run the *Chronicle* as its editor. Horniman, a Briton who had taken up residence in India, had a well-earned reputation as a moderate, though in truth he held a much harsher opinion of his home country and its methods of governance than his new-found employer. His sympathies lay with those calling for more lasting and widespread changes, like Tilak and Annie Besant. When Mehta died in 1915, Horniman felt free to express his opinions more openly. Once the Home Rule Leagues got off the ground, Horniman joined Besant and served as vice president, and the *Chronicle* started mirroring its editor's fiery anti-colonialism.[61]

Hossain was dapper and debonaire, the son of a scholar and the grandson of Nawab Abdul Latif Khan Bahadur, a decorated Bengali educator. He was preternaturally gifted with words, both written and spoken. Working together with Horniman, he helped make the *Chronicle* a respected, admired and feared brand.

Hossain too got involved with the Home Rule League. Annie Besant selected him to participate in a mission to the United Kingdom in 1918, where he was to help deliver the League's message directly to the British people. But the delegation never completed their trip. They were halted en route by British forces and arrested. Hossain had his passport impounded, and he was sent back to India.

Motilal, meanwhile, had gradually strayed from his moderate roots as well. He held Gandhi in high esteem and found himself drawn ever deeper into the world of politics.[62] By early 1919, he decided to establish a new newspaper to help further the greater cause. He turned to Horniman for advice and assistance.

No expense too great, Motilal poured money into the new venture, the *Independent*, offering stratospheric salaries to lure established journalists from other papers.[63] And with Horniman's blessing, he hired Syud Hossain away from the *Chronicle*, as the new newspaper's editor.

Hossain moved to Allahabad to work on the paper and immediately made waves. He had a flair for eye-catching headlines, and even more incendiary prose, both of which attracted government attention.

His work brought him into frequent contact with Motilal, who soon invited the young man to stay in Anand Bhawan as he adjusted to life in Allahabad. And that is how he came to Nan's attention. His elegance and eloquence were characteristics she revered, and the two struck up a passionate relationship, though he was thirteen years her elder. The attraction was powerful and mutual. Within three months the two decided to get married.⁶⁴ 'In an era that proclaimed Hindu-Muslim unity and belonging to a family that had close Muslim friends, I must have thought it would be perfectly natural to marry outside my religion,' Nan later recalled.⁶⁵

The ceremony was intimate and 'informal', as Hossain confided to Sarojini Naidu.⁶⁶ There was none of the usual Nehru fanfare. In fact, none of the family had even been informed. But once the formalities were completed, the newlyweds then made their way back to Anand Bhawan to share the news, only to find unyielding opposition to their union.

Motilal was upset with both of them, but particularly with Hossain for betraying his trust. But he also wanted to handle the matter delicately. Hossain was asked to step down from the *Independent*. '[I]n matters such as marriage the times were deeply traditional,' Nan wrote, 'and I was persuaded that this [marriage to Hossain] would be wrong'.⁶⁷

Swarup Rani was just as taken aback by the entire affair as her husband. She 'felt . . . [Nan's] Western-oriented upbringing encouraged . . . [her] in unorthodox ways'. Both parents agreed that some kind of intervention was required, and so they sent Nan and Hossain to stay with Gandhi, now widely known as the Mahatma (Great Soul) at his ashram on the banks of the Sabarmati River in Ahmedabad.⁶⁸

Once the two of them were securely under Gandhi's care, he began to lecture each of them on their choices, and their broader duties. 'How could you . . . regard Syud in *any* other light but that of a brother—what right had you to allow yourself, even for a minute, to look with love at a Mussalman,' he asked her. 'Out of nearly twenty crores of Hindus couldn't you find a single one who came up to your ideals—but you must . . . pass them all over and throw yourself into the arms of a *Mohammedan*!!!'

Nan blanched at these arguments. 'Poor man! To him it is inconceivable for a Hindu and a Mussalman to marry and live happily,' she wrote to Padmaja Naidu. Gandhi persisted, telling Nan how he would have behaved in her place. This 'didn't carry much weight' with Nan. She sarcastically declared after parroting certain lines: 'Ahem! Isn't that a nice, ladylike speech and worthy of a Hindu girl—the descendant of a thousand Rishis?!!!' She told Padmaja: 'if

I started telling you the good Mahatmaji's objections I should fill a few hundred pages.' Gandhi conjured a world of rules and norms, of patriarchy, and of conservative politics, none of which Nan could abide. It was the world, and India, as it for the most part was, but not as she saw it or wanted it to be. To her, in that moment, the Mahatma was regressive and reactionary, and so simply could not be taken seriously.[69]

~

Nan did not adjust easily to ashram life with its rigorous simplicity. She was shorn of her luxuries. There was no staff to assist her through her day. In fact, here she was required to conduct chores throughout the day, which began at 4 a.m. with prayers.

Mornings were spent sweeping, cleaning and doing laundry by the river. Everyone at the ashram was required to clean the latrines, which was of high symbolic value. Throughout the region, the task was generally restricted to select communities who then suffered for performing it, as part of widespread caste discrimination. Gandhi wanted to show the value and dignity of the work and the absurdity of relegating people to a lower status for doing it.

Such ideals were far from Nan's mind when she saw what had to be done. To ease her into this very different lifestyle, Gandhi initially exempted her from this work, for which she 'offered thanks to the Almighty'.

Afternoons were spent on a range of other matters. She was required to study for some time, and then assist with errands and other small tasks in the office, from where Gandhi published his newspaper *Young India*. The dairy needed looking after, to take care of animals, clean quarters, or draw milk. And there was a daily allotment of spinning.

When replicated many times over, spinning was an act of mass defiance and self-control, illustrating the key Gandhian precept of *satyagraha* (Truth Force). Gandhi believed that injustice would retreat in the face of itself, because people generally, deep down, wanted to be good, and perceived themselves that way. Satyagraha was pursued every day and in every way. It served as the basis of daily routines, and of large-scale campaigns against systemic, social ills.

Perhaps food was the most challenging aspect of the ashram life for Nan. She was used to the finest of delicacies and especially loved the art of preparation. She saw the ashram as wanting 'to kill one's desire for food'. Meals were limited to steamed vegetables with hand-ground chapatis (unleavened bread) or unpolished rice. There was no tea or coffee or salt or sugar or spice or butter. 'Certainly no one in the ashram was in danger of putting on weight,' she wryly observed.

At 6 p.m., everyone participated in multi-faith prayers. Gandhi drew from the Bhagavad Gita and the Quran as well as Christian, Parsi, Buddhist, and Sikh sources.

Nan stayed with Gandhi in his hut, and the two would sleep out on his veranda at night, spending hours discussing theology and matters of Hindu faith.

Despite the time they spent together, she mostly found him stubborn and impossible, and committed to a range of practices she simply could not condone. Aside from his obdurate interventions in her own affairs, which she found antediluvian, she recalled years later that two young people stayed at the ashram, fell in love and slept together. Gandhi saw this as a sin and demanded penance. Nan could not recall how the young man was punished, if at all, but the young woman's hair was shorn. Gandhi himself fasted for several days in atonement. Nan saw sex as natural, and human intimacy personal and beautiful. She cringed at Gandhi's 'primeval' notions, and the two had many arguments. It would take more time for her to develop appreciation and affection for the Mahatma, or for her to see the value in the Spartan lifestyle she was forced to endure in the ashram.

After suffering these trials, she returned to Allahabad, single and sullen. 'Serious trouble' emerged between Motilal and Nan, each equally unhappy with the other in very deep ways. Reconciliation would take time. Things only changed months later when she found herself once more in the thrall of a mysterious stranger.[70]

CHAPTER TWO

# The Portrait of a Lady

Nan found life complicated on her return to Anand Bhawan. Dewan Bahadur Narendranath, the father of Nan's childhood fiancée Anand Kumar (and of his sister, Rameshwari Nehru), broke off the pre-arranged engagement.[1] Rumours of her relationship had begun to spread. Both Nan and her father wondered what impact the gossip might have on her reputation, and if the consequences could be long-lasting and harmful.[2]

With Gandhi's backing, Motilal decided to engineer a solution. Jawaharlal had a steadfast friend and admirer from Trinity who had returned to India and become a barrister. He was elegant and athletic, with the soul of a scholar. He was also a Saraswat Brahmin like Nan, though from Maharashtra. Motilal thought he might make a good match for his daughter, within the overall norms but perhaps just transgressive enough for her tastes. He invited the young man to visit Anand Bhawan.

Ranjit Sitaram Pandit arrived in Allahabad late one evening in November 1920 but was up so early the next morning that he was the first at the breakfast table set up on the veranda. Once the larger family had finished their meal, he was able to speak to Nan alone. 'Do you like Sanskrit poetry?' he began.

They chitchatted for a bit more before he confessed, 'You are very beautiful, and I have come here only to meet you. I suppose you have guessed that.' She relaxed a bit at the honesty.

It was the perfect day: clear blue skies with a magnificent sun, flowers all around in bloom. The two toured the gardens and got to know each other. He told her about himself, and of his family, interspersing verse now and again for effect.

She decided to show off a bit too, and suggested they go riding. She was pleasantly surprised to learn that Ranjit was as good as she was.

They developed a fast repartee, even amidst all the hubbub of Anand Bhawan, which was busier than usual with guests to celebrate Indira Nehru's third birthday. When there was finally a quiet moment, Ranjit proposed: 'It is only two days since we met, but I have thought about you for a long time and feel as if I know you. It has taken me some courage to come from far-off Kathiwar to the home of the Nehrus to meet a daughter of Kashmir. But I have traveled with hope. Could you trust me enough to travel in hand in hand with me through life?'

Nan had not discussed the matter with Motilal or Swarup Rani, but she had surmised that Ranjit's visit had been arranged by her parents with the prospect of marriage in mind. She clasped his hands and said, 'Let us always travel together.'[3]

~

Some in India saw the breakup of the Ottoman Empire, and the removal of the caliph, as an expansion of Western imperialism. Following the end of the Great War's hostilities in 1918, and because of the secret Sykes-Picot agreement, Britain and France came to occupy and partition Ottoman lands, triggering in 1919 a war of independence. The status of the Ottoman caliph was threatened by this turn of events, despite an initial promise by the victors in the Treaty of Versailles to protect his position.

The brothers Mohammad and Shaukat Ali joined with friends to establish the All-India Khilafat Committee in Lucknow, approximately 200 kilometres north of Allahabad. They urged people to come to the aid of their fellow Muslims. The call quickly caught fire, and a movement to save the caliph was born.[4]

Gandhi lent his support to Khilafat, creating synergy between that campaign and his own. The non-cooperation movement—launched in 1920 in response to the Montagu-Chelmsford reforms, the Rowlatt Bills, and the Jallianwala Bagh (Amritsar) massacre—catapulted Gandhi to fame. People all over the region came to see in him not just a champion, but a saviour.[5]

The Indian National Congress shed its moderate beginnings and embraced Gandhi's new agenda and radical call to action. Simple petitions and restrained smoking-room debates were out, replaced by public engagement and showy demonstrations of resistance. Motilal and Jawaharlal now were at the forefront of a revolution.

~

Nan and Ranjit spent the months after their initial encounter and engagement getting to know one another, enjoying each other's company. While national affairs were never far removed, the young couple did their best to focus their attention on their budding relationship.

Much to Swarup Rani's chagrin, Ranjit had given Nan a worn copy of the Bhagavad Gita as an initial engagement present rather than a diamond ring or other ornament (though these would follow later). Years later, Nan came to see the Gita as a kind of talisman, collecting various editions as gifts over the years and embodying in many ways its call to action. As he handed it to her, Ranjit noted that this was his most precious possession, for it had belonged to his father.[6]

Family stories held that the Pandits had originated in Kashmir, the same as the Nehrus. But they migrated to Maharashtra through the Konkan region on the western coast and settled there. Sitaram Pandit was the middle child among twelve other siblings. Brilliant, he secured a scholarship to study in England, where he passed the bar. Upon his return home, and following marriage, he shifted for work reasons to Rajkot, the capital city of the princely states agency of Kathiawar, in what is today the Gujarati peninsula.

Sitaram was much like Motilal: gregarious, big-hearted and generous to a fault. While he did not share the Nehrus' sense of grandiosity and instead preferred much more simple living, this did not diminish the flow of visitors through his home. He doled out money, especially to educational institutions from various faiths, and to famine-relief agencies.

The rest of the family was equally talented, possessing renaissance abilities: they were generally scholarly, modern in outlook but with deep mastery of classical traditions, and terrifically athletic.[7] Ranjit's uncle, Shankar Pandurang Pandit, was a renowned scholar who spoke eighteen languages and served a stint as *dewan* (prime minister) of Porbandar, the princely state on the west coast where Gandhi was born. Gandhi's uncle had also served as a dewan of the state, and the two families were close. Shankar Pandit's son, Ranjit's cousin Vamanrao, was a talented artist trained at Vienna, Dresden, Venice, France, Hungary, and ultimately the Royal Academy in London.[8] He painted several portraits of the aristocracy from across India.

Women in the household embraced this moderately bohemian lifestyle: Ranjit's mother also learned to ride horses so she could accompany her husband on his work journeys. His cousin, Vamanrao's sister Kshamabai Row, was a Sanskrit scholar and writer. Yet traditionalism also led the family to celebrate a fraught legacy: Ranjit's great-grandmother was lauded and commemorated for committing *sati* at the death of her husband, immolating herself alive on his funeral pyre.

Like his father and much of the rest of his family, Ranjit himself was a polymath. He graduated from Bombay University with distinction, earning him the right to study abroad. He chose a more unusual route than many of his peers, for though he began as many of them did with an Oxbridge education, at Christ Church Oxford, he went on to study at the Sorbonne and the University of Heidelberg, acquiring a more continental perspective and temperament. He was soon called to the bar by the Middle Temple in London, and thereafter returned to India.[9]

Gifted in both Indian and European musical traditions, Ranjit was also a singer of some merit, and played the violin as well. His equestrian skills were exceptional, matching Nan's, and he was also handy with a rifle. Above all, he adored history and the study of classical texts, Sanskrit being the favourite of the eleven languages he spoke fluently.[10]

Ranjit Pandit's calm nature and wide-ranging talents complemented Nan's insatiable curiosity and high-octane personality. They fell deeply in love with each other.

~

The wedding was fixed for 9 May 1921, the sixty-fourth anniversary of the Rebellion. The buzz around the event was very high, not only because it was another Nehru wedding, but also because the Indian National Congress executive, its Committee, was meeting in Allahabad at the same time. Edward VIII, the Prince of Wales, was scheduled to visit India that November, and the Congress High Command had to decide how best to respond. Most of India's political leadership descended on the city and were in turn invited to the wedding. Nan later described the whole thing as 'a simple affair'.

In the weeks leading up to the ceremony, gifts for the young couple, including Irish linens, Italian embroidered tablecloths, and an array of furniture and silverware, began to arrive from all quarters. Motilal tossed in a few small tokens of his own, like a new horse, and a new car as well. Swarup Rani assembled a magnificent trousseau for her daughter: 101 lavishly tailored saris, many of them gem-encrusted, and complemented with a range of other ornaments and gold jewellery.

Swarup Rani paid the greatest attention to Nan's wedding sari. Kashmiri women traditionally wore pink, silk saris, with heavy embroidery, for weddings. The grandeur of the sari was meant to reflect the resplendence of the bride. So it came as a shock to the family then, when Mahatma Gandhi informed them that Nan should wear *khadi* or homespun cotton.

Since his arrival back in India in 1915, Gandhi had spent time travelling around the country, seeking to understand the nature of life for everyday people. Over time, he deciphered key mechanisms of British administrative and disciplinary control and came to better understand what kept the local population in bondage. He saw that the imperial structure thrived off an intricate system of economically exploitative controls that actively impoverished people in the subcontinent while enriching colonial masters. And it was Indian consent that facilitated all of this, driven by fear, but also freely given. The non-cooperation movement developed from these insights. If Indians would just stop building their own prisons, they could be free.

Peasants throughout India were forced to grow various cash crops, including indigo and cotton, manipulated by landlords, taxation policies and import/export rules. The net effect was to reduce subsistence farming and destroy arable land in the process, thereby creating millions of destitute, starving souls. Gandhi saw reducing consumption of foreign cloth, and empowering every person, large and small, to manufacture textiles, by spinning raw material on small handlooms, as an active form of resistance that negatively impacted the imperial bottom dollar. It had the added benefit of giving hope to the despondent and building the kind of pride that comes from productive, self-satisfying community-building work. Just as importantly, spinning built character and skills: it required patience, perseverance and stamina, and fostered determination and resilience.

But homespun lacked finesse. It was often produced in small strips, generally was very coarse, and could not hold dye. It was not at all appropriate for a bridal sari. Swarup Rani grew angry at Gandhi for interfering in what she saw as a deeply personal family matter. She saw those she loved being drawn ever closer into his orbit, and the world she knew fading away. Politically, this may have been okay, but there had to be limits, she thought, especially on internal family matters.

So, the small package that arrived a few days later was a welcome surprise. Kasturba Gandhi, the Mahatma's partner and wife, had herself spun and handwoven a delicate cotton sari of the requisite width and length. It was perfect for dying pink. The gift conveyed affection and respect, and was princely in an obverse way, a mark of hours of labour and master craftwork that carried with them the aspirations of an impoverished country on the move.

On the big day, Nan was decorated with flowers—her fancy ornaments were forbidden as well. There, in her majestic home, surrounded by friends and family, and before a congregation of eminent personalities, Nan married Ranjit.

The large, political crowd gathered on the prominent estate on the anniversary of a historic uprising alarmed local officials, who feared a new plot of some kind was afoot. The police were alerted, and so they too, in a way, attended the wedding, as uninvited observers, keeping a close eye on all the commotion.

The ceremony lasted several hours, the *muhurthum*, or auspicious moment at which the official joining rituals were performed, occurring after midnight. Gandhi, who was in attendance, had kept to his schedule and gone off to bed early.

The newlyweds awoke him after the ceremony to seek his blessings. They were easily given, but then the Mahatma began to speak of the country's needs and the great challenge before them. Personal control, the command of the self—swaraj—these would give the *satyagrahi* the inner powers needed to triumph, he said, linking individual puritanism with national and global awakening.

What all this boiled down to in that key moment: Gandhi started talking about the virtues of chastity. Nan found herself falling under the old man's spell, just as everyone seemed to, and noticed that Ranjit was perhaps even more easily seduced. She jolted back to her senses. 'Why did you give your permission to our marriage if you thought it was wrong for us to live together as husband and wife? I love Ranjit and I want a normal married life,' she snapped. Stunned at her own insolence, she stared out in silence, awaiting the harsh admonition she felt was sure to come.

Gandhi instead sighed and smiled lovingly. 'So, you love Ranjit,' he asked triumphantly. See to it then that you do not distract him from his duty!' He smacked her cheek gently and dismissed the couple.[11]

~

As part of the elaborate rituals, Ranjit's family gave Nan a new name, one that signified the union with her new husband, and the complementary relationship they were to share. Ranjit meant 'the victorious', so something was to be chosen that could embellish this idea.

Nan had always disliked her given name and so embraced this opportunity to refashion herself. Sarup Kumari Nehru was no more. While she would remain Nan to all who knew her personally, thenceforth for 'all public and official purposes' she was, after the Goddess of Victory, Vijaya Lakshmi Pandit.

~

Shortly after the wedding, Nan and Ranjit travelled together to Calcutta, where Ranjit practised law as a junior team member of prominent advocate, Sir B.L. Mitter. They acquired an apartment and rented out several blocks of rooms at the Grand Hotel, a spectacular establishment on Chowringhee Road in the heart of the city that truly lived up to its name.

Ranjit's family was keen for him to continue in his career, and to achieve great things through his work. He himself had not yet decided whether that was what he truly wanted, for he felt there was a larger calling. Still, young and newly married, he and Nan did not want to worry about their responsibilities, and so they initially continued with the lavish lifestyle they were used to. To keep up their resplendent surroundings, they maintained a small staff that included a maid, a valet, a chauffeur and a colourfully uniformed attendant.

Just three months later, after the court adjourned for the summer, the Pandits decided to travel to Rajkot on the opposite coast to stay with Ranjit's family. While there, they confronted a difficult decision: Gandhi had called on lawyers to stop participating in the court system, arguing that the legal structure did not serve the interests of the people at large under the current conditions. Obeying this command meant a loss of property, which Ranjit shared with his brother Pratap, and very likely the end of a highly lucrative career. After much debate and consternation, Ranjit realized that he knew what he was going to do all along.

~

Back in Allahabad, Motilal too faced the same choice, and like his son-in-law, he wondered if he might not best serve the cause by continuing in his practice and donating money. 'But it is you I want,' Gandhi replied. And so it came to pass. Motilal, who prided himself on his zest for the finer things in life, now turned his back on it all, to follow in the footsteps of the man he now accepted as the Mahatma.

Just a few weeks later, Motilal and Jawaharlal were arrested and sentenced to six months imprisonment for boycotting Edward VIII's visit to Allahabad, in keeping with the instructions of the Congress Committee. Many of their friends and associates were also rounded up.

Nan and Ranjit raced back from Rajkot once they received the news. Nan felt the multi-day journey interminable, and so was understandably bothered when she found out that her sibling and father had been taken to Lucknow, resulting in a journey of several more hours. Swarup Rani, along with Kamala and Betty, was there already.

The family fretted about how Swarup Rani would handle the entire affair, her beloved family torn asunder, and she put in a position she never imagined. After a week in Lucknow, Nan and Ranjit brought the rest of their family back to Anand Bhawan, in the hope of returning her mother to some semblance of stability. But the world they knew was gone.

They downsized staff and shuttered portions of their great house. Motilal and Jawaharlal had been ordered to pay some fines, amounting to Rs 1000. But Gandhi had ordered that no such fines were to be paid. Satyagrahis were to bear the full brunt of punishment for their just but illegal actions, for only then could the injustice of the entire system be revealed. Gandhi believed that unjust suffering, borne willingly and openly, without resistance, could penetrate the hearts of people shrouded by lies and deceit, and thereby, eventually, bring about holistic non-violent change. Since the fines were not paid, the police were ordered to enter Anand Bhawan and seize property as recompense for the violation. This too no one was to oppose in any way. Thus, given a free hand, the police who subsequently entered the premises behaved boorishly, ransacking the house. All of the fine things that had been so tastefully arranged—'carpets, pieces of furniture, and ornaments'—each hand-picked to complement the other, were hauled off to auction.

Nan stood by watching all of this. Over the coming years, she would occasionally find her family's things in the homes of various acquaintances, and though she would say nothing directly, she could not help but observe that none of them had any real 'appreciation' for what they had, as she later confessed.

The elegance was replaced with a new egalitarianism, the soirees and salons giving way to sober-minded Congress volunteers consumed with their work. Anand Bhawan went from an opulent private residence to a rebel base almost overnight.

The family adopted the uniform of the general worker, khadi. Bedspreads, sheets and towels, all had to be of this material. But for all of this to have a meaningful impact, Gandhi had also called for boycotting foreign cloth, to strike directly at a key British money-making enterprise upholding the colonial system. Gandhi especially called on women to participate in this campaign, to picket local shops that continued to sell such merchandise. Betty and Kamala signed on.

The Nehrus further responded by destroying all they had collected in their wardrobes over the years. The stunning saris, perfectly tailored dresses and Motilal's fabled Saville Row suits were carted out in trucks to be publicly burned. Swarup Rani thought all this was too much. Even Ranjit, madly devoted to Gandhi and Jawaharlal, opted to keep his Middle Temple blazer out of sentiment. Nan, still finding her voice, and her place in all of this, said nothing, but secretly applauded her mother and husband for not going along quietly. When she looked back on all this years later, she laughed at her innocent churlishness, knowing by then just how important the purging was.[12]

The changes in daily routine were dramatic. The family was accustomed to tennis, hunting, and great banquets, but gave them all up. Most of them became vegetarian and experimented with skipping meals. Ranjit struggled with all of this, his mind willing but his body unable to cope, so he, like Motilal, continued to eat meat. But this was the easy part. He had given up his practice and so had long, unscheduled days to fill. He could neither work nor play, and quickly grew bored and irritable, and he and Nan began to squabble over minor matters, idle minds turning the trivial into the terrible. Gandhi again intervened and urged the Pandits to take a role in his constructive programme, to go back to Rajkot to expand khadi operations, and to lead a campaign against one of India's deadliest blights: untouchability.

~

Gandhi began writing about the problem of untouchability, and of broader social discrimination in 1920, just at the outset of the non-cooperation movement. He did not find the idea of caste in and of itself to be a problem, since he saw organizing around kinship and work as an extension of the family unit and ergo, at least in the abstract, as having a 'scientific basis'.[13] But he saw any discrimination based on one's caste as something to be repudiated and accepted that this had become a key component of the caste system, even as he called on people to embrace their respective identities. Untouchability, above all, he thought was evil, and something that had to be fought against with all due diligence. As Gandhi began talking about these issues, then at the height of his universal appeal throughout the region, his opinions were read as radical and just, furthering the saint-like image he had begun to acquire.

Very few at the start of the twenties could imagine strong opposition to Gandhi's position, or his claim to stand as a champion of caste equality, yet a new representative of the downtrodden was even then making waves with his much more searing critique of caste and its causes. Just over a decade later, Dr B.R. 'Babasaheb' Ambedkar would come to see Gandhi as a recalcitrant conservative and a great foe of a truly egalitarian India.

~

Ranjit found a renewed sense of purpose back in Rajkot. Nan, on the other hand, felt more uncertain than ever about her path, wanting to contribute to the larger political effort, but also wanting to enjoy life with her husband. Torn between these two things, and still young at heart, she leaned into the more frivolous aspects of her life. She found the work 'dull', at least initially.

Even so, out of a deep sense of loyalty to her family and Gandhi, she dedicated herself to the tasks at hand. Together, she and Ranjit 'organized spinning and weaving centres', their star power attracting locals to the cause as well.

Over the course of the next year, talking to ordinary workers and farmers whose lives were far removed from the glittering estates of Allahabad's Civil Lines, the Pandits 'came to know . . . [the] people and problems . . . [they] had not previously spent much thought on'. They built schools and launched a series of initiatives 'to arouse social conscience and open up opportunities' for those suffering caste discrimination or who were otherwise 'underprivileged'.

Just as Nan and Ranjit were settling into this work, Gandhi called an end to the non-cooperation movement at the national level, after a protest in the Gorakhpur district of the United Provinces turned violent, resulting in police deaths. Though he was not to blame, Gandhi assumed responsibility for it. Motilal and Jawaharlal were upset when they learned from prison that Gandhi had called off the movement, and they wrote to him expressing their concerns. Gandhi replied, sending his letter to Nan, and it was she who in turn travelled to Lucknow to read the letter to her father and brother. 'In this letter,' she recalled, 'Gandhiji explained that if he had not ended the civil disobedience movement the struggle would have lost its character and become a violent one all over the country and that the national cause would prosper as a result of his action, however illogical it seemed.'[14]

Within a few weeks, Gandhi was arrested and charged with sedition.[15] At the famous one-day trial that followed, Gandhi said 'he was in court to submit cheerfully to the highest penalty which could be inflicted'. The judge, Gandhi said, could 'either resign if he felt the law he was called upon to administer was evil and Gandhi was innocent or to inflict the most severe penalty if he believed Gandhi's activity injurious to the public weal'. The judge replied that 'it was impossible to ignore the fact that in the eyes of millions of his countrymen, Gandhi was a great patriotic leader and a man of high ideals leading a noble, even saintly life', but it was nevertheless his 'duty' to 'judge him as a man who admitted he had broken the law'.[16] Gandhi accepted the verdict of the court just as he advised his compatriots to absorb physical blows: willingly and with gladness in his heart.

This incredible turn of events shook the country, but Nan had more pressing matters to attend to. She was now pregnant with her first child. She continued with her work with Ranjit in Rajkot, before travelling back to Allahabad in January 1923 for delivery. Motilal hired a doctor decorated with many degrees and had all the latest hospital equipment brought into Anand Bhawan. Despite such great care, Nan developed sepsis and almost died during the 'prolonged and very difficult labour'.

Nan gave birth to a baby girl on the twenty-third. She and Ranjit named the child Vatsala (Beloved) after Ranjit's recently deceased mother. Nan and Ranjit were thrilled by the new addition, and doted on her, but their joy was not to last. Just nine months later, with her parents on either side of her, the baby lay very still. 'Suddenly she turned toward me,' Nan remembered decades later with crystal clarity. The baby 'looked into my eyes—her own were meaningful and were conveying a message as clearly as if she had spoken. She was saying good-bye. She looked at Ranjit the same way, and I saw two tears roll down his cheeks. Vatsala died a few minutes later'.[17]

~

Nan was about three months pregnant at the time of her first child's passing. Six months later in Bombay, she gave birth on *Shivratri*, the Night of Shiva, and named her daughter Chandralekha (Crescent Moon), to honour the God also recognized as the protector of the moon.

Gandhi, as it happened, had had an emergency appendectomy while serving his prison sentence at Yerawada in Pune and was released on medical grounds. He came to Bombay to recover by the sea. Motilal, himself out of prison, Kamala and Betty all travelled to the resort of Juhu to look after their friend and leader, and Nan joined them as well, appreciating the opportunity to be together with her newborn and family. Motilal wanted to take advantage of the second wave of Montagu-Chelmsford reforms, which now allowed Indians to run for election to local legislative councils. Gandhi was not convinced that any of this would be meaningful, but he gave Motilal his blessing to launch the Swaraj party under the larger Congress umbrella, in order to field candidates for the newly opened positions in what came to be known as the Council Entry programme.

Nan for her part wanted to focus on her young family. She and Ranjit bought a house at 9 Cawnpore Road in Allahabad, close to Anand Bhawan, and looked to settle into some semblance of domestic life. But being a Nehru meant that larger political affairs were never too far removed.[18]

~

In 1925, a growing animus between Hindus and Muslims manifested in a series of riots in major cities all over northern British India, including in Allahabad. Gandhi intervened to calm the situation. He believed that all people were connected, and shared a bond of Love, which he saw as equivalent to Truth and the Divine. He thought that an act of self-sacrifice or self-harm, done out of true affection for other people and in service of them, would tighten the bond they shared, and compel them from within to act righteously. He thus declared a twenty-one-day fast, out of remorse for what was transpiring and to atone for it. Gandhi's actions had an immediate salutary effect—just as they had before and just as they would again in the future in an even more spectacular manner—and the situation, at least temporarily, calmed down. Nan was with Gandhi when he broke his fast.[19]

~

That December, Sarojini Naidu was elected president of the Indian National Congress, succeeding Mahatma Gandhi, and becoming the second woman in the post after Annie Besant, and the first Indian woman. Gandhi wryly observed that 'a mere woman displaces a mere man'.[20]

Following her inauguration, Naidu threw herself into 'Congress work'. She toured around northern India as part of her presidential duties, using Anand Bhawan as a command post. Nan often accompanied her around Allahabad, soaking in her ministrations, perspicaciously picking up on every heartfelt gesture, every humorous deflection and every sing-song word.[21]

~

Nan and Ranjit had not yet had a honeymoon and planned a trip to Europe. The Pandits left Chandralekha, now called Lekha for short, with Swarup Rani so they could focus on each other, and all that Europe had to offer. But just as they were preparing to go, they learned that they would have some company for part of their journey.

Kamala Nehru had only a few months earlier fallen 'seriously ill and lay for many months in a Lucknow hospital'. She had advanced tuberculosis, and doctors recommended that she travel to Switzerland for medical care and the benefits of the climate. Jawaharlal felt quite depleted from all he had endured over the past several years and decided to leave India for a bit. Jawaharlal wrote that his 'mind was befogged, and no clear path was visible; and . . . [he] thought that, perhaps, if . . . [he] was far from India . . . [he] could see things in better perspective and lighten up the dark corners of . . . [his] mind'.[22] He decided to take his family, including nine-year-old Indira, abroad to help Kamala recuperate and booked themselves on the same liner his sister was taking.[23]

They travelled with Lloyd Triestino (formerly the Austrian Lloyd, and now Italia Marittima), then known for its elegant and glamorous passenger ships.²⁴ Nan felt comfortable doing so, writing later: 'We were still not used to austerities, to wearing coarse clothes and buying India-made goods no matter how poor in quality, when all our lives we had had the best. It seemed to me, young as I was then, that everything gay and lovely had been cut out of my life.'²⁵ The Pandits intended to treat themselves without consideration of cost. They wanted to be carefree.

~

Once they reached Europe, the Pandits and the Nehrus parted company, reuniting only briefly when Nan and Ranjit visited to check in on Kamala.²⁶ Jawaharlal and his family had gone to Geneva to get his wife into a treatment programme as quickly as possible.

The Nehrus ultimately stayed abroad for one year and nine months, splitting their time between the Alps and the mountains of Montana in the United States. Other family would visit over this time, while Nehru took every opportunity to meet individuals like Romain Rolland and Madame Sun-Yat Sen, and to get involved with an organization soon to be known as the League Against Imperialism.²⁷

The Pandits, meanwhile, played no part in this. They were in Europe only for the first six weeks, during which time they travelled to England, France, and Germany. They made sure to stop in between in Switzerland to check in on Kamala and Jawaharlal as well.

In London, Nan and Ranjit attended a 'gala automobile show' where they ordered a Rolls Royce without thinking. It took a letter from home to remind them that such a thing could not be brought back to India.²⁸

If their dreamy vacation was briefly interrupted by the realities of life in their country, events in Italy shortly thereafter would rudely awaken them to changing international circumstances as well.

Benito Mussolini had spent the last several years eliminating his opposition and consolidating his power. He had become the prime minister in the early 1920s with the support of armed enforcers, the Blackshirts, and gradually tightened his vice. Through an alchemy of bluster and buffoonery, he emerged by the late twenties as Italy's strongman, his fascist party now in total control.

Nan and Ranjit were oblivious. They had come to Rome to soak in as much art and culture as possible, practically living in theatres and concert halls. On 7 April, they visited the Palazzo Nuovo in the spectacular Michelangelo-designed Piazza del Capidoglio. A short while later, Nan found herself in police custody, a suspect in the attempted assassination of Mussolini.

~

Violet Gibson was an Irish Catholic converted from Protestantism. She had led a migratory life, hopscotching around Europe, before landing in Italy in the twenties. She had been wrestling with the meanings of violence and morality, receiving medical attention for her homicidal nature. What exactly drove her that afternoon remains unclear, since she also appeared to have anti-Fascist leanings, but as Mussolini walked past her on Capitoline Hill, she drew a revolver and fired. At just that moment, Mussolini leaned back to wave at the thronging crowd, escaping the bullet. It grazed his nose. Describing the incident a 'trifle', he had his nose bandaged, and continued with his appearance, to the rapturous delight of his admirers gathered there. Violet was arrested, and eventually deported to the United Kingdom where she was locked in an asylum for the rest of her life.[29]

Nan and Ranjit had gotten locked inside the museum when this incident occurred. While everyone else was released soon after, the Pandits were taken in for further questioning of their possible role in the attack on The Leader (Il Duce). Ranjit, fluent in Italian, 'explained . . . we were just tourists and not interested in attacking . . . anyone'. The Italians were not persuaded.

Facing the risk of the accusations becoming more serious, they made the tactical decision to contact the British Embassy for assistance. This was a difficult choice, since 'they had ceased to recognize' the legitimacy of British rule. Yet their imperial passports made this their only option. It felt humiliating to ask for help, but they were also nonetheless grateful when they walked free.[30]

~

International affairs suddenly seemed much less remote. Nan and Ranjit sensed that they had a narrow window to enjoy some semblance of family life, if ever they were to. Back in India, they settled into their home at Cawnpore Road, and devoted themselves to each other, and to their growing family. A few months after their return from Europe, Nan was carrying again, and on 10 May 1927, gave birth to their second child. They named her Nayantara, Star of the Eyes. Two years later, their third daughter, Rita, meaning Truth, completed their family.[31] Nan relished motherhood and showered affection on her children. The Pandit household was filled with love and laughter, and true happiness.

~

Nan and Ranjit were consumed by domestic bliss. They saw out the twenties primarily concerned with the needs of their young girls and other matters of the home. They also contributed to Congress matters in Allahabad and general village engagement work.

But political affairs in India took a dramatic turn in this period. The British reneged on a promise to properly revisit the 'principle of responsible Government', setting off a firestorm of protest throughout the subcontinent.[32] The government responded with a heavy hand, resulting in the deaths of some demonstrators, including the prominent old-guard nationalist, Lala Lajpat Rai. This enraged the population further and led to an opening for more radical responses. Jawaharlal Nehru took a more active role in protests, even taking body blows of his own.[33] He began to call explicitly for independence and grew in popularity as a result. But his relationship with his father, still the moderate, suffered.[34]

In December 1929, when Gandhi turned down entreaties to take the post, Jawaharlal was elected president of Congress. Nan, in attendance, beamed with pride at her brother's elevation.

The Congress immediately adopted a resolution calling for *Purna Swaraj*, or total independence, to be marked on 26 January.[35] They supported calls for a campaign of civil disobedience from Great Britain. In the weeks that followed, Gandhi targeted the country's salt tax and organized a major march to the sea at Dandi.[36]

Viceroy Lord Irwin ordered widespread arrests. Jawaharlal was picked up a week into the campaign and packed off to Naini Central Prison just outside Allahabad. Gandhi was incarcerated in May, and Motilal in June.

Meanwhile, in the north-west, the Pathans, led by Khan Abdul Ghaffar Khan, declared a common cause with Gandhi. As they organized in civil disobedience, Khan and his followers were arrested in keeping with Irwin's broad orders to sweep the Congress leadership off the streets. But people continued to assemble throughout Peshawar city, ultimately choosing the Qissa Khwani Bazaar (Storyteller's Market) as a central gathering point in April 1930. British troops were called in and, in an echo of the Amritsar Massacre from the decade previous, ordered to open fire with machine guns on the crowd following some minor scuffles. The Pathans held to their Gandhian vow and did not fight back, martyring themselves for the greater good.[37]

The Congress appointed a committee to investigate the incident, and named Sardar Vallabhbhai Patel, Gandhi's right hand, to chair. Ranjit was asked to serve as secretary. They departed on their fact-finding mission within weeks.

~

Lord Irwin had hoped that mass imprisonments would crush the resistance. But as men disappeared from the scene, whisked away into the dark, women stepped into the breach. The Nehrus led the way. Betty, Kamala and Uma took charge of various matters, organizing pickets and mobilizing others to join in. Even Swarup Rani got into the act.[38]

Nan's three girls were her immediate priority. She was reluctant to divert her attention, even as she felt compelled to get off the sidelines. Hesitantly, she helped organize a procession to signal continued opposition to the government's reform-proposing Simon Commission (because it lacked any Indian representation). But on the very evening of the march, news spread that an eight-year-old child named Rajpal, a child activist from Lahore, had been 'found drowned [of suspected] foul play'. Nan and others organized an even bigger demonstration the next day. This time, about 600 children were out front, led by six-year-old Chandralekha carrying a flag. Some 400 women and 4000 men followed. Nan delivered a speech to the crowd as they gathered afterwards, exhorting 'all students of whatever age to leave schools and help'. In an instant, she found herself 'definitely committed'.

She pulled Chandralekha from government school in an act of defiance, and now threw herself into work. 'I haven't a second to call my own,' she wrote to Ranjit. '[I] am rushed off my feet from the moment my eyes are opened in the mornings until I go to bed.'

As she started making appearances, Congress handlers sensed star potential. They proposed that she tour across the United Provinces, covering Cawnpore, Benares, Agra, Lucknow and Meerut. Nan found this exciting and agreed. She wrote Ranjit to excuse herself from joining him out in the north-west on his assignment investigating the Qissa Khwani massacre. Instead, she said, she would wait at home for his return, whereupon they would swap places. He was then to watch the children while she took to the road.[39]

~

Motilal Nehru fell seriously ill in 1930.[40] Medical examiners concluded that he was in distress and ordered his early release from prison, just two and half months into his sentence. He returned to Allahabad but not to his old home.

Motilal and Jawaharlal had met up with Gandhi in the middle of the salt march and spent an evening with him. There, Motilal had announced his decision to hand over Anand Bhawan to the national movement and to formally convert the grand old house that once stood for private wealth into a literal symbol of the public trust. Motilal had at once taken care of the preliminary formalities (though it would be another year and a half before the transfer was officially completed). Anand Bhawan was rechristened Swaraj Bhawan, and a smaller but still massive house designed and built elsewhere on the estate—quaintly referred to as a 'cottage'—became the new Anand Bhawan.

~

Almost as if in exchange for Motilal's return, Ranjit was picked up for 'seditious activity'— for his role in documenting the slaughter at Qissa Khwani. Nayantara, then three years old, recalled the episode with such vividness, she later named her first memoir after it. The police arrived while the family was having chocolate cake, rather than their ordinary bread and butter, with their afternoon tea. When the children asked what was happening, Nan told them matter-of-factly that the officers had come to take their father to prison, but that it was alright because Ranjit wanted to go. So, they kissed their father farewell, 'cheerfully' chatted with the police, and continued unbothered with eating their special treat.[41]

Nan was more shaken than she let on. It was Gandhi who gave her courage, writing: 'Ranjit's arrest could not have possibly caused you uneasiness! When you meet him give him my blessings.' Ranjit and Nan corresponded regularly, and he reassured her that he considered his term 'a windfall' as it gave him the chance to spend time with Jawaharlal and learn directly from him.[42] She was glad that he had at least been made a 'Class A' prisoner, which allowed for extra 'interviews' with loved ones, and more letters as well (perks that were the result of an earlier hunger strike by a young revolutionary named Bhagat Singh).[43] But she missed him 'terribly' and felt 'so lonely', unable to enjoy anything without him.[44]

Motilal's condition, in the meantime, grew worse. The family decided it best that he retreat to a better climate, to Mussoorie, a spectacular mountain retreat in the foothills of the Himalayas, proximate to Dehra Dun, and a favourite destination of India's rich and royal. Motilal and Swarup Rani went first while Nan packed up the children and joined them shortly thereafter. Indira came along as well.

It was a pleasant sanctuary, and Motilal was surrounded by staff and doctors, but his health continued to decline rapidly, nonetheless. He passed numerous blood clots. Nan and the children at least improved his mood, and the family shifted to slightly nicer quarters in the shadow of the English-Gothic castle-like Savoy Hotel.[45]

While the Nehrus' attention was primarily on hospice care, and they were grateful for creature comfort, they remained keenly attuned to national affairs. Motilal received a stream of visitors who sought his input and assistance. Nan for her part managed the house as best she could. In keeping with ongoing boycotts, she avoided British goods as much as possible, though this was made difficult in certain instances by the medical necessities of Motilal's bland dietary requirements. Khadi was the cloth of choice.

As the days passed, Motilal proved a challenging patient. He coughed up blood regularly and suffered from bouts of malaria and insomnia. Allopathic and homoeopathic doctors argued about which treatment plan he should follow. A local church held a special service to pray for his well-being, causing a minor sensation in the town, the vicar drawing a rebuke from the local authorities. Nan grew sick with worry about everything and dreamed of Ranjit.

She wanted to visit him in Naini but had to forego meeting him to stay by Motilal's side. Betty went in her place. Ever the encouraging and sympathetic husband, Ranjit soothed his wife's guilt, announcing that he intended to use his time for scholarly pursuits. He intended to translate an important twelfth-century text on Kashmiri history, the *Rajatarangini* (River/Waves of Kings), from Sanskrit to English. As a hobby, and to spruce up the conditions of his confinement, he also planned to plant a small garden. Nan was thrilled by this news and began exploring ways to send necessary books and seeds.[46]

Motilal's mind, however, was on Jawaharlal. He wanted to see his son. Nan conveyed the message through a letter to Ranjit. As it happened, Jawaharlal was 'released suddenly . . . on the expiry of six months' sentence' and managed to spend a few days with Kamala and his father. But he was rearrested soon thereafter and sentenced to do 'rigorous' time.[47]

~

The reimprisonment of Jawaharlal Nehru incensed the Congress. Doubling down on non-cooperation, they announced 'Jawahar Week', to symbolize their president's presence in absence. Nan stepped forward to lead. Together with her sister (-s-in-law), she organized massive processions, some by students and some by women. English ladies took note of all the activity: 'its [sic] too interesting', they declared.

In between organizing and marching, Nan darted back home to look after the kids, ensuring that the little ones were asleep by 8 p.m. Her children remained her top concern: she worried incessantly about them and felt tremendous guilt for not giving them her undivided attention. She wrote Ranjit that she 'can't look after them these days as they should be looked after'.[48] Her eldest was just at the age for Nan to feel a universal parental desire: 'I do so want Chand to be my friend + and not only my daughter.'[49] She felt anguish when an acquaintance accurately assessed the bargain they had made: 'our children may thank us for having made them free but I am sure they will always blame their parents for the way they were neglected'. The children, however, found protests and jail and campaigning for the greater good entirely normal, for the most part. When Betty asked the two older girls what they would do if their mother was arrested too, Nayantara responded: 'let them come. We will take our Mommy back from them.' Chandralekha, on the other hand, said she would sit and cry.

But there was no turning back now. Uma Nehru had fallen ill, and Nan had taken charge of the Devika Sevika Sangh in her place. She spent her afternoons enlisting women in the fight. She also set about decorating a swadeshi showroom, to help promote khadi and show that it could be elegant as well as functional.[50]

Every now and again, she would crumple in a corner incapacitated by her longing for Ranjit, though she now saw him in brief interviews. 'I miss you more than I can ever tell you,' she confided in him. 'It is a horrible thing to miss a person as much as I am missing you . . . I long to have you here in this room with me . . . What lovely evenings we have had . . . + what terrible quarrels too,' she admitted. '[B]ut somehow the quarrels + misunderstandings have all vanished + the happy moments alone remain and make me miss you all the more.' 'We have been together so much ever since our marriage that I had almost forgotten that the time would come when we would have to be apart.'[51]

But there was no time for their sorrows. Jawahar Week culminated in a 'huge procession + a monster meeting'. Kasturba Gandhi and Mahadev Desai, the Mahatma's wife and personal secretary, as well as Sardar Patel, all came to Allahabad in a show of support. Kamala Nehru delivered some remarks in her husband's name, and Nan and the others sold pamphlets and marshalled the crowds. Both braced for their imminent arrest. Nan packed a suitcase to get ready for the eventuality.

But the British were perplexed by mass demonstrations by women and uncertain how best to respond, for fear of breaching an unwritten code of etiquette. Elsewhere, of course, they did not hesitate in repressing Jawahar Week activities.

Kamala and Nan pressed their advantage.[52] They 'decided to start picketing in the Civil Station' part of town, targeting the sale of foreign cloth. At first, they sent men into the protests, but all were arrested within twenty-four hours. Nan and Kamala then prepared a team of *sevikas* (women service volunteers) and headed over to lead the picket themselves. But when the group reached the Civil Station, they were shocked to find the cloth shops closed. The 'cloth merchants . . . said they would suffer any loss rather allow a single woman to be arrested on their account'. Kamala ordered them to 'get all their foreign cloth sealed' within a week.[53]

News of Allahabad's mass demonstrations spread, making the European papers. They carried pictures and accounts of everything.[54]

~

Motilal had watched all of this with satisfaction. But he continued to deteriorate. By early December, he was resting in Calcutta, 'very weak and depressed'. Nan rushed to his side, leaving the children with Indira in Anand Bhawan. Motilal 'had difficulty breathing' and 'looked ghastly'.[55]

Soon, he was brought back to Allahabad, his face 'even more swollen', unable to speak properly, his mind 'not always quite clear'. As his body began to shut down, a stream of visitors from all over the country began to descend on Anand Bhawan to see him one last time. Jawaharlal, Ranjit and Gandhi were all released from prison and rushed to his side. Motilal Nehru died a few days later, in early 1931.[56]

~

Nan took some time to reflect on her loss and to recuperate from the toll caregiving had taken on her. She spent time in the hills of Mussoorie with Betty and the children that summer. She read books and worked on her French.[57]

In anticipation of further arrests, the executive Congress Committee in the meantime prepared a list of names of potential leaders. If one was put in prison, the next in the chain was automatically to take their place. The frequency of the changes did not allow time or resources for elections, so an appointed leader was called a 'dictator'. 'A "dictator" therefore had full powers to issue orders for noncooperation activities and all congress men and women obeyed such commands.'[58]

Soon after she returned to Allahabad rejuvenated, Vijaya Lakshmi Pandit found herself a 'dictator' of the city. In 1932, she was responsible for organizing ceremonies on 26 January to mark Independence Day. Activities included hoisting the flag and reciting the pledge of swaraj. A public meeting was held in Purushottamdas Park. It was 'crowded to capacity'. The 'police . . . [were] present in full force' but everything proceeded uneventfully, and the crowd dispersed peacefully when it was over. But that night, the police nonetheless came for Nan.

CHAPTER THREE

# Knowing Why the Caged Bird Sings

The Allahabad District Jail was 'a collection of mud houses in a large yard enclosed by a dilapidated wall'. It was just a way station for prisoners about to begin their terms, or for ones about to be released. Nan was confined to the female barrack, which was a long hall 'with gratings in the wall at intervals of four feet'. There was an inner courtyard 'with one gigantic banyan tree in the center'. Most of the others in lockup were 'prostitutes, with a sprinkling of those who were charged for petty thefts'. Nan found their 'habits, morals and language' distasteful.

A matron and some assistants oversaw the entire operation, usually spending the day in the courtyard. Nan and the other political prisoners—including Betty, who had also been arrested—were free to move about the facility during the daytime, but they stayed in the barrack to avoid the matron. At 6 p.m., everyone was locked in their barracks for the night. Nan found this a jolting and disturbing experience. There was only one 'hurricane lantern suspended from the roof', its 'flickering wick' providing dim, pale light. The sound of snoring was interspersed only by the warden's booming hourly roll call. Unable to sleep, Nan found herself in a waking 'nightmare'.

After three days, Nan was hustled off to a trial she likened to 'comic opera'. She was sentenced to one year of 'rigorous imprisonment', which meant that she would have to work while in prison, though she could, in turn, earn time off for good behaviour. She was additionally subjected to a Rs 1500 fine that would add six months to her term if left unpaid.

Every prisoner was placed into one of three categories, A, B or C, the last for 'ordinary criminals' and the former two for political prisoners, the further division made based on 'social and financial status' and '[s]ometimes a university degree'. The magistrate was flustered by the fact that Nan was a woman, and further that she was a Nehru. He inquired about her background, but when she refused to answer, he presumed she met every standard, including studying at a 'foreign University', and so awarded her A status.

She returned to Allahabad District Jail, grateful that she at least had Betty by her side, facing the same circumstances. After a short stint there, the matron informed them they were being transferred to Lucknow Central Jail, about 200 kilometres away. The police superintendent was personally taking them by car to the train station under the cover of night, the gesture not so much a courtesy as a hurried means to get them out of the city before the masses found out. This was to no avail as a massive crowd gathered and 'cries of Jai! [victory!] rent the air'. People threw flowers and garlands. Nan felt a surge of pride. 'It was a triumphant sendoff.'[1]

~

Prison was a kind of family reunion, filled with relatives and close friends who were all part of the civil disobedience campaign, but it was a 'far cry' from Anand Bhawan. Prior to the arrival of political prisoners, girls up to the age of eighteen were the only females confined there. A, B and C class inmates were each kept apart. The women's barrack had a similar layout to the Allahabad quarters: a long hall, now jammed to double capacity, filled with rows of beds, each with an accompanying stool and tin box for garments. At one end was the entrance, and at the other was the toilet, 'a raised platform with a hole in the center' partially covered by a curtain. No one wanted to sleep near the platform because of the smell, but Uma Nehru convinced everyone to share 'disabilities like privileges'.

Recalling the experience in her memoirs, Nan wrote cagily that she 'soon discovered that . . . [she] was Indian only by fact of birth', seemingly to imply that she could not relate to the ways other social classes lived. In fact, it was those who shared her background but who desperately clung to their traditions and customs who suddenly seemed distant and unrecognizable to her. 'Among our group were two ladies from one of our great families, the Malaviyas. They belonged to the period when caste and class had strict meaning and they continued to adhere rigidly to the letter of Hindu orthodoxy, fashioning their lives, even in jail, after the conservative pattern of their homes. They suffered endlessly in consequence and the rest of us suffered from the effects of their irritation. I do not know what urge led them to participate in a movement, the whole purpose of which was to break down caste barriers and create a new social and political order.'[2]

Everyone in Class A enjoyed a series of perks, small on the face of it, but significant in the context of a strictly regimented and restricted life. They could receive visitors for monitored thirty-minute interviews, though no embrace of any kind was possible. Guests could bring small gifts of food, like bread or jam. Books were allowed.[3] And prisoners could send and receive censored letters.

In some ways, these perks bothered Nan the most, because they regularly reminded her of what she was being denied: contact with her husband and children. Still, she took advantage of what she could, and exchanged letters with her family as frequently as possible. This too put a strain on her, as she came to anticipate correspondence at certain times, and found it 'dreadful to go on expecting a letter that doesn't come'. She wanted to regulate the process, especially with Ranjit, so that she could better plan, and better control her feelings. 'I have always admired the nice placid people who go through life with a perpetually smiling face. I don't seem to be able to shake off my moods even in prison—It's a sad case! But then Ranjit you can console yourself by thinking how deadly dull it would be for you if you had a wife who always . . . [agreed] to what you said + approved of what you did. As it is—in spite of eleven years of marriage + the many disagreements, I think we can still find a thrill in "looking at the Alhambra by moonlight" together –After all it's a jolly old world— there's quite a lot of beauty knocking about if only you try + look for it—so why grumble!'[4]

Most of what Nan shared with Ranjit concerned the children. They visited her only once in the prison. Nayantara recalled years later, when she was yet to become one of India's most celebrated writers, that they were allowed 'as very young children . . . to go into the barrack instead of seeing her in the superintendent's office'. 'It was hard enough to accept the fact that we could not see Mummie again until her release, but to picture her there in that dingy, airless place, wearing coarse clothes was harder still.' She continued: 'We had always associated our mother with the ordered beauty of home. We were used to seeing her early in the morning on the veranda, where she would be down on her knees among the freshly cut roses, arranging them with care in the vases arrayed before her. We were used to hearing her silvery laugh float out from the drawing-room on evenings when there were parties in the house. We were used to hearing friends and strangers who had never seen her before exclaim: "Is that your mother? Isn't she lovely?" How unfair that she of all people should have to go through this ordeal!'[5]

Soon after this farewell meeting, the girls were sent to Poona (Pune) to be looked after by the Vakils, family friends who charged nominal fees to cover some of the basic expenses.

Padmaja Naidu checked in on them every so often. Nan wrote regularly about the girls' eating habits and weight, expressing relief and gratitude that they were keeping fit. As she described it, they were also happy, picking up new languages like Gujarati, travelling to Bombay and spending days at the beach. Recalling all of this decades later in her memoirs, she noted with pain and regret: 'I have never quite forgiven myself for that first jail term which broke up my home when my children most needed its security and comfort. To stay at home and look after them would have been dull. Perhaps I was envious of my friends who had broken away from their ties and placed the burden of personal responsibilities on others; perhaps I had a too-lenient husband who seldom, if ever, interfered with my decisions. Whatever the reason, I am now sure that I acted selfishly, thinking in vague terms of personal political achievements rather than the satisfaction I could have gained through domestic duty honestly performed.'[6]

These guilty thoughts roiled her mind during the long days, and kept her up many a longer night. To distract herself from the heavy burden of her worry, she wrote and read. 'It is [like] going through the university of life . . . there is so much to think about—the Past with its hosts of memories, sweet + sad, that come crowding into the mind unbidden—the Present, + above all, the Future.'[7] She ploughed her way through works on the 'French and Russian revolutions and Gibbon's *Decline and Fall of the Roman Empire*,' as well as Ernest Toller's *Which World-Which Way*, comparing the United States and Russia.⁸ Among the 'most amazing things she read' was Aldous Huxley's *Brave New World*.⁹ She read poetry by W.H. Auden and T.S. Eliot, a discussion of Plato and writing by the esteemed Spanish diplomat Salvador de Madariaga.¹⁰ She made a habit of reviewing parts of the Bhagavad Gita and reciting bits of the Ramayana. 'She also read Vivekananda . . . St. Augustine, Thompson's *Rise and Fulfilment of British Rule in India*, Dickens, Shakespeare . . . and a great deal of Chinese history.'¹¹

One work made a big impression. It was a novel that had just been released—*Free Love*, by Alexandra Kollontai. The Russian author achieved fame in 1919 when she became the first female government minister in Europe, and again in 1923 when she became the first woman in the world to be appointed an ambassador.¹²

Aside from intellectual pursuits, Nan passed her time in the yard, walking and gardening. She had a marvellous green thumb and put its magic to work growing flowers in gravel.

The women's barrack more generally amused themselves through distant flirtations. 'The girls were hungry for men and made no effort to disguise the fact.' They were separated from the men's quarters by a high wall but communicated with the other side through song and signals. The men in turn would toss over a newspaper, sometimes inscribed with a message. Since the prisoners had access to papers of all kinds already, this was all a game to see what kind of small capers and hijinks they could pull right under the nose of the wardens. When they actually had direct contact with men, as when they were routinely weighed by a young doctor, 'the girls were in a state of excitement amounting almost to hysteria'.¹³

~

The jail was far from a pleasure palace, of course. Nan's strong will and colourful imagination helped see her through the day-to-day tedium. But the conditions took their toll, especially on her health. She had limited food: some lemon water in the morning; a lunch consisting of 'boiled spinach, dahi [yogurt], bread + butter + fruit'; and a 'dinner consisting of fruit + milk or "khir [rice pudding]"'.¹⁴ She tried to stay fit with a regimen of yoga but had to give it up when she 'lost consciousness' due to the terrible heat (clocking in at 40 degrees Celsius she heard) and suffered from a terrible headache as a consequence.[15]

In a memorable moment, Nan woke one day to a severe toothache. Readily available salves brought no relief, so the next day Nan asked to see a dentist. 'This simple request fell on the prison like a bomb.' The warden did not know what to do, as there was no such person on site. Soon, Nan's 'face . . . was swollen beyond recognition'. After some to do, the superintendent authorized an outside visit, though on the next working weekday, two days later. 'I was so angry I forgot my pledge of nonviolence and threatened the jail authorities with dire consequences as soon as the Congress came into power,' she amusedly recalled years later. Her tantrum had a salutary effect, however, and she was promptly taken to a dentist who dealt with the 'offending tooth'.[16]

The dental problems further narrowed her diet, and Nan was left to 'drinking large quantities of buttermilk [matha]'. Mangoes, which comprised most of her fruit intake, were 'forbidden' because they were 'said to irritate the conditions of the gums'. She was told she could eat oranges, but none were available. She maintained good humour through it all, talking up the benefits of her complexion and weight with Ranjit. 'I look elegant in the extreme,' she joked.[17]

Prison was taxing mentally and physically, so her correspondence had therapeutic value. It stung more, then, when even this small outlet for joy was closed off.

The government had decided to subject Ranjit Pandit to a harsher penalty, stripping him of his privileges for three months. He would no longer be allowed letters or interviews during this period. Nan found the punishment capricious, 'utterly stupid and barbarous'. She was 'intensely annoyed at the unjustness of the whole proceeding' and just could not 'follow the workings of the Govt mind'. In protest, she too gave up her correspondence and interviews. Betty joined in in support, but soon succumbed to the harsh environment, falling sick with a malaria-like illness followed by an 'attack of flu'. She became 'very weak + run down' and lost weight due to a lack of appetite.[18]

To add to Nan's stress, she battled 'depression' in mourning for Motilal. 'The anguish of the loss' seemed 'greater' a year in. In a classic sign of grief, Nan made herself 'ill with fretting' that she 'didn't feel as bad as the last year', and that any happiness she allowed herself might somehow sleight the memory of her father.[19]

~

Roughly one month after Nan objected to her husband's treatment, the superintendent informed her that all suspended privileges would be restored. She was unclear if her actions had had a direct effect on the situation or not.[20] But it was a victory either way.

Once back in touch, Ranjit encouraged his wife to take some time for herself once she was released and suggested she consider taking a trip to Europe. 'You seem determined to get me out of India! Don't tempt me too much or I might go - + who knows when I should return?' she replied, amused, before seriously adding that she would only want to travel with him by her side.[21]

She shared stories about their children. She was especially proud of precocious eight-year-old Chandralekha, who had grown interested in Rabindranath Tagore's poetry. She feared her youngest, Rita, might forget her and so had a tricycle delivered for her birthday. The real present, though, was promised when they returned to Allahabad: a pony.[22]

~

Nan's release from prison drew closer—it was to be in a month.[23] She felt a surge of joy, but it was accompanied by nostalgia for a life that now seemed behind her. 'I'm afraid there will be no 9 Cawnpore Road or log-fires or cocktails for many a long day to come. Ah well! Such is life,' she told her husband.[24]

She was very pleased that Ranjit had made 'good progress' on his translation of the *Rajatarangini*. 'With regard to your imprisonment,' she told him cheerfully, 'it can certainly be said "out of evil cometh good".' She told him she had started to dream of seeing his work sold in bookshops.[25] She added that she had 'blossomed . . . as a writer' herself, wickedly promising him 'all sorts of surprises' with her new-found skill at 'witty . . . limericks'.

As her upcoming reunion drew nearer and more real, she took stock of what had gotten her family through the year. 'People have been so wonderfully good to us since we came to jail, + to the children, I really don't know how we can ever repay their kindness. I shall however see how I can show my gratitude to our many friends when I get out'.[26]

~

Most of Nan's close friends and associates, including Betty, were released shortly before she was, though when her turn finally came, a few remained, like Prabhavati Narayanan, the wife of the American-educated leftist Gandhian, Jayaprakash. Nan 'hated the idea of leaving her' but 'there was nothing to be done'.[27] She hurried west to see her children.

'Chand + Tara at once ran up to be kissed but Rita hung back'. The youngest Pandit had grown very attached to her surrogate family. Nan was just relieved and thrilled to hold her girls again, and revelled in their company, amazed at how much they had grown, and tickled by the Marathi and Gujarati that Rita especially had picked up, even if it was to the detriment of her Hindi skills.

While she was in Poona, Nan went to visit Gandhi in his jail cell. He looked 'bright + cheerful as ever' and told Nan 'now he was really proud to accept' her 'as a daughter'. This was not only because she had blossomed into a full-fledged freedom fighter but also because he could now speak his mother tongue (Gujarati) with her children,[28] he joked.

When it finally came time to leave for home, 'dozens' of Rita's friends 'turned up with toys + flowers + sweets! Everyone was in tears because the little lady was not [going to be] returning to school again'. The little girl loved all the attention until she had to say goodbye. Then, 'her big eyes full of tears', she started wailing. It took a chicken sandwich from their lunch basket to finally quiet Rita down once the journey had begun. 'At three years food is an important factor in bringing solace', Nan amusedly noted.[29]

~

Back in Anand Bhawan, the stress and tension of the past year seemed to have washed away. The great house—the new one built by Motilal after the rechristening of the old one as Swaraj Bhawan—was 'full of song' thanks to the musically-inclined children, who serenaded their mother 'from morning to night'.

Ranjit was still missing, but he too was due to be released soon. Chandralekha told him that it was 'so nice to be home again', and that she was 'very proud' that he was 'serving India'.[30]

Indira joined the Pandits. Nan had been worried for her over the previous year, feeling she was developing bad habits, but now decided her worry was for nothing. 'She is a "darling", she told Ranjit. 'She has put on some flesh at last + looks very beautiful + so chic in her smart clothes'.[31]

Surrounded by her beloved family, Nan now turned her attention to pressing health concerns. Betty had 'had a hard time' in prison. While she was at last 'improving', the damage seemed severe. 'She does not go out anywhere without me—hardly ever speaks to anyone except myself . . . She behaves at present as if she were one of my babies—all her old independence etc seem to have vanished. I don't like it.' Nan decided that when she returned the children to school a few weeks later, she would take Betty along and 'give her a good time'.

Nan herself managed to see a doctor at the hospital, to investigate some chronic pain she had had ever since a small operation she had undergone in Calcutta well before her arrest. The doctor discovered an inch-and-a-half stitch that had not been properly removed and buried two inches deep. He removed it with 'the greatest difficulty + pain' and told Nan that she should sue the previous surgeon for malpractice. Nan was also told she needed a 'slight operation' to remedy an 'old trouble', and so scheduled this for a few weeks later.

Reviving health took more than medical care, however. Nan decided to take Betty to visit Bombay. They would stay with Ranjit's cousin Kshamabai Row.[32] Kshama by then had become one of India's greatest women tennis players, having won the 1927 Bombay Presidency Hardcourt Championship. Kshama's daughter Leela was on her way to surpassing her, winning her own title in the All-India Championships in 1931 in straight sets against Lena McKenna. This created a rivalry in the Row household.

Nan watched Leela play in the '33 Bombay tennis tournament. 'Leela played very well the first few days' Nan observed, but came up short in the finals match 'through nervousness + partly because

Kshama . . . [went] on instructing her throughout the game'. Nan thought Leela's mother's imperiousness was 'a severe handicap'.[33] Even so, Leela would go on to become the first Indian woman to win a match at Wimbledon, achieving this distinction the following year, and going on from there to win six national titles from 1936 onwards as the number one women's tennis player in the country.[34]

At the match, Nan was 'introduced to Conte di Bonzi' who invited her 'to visit him' in his castle in Milan whenever she was in Italy. She was 'thrilled' until she learned 'by accident, that similar invitations had been given to nearly all the "females" who were passably good looking', she informed Ranjit mischievously.[35]

Even so, the count's flirting seemed to awaken Nan's more vivacious side. She spent the next four days having fun at Juhu beach in 'a delicious bathing suit about the size of a postage stamp'. Her nights on the town ran into the wee hours of the morning. Kshama took all this the wrong way and called Nan 'uncultured, uneducated, + a vamp'.[36] She demanded Nan leave her home. Nan thought the whole thing a 'storm in a teapot', but obliged and transferred to another friend's house.[37]

~

Nan had gotten 'busy with untouchability work in Allahabad' nearly as soon as she had set foot in Anand Bhawan. She focused on a nearby village that was home to 'sweepers + pasis'.[38] She aimed to 'make it into a "model" village'. Rather than focusing on the systemic structures that upheld and legitimized caste discrimination throughout society, including social norms and religious practices, Nan's efforts were structured by the Gandhian idea of upliftment. She hoped to 'Get sanitary dwellings put in place of the old huts—start a night school + a workshop—see that the babies are kept clean + that the liquor shops . . . [were] removed from there . . .' She was so successful that she was asked to 'take charge' within just a few weeks of getting re-involved.[39]

She refused but was open to other possibilities. So, once she returned her children to school in Poona and Bombay, she met with Gandhi for four hours to discuss his agenda. He set her on a new mission.

She was told to travel immediately to Kathiawad where she was to use her 'powers of persuasion' on communities that opposed lower caste entry to temples in the region.[40] She was also to rally princes to the cause, using the connections she had through Ranjit's side of the family. As the Mahatma had predicted, Nan soon won converts wherever she went, facilitated by advance letters Gandhi had dispatched informing the states that Vijaya Lakshmi Pandit was his personal emissary.[41]

In Rajkot, she held a 'very successful public meeting' even as opponents showed their strength in a 'large gathering'.[42] The tour gave Nan a new-found appreciation of the absurdity and awfulness of caste discrimination. 'It is ridiculous that these people are deprived of the rights of human existence', she concluded.[43]

~

At the tail end of her travels, Nan discovered that Ranjit's father, 'convinced that he [had] . . . only a few months to live', had paid his son's fine so the two could see each other 'at an earlier date'. Nan thought the news was 'disagreeable', but 'useless' to fight since 'the fine had been paid'. She was happy that she was, at last, going to have her husband back.

But her joy was short-lived. Just as the release took place, Gandhi announced a major fast against untouchability. This was to be his third in the previous nine months—Nan's tour taking place against this backdrop—the first as notably successful as it was controversial.

Gandhi had met Ambedkar in 1931 and, though he praised the great anti-caste champion as a 'patriot of sterling worth', the two did not leave that meeting on good terms. Ambedkar had a very different view on the plight of his people, and on his relationship with the country that allowed such treatment. The two met in England as they attended the second Round Table Conference, Ambedkar having the year before critiqued 'paper rights' guaranteed by a constitution, saying they were worthless unless stringent penalties were imposed on people who infringed on those rights. Gandhi wanted change to begin in the hearts of oppressors.

Drawing from the discussions that took place at the second conference, British Prime Minister Ramsay MacDonald announced the Communal Award a year later, granting separate electorates to various communities, allowing each to vote for their representatives. While Gandhi was willing to agree to these conditions for minority Muslims, he was adamantly opposed to it applying to caste, arguing that it would divide and break the Hindu community. Ambedkar on the other hand applauded the move and saw it as an important way to advance the cause of his people, whom he called 'Dalits', 'the ground to pieces'. Gandhi, who was still in jail, announced a fast in protest, and continued it even after his release. Ambedkar was forced to compromise, agreeing days later to the Poona Pact, which provided for Depressed Classes reservations in lieu of a separate electorate.[44] What that meant was that, for certain seats, all voters could choose between candidates that came from under-represented communities—the seats were 'reserved' for members from those communities. Ambedkar never forgave himself, or Gandhi, for this, what he took as a great betrayal.

Gandhi, for his part, saw his own position as entirely consistent. He was opposed to discrimination based on caste and accepted the urgency of changing ground conditions. Now in 1933, the Mahatma felt he had to do more, to make his commitment to the cause known, and declared another major fast, this time to explicitly protest untouchability itself. Ranjit went to stand by his side.

~

Nan was worried. 'What is going to happen,' she fretted.[45] She, the children, and Betty had by then all come up to Mussoorie to escape the scorching summer heat of Allahabad, halting only briefly in Dehra Dun while en route to spend some time with Indira and Kamala, whose health remained skittish.[46]

On the day Gandhi started his fast, all the Pandits joined in in solidarity. With so much going on, Nan went to visit her brother in prison. Jawaharlal, 'pale but otherwise fit' convinced her that all was for the best. 'I think that is true', she hesitantly agreed. 'There could be no more perfect ending to Bapu's life than that he should pass away while fasting--+if he survives he works another miracle. So in any case all is well'.[47] She tried to convince herself, but days later broke down in panic. She telegrammed Ranjit saying she was 'extremely upset' about Gandhi's condition and was considering making a trip to Poona to be by his side.[48] In response, 'Bapu had a letter written . . . asking us not to worry about him + saying he is getting on very well + is going to get through'. 'Wasn't it just like Bapu', she noted admiringly. 'I thought it was so very kind of him'.[49]

National affairs by now had fully intruded into her personal life, and they were not separated any longer. She celebrated her wedding anniversary from a distance. 'I hope dear Ranjit the next 12 years of our life together will be better than the preceeding ones + that we shall grow closer friends as the years pass'.[50] When he didn't respond right away, it irritated her already raw nerves. She sent him a 'nasty postcard' before thinking better of it. She told him affectionately it was his fault for not writing, adding: 'You have no idea how much your letters mean to me. I wait for them almost as eagerly as I used to wait for your letters in Calcutta in 1921, so please don't deny me that pleasure. I love you terribly Ranjit. [It] . . . leads to all sorts of complications but I just can't help myself'.[51]

Nan decided she really needed to just take a break from everything and pamper herself a bit. The doctor told her that she was 'run down' and suggested that 'the best tonic in the world' would be having another baby. She 'told him he was an idiot'.[52] She chose instead to relax among the picturesque mountains and spend time with old friends. Once she opened her social calendar, however, she was inundated with appointment requests. 'Why am I getting all this attention at this time of life', she wondered when 'every body [sic] in Mussoorie . . . [was] simply tumbling over everybody else to do things for' her. 'I refuse most invitations + always return the presents but they continue to come + from all sorts of unexpected quarters', she dutifully reported to her husband.[53]

The mental and physical fatigue seemed to immediately lift once she received word that Gandhi broke his fast. 'Rejoice Bapu emerges stronger from another ordeal', she exclaimed. 'We went mad with joy + sent a joint telegram from ourselves + the kids telling the old man how happy we were'.[54] Nan decided to celebrate the all-round good fortune with reckless abandon.

She allowed herself some real luxuries at last. 'I ride sometimes—it's expensive unless someone else provides the horses—which usually happens in my case!' She exuberantly confessed: 'I'm the best rider here + I'm quite well known!!!' Old royal acquaintances like Pratapsingh Gaekwar (Gaekwad, son of Sayaji Rao) and the Rani of Rajpipla reconnected. 'Then there are the Nepalese boys—Kapurthalas, Indores, etc etc . . . If Bhai [Jawaharlal] knew that I was moving only amongst Princes he would I am sure be horrified but I am sure you won't be', she told Ranjit self-assuredly. 'Besides, since I do not consider myself anything but a Princess I can't go about with anyone else', she confessed, tongue partially in cheek.[55]

Nan knew this was a momentary bit of silliness. She knew too what was going on all around her, what was at stake, and what was expected of her. She was ready to turn her attention back to more serious matters. She told Ranjit that they needed to re-establish a home base and expressed a longing for their old place at 9 Cawnpore Road in Allahabad.[56] As luck would have it, a nearby house on the same street was available, and number 6 became the new Pandit residence. They moved in within the month.[57]

~

While they had been in Bombay, Betty had met a young man named Gunottam 'Raja' Hutheesing at a party one evening. 'He looked somewhat different from all the others there, with a detached and rather superior air about him . . . He sat silent and aloof, smoking a lovely meerschaum pipe.'[58] They saw each other later at Juhu Beach and spent an evening discussing politics and books. Nan had mixed feelings about the meeting, which had been set up with 'an idea to marriage' by Kshama. But there was 'no doubt that B[etty] was inclined towards him . . . —she was with him all the time, morning to evening except when he went to work'.[59]

Once the family returned from Mussoorie, Betty decided to make a trip to Ahmedabad via Bombay and saw Raja again. They spent the week together before he asked her formally to marry him. She was a bit unsure about her feelings and left for her onward journey. A few days later, she returned to the great city having thought it over and accepted his proposal. Betty asked Nan to keep the news a secret until their mother, temporarily ill, felt well again. In September, once Swarup Rani had recovered somewhat and Jawaharlal was out of prison, Raja was introduced to the whole family, including Gandhi, who knew the Gujarati, Jain Hutheesing family quite well. Everyone gave their blessings and the wedding was fixed for the very next month in Anand Bhawan.[60]

It was a simple civil ceremony of just a few hours, in 'great-contrast' [sic] to Nan's 'celebrations . . . [of] a week or more.' Just a few friends and family were able to attend. Still, the family managed to generate a small controversy when Jawaharlal had 'invitations printed in Hindustani written in the Roman script', some riled by a break with tradition they found 'unacceptable'. But Betty and Raja were happy and moved together to Bombay shortly thereafter.[61]

~

Even as one sister appeared to grow up overnight, Nan's other, by law, began an equally rapid decline. Jawaharlal wanted to spend some quality time with Kamala, knowing that her health was failing. They made a trip to Calcutta together, and there, had a few consultations with doctors. Just before they left, a major earthquake struck North-Central India, so as soon as they returned from their trip, Jawaharlal joined relief work and, in the process, critiqued the government for its inefficient and incompetent response. Together with widely read and translated articles situating India in world affairs, he soon attracted the ire of the authorities once again. He was re-arrested on 12 February 1934, just '[f]ive months and thirteen days' since his release, with catastrophic consequences for Kamala's well-being.[62]

The doctors expressed deep concern for the young woman, only thirty-four years old. Within just six months, they feared for her life. Jawaharlal was initially imprisoned in Alipore Jail in Calcutta but had been transferred in May to Dehra Dun. In July, he was suddenly escorted to Allahabad, and informed that he was being temporarily released to be with his wife.

'There she lay, frail and utterly weak, a shadow of herself, struggling feebly with her illness . . . Surely she was not going to leave me now when I needed her most? Why, we had just begun to know and understand each other, really; our joint life was only now properly beginning. We relied so much on each other; we had so much to do together.' Jawaharlal was allowed eleven days to reminisce and ruminate like this before the police took him back to jail, this time to Naini prison.

Within a few weeks, Kamala's medical team recommended that she be moved to a TB sanitorium in Bhowali, just outside the resort town of Nainital, nestled among the lush lower Himalayan Kumaon Hills. It now fell to Nan to oversee Kamala's care and treatment. Jawaharlal felt terrible guilt for the burden he had placed on his wife and sister, regretting all the small irritations common to everyday interactions. He wrote to Nan with gratitude and encouragement: 'You have a rare quality—tact and savoir faire. Do not forget it or put it by. Keep it with you light and shining and you will find that it will not only help others but yourself.'[63]

Nan looked into living arrangements for her sister-in-law and coordinated matters with the rest of the family, acting as an intermediary between her brother and the rest. Jawaharlal was transferred to a prison in Almora, a town proximate to the Bhowali facilities, once Kamala made the move in October.

Meanwhile, Swarup Rani's health continued to fluctuate as well, and Nan had to attend to her too. This was made more difficult because of her mother's addiction to certain bad habits. 'The doctors have given very strict instructions about diet, outings, etc and all tobacco is absolutely forbidden. We have had great difficulty in breaking her tobacco habit and although the doctors have explained how dangerous it is for her to take it and she has again and again promised to give it up still, when she gets a craving she manages to get a little from the servants and each time her pressure has shot up to 190 and she has a sort of relapse each time. The doctors are definite that tobacco may bring about another stroke [following a paralyzing one she had in January] which will prove fatal.'[64]

Jawaharlal had planned for Kamala to stay in some private cottages near the treatment facility, but this quickly proved inadequate. By March 1935, she needed to be moved into the main building. The family then made plans for everyone to rotate through.

~

As the Nehrus and Pandits got acquainted with Bhowali, Ranjit fell deeply in love with the surrounding hills. Nan had indicated repeatedly her interest in acquiring a house in the general area, once flippantly writing: 'Why shouldn't we renounce the world, the flesh, + the devil + live in Dehra Dun?'[65] So Ranjit set his sights on purchasing a small property that Gandhi had acquired and turned into an ashram in the nearby town of Binsar.⁶⁶ 'While at Wardha I had a long talk with Bapu on this subject,' Nan confided to her brother. Within just a few weeks, the transfer was complete. Nan was excited about the new getaway and the prospects for vacation. But she also worried that Ranjit was considering a permanent move to the hills, fearing that they 'would be completely cut off from everything that was going on'.⁶⁷

Ranjit formally named their new estate Ritu-Samhar—the Festival of Seasons—after one of the great Sanskrit master Kaildasa's poems that he liked.⁶⁸ But everyone soon came to know the property simply as Khali (Empty).⁶⁹ For the children, as for Ranjit himself, this place, accessible only 'on foot or horseback', was as close to paradise as possible, leaving long lingering memories 'of the fields covered with golden, ripening wheat, of the thriving poultry farm, of the flourishing grapevines brought from Quetta and Kashmir, and the trees loaded with apples, cherries, and figs, of the masses of wild raspberries, strawberries, and mulberries, of the primary school he had started for the hill folk's children, and the tannery he had set up'. Nayantara recalled nearly two decades later that 'Khali became the symbol of happy family life. It was one of the few places where we could all be together and our parents could rest from responsibility, work, and worry'. She waxed nostalgic: 'Khali brings to mind early suppers eaten on the porch, from which we watched the sunset casting a rosy glow over the snow peaks of the Himalayas; fragrant pine-cone fires crackling every evening in the living-room; picnic lunches taken to the many beauty spots in the forest around the house; pure, sweet, icy, sparkling water drunk from the mountain streams; the walled orchard of . . . apricots, and peaches where we played; the lonely mountain paths where more than once we saw a graceful tawny panther prowling at sundown; and above all, like a constant refrain, the look, the smell, the soft regular swish of the slender pines with their spicy-sweet dry odor'.⁷⁰

Just as the land in Binsar came into their hands, the Pandits received some long-awaited news. Ranjit's magnum opus, his translation of the *Rajatarangini* was to be published in late May.⁷¹

~

But as long summer days stretched out before them, Kamala took a dramatic turn for the worse. The doctors in Bhowali, who had been administering cutting-edge treatments, concluded she was now beyond their care. As a last resort, they recommended that she travel to Europe.

The family immediately made arrangements for Kamala and Indira, who was studying at Rabindranath Tagore's Shantiniketan University, to make their way to the Black Forest in Germany. In September, Jawaharlal was suddenly released from prison so that he could attend to his wife, and he immediately flew to Badenweiler to join her. He 'was shocked' when he saw her, for the radiance he normally saw in her face had dimmed so considerably.[72]

~

Nan watched over the entire Pandit and Nehru clan from 1934, becoming the de facto head of household, handling bills, attending to school matters and planning various travels, even as she also served as caretaker for her mother and sister-in-law. Her children's education continued to consume her, and she worried about what to do. She thought the 'standard of Indian-language schools was poor', while the 'local [English-medium] convent did not prove satisfactory . . . [because] all three girls hated it'. Nayantara described the experience as 'torture'.[73] For a time, Nan wanted to send at least her older kids to Switzerland, but ultimately 'decided against this'. Finally, she came across 'an American Methodist School called Woodstock, in Mussoorie', and, after a trial run, officially enrolled the children in 1936. 'Some of our parents' acquaintances raised startled eyebrows at the idea . . .' Nayantara recalled. '"Do you want your girls to learn hiking instead of arithmetic?" a lady asked . . . [their] mother sourly.'

But the environment was nurturing and all three girls thrived. Nayantara's 'marks soared' and she 'became a prize student'.

One reason Woodstock proved to be such a good fit had to do with Nan's and Ranjit's political sacrifices. Nayantara wrote fondly nineteen years later:

> During the first few days at Woodstock I suffered a slight setback when, during a recess, an eight-year-old classmate asked me: 'Say, is it true your folks have been to jail?'

I nodded nervously. How explain to him all the background that I took so much for granted? And what would my new friends think of me now?

My questioner bounced his Yo-yo back and forth unconcernedly. 'What for? Did they steal something?' 'Oh no,' I said hastily, 'it's not like that at all.' I strove anxiously for the right words. 'You see, it's just that they want the British to leave India, and when they say so, they're put in jail.'

'Aw—that's not fair,' he sympathized, and then went on earnestly: 'You know what? The British used to be in America too, but they aren't there any more. I guess it'll be the same way over here.'

My class mate must have explained our position to the rest of the class, for no more questions were asked.

Nan came to have a deep appreciation for the 'fine men and women' connected directly and indirectly with the school, and what she perceived to be the authentic American way of life. She considered them true friends, her own and India's as well.

~

The Nehru-Pandits by then were prepared for their every interaction to be affected by the heat of national politics. But, as they had sensed even during their last trip to Europe, international affairs were changing quickly and growing in importance—a massive thunderstorm now gaining strength. This seemed to cast a long shadow over all that they did as well.

Jawaharlal was familiar with the interplay of light and darkness from the sunbeams that had penetrated the small jail window. They bounced around his gloomy cell to create theatre out of dancing silhouettes. So as he gazed out at the gathering clouds, he saw in them dangerous shapes.

There was the ferment in France resulting in fascist riots and the formation of a 'National' Government. And, far worse, in Austria, Chancellor Dollfuss was shooting down workers and putting an end to the great edifice of social democracy there. The news of the Austrian bloodshed depressed me greatly. What an awful and bloody place the world was, and how barbarous was man when he wanted to protect his vested interests! All over Europe and America fascism seemed to be advancing. When Hitler came into power in Germany, I had imagined that his regime could not possibly last long, as he was offering no solution of Germany's economic troubles. So also, as fascism spread elsewhere, I consoled myself that it represented the last ditch of reaction. But I began to wonder if my wish was not father to my thought. Was it so obvious that this fascist wave would retire so easily or so quickly? And, even if conditions became intolerable for the fascist dictatorships, would they not rather hurl their countries into devastating war rather than give in? What would be the result of such a conflict? Meanwhile, fascism of various kinds and shapes spread . . . Everywhere Liberalism showed its utter ineffectiveness to face modern conditions. It clung to words and phrases, and thought they could take the place of action. When a crisis came, it simply faded off like the end of a film that is over.[74]

Nan, Ranjit, and Jawaharlal corresponded regularly about these matters, their concerns growing in intensity with each passing moment. When Italy invaded Ethiopia in 1935, Jawaharlal wrote to his sister: 'The actual coming of war makes my brain work in all manner of directions and I am troubled at the absence of real understanding of the situation in India.' He connected the fascist expansionism with imperialism generally and saw the latter force as the underlying driver of unfolding events.[75]

Nan shared her brother's fears, and she discussed the issue extensively in her house. She knew her children were world-wise, but she was taken aback by just how closely the little ones were paying attention to all that was going on far beyond the walls of their home. Twelve-year-old Chandralekha demonstrated this most dramatically. 'She abused Hitler . . . then swore at Mussolini—discussed the Spanish war + the possibility of a world war arising out of it. Wanted to know about the Palestine problem + why Congress sympathized with the

Arabs + not the 'poor Jews'. Called Ramsay Macdonald a traitor to his party + discussed the chances of Roosevelt's reelection.'[76]

From Badenweiler, Jawaharlal saw 'Europe in turmoil, fearful of war and tumult and with economic crises always on the horizon.' As he stood in the sanctuary of the Black Forest, he watched 'the mists steal up the valley and hide the distant frontier of France and cover the landscape . . .' And he wondered: 'what lies behind them?'[77]

CHAPTER FOUR

# The Awakening

The All India Women's Conference had been established in 1927 by Margaret Cousins, the Irish suffragette and international peace activist who had been working closely with Annie Besant since her arrival in India more than a decade ago. Cousins was involved with the anti-colonial cause and had set the Indian poet Rabindranath Tagore's 'Jana Gana Mana' (independent India's national anthem) to tune. With Besant and Dorothy Jinarajadasa, she had started the Women's Indian Association, and was part of the delegation, with Uma Nehru, who had met with Lord Chelmsford to discuss the right to vote.[1]

The year after the AIWC was created, Cousins travelled to Hawaii for the Pan-Pacific Women's Association Conference and decided that there needed to be an Asian equivalent. So upon her return, she rallied several members of her new Indian organization to get involved, including Sarojini Naidu, Rajkumari Amrit Kaur and Lady Abdul Quadir. Together, they organized the All-Asian Women's Conference in 1931, and advocated for a certain kind of pan-Asianism inflected by a kind of cultural nationalism that privileged the Indian experience over other regional ones.[2]

Nan knew virtually all these women personally, either as mentors or as friends. While she had been a member since the AIWC's inception, she got more formally involved in 1935.[3] Though she shared the elite status of the other participants, what set her apart in some ways was her intersectional interest in—her empathy for—those with backgrounds entirely different from her own. Her view was framed by Gandhi's outlook, and her brother's, but also tinted by her own unique perspective. Jawaharlal, with a hint of pride in his sister, noted that she was a 'shining light' in the group, and gently prodded her to assert her own views more strongly: 'I am glad you are taking an interest in the AIWA. It is a very feeble and ladylike body and overfull of reactionaries, but it is the only effective women's organization in the country and it is in touch with international women's societies etc. I think it will grow and move in the right direction. The pace has to be quickened and the reactionaries suppressed.'[4]

~

In the late spring of 1935, Margaret Sanger, the leading Western advocate of birth control, began coordinating with both British suffragette Edith How-Martyn and AIWC founder Margaret Cousins about how to make a trip to India. How-Martyn, an ally of Sangers, had just returned that March from a tour campaigning for birth control in India, during which time she had met and spoken with Gandhi. Sanger and Gandhi had begun corresponding in the midtwenties, politely disagreeing on various matters related to sex and women's bodies.[5] She had issued a forceful public rejoinder shortly thereafter and was delighted when Rabindranath Tagore expressed support for her views.[6]

Sanger was extremely sensitive about coming across as an imperialist—she wrote to Cousins saying that she did not 'want the Indian people to think that we are imposing this idea on them'.[7] Given what she knew of Indian birth-control pioneer R.D. Karve's groundwork, Tagore's views, and grand debates the All India Women's Conference had had the preceding years, she felt that India actually was ahead of most other places in the world on the issue.[8] She was convinced that the country and its people could play a critical leadership role. She asked Cousins for her help in securing an invitation to visit the country from Indian women themselves. This invitation, she claimed, 'would inspire our own women here [in the United States and the West], have a great influence on government officials, [and] would impress legislators as well as women's groups in Egypt, Persia, and other countries . . .' 'Altogether,' she emphasized, 'it would make the Indian women, by comparison, with their vision and foresight seem 100 years ahead of the rest of the women of the world.'⁹ Cousins, herself still involved in the executive, reached out to her colleagues in the current leadership of the AIWC and asked if they would be interested in having Sanger attend their next annual meeting, to take place at the tail-end of that year and the start of 1936.

Nan was by that point serving as the vice-president of the Allahabad chapter of the AIWC and as a member of the group's national Standing Committee.¹⁰ In those positions, she and her associates quickly approved Cousin's proposal, agreeing in August to invite Sanger to visit India and to attend their meeting as a 'Special Visitor'.¹¹ Sanger immediately started planning her trip, packing it with as many events and interactions as possible. She was especially keen to meet with Tagore and Gandhi and to have them each present their viewpoints in open dialogue.¹²

On 23 October that year, Sanger set sail on the S.S. Normandie bound for London, where she hoped to spend a few days raising money for her India tour. While there, she learned that Jawaharlal Nehru too was in town, staying at the Mount Royal Hotel. Jawaharlal was in Europe on release to tend to Kamala in her last days, officially instructed to stay out of India until his prison sentence ended in February 1936 or to face reimprisonment. Sanger immediately sought out an interview and was thunderstruck when she finally met him. She noted in her diary later that he 'kept popping up in . . . [her] mind' and that she found 'his face & bearing very convincing'. Jawaharlal instructed Sanger to meet with Nan when she (Sanger) arrived in India, giving her his sister's address.¹³ He wrote to Nan, describing Sanger as 'the famous leader of the Birth Control movement in America', and 'a dear old lady'.¹⁴

Sanger arrived in Bombay on 25 November, received by How-Martyn, who had travelled to India in advance and who had also been in touch with Gandhi to discuss Sanger's visit. When she finally met the Mahatma, she was awestruck: 'He has an ↑ [*inward*] ↓ light that shines in his face! that shines through the flesh! that circles around his head & neck like a mist, with white Sails of a ship coming through. It lasted only a few seconds but it was there.'¹⁵ She gushed to her husband soon thereafter that Gandhi was 'a remarkable personality'.¹⁶

After visiting Tagore at Shantiniketan, Sanger made her way to Allahabad, where she stayed at Anand Bhawan as Nan's guest.

The Pandits were still living at 6 Cawnpore Road, but Nan, as the de facto head of the Nehru clan, looked after the family property as well. Sanger was wowed by her hostess and by the great mansion as well. Even though it was relatively new and much smaller than the original, she described it as 'old and spacious'. More pertinently, she felt Nan's home 'a nucleus of intellectual thought and activity'.[17]

Nan arranged two major events for Sanger, one to a group of students and the other to the city's women's association, known as the Purdah Club.[18] Six hundred people attended the first session, and Sanger took note of their ecumenicalism, their effort to bridge multiple worlds to create an altogether new reality. She found the students 'extremely sensitive'. 'At the Purdah Club, the audience ... was entirely women; many, in their early twenties, already had large families. They were little accustomed to frank examination of such subjects, but, on the other hand, did not want mere theories. By the time the questions were in order they had recovered from their giggling and were ready to talk seriously'.[19]

Sanger concluded her trip several weeks later by attending the AIWC meeting in Trivandrum. Nan had been planning to attend but backed out at the last minute for personal reasons.[20] Still, she followed the proceedings closely. The big news out of the meeting was that the AIWC had 'decided to get itself affiliated to the International Alliance of Women for Suffrage and Equal Citizenship' further proclaiming that the 'Conference has always upheld the ideal of International Co-operation and friendship as an indispensable factor in the ultimate unity of all women in the service of humanity'.[21]

To top this off, Sanger worked with the standing committee on which Nan sat in absentia to draft a resolution to have birth-control access dramatically expanded, tying it to widespread municipal board practice to send medical teams of 'midwives, doctors and nurses to the poorer classes'. 'No Indian women were against it', she later recalled. It passed overwhelmingly.[22]

~

Kamala Nehru died in February 1936, a few weeks after Sanger left India. Jawaharlal had been hopeful that she would recover, thinking right up until a week before her death that she was improving.

The death, even though not entirely unanticipated, therefore came as a shock.

Jawaharlal, who had been feeling the family's property a burdensome nuisance for some time, had trouble returning to Anand Bhawan, as full of ghosts as it seemed to him. He had just about a year earlier written to Nan suggesting that she and her family move into the great mansion, echoing one of their father's last wishes. Nan and Ranjit had resisted this, feeling it improper, and had continued to maintain their residences, first at 9 Cawnpore Road, and presently at number 6. But the Jawaharlal who returned from Germany was forlorn and could not envision staying alone in such a place. He was also concerned about the expenses he had incurred over the past year. While he had originally proposed selling a cottage on the property to generate some cash, he now thought that perhaps he should sell the Anand Bhawan estate in its entirety. Nan and Ranjit thought this unthinkable, and so at last gave in to family pressure. They agreed to move in and take over the management of Anand Bhawan, sharing expenses with Jawaharlal as appropriate.

Living together proved mutually beneficial immediately. Jawaharlal was rescued from his grief and freed of responsibilities he found tedious, while the Pandits found 'great joy' in having their hero home. Anand Bhawan sparkled once more.[23]

~

In the same month that Sanger received her invitation from the AIWC and finalized her plans to come to the subcontinent, the British Parliament passed the Government of India Act, which served as a kind of proto constitution for the colonized country. It undid the idea of dyarchy that had been in place since the Montagu-Chelmsford Reforms of 1919 and supported greater local autonomy. There were many concerns with the new measure, for it allowed for separate electorates for Muslim communities, but not for Dalits, and it contained no reference or commitment to fundamental rights. While protests were lodged, it did spur greater interest and participation in local government, which was now given greater policy-making powers.

Indians were allowed to run for seats on local boards to 'try to improve civic life', and the Congress decided now to allow members to contest, even though they were formally protesting the 1935 Act. Nan was constrained by her family obligations and her additional responsibilities with the AIWC, but her sense of duty to uplift those less fortunate than herself drove her to stand for the Allahabad Municipal Board. She informed her brother of her decision and inquired about his views on the election. He replied that he had himself been approached to run for a seat but had declined. 'But that is no reason why you should not stand,' he said supportively to his sister, declining to offer any further advice one way or the other.[24]

The Congress put up thirteen candidates. Just before Sanger had come to stay with her, Nan had been informed that she, Ranjit and some other members of the Congress were among nine winners.[25] Still in Germany, Jawaharlal said he was 'interested' in the news, which he described as 'exciting happenings'.[26]

While other women had previously served on the Board—Nan's cousin Uma had helped pave the way—Nan immediately made waves by refusing to defer to the ossified corps of men that had long dominated the council. 'Some of them had been there for years and were rigid in their attitudes . . . The seat allotted to me was between two old gentlemen who, quite obviously, were women haters as well as being anti-Congress,' she recalled later, 'I did not feel like the emancipated young woman people imagined me to be.' Nevertheless, she persisted. She 'was elected chairman of the Education Committee . . . This committee was controlled by the conservative elements who had a vested interest in it . . . A more narrow-minded, backward group of men I had never met before. Hindu and Muslim alike, all belonged to a feudal age. Their ideas on education were vague, and one and all they disapproved of the education of girls though they could not, under the rules, abolish the few existing primary schools'. But this was only a small mercy. For the 'buildings of the municipal schools were almost dilapidated and ill ventilated. The teachers were so ill paid that they were barely able to keep alive . . . It was not possible for them to be interested in their work as their main preoccupation was in trying to keep out of the moneylenders' clutches'.[27]

Nan soon discovered that the situation was due not just to the close-mindedness of committee patriarchs, but to a mendacity and vindictiveness that had seeped its way deep into the entire bureaucracy. The school superintendent had primary power, not Nan's committee, and he maliciously lashed out against anyone who crossed him, while putting up pretences whenever she inquired into affairs. During her 'first visit of inspection', her 'surprise and concern at the appalling conditions were equaled only by the shock of seeing how subservient the teachers were to the superintendent and how he, in turn, groveled before' her. She saw right through all of this.

So, much to the superintendent's dismay, she decided to visit all primary schools under her jurisdiction 'immediately', and then regularly thereafter with groups of teachers in small batches. The committee and the superintendent objected vociferously, arguing that the men would be 'rude', and that the women were from a 'low social class' that she should not mix with. The committee added that the women teachers' world was so far apart from Nan's that they simply would not be able to understand anything she had to say.

Nan pushed ahead, inviting teachers into Anand Bhawan to share their stories and their problems with her. She was quick to see how men and women behaved very differently. Male teachers were 'pleased to have been asked' their opinions on matters, and generally were ready to offer their thoughts on a range of subjects without hesitation. The women, on the other hand, proved more reticent. Many of them were child widows who had become teachers 'because it required little training and because it carried a certain prestige, though they were exploited by the men who controlled their working destiny'. They were 'suspicious' of Nan at first, unsure what her intentions were. It seemed unbelievable to them that anyone, particularly someone of her stature, should care. With 'a great deal of patience' and perseverance, Nan gained their trust, at least to a degree, convincing them, in what was to become her trademark talent, of her 'genuine interest in their work and in them as human beings'.

Making this connection was important, but Nan was very aware that it was hardly revolutionary. The women teachers' predicament was the product of a 'warped social system' that was international, with national, regional and local manifestations. Nan could only do so much from her position but was determined to make the most of it.

One of the first things she gleaned from these discussions, complementing the observations she made during her site visits, was that the poverty and hunger of students were just as serious an impediment to their successful education as crumbling buildings and underpaid instructors. The children 'came in tattered clothes and with bloated bellies.' Many were undernourished and faced endemic diseases like tuberculosis. A 'periodic medical checkup' was to identify students at risk, and to provide those in need with milk as a booster.[28] The milk was usually diluted and quickly thinned out when distributed, leaving many children with nothing. Nan identified 'the first problem' as money. The municipal budgets were simply too meagre to do anything meaningful. It was not within the Board's power to change revenue since that power resided with higher-ups in the British administration. As a workaround, Nan proposed that they raise money 'through donations from the wealthy people in the city', specifically targeting 'wealthy bankers and businessmen' in the Indian part of town who, she felt, owed it to their community and their country to help. She was under no illusions about the likelihood of success: 'Unfortunately, their money was spent either on erecting temples or, under pressure from the Collector, for some scheme in which the Governor's wife was interested. For this, if the amount contributed was large enough, the reward came in the shape of a title . . .'[29]

The men of the Municipal Board were apoplectic. One warned her direly: 'Sister, you must realize the consequences of this dangerous proposal. Giving these children milk today—perhaps better educational facilities tomorrow—simply means that the day after tomorrow they will demand to sit in our places—Then what?' Nan responded squarely: 'You have summed this up correctly. That's exactly my idea.'[30]

Nan was met with stunned silence, not only from those in the boardroom but from the city's high and mighty. With no one supporting her, she 'issued an appeal ward-wide for one penny from each home every month to build up a milk fund'. The 'pennies poured in and filled to overflowing the little wooden boxes we had put up in each *mohalla* [district], and the milk scheme was inaugurated'. Ranjit and Jawaharlal, in addition to several family friends, bolstered the coffers with sizable personal gifts, which together with the pennies made the milk scheme a success.[31]

Nan also turned her attention to night schools aimed at adults. Again, she was amazed at the shoddy implementation of a well-meaning policy. Classes were held 'irregularly in a shack or broken-down mud hut with a flickering hurricane lantern.' Few attended, and those who did rarely learned anything. Nan assessed the situation. There could have been many factors keeping men and women from the school, including curriculum and community factors.

She discerned that locals needed to see a social value in coming to night school. Moreover, material had to be taught in culturally familiar terms, to be relatable to everyday people. This was a much larger problem, in fact, with primary school students being taught using readers featuring King George V on the cover. 'The first lesson was about Nelson and ended with his famous words at the Battle of Trafalgar! A picture of Nelson in his admiral's uniform accompanied the text. The dress was unfamiliar to the children and England meant nothing to them.'

Nan was unable to do anything about the primary school curriculum, since that was dictated by British administrators, but she was able to address the problems of the night schools because their core mission was literacy, not mastery of subject matters. She converted each of them into clubs—happening places for the community to gather. Activities included singing, reading from newspapers, and reciting epic stories. 'Together with all this, reading and writing were also thrown in and accepted without fuss.'[32]

~

In late 1936, about a year after her election to the Municipal Board, Nan was selected, along with Ranjit, to run for a seat in the state legislature, now made possible by the Government of India Act of 1935.[33] While she was enjoying her work at the local level, she could not resist the challenge the new position presented. 'Difficulties, opposition, criticism—these things are meant to be overcome, and there is special joy in facing them and coming out on top. It is only when there is nothing but praise that life loses its charm and I begin to wonder what I should do about it,' she recalled about two years later.[34] She was about to get her wish.

Nan was slated to run in the Cawnpore-Bilaspur (Kanpur) women's constituency, facing off against Lady Srivastava, whose husband worked in the Viceroy's Council.[35] Like most others opposing the Congress candidates, Lady Srivastava was a powerful elite who generally was pro-British, or at least accommodational, and backed by money. While Nan herself did not lack money or clout, Congress candidates by and large were underdogs, easily outspent by their rivals. To compensate, they had to engage in granular politicking—to spend time with individuals and communities they were hoping to represent.

Nan's constituency was a 'rural one and very spread out'. Standing for this election was altogether different from her previous experience, where she was able to contest from the comfort of her own home. Now she had to plan extensive travel, with days away from Anand Bhawan. Accompanied by several male colleagues, Nan set out by a Ford car, 'which had seen better days'.

Nan's first night on the trail was spent in a little village. After dining with the locals, she was escorted to her bed, which was laid out in a tidy school, right next to those of her companions. This shocked her, since she was wearing a coarse cotton, khadi sari, and usually slept in something much more comfortable. But there was nowhere private to change. With nothing for it, she laid down and fell right to sleep.

The next morning was hardly better. She discovered she had to bathe 'with one's clothes on in the traditional open-air manner of the Indian peasant'. Again, the thick khadi got in her way, and she felt the task of cleansing herself this way difficult. But Nan was determined to make the best of things, and to adjust as necessary, her experience in prison having prepared her for life beyond the comforts with which she had grown up. She came to love life on the road, and the people she met along the way. She instantly connected with each of them in a personal way.

That night, she spoke with Ranjit by telephone. His constituency was Allahabad itself, so he remained at home with Jawaharlal. When she told him that she had 'slept with the boys' since she had no other place, he roared with laughter at his wife's predicament.[36]

While Nan, Ranjit and other candidates concentrated on their specific races, Jawaharlal, now known widely simply as Nehru, traversed the country encouraging people to vote. He called on them to treat a trip to the polls as 'a pilgrimage' and to resist temptations offered by those hoping to shore up the existing system. He declared: 'We go to the legislatures not to co-operate with the apparatus of

British imperialism, but to combat the Act and seek to end it, and to resist in every way British imperialism in its attempt to strengthen its hold on India and its exploitation of the Indian people.'[37]

The competition was fierce, the *Times of India* noting the 'unusually large number of candidates' in the field. Very few incumbents were returned unopposed, but Sir J.P. Srivastava, the husband of Nan's opponent, was among them.[38] In late December, an objection was raised to Nan's candidacy in the hopes of derailing her chances.[39] But nothing came of it.

Voting stretched out over the first two months of 1937. Polling day in the United Provinces, where the constituencies of Nan and Ranjit were located, was slated for 8 February.[40] As predicted, the opposition candidates—that is, those representing the establishment and status quo—offered rides to polling stations, and luxurious food and drink as rewards. But the people turned away from this, not to be fooled, and instead cast their lot with the insurgent Congress. Surveying the landscape, Nan recalled herself thinking 'These are the people of India. They and they alone will give the final answer. I will never forget this day. How right Bapu is—we must never forget them.'[41]

Congress won major victories throughout the country, in eight out of eleven provinces, and so were 'invited by the governors to form ministries'. As soon as she learned her fate, Nan dashed off a telegram to her children, who were at home in Anand Bhawan with Swarup Rani and Bibima. Upon receipt at mealtime, '[Chandra]Lekha tore it open and read: "Yes for Mummie." She and her sisters looked at each other "bewildered". Suddenly Lekha shrieked: "Yeah for Mummie!" It means: "Yeah for Mummie". "Mummie's won the election"!' With amusement, Nayantara later recalled the incident and explained: 'Resigned to our use of American slang [picked up through their time at the American Woodstock School], Mummie had obviously thought "Yeah" would be the most apt way to announce her victory to us, and the telegraph office had of course changed the word, thinking it was a mistake. We dropped our forks and joined in a wild dance around the dining-table.'[42]

Nan herself swelled with pride, in what she personally had accomplished to a degree, but more so for her country and its people. '[A]las for us and for India,' she reminisced regretfully decades later, 'we keep forgetting them [the ordinary people], letting them down when personal opportunity beckons us, running to them when their aid can tip the political scales in our favour. In every crisis in India the faceless multitude has rallied to uphold the great ideals on which our civilization has been based, but in the continuing crises in *their* lives what have *we* done, the so-called leaders, the educated, the "upper classes"?'[43]

~

Once the Congress won the elections, they had to decide whether they should actually enter the legislatures, the question known as 'office acceptance'. Local Congress committees met to discuss the matter, each coming to their own conclusions and forwarding those on to the central All India Congress Committee for deliberation. Nan and Ranjit participated in the Allahabad District Congress Committee on 20 February, shortly after their victories had been announced.[44] A week later, the Congress Working Committee met to discuss the issue as well. Gandhi attended this gathering, and while he did not choose sides, he tacitly gave his consent to participation, suggesting that Congress candidates be allowed to enter provincial legislatures and form governments on the condition that the local governors agree not to interfere. They had the legal power to do so under the new scheme, and the Congress saw this as an effort by the British government to effectively limit any true autonomy. Asking for this stipulation seemed like a reasonable compromise to him.[45]

Gandhi's reluctance to definitively take a stance on the matter allowed local Congress bodies to debate the matter and come to their conclusions. The United Provinces Provincial Congress, of which Nan and Ranjit were a part, thus voted in open session against office entry, seventy-one to forty-nine.[46] But they were in the minority, with most divisions approving of participation.

The Congress then convened nationally a few days later in Delhi to decide on a course of action. The Working Committee, under Nehru's guidance, moved forward with what seemed like a reasonable balance of different views. Congress candidates could accept offices though British-appointed governors had to assure 'non-interference'. The objective of Congress participation, though, was to resist and reject the constitution of the 1935 Act and have it replaced with a new one formulated through a Constituent Assembly.[47]

From the Working Committee, the matter now moved before the full All-India Congress Committee, the executive body of the organization. The Congress Socialist Party was a somewhat new faction within the larger group, started only three years previous by Jayaprakash Narayan and others. JP, as Narayan was commonly known, opposed office entry and submitted an amendment to that effect, essentially a line-item veto of the larger Working Committee's proposition. Nan rose to second the motion, 'so intent' to speak her mind in rare open defiance of her brother and Gandhi. There were murmurings throughout the assembly, for this was no small thing. 'I felt he treated me rather unfairly,' she later wrote of her brother's actions at that moment, 'ringing the bell even before my time was over. But I stuck to my guns and said what I had to say'.[48]

The committee discussed the amendment for thirteen hours, before sending it down to defeat 135 to seventy-eight.[49] Some technical wording was instead altered to ensure the proper autonomy of elected Congress officials. With that the Working Committee's resolution advanced, sending all further amendments down to defeat, and carrying the day 127 to seventy. The Congress was ready to enter provincial governments and form new ministries.[50]

The British did not make things easy, refusing to promise non-interference. Without that, the Congress could not move forward. The stalemate led the British to appoint interim ministries for a few months, though these lacked any legitimacy. By July, with matters coming to a head, the Congress Working Committee agreed to move forward according to their original stipulations, regardless of whether the British formally agreed or not.[51]

~

On 12 July 1937, Pandit Govind Ballabh Pant accepted an offer from the governor of the United Provinces to form a new government, announcing that he would name his cabinet within four days.[52] Pant then huddled at Anand Bhawan for intense discussions with Nehru and Maulana Abul Kalam Azad about ministry appointments, and rumours that women might be included began to circulate.⁵³ Buzz surrounded Nan as a possible appointment.

The next day, Nan found her name splashed across papers around the world. Reuters heralded 'India's First Woman Cabinet Minister,' while papers from the *Manchester Guardian* and the *Scotsman* to the *Times of India* and the *South China Morning Post* all ran variations. The achievement was considerable.⁵⁴ Nan was only the fourth woman ever named to a Cabinet post in the British Empire.⁵⁵

Nan had initially been in a 'dilemma' about what to do about Pant's offer. 'I did not want to join the Ministry. In my opinion,' she wrote two years later, 'the decision to accept office had been wrong and I was not in favour of it.' But, she felt that she should go along with the final Congress decision. 'Besides this . . . the offer had a certain significance' that was not lost on her. 'In offering me a seat in the U.P. Cabinet the Congress was accepting the principle of equality between man and woman.'⁵⁶ This sealed her decision and led her to accept the offer.

The swearing-in ceremony proved a challenge when Nan realized that she would have to declare her loyalty to the King-Emperor. She wondered what to do, since she, and the people she now represented, avowedly did not accept such authority any longer. Ultimately, she decided she had made the choice to accept the office, and so had to take the requisite steps. 'But when my turn came I could hardly speak,' she recalled. 'It was a most difficult five minutes. Shaking hands hurriedly with the Governor, Sir Harry Haig, whom I had known since I was young girl and he the Commissioner of Allahabad, I followed my colleagues to the next room where soft drinks were being passed. As I picked up a glass the aide-de-camp to the Governor asked if I was feeling well. "Thank you, I'm well," I answered. "It's just that the King is stuck in my throat." "Well, you must wash him down, then," said the Englishman with a smile.'⁵⁷

Nan gasped when she saw her garish office at the Central Secretariat. There were all kinds of chairs and tables and bookshelves strewn about. She felt it rather resembled a 'a second-hand furniture dealer's shop'. A garish pink carpet clashed with the 'apple green . . . walls' of the room. And everything was covered in dust. As soon as she learned that she was allowed to make some basic stylistic modifications to make herself comfortable in the space, she exchanged the pink carpet for 'a delightful beige and bluish green one', and hung 'restful blue-green curtains' she had brought from Anand Bhawan. The extra furniture was sent to storage, and the room was reset in a manner that more suited her tastes.

As she surveyed her handiwork, she thought the room needed one final touch: some freshly cut roses placed carefully in a green ceramic bowl. The 'request was met with a horrified silence'. 'But Madam,' her P.A. said in a hue matching that of her redecorated room, 'you can't have flowers in here, it has never been done before.' 'Then it's time someone began,' Nan replied, 'I think I shall go down to the garden and pick some now.' From that moment forward, fresh flowers always adorned her workspace.[58]

~

The first few weeks were a period of serious adjustment. She felt a heavy responsibility, and she 'frequently cried . . . [herself] to sleep, wondering if . . . [she] would be able to do credit to the family and the country.'[59] A telegram from her brother helped snap her out of it. 'Remember the Chinese philosopher with four sons,' he counselled. 'The first was clever and trained to be a poet. The second was brilliant and learned the arts. The third went into the army. The fourth was the despair of the famous father who consulted many friends. Their advice was that the boy's intellect was limited so he might do well as a cabinet minister.' He signed off with love and good wishes, and Nan took the good-natured ribbing as an important reminder to keep her ego in check. 'As I look back to earlier days,' she recalled decades later, 'I am struck by the fact that no matter how our fortunes fluctuated our sense of humour remained, helping us to see things in perspective. This was the anchor that kept us, especially me, in safe harbor.'[60]

Ministers were given several perks tempered by a certain Gandhian asceticism: Rs 500 per month, a car and a house, but rail travel was restricted to third class, with a small number of exceptions permitted. Nan had to shift to Lucknow from Allahabad and planned to have a look at the available houses, so she might choose one to her liking. She was taken aback when Pant did not permit this, instead demanding that she stay with him and his family in his own bungalow. Nan looked on Pant with affection and respected him a great deal but thought this utterly ridiculous. She protested, eventually getting him to agree to her terms for only a month's time. Some of her more enlightened colleagues 'teased . . . [her] mercilessly about having to be chaperoned', but all agreed that some like Pant would have to be 'converted to new ideas of women's freedom as gently as possible'.

Once her probation was over, Nan moved into her allotted house. Ranjit would stay when the legislature was in session, and the girls would also visit during school vacations. But for the most part, Nan was on her own.[61]

While she thought her new home was aesthetically the best one, it was also the one no one else wanted. She wrote: 'It was on the banks of the Goomti River, with a lovely well-cared-for garden, and was situated in a park, part of which was a zoo. I soon became accustomed to waking up when the lions roared and it seemed as if my bed was being shaken.'[62]

Once settled, Nan began to regularly entertain in the evenings, as she had always done. This drew the attention of Pant, who inquired after the many male visitors she seemed to have. Nan amusedly sought to reassure him that they were mostly extended family or close friends, but he remained sceptical. '[Y]ou are much too good-looking to be living alone,' he exclaimed. Nan took this in stride, determined to live her life on her terms, pushing for change where possible, and accepting that it would not come as fast as she wanted.[63]

~

Nan was given the 'portfolios of Local Self-Government and Medical and Public Health'. From her very first day, she realized what an enormous task she faced. Her predecessors—vassals of the British Indian administration—had mostly looked on such posts as ceremonial, and opportunities for their own benefit. Work that was meant to benefit the people in any meaningful way for the most part had not been done.

Nan faced a desk full of files, many of which simply had been signed by the previous minister without any action being taken at all. As she worked her way through them, she soon developed a rhythm, advising on what to do where appropriate. But she soon realized that the rot went deep, and unaddressed piles of files were simply symptomatic of complete dysfunction. 'The state of affairs in the municipal and district boards in the province were deplorable. Few of the duties of the City Fathers were performed, and the bribery and corruption shocked me because they were part of the accepted pattern . . . Work in the Public Health Department was equally slack. There were all manner of reports of work done, reports that were grossly exaggerated. Here, too, though the scope for patronage and corruption was not so great as in the Local Self-Government Department, plenty existed.'[64]

Just as she had done while on the Allahabad Municipal Board a year earlier, Nan decided to tour the areas under her jurisdiction, and to conduct surprise spot checks and site visits of schools, utilities and hospitals, while monitoring basic infrastructure like roads along the way. She wanted to understand the needs of the people as best as she could and, again drawing on her previous experiences, planned out interactive encounters. During one visit in October to Bundlekhand, she opted to go by 'cart', and to stay with ordinary peasants while there.[65] Where possible, she threw her support behind local initiatives aimed at welfare improvement, backing for instance a literacy campaign in the Lucknow district proposed by a students' federation.[66] These simple steps immediately endeared her to people throughout the United Provinces.

Part of her job entailed visiting the local Municipal Board, where she was to be welcomed with a speech and then provide a perfunctory statement of her own. But 'a few days before my visit', she wrote two years later, 'I received a copy of the . . . Board's address together with suggestions for the reply I was to give.' The visits were nothing but a sham, she realized, everything prefabricated to give an appearance of efficacy. She declined to play along, informing her hosts that she would instead deliver her response '*ex tempore*', a commitment she then carried forward from then on to many of her public addresses.[67]

At the actual event, she was 'presented with a beautiful tray decorated with Kashmir engravings', in keeping with the usual practice of giving such gifts to ministers as a reward for their looking away from instances of mal- practice and feasance. Nan took the stage by announcing that the point of the Congress government was to 'bring clean and efficient administration to the towns'. There was 'much to be done', she declared, and 'a lot more to be undone'. Board finances had to come under scrutiny. This was dramatic, but she topped it when she pointed to her new tray and proclaimed her intention to auction it right off, to raise money for the local hospital. Her hosts were aghast. But the stunt was effective and powerfully symbolic. Her Rs 250 tray brought in Rs 5000, the 'landed gentry . . . outbidding themselves . . . to keep . . . [her] from prying too much into things'.[68]

Within a few months, she had a basic understanding of how services under her departments were delivered: they simply were not. She noted that 'roads lacked repair, drainage was bad, electricity inadequate, schools in a shocking state, teachers unpaid for months, and money for parks and other amenities diverted illegally for other purposes'. Hospitals were even worse off, working overcapacity with no money and improperly trained staff. Nan had discerned that the problem lay in oversight since the supervising director always announced his visits and was thus misled, perhaps willfully, about actual affairs. By dropping in unexpectedly, Nan was able to see what was going on: an abysmal abdication of the actual avocation. 'The poor, especially the women, were terrified at the idea of going to a hospital . . . Once admitted, they were more or less left to fate.'[69]

~

Nan had a parliamentary secretary and two departmental secretaries for each of her portfolios, in addition to her personal assistant and managerial staff. Men held all of these positions, and Nan soon recognized that they would often go out of their way to facilitate her work or to help her. She chalked this up to her pathbreaking role: men were simply not used to being in a subordinate position to women, and she felt it natural that some would take a 'chivalrous' attitude to the experience, even as others vociferously objected to the very idea of an inverted relationship. She developed a close bond especially with A.G. Kher, who would go on to become the speaker of the U.P. Assembly.

Still, Nan also knew that Kher and the others were emblematic of the existing patriarchal structure, and their imagination was limited in many ways. The men's 'chivalry' often translated into misguided efforts to shield Nan from the cruel realities of the world, particularly anything that was seen as unbecoming of someone of her class and upbringing.[70]

But Nan had become a hero to the poor and working class, and to women throughout the province. And they wrote to her in droves, sometimes simply to send blessings or sing her praises, but just as often to appeal for assistance. 'Sometimes they were pathetically urgent in their need for help,' Nayantara recalled, 'and [they] confusedly began: 'Dear Sister: You are my father, and my mother. If you cannot help me, no one can.'[71]

One of the letters Nan received expressed this sentiment in flowery Urdu, which neither Nan nor her staff could read. They had it read to them and discovered that some women in town (Lucknow) were being forced from their homes by the local board. Nan decided that she would go visit to assess the situation for herself and to see how she could help.

'This matter can be looked into by one of us, and there's no need at all for you to go,' she was told by Kher. When Nan insisted, Kher protested that Pant would not want her to go. Baffled and exasperated, she asked how the chief minister was involved in the matter at all. The next morning, as planned, she went to her car to be taken to the house in question. The driver shamefacedly told her that he could not take her. 'Well, I must drive myself,' she said self-assuredly.

Once it became clear that she was determined to go, her chauffeur and Kher got in the car with her and explained, astonished that she had not yet realized, that she was headed to a house for courtesans. The women did not wish to move because they feared it would be detrimental to their business. Nan and the others were politely received, and Nan promised to bring the matter up before her superiors, though she knew that nothing would be done on a matter involving prostitution. But just as she was leaving, Nan was informed that one of the women in the home was sick and contagious. Nan visited with her and promised to get her aid, which was being denied to her on account of her profession. Kher found this too much. But Nan pursued the matter and found that even with her intervention, no one would help the woman in need, who was infected with syphilis and was also pregnant. Nan then issued a formal order requiring her care, securing a bed in a hospital and proper treatment. 'When I look back on my life there are a few incidents that give me satisfaction. This is one of them,' she wrote many decades later. Realizing that the young woman was but one among many, Nan then pushed to establish a clinic for pregnant women. Though many opposed this, including Pant, she eventually succeeded in creating what was a first-of-its-kind facility. For years afterwards, the young woman Nan saved would write to her on her birthday and send a Banaras handkerchief as a small token of gratitude.[72]

A few months later, Nan took to the radio to deliver a scathing takedown of patriarchy, identifying the 'cult of domesticity' as a systemic element of generational suppression. 'In the course of time, a system of female education has been perfected, which is designed to persuade the woman that she is in need of protection, but . . . only . . . if she will abide by certain rules,' Nan said. 'While [her brothers] . . . were allowed interests outside the home, she must remain inside. Thus a separation of male and female thought and activity has grown up, and it becomes increasingly difficult not to think in terms of this tradition,' she went on. 'Brought up in this tradition, the Indian woman gradually became what she was intended to be . . . not an individual with any independent ideas, but [someone who] had to express her contribution to life in terms of contribution to the man [father, husband, son/s] who owned her . . . Generations of unthinking action on the part of woman have succeeded in drawing the chains that bind her closer, and now when darkness is giving place to dawn she hesitates on the threshold of a new and free life, and is afraid to step forward,' she added. Then she closed: 'People tell me that the modern woman is aggressive. I wonder if this is true. But if it is, she has good reason for it . . .'[73]

~

In late December 1937, Nan was invited to deliver remarks at the annual meeting of the national All India Women's Conference. Her path-breaking role in government now catapulted her to a new kind of fame, outside the shadow of her illustrious family. The official proceedings of the meeting took note of the 'unique magnificence' of the atmosphere at the gathering, singling out Sarojini Naidu, Nan and English representative Grace Lankester for their presence. It was quite the welcome for Nan, in attendance for the first time. She was further feted during the opening delivery of the annual report, the organizing secretary taking note of all the women elected in the recent elections.

Shortly thereafter, Nan was 'greeted with loud cheers when she rose to address' the body. She began by noting that she had not really stayed away from the national meetings by accident, but rather because she had been involved in the political field while 'this Conference has always endeavored to keep away from politics'. She commended the organization for its achievements, and for its larger objectives, but also urged her compatriots to join the larger anti-colonial cause. 'It seems to me that in a country like ours and with conditions as they are, we cannot achieve what we have set out to do by merely passing resolutions . . .' Moreover, she went on, what was taking place in India had to be seen in a larger, global context. 'Our difficulties are increased by the tragic aspect of the world situation and the question of Women's rights is getting merged in the large and more important one of the rights of humanity. This makes it immediately necessary for women of every nation to unite and strengthen the causes of democracy and peace of which the women's cause is a part. The terrible sufferings inflicted in Africa, Europe and China must inspire all women to further effort. The struggle for equal rights may continue, but the urgent need is for us to restore to the world its balance and give back to men a true sense of values. The terrible shadow of war must not be allowed to increase . . . Let us work for equality and freedom for our sex by all means, but let us not forget the more important issue of equality and freedom for humanity, and by joining our forces to those who work towards this, let us help to make the world beautiful to live in.'[74]

Several other speakers followed Nan that opening day of the conference, culminating in some remarks from Sarojini Naidu. It was a moment Nan's younger self could never have imagined would come to pass, though she had dreamt of it just the same. In the poetic singsong that was her trademark, Mrs Naidu heralded Vijaya Lakshmi Pandit's achievements: 'Do not be deceived by that gentle voice and those appealing eyes. Do not be deceived by something like "abala" [Telugu for a weak woman] speaking to you; it is the voice of the woman of India returning into her accustomed inheritance of Shakti [female/power], the power that creates and the power that destroys, and we thank her for being herself to-day the symbol of many lovely and brave things for which the women of India stand.'[75] This was high praise from the High Priestess of Homilies.

Nan made one further contribution to the conference, when the body reconvened the following day. The members were asked to consider a resolution calling for free and compulsory primary education and the creation of a corps of trained, women teachers. Nan took the floor to say, re-emphasizing the point she had made in her formal presentation, that such resolutions had so far failed to achieve anything meaningful as the matter was ultimately a political question. Governments had to be forced to live up to their obligations, including providing children with basic healthcare and education, for these were their rights. She implored the attendees to therefore see fruit in political agitation, and to get more directly involved.[76]

~

In January 1938, Nan returned home to Anand Bhawan for a brief stay. Time paused, and the whole family was able to enjoy a reunion of sorts. Chandralekha, Nayantara, and Rita were home from school. Jawaharlal, Ranjit, Swarup Rani and Bibima were all in town as well. Together, they celebrated each other's achievements, and enjoyed one another's company. Nan had been profiled just three days before in the *Christian Science Monitor*, which celebrated her pioneering role in government. The essay introduced Nan to a much wider audience, significantly bringing her to the attention of many in the United States. 'Tall and graceful, Mrs Pandit has in abundance the wit and intelligence of her father, the courage of her brother, and the charm of a cultured Hindu brought up in luxury,' the correspondent glowed.[77] 'She has been one of the first of her sex in India to court imprisonment in a political cause. Now she wears only khaddar and leads an extremely simple life,' they added.

On 10 January, the family busied itself for their anticipated departures. Nan was leaving that night for Lucknow and Jawaharlal two days later for some extensive travel. Swarup Rani was agitated by all of this, and 'seemed depressed'. Nan suggested that she come up a few days later and stay with her for some time. Swarup Rani brightened at the thought. Around 9 p.m. after dinner, Nan went to hug her mother goodbye. 'She put her arms up and as she did so she suddenly collapsed.' She had suffered a stroke, and by early morning had died.[78] In its obituary for the Nehru matriarch published the next day, the *New York Times* noted that she was 'an ardent supporter of the nationalist cause . . . and welcomed her husband's decision to give their palatial home to the party and live in an outhouse.' The *Times* added that she had presided over a meeting once, where she was injured by police called in to break it up.[79]

On 11 January, Swarup Rani was cremated and her ashes were immersed in the holy Ganga River, on the outskirts of Allahabad. When the family returned home, Bibima said she wanted to go right to sleep. She wrapped herself in a shawl and laid down right on the floor. 'We thought it best to let her sleep, but, when she was not up four hours later, Bhai went to wake her and persuade her to take some nourishment. She was dead . . . It was certainly a case of dying of a broken heart.'[80] In a flash, the Nehrus lost two women dear to them, who represented strength, resolve and compassion.

~

In early April 1938, Nan set out for the Hindu holy city of Hardwar, in the northwestern point of the United Provinces (now the state of Uttarakhand), nestled amongst the Himalayan foothills near Dehra Dun. The city was (and continues to be) home to one of the largest religious celebrations in the world, the Kumbh Mela, where people came from all over the subcontinent to bathe in the mountain-pristine aqua-emerald waters of the Ganga River. The site was one of four spots where a drop of the godly nectar of immortality (*amrita*) was said to have fallen, and where, in its diluted state, it was said to heal those in need in lieu of granting them everlasting life. The festival was (and continues to be) held only once every twelve years, its rarity combined with its promise of deliverance to make participation highly valued and desired.

Nan's visit was related to the opening of the great festival, to meet local religious authorities and to ask for their assistance in maintaining sanitary and safe conditions throughout the get-together. While in town, Nan also planned to open a swadeshi (home-spun) exhibition.[81] But feeling 'happy as a child going to its first party', she suddenly found herself obsessed with the idea of immersing herself in the special waters of the region, even though her hometown of Allahabad too was bordered by the Ganges and was one of the other three homes of the great festival (held on a different cycle). Despite her enthusiasm, she could not work out proper scheduling and had to cancel her plans to participate. Her mood soured from this and she made the journey into the holy city scowling at all who came near her. As they neared their destination, though, the multitudes thronged all around them—over one million visitors were estimated to be in the small city—and Nan found herself enthralled. Just then, a 'young fellow-traveller' from Punjab noted with alarm and disgust how some took advantage of the celebration for their own ends, observing that 'these great vulgar men marching nude through the streets of Hardwar without any religious motive—just showing themselves off, making suggestive gestures—marching in a brazen-manner, thwarting the authorities in the knowledge that they were supported by the ignorant to whom their flaunted nudity was a symbol of sainthood—and the women . . . , old and young, rich and poor, throwing themselves at the feet of these rascals, fighting with each other in a desperate effort to . . . receive the blessing . . .' Nan felt jolted awake. India had many great traditions, beliefs, and festivals. But devious and deeply deceptive men, corrupt and conniving, had ensorceled people, enticing and then ensnaring them through trickery. She could suddenly see through the illusions. 'I saw before me,' she recalled the next year, 'an enslaved people, poverty-stricken and down-trodden,—their weak undeveloped bodies being a correct outer shell for their weak and undisciplined minds.' Crooks and con artists exploited ill-informed people in terrible need, feeding their depraved cravings in the name of offering divine assistance. 'To-day India was a land divided, where brother fought against brother, where each one strove for his own selfish end, and where the ignorance and superstition of women was in no small part responsible for the downfall of the race. But . . . a new hope was born within me,' she went on. 'If there are quarrels, there is also much unity. If there is ignorance, knowledge also exists. And if superstition still stalks the land, is it not equally true that enlightenment pursues it and seeks to drive it out?'[82] As these thoughts gained coherence, so too they helped shape Nan's new sense of purpose.

These contours were made further visible when the city's local religious leaders, the pandas, came to pay her a visit at the little rest home where she way staying, following up on the official meeting she had just held with them. The pandas were 'enormously wealthy', with some the 'heads of big religious foundations'. They were powerful and privileged. They brought Nan a written petition asking that cow slaughter be banned in the city, their request coming on the heels of a 'Cow Protection Conference' held the week before in the city under the auspices of the Sanatana Pratininidhi Sabha of Punjab, a right-leaning religious organization that had had ties with Lala Lajpat Rai.[83] Thinking the appeal was generally a not unreasonable request given the city's special sanctity for Hindus, and cows holding a special place of significance, Nan signalled an initial willingness to assist. But as she read through the petition, she blanched. The request was only to ban cow slaughter in one district within the city, one home to a small community of 'Muslim butchers and vegetable sellers'. Nan grew 'furious', realizing that this was little more than a thinly veiled effort to attack the local minority population. Nan asked why they simply did not want to enact the ban on the whole city, and when they replied that they felt it easiest to begin one district at a time, she bluntly asked if they felt no shame in taking away the livelihood of poor people. 'At this they lost their temper and started to shout abuse at me and at the Nehrus for being traitors to the Hindu creed,' she later recalled. Things grew heated quickly and the staff had to ask the panda delegation to leave. As they left, they warned they would 'return with the whole town'. The local police chief suggested placing the house under the protection of his men, but Nan politely turned all of this down, feeling it not in keeping with the ethos of her family. Moreover, she added, she 'was a popularly elected Minister and if those who voted for . . . [her] wished to demonstrate against . . . [her] it was their privilege to do so'.

The pandas were true to their word. 'Within an hour the shouting of slogans gave us warning that a large crowd was approaching. I gave orders that all the doors and windows should be closed, and the crowd soon surrounded the house screaming vile abuse and threatening to break down the doors. They did shatter nearly all the window panes,' she recorded. The situation was deadly serious, and the officials accompanying Nan started to fear for their safety. Nan decided that she had had enough. 'I flung open the door and surprised the shouting crowd. For a moment they were silent, shocked at seeing me, and I climbed onto a chair,' she wrote. In dramatic fashion, she removed her watch and held it aloft, declaring that everyone had but ten minutes to come to order and share their concerns. Her keen instincts helped her to calibrate her message for the ultra-orthodox crowd, and to play into their conservative mindset: 'If they wanted to harm me, I told them, it was their privilege to do so, but such an act would only hurt them. Here, on the banks of the holy Ganga, an assault on a [priestly caste] Brahman [sic, Brahmin] woman would hardly be to their credit.' The rage dissipated. She stated again that she would discuss their petition at an all-Hardwar level or not at all. She stood there as they stared at her, then at one another, and then turned to go home.[84]

~

Nan reflected on her experiences in office, and on how they mirrored broader trends in society. One of her favourite childhood books had been *Princes and Princesses*. She found the historic stories found in the volume to be 'thrilling' and grew particularly fascinated with Marie Antoinette, the famous queen who would meet her end by guillotine during the French Revolution. As a girl, she idolized the beautiful and powerful ruler, and found her story tragic and unfair. She frequently imagined herself in royal roles, her real-life upbringing not all that far removed from the fairy tale.

While Nan was in office, she was pleasantly startled to learn that Marie Antoinette's tale had been readied for theatrical release, and she excitedly made plans to see it. As she watched, the 'charm of the film entirely vanished, and the famished people of France [in the pre-Revolutionary period of the late eighteenth century] were replaced in . . . [her] imagination by the hungry millions of India, striving towards that same liberty, equality, and fraternity . . .'

She who had very much been a part of this class abruptly felt a sharp revulsion at the way those with social and financial privileges lived their lives in India, far removed from the terrible sufferings of ordinary people. 'Tennis tournaments are played, parties attended, festivities enjoyed, while far away in the distance, for those who wish to hear, is the cry of the oppressed and the hungry . . .'

As she was ruminating over these matters at home one evening, Nayantara walked in and tossed onto a table the worn copy of *Princes and Princesses*, which she had pulled from a shelf in her mother's library. 'What utter rubbish you must have read when you were a child, Mummie? These stories are stupid, and besides who is interested in Princes and Princesses, I should like to know,' she said dismissively, before dashing out of the room. Nan wrote knowingly: '"Princes and Princesses" lies abandoned in its now shabby cover—the once glittering letters are dull and even the child of to-day has no use for the stories it tells. And so the world moves on.'[85]

It was time for Nan to shed her youthful fantasies, for she now felt drawn to a higher purpose. Not only did the British colonial system need to be demolished, but so too did all social strictures that perpetuated discrimination and egregious inequity. While class was a key category that impacted people's opportunities, Nan also came to develop a finer appreciation for the role other categories like gender could play, sometimes in parallel, sometimes intersecting.

She wrote: 'A myth has persisted that, in spite of purdah and other social handicaps, the Indian woman was the real power inside the home . . . This is, in my opinion, an entirely wrong representation of the case and is the argument used by those men whom though outwardly educated, have not been able to uproot from their minds the inherited superstition and tradition of ages.' The worst example of this was of the man who took child-brides and otherwise mistreated his wife, all in the name of his mother's wishes. 'This mother or wife, as the case may be, was seldom seen but was a useful person to have in the background, and the myth of her power helped many a weak man out of uncomfortable corners.'[86]

Nan wrote approvingly of Gandhi's appeal to women to come out of the home and into the public sphere, to get involved actively in political matters that affected their daily lives.[87] Yet, in more abstract terms, her conclusions were scathing. 'I read with amazement the articles . . . in the press on woman . . . The writers are, in every instance I have come across, men, and with the confidence of those who are above reproach . . . They are so definite about all that concerns women. They appear to know so thoroughly what the requirements of women are and they are so ready to offer help and advice that it seems a pity to contradict them and shatter their illusions.'

'From the moment a woman desires sex, society compels her to become dependent on some man. If a woman, working for her living, is discovered to be immoral [i.e., to have sex outside of marriage, with or without her consent], she will be immediately discharged, no matter how efficient her work may have been. She is given no quarter at the hands of those who constitute themselves the guardians of the world's morals, and often ends her days as a prostitute. Put bluntly, even in this modern age a woman must choose between slavery and starvation.'

'Woman . . . must not try to see things as they are, or give expression to the urges within her . . . [Men and the women they have mesmerized] beg woman not to throw away her modesty and become unsexed and shameless. They entreat her in the name of India's past glory not to discard those virtues which, it is said, made the woman of a past age great. What these people really wish to preserve is neither virtue nor chastity, but the ignorance which has kept woman enslaved through the ages and which is now giving place to the light of knowledge. Once that light spreads, no power can prevent its reaching women, and they will shake off all restraint and fear and go eagerly forward with men to establish a better order of things.'[88]

Despite her individual achievements, Nan saw the way endemic patriarchy sought to caricature and thereby contain her. She noted that the 'interviews . . . men journalists produce generally begin with a description of my dress which varies with every account according to the mood of the writer. If he is of the socialist school of thought, I am dressed plainly, due emphasis being given to some aspect of my work. If, however, the writer represents either the popular press or the conservative view, I am clothed with all the magnificence of the Orient, from the 'red enamel caste mark' on my forehead to my "scarlet lacquered finger and toe nails".' She compared this treatment with that tendered to her brother: 'What straight, clear and intelligent questions are put to him, and yet I, who also attempt to do public work, am treated as if my interests were confined to clothes and children and those petty social activities in which the lady of means and leisure engages in order to allay the prickings of her conscience.'

This could not stand, she declared assuredly. 'Tradition dies hard and the world moves slowly; but slower still is the progress of human thought. Woman, though theoretically now the equal of man in most advanced countries, is still regarded in fact as the lesser being even by those whose public appearances would make it appear that they had accepted an equal partnership. But the advancement of woman cannot now be kept back in this way. She is now going forward, not because of the courtesy or chivalry of man, but because it is an accepted fact that in her advancement alone lies the future progress and prosperity of the world.'[89]

~

Just as the Kumbh Mela came to an end in Hardwar, virulent cholera broke out in the city and quickly spread. Within the first few days, there were 200 cases reported, with seventy-two deaths. Just two days later, there were about 150 cases in one day, all resulting in death.[90] The director of public health, who served under Nan, was dispatched to the city and oversaw 'house to house visits . . . to detect cases of infected persons'. Sick people were sent to the hospital, while others were vaccinated, with upwards of 20,000 people receiving protection. This helped somewhat to control the epidemic in the city, but it failed to contain it.[91] By the start of May, people were dying at the rate of 100 a day, primarily in the city, but elsewhere in the United Provinces as well.[92] Within a month, the crisis was declared the worst seen in the previous ten years, with 15,000 dead.[93]

As minister for public health, Nan was responsible for the government response. In advance of the Mela, she had tried to have the population inoculated enough to reach herd immunity. Once the disease struck, she called on all available medical personnel to assist. But superstition and stubbornness kept many from receiving prophylactic treatment—even the state's Assembly speaker, Purshottamdas Tandon, refused, leaving Nan exasperated. To make matters worse, many people believed that the dead had to be disposed of in the river, which was also a site of ritual bathing and the primary carrier of cholera.[94]

Nan decided she had to intervene in a more personal way, and so in early July, she began touring all affected areas herself, accompanied by her director-general. Even with protection, she placed herself at considerable risk while doing so, but she thought it necessary to be able to fully understand what was happening, and to allocate resources accordingly. By that point, they were seeing over a 1000 deaths and just under 2000 seizures a week throughout the province.[95] Together with volunteers, Nan and her staff managed to bring the 'terrifying' threat under control, but at considerable cost to her own health. She suffered a (near) nervous breakdown from the strenuous effort.[96]

Her brother was by then in London, to visit with Indira, now there for her higher studies. Nan had kept him informed of her doings. In the weeks leading up to her efforts to contain the outbreak, she had already faced deteriorating health for a recurring condition and required another operation to fix the matter. Jawaharlal had written then: 'One need not be anxious about this [an operation] but is . . . desirable to take all precautions and to have the best medical aid available. Purandare [her local doctor] is no doubt good but, everything considered, it seems to be obviously better that you should have the operation in Vienna or elsewhere in Europe. I want you to consider this. The question of your ministerial work need not come in the way much as in any event you will have to suspend it if you have the operation. I do recommend strongly that you should come to Europe soon.'[97] Two days later, he wrote again from Goodfellows, the country estate of British politician Sir Stafford Cripps, where he had been invited for a short stay. He repeated his wish that Nan come to Europe, reminding her that medical care was a necessity and that she would, as a result, need time away from work to recuperate. The children would all be in school in Woodstock, he also noted, so Nan was free in every way to travel.[98]

Once Nan indicated that she had to attend to those taking ill across her state, Jawaharlal wrote back with encouragement and concern: 'Obviously you had to go to the cholera-stricken areas. One cannot keep away whatever the risk—but I am worried about your general health and I do think you should get rid of your general troubles.'[99]

Nehru grew more alarmed as the days passed, as Nan told him of the toll her daily battles were taking. 'From what you write to me it is clear to me that you must take yourself in hand or else you will have to face greater trouble. I appreciate all your reasons [for wanting to continue to work]. But you cannot possibly carry on in this fashion. You will grow increasingly inefficient even in your work and may have to stop suddenly. My strong advice to you is to have a frank talk with Pantji and your other colleagues and take leave for treatment, and then come over to Europe, say for three months.'[100]

Nan put on a brave face and reminded her brother that she was more than capable of handling matters, even as she expressed frustration at the epidemic's endurance. Jawaharlal responded: 'I am worried over the . . . situation in the UP. What a terrible burden this must be on you. I suppose you know best what to do about your health. But do look after it.'[101] Just a few days later, after her public health measures finally forced cholera into retreat, fatigued mentally and physically, Nan told her brother that she planned to follow his advice and take a few months' leave of absence from work.[102]

Two weeks later, she departed by air for Europe, for what she hoped would be some much-needed respite.[103] But dramatic events were just unfolding that would make the trip much more consequential than she had imagined.

CHAPTER FIVE

# The West with the Night

With Ranjit and the kids stuck in India for work and school, Nan tried to coordinate her trip with her brother, but he by then had a complicated schedule, with obligations to attend a conference in Paris, to speak with a wide range of other European figures, and to travel to Normandy, Munich and Czechoslovakia. Nan's itinerary was fixed so that she and Nehru would at least overlap in one place briefly.[1]

After splitting her portfolios between Rafi Ahmed Kidwai, the UP revenue minister and Hafiz Muhammad Ibrahim, who ran communications, Nan departed Lucknow on 18 August by the Dutch airline KLM. Her first port of call, by way of Karachi, was Budapest.[2]

Nan desperately wanted to decompress with her brother.[3] She had been looking forward to spending time with her beloved sibling, and to simply relaxing and focusing on building her strength back. Unfortunately, by the time she got to Budapest, Indira was sick with pneumonia, accompanied by pleurisy. Doctors reassured them that the condition was 'not in the least dangerous', and that she was expected to make a full recovery. Nonetheless, Nan and Nehru spent their brief reunion in anxious worry.[4]

She soon dashed off to Prague as the guest of its government. Though she was in Europe for her health, she had nonetheless mixed in some work assignments.

Tensions there were running high. Czechoslovakia was a new state carved out of the old Austro-Hungarian Empire at the end of the Great War. Its western flank, called the Sudetenland, was dominated by a German-speaking ethnic minority which had grown increasingly opposed to central-governmental control.

A few years earlier, Adolf Hitler had manipulated a fire at the German Reichstag (parliament) to assume dictatorial powers, advocating a strident ethnic nationalism purged of all 'alien' influences. Hitler stoked longstanding resentments about the post-war peace and talked of returning his people to greatness. He exploited strict rules in place since 1919 to protect national minorities in the newer European states, arguing that they comprised part of a larger organic whole. Germany had an obligation to protect and, in fact incorporate, Germans wheresoever they may reside, he claimed. Nazi propaganda helped spread these views, unsettling surrounding countries.[5]

Local politicians affiliated with the Sudeten German Party (SdP) liked what they heard and allied themselves with the Nazi cause. The British had kept a close eye on developments and grew increasingly alarmed over 1938, fearing that the simmering dispute could lead to an outright crisis. With the Great War still fresh in their minds, they wanted to avoid another costly conflict. So in early August, they dispatched Lord Runciman on a diplomatic mission to Prague to help forge some kind of agreement between the SdP and the Czech government.

Upon her arrival in the city, Nan took up a room at the 'chic' Hotel Alcron, where the Runciman Mission was staying. Lord Runciman himself was her immediate neighbour, and he called on her within a few days to apologize for all the disturbance he was sure he was causing.[6]

Nan was officially received by the secretary of the minister for public health, who put their offices and the services of a car at her disposal for the duration of her stay. On 31 August, the minister and his wife threw a tea party in Nan's honour. She made quite a sensation, many astounded that one so young could hold a Cabinet rank already.[7]

That same day, the Indian Czech Association hosted a luncheon for her. The ICA had been established on 4 May 1934 as an affiliate of the Oriental Institute in Prague, at the behest of Moritz Winternitz, Otakar Pertold and Vincenc Lesny, scholars who thought of themselves as 'friends of India', and who maintained contact with Nehru, Tagore and others. Subhas Chandra Bose had personally attended the inauguration of the ICA in Prague. Lesny had a warm conversation with Nan and talked with her about Ranjit's translation of the *Rajatarangini*. He told Nan that he hoped her husband would eventually make the trip out there as well.⁸

Nan ended her Czech trip with a visit to the Masaryk Homes for Social Workers and Labourers, where she spent an hour in conversation with Foreign Minister Jan Masaryk. This encounter stuck out to her.⁹ When she was asked for her thoughts on the Sudeten crisis a few days later, Nan demurred, replying that Czechoslovakia's 'magnificent' welfare work was the real focus of her trip. Still, while saying she did not want to get into the details of the 'Central European Situation', she affirmed that she felt 'that the people, although just as averse from war as any others, seem reconciled to the prospect of having to fight one day for their independence'. This made them seem even more determined, she observed with a touch of despair, 'to have as good a time as possible while it lasts'.¹⁰

~

The UK Ministry of Health sent Nan an official letter of welcome, and the press received her with laudatory coverage: 'As Minister of Public Health in the United Province she had to cope with the arrangements for the mela, in Haridwar, a festival held once in several years and attracting huge crowds. This year the visitors numbered over three million, and despite every possible precaution cholera broke out in epidemic form soon afterwards. Mrs. Pandit earned the admiration of all India by her gallant fight against the pestilence, touring the afflicted areas, fearlessly mixing with the afflicted, and by her example encouraging the mere men of her department to redouble their efforts. Her own health stood the strain remarkably well, but doctors ordered her to take leave immediately if a breakdown were to [be] avoided.'¹¹ The *Manchester Guardian* gave her a major biographical profile, complete with large picture. 'Until last year,' they began, 'only one woman in any part of the British Commonwealth had ever held Cabinet rank. Mrs. Vijaya Pandit . . . is Miss Margaret Bondfield's first successor, but, unlike Miss Bondfield, she holds two Ministerial posts in the . . . United Provinces . . .' The story talked about her pioneering work and her popularity with women, taking special note of a major initiative she had pushed through just before she departed for Europe. 'Mrs. Pandit . . . recently started a training school for nurses, and [when she returns] she wants to establish a nursing service for the poor and for middle-class people in their own homes,' it concluded admiringly.[12]

She attracted attention wherever she went. She was 'swamped by photographers as all the Art Editors and agency men in the country seemed determined to get their own photographs of so good looking a Cabinet Minister'.[13]

But Nan knew that she needed treatment urgently. To a room of reporters 'mainly of Indian newspapers', she made plain that while she was fully attuned to both domestic politics and international affairs, she was going to clear her calendar of all public engagements for several weeks to address 'the matter of her health'. She felt uncomfortable with the laudatory coverage she had thus far received for being a trailblazing woman in government because it implied that Britain's provincial autonomy arrangements too deserved praise. She urged everyone to focus on what was really at stake for India and elsewhere in the world: freedom and real democracy. Those were the causes for which she stood.[14]

She felt lucky to be in the care of her friend, Agatha Harrison. Harrison was the daughter of a Methodist minister and considered herself an avowed champion of women, of peace, and of India. It was she who had helped arrange Gandhi's visit to England in 1931 for the Second Round Table Conference. Since then, she had only grown closer to the Mahatma, and to the cause of subcontinental freedom.

Harrison advised Nan to enter a private nursing home in Broadstairs, Kent, on the south-eastern coast of England. Nan found it 'a delightful place—lovely rooms –good food + absolute quiet'. She enjoyed the 'lovely weather' and 'spent long hours by the sea', along with visits to the nearby towns of Ramsgate and Margate. But the real highlight was a tour of the renowned Bleak House, the former home of Charles Dickens, and popularly regarded as the real place behind his eponymously named novel.[15] It was also where he wrote *David Copperfield*. This all struck a chord with Nan's literary sensibilities, but she was most impressed by the way the property had been maintained for the public by the government.[16]

Despite the relaxed atmosphere, Nan's health did not improve. Part of the reason could have been her concern for Indira, who had joined her in England with her father. Shortly after Nan had departed for Broadstairs, Nehru had left London to get his daughter further care in Switzerland.[17]

On the advice of two different doctors, Nan checked herself into the New Lodge Clinic, a massive Tudor-Gothic mansion with castle-like turrets situated in Windsor Forest in Berkshire. The house had originally been built in the nineteenth century for the Belgian ambassador, a friend of Queen Victoria. Dark wood panelling, exquisite mouldings, a richly carved staircase and stained-glass windows lent further grandeur to the establishment.[18]

Nan was tended to by Sir Arthur Hurst, a pioneer in the field of neurology, who the year before had co-founded the British Society of Gastroenterology.[19] Although she found her accommodations 'posh', and managed to get to the theatre every now and again, she was not at all happy. 'I hate being here + find it difficult to submit to hospital discipline + be treated like an invalid but I suppose I shall have to grin + bear it,' she morosely informed Ranjit.[20]

~

Nan paid close attention to the international developments taking place in Europe and grew increasingly uneasy, distrustful of both German and British intentions. She wrote to Ranjit that she felt 'Britain as usual' was 'trying to play a double game'. She joined leftist critics in a 'bitter + scathing' assessment of the situation, and feared that Czechoslovakia was about to be sacrificed.[21]

She was proved right. After negotiating with Hitler following Runciman's recommendations, UK Prime Minister Chamberlain waved the agreement in the air in front of a crowd of supporters in London and declared that he had secured the 'settlement of the Czechoslovakian problem'.[22] He had given in to many of Germany's demands in the Munich Pact.

People poured into the street, and the international press went wild. Chamberlain proceeded to Buckingham Palace, and then returned to 10 Downing Street, where he was greeted by thousands of adoring citizens grateful that war had been averted. He 'stood for a few moments on the doorstep', before heading inside. A few moments later, in an iconic moment, he peered out a first-floor window and declared 'peace for our time'.[23]

Nan, just back from Windsor Forest, stood solemnly alongside her also just-returned brother, they amongst the thousands outside the prime minister's home that night listening intently to his words. The Nehrus 'watched the rejoicing with which Mr. Chamberlain's words were greeted'. 'It was perfectly understandable but sad,' she later recalled, 'for one could see that peace was farther away than ever before. For hours that night we wandered around London. The churches had been kept open and were full of people, mainly older women, on their knees thanking God for deliverance from war. I was near to tears and wanted to join the worshipping throng, to pray that in spite of all the signs to the contrary peace might still be possible.'[24]

~

Chamberlain's speech took place late on a Friday night. It was front-page news the next morning, stories reflecting the widespread relief that war had been avoided. Chamberlain was lauded as a visionary and hero.

As it happened, that same day the papers announced that on Monday, the India League was going to hold a public meeting headlined by Vijaya Lakshmi Pandit. Also listed as speakers were Nehru and Labour leader Ellen Wilkinson, the latter having achieved prominence for drawing national attention to the plight of the working class during the Jarrow March two years previous.[25]

The India League had evolved from Annie Besant's Home Rule movement and was a Britain-based organization with multiple chapters throughout the country, all run by a sharp-tongued lawyer: V.K. Krishna Menon. Menon had been in England since the twenties. The scion of a Travancore dewan (that is, the prime minister of a premier princely state), he found himself inspired by Besant. Supported directly by her, he had come to study at the London School of Economics (LSE) following a course at the Madras Law College (now Dr Ambedkar Government Law College). At the LSE, he had come under the tutelage of Harold Laski, a prominent political theorist and Labour partisan.[26] Nehru had met Menon just a few years before, when he had been in Europe to tend to Kamala and had made a short trip to London.[27] The two men had a connection almost immediately, bonding over their shared intellectualism.[28]

Menon had a powerful, left-leaning network of writers, scholars, journalists and politicians that he deployed effectively to argue for India's independence from the early thirties forward. Together with Wilkinson, he had published a book of investigative findings of political repression in India in 1932. Once he met Nehru, the India League became closely aligned with the Indian National Congress, effectively serving as an overseas arm of the organization.[29]

The Monday reception in Nan's honor was a public event, but Menon made sure to extend a special invitation to some important guests. Among those who graced the occasion were Ronald Kidd, the founder four years before of the National Council of Civil Liberties, and renowned suffragette and Labour activist Emmeline Pethick-Lawrence.[30]

Nan knew she was being given a powerful platform. She planned to make the most of it. The event was held at Friend's House, the headquarters of the Quakers, a Christian denomination dedicated to plainness and pacifism. The red 'brick and Portland stone' building, with 'a colonnade of Doric columns' at the entrance, was designed especially for large meetings.[31]

Pethick-Lawrence heralded Nan at the start as a 'fighter for freedom'. 'We wish India could lend us a stateswoman like Mrs. Pandit at the present time,' she emphatically proclaimed. Nan boldly used the opportunity in front of a big audience to deliver a stinging rebuke of Chamberlain and the Munich Pact. 'The fate of Czechoslovakia has made us more determined than ever to achieve our aim, and to sever connection with a Government whose ideals differ from ours ... Since coming here I have heard much talk of self-determination. That is what we fight for in our country to-day ... We feel that in achieving it we shall have contributed to the freedom and self-determination of the world ... In Europe to-day we find utter degradation in the political field, violence, and blackmail, and people are resorting to such methods who are called saviours of their country. I have lost faith in words since I came to England. Listening over the radio I heard words that were sacred to me, democracy and freedom, uttered by a man who, in my opinion, has perpetrated the greatest betrayal.' Nehru added: 'What has been done at Munich will be remembered by millions of people all over the world to the shame and dishonor of England and France.' Nan's speech, along with notes on the rest of the event, received coverage in the papers on the morning of 5 October, the *Manchester Guardian* headlining its story 'The Shame of England'.[32]

Later that very evening, Winston Churchill stood in the House of Commons and inveighed against the policy of appeasement, in what has since come to be considered a landmark speech. Although Churchill had been from the early thirties one of the fiercest opponents of any loosening of British control of India, his remarks that night uncannily paralleled the views of the Nehrus, even as he remained ironically oblivious to any critique of colonialism his own words carried. Churchill lamented the 'total and unmitigated defeat' his country had just suffered. Then in a strange echo of Nan, he added: 'We in this country, as in other Liberal and democratic countries, have a perfect right to exalt the principle of self-determination, but it comes ill out of the mouths of those in totalitarian States who deny even the smallest element of toleration to every section and creed within their bounds.'[33]

The emboldened nationalist press in India unleashed a wave of stories that chided Chamberlain for his 'betrayal' and '[c]omplete surrender to Hitler'. *The Leader* said that the Czechs had been 'offered as a sacrifice'. *The Hindu* pointed out that 'the blessed name of self-determination is being invoked to support Nazi ambitions, and we have the odd spectacle of Wilsonian idealism harnessed to the rule of strong'. The *Pioneer*, based out of Nan's home state of UP and headquartered near her government office in Lucknow, called on its readers not to 'forget that it is laid down in [Hitler's] "Mein Kampf" that such a pact [as the Munich agreement] is essential as a preliminary to the destruction of France, and Britain's turn is to come afterwards'. So universal and severe was the criticism that the British press was forced to take notice.[34]

~

Nan threw herself back into her work and arranged an 'extensive programme of visits to hospitals and other institutions in England'.[35] She restated that she wanted 'to take stock of the means provided on the preventative side of public health', so that when she returned home, she could help her state develop better and more effective policies and services.

*The Christian Science Monitor* interviewed her again for another lengthy profile. Nan was frustrated and concerned that the attention she was receiving—for her leadership, for the projects she spearheaded, for her looks—was being construed as an endorsement of British self-governance policies stemming from the 1935 Act. As she had several times over the course of her trip, she reiterated that the 'heavy' workload she had taken on was really 'a means to an end [rather] than . . . an end in itself, since all work undertaken under the present governmental regime in India appears to many Indians unsatisfactory'. Nan further stipulated that 'Congress Ministries are "doing the best they can." Sooner or later they will come to a stop, and a better means of government will be brought in . . .'

Nan spent the rest of the interview discussing her specific role and the new opportunities for women in public service. She credited changing gender dynamics in India primarily to indigenous anti-colonial efforts: Gandhi's call for women to participate in his salt campaigns in 1930 and an agreement the year later at the Karachi Session of the Indian National Congress that there should be no bar to office based on sex. She observed that some women, including herself, had had some general interests in politics beforehand as well.

The profile focused on pathways available to women, and walked readers through Nan's personal journey, interweaving the two enough to indicate that she had achieved her position through struggle and not partiality. 'The whole affair . . . begins by being a primary member of Congress and, in time, being elected to a town or district Committee. From such a Committee, a woman, like a man, may be sent to represent her district at an annual meeting of Congress where, in turn, she may be elected to the All-India Congress Committee from which, again, she may rise to membership in the Congress Executive, which changes its members each year.'[36]

The interview was just one of several ways Nan continued to be feted during her trip. About a week and a half after her speech at Friend's House, Nan was again honoured by the India League, this time in the friendly territory of Finsbury in northern London. In the late nineteenth century, it was this township that had elected Dadabhai Naoroji the first Indian member of Parliament, as part of the Liberal Party. The reception for Nan was held at the opulent Town Hall, a triangular building designed in an 'eclectic "Free

Renaissance" composition in a Flemish-inspired manner'.³⁷ With its 'art-deco canopy entrance, [and] beautiful stained glass . . . adorned with chandeliers', it was quite a contrast to the simple-ness of the site of her previous event.³⁸

About 'three hundred people, nearly half being English men and women residing in the Borough of Finsbury' came out to meet Nan.³⁹ The outgoing mayor, Charles Alfred Allen, was present. He would be replaced within a few weeks by Chuni Lal Katilal, Britain's first South Asian mayor.⁴⁰

She addressed the crowd for about fifteen minutes. She brought up Czechoslovakia, distilling the problem to the acceptability of imperialism as a principle. She talked of Indian independence and of the work of the Congress government in UP. In addition, she 'expressed her amazement at finding a supreme lack of interest in Indian problems among the ordinary people here, and even those who were interested were not fully informed about the recent developments'.⁴¹

~

Nan had made a two-and-half-month trip to Europe to deal with her mental and physical health yet had only managed about three and a half weeks of serious treatment. Fast-moving international events weighed heavily on her conscience and forced her to intervene however best she could. Guilt about taking time off when the people of India were in such desperate need and a desire to be gracious with all who sought her company combined to drive her back into meetings and professional tours. She simply was not yet ready, and she fell very sick immediately after her visit to Finsbury.

Personal matters brought her down further. She learned that one of her assistants, Shivlal Panachand Shah, had died rather suddenly.⁴² She told Ranjit she was 'deeply distressed' by the news and asked him to write a letter to Shah's wife in the bereaved family's native Gujarati on her behalf.⁴³ Indira continued to fare poorly, and Nan 'worried' for her, and for all the 'burdens' her brother had to bear. And to top it off, Ranjit had been asking her to consider purchasing a plot of land to build a house. She begged him not to do it, saying, 'things are happening so fast one never knows where one will be'.

Nan quietly confessed to her husband that she was 'very unwell'. She checked herself into a hospital and postponed her travels by an additional two weeks at the behest of her doctors.[44]

Nehru had been closely monitoring the situation. He cabled Pant back in UP to inform him of Nan's relapse and of the new delay. Pant wrote back on the twentieth with 'much concern', saying he found the news 'very disquieting'. The two had been in regular touch, and Pant reassured Nehru once again that Nan should not feel any 'urgency' to return immediately to work: 'she need not start until she has entirely recovered . . . We are carrying on her work as well as we can in her absence. It is a pity if after having incurred all this trouble and expense she comes back without regaining her health completely.'[45]

About a week later, Nehru, with Indira in tow, left England and headed to an international peace conference in Cairo via Paris. As he was departing, Nehru wrote to his sister: 'I am leaving you now and hope to meet you in Allahabad in about three weeks' time. I am glad to see that you are getting on well and will soon pick up strength. You have had a stiff time during the last fortnight but I think that it has been as well that you passed through this shake-up to your system. I think this will clear you up and put an end to many things that were troubling you. You will, I am sure and the doctors assure me, be in better health and fitter now than you were when you came to Europe. You need not worry at all about your work in India. Pantji cabled to me that you should get well and not bother about work. Your bills etc in the Assembly have been postponed and will not be taken up during this session.'[46] Clearly anxious, he telephoned and wrote often over the next several days, reassuring his sister, and himself, 'not to worry about the slowness of recovery . . .'[47]

On 9 November, Nan finally left London for Amsterdam, seen off by Krishna Menon, and from there onwards back to India.[48] The press followed her travels breathlessly, reporting on each pitstop along the way.[49] They also noted that she 'appeared to have improved in health', though in truth she was quite frail and still needed time to regain her strength.[50] Her doctors had 'telegraphed instructions to . . . K.L.M. for special treatment . . . and accordingly at all hotels *en route* special arrangements were made for her conveyance and diet'.[51]

Nan finally reached Anand Bhawan on the fourteenth and was received by 'a large number of friends and Congressmen', all thrilled to have her home.[52] After a daylong stopover, she headed back to Lucknow. 'Practically the whole of the U.P. Cabinet was present at the station to welcome her . . . besides a large number of prominent persons.'

People quickly observed that 'Mrs. Pandit appeared weak and had to be helped by Mr. Pandit while crossing the overbridge.'[53] Still, she was determined to get back to work. Despite entreaties from Pant and others to take it easy, she attended the Assembly and assumed charge of her portfolios right away.[54]

~

Nan struggled to push through her difficulties. Shortly after resuming her responsibilities, she accepted an invitation to address the Agra Constituency Women's Conference at Allahabad, but just could not withstand travel again so soon. So instead she delivered her remarks in absentia. She connected local concerns and women's rights with the larger international scene: 'I have only just returned from Europe and was a personal witness to the shameful betrayal of a gallant nation in her hour of need by one who posed as a friend . . . I have also seen the terrible distress that is inflicted on members of a suffering race by the Totalitarian States . . . And through all these things the only hopeful sign has been that women in every country are realizing the terrible danger by which humanity is beset and are trying to form themselves into one unit in order to fight this great calamity which draws nearer and ever nearer.'

'We in India are far away from war and its consequent dangers and therefore cannot quite realize the horrors with which people in Europe are faced. But no war of the future can leave us entirely unaffected and so long as any mother's son is in danger of injustice, humiliation or death, it is the duty of every mother, no matter where she be, to raise her voice and join her strength to that group, which fights to restore peace and justice to a weary world.'[55]

~

Nan started to feel better in early December 1938. She suddenly dashed about with renewed vim and vigour and seemed to be everywhere at once.

She tended to matters large and small. During one meeting of the UP Assembly session for instance, she addressed the 'Simian invasion of Bareilly', aware that 'the upper storeys of houses had become uninhabitable and that the monkeys were a constant threat to women and children living in the invasion areas'. She announced that the government had increased its expenditure by almost two-thirds from the previous fiscal year when virtually every rupee allocated had been spent successfully 'capturing and transporting 1,168 monkeys'.[56]

One of her primary concerns was expanding access to high-quality healthcare, which she now approached with new urgency. She introduced legislation to regulate the practices of medicine in the state to 'control' common 'quackery' and bring local options, like the Unani and Ayurvedic systems, up to international standards.[57] She expanded the number of women professionals, while arguing in favour of bringing in experts from outside the country 'to help to train our own people'. Many of these doctors were Jewish, Nan cognizant of the 'unfortunate' circumstances they were then facing in Europe.[58]

Together with her eldest daughter Chandralekha, she challenged long-standing customs like *purdah* that all too frequently kept women from getting medical help as required. This harmed public health overall, they argued, facilitating diseases like tuberculosis.[59] When Nan presided over a small convention of doctors and local and state officials sometime later, she announced that the government 'would nominate a board . . . to devise ways and means to counteract epidemics.'[60]

She also proposed a scheme to provide 'mobile hospitals' throughout the state, so those in rural areas could also be properly serviced. After launching one bus with government funds, she secured three more from donors, prodding the government to support a further two, meeting the immediate needs of six districts. Though she had forty-two more she wanted to cover, it was an impressive start.[61] Nan's efforts drew commendation from the Countess of Dufferin's Fund, a welfare trust focused on women's health.[62]

Amid these activities, Nan re-joined her old friends and colleagues, including Agatha Harrison, at the annual meeting of the All India Women's Conference, which took place at the turn of the year in New Delhi. This time, though, Vijaya Lakshmi Pandit was considered one of the most distinguished and important names in attendance.[63]

Nan was well aware of her increased stature and parlayed it into headline-grabbing news. In a bit of rhetorical jujitsu, she called on the thousands of delegates to take an anti-war stand, slamming the West's peace moves in Czechoslovakia as bringing annihilative conflict ever closer. She 'witnessed a real panic in London, a panic due to fear of war'. While 'she saw British people genuinely relieved when they were told that Mr. Chamberlain had succeeded in averting war . . . [the] moral . . . was that a great Power did not honour its obligations towards a weaker state when there was a real threat of war'. The West's 'greed for power and possessions' was poisonous and destructive, she went on. These forces 'of reaction and oppression' had to be resisted. War could still be stopped, but only if right action was taken. 'Women of India could make a stand and create a world 'united front' for liberty. They in India had set their faith on non-violence,' she said, linking the women's movement in India, Gandhi's interventions and international affairs in one fell swoop. 'Non-violence was not pacifism,' she clarified, adding that she 'had no doubt that the women of India would today send out a message to the oppressed nations of the world, which would bring them faith in justice and equity'.[64] The resolution demanded the creation of a 'new order', and condemned the Anschluss and Munich Pact, the 'merciless persecution of the Jews' as well as 'the deplorable interference and cruelties in Palestine, and the unjustifiable aggression in China [by Japan]'.[65] *The Manchester Guardian* called her resolution 'easily the most important' tabled at the entire event. The paper singled Nan out for her moral clarity and her visionary protest 'against war as an instrument for the settlement of international disputes,' foreshadowing the basis of the world organization with which she would later be so associated.[66]

In August of 1939, she took on yet another responsibility by joining the new National Planning Committee under the chairmanship of her brother, which was tasked with looking into questions of 'labour, manufacturing industries, crop-planning, insurance and animal husbandry'.[67] It was the brainchild of Subhas Chandra Bose, who had proposed it in his Presidential Address the year before.[68] Nan took subcommittee assignments dealing with the role of women in a planned economy and with overall population matters.[69]

~

On 1 September, on orders from Adolf Hitler the previous day, German troops began a full-scale invasion of Poland, a move that would complete the fascist state's expansion along its entire eastern frontier. Within days Britain and France declared war on Germany.

The Indian press was virtually unanimous in its condemnation of the invasion. The *Amrita Bazar Patrika* called it a 'war for the extermination of the human race'. *The Hindu* discussed 'the shameful story of duplicity and suppression that preceded the rape of Poland'. The *Hindustan Times* called Hitler 'a lunatic' who took 'sadistic delight in human suffering'. The *National Herald*, associated with Nehru, stated that 'the reply of Germany's antagonists can only be that they will not lay down arms till the Hitler dynasty is completely wiped out'. Some called for India to be made free so that it could righteously stand together with Britain as an equal and face down fascism.[70]

India had been included in Britain's war declaration on the third. The Congress High Command met about a week later to discuss the stand they should take. They strongly condemned the Nazis and placed the blame for the situation squarely on Hitler's shoulders. But they also strongly disapproved of the continued suppression of democracy in India and demanded that the people have a say on participation in the war effort. 'A free, democratic India will gladly associate herself with other free nations for mutual defense against aggression and for economic cooperation. We will work for the establishment of a real world order based on freedom and democracy, utilising the world's knowledge and resources for the progress and advancement of humanity.'[71]

The British only gave a perfunctory response, saying they would be willing to discuss all matters upon the successful conclusion of the war. The central government's intransigence put the Congress ministries in a difficult position given both popular and organizational stands on independence. Nan herself had always been ambivalent about her own participation, fearing that it simply further legitimized British rule. She had grown increasingly discontent over 1939, angry with Britain for its failures in Europe and worried about the conflict she saw looming on the horizon. Once war was declared, she knew there was no choice. In late October, she and her colleagues in UP took up discussion of the matter. Nan moved the resolution, which stated: 'This Assembly regrets that the situation in India has not been rightly understood by His Majesty's Government when authorizing the statement which has been made on their behalf in regard to India, and in view of this failure of the British Government to meet India's demand, this Assembly is of the opinion that Government could not associate itself with British policy.' After several days of discussion, the Cabinet resigned.[72]

CHAPTER SIX

# The Time in Between

For a few months, an eerie calm descended on India, as if collectively the country was drawing a deep breath waiting for a great confrontation they knew was coming, but that still seemed just far enough away. Daily life carried on as normal, though now the routines were more about the comfort of predictability in uncertain times.

In place of ministerial duties, Nan devoted herself to her other professional obligations, taking a keen interest in her work on the Planning Committee and in preparations for the annual All India Women's Conference. There was considerable overlap between the two, not only because Nan held a position in the former on the Subcommittee on the Status of Women in a Planned Economy, but also because she shared both platforms with others like Sarojini Naidu, Rani Lakshmibai Rajwade and Begum Hamid Ali, two former presidents of the AIWC, and one current one. In mid-December, Nehru inaugurated Nan's committee in Bombay, and deliberations began immediately.[1] Within a few days, the committee had drafted a resolution that proclaimed that women had to be given 'not only theoretical equality of opportunity', but actual 'training and particularly employment' as well.[2] Nan and the others carried this forward to the full Planning Committee as it met several months later, and ensured that the language was adopted.[3]

Once the planning subcommittee had completed its initial work, Nan shifted gears to focus on the fast-approaching women's conference, set for the following month. She had been selected to chair the reception committee, so had to play a significant organizational role. This was further magnified by the fact that the annual affair was taking place in Nan's hometown of Allahabad.

Nan gave the formal welcome at the opening session. She updated the delegates on the work of the Planning Committee's subcommittee, informing them that a formal report would soon be ready. 'Efforts had been made to tackle important questions relating to women's disabilities in the social, economic, and legal spheres,' she announced.

Then she did something quite unusual and took her colleagues to task for failing to make the AIWC meaningful to ordinary people. She implored them to make the body 'truly representative' of the women of India 'and not only of the educated and leisure classes'. She pointed to ways barriers to such an inclusive approach could be torn down, proposing for instance that delegates try to hold meetings in provincial languages to better understand the concerns of local people, to address their needs, and to communicate their ideas.

She called on the conference to help foster a 'civic consciousness' amongst the people. She charged that malicious forces were sowing discord and division throughout society and harming 'the spirit of tolerance' needed for national progress. She condemned separate electorates 'as the greatest stumbling block' to 'harmony' in the country between all different communities.[4]

~

Ramsay MacDonald's Communal Award of 1932 had established separate electorates based on the deliberations of the Second Round Table Conference, and extended a principle originally put in place by the Morley-Minto Reforms of 1909. Gandhi had acquiesced to them for the Muslim community, even as his fierce resistance to their extension to Dalits created reservations for that group instead.

Muslims were heavily concentrated in the north-east and north-west provinces of the subcontinent and were divided over the need for joint electorates. Those in Bengal favoured them while those in Punjab were more fearful since they were there outnumbered by those of other religions.

Muhammad Ali Jinnah had only recently re-entered the political fray, after spending the twenties in a self-imposed exile out of disgust for the way things were being handled in the subcontinent. He took over the reins of the Muslim League but expressed skepticism of separate electorates, realizing the potent factionalism and provincialism that was also in play. He had entered discussions with the political leadership of Bengal and Punjab, but overall was very disappointed with the results of the 1937 elections, where the League did very poorly.

To turn things around, Jinnah had begun a series of surgical political strikes that soon gained mass attention. The Muslim League gained traction in the United Provinces, setting off frequent protests against the Congress-led government and its various ministers.[5]

Nan thought all this part of the overall business of democracy. Every so often, overprotective handlers would prevent her from attending a particular event for fear that she might be met by angry citizens. She found this overbearing and frustrating, and an interference with her job. Towards the end of 1939, shortly before the mass Congress resignations, she had asked Pant to intervene, and to make clear that ministers' travel was not to be curtailed on the account of protests.[6]

Nonetheless Nan was growing increasingly uneasy about deteriorating Hindu-Muslim relations. She had been watching this first-hand in Allahabad itself, with those intent on provoking conflict acting ever more aggressively. In April of 1938, for instance, someone had placed a pig's head on the stairs of a local mosque, enflaming embers of anger that were already hot. Only the tireless interventions of Nehru, in coordination with Nan, had managed to cool these flare-ups, if only temporarily.[7]

Nan spoke out on the issue in late December of 1939, fearing that passions were on the rise. She spoke before a large, open-air gathering in Ahmedabad in western India. She 'declared that the Hindu-Muslim problem was engineered by interested persons', and that it was 'false propaganda' to suggest that Hindus and Muslims were historically 'disunited'. She argued that everyone had a right to freedom and pleaded for people to work for national interests rather than those of particular communities.[8]

~

Nan had time to consider what all she had accomplished during her time in office. She wanted to document her experiences in some fashion, because she felt that transparency was a hallmark of good governance, because she felt she had been part of something of interest to history, and because she felt an acute desire to write a book as a reflection of her own literary merits. So she penned a collection of essays and released them at the turn of the year under the title *So I Became a Minister*.[9]

In its review in early February, the *Times of India* heralded Nan's 'fresh and spontaneous' writing but applauded even more strongly the life that served as the basis of such an account, saying that 'Vijaya Lakshmi Pandit ... has probably done more than any Indian woman, with the exception of Mrs. Sarojini Naidu, to break down ancient taboos preventing women from entering public life'. It called her book 'a record of a brave and useful pioneer life' that would serve as 'an inspiration to all progressive women in India'.[10]

~

The war loomed large over the Pandit household. The young children, though safely ensconced at Woodstock in 'the peaceful Himalayas', followed every development on the radio, and grew increasingly concerned about the future. The insistently inquisitive twelve-year-old Nayantara wrote her father in hopes of getting some answers. 'Do you think that India should help England,' she asked, reasoning that if 'she did, then Germany would be squashed, which would be a good thing. If she didn't,' she went further, 'England might be beaten, and then Germany and Japan would together march into India. What good would non-violence do then?' She concluded: 'I don't know when non-violence has done any good. I suppose it has, but it certainly won't if Germany and Japan get into India. Then we will have to either fight or slave for them. I think we jolly well ought to fight, like Patrick Henry, "Give me liberty or give me death". What do you think about it? [Also] Will you please explain to me what "communism" means?'

Ranjit responded in his typically patient, kind and nurturing way. He told her that the people of India 'do not want to see the spread of triumphant Hitlerism'. He explained what the Working Committee had thus far done and the significant role her uncle had played. 'We stand for freedom, peace and progress,' he told her. 'We are against wars to destroy the freedom of weaker nations by violence and force. If England is in favor of the freedom of the nations, then she must not forcibly occupy India, and keep the people of India in bondage. Such freedom must be for all countries, including countries in Asia and Africa.'

He assured Nayantara that non-violence was 'good', explaining that wars ended with discussions on the nature of peace anyway, and that diplomacy therefore seemed the much more rational path to resolving disputes than armed combat. 'If, however, our country is invaded by cruel people, we cannot save it by talking of non-violence. Force must be resisted by force. But we must use only as much force as is necessary for defence, otherwise there is the danger of being ourselves brutal and cruel.'

And to her final question, he responded, 'Communism means working together in common and sharing benefits in common, with equal justice to all . . . That is to say where there are no rich and high and mighty who have all the good things in the world and more on the one hand, and, on the other, a vast mass of ill-clad, ill-fed, ill-housed humanity . . . This is the theory of Communism. But between theory and practice there is a world of difference. You know the Sermon on the Mount . . . Now watch what the Christian English, French, and Germans, and others are doing, and how different their conduct is from what it should be. And so it is with Communists.'

He symbolically put his arm around his daughter and gently advised her to keep 'calm'. She had to steel herself for what was to come. 'The war may last long, for several years, and we shall need strength, physical and mental, for a long time, so that we can help others.'[11]

~

As the months dragged on, Congress patience with British delay in dealing with India's concerns began to wear thin. The leadership felt a growing sense of urgency, a deep foreboding of what was soon to come in Europe and an anxiousness to move to an agreement that would allow India to independently decide its future and Britain to gain an ally in the war. Journalists wrote plainly in the Western press, trying to convey the message. B. Shiva Rao, for instance, wrote as a foreign correspondent for the American paper, the *Baltimore Sun*, that no one in India 'however extreme in his political views, has the slightest sympathy with Nazi methods and all that Hitlerism represents'. Rao wrote of the 'enormous difference' the war had made, saying Gandhi and others welcomed negotiations and were open to compromise regarding transitions and timelines, so long as the basic principle of self-determination was respected.[12]

Gandhi was explicit about the role Rao and the others were playing, writing in the *Harijan* that India had to 'educate the world as to what we stand for'. He reiterated his willingness to work with the British on friendly terms, and to hold off on any civil resistance as conversations for a settlement continued. He emphasized though that 'India cannot . . . partner in the exploitation of the non-European races of the earth'. He saw any talk of 'dominion' as fundamentally part of this enterprise, and demanded independent status determined freely by Indians alone to ensure that the country would not be 'co-sharer in the exploitation of the Africans and the degradation of our own countrymen'.[13]

Nan had always had an outsized interest in the affairs of the Congress because of her family's various activities. She had, however, started out merely an observer as a young girl and had gradually earned her stripes, rising through the ranks from the local to the national scene. Only occasionally had she even sat in on discussions of the High Command when it met in Allahabad or some other proximate location. Now she found her voice greatly enhanced by her breakthrough role in the UP Cabinet, and the international attention she had received for her work.

In early 1940, as frustration with British intransigence grew starker with each passing day, the Congress knew it was time to consider their 'next struggle'. Nan was officially elevated to the status of regular special guest of the Congress Working Committee, informally joining the ranks of Gandhian lieutenants Sarojini Naidu, Acharya Kripalani and Vallabhbhai Patel in the inner circle.[14]

Things took a dramatic turn in April and May when Hitler finally unleashed the full force of his fury on Western Europe. As Holland and Belgium fell to the blitzkrieg, Chamberlain was replaced by Churchill. Just days later, the new prime minister thundered that the UK would 'never surrender' following the retreat and rescue of British and French forces off the beach at Dunkirk. He reassured a terrified domestic audience that even if the island were to be subjugated, the rest of the Empire would continue the fight until such time as the United States could ride to the rescue.[15]

The Indian Congress knew what was now at stake and raced to formulate an appropriate response. Churchill's words rang around the world, but while they were inspirational to all who feared and opposed the fascist march, they resonated in a unique way in the subcontinent. Hundreds of thousands of South Asians were already fighting in the British Indian Army by then, the numbers increasing every day, and with forces deployed in various theatres by the imperial government. Although the soldiers were all volunteers, their forced participation in the war was indicative of the larger problem, that India was in the war not of its own volition. The High Command thought it not only eminently reasonable to ask that the country be set free to chart its own course, but necessary for the war effort itself, which was framed as a battle between the forces of liberty and those of tyranny. At the same time, everyone recognized the serious threat that Germany posed to Britain, and they wished to do nothing to undermine the United Kingdom's position. The Working Committee released a statement to this effect: 'The problem of the achievement of national freedom has now to be considered along with the allied one, its maintenance and the defence of the country against possible external aggression and informal disorder.'[16]

Gandhi's perception of the threat that Hitler posed had meanwhile grown spottier. He saw the destruction Nazis were intent on bringing but remained convinced that non-violence was the best way to counteract it all. While he penned an essay that appeared in *Harijan* calling for resistance to German aggression, he insisted this had to be done without force and bizarrely praised the surrender of France as an act of bravery.[17]

The High Command immediately but delicately distanced themselves from this position. They announced that they were 'unable to go the full length' with Gandhi, but accepted his commitment to his ideals and absolved him of the course of action they were prepared to choose, implying their readiness to declare war against Germany should they come to an agreement regarding independence from the colonial regime. 'The critical attention that faces the world today requires vigilant attention and action whenever needed. For this purpose, the Working Committee will meet at frequent intervals and all members must keep in readiness to obey urgent summons.'[18] They authorized a committee staffed by Ranjit, Patel, and representatives of Khan Abdul Gaffar Khan's Kudai Kitmatgar movement to 'encourage . . . and promote . . . trained volunteers for national service.'[19]

This was all a delicate balancing act. Nehru and the others wanted to pressure Britain to agree to some basic terms on the transfer of power while simultaneously signalling their sympathy for the war effort and their intentions to join the Allies.[20] This willingness to fight put them at odds with Gandhi, who nonetheless remained their most powerful negotiator and the one who could exert the most suasion on the viceroy to make concessions.

But the government's eyes were on Europe, and the harried British administration in India felt it had neither the time nor the resources to attend to domestic concerns at that moment. The Congress felt that they needed to attend to Indian concerns for the very same reason.

~

Nayantara, Chandralekha, and Rita remained unconvinced about either the righteousness or the unstoppable power of non-violence, though they tried to talk themselves into believing. They wrote to their parents about their ambivalence. Ranjit responded that 'that was exactly the question before the Working Committee of the Congress and Gandhiji. Briefly, the former thought not. Gandhiji was quite sure, and still is, that non-violence is the way'. He expressed pride and happiness in his children's interest, and in their philosophical need to understand what was happening around them. He suggested that they form their own Working Committee in the house. 'As Gandhiji's views are known to me for over twenty years, perhaps I shall be able to put his points, and the rest of you may argue against them. I shall be happy to hear you argue and to learn from you and, if necessary, to change my view and vote with you. And perhaps you may do the same after hearing me. There is also a third possibility—we may say to ourselves, "Much may be said on both sides" and may keep to our views!'[21]

Meanwhile, the real Working Committee met throughout the summer and into the monsoon in the hope that a deal with the colonial government would soon be forthcoming. But as the rains began to taper off and winter neared, it became clear that the two sides just did not see eye to eye. The British were simply too distracted. The High Command considered their alternatives. They needed to capture attention, but yet do nothing that would imperil the fight abroad.[22] In September, when their proposed deal with the government was finally formally rejected, they decided to reverse course and once more reaffirm their faith in Gandhi and his ways, while at the same time making clear their continued support for the war overall.[23] The Mahatma immediately took charge and called on people to steel themselves for what was to come, calling on them to follow all laws as a matter of discipline. Nehru announced to the press that the country was 'on the verge of a great crisis'.[24]

The plan was for 'individual satyagraha', as opposed to a mass campaign, with hand-picked, high-profile people resisting British authority. This was just symbolic, but in a war setting where every ounce of information was controlled, and actions especially restricted, no less potent for it.[25] In mid-October, the Working Committee was called into an emergency meeting to lay out a plan of action.[26] With international fanfare, Nehru and Vinoba Bhave were announced as the first two to court arrest, as both were considered Gandhi's closest and truest followers. Gandhi announced that the Indian intention was 'to demand a [British] change of heart and mind . . . [but not to] pray for their downfall. Defeat of the British would connote a Nazi victory, which we do not, and must not, desire'.[27]

The next day, Gandhi clarified that although he had 'sole charge of the campaign', he kept in constant consultations with the Working Committee. He now stipulated that Bhave was to offer non-violent direct action first and took note of the fact he represented those who resisted the war in broader terms than others. For Gandhi, Bhave and the whole campaign was conceived as an effort to unify the Mahatma's own seemingly divergent views as much as it was meant to bring together an increasingly fractious population. He proclaimed that Bhave, and he himself, had to fall if they did not truly represent the whole Congress, and indeed all of India: both those who were opposed to 'war as war' as well as those more narrowly concerned with India's illegitimate 'participation in the present war'. If the people were with them, though, Gandhi asked that they show their cooperation by leaving resistance to those specially selected. Everyone else was to cooperate in the constructive program by dedicating themselves to daily spinning of cotton, to the 'complete disappearance of untouchability and increasing friendliness between the communities and an increasing sense of justice in every walk of life'.[28]

On 17 October, Vinobha Bhave made a speech in Nagpur criticizing the war with all of this in mind. He was immediately arrested.[29]

Roughly two weeks later, Nehru huddled with Gandhi at Sevagram to plot out the second act of defiance.[30] Just as he was travelling later that night, he too was picked up by the police in anticipation of remarks that he had announced he intended to deliver.[31] The government used an earlier speech he had given at Gorakhpur as the basis for their charge.[32]

The Congress Working Committee was immediately called into an emergency session to consider what to do next.[33] But before their planned meeting, Nehru's trial got underway. Nan and Ranjit rushed to Gorakhpur to be by his side. The Pandits were 'deeply moved' by their beloved sibling's passionate courtroom statement. He made no defence and instead claimed that 'the British Empire itself . . . is on trial before the bar of the world'. He added with a flourish: 'Seven times I have been tried and convicted by the British authority in India, and many years of my life lie buried within prison walls. An eighth or a ninth, and a few more years make little difference. But it is no small matter what happens to India and her millions of sons and daughters.'[34] Nehru was sentenced to 'four years of rigorous imprisonment' in Dehra Dun Jail.[35]

After this, the campaign widened a bit to include about 1500 prominent individuals from the Working Committee, the All-India Congress Committee, and legislative members from provinces around the country. Patel, Mrs Naidu, Ranjit, and many others swiftly found themselves behind bars.[36] Nan's turn finally came on 5 December.[37]

~

From the moment that Nehru was sentenced, Nan had known what was coming. And while she welcomed it, she again fretted for her children and worried about abandoning them. She raced hither and thither to get things in order, since she had no way of knowing how long they would remain forcibly separated. Chandralekha, the eldest, was completing her upper secondary studies, so Nan had to set up her transfer to Isabella Thoburn College in Lucknow. She also arranged for Nayantara and Rita to stay at Anand Bhawan under the care of their longstanding nanny, Anna, their education now the purview of private tutors. Then she wrote each of her daughters a letter explaining the situation, comforting young Rita with the most details and loving, inspiring reassurance.

'Mamu [Nehru] has already gone. Papu [Ranjit] is going in a day or two, and my turn will come next week. You and Lekha and Tara will remain out, but you will be satyagrahis just the same as we, and you will do your bit by keeping the flag flying over Anand Bhawan . . . It will be a bit lonely sometimes, but if you remember there is a war on, and how many little boys and girls have had to leave their parents, you won't mind . . . Soon we shall be home again . . . We want smiles and grit to win through in this fight which will mean freedom for us all, and for this great, big, beautiful India of ours.' She concluded encouragingly: 'Think of it, darling, you and I and Papu and Mamu are helping to make her free. Isn't it something to be proud of and very happy about?' Nayantara later recalled with pride that 'If there were tears in Mummie's eyes when she wrote that letter, and during the many months she was separated from her children, we never knew it.'[38]

Indeed, Nehru, Ranjit, and Nan took extra steps to keep the children's spirits up and to ensure that they never felt too worried about what was happening. Soon after Nan was picked up, Nehru wrote to Chandralekha as 'the responsible head of Anand Bhawan now'. He lightheartedly wrote: 'We are flourishing, Papu [Ranjit] and I, and busily occupied with reading and writing and looking after our little household, and spinning, and standing on the head [that applies to me only] and sleeping.' Teasingly, he then asked her to convey to her mother a very important Chinese poem written by Su Tung-p'o during their next official interview: 'Families, when a child is born, Want it to be intelligent. I, through intelligence Having wrecked my whole life, Only hope that baby will prove Ignorant and stupid. Then he will crown a tranquil life By becoming a Cabinet Minister.'[39]

~

Nan's arrest made news around the world and drew international criticism, just as Gandhi and the High Command had planned.[40] The *Manchester Guardian* wrote that the news was 'received with great regret by the many friends this brilliant woman made during her visit to England in 1938'. Still, the paper noted that many in Britain, including those that considered themselves India's allies, found it confusing that one who had spoken so eloquently and passionately about the menace posed by Hitler was now protesting 'any effort' to challenge him. Krishna Menon explained with some success the razor's edge that India was trying to walk.[41]

When Nan was sentenced to four months, an influential group of twenty-three prominent British women wrote a letter to *The Times* expressing their outrage.[42] The signatories included the first woman ever to hold Cabinet rank in the UK, Margaret Bondfield, who was symbolically linked to Nan through the history that each had made. Allies Agatha Harrison and Emmeline Pethick-Lawrence added their names, along with other friends and admirers, including the acclaimed writer Vera Brittain, Dame Elizabeth Cadbury (of chocolate fame), pioneering doctor Hilda Clark, suffragette Kathleen Courtney, and renowned Shakespearean actress Dame Sybil Thorndike. 'The present situation in India has been brought home forcibly to us,' they wrote, 'by reason of the imprisonment of some leading members of the All-India Women's Conference—Mrs. Vijaya Lakshmi Pandit, for example.' They called out the unjustness of it all: 'We are fully aware of India's generous help to the war effort in terms of men, material, and money. But alongside this comes the disturbing news of the imprisonment of outstanding national leaders.' They urged the release of all political prisoners and called on their government to find a solution to the 'constitutional deadlock'.[43]

~

Nan's second stint in prison passed much less eventfully than her first. This was because of the worldwide elevation of Gandhi to saint-like status, the sense that independence was nearer if still out of reach, the context of the global war, the Nehru-Pandit's own achievements, and because the sentence generally was much lighter. Nan was taken to Naini Central Prison, one of the country's largest such facilities located just outside of Allahabad where her brother had previously been incarcerated. 'This time there was no overcrowding in the barrack and there was less vigilance. The matron knew that political prisoners would not try to escape and spent time chatting with' everyone.

As was true before, Naini was home to different kinds of inmates, including those incarcerated for violent crimes, each classed differently with different perks. Some women who were jailed brought their young children along as well, 'not having a home where they could be left.' The 'rules did not permit a child [over the age of three] to accompany the mother'. Since all prisoners were required to work in some way, Nan offered to look after the toddlers on-site, seven total. She saw to it that 'a small barrack in the political ward was cleaned and whitewashed', and she turned it into a daycare centre of sorts. She gave them regular baths, washed their clothes, fed them, and otherwise entertained all of them every day from morning until lockdown in the night. 'It sounds easy enough,' she later recalled with amusement, 'but some days those babies nearly drove me out of my mind.'

Nan's supervision of the children facilitated conversations with women throughout the ward across the crime-class divide. She found herself learning many new things, and thereby chanced into a surprising mentoring relationship. A young twenty-two-year-old woman named Rajkumari was on death row and wailed in fear and anguish every night for what had happened and what was to come. 'She had been a child widow and, after the death of her husband, had had an affair with a married man who persuaded her to part with her jewelry, which he gave to his wife. Thereupon she found a suitable opportunity to murder him.' She told Nan 'with great relish that she cut him up in little pieces and put him in a sack'.

Even so, Nan took pity on her unfortunate life, and tried her best to comfort her. Rajkumari had an appeal pending, though everyone believed nothing would come of it. So she appreciated Nan's reassurances and took to calling her 'mama'.

Towards the end of Nan's term, Rajkumari received news that the high court had, in fact, granted her appeal, and the prison staff went about preparing for her release. The young woman sat 'outside her cell howling and swearing', demanding that she be allowed to stay with Nan. When no amount of cajoling moved her, Nan had to intervene with some embarrassment. She phoned a cousin and the district magistrate asking that Rajkumari be released into the family's care. The magistrate was particularly upset at having had his tennis game interrupted, but he, along with everyone else, complied. Nan assured her cousin that she would take over responsibility within six weeks, once she too was freed from prison. 'But in six days Rajkumari had run away . . . and settled herself in the red-light district of Allahabad, having first stolen whatever she could lay her hands on.' Nan would forever after remember all of this as 'an interesting experience'.[44]

~

By January 1941, rumours began to swirl that Gandhi himself might face arrest, and some also speculated as to who might replace him in such an event.[45] Suspicions of skulduggery seemed to breathe extra life into the whispers. Subhas Chandra Bose had broken with the Congress the previous summer and launched his own protests against the British occupation of India. When he was jailed for it, he went on a hunger strike that ultimately prompted his reassignment in December to house arrest in Calcutta. Then, suddenly, in late January, he disappeared mysteriously, simply vanishing from right under his captors' noses.[46]

The Mahatma publicly paid this no heed and carried on with his overall campaign. In early March, he visited with Nan in prison, and spoke with Maulana Azad and some others, but this only set off further conjecture. He told people not to read anything into what were merely friendly visits.[47]

Nan followed up by visiting Gandhi after her release on 3 April.[48] At his behest, but also after personally consulting with Nehru and Ranjit in Dehra Dun Jail, she assumed some lieutenant responsibility, ordering nationalist papers to shut down in protest of wartime censorship.[49] At the same time, Gandhi appointed her an 'exempting authority' for her province. Although it had been limited in scope, people were disappointed in this satyagraha's results, and some were asking not to go to prison even if called upon. Nan and others in her position were asked to judge the merits of such requests and, where warranted, to forward a matter to Gandhi for a personal decision. She felt the broader strategy needed to be rethought. But for the time being, she went along with what she thought was 'the most difficult and fruitless task' she had 'ever had to perform'.[50]

~

Nehru first visited China in August of 1939 and quickly forged a strong rapport with nationalist party leaders Generalissimo Chiang Kai-Shek and his wife Madame Chiang.[51] The Chiangs and the Nehrus (Jawaharlal and Nan) began to correspond regularly from then on, and the two families began to encourage closer ties.[52] Within the year, Nan had succeeded in establishing a relationship between Madame Chiang and the All India Women's Conference. In October 1940, news that Nan was to lead a women's delegation to China went public.[53] The planned exchange, however, was derailed by Gandhi's individual satyagraha campaign. Chinese communists, meanwhile, acted more cautiously, but when Nehru was arrested in November, the official organ of their party, the *Hsin Hua Jih Pao*, called him a 'great friend of China' and demanded his quick release. Mao Tse-tung, Chow En-lai and others, all party generals, 'cabled Nehru expressing sympathy'.[54]

Nan's trip was revived when her second prison term came to an end.[55] She immediately applied for a passport and began making plans, her trip generating considerable enthusiasm in India.[56] But at the last moment, everything had to be cancelled once more because 'the bombing' was 'worse than ever before + already two planes carrying visitors' had 'been completely destroyed'. The Chiangs did not want her to take the risk and the trip was postponed indefinitely.[57]

~

Nan's disappointment at having to shelve her China plans for the time being was tempered by some other news that arrived at just the same moment. She had been elected the president of the sixteenth session of the All India Women's Conference.

She had just fallen ill with 'a mild form of heatstroke' from her frequent travel between various cities and towns and needed to take a few days off to recuperate from 'severe headaches + fever'. Under doctor's orders, she had cancelled a planned trip to Bombay where she had hoped to meet up with Rameshwari Nehru, Rajkumari Amrit Kaur, and 'all the other luminaries'. She had hoped only that her absence would not 'be attributed to any incorrect reason'.[58] So word of her election took her somewhat by surprise. 'Every province except my own voted for me!!!' she told Ranjit bemusedly.[59]

A few days after Nan was named to her new position of leadership, a group of prominent British women who considered themselves friends of India, feminists and activists in the cause of peace, delivered an 'open message' to the women of India, stressing British friendliness, urging them to realize India's peril, and pleading with them to embrace the war effort fully. Several of these writers were the same ones who had criticized the British government over Nan's arrest. But this was a broader group that included the likes of Lady Violet Bonham Carter, the daughter of a former British prime minister and close companion of current PM Winston Churchill (and later grandmother of celebrated Hollywood actress Helena). 'We know how passionately you hate war. We hate war too,' they wrote, saying it was a 'terrible indictment' of their generation that 'brute force [was used] as an instrument of policy'. Nonetheless, they felt the Axis were an existential threat that had to be fought and they warned of what was to come to the subcontinent if the Allies did not soon prevail. 'We are told that some of you say that this is the war of British Imperialism, and that therefore Indian nationalists can have no part in it,' they wrote with disbelief. They quoted a recent FDR broadcast that the whole world stood 'divided between human slavery and freedom', and begged India to set aside political differences for the moment and join the fight for the side they knew it stood for. 'Without victory for the democracies there can be no Indian freedom, and we assure you in all sincerity that never was there so much sympathy with Indian aspirations, as is to be found in Britain today,' they ended.[60]

Though the letter was well-intentioned, it was not well-received in India. Many took umbrage with the writers' ignorance of ground realities. Nan herself was outraged and dashed off a reply 'straight off without thinking of its suitability . . .'.

Right after posting it, Nan was contacted by Rajkumari Amrit Kaur, who asked if she would sign on a joint statement critiquing the

British women's appeal. Sarojini Naidu, Rameshwari Nehru, Rani Laxmibai Rajwade, and a few other leaders of the AIWC had also been asked to co-sign. Nan thought the rajkumari's response 'milk + water', especially when compared to her own, but added her name in any event.[61]

They wrote, they said, in their individual capacities, but also as representatives of the women's conference and of 'the conviction of a large body of India's women'. They called out the white privilege, condescension, and willful blindness they saw in the open message. India was already fighting on behalf of the West, so such a plaintive plea was just cover for the further denial of Indian self-determination. Prime Minister Churchill, Nan and the others pointed out, had 'no misgivings about the status that India occupies in the British mind. It is a dependency, which can be, and is being, utilized at the British will. He knows that he does not need the consent or co-operation of India's thinking sons and daughters in anything that Britain wants for fighting the war'. The British used Indian soldiers as well as taxation and 'so-called voluntary contributions' to claim any amount of money they wished. 'The fact is,' the AIWC team wrote bluntly, 'you are wholly wrong in your estimate of things . . . You quote today that the whole world is divided between human slavery and human freedom. The fact is that there is no such thing as human freedom for the Asiatic races, certainly not for India; nor is there any for the virile Africans. The result, whatever it may be, of the war will not alter their condition for the better, save through their own efforts. As we see the realities it is this. It is a war between the British Empire and the Nazis and Fascists for world domination, meaning in effect the exploitation of the non-European races. We cannot be in love with Nazism and Fascism, but we may not be expected to be in love with British imperialism.'

It was the sanctimoniousness of the British appeal the Indian women found most irksome. 'Lastly,' they wrote, 'let us point out the anomaly of British women asking India, though a slave nation, to help a slave owner in distress, instead of asking the slave owner to undo the wrong, and cure himself of the initial sin and thus ensure the moral justness of his position. This presentation of the picture may appear unpleasant to you, but it is, nonetheless, sincere, and we could not answer your sincerity except by being equally sincere.'[62]

The independently crafted response was published first, followed several days later by the collective petition. Nan 'received letters of congratulation from different parts of India' for her efforts.[63]

~

As international and domestic affairs demanded more and more of Nan's attention, she grew proportionally more defensive of her private time. She felt that her family life had already suffered from the public commitments she, her husband, and her brother shared. This was a cost she had been willing to bear in service of a larger cause. But this also made every moment she could carve out for personal matters more precious. She treasured her immediate and extended family and found ways small and large to create a grounded, comfortable and loving sense of home for them.

Just weeks after Nan was freed from prison, Indira returned to India from Europe. She had been in Switzerland when the war broke out and found herself stranded. She eventually decided to make her way out by hazarding a dangerous journey through unoccupied France, Spain, and Portugal to get back to London, where she experienced the terror of the *blitz*. Indira claimed to take all of this in stride. But Nan felt a bond with her niece, worried constantly about her health, and felt a special responsibility to look after her with Nehru still in jail.[64]

This was perhaps made all the more vivid by the fact that Nan had just taken a position as secretary of the Kamala Nehru Memorial Hospital, which was now run out of a wing of Swaraj Bhawan (the original Anand Bhawan).[65] She thought of this as a way to help out and to honour the memory of her sister-in-law, though the obligations quickly proved heavier than she expected. 'It is a wholetime job' she complained to Ranjit.[66] But overall she was pleased that the 'Hospital is functioning well'. She added that it 'was such a joy to feel we are able to give some relief to those in need of it'.[67]

Nayantara and Rita, who were home for the holidays, looked up to their 'big sister' (cousin) Indira, and 'followed her around the house admiringly, imitating her in every way . . .' Nan decided to put together 'a little celebration' for Indira's homecoming. 'It was a standup affair on the roof + Anna decorated it very prettily. She shaded lights + flowers gave it a lovely fairy like effect. Indu [pet form of Indira] wore pale pink + silver + looked like the Queen of the fairies. It was a very successful party,' she told her husband, even as she confessed that she missed him and her brother 'every minute of the evening'.[68]

Ranjit had meanwhile kept himself quite busy in prison producing a scholarly translation of the *Mudra Rakshasa*, a Sanskrit work of historical fiction about Indian emperor Chandragupta Maurya's rise to power. The play focused on the salubrious machinations of Chandragupta's aide-de-camp, Chanakya, often compared in modern times anachronistically to the Renaissance-era Italian, Niccolo Machiavelli. Ranjit complemented the main translation with explanatory and analytical essays.[69]

Nan assisted her husband with his work where possible. This involved handling the exchange of books and other materials back and forth from Anand Bhawan. She had the *Mudra Rakshasa* typeset and began corresponding with potential publishers. Oxford University Press and the New Book Company both expressed strong interest.[70]

Meanwhile, Nan was determined to carve out some time for her children to play and grow—to be children. After settling Indira in Mussoorie, she arranged to spend the summer in Khali, sending the children ahead as she wrapped up loose ends in Allahabad. Nayantara, just discovering her literary powers, immediately told her mother that she found the estate 'so lovely' that she tried 'to capture the beauty of the sunset + the magic of the moonbeams in words', before adding in a more typical teenage fashion that her efforts were hampered by her younger sister. 'Rita is always around + these things have no meaning for her + she delights in worrying me.'[71]

Nan was shocked to find on arrival a few days later that Khali had fallen into disrepair. Nan quickly went about cataloguing everything and updated Ranjit on the state of affairs. Although finances were tighter than before, she also decided that she now had to get things in order. Still, no matter how much she cleaned things up and how graceful she made her home, she could not seem to get rid of a melancholy that lingered in the air. 'Khali is so full of memories of you,' she wrote Ranjit sadly, 'that living here without you has become almost painful!'[72]

The older girls, for their part, threw themselves into their studies, while Rita grew more serious about dance. 'Everyone now seems hard at work + other things are incidental. I suppose they are growing up + beginning to take their responsibilities more seriously,' Nan informed their father.

Even so, they rested and took in the sunshine. They went hiking and hunting, rode ponies, ate fruit right off the tree, and marveled at the natural beauty of the place.[73] 'The grass is thick with daisies + crocuses + looks like a pink + white carpet under trees. The hydrangeas are masses of deep blue + give wonderful colour effects . . .' The family decided to eat only locally sourced food for the remainder of their stay. 'There is homemade dalia, delicious Bread + biscuites [sic], chappatis, vegetables, dahi, eggs + plenty of apricots + plums with a few early peaches thrown in . . . [and] there is the Honey + the fresh jam we have made.'[74] Various friends dropped in every so often, and a few, including future prime minister Lal Bahadur Shastri, stayed on in 'Paradise' for several days.[75]

One evening, Nan met Uday Shankar, an Oxford-educated international dance impresario who ran a nearby school of performing arts, and who would go on to become one of India's most acclaimed performers and teachers, his own accomplishments outshined only by those of his sitar-playing younger brother, Ravi. Shankar praised Rita's abilities and suggested that Nan enrol her in his school the following summer.[76] Ranjit was tickled by all of this and encouraged his daughter to pursue her passion. Within a couple of weeks, Nan informed him that 'Rita is so obsessed with her dancing that she practices for hours at a time + is completely content.' The members of her household staff were horrified by all of this and begged Nan to put an end to it all, pleading 'almost in tears' not to let the young girl 'bring disgrace on the family'. 'I had to spend an hour in explaining very gently how changing time required a new adjustment of ideas etc.,' Nan bemusedly told Ranjit.[77]

Rita was not the only one to have little patience for traditionally defined roles. Chandralekha had become 'a book-worm', and 'the first object of her life now . . . [was] to get a first division in every examination + as many prizes as she can possibly compete for'. Nan worried about how many hours she spent studying, but her daughter assured her that she was doing what she enjoyed. Nayantara modelled herself after her big sister and precociously announced her intention to stand for the matriculation examination (equivalent of tenth grade), a tough challenge because of the high level of Hindi that was required and because she was still only in the middle of the ninth standard and more than a year too young.[78]

When a male cousin asked Chandralekha what she would do about housekeeping once she was married since she professed disdain for the task, she replied that she 'would only marry on the express understanding that the house looked after itself'. Nan thought her the epitome of the 'modern young woman'.[79]

Mother and daughters bonded during this time, the girls affectionately calling Nan 'the honourable ancient one'. 'I can assure you,' Nan told their father, 'the tone in which this is said makes me feel ancient, even as I don't feel too honorable.'[80]

~

Nan and the children returned to the dusky heat of the UP plains several weeks later. Nayantara and Rita enjoyed the late summer days, cycling and swimming and otherwise occupying themselves. Chandralekha went back to college, while her mother fretted over the terrible dorm conditions and the awful food, like parents everywhere.[81]

Nan's birthday was coming up on the eighteenth on the Gregorian calendar and on the fifteenth on the Indian one. So the family decided to have two separate celebrations. On the first one, she travelled up to Dehra Dun Jail to spend it with Ranjit and Jawaharlal.[82] She enjoyed this very much, and shortly after told her husband that he had 'no idea' what it was like to live alone in Anand Bhawan '+ not having anyone to fuss over'. 'The days,' she groaned, 'simply stretch out into eternity.' The children did their part to cheer her up. For the second party, Chandralekha and Nayantara put together a fancy lunch, while their youngest sister arranged the 'marvelous' supper. 'We had to go in fancy dress. Rita was Princess Padmini of Chitor [sic] complete with all the family jewels—Chand wore Kathiawadi dress, Tara wore an evening frock, Anna [the nanny] was a gypsy + I was dressed up by Chand in Burmese costume!' she reported. Rita set the table with the home's little-used Venetian glass and French crockery and entertained everyone 'as if she were 25 years old instead of ten!'[83]

All the frivolity seemed to make Nan nervous, and she grew increasingly anxious about everyone's well-being. Nayantara was inexplicably losing weight and had to be sent off to Lucknow for tests. The doctor forbade her from sitting for the matriculation exam, which caused a good deal of upset.[84] Ranjit too had been mysteriously ill. Despite reassurances to the contrary, Nan was overcome with an ominous sense of foreboding. 'It is not enough to say there is no cause for anxiety,' she warned her husband.[85]

~

In September, Nan made another pilgrimage to Wardha to see Gandhi. 'A visit to Sevagram is not only rejuvenating—it does to me what a cocktail does to other people—gives me pep + vim + vigour + all the other American terms combined.' En route, she bumped into Sarojini Naidu, who shared so much gossip with her that Nan feared she herself might be the next victim of such stories.

The visit to the ashram went as she had hoped. 'Bapu . . . was very kind + gave me a lot of time—He fed + looked after me in his own inimitable fashion . . . In a moment of weakness I have promised to drink a glass of milk every day! So you see what one can do for Bapu!' she joked while describing her trip to Ranjit. Nan and Gandhi discussed ongoing political matters and her role, and she emerged with a 'much clearer' understanding of what she needed to do. Gandhi asked her to come see him regularly, once a month if possible.

Over the years, the two had grown very close, he almost a substitute father for her by this time, when she had long since forgiven whatever had happened in her youth. In a sense, though, Gandhi's attitude had remained constant from then through this moment: he was paternal and paternalistic. When Nan spent one evening out late speaking with another guest, 'Bapu sent out a search party + was terribly worried. He still treats me as if I was a two year old. It is embarrassing,' she wrote.[86]

~

Just as she was visiting with Gandhi, Nan received word that she was up for the post of vice-chancellor of Lucknow University. She consulted with Ranjit, who lent his 'moral support' for the idea. But as soon as canvassing on her behalf got underway, Nan found she did not have the stomach for it. The position was a full-time commitment and she had too many other responsibilities. But the post also 'required a capacity for intrigue etc which . . .[she] neither possessed nor desired to cultivate'. She felt sullied by the whole affair. 'Of course I felt just a wee bit sorry to say "no"—who wouldn't enjoy being the first woman V.C. in the world,' she confessed to her husband, before self-effacingly adding '+ getting there without any educational aids!!!' Despite the allure of making history her story, she went with her gut, and the sensible advice of Chandralekha who also strongly advised her against accepting. Once she formally declined, however, letters 'from many parts of India' came flowing in 'saying how much people were looking forward to . . . [her] acceptance of the post'. 'Its [sic] a queer world,' she observed.[87]

Nan did not have much time to worry about any of this. Her brother in 1938 had started a new newspaper based out of Lucknow, the *National Herald*, as a platform to consider the most pressing issues of the day, against the backdrop of colonialism and war. It achieved a fair amount of attention almost overnight, in part because of its stirring banner appeal: 'Freedom is in Peril. Defend it with All Your Might.' Despite its fame, the paper was in debt and on wobbly financial footing and found itself in a particularly precarious position in late 1941. The board of directors wanted Ranjit to stand surety, to guarantee the repayment of its loan and to help stabilize the paper. They tried to convince Nan to go along, assuring her that Ranjit had already given his approval. With difficulty, she resisted efforts to force her to acquiesce, ensuring she had the time and scope to properly talk matters out with her husband. Once she had done so, she was of course on board with protecting the paper. 'I think in the circumstance we should risk something. It is difficult to refuse when outsiders are helping,' she wrote encouragingly to Ranjit.[88]

Then she was on the move again. As 'heaps of invitations [came] pouring in,' she headed out for another tour, this time through the state of Bihar, with visits to Patna, Gaya and Chopra. From there, she had further travel to Udaipur in Rajasthan, before she needed to attend the annual women's conference. She tried to talk Ranjit, soon to be out of prison, into joining her on a trip down to the south, wistfully reminding him that they had not 'been together in ages'. She begged him to say yes, before having to drop the entire idea. They would instead just spend a little time together at home. She thought seriously about retiring.[89]

~

The sixteenth session of the All India Women's Conference was held in late December 1941 in the southern coastal city of Cocanada (today known as Kakinada). In entering the name of her cousin-in-law as president for the coming year, Rameshwari Nehru began the meeting by highlighting Nan's signature achievements to date, heralding her as the most popular minister in her province. 'She is well-known for her tact, for her discrimination, for her grasp of things and for her ability to work with all kinds of people and in all kinds of situations. She knows how to tackle difficult problems and in her dextrous [sic] hands they become easy of solution. It is . . . her capacity for hard work which has given her the position in public life of the country which she holds today,' she said in praise. Other opening remarks were just as laudatory. Margaret Cousins declared that Nan's presidency 'crowned with success' all that Cousins had fought and stood for her over the past decades.

A princess from a small, local *zamindari* (princely) state, Yuvarani Vedavathi of Pithapuram, then, in the same capacity that Nan previously had, formally welcomed the delegates to the conference by drawing attention to global events. 'The All-India Women's movement is not an isolated movement. It is part of a great world movement. We are seeing with what heroism and strength of conviction, our comrades, the women in China, Russia, Britain and America are facing the cruel vicissitudes of fortune. In all likelihood we may have to face a similar fate,' she noted.

'Now the time is come when we are confronted with problems that are not limited to the exclusive spheres of the woman or the man alone. They belong to the common humanity . . . [and] demand a solution. Perhaps the perfect solution will never be possible in the sphere of human activities, limited as the human being is in his intellectual and physical capabilities. But nevertheless, a solution of the problems is an imperative need, if a belief in a better future is to be maintained . . . This conception is not Utopian, it is practicable . . . It is an effort, a great and worthy effort. Disarmament, greater peace, a more sensible economic rehabilitation and a better and more equitable distribution of world's natural resources, a more human view of science, education, and art, are all factors in that effort.'

Nan's keynote address, delivered shortly thereafter, echoed many of these sentiments. She too drew connections to women around the world, and to organizations fighting for interrelated causes. She started by lamenting the absence of British writer and peace activist Vera Brittain, who had been invited but had been unable to come due to the war. Nan then talked of her association with the Women's International League for Peace and Freedom, an organization devoted to understanding the root causes of war and developing mechanisms for a perpetual peace.[90] The American icon Jane Addams was one of the founding figures of the WILPF during World War I and had won a Nobel Peace Prize in the early thirties for her efforts. Brittain had served as vice-president in the years that followed. At the AIWC, Nan said: 'The great forces arising in the world today will ultimately help shape the new world which will come into being after the war. It is in planning for a new world order that women should take their share . . . The Women's International League for Peace and Freedom . . . has declared itself in favour of a world order based on a "new attitude of man to man and nation to nation with a realization of interdependence and a renunciation of exploitation and profiteering". But declarations to be effective must be implemented by action.'

She continued: 'We must decide whether we shall ally ourselves to the forces of life, or those of death . . . [S]hall we raise our united voice in favour of a brave new world where human life and human liberty receive the respect which is their due, where progress and security are within the grasp of each individual . . .? The future, not for women only but for humanity as well, is what the women of India make of it.'

'Today woman faces the world as an individual for the first time. Her problems are the problems of society, and while fighting for those legal, civic, and economic rights, which are still denied to us let us not forget that the whole question of rights for women is closely linked to the social question which, in its turn, is part of the larger political question.'

Nan mildly chastised the delegates for trying to take on too many tasks at once. As a result, they had wasted too much time passing resolutions to no meaningful effect. Nan called on them to tackle one problem collectively over the coming year: illiteracy. 'A mass drive . . . started by the Conference would instantly invoke a response from other progressive groups and would help us to establish closer contacts with the villages and with the workers in the fields and factories.'

By way of ending, she first praised efforts to codify the Hindu law of succession, which sought to address deficiencies in the way women inherited property. She noted that 'the codification of the whole of Hindu Law' was 'urgently required' 'based on the equality of status between man and woman'.

Then she closed by appealing to her friends 'to remove the hatred and suspicion which have crept into our midst'. 'India belongs to all of us,' she reminded them. 'Her greatness is the result of that culture to which each sect and religion has contributed. Her past glory as well as her present fallen condition are the handiwork of her children . . . Some of the work we have done may have value, but if we can contribute even a small measure to the unity of India we shall not have lived in vain.'[91]

~

Moments before Nan delivered her remarks, Kamaladevi Chattopadhyay, a founding figure of the AIWC and herself a pioneering political figure who had helped lead Gandhi's salt satyagraha, was welcomed home with an ovation. She had just returned from a world tour to advance India's cause abroad, with prominent trips through the United States and China. She had brought back a small token from her time in Chunking, a gift from Madame Chiang. It was a canvas of a majestic bird entitled 'Eagle', she said, that had been 'prepared in the course of air raids . . . [and] mounted up in an air raid shelter while the bombs were dropping on around from above. It is why you will find a few black spots on it'. The picture was inscribed with an ancient Chinese verse. In English, it read:

> When and where is the eagle to be seen at his noblest?
> In the mountain forest when the mist covers
> His feathers with rain drops.
> When his threatening beak looms through the high clouds
> In the late autumn when he faces peril and danger.[92]

CHAPTER SEVEN

The Night Watch

On New Year's Day 1942, following the Japanese sneak attack on Pearl Harbor, the United States, Great Britain, and the Soviet Union joined together with China to sign the Declaration by United Nations, a statement of joint principles and objectives grounded in the Atlantic Charter, signed shortly beforehand to essentially extend FDR's Four Freedoms (freedom of speech and religion and from fear and want—together the basis of all freedom) to people around the world. The very next day, forty-seven other governments, including India's, signed on to the new UN. The only problem was that India was itself not free, the only one among the signatories brought in under such circumstances.

The swiftly changing reality forced the Congress to again alter some of its calculations. By this point, there was a pronounced rift between those who opposed all war, no matter the circumstances, and those who thought that, at least in certain narrow circumstances and when otherwise unavoidable, war might be necessary. Gandhi pledged himself to the former, while Nehru and most others fell in the latter camp.

Gandhi had already tried to bridge the divide with his individual satyagraha campaign, which had begun symbolically with Vinobha Bhave and Jawaharlal Nehru each representing the divergent points of view. They had hoped to encourage Britain to free India, so that the nature of its assistance to the war effort could be determined thereafter. Gandhi, for his part, was willing to support non-violent resistance. But the campaign had failed.

The Congress Working Committee met in late December 1941 to fashion a way forward. Extraordinary secrecy surrounded their deliberations. Finally, on the thirtieth, they recommitted to their Bombay resolution from September, announcing that while 'there has been no change in British policy towards India, the Working Committee must nevertheless take into consideration the new world situation that has arisen by the developments of the war . . . The sympathies of Congress must inevitably lie with peoples who are the subjects of aggression and who are fighting for their freedom, but only a free and independent India can be in a position to undertake the defence of the country on a national basis and be of help in the furtherance of the larger causes that are emerging from the storm of the war'.[1]

If this seemed a distinction without a difference, simply a repetitive restatement of their long-standing position, Gandhi made sure the divergence was made plain. In a letter to Maulana Azad, then serving as Congress President, Gandhi wrote that it was now clear that he had 'committed a grave error' in his earlier interpretation of the Bombay Resolution. He had believed that the Congress had earlier called for opposition to all wars, including the ongoing one, on the grounds of non-violence. He realized now that he had projected this meaning onto the official pronouncement, and that there were some who did not oppose the war at all. Gandhi inverted the logic of this to defend his position. 'The resolution contemplated material association with Britain in the war effort as a price for guaranteed independence of India. If such was my view, and I believed in the use of violence for gaining independence and yet refused participation in the effort as the price of that independence, I would consider myself guilty of unpatriotic conduct. It is my certain belief that only non-violence can save India and the world from self-extinction.'[2]

Gandhi resigned from the leadership of the Congress as a result. Congress authorized the use of armed resistance against the Axis, and signalled its readiness to enter the war effort if India was freed to make the decision independently.[3]

Days later, the All-India Congress Committee adopted the new policy.[4] To put to rest speculation about what had happened, and to make his wishes for the future perfectly clear, the Mahatma then declared: 'Jawaharlal Nehru is my legal heir . . . I am sure that when I pass away he will take up all the work that I do. He is a brave and courageous man. He often quarrels with me, but when I am no more he will know how to carry on my work.'[5]

~

Nan brought the annual meeting of the All India Women's Conference under her presidency to a close on 1 January with three resolutions that spoke directly to these tumultuous events. 'This conference is of the opinion (a) that permanent peace cannot be achieved except on the principles of freedom and justice equally applicable to all nations and races and without an immediate and fundamental change in the present structure; for a post-war world can be reconstructed only out of policies initiated and operated during the present war . . .' they declared, before adding '(b) that Britain's statements regarding her war aims cannot make any moral appeal to the peoples of the world so long as she refuses to alter her present policy in regard to India.' Moreover they proclaimed, their 'Conference reiterates its abhorrence of war and declares that if war is persisted in it must inevitably lead not only to meaningless destruction but also to the deterioration of moral values. It, therefore, firmly believes that human progress is possible only in a world free from military domination and based on the acceptance of international disarmament.'[6]

Such denunciation of war conceptually, however, was not meant to challenge the necessity of the ongoing global conflict against the Axis, but rather to stipulate the parameters for the world that was to emerge thereafter, premised on an end to the old imperial order. This was made clear in another of the conference's major resolutions, establishing a voluntary corps to prepare for the fallout from catastrophic violence. 'In view of the critical times and the danger of air attacks, such as Rangoon has experienced recently [with Japanese advances to the very borderlands of the subcontinent], to all parts of India, this Conference resolves that instructions be issued to all its Branches to concentrate in the immediate future on training their members for humanitarian work' in times of crisis. These volunteers were charged with 'allaying panic among the masses . . . assisting in the evacuation of women and children from threatened areas . . . arranging for first aid and emergency nursing courses . . . facilitating the distribution of food and other necessities in affected areas . . .

helping in protective measures after air attacks, and . . . tackling internal disruption.'⁷

The war threatened more than everyone's physical safety though. It undermined the very basis of a just society—civil liberties—asking people all over the world to trade in their freedoms in the name of security. This was a devil's bargain, the conference discerned, that would burn down both things and leave people completely defenseless. 'In these times when the encroachment on personal freedom threatens to destroy these inherent individual rights which are so precious a heritage of civilization, this Conference associates itself with such organizations all over the world, as are striving to preserve the fundamental rights of all human beings . . .' The third resolution named a few for illustrative effect, including the freedom of religion and speech, and from fear (which they termed the right to personal security, including from a rogue state).⁸

~

The Chiangs made headlines around the world in early February when they made a surprise visit to India after traveling 'incognito'.⁹ Officially, Chiang Kai-Shek was in the subcontinent with his staff officers to consult with the government and the Allied Command about military strategy. But the BBC reported on the very day of his arrival that he was also there to consult with both Gandhi and Nehru.¹⁰ Chiang was hoping to use his friendship with the Nehrus to persuade them to give their blessings to the war effort, and to hold off on any other anti-colonial campaigns for the time being. He knew that he had to engage with Gandhi as well, who remained respected and revered, and represented the unrelenting opposition. Chiang had consulted with Roosevelt beforehand and unofficially planned to reassure the Indian leaders of American and Chinese support for Indian independence, and to promise to nudge Churchill towards this goal if their commitment was secured.¹¹

At the official ceremony hosted by Viceroy Linlithgow, Chiang announced: 'We pledge to our valued ally, who occupies an important and unique position, our friendship and co-operation in defeating the common foe, prepared to defeat aggression and ensure victory for the democratic front.' Chinese troops by then had been moved into position to defend Burma and India from Japan's assault. This, he hoped, would both underscore his sincerity and give him leverage with both the British and Indian sides of the bargaining table.[12]

The visit seemed to have an immediate salutary effect, serving as a much-needed morale booster to Allied forces around the world. Linlithgow made plain why: 'This meeting sets the seal upon the comradeship-in-arms of two great nations which between them number 800,000 souls, one-third of the world's population . . . [and] which bodes our enemy no good.' The Western press breathlessly reported on Chiang's ninety-minute meeting with his 'old friend' Nehru the next day, hoping for a breakthrough announcement on reconciliation and a 'map [of] aid for Britain'.[13]

~

Nan travelled to Delhi to meet the Chiangs in person.[14] She had been looking forward to this for so long and was filled with anticipation. Before beginning her journey, she dispatched a telegram of preliminary welcome: 'On behalf of the women of India,' she began, addressing herself to Madame Chiang, 'we welcome you and send you and the Generalissimo our heartiest greetings. We request you to convey to the women of China our deep admiration for their courage and endurance and our belief in the victorious outcome of the struggle for freedom.'[15]

Nehru introduced her to the visiting delegation on her arrival. The two families spent time together before the women headed out for the evening.[16]

Nan organized a gala reception in Madame Chiang's honour on 12 February under the auspices of the All India Women's Conference and arranged 'Indian music and dancing' as entertainment. She presented her guest with a 'white silk banner' with 'freedom, peace, progress' written in red embroidery.

The event was the only one where Madame Chiang was scheduled to speak publicly. Nan shared the platform with her guest and began: 'You have come here unexpectedly and unannounced and only a few of us have been able to gather in this ancient city of Delhi to bid you welcome and to draw inspiration from you.' Then she turned to the historical connections shared by the two vast Asian neighbours: 'For thousands of years China and India have been sister nations, very old and yet always renewing their youth, bound together by innumerable ties. Today we see again a renewal of those ancient bonds, and in you and in your comrade through life's journey, that great man who is leading China to victory, we see the living symbols of the future that is to be—India and China closely associated together in freedom and friendship for their own good, for the good of Asia, and for the good of the world.' Nan drew parallels between women's lives in both countries and spoke of the inspiration Indian women drew from the role their counterparts in China were playing 'in the reconstruction of their country'. In closing, she referenced the gift that Kamaladevi Chattopadhyay had brought to Cocanada. 'Members of the Women's Conference have been deeply touched by the gift of the silken banner which you recently sent to the women of India. That banner will ever symbolize for us the courage, the calm determination, and the spirit of sacrifice of the women of China, and in the hard and difficult days ahead of us it will give us strength and hearten us.'

When her turn came, Madame Chiang echoed many of the same sentiments: 'The urge to come to India has been mine for a long time. Now I am here and I am glad to stand in the midst of the women of India . . . There are ancient bonds of history which unite the people of China and India as brothers. China and India are the two pillars supporting the economic and social edifice of Asia and both are playing their part in making the world safe for democracy.' Then she dispensed with the pleasantries: 'War is at India's doorstep . . . You must prepare. It is futile to hope for victory unless you prepare. Chinese and Indians are realists and know that the enemy is treacherous.' She bemoaned the fact that earlier calls she had made had gone unheard. 'Pearl Harbor and Singapore are proof that my warnings were not figments of a war-torn mind.'

Nan knew there was truth to what Madame Chiang was saying. But so was the fact that the people of India were being prevented from making any defensive decisions for themselves.[17]

The Chiangs continued to press their views on the war for the remainder of their trip. At a press conference, Nehru reassured everyone that all aggression, 'whether Japanese or German, would be resisted by Mr. Gandhi and Congressmen'.[18] The Mahatma, wanting to go the extra mile, travelled over 700 of them from Wardha to

Calcutta to meet with the Chiangs, and spent a pleasant afternoon talking things over with them, with Nehru facilitating.[19]

Nan meanwhile accompanied Madame Chiang to the Taj Mahal and started to develop a bond with her.[20] The two women talked about a range of subjects, Chiang taking a keen interest in Nan's affairs. After listening intently to some family stories, she inquired why Nan did not consider sending her daughters to study in the United States, and she offered to assist at her alma mater, Wellesley College.[21]

~

Anand Bhawan was abuzz with excitement. Indira was about to wed, and everyone hustled about in preparation.

The groom-to-be was a young man named Feroze Gandhi. The young couple had gotten involved with each other in the mid-thirties. As he came closer into the Nehrus' orbit, however, Feroze had initially grown correspondingly distant from his own family. This had created a fair amount of tension between the two clans. It was Nan who had engineered a rapprochement. Nehru had been preoccupied with Kamala's illness and was in and out of prison. So he had tasked his sister with visiting the Gandhi family (no relation to the Mahatma) and apologizing to them for any trespasses.[22]

Just before Nan had left on her European tour, Feroze wrote her a lengthy missive in which he expressed regret for any past hurtful actions, asking that they be chalked up to childish behaviour. He told her how much he admired her and asked if she might serve as a trusted friend. Then he confessed: 'There is something else I ought to tell you. It is about Indu and myself . . . we love each other.'[23]

Only Nehru had known about Feroze and Indira till that point. He had had many reservations about the relationship and conveyed them regularly to his daughter. But she repeatedly dismissed his concerns. She and Feroze had decided to marry while they were at Oxford, and he had stayed by her side through their treacherous journey back to India. Indira informed her father of her decision upon her return, while he was still in jail.

Both the Nehrus and the Gandhis (Feroze's family) doubted the match, and the Mahatma was asked to talk some sense into the youngsters. But once it was clear that there was nothing that could be done about it, everyone embraced the union. After some discussion, they decided to have a Hindu ceremony rather than a spartan civil one, as Betty had last had. But Jawaharlal was wary of ostentation, and wanted things kept as modest as possible. Ranjit was asked to officiate, keeping only the rites that were 'essential' enough for the service to be 'meaningful'.

Presents began to pour in from all over the country once news of the celebration was announced. There were 'gifts of silver and crystal, lovely saris, and occasionally a velvet-lined casket containing a jeweled ornament'. The Nehrus were grateful for this outpouring of affection but made sure to return anything that came from people who were not close friends.

The ceremony took place on 27 March, at the veranda adjoining Swarup Rani's and Bibima's old quarters. An empty mat was placed on the ground to evoke Kamala's presence. Indira wore a 'shell-pink sari made from yarn spun by her father and edged with delicate silver embroidery'.

A carpet was placed towards the interior entrance where guests were to be seated. But the event generated so much excitement that hundreds of uninvited people showed up as well, hoping to catch a glimpse of things. Even the trees outside were filled with spectators.

Mixed in among the crowd were some of India's most prominent citizens. Sarojini Naidu, Govind Ballabh Pant, Rajendra Prasad, and Sir Tej Bahadur Sapru all graced the occasion. Madame Chiang sent a special cablegram of congratulations and good wishes.

After stepping in to assist with certain rituals where needed, Nan sat to one side, by a grey stone pillar lining the veranda. Uncharacteristically, tears started to roll down her cheeks. Nayantara caught notice of the unusual sight, and wondered what it was that had her unflappable mother so emotional.[24]

~

Sir Stafford Cripps arrived in India to much fanfare just a few days before Indira's wedding.[25] But the hopes generated by the visit quickly turned brittle and crumbled to dust. His proposals for future governance pressed heavily on existing fissures in the subcontinent's leadership, causing further fracturing between the Muslim League and the Congress. For the latter, Cripps's idea that provinces could refuse constitutional arrangements essentially endorsed the kind of factionalism they thought was being advocated by Jinnah and his organization. But it was the matter of India's place in the war effort that concerned them the most.

Nan thought of Cripps and his wife Isobel as 'personal friends' and invited them to stay for two days at Anand Bhawan during the talks. She treated both as proper guests, sending for Kabul melons and Quetta grapes, delicacies with special meaning for Sir Stafford, who was fond of fruits.[26]

Cripps tried mightily to win the day, bringing all his powers of persuasion to bear on the parties concerned. For a moment, success seemed within his grasp. Maulana Azad was ready to concede on the provincial arrangements provided the British were willing to grant them command of their defences. And Cripps got Churchill to agree to these terms.

Linlithgow, however, had other ideas and knocked Sir Stafford off balance by refusing to concede any meaningful wartime authority. Startled by this, and with his deal teetering precariously in balance, Cripps began to race around clownishly trying to keep all his teacups from crashing.

In the middle of this circus arrived Louis Johnson, Roosevelt's personal representative in India.[27] Johnson tried his best to stabilize things, bringing the full weight of the American President to bear on the situation. FDR was especially keen to see the India problem resolved. He saw 'great danger' in the lingering status quo and wanted Britain to relinquish control so that India could properly join the Allied cause.[28] Chiang, distressed at the failure he sensed looming, intervened as well.[29]

But it was all for naught. Linlithgow insisted that Archibald Wavell retain all power as commander-in-chief, the one thing the Indians would not abide. Working together, they torpedoed any possible diplomatic rescue of the situation. Sir Stafford's hopes sank. Within ten days, the smoking ruin of his diplomatic efforts was all that remained of Cripps' mission.

~

Nan was summoned by Maulana Azad to a meeting of the Congress Working Committee to discuss possible actions they should take.[30] Nehru set the parameters at a press conference shortly after holding follow-up discussions with Johnson. 'We are not going to embarrass the British war effort in India or the efforts of our American friends who may come here . . . We want that (British and American) action to whirl full speed ahead.' He noted ruefully that he had 'wanted 1,000,000 Indians in the army,' backed by 'every man and woman doing something, making it a popular war'. He warned of a looming 'tragedy' if Germany and Japan were to win and spread their dominion across the lands. He pledged to organize an Indian war effort on the 'basis of a free and independent India'.[31]

The Congress was riven with internal divisions on how to proceed. Amid such turmoil, members again began to clamour for Gandhi's leadership.

The Mahatma agreed that the Japanese, now threatening the south-eastern coastal city of Madras, had to be resisted. But he remained steadfast in his core belief that non-violence remained the supreme weapon.[32]

The debate stretched out over the next few months. Then, slowly through the summer, a plan began to take shape.

~

Nan felt the world closing in. She decided to get away to Khali with her family, sticking to their usual plans. It was a fortuitous decision. This would be the last time they would ever all be together.

~

The Almora Hills seemed especially beautiful that May, starkly so. Nayantara rolled this thought over in her mind as her eyes gently bobbed along the ups and downs of the terrain.

They had journeyed from Allahabad halfway by train before switching to a car at the base of the mountains. As they rose through the cooling mists, the girls felt a thrill as the car swerved sharply in this and that direction and hurtled along 'narrow and winding' roads. They loved the fact that their father was driving most of all.

Lunch was at a small one-room rest stop. The food was simple, fried puris puffed up like small flying saucers, served on a brass thali (a large round plate) with accompanying vegetables and yoghurt. They washed it all down by drinking straight from a small waterfall. For some reason, the meal lodged in Nayantara's memory.

They covered the last mile up to their estate on foot. And there, in paradise, the girls relaxed and played together as summer children, running through fields covered in daisies and wild orchids. They marvelled at the honeybees their father gently nurtured, climbed trees and ate berries by the fistful.

Chandralekha later joined some cousins to trek out to the Pindari Glacier for two weeks. So Nayantara and Rita enrolled in Uday Shankar's dance academy nearby, as Nan had wanted since her first encounter with the great master. The girls were given the option to learn Manipuri or Kathakali styles and picked the former, appreciating its freeform grace. Nayantara recalled her teacher saying to them: 'you must treat . . . [[t]hese movements which I show you] like flowers, for . . . [they] are just as fragile and delicate.'

The images her dance instructor conjured with the mere flutter of his arms and legs were vivid, and breathtaking to behold. But they hovered only an instant before disappearing back into the ether, leaving observers with a painful yearning for that which could not be held. Years later, Nayantara would look back on this fleeting, family summer holiday of joy with much the same feelings.[33]

~

In July 1942, the Congress Working Committee met at Sevagram, Gandhi's ashram at Wardha, to lay out a course of action.[34] They decided on 'a fight to the finish'.[35]

On the fourteenth, the Mahatma met with the press and announced 'open rebellion' against British rule. Representing the Congress, he flatly demanded that the United Kingdom 'recognize India's independence'. The Working Committee formally resolved not to hamper the war effort in any way, and repeated its long-held position that India would marshal all its might against the Axis if it were given a chance to do so of its own volition. Should Whitehall remain unwilling to surrender its authority, however, they warned that they were prepared to back a non-violent struggle for the 'vindication of its political rights and the liberty of India under Mr. Gandhi's leadership'.³⁶

The All-India Congress Committee was scheduled to meet on 7 August in Bombay. Nehru carefully crafted the formal resolution calling on Britain to 'Quit India'. He wrote that the 'future of the war and the success of freedom and democracy' were at stake. 'A free India will assure this success by throwing all her great resources into the struggle . . . against the aggression of Nazism, Fascism, and Imperialism,' he promised. 'This will not only affect materially the fortunes of the war, but will bring all subjected and oppressed humanity on the side of the United Nations . . .'³⁷ The resolution went on to outline steps that India would take upon independence to organize itself fully and effectively against Axis forces and laid out a vision of the world that should come after.³⁸

The British, desperate now to ward off a distracting insurrection, tried to undermine Gandhi, raiding AICC headquarters in Allahabad and seizing a trove of documents just days before the group's official meeting was set to begin. The government quickly sealed the materials it had taken and selectively released small statements of a resolution Gandhi had drafted back in April to make it appear that he wanted negotiations with Japan. They branded him and the Congress as appeasers.³⁹ Nan and Nehru, who had consistently sounded the alarm over Chamberlain's actions, found this a bit much to swallow.

Gandhi denounced the actions of the government as 'reprehensible' and said efforts to 'discredit' the Indian anti-colonial cause would fail. He called on Britain to cleanse itself of this 'taint' and pleaded with America to compel its ally to do so if it would otherwise not.⁴⁰

Despite British machinations, the AICC Working Committee passed Nehru's revised Quit India Resolution on 5 August and placed it on the agenda for the full meeting days later. After the Mahatma's opening remarks on the seventh, Nehru placed the resolution before the body. Sardar Vallabbhai Patel, Gandhi's right hand, seconded the motion. It was adopted late on the following evening.⁴¹

~

'Well, it has begun,' Nan said as the family sat for dinner at Anand Bhawan, listening to news of the Congress vote break on the radio.⁴²

Nan had gone to the Allahabad city Congress office that morning. It was a hive of hurried activity as frazzled workers prepared for the fallout from the final campaign. They hurriedly burned papers and sent equipment away to secret locations for safekeeping. Nan met with various officials who had not attended the AICC to discuss what to do. She was tasked with overseeing the response of university students.

Shortly after dinner, she received an urgent message that her ward, Mehrtaj, the daughter of Khan Abdul Gaffar Khan (the Frontier Gandhi), had taken 'seriously ill' in Lucknow, where she was in college. Nan rushed to be by her side. In the hospital the next day, she learned of arrests in Bombay. She immediately booked her return journey on that night's train.

Fearing arrest, the stationmaster quickly escorted her on arrival to her compartment, where the other passengers hid her under the covers. With their assistance, she reached Allahabad at 5 a.m. on the morning of the tenth. She got off at a way station on the outskirts of town to avoid any unexpected confrontations and travelled the rest of the way home in a horse-drawn carriage.

As soon as she walked in the door of Anand Bhawan, Chandralekha, Nayantara, and Rita rushed to welcome her, their eyes wide with excitement, each bursting with the big news. Mass student processions were planned for that day. Stories of all the rumours and whispers practically fell from the girls' lips.

Nan exchanged a word with the vice-chancellor of Allahabad University, who was in a state of panic. The students were riled up, he told her, and he feared that the police might respond with violence. Demonstrations were taking place around the country and the government was bent on stamping it all out quickly.

Nan walked over to the campus, which was nearby her house, and met with student leaders, calling on them to remain calm and to follow Gandhian protocol. But the tension in the city was palpable. The other Congress leaders whom Nan had met for discussions on the eighth had all already been incarcerated.

But that day, and the next, the marches went off without any major confrontations, though the police were prepared for one. Nan in the meantime had received word that several Congress leaders had escaped arrest in Bombay and had gone underground. Two of them turned up at Anand Bhawan in the deep night of the eleventh, one being the diminutive but feisty Lal Bahadur Shastri. The police were on the lookout for him.

Nan whisked her two guests into an upstairs bedroom and locked them inside, hiding the key away in the folds of her clothes. They set up shop and began 'typing and cyclostyling instructions to be sent to the villages'.[43] Nan planned to take them meals herself, only at night, so that no one save for herself and her children would know about the visitors hiding in the caverns of the great mansion, not even her trusted household staff.

On the twelfth, the vice-chancellor telephoned Nan. He was frantic. He had heard that the police planned to lathi-charge the students that day and were prepared even to shoot at them. He begged her to use her influence to have the students call off their planned activities. She had visited with the students over the previous days and had felt their anger and frustration. She had exhorted them to follow in the footsteps of the Mahatma. She told the vice-chancellor that nothing further could be done.

Nan herself was anxious. Mothers had been stopping by to berate her for getting their children mixed up in politics. While she reassuringly told them that they were 'all in it together', she was wracked by guilt, and worried incessantly over the safety of all the children involved, including her own.[44] Chandralekha and Nayantara, the latter only fourteen, were now old enough to participate as well, and both had decided to march.

In anticipation of casualties, Nan informed the Kamala Nehru Hospital 'to be ready for any eventuality'.[45] Emergency preparations were made.

The march was split into two branches, each winding its way through a different part of the town before terminating at a common rally point. Nan sat on her veranda and waited. The time seemed to stretch out and then melt in the glare of the noonday sun, the minutes drip-drop-drooping into a Salvador Dali-like puddle.

Nan was jolted from her stupor around 2 p.m. by the sound of machine-gun fire. She could suddenly hear the chanting of protestors. Just as she got outside, a car pulled up and 'three lawyer friends' got out and ran up to her. One of the marches had been fired upon. Chandralekha had been 'gravely injured'. The men were there to take Nan to her daughter's side. Nan's 'heart almost stopped beating' and she felt 'giddy and sick'. But just then, another acquaintance came running from another direction to say 'that the boy leading the [other] procession in front of the university had been shot dead'. Nan was momentarily paralyzed. Then, in her mind, she heard Mahatma Gandhi command her: 'do your duty.' She turned towards the university side, asking her friends to find her daughter and look after her as best they could.[46] Nayantara would later think of this as her mother's 'moment of supreme courage'.[47]

Nan walked into a disaster zone. Students had been shot and lay bleeding on the streets. Their peers were screaming 'Murderers' at the police who had surrounded them. Nan found her path blocked by the on-scene officers and pleaded with them to let her through but was denied. The youthful crowd took notice of her arrival and roared with approval, the crowd surging forth with renewed energy as students stretched out to receive her. Nan made her way into the thronging mass of people. She climbed on top of a car to take a command position and negotiate an end to the skirmish. She asked the students to back off so that those who were injured could receive medical care. She pledged to the police to calm the situation if only they would withdraw. As all complied, she rushed to aid the fallen. As she attended to one after the other, helping 'to pick up and remove [each] to hospital', the image of one boy 'whose testicles had been shot . . . [and who] screamed in agony' seared itself into Nan's memory.[48]

~

It was only that night that Nan learned about Chandralekha escaping unscathed during her procession's encounter with the police. But there was no time for celebrations. Indira snuck through the gates that night, weary after travelling from Bombay. She had been at home there when the police arrived to pick up her father and had mistaken them for an American film crew when she let them into the house. Though her father welcomed the arrest once it became clear what was happening, his daughter felt guilty for her naiveté. Once inside of Anand Bhawan, she practically collapsed. Nan and her children were equally wiped out from the day's events, and they too 'went weary and heartsore to bed'.

~

Nan woke with a start at 2 a.m. The night watchman had gently prodded her awake and leaned over to tell her that the police had surrounded the premises.

Nan moved deliberately then, heading upstairs first to alert the two fugitives she was harbouring. The two men hastily tried 'to dispose of certain important papers' by flushing them down the toilet but were stymied when the facilities immediately clogged up. 'What a time for the plumbing to go wrong,' Nan groaned.[49]

Meanwhile printing machines needed to make other pamphlets were wrapped up in 'soiled sheets', to look 'like a dhobi's [washerman's] normal bundle of laundry'.[50] These were then sent over to the Kamala Nehru Hospital and mixed in with the regular washing.

She took the remaining flyers to Chandralekha's bedside and nudged her awake. With her help, she slid the proscribed papers under her mattress, confident that her daughter would know how to get the materials to other student leaders, and out into the countryside.

Nan took a wistful glance at her younger girls sleeping peacefully out on the veranda. Then she went to the front door and walked outside. 'The City Magistrate, the Deputy Superintendent of Police, and half a dozen armed policemen' stood menacingly outside. When she turned the lights on, she was startled to see the lawns swarming with 'plain-clothes' officers. Some were brazenly standing uninvited on the outer veranda. She glared at them before witheringly telling them to step back into the garden. They shrank at her order, and she turned to the magistrate, her bearing now imposing. 'Why is it necessary for so many armed men to come to arrest one unarmed woman at this amazing hour?' she asked tartly. The magistrate was 'ill at ease', but responded that they had a warrant to search the place and to take her into custody.[51] Nan nodded her assent and granted them permission to enter. She turned around to prepare some things for prison.

Nan's posturing belied her own doubts. She did not know Ranjit's whereabouts. He had been in Bombay for the all-India meeting, but she had heard nothing once the campaign had been announced. Was he too on the lam? Or had they already captured him?

To make matters worse, she had been 'taken by surprise' by this midnight turn of events.[52] She had herself not been at the AICC meeting and had been moving freely through Allahabad, interacting regularly with law enforcement. Her clandestine nighttime train journey from Lucknow had started to feel like paranoia.

She knew better. She was harbouring wanted men and participating in banned political activities. Though she had played no direct role in coordinating the student protests, she had nonetheless been constantly behind the scenes.

She gathered herself together and headed back up the stairs to wake Indira. Once her niece had shaken the sleep from her eyes, she apprised her of the situation, and then walked over to the verandah where Nayantara and Rita were sleeping. She took one last heavy breath and she woke them.

The children 'immediately grasped' what was happening. They asked 'no useless questions', put up 'no fuss', and were 'brave as always'. They resolutely set about helping Nan to pack some necessities: undergarments, toiletries . . . and books. Rita glanced around as they moved about, her 'big eyes' catching her mother's attention. Suddenly, the warrior's 'courage began to ebb'. 'She was so little and the world was so big,' Nan sorrowfully thought to herself about her baby, 'who would take care of her?'[53]

Rita swung around and smiled. 'How wonderful to live in these days Mummie. I wish I could go to jail too.' Nan's heart swelled with pride as relief washed over her. Things would be alright. She leaned over and kissed her little one.

'Let's say good-bye to you outside Mummie,' Nayantara piped in. 'I want the police to see how we take these partings.'

On the porch, Chandralekha gave her mother a 'tight hug', and whispered, 'Darling don't worry. Everything will be fine. I will look after the kids.'

Nayantara 'held her head high' and announced that they would 'keep the flag flying'. Rita ran up to her mother for a lingering embrace before she reassuringly told Nan to 'take care' of herself. 'We shall be fighting the British outside while you are in,' she declared fearlessly.[54]

The unusually large army of police stood there ridiculously. Nan took a last look around before allowing them to escort her into a waiting lorry. The children marched back into the house and went to sleep, using the secret documents the police were still looking for as extra padding in their mattresses.[55]

~

Nan's third stint in prison began most unceremoniously. Allahabad had been placed on curfew earlier that evening, and the military had been called in. Yet no one at Naini Central Prison on the outskirts of the city seemed to think anything was out of the ordinary. The jail was dark as the police caravan pulled up, and it took the prison staff thirty minutes to finally open the gates. By the time Nan was finally back in her old barracks, it was 3.45 in the morning. As she drifted off to sleep, thoughts of the past few hours rolled over in her mind. Chandralekha had long anticipated joining her parents in the fight for freedom, yet she was overcome by the reality of British colonial violence when she finally saw it with her own eyes. 'It will take a long time for me to forget what I have seen,' she had confided in her mother, 'and it will be longer before I can root out the hatred which is growing in my heart.' Then she said with absolute conviction, 'there's no going back for us. We must go straight to the end, whatever the end may be.'

The weight of history was on them all. The next day, her daughter's words ringing in her ears, Nan decided to keep a record of things in a diary.[56]

The jail had a gloomy familiarity. As she acclimated slowly over the next several days, Nan was surprised to see how much further things had deteriorated since her last stay. Never particularly well maintained, Naini was now literally falling apart. 'The ceiling falls in chunks every day and makes a mess all over my bed and on the floor. The tiles are badly placed and sun and rain come in as they please... The floor is so uneven that one cannot walk across the barrack at night without stumbling.'[57]

It had taken the staff nearly two full days to provide her with some basic supplies. 'There was no water, no sanitary arrangements—in fact nothing at all.' As opposed to those in for criminal charges, who were given (nearly inedible) cooked food, political prisoners were given a daily allotment of fresh vegetables for cooking.[58] But this time around, the food was rotting, mixed in with 'grit and dirt' and the 'odd spider or two' and without proper kindling or charcoal for cooking.[59] She figured out quickly that this term 'was going to be different from past ones'.[60]

On her birthday, 18 August, she was informed that most previous privileges would not be accorded to her or other political prisoners this time. They were not going to be given access to 'newspapers, letters or interviews or any article from home' and their daily spending allowance was reduced by one quarter, to 9 annas from 12.

The living conditions were terrible. The prison was overrun by frogs, 'great big ugly creatures and incredibly foolish looking'. They were everywhere, hopping about inside and out. Nan even stepped on a frog one morning as she got out of bed. Their croaking was incessant in the evenings and enough to drive anyone to distraction.[61]

But the frogs were the most benign of the pests that plagued the prisoners of Naini. Mosquitoes, flies and gnats flew about in great clouds, each adding their unique sound to the frogs' noise to create the most discordant of symphonies. They plagued the humans of Naini, flying in and out of all manner of crevices, feasting on flesh.[62] But to make matters worse, the insects drew many bats, which also flew about the barracks keeping the inmates 'in terror'.[63]

Nan was placed in the same hall that had previously been her home, and as she settled into her new term, it suddenly felt to her that she had been there all along—one continuous stay. Her barrack was rectangular and was made to hold twelve prisoners or so. There were two commodes, one on a small, raised platform on one end, and the other in a tiny bathroom, the latter only accessible during the day. Nan was given 'a *moonj* jail cot and a small rickety iron table'. The first thing she did was move her belongings to the end furthest from the stench of the latrines.[64]

Every so often, Nan would bring her cot out into the attached yard to sleep under the stars. It brought her a certain peace of mind, but also subjected her to nature's whims. She sometimes woke in the night soaked through 'the rain coming down in torrents'.[65] She did not mind this so much though, since the inside was hardly any better. The spotty roofing allowed water to pour in during heavy storms, quickly filling the barrack with so much water that she felt her little bed a tiny island standing in the middle of a lake.[66]

The wall of Nan's hall was spotted with window gratings, the one by her bed looking over the yard and onto the main gate. There was another barrack in the same yard, as well as a separate yard and barrack where most of the criminal convicts were housed. Facilities for solitary confinement were also located there, a fact that disturbed Nan's deeply felt belief that such treatment was 'unfit for any human being'. In total, Naini was made to hold about forty-four women, a 'very small jail'. This allowed for a certain intimacy between the prisoners, and between some of them and the jail staff. The twin yards were connected by a door that was regularly kept open, allowing everyone to mingle. Nan met old acquaintances and found new friends.[67]

But as she reconnected, she was forlorn to discover eliminated the nursery she had made to look after the children who were forced to call Naini their home by unfortunate events. It had been converted into a 'half-store-room, half-office'. The bright murals 'had almost faded out . . . the clay toys . . . were broken and lying in bits on a shelf, the straw mats on which the children sat had disappeared, and the blackboard was broken and lay covered with dust in a corner'. The young boys and girls, meanwhile, had suffered, going feral from neglect. They were malnourished with stunted growth and decaying teeth, their lessons long forgotten. Their mothers too had given up on studies. Nan despaired at the hopelessness of it all, the multi-generational downward spiral now set in motion.[68]

Many of the wardens took advantage of the inmates' pitiful predicaments. One incident perfectly illustrated the benighting effects of the entire institution of which they all found themselves a part. When a poor man came to visit a relative locked up in Naini, he was told he first had to pay a small fee. When the bribe had been fully extracted, the warden brought the woman out halfway, only to turn her around and send her back to her cell after finding fault with some minor infraction. Nan was overcome with disgust.[69]

For solace, she turned to the books she had brought with her, and to the few that somehow made their way to her through the various barriers of prohibition. These set her mind free, and it wandered through myriad literary landscapes. She was drawn to the power of words themselves, to their ability to provoke and alter perception. As she sat looking about the iron bars and the world of the women and children confined by them, she recalled lines from a little book on jail life she had once read, astounded by the astuteness of writer Geffray Mynshul's seventeenth-century observations: 'A prison is a grave to bury men alive, a place wherein a man for half a year's imprisonment may learn more law than he can at Westminster for a hundred pounds. It is a microcosmos, a world of woe, it is a map of misery, it is a place that will learn a young man more villainy if he be apt to take it in one half year than he can learn at twenty bowling alleys . . . It is a place that hath more diseases predominant in it than the pest house . . . and it stinks more than the Lord Mayor's dog-house in August.'[70]

~

'It is absurd to keep human beings locked up in this fashion—it solves no problem and creates new difficulties,' Nan thought to herself as she sat watching 'the stars twinkle' through her window grating.[71] That night, she found herself in solitary confinement, her head throbbing in pain from coins dropping on her head like raindrops. She awoke from her nightmare in terror, drenched—rain was pouring in from the patchwork ceiling. As she sat there floating in her waterlogged bed, lines from a nineteenth-century poem by Samuel Taylor Coleridge surfaced in her mind:

> As he went through cold Bath Fields
> he saw a solitary cell
> And the Devil was pleased, for it
> gave him a hint
> For improving the prisons in Hell.[72]

Several days later, Nan watched as a newly arrested woman was 'bustled out of the yard' and into solitary confinement on the charge of arson. All too aware of what this meant, Nan rushed to intervene. 'There was no reason at all why two women arrested for the same offence should be treated differently,' she successfully persuaded the matron, citing the case of another inmate allowed to stay in the regular barrack.[73]

~

Nan's mood improved significantly about a week into her term, when she found her close friend Purnima Banerji among those hauled in on political charges. Banerji, whom the Nehrus affectionately referred to as Nora, was the secretary of Allahabad's Congress Committee and a veteran, along with her prominent older sister Aruna and brother-in-law Asaf Ali, of several anti-colonial campaigns, including Gandhi's famous Dandi march.[74] She and Nan stayed awake late into the night huddling and chatting like schoolgirls.[75]

About a week later, Nan was sluggishly still rousing herself for the day, reading just after tea at 9 a.m., when Purnima pointed to some commotion in the yard. There, beaming under heavy garlands of flowers, stood Chandralekha.

Nan was dumbfounded. She wondered if she was about to be released before she realized that the unthinkable had happened: her daughter had been arrested for political protest. 'Why surely Lekha was only a baby still—not nearly old enough to understand politics, let alone live them,' she thought. Her child's life flashed before her eyes. And she now worried for her youngest, left all alone in the great halls of Anand Bhawan.[76]

The shock wore off as Chandralekha hurriedly shared the details of her own rather 'comical opera': the CID (the Criminal Investigation Department, equivalent to the American FBI) showed up late in the evening to pick her up but were informed that she and her siblings had all gone out. So they used a warrant to search the premises, found nothing and left. The next morning, they returned for their quarry. Chandralekha was 'seething with excitement' but in an effort to emulate her beloved uncle's most recent arrest, ordered an extra piece of toast for breakfast 'to make the police wait and show them that . . . this event [w]as of no special importance'.[77]

On 11 September, Indira too waltzed into the barracks, though not in the triumphal manner that her cousin had done. She had been at a meeting with some other women when the police stormed in.

'Indu was pulled about and bruised and had her clothes torn', in the ensuing 'scuffle'.[78] She brought with her some important news: Ranjit had taken ill and had stayed back in Bombay unable to travel. It was the first news Nan had of her husband. She assumed that he would head to Khali to recuperate, but a week later he too was arrested shortly after he arrived at Anand Bhawan.[79] In a pleasant surprise, he was brought to the men's barracks at Naini prison, and the two old lovebirds found themselves nesting next to one another again, this time separated by a wall.[80]

Nan relaxed a touch with her family in proximity. It helped that Chandralekha and Indira took the situation light-heartedly, drawing up extensive meal plans 'with as much enthusiasm as if . . . [they] were dining a la carte at a French restaurant'.[81] Nan was tasked with cooking lunch while the girls took charge of dinner.[82] The barrack was divided into named districts: 'Indu's was Chimborazo and Lekha's, Bien Venue.' Nan's zone was the bleak 'Wall View.' The central area was dubbed the 'Blue Drawing Room' for meals, gatherings and the occasional party celebrated with saved-up rations. The girls also used their imagination to conjure a host of kooky resident apparitions. 'A bottle with a broken top was known as Reckless Rupert the Headless Earl.'[83]

Occasional short visits with Ranjit were also permitted, and Nan looked forward to such 'interviews' with great anticipation.[84] These moments of intimacy, however brief, recharged her soul.[85]

One meeting, however, turned out rather unexpectedly, when she discovered that Rita, who had only recently turned thirteen, had come to visit. The officials turned her away at the gate, without ever letting the mother catch glimpse of her daughter. Nan was distraught and approached the superintendent for an exemption but was denied. Ranjit walked in at that moment and Nan broke down in his arms. When he learned what had happened, he asked; 'Do you mean to tell me you actually asked for permission to see Rita . . .? You mustn't let your feelings get the better of you. You are much too big a person, my dear girl, to ask favours from anybody. Pull yourself up.' Though she was hurt, Nan noticed that some of the Indian jail staff were inspired by Ranjit's words, and she too took courage.[86]

~

Every so often, American planes would circle overhead as part of their patrols, reminding everyone of the danger they still faced from the ongoing war.[87] Air raids over Calcutta by year end reinforced this dread reality.[88]

This lent a particular absurdist quality to life in prison. Rain continued to seek out cracks and crannies in the ceiling, caressing and cropping every opening, before rushing through in mad glee.

The consequences were constantly felt, as bits of the roof would cave in and drop down into the barracks. One night, Nan found herself in the line of fire, as small chunks kept falling on her as she tried to sleep. After shuffling her cot to find a place free of debris, she finally managed to secure some sanctuary, and was just dozing off when Chandralekha shrieked 'and bounded out of bed'. Something had dropped right onto her chest. Only it was not building detritus. It was, instead, a large, frightening-looking bat. Everyone stayed awake the rest of the night as their visitor flitted about the great hall.[89]

'If . . . [a] rainy day can upset the organization of a Central Prison in this way,' Nan noted about their general situation, 'I shudder to think what would happen in the event of an enemy invasion!'[90]

~

Nan and Ranjit sent each other parcels of reading material every so often. She and Chandralekha read Bernard Shaw, Lin Yutang's *A Leaf in the Storm*, and Plato together, as well as quite a range of work in Hindi and Sanskrit. Indira helped her cousin with French. They all laughed over comedic stories of families much like their own.[91]

Nan was particularly struck by some lines from the English playwright Laurence Housman's autobiography *The Unexpected Years*: 'Defenders of the public school system—as it existed in my days, and as they would like it to continue—maintain that the bullying of small boys is good for them and has a healthy and hardening effect on their characters. It may be so, but what of its effects on those who do the bullying? It seemed to me a cowardly and despicable thing for the strong to afflict the weak: and I am inclined to think that the right of Imperialism to swagger through the world exploiting subject races for their supposed benefit has very largely had its origin in the bullying . . . [which has] been countenanced in our public schools.'

And, 'Would you know a man, give him power. Wherever I have seen power in operation—the kind of power which its admirers are fond of describing as 'benevolent despotism' its effect has always been to show very plainly the true character of the man—the good and the bad of him; and very seldom indeed have I found human nature capable of sustaining the burden without moral and intellectual deterioration both in the operator and those on whom he operated. The atavism of cruelty is far too deeply ingrained in the human race for even saints to be entrusted with uncontrolled power over the lives of others.'[92]

These thoughts rolled around Nan's mind for a few months until she read *Dragon's Teeth*, Upton Sinclair's novel about ordinary people navigating the terrifying rise of the Nazis. His writing brought back memories of her travels through Europe in 1938 and rang true of many stories she had heard at the time. She concluded that the 'world today seems to have shrunk and consists of only two groups—those who suffer for an ideal and those who inflict the suffering . . . Sitting here [in prison] I find it difficult to understand or excuse that group of people which live between two worlds—the world of conflict for the sake of ideals and that other world which seeks to crush truth and light and beauty and lowers human dignity and makes a mockery of civilization. Such people seem to grow in numbers. Neither the tragedy of their own country nor the terrible world conflict seems to affect them'. The words of American Labor activist Ralph Chaplin rang in her ear:

> 'Mourn not the dead who in the cool
> earth lie, dust into dust
> The cool sweet earth who mothers those
> who die, as all men must.
> Mourn not your captive comrades who
> must dwell, too strong to strive
> Each in his steel bound coffin of a cell
> buried alive,
> But rather mourn that apathetic
> throng, the cowed and weak
> Who see the world's great sorrow and
> its wrong, and dare not speak.'[93]

CHAPTER EIGHT

# The Good Earth

Prisons exacted a heavy toll on inmates, stealing from them time, dignity and morale, as Nan had been observing since her first incarceration. But the most difficult thing to take was the cost to one's health. Subjected alternately to blazing heat, torrential rain, or freezing temperatures, swarmed by insects day and night, and without basic meals, Nan and the rest quickly began to deteriorate physically.

Nan had regular bouts of headaches and would frequently feel listless. Occasionally, exhaustion would set in, and she 'could hardly sit up'. Within two months, she was suffering from neuritis, causing debilitating nerve pain.[1] Her weight started to drop precipitously.[2]

The children, too, faced challenges right from the time of their arrival. They both had trouble sleeping in such conditions. Indira ran a constant, low-grade fever. Chandralekha broke out in boils.[3] Then she found a lump under her right arm, which her mother diagnosed as 'hard glands'.[4]

On New Year's Day, 1943, rumours began to circulate that Mahatma Gandhi was going to launch a new fast to protest his unjust internment. The government was put into an awkward position. Gandhi had now transcended the status of ordinary politician, and was widely thought of—in India, the United States, and even in Britain—in saint-like terms. The British had taken this into account when they had chosen to confine him not within an ordinary jail, but instead within the Poona-based luxury palace of the Aga Khan, with its vast lawns, colonnaded outer hallways and Italian arches.

On 9 February, officials were informed that Gandhi would go ahead with his plans and begin fasting the next day. The fast was to be limited in scope—three weeks, supplemented by water lightly flavoured with citrus juice. But for the frail seventy-three-year old, this assault on his 'skinny frame' had the potential to turn deadly at any moment.[5]

Nan happened to have a regularly scheduled interview with Ranjit that day. Everyone was 'distressed' as they discussed the matter. Ranjit confided that all the men planned to undertake a twenty-four-hour sympathy fast the next day in support of their heralded leader, as well as for the cause he stood for. When she returned to her barracks, Nan discussed the matter with her fellow inmates, and they all decided to join in as well.

The next evening, following the success of their small campaign, the women in Naini 'joined together in prayer for a few minutes.' But the 'strain and suspense' of what could yet happen to the man most revered as 'father' was intense. Nan held her breath as a gloomy grey consumed her vision and her nerves frayed.

Gandhi finally ended his fast on 3 March. Nan let out a huge sigh of relief, and, looking around, seemed to glimpse the world in colour again. 'As if rejoicing over the event, some of our flowers are coming out,' she noted happily.

But in the days that followed, she suddenly found herself consumed with new worry, as she learned that the governess looking after Nayantara and Rita was having some difficulties. Anxiety immediately overtook her again.[6]

Jail officials grew concerned about her condition, and after some internal deliberations, decided to release her on a temporary one-month parole, to help her recuperate. She 'hate[d] leaving Indu and Lekha', but thought she could take advantage of the opportunity. Most of all, she wanted to avoid the kind of health crisis she had faced a few years prior.[7]

~

Nayantara had become the lady of Anand Bhawan in the absence of her elder guardians. The Pandits' long-time governess, Anna Ornsholt, had left their employ for a life in South India, though she remained in touch with the family. In her place, Nan had hired a Chinese refugee from Singapore, whom the children knew as Mrs Chew.

In early November of 1942, about two months into Nan's prison sentence, Nayantara managed to get a letter to her uncle, who was then in prison in Ahmadnagar Fort.[8] Nehru was as ever in good spirits, though he had had no news of his family's health or whereabouts, deprived as everyone else was of prior privileges on account of the war. The lack of information bothered him, as he thought often of everyone, but he had long since trained himself 'sufficiently not to worry overmuch and to accept the vagaries of life'. He kept himself pleasantly distracted with regular exercise and general conversation, surrounded as he was this time by 'more company' than usual. Important figures like Maulana Azad, Kripalani, Sardar Patel, Asaf Ali and Pant were all in lock up with him.[9]

Nayantara wrote reassuringly, trying to convince Nehru that she was 'cheerful and happy' and that all was being looked after at Anand Bhawan. But he saw through her pretence immediately, perceiving his niece to be filled with both normal teenage and extraordinary angst.

He wrote back with encouragement, telling Nayantara that she and her younger sister too would have a role to play in the future, and that for now, they each had to develop a 'body that is fit and a mind that is sensitive and keen as the edge of a sword and a character that is firm and steadfast and wedded to high ideals'. As she got older, she could look to engage the world, relying on India's long tradition and history for inspiration. He reminded her, though, that she would always also have to 'learn from other countries also—from China with her equally ancient and splendid culture and history, from Europe, from America'.

She asked whether he believed in God and proudly proclaimed that she was working her way through his *Glimpses of World History*. He told her: 'It is important to know, if it is possible, what to believe and what not to believe ... not an easy matter. It is more important to know what to do. If we have worthy ideals and try to live up to them we shall not go far wrong, whatever our other beliefs might be ... We have a big enough job in this world, to understand it and our fellow creatures and to work for its betterment.'

In January, Nayantara wrote again, sheepishly confiding in her uncle that she thought herself strange and unlovable, and indicated that she felt out of place in the world. He said sympathetically: 'The fact of the matter is that the world we live in is all awry and upside down and it is not an easy matter to fit into it, especially for those who are sensitive.' What she felt, he clarified, was that things were not right. They needed to be corrected, not she. 'It is not normal for most of us to spend our lives in prison cut off from our families and dear ones. It should not be normal for intelligent human beings to spend their strength and energy in killing each other off, as they are doing today all over the world. It should not be normal for people to starve and others to get indigestion through overeating.'

But such ferment carried one major advantage, he pointed out. 'Those who are lacking in courage and are poor in spirit fear such times for they love security above everything. But for others, new ways and avenues open out, which, though full of risk and danger, yet carry the promise of a better world . . .'

He spent the rest of his letter telling her of Byron and Shelley, and of late Mughal history, and inquiring after her father's Sanskrit translations. It was all just what the young girl would have needed to hear. But the colonial censors deemed such discussions dangerous and withheld the letter. Nayantara was left to grapple with her existential concerns on her own.[10]

Gandhi's fast helped bring her mind out of the clouds and back to ground realities in India. She thought carefully about what she could do and decided on a plan of action.

Together with Rita, she sought out the superintendent of Naini and asked if they might send their mother some basic household supplies, like soap and toiletries. Permission was granted since restrictions were on letters, news and actual meetings. So the children ingeniously wrapped clippings of the latest reports of the Mahatma's health around a tube of toothpaste and hid them back in a box that they sent inside the prison. 'And so . . . [their mother] got an actual account of the fast, though the news had reached her through inevitable jail gossip.'[11]

~

Nan arrived to quite a scene as her *tonga* (horse-drawn carriage) trotted up to Anand Bhawan. She had taken pains to ensure that no one knew of her impending arrival, so was startled by all the commotion.

As she entered the grounds, she found a legion of police officers ransacking the house. 'Cupboards had been forcibly opened, clothes thrown anyhow on the veranda and in the garden, books taken out of shelves, and furniture and carpets piled on the lawn. It was as if a tornado had hit . . .' She strode up to the district magistrate, who was on site monitoring the whole operation, and demanded to know exactly what was going on. They had orders, she was told, to find a letter that Nehru had written to President Roosevelt some time before he had been arrested in August.

'Please take my assurance that I know where that letter is,' she announced icily. 'I also know that you will not find it, because it is not in Anand Bhawan.' She reprimanded the official and his men for their behaviour and ordered them to put everything back as it was before they departed. Her property was damaged all the same, and though there was nothing really to be done about that, she penned 'a letter of complaint' to the UP governor, Maurice Hallet, with whom she had worked as a minister.

Nan's show of defiance had the desired effect, and order was soon restored to her home. She breathed a sigh of relief. She had kept the letter, or the copy of it in her possession, safe.

Nehru had drafted his missive on 12 April, soon after the Cripps Mission crumbled apart. He had then given it to Louis Johnson, who immediately conveyed it to FDR. Nehru conveyed his disappointment at British intransigence and pitched the need for Indian independence in war time terms. 'We are a disarmed people,' he admitted. 'But our war potential is very great, our man power vast and our great spaces, as in China, would have helped us. Our production can be speeded up greatly with the cooperation of capital and labour.'

He signed off: 'Our sympathies, as we have so often declared, are with the forces fighting against fascism and for democracy and freedom. With freedom in our own country, those sympathies could have been translated into dynamic action . . . To your great country, of which you are the honored head, we send greeting and good wishes for success. And to you, Mr. President, on whom so many all over the world look for leadership in the cause of freedom, we would add our assurances of our high regard and esteem.'[12]

Roosevelt responded immediately through Johnson, telling Nehru that he appreciated the letter and promising that India could count on American support in the event of a Japanese invasion. The US also let it be known that the President had also earlier attempted to personally intervene with Churchill.[13]

~

Soon after she arrived home, Nan sat down for an extended interview with the foreign correspondent of the *New York Times*. He was trying to get a better understanding of the situation in India, and where exactly people stood on the war effort. He was having trouble reconciling Gandhi's recent efforts with other statements that seemed more attuned to the desperation the Allies were feeling.

Nan spoke frankly, admitting that there were different points of view. One thing that worried her, she confessed, was the role that India might play in creating a post-war order. For India to claim its proper place in negotiating the peace that was to follow, it would have to be clear that it had always stood for the right values, including being unequivocal in its opposition to fascism.[14]

~

The government relaxed a host of restrictions during the first quarter of 1943 and allowed prisoners access to books and letters again. Nan and Nehru, as well as he and the children, began to exchange correspondence once more.

As soon as he learned some of the details of her release, Nehru wrote to express concern about Nan's health. He told her to 'do what she can about it' and hoped that her planned treatment would do 'immediate good'.

But he was overall relieved to learn what had all gone on since they had last been in touch. He was especially moved by the way the children had humorously coped with life in Naini.[15]

Now free to do so, he also dispatched parcels of reading material to his incarcerated daughter. He told his sister that she could distribute anything to Feroze or Ranjit as she saw fit, before having everything eventually deposited back at Anand Bhawan.[16] When Chandralekha told him that she had been studying quite a lot, he chided her for spending all her time reading 'textbooks', which he belittled. She wrote back with 'indignation', telling her famous uncle off for making assumptions. He wrote back approvingly, indicating that she had put him in his place.[17] He admitted separately to Nan that he himself had 'not read very much' in the eight months he had been in Ahmadnagar, only managing to get through about 100 books.

The siblings also discussed the management of the great house. Nehru had worried for some time about the health and security of the staff, whom he looked on as family, and as workers who required proper treatment. He had asked his cousin, Ladli Prasad Zutshi, to assist with accounting while the family was in detention, somewhat to the chagrin of the young Nayantara, who asserted her confidence in looking after matters.

Now that Nan was out, even if temporarily, he asked her to look into 'salaries and allowances' and requested that she consider being 'generous', noting that 'the rising cost of living and the high prices' might otherwise 'fall heavily on them'. Giving one example, he recommended a large 25 per cent salary increase, in addition to bumps in other perks.

When Nan pointed out that everyone felt 'fairly treated', he pointed out that this was 'not enough'. 'They are so used to terribly low standards that they dare not think above them . . . I would try to make big changes. I think all of us pay our domestic servants, or some of them, at a terribly low rate. I should like to remedy this in so far as I can.'

He confessed that he was in a 'sorry mood', upset for Maulana Azad, who had just lost his wife to aggressive tuberculosis, and for the state of the world generally. 'Tragedy is bad enough but what makes it worse is the vulgarity and falsehood and ballyhoo that accompany it these days. All dignity and self-respect and restraint seem to be vanishing and only violence and vulgar self-assertiveness and an unctuous and odious self-righteousness survive.'[18]

~

Chandralekha was released from prison for lack of evidence about a week after her mother had settled back into Anand Bhawan. Nayantara went to Naini to pick up her sister, but while waiting outside caught a glimpse of her father, just out of reach, in the

Superintendent's office. Suddenly, the brave face she had put on publicly for so long fell—she hated being forcibly separated from her family, the trauma inflicted on her young mind all too evident—and she began to wail in utter distress. Ranjit was permitted to come to the entrance to try to calm his daughter, though the 'iron bars' of the prison remained unbending. 'We mustn't let these people see us cry,' she later remembered him telling her. He complimented her on her new sari and earrings, selected to make Chandralekha's homecoming special. She asked her father when they would let him come home. He had no answer and so promised that they would discuss everything once they finally did. He turned to be escorted back to his cell, his child shrinking behind him, her nose glowing red from blowing it into his rough, khadi handkerchief.[19]

~

Once the children got back home, Nan broached the delicate subject of further studies with her eldest and suggested that she consider pursuing college in the United States. Chandralekha was reluctant to leave either her family or her country in their hour of need and felt strongly that she should stay. But Nan argued that 'education in a free country' provided students with the benefits of 'wider vision', as well as with 'contacts with worthwhile people who are doing things'. She also pointed out that Chandralekha would have to pledge to forego political activity if she were to remain in India.

This did the trick. After her eldest finally relented, Nan decided to send Nayantara along as well. Relying on the advice and assistance of Madame Chiang, and with the full backing of Ranjit, Nan cabled Wellesley to request admission for her children, modestly boasting that Lekha 'stood among the top ten students in the province, and that Tara had just secured first division in her matriculation'. She was a bundle of emotions when Mildred McAfee, the president of the famed school, responded within forty-eight hours: 'Wellesley College proud and pleased to welcome your daughters.'[20]

Over the next few weeks, Anand Bhawan was a flurry of activity, as Nan raced against the parole clock to prepare everything for her children's departure. She made financial arrangements with her bank to handle the expenses involved. Madame Chiang also took care of matters with the US government, to ensure that they would have no objection to the girls' stay.²¹

Nan spoke with the former principal of Woodstock as well, to get a better sense of what the United States might be like. And she reached out to well-known journalist Frances Gunther, whose partner John was also a journalist of repute. Frances had become an acquaintance of her elder brother the previous decade, and then a friend and correspondents as she grew increasingly smitten with him.²² Frances helped facilitate matters and agreed to serve as the girls' guardian when they reached the States. Nan and Frances Gunther also looped in Richard Walsh, the publisher of Nehru's books at John Day, and his wife, the Nobel-prize winning author Pearl Buck, who had already taken an active interest in the affairs in India.²³

That left the biggest hurdle: how to get the two girls out of a locked-down country and halfway around the world. Nan wrote to the government and asked if they would help arrange air transport for her children, but nothing of the kind was available due to 'the prosecution of the war'. She also requested them to provide her children with passports and the necessary approvals to allow them to travel.

The government deliberated internally over the matter, observing that Chandralekha had been 'detained' for the 'dissemination of leaflets in Allahabad', and mulling over the possibility that the 'two girls might become the centre of anti-British agitation in U.S.A'. Ultimately, though, they 'saw advantage in moving them from [the] present political atmosphere'. They concluded that 'stringent action against school-girls' would invite 'adverse publicity' against the government that would outweigh any risks stemming from similar activities based in America. Permission to travel and all required documents were granted.²⁴

Betty had to handle the final arrangements, taking care of the children in her flat in Bombay and figuring out how precisely to get them to the other side of the world. Nan decided to send Rita to her sister's as well.²⁵

~

Just before they headed out on their journey, the departing siblings were permitted a half hour interview with their father. Nayantara watched as he stooped to pass through the low-framed door to enter the 'dingy' superintendent's office. 'He was nearly six feet tall, and very brown, with the bronzeness of a man who loves an outdoor life. His thick hair was crisp, curly, and black, with hardly a gray hair visible. He was dressed as usual in a white khadi kurta-pajama, and wore brown leather sandals on his feet.' She looked closely at his 'sensitive hands', 'determined chin', and 'contemplative eyes'. She thought him the 'handsomest, the most lovable, kind, and understanding person' in the world. Her eyes welled with tears.

They sat together on a small bench, the room sterile and cold, empty save for the superintendent at his desk and the guard standing by. The Pandits had had good relations with the jail officials, and they all behaved cordially, even respectfully to one another. Ranjit leaned in and asked permission to sing. As they began, the jail gong went off, and the whole gang broke into a gleeful, raucous chorus, interrupted by fits of laughter.

He looked on his children warmly and told them they had 'nothing to worry about'. 'Buy up all Fifth Avenue . . . What is the family fortune for,' he said in jest. 'When I was going to Europe for the first time as a young student . . . my father said to me: "I'm not going to tell you not to smoke, because I know you're going to smoke, but see that you smoke the finest tobacco!" That was the only advice he ever gave me. So, like him, I can only say: "See that you have the best time possible."'

Though he let them stay well past their allotted limit, the superintendent soon enough had to bring their farewell meeting to an end. Ranjit gave each of the girls a goodbye kiss and they were forced apart. It was the last time Chandralekha and Nayantara would see their father alive.[26]

~

Nehru learned of the decision to send his nieces to the United States from Betty. It was surprising that Nan had taken such a momentous decision without consulting him, but he was unfazed. He wrote encouragingly back to his youngest sister, and then to his eldest niece. He told Chandralekha: 'I thought over this proposal and I liked it. Indeed I like it very much.' He added: 'In many ways America is the land of tomorrow—in a different but a very real sense Russia is also the land of tomorrow. All other countries—in Europe or Asia or elsewhere—are lands of yesterday, trying hard to fit themselves into today, and for the moment not succeeding.'

'So to go to America, to understand her and learn from her, is to fit oneself for tomorrow, which will surely come upon us, whether some of us approve of it or not. I rather envy you your visit to the United States. I have long wanted to go there but the fates have conspired against it thus far.'

He talked of the exciting adventure that awaited her, and then recommended she look up one friend in particular when she got to her new home, 'a very charming and clever woman' who had written *European Spring* and *The Women*, which had recently been made into a moving picture. Her name was Clare Booth Luce.[27]

~

Nan returned to her barrack at the end of April, her health still quite poor. Thanks to the relaxed rules, she continued corresponding with various people regarding her daughters' upcoming trip. The flurry of activity was substantial, the letters 'endless', and she worried about grating on the nerves of the jail officials, who otherwise were of 'good temper'.

'I can't say what I feel about it all,' she noted in her diary. 'I want the girls to go. It seems in their best interest as far as I have been able to figure it out and yet as the time of their departure approaches my heart is heavy with anxiety and like every mother from the beginning of time, I am torn in two by my desire to ensure the safety and well-being of my children and also to do the best I can for their future. Life is so difficult...'[28]

~

Nan had spent many days the past few months worrying about her husband, but comforted herself knowing that he was nearby, just on the other side of the wall. She cherished her regular visits with him, however brief they were.

So she was alarmed to learn shortly after her return to Naini that Ranjit was to be transferred to Bareilly jail, a 'notorious place' that had had a devasting impact on his health when he had been placed there in the early thirties. He had already developed breathing difficulties, a problem he faced on a recurring basis. Bareilly was 'badly located', was known as 'one of the worst prisons in the province', and 'constantly filled up with smoke from a neighboring factory'.[29]

'He is such a very sensitive person and his surroundings affect him,' she thought. 'He is not meant to be in the rough and tumble that is Indian politics. With his wealth of learning and fastidious scholarship, his love of art and of all those finer aspects of life which are understood by so few people, this association day after day with crudeness and ignorance is a process which is breaking him down physically. It is a slow daily sacrifice which can be so much more deadly than some big heroic gesture made in a moment of emotional upheaval.'[30]

Her feelings got the better of her as she contemplated their relationship and the true love they had forged over the years. She recalled with amazement the 'sense of oneness' the two had had, despite all their years apart.[31]

~

After considerable hullabaloo, Betty finally secured passage for the girls on board the USS Hermitage, a luxury Italian ocean liner previously known as the Conte Biancamano that had been seized by the Americans and converted into a spartan troopship. Just before the war had begun, the vessel belonged to Lloyd Triestino, and so, in a sense, the girls were making their first trip abroad on board a vessel that echoed the one their parents had taken together to Europe all those years before.[32]

Nayantara and Chandralekha hurriedly completed their shopping to ensure they would have the essentials. As she bid them farewell at the docks just prior to boarding, Betty garlanded them with flowers, placed red tikka on their foreheads, gave 'each a coconut for good luck and a little box of carved wood containing a handful of Indian earth' to ward off homesickness. She did her best to gin up excitement by telling them stories of her own earlier travels, but her fear for their safety nonetheless was apparent.

'The thing to remember,' she told them in parting, 'is to look helpless, but be efficient. That way everybody gives you a helping hand, and if everybody doesn't, you can take care of yourself anyway.' Nayantara thought this especially wise advice, though she dryly observed that it 'it did not work out so well' for her sister. 'I always looked helpless and she was forced to be efficient.'

Everything about their trip was secret. They did not know where they were headed or by what route. They had not even known their exact date of departure. So they were given a few days once onboard to explore their new, temporary home. They quickly discovered that they were among 'fifty regular passengers . . . [and] many servicemen' as well as 706 Polish refugees, including 200 children, who had received sanctuary in India.[33]

Nayantara found the muster drill particularly amusing. The lifebelt she was given did not quite fit and she had to wear it across her shoulder in an altogether ridiculous fashion.

She also had a chance to see the captain, who informed everyone that they were under his direct command and that they had to obey his orders at all times. Everything that went on was at his discretion.

The passengers were all divided into two categories—officers and troops. The refugees were all classified as troops and were housed below deck in cramped quarters, with cots to sleep on. The regular passengers inversely were classed with the officers and given cabins on the upper deck. The Pandits were given a four-bunk room with two other women and a small bathroom with 'rusty yellow' water. No one had much privacy. Everyone ate together in the common mess hall, meal time signalled by a call to 'Chow'.

There were no conveniences on board—no 'tennis, swimming, dancing, cinema shows, or any of the other amenities of travel by sea'. The captain warned that enemy submarines posed real danger.

The girls got a thrill from all this. As they gazed out onto the vast expanse before them, and beyond onto the distant horizon, great adventure beckoned.[34]

~

Nan and Indira were released from prison on 13 May, though under restricted conditions. This was especially good news for Indira, who was down with a fever and cold. While Nan herself remained in frail condition, she opted not to 'comply with the externment order' that had been served on her, feeling the rules unacceptable enough to warrant light civil disobedience. The authorities had decreed that she proceed straight to Khali, where she was to submit to regular observation by the deputy commissioner of Almora.[35] When she disobeyed, she was ordered back to Naini within roughly two weeks.[36]

In the interim, she had learned that Nayantara and Chandralekha had set sail. The frenzied activity that had occupied her for the previous few weeks came abruptly to an end with this news. 'All this time I had been planning and arranging for them to get away and now when they have left I feel unhappy,' she wrote in her diary. 'The days will be heavy with anxiety until I hear of their safe arrival.' She reflected on her own mother's behaviour in similar circumstances, when Jawaharlal used to study abroad, and remembered with bittersweet irony how she used to chide her for her worry. Purnima stayed close by Nan's side and gave her courage.

About a week later, Nan saw some much-needed news in the paper. The girls had reached Australia.[37]

~

The winds shifted over Naini, as a multi-day heatwave crescendoed in a thundering hailstorm. 'Enormous' balls of ice 'filled the yard and smashed the tiles of . . . [the] barrack and killed . . . [the] flowers. The whole place was transformed into a place of glittering white.'

Nan hoped the change in the weather would have a corresponding impact on her mood, to help ease her fears. But then military lorries started rumbling by the jail gates, headed for Calcutta, and the Japanese forces felt closer than ever.

~

'The news from Bengal is bad,' Nan concluded as she sat surveying the latest papers. 'The effects of the Midnapore cyclone are not yet over and now a food-crisis seems to be developing. The *Modern Review* predicts a hard time. What a mess everything is in, and those who might be unravelling the tangled skien are behind bars.'

Her own condition was worse than ever. Soon she was completely beridden. Doctors came in and out to see her, pumping her full of medication, but to 'no effect'.

Fearing the repercussions of further decline, especially considering the continued interest of the international press in her well-being, the authorities decided to release her 'unconditionally' on grounds of health. They also lifted the injunctions they had placed on Indira.

Feeling victorious but depleted, Nan immediately made plans to head out to Mussoorie after a brief stop-over at Anand Bhawan. She hoped the secret power of her beloved hills could yet rescue her.[38]

Nehru read about his sister's release in the papers and dashed off a letter to her excitedly. She had in the previous few weeks finally told him the details of the decision to send the girls out of the country for college. He had approved of this choice from the moment he had first heard about it from Betty. He wanted to be encouraging. 'There is no lack of friends in America who will go out of their way to help them,' he surmised before adding half-jokingly: 'Indeed there is a little danger of this being overdone.' He told Nan to rest well in Mussoorie and to get seen by competent doctors.

~

Nan nestled into her suite of rooms in the Savoy Hotel, glad to be back among her familiar haunts. The food situation in the hill station, however, was quite bad, a product both of wartime restrictions and of growing dire conditions in Bengal. The All India Women's Conference, where she remained president, submitted resolutions to the Viceroy's Executive Council warning of the 'increasing panic and threat of imminent starvation in the country due to shortage of food'.[39] This made any effort to stay alone in a house practically impossible, leaving a staffed hotel her only real option. Nehru wrote his sister approvingly, telling her to take the time needed to heal.[40]

She reached out to an old friend, Colonel G.R. Oberai, who had previously been the superintendent of Naini but was now the in-charge of the Lucknow Military Hospital. Through him, she managed to have a telegram dispatched to her older daughters updating them on her situation and her temporary home, telling them not to worry, and reinforcing that everyone back home was very supportive of their opportunity. The transmission did not escape the attention of the Intelligence Bureau, which recorded the contacts and appraised others in the Home Department of the activity. The government had lifted their order that Nan submit to surveillance only to impose it clandestinely.[41]

But she was unaware of any of this, and so carried on normally. For the moment, another matter had aroused her pique. Nehru had inquired after her writing—she planned to publish an account of her life—and mentioned in passing that Betty was putting 'the finishing touches' on her own work, which was also autobiographical. He quipped that the whole family were odd for wanting to tell their stories, following his 'catching example'.[42] Unintentionally, his words brought to the fore long-simmering sibling rivalries. For the most part, these still remained minor and not beyond those of most other families.

Betty had not wound up in public life the way her more prominent brother and sister had, and this rankled her. Her book, *With No Regrets*, was thin, with relatively wooden prose, and suffered from an impulse to project its author into the centre of activities in which she had actually played a much more peripheral role.[43] Nehru looked on his youngest sister with fraternal affection and so tried his best to phrase his views positively while yet remaining honest. He tried to convince Nan: 'Inevitably, everyone of us, consciously or unconsciously, puts on a pose and, as in life itself, we try to appear not as we are but as we would like to be or at least as we imagine we are . . . It is the impression of sincerity which a piece of writing creates that goes a long way towards making it worthwhile and good.' Still, he admitted, 'Betty has a tendency to become sentimental and if this appears in the written stuff, it makes it weak . . . [though she nonetheless] had the capacity to write well.'[44]

Nan let things lie, though she later confided to her old friend Padmaja Naidu that she privately 'howled' at her brother's assessment.[45] Nan loved Betty dearly, but could not quite understand her behaviour, nor her desire to try her hand at things at which she did not appear to have talent, like writing. Her brother correctly summed up their strange-yet-normal relationship: 'It is odd how we three—a brother and two sisters—differ from one another and yet have common features. That is always so. The abnormality of our lives has emphasized all these common and uncommon features. Yet, on the whole, we have not been unsuccessful in our joint or separate ways.'[46]

~

Nan felt uneasy about her family, all of them save for her youngest so far away. The bits of news that trickled in about her elder children were welcome, but sometimes only made matters worse. When she saw a short letter her elder daughters had written to Rita, talking about the chilly weather while they were in Melbourne, she nearly panicked, even though the letter arrived after they had already reached the United States. 'That night I dreamt that both the girls were sitting naked on an iceberg + I was standing up in a row boat in the open sea holding two coats in my hands + begging some invisible person to row me to the iceberg!!!' Rita internalized all of this and showed signs of 'nervous tention [sic] + strain'. This in turn led her mother to worry even more in fear that her child might have a 'serious breakdown'. Rita improved, but at such a slow pace that Nan did not feel appreciable relief. 'Tante' Anna Ornsholt returned to care for the Pandits in their hour of need.[47]

Ranjit's health, in the meantime, was taking a beating. The conditions in Bareilly were exactly as his wife had feared. In late June, he was transferred for several weeks to the nearby Balrampur Hospital for treatment and there slowly recovered some strength. Nan thought it 'very depressing' that he would immediately be sent back to jail, even if it was to be 'under observation in the prison hospital'.[48]

This and her other worries started to exact a tax on her. Nan's blood pressure dropped, and she suffered from a fainting spell.[49] She wrote to Padmaja that she felt 'very tired all the time'.[50]

She tried to focus on some simple routines. She was glad for the well-lit rooms she had and for the view overlooking the garden. Friends regularly kept her place decorated with lots of flowers. She went out for walks every day. She 'swallowed every vitamin from A to Z + had millions of injections . . .'.[51] Towards the end of August, she began taking instruction in yoga, hoping to master a few easy *asanas* (postures) to target areas of need.[52]

But she grew quite upset when she learned that Betty had 'told people in Bombay & Delhi that . . . [a] visit [Betty had made] to Delhi was for the purpose of securing Ranjit's parole for treatment'. Nan, already raw from all that she was enduring, found herself unable to show her normal restraint. All the feelings she usually kept bottled up inside came tumbling out. 'Why does she do these things to injure us?' she asked Oberai heatedly. 'We have not ever done her any harm. If . . . [Ranjit] ever hears he will be furious. Surely if parole was required I could do the needful—I managed for myself and I could manage for my husband without Betty's help. I try so hard to be fair about everything and not to loose [sic] control of myself, but if this sort of thing goes on I am afraid I shall burst out one day.'[53]

She sorted through her jumble of emotions. She was grateful her children were safe, worried sick that they were so far away, unsure if she had done the right things, happy for their opportunity, upset about her husband's treatment, angry about the state of her country and fearful of the future.

Nan decided it was time for some tough decisions. A house she and Ranjit had purchased at 5 Edmonstone Road was just coming off rent, and so she felt it time to shift back there from Anand Bhawan. She wanted to give Indira and Feroze the freedom to run their own home. Shifting her centre of operations helped her to be more sure-footed.

Gradually, she got her bearings and started to feel more like herself. As she felt her mind clear and life return to her limbs, she grew increasingly aware of her surroundings, and of happenings elsewhere. The food shortage she had read about earlier had spread far and wide, and there was distress at every turn. Suddenly, the amenities with which she had surrounded herself, which till then had brought her a sense of serenity, now felt grotesque. 'The vulgarity + utter superficiality of Mussoorie jars on the nerve,' she told Ranjit. She decided that any further inaction amounted to 'criminal folly'. Though she had been sending money to help those in need, she now thought this insufficient. She herself had to get directly involved.

She told Ranjit that she was 'haunted by the hungry eyes of starving children.' She had to 'go to them if only to thank God that . . . [their own] children . . . [were] free from want'.[54]

~

The epicentre of the crisis was Bengal, where hundreds of thousands of people were suffering from the spreading scarcity of food. The state had a total population at the time of around sixty million people.

India had seen several major famines over the years, five sequential ones in the late nineteenth century, and a very widespread one in the eighteenth. The earlier tragedies had all been caused by draught, so many assumed it to be the root of what was happening again. There had been deficient rain during the previous few years, so many attributed the current problem to natural causes. Yet the rains had returned rather forcefully that year, quenching the thirst of the parched earth and revitalizing it.[55]

But by then the situation was already very grim. England was essentially using India as a reservoir for various goods and services, generally to help with the war effort. So where the state of Bengal had imported just under 300,000 tons of rice in 1941, it was exporting 185,000 tons the year later.[56] This move combined with poor rains and low crop yields caused the price of rice to skyrocket. Speculation and hoarding predictably followed, adding to the problem.[57]

By the start of 1943, both the viceroy and the secretary of state for India knew that they were facing a disaster, and that the country required at a minimum 600,000 tons of wheat to get through it. Prior policies had created a shortage of this essential grain as well. The importation was necessary to maintain the country's own war efforts and its role in the supply chain just as much as it was to feed the local population. But even this calculation woefully underestimated the situation. Other Government of India figures showed that rice production was short consumption needs by a staggering two million tons in Bengal alone, and by 3.5 million countrywide.[58]

While in previous instances, necessary imports could have been arranged with Burma, the Japanese occupation now took that option off the table. It meant, essentially, that India had to look to London to have needed food stuffs shipped into the country. Over the next few months, Linlithgow, Amery and incoming Viceroy Wavell, just ending his stint as commander-in-chief of British forces in South-East Asia, tried their best to persuade the War Cabinet of the urgent need. Churchill, however, was adamantly opposed to allowing this, making a series of dubious claims about Allied war requirements to defend his choices. Much of it boiled down to the fact that he was simply unable to see Indians as people, blinded as he was by a racist worldview. And about three million people died as a result.

~

Nan was shocked by the magnitude of the catastrophe. She took stock of her surroundings as she toured around aid centres that had been set up to take care of the indigents and to provide them with some basic nourishment. 'I have read and thought of India's starving millions, but until I came to Bengal this time I did not realize the significance of these words,' she reported to the press.[59]

What she saw sickened her, a 'scene . . . of horror, extreme suffering, and despair'. In the villages, young children who could not find their parents, likely because they were deceased, were placed in camps before being transferred to Calcutta for medical treatment. Even babies were included. But the situation in the great metropolis was no better, as 'streams of peasants' flowed into the city from the surrounding regions, walking many miles to seek sanctuary. Along the way, families were separated and the old and weak perished.

'Cholera, dysentery and other diseases' broke out in 'epidemic form in rural areas', compounding the misery. Dead bodies could be seen floating on the local river.[60]

Nan got to work. She contacted members of the All India Women's Conference to organize relief. Together, they worked with a local bank to secure just over 16 ½ acres of land for a home for displaced and orphaned children in the Entally neighbourhood in the south-central part of the city (and where a young nun named Sister Teresa was living after recently taking up her vows). This was to be the first in a chain of such facilities, open to boys and girls, providing avenues for work and play, with care supplemented by the Indian Medical Association. Nan inaugurated the building at the end of the month.[61]

~

Nan returned to Allahabad in mid-October after her first tour of Bengal. She had by then launched 'about half a dozen' additional homes for famine-afflicted children in the intervening weeks. She spoke to reporters about her experiences, narrating harrowing stories of 'parents having sold their sons and daughters for only a handful of rice'. She wanted to create a foster system to look after children left alone, even as she pleaded for further action from the state before it was too late.[62]

The New York press took notice with the *Herald Tribune* running a feature on her activities. 'Relief work in starving Bengal gives India women a new job,' blared the headline. 'Led by Mrs. Vijaya Lakshmi Pandit, Nehru's sister, they establish free kitchens, open homes for waifs and alleviate disease.' The article further talked about the history of the AIWC and the transforming roles of women in India but noted that change was slow. 'A daughter [still] does not inherit from her father and a woman has no legal claim to her husband's estate.'[63]

~

Ranjit had been released from prison unconditionally just as Nan had departed for the North East. He had come back to Allahabad but was ailing and desperately needed care. Even so, the very first thing he had done while still in Bareilly was to write a check for Rs 1000 to the *Hindustan Times* Bengal Relief Fund.[64] Just as they had with his wife, the American press reported on his condition.[65]

As he had done during his previous stints in prison, Ranjit had spent his time in study and scholarship, translating Kalidasa's Sanskrit poem, the *Ritusamhara*, into English. The subject matter concerned lovers in changing seasons.

Nan was glad to have her beloved husband home. But 'he looked thin and his voice was weak'. He seemed like a tall, slim tree, usually bountiful, losing its colour in late autumn. Nehru wrote in concern and suggested that his brother-in-law 'take things easy' and consider getting out to Khali for rejuvenation.[66] Ranjit thought this over and decided it was a good idea. He would go after a brief visit to Bombay.

~

Nayantara and Chandralekha started college at Wellesley under the watchful care of Pearl Buck and her husband, Richard Walsh.[67] In mid-October, Chandralekha and Nayantara were invited to stay at the pristine Beeches estate in Enfield, Connecticut, as guests of Eslanda and Paul Robeson. Paul was a celebrated African American actor and singer who had had achieved international renown for his roles in the musical *Showboat* and the Shakespearean play *Othello*. Eslanda, better known as Essie, was equally larger than life, having started out as a pioneering histopathological chemist before becoming a writer and actor. She served as her husband's business manager while also studying for her PhD in Anthropology, following some earlier work at the London School of Economics. Together, the power couple had helped co-found the Council on African Affairs two years earlier, where they worked with luminaries like W.E.B. Du Bois and Ralph Bunche to advocate for racial justice, international solidarity and anti-colonialism.[68]

Nan had first met Paul with Ranjit after one of his performances in London in 1932. She met Essie a few years later in 1938 in the same city and immediately told her that she felt they were somehow 'old friends'.[69]

Essie arranged for the girls to visit her current educational home at the Hartford Seminary. They sat in on classes about India, toured the campus, and attended a tea and lunch held in their honour. They also spoke with other students about their experiences, and shared their own, highlighting the influence of 'their mother, described as beautiful and well-versed in politics, and their father, a distinguished linguist'.[70]

~

Nan returned home long enough to have a brief reunion with Ranjit before each headed out in opposite directions again, he to the West coast to convalesce, and she to the East to once more fight against the famine. After arriving in Calcutta, she toured the western part of Bengal before swinging back to the city, witnessing ground reality in the district of Midnapore, which had not long before been the epicentre of a devastating cyclone.

Conditions were worse than ever. She witnessed the unthinkable. In one instance, a mother was caught trying 'to bury her living child'. The child was rescued, but her condition was so poor, Nan could not help but wonder, despite herself, 'whether death would not have been more merciful than life'.

As awful as this was, matters were far worse in remote villages. 'Some of these have been entirely abandoned and the empty huts tell a pathetic tale. Everywhere people are attacked with malaria and lie down with patient resignation to die. Responsible people outside official quarters have assessed the mortality in some sub-divisions as 700 a day,' Nan announced. She ripped into official claims that things were getting better as food and medical supplies were increasing. 'The reverse is the case, and unless immediate steps are taken the province will be faced with another catastrophe in the form of epidemic disease . . . Months, if not years, of continuous effort will be required to restore normal conditions.'[71] Her comments drew critical international coverage from the likes of the *New York Times*.[72]

Lord Wavell, who had started his tenure as Viceroy earlier that month, visited Calcutta the next day. News organizations demanded that he and others pay closer attention. 'The warning by Mrs. Pandit . . . is justified,' they proclaimed.[73] She continued to press her case, utilizing her previous experience as a minister for public health. She pleaded for quinine and mass inoculations to stem the spread of sickness.[74]

The AIWC had just that month launched the Bengal Relief Fund. Several major donations had just come in: Rs 9000 combined from the Maharanis of Travancore, Baroda and Indore, and an additional Rs 3500 from Sarojini Naidu.[75] These were sizable sums, but nonetheless amounted to mere pennies in the well of what was needed.

Nan further activated her extensive network. Clement Davies, a Liberal member of Parliament in Great Britain, mobilized the Indian Relief Committee to collect funds. The monies were then sent to Nan and the head of the All-India Trade Union Congress. Together, they coordinated the disbursement of funds.[76]

~

Some friends of hers, the eminent lawyer Tej Bahadur Sapru and the scholarly Pandit Hridya Nath Kunzru, had grown increasingly interested over the previous few months in the need for an Indian perspective on world affairs. They held a conference in late November in Delhi and inaugurated the new Indian Council on World Affairs. Its 'main object would be to study international problems and suggest their application to Indian conditions'. The organization was meant to be non-partisan and open to anyone of any background. At their first meeting, they established a rules committee, which was to help set parameters and plan future programming. Nan was asked to serve.[77]

She was in the capital primarily to further her relief efforts. A few days later, she held a press conference and made headlines around the world when she indicated that not only was the death toll in Bengal at 100,000 per week, but that she shockingly thought this number to be a 'quite modest' estimate. She elaborated that cholera, malaria, and beri beri were compounding starvation deaths even further. She and Kunzru had worked out the mortality figures together without factoring in the impact of disease.

She announced plans to create a trust of '30 leading men and women' to manage relief funds, which now stood in the hundreds of thousands of rupees, while small sums continued to trickle in. And she also raised a new concern, that young women in Bengal were disappearing, captured and forced into prostitution. Women volunteers had to struggle to overcome this evil.

In closing, she applauded the creation of the new United Nations Relief and Rehabilitation Agency (UNRRA), under the assumption that such an organization would obviously be concerned with what was happening in Bengal. But whatever UNRRA might ultimately be able to do, it was not going to be able to act in time. '[I]mmediate help for India' was required. The need was so acute that, even monetary donations led to unacceptable delays. The people needed direct transfers of food.[78]

But just as this was getting going, Nan received an urgent message from Betty. Ranjit had taken a dramatic turn for the worse in Bombay.

~

Betty had been watching over her brother-in-law since his arrival in the great coastal metropolis. He had not looked well from the start. Within a few days, it was clear that he was quite sick, and everyone surmised that he had had a relapse.

Betty kept in contact with her sister, but the situation further strained their relations, the youngest Nehru upset at the price politics was exacting on someone she held so close to her heart. Nan for her part was already quite angry with her younger sibling for her efforts to project herself into matters with which she was not directly concerned. She finally admitted her feelings to her brother in several letters in late October. Nehru was taken unawares. But he nevertheless wrote soothingly, talking about the 'stress and strain' the family had endured, and the unique impact it had had on Betty, who had never known anything different. She was bound, he said, to feel left out.

Nan revealed that Betty had been writing her letters taking issue with some of her choices, and Nehru suddenly saw some exchanges he had had in a new light. Betty, for instance, had told him that she disapproved of Chandralekha and Nayantara travelling to the United States, and soured further when he disagreed with her. He told Nan that 'it is the people we care for, with whom we are intimate, who have the capacity to hurt us. Even their gestures may irritate us—and words when lightly or thoughtlessly used, are dangerous for they rankle'.

Then he reminded her of her special gift, 'to win over people'. This, he suggested, could do much to improve not only this situation in their own lives, but more generally to ameliorate the 'lives of others'.[79]

But even as this bit of family drama was playing itself out, Ranjit started to complain of acute chest pain. He was diagnosed with pleurisy with pleural effusion and was rushed to Lucknow, where he could stay in the home of Colonel Oberai and remain under his watchful eye.[80]

Nan cut short her tour of Bengal and returned to UP to manage matters. Once there, she focused her attention on him and minimized her other obligations, though she continued her work related to the famine and allowed herself proximate travel as required.

~

Nehru was troubled by the news of his brother-in-law's declining health. Nan had written to him soon after she herself had learned the details of Ranjit's situation. Nehru expressed shock that such a condition had gone unnoticed and undiagnosed for so long, and he speculated about possible underlying causes. His core message, though, was that everyone had to focus on future steps rather than past mistakes. And he expressed great admiration for Ranjit's reservoir of strength and 'vitality', which had given him the ability to endure terrible pain.[81]

By mid-December, Nan thought there was a glimmer of hope. Ranjit had perked up a little, under the rigorous care of his doctors. Nehru was pleased to hear the news, but wary that his sister's husband was far from normal. He recommended that Nan take him to Calcutta once he was strong enough to endure travel, for only there could he receive the quality of care he needed in an amenable climate. He knew of course of the grim situation in Bengal, but thought this the best location nonetheless.

Calcutta would afford Nan the additional benefit of getting back to 'the very important work' she was doing there—combatting the effects of the famine. Nehru talked about the size of the problem, the role of government policies, and the place for private interventions. He talked of the value of feeding those who were starving and giving medicine to those who were ailing, the immediacy of the peril giving 'primary importance' to such acts. But he also talked of relief work more broadly, drawing attention to the Quakers and holding them up as examples of effective providers of assistance. The point, he said, was to lift people up and get them back on their feet, to give them back their independence and their freedom. He praised the work of the Ramakrishna Mission for a 'spirit of quiet . . . and unostentatious service' that he thought others should emulate. And he talked about the impressive work the AIWC had been doing under his sister's leadership.[82]

Nehru's overall message of support was welcomed, but it quickly became clear that his assessment of his brother-in-law's condition was too optimistic. Ranjit's chronic asthma made recovery difficult. Nehru tried to hold out hope, and he continued to suggest additional doctors who might be approached. He also recommended a visit to Puri, where the clean, fresh air could help with the healing.[83]

But it was not to be. Ranjit developed pneumonia and declined rapidly. He died on 14 January 1944.[84] Nan was by his side.

~

It was especially challenging at that moment to be so far away from her eldest daughters. Rita had taken the news especially hard, crying hysterically. Nan so wanted to call Chandralekha and Nayantara to her side, or she wanted to run to be by theirs. She sadly cabled the girls in the United States and informed them that their father was no more. The girls, staying with friends in New York at the time, responded with the grace and compassion that had already come to define them: 'We are with you in spirit,' they told their distraught mother. 'Do not grieve. Papu lives on in us.'[85]

~

Ranjit's body was brought back to Allahabad by car, with Nan, Rita, Indira and Feroze, and a few other close friends and relatives, all riding alongside. Once there, his body was draped in the tricolour flag, the symbol of the Congress and its campaign for independence. He was cremated on the evening of the fifteenth.

~

The next few months proved extraordinarily difficult for Nan. Ranjit was the centre of her life. She had worried about him incessantly, cared for him, fought with him, dreamed with him, loved him passionately. He had always known exactly the right thing to say. They had so many plans. Now, suddenly, he was gone and Nan felt adrift.

Anand Bhawan was no longer home, and she could not manage the Edmonstone Road property alone. So she was grateful when Oberai allowed her to stay in a small house he owned on Mukerjee [sic] Road. Her longtime staff moved in to look after her.[86]

Nehru tried to console his sister as her mind wandered and purpose and presence seemed to leave her. 'I have myself found that work, hard continuous work, is the best occupation and antidote for a disturbed mind,' he wrote encouragingly. He told her to take rest, and to think about escaping for respite to Khali, or some other 'cooler climate'. Once she felt 'well enough', he suggested that she then could 'get back to work'. Her relief effort in Bengal was a 'vast enterprise' that required 'all energy and effectiveness'. A 'finer and more worthwhile activity,' he coaxed, was 'difficult to imagine'.[87]

Though these were soothing words, Nan took the most amount of solace in the message she had received from Chandralekha and Nayantara. Nehru agreed, calling their response 'beautiful'. 'They are growing up well and show every promise of being worthwhile in the future,' he added.[88] Nan thought longingly of her children and parcelled off some saris to them, gratefully acknowledging that she had found their telegram of 'great comfort'.[89]

She thought tenderly about her girls, about how wise and empathic they were. She longed to talk with them in detail. It suddenly occurred to her that she had had no actual letter from them since the middle of December. After mulling over this for a few weeks, she wrote to the government to inquire if her mail was somehow being withheld. 'I am not in a position to send frequent cables which are expensive,' she told them, explaining that she was struggling through a period of great 'strain and sorrow'. The government replied after an internal review that while all correspondence was subjected to military censorship, she was not being subjected to any extraordinary restrictions. There simply were no letters.[90]

Nan was overtaken by grief and anxiety. She felt lonelier than ever. And to make matters worse, her extended family was behaving very oddly.

Ranjit's brother, Pratap, and his wife, Saraswati, had travelled all the way to Allahabad, yet had not attended the cremation ceremony or performed the last rites as was custom. Then, even more concerning, Pratap refused to collect Ranjit's ashes from the banks of the Ganga several days later. The task was left to Feroze Gandhi and Ladli Prasad Zutshi, and close family friend P.N. Sapru, the son of Tej Bahadur.[91]

In the days after, Nan tried to acquire the necessary documents to handle estate matters related to the death but ran into difficulties right away. Ranjit had not left a proper will, or any 'other satisfactory arrangements' to ensure the financial security of his family. At first, this appeared little more than a 'temporary nuisance', but it turned out to have serious consequences.[92]

Pratap asserted control over his brother's family's assets and froze all of Nan's accounts, including those which had been hers independent of her husband. 'What had happened was that . . . Pratap had given instructions which, under the existing Hindu law, were valid. As the widow of a man who died intestate and was a member of a joint Hindu family, and because . . . [she] had no "offspring", meaning son . . . [she] was not entitled to any part' of their assets. All of this came as a shock, since Nan had never before had any familial constraints placed on her personal freedoms.⁹³

Nehru confronted the 'new thought' that his sister now would 'not have much money or property'. He had mistakenly assumed that she and her children would simply be able to 'carry on' as before. He talked of money in the abstract, and of their father's wise planning. He promised Nan that anything he had, she could share.

She thought of accepting her fate, ridding herself of staff and commitments, and accepting her new-found place. But when she consulted with Gandhi, he brushed this aside, saying she was in fact under no such obligation to 'observe rigid orthodox conventions'.

Nehru agreed. He told his sister to keep her staff and plan her travels, both generally necessary for her health, and Rita's as well. And he again returned to his previous recommendation, that work could afford her a way out. He noted that she might not have many opportunities under present conditions but implied that this could change soon. In the meantime, he talked up her work in Bengal again and suggested that she get back to it.⁹⁴

~

The Pandits had been taken aback by the interest American society had taken in their daughters. Nan especially grew concerned by the media attention they had started to receive. She worried about their exposure—they were only young children after all, and she wanted to 'protect [their] . . . privacy and dignity'. She had sent a telegram to Pearl Buck and Richard Walsh immediately, asking them then to watch over her daughters and to ensure that both maintained decorum. Walsh had written back ensuring her that the girls would be well cared for and that public profiles would be kept to an absolute minimum, with the caveat that interest in them, and in the family and country they represented, was very high.⁹⁵

Over the course of the fall, as Ranjit's condition was worsening, things for the girls had largely settled down, and Walsh wrote a follow-up letter reassuring Nan that everything was under control.

He and Buck were looking after matters, and publicity as a result 'had been held down as much as possible'.

It was not actually easy. The girls were much sought after, and Walsh admitted that he regularly had to fend off radio stations requesting interviews, as well as offers to have Chandralekha and Nayantara go on a lecture circuit.[96] This had had the reverse of the intended effect, however, as demand for all things Pandit soared.

On New Year's Day, the girls had been feted at a society reception in Chicago, headlining an event featuring community leaders from the city.[97] In February, they were featured in a photo shoot in *Vogue* magazine, which described them as 'fighters from a fighting family'. Vijaya Lakshmi Pandit, the profile added, was 'the most important woman in India'.[98]

But despite the upkeep of appearances, and what they had reassuringly told their mother, both girls were devastated by the loss of their adored father. Chandralekha indeed had taken the loss little better than Rita, breaking down in tears. Nayantara found herself unable to expunge her pain by crying, the sorrow instead flowing deep inside of her, where it would forever remain. Neither girl would ever truly get over the heartbreaking loss.[99]

~

Nan pulled herself together slowly. Just a month after Ranjit died, she had learned that Mahatma Gandhi's longtime partner, his wife Kasturba, had also passed away. Gandhi too was distraught, and she was allowed the opportunity to speak with him. The two consoled each other, though it was she who needed him most at that moment.

She added her name to an appeal to raise funds for the new Kasturba Gandhi Memorial Fund.[100] The money was going to go to the creation of a new trust dedicated to the upliftment of rural women and children.[101]

At the start of April, Nan headed over to Bombay for the annual meeting of the All India Women's Conference. There had not been a meeting in over two years on account of all the imprisonments and wartime disruptions and so she had held the presidency for an extended time. But the time had come for her to turn over the gavel to her successor, Kamaladevi Chattopadhyay.

For the next several days, she was back in the swing of things. She opened an arts and crafts exhibition that 'showcased handicrafts produced by women' on the evening before formal proceedings began.[102] In her welcome remarks, she praised cottage industries as a potential solution to unemployment issues and a tool that might be used to help fight the toll of the famine.[103]

But the behaviour of her brother-in-law was never far from her mind. She felt wounded, and also angry at the unjustness of it all. What was happening to her was, after all, systematically harming women throughout the country. Working with her successor and the other delegates, Nan helped marshal the AIWC to carry on an extra day and pass a number of resolutions 'embodying the women's point of view on social, economic, and educational problems'. Specifically, 'the conference felt that there should be some provision for the dissolution of marriage under specific conditions and demanded equality of treatment between daughters and sons in the matter of intestate succession.'[104]

Nan also utilized an event hosted by the National Council of Women in India and the Bombay Presidency Women's Council to appeal to all women's organizations to 'come together and coordinate their efforts' for better impact. 'Women in India wanted nothing but the rights of human beings,' she declared.[105]

~

Things with Pratap only got worse. Initially, it appeared that he planned to set up some formal trusts for the children and appeared interested in assuming guardianship of the two younger children. Nan had hoped to meet him personally and bring matters to a resolution while she was in Bombay for the women's conference.[106] But instead, he hardened his stance and asserted even greater control over Ranjit's assets. Nan reacted with shock, horror and disgust. Nehru was astounded by his sister's unfortunate circumstances but counselled her to take things in stride. While she had to stand up for what was right, he also told her not to worry too much about money, for that was something she could always earn back through work. He assured her over and over again that she could share whatever he had, or at least take loans from him as required if she so preferred.

But by then, motions had been filed in court. Tej Bahadur Sapru had taken up Nan's case and vowed to fight it through to the end. The odds were not in her favour though, as women did not have standing to inherit joint family property. Moreover, Pratap had retained P.R. Das, another eminent, high-powered lawyer, a signal that he was prepared for a ruthless fight to the finish.[107]

~

Mahatma Gandhi was released from prison into the care of Lady Vithaldas Thackersey in early May. He had taken ill with malaria a few weeks earlier and was in very poor health. The British feared that he could be close to death.[108] Nan came to him in Poona straightaway.[109]

Within a few days, Gandhi and his entourage shifted to the home of industrialist and friend Shantikumar Morarjee, in Juhu in Bombay. Those attending to him hoped the sea air could help boost his recovery. Nan stayed by his side, and was joined by Padmaja and Sarojini Naidu, as well as several others.[110] She and the Naidus took up residence on the property right next to Gandhi's quarters. Mindful that he needed rest and relaxation, they clamped down on visitors, though people soon started to arrive from all over just to catch a glimpse of the sainted old man.[111]

Nan welcomed the respite. Gandhi asked her to stay on for a bit, and the two spent time in each other's company, sharing stories old and new.

~

The All-India Friends of the Soviet Union had been established in 1941 in Bengal. The Comintern in 1926 had encouraged the creation of national advocacy arms to foster relations between the USSR and the world, and various 'Friends of' groups started to emerge as a result. Generally, these organizations were meant to push positive views of Soviet activities and of communism more broadly. But they also served as intelligence gathering operations where the Communist Party could learn about political conditions in various societies.[112]

The AIFSU had held only its second meeting in April but decided to go national immediately by holding a major conference in Bombay at the start of June. Nan was asked to preside over the function, which included important figures from across the ideological spectrum.

During her keynote, she spoke of Russian achievements in the war against Germany and commended the bravery of soldiers on the battlefield. She thought their 'well-organized discipline' something her fellow Indians would 'do well to emulate' as they fought for their cause. This, she urged, had to be seen in more internationalist terms. 'India's freedom is not the freedom of merely one-fifth of the human race—it is more than that. It is the freedom from exploitation of all oppressed peoples everywhere and, therefore, it ceases to be a narrow patriotic issue and becomes a part of that wider struggle for life and liberty for the whole human race.'[113]

~

Nan concluded that she could not wait any longer to see her elder children. As relations with Pratap took their unfortunate turn, she felt desperate for escape and to once again feel the embrace of her loving family. She reached out to Frances Gunther and the Walshes and asked what they thought of her visiting the United States later in the year.[114]

Walsh reported back to her in early May that there was 'great enthusiasm in many quarters' for the idea and that the US State Department would make no objections to her visit. He had convincingly argued that she 'might contribute greatly to the cause of common understanding among the United Nations and between us as allies in the war effort'.

Nan had received an invitation back in November from a prominent booking agent keen to have her on a lecture tour of the country. She had rebuffed the idea then, but it now seemed worth reconsidering. The agent was Clark Getts, a former journalist who had spent time in China. He and his wife, former client and filmmaker Osa Johnson, were a well-connected couple, who had originally reached out after discussing the matter with Frances Gunther. He had promised to get Nan 'the best audience and fees.'[115]

Walsh had not brought these details up with American officials. Instead, he had told them that Nan should be allowed to make the trip so that she could visit her children on account of the death of their father. The trip would also afford them the opportunity to work together on famine relief and on publishing Nan's autobiography. Encouraged by the reactions he received, Walsh counselled Nan to approach authorities in India.[116]

British intelligence got wind of this right away. All international correspondence had gone through military censors, and they had records of each of these exchanges on file. In themselves, they had not amounted to much. But once Walsh approached Britain's ambassador in Washington, Lord Halifax, they became newly relevant.

Halifax had immediately discussed the matter with the viceroy's local representative, Agent General Sir Girja Shankar Bajpai. They both agreed that such a visit would not be in Britain's interests and cabled back to India to inform them of their judgement.[117] Vijaya Lakshmi Pandit, they wrote, could be counted on to 'indulge in embarrassing propaganda' if given the opportunity.[118]

Unaware of any of this, Nan wrote in July to Maurice Hallett, the governor of the United Provinces under whom she had served as minister, to ask for a passport and permission to travel. She indicated that she wanted to take Rita along with her and that she intended to leave Rita behind in the United States to study along with her sisters. She followed Walsh's advice and listed only personal reasons for making the trip.[119]

The request sent the Home Department into a flurry of activity, as they reviewed the risks involved. The director of the Intelligence Bureau of the Home Department, D. Pilditch, noted that wartime considerations mandated that 'anti-British persons' be prevented from visiting the United States. There had been to that point only one known exception made to this rule: for Chandralekha and Nayantara.[120]

Hallett did not make much of these concerns himself. He pointed out that the daughters would 'likely make capital' out of a situation in which their mother was refused travel and that whatever her motives, Vijaya Lakshmi Pandit had to be allowed to go. He had earlier personally recommended that the elder children be granted permission to study abroad. 'Even at that time, there were some who thought that they might stir up anti-British feeling in America,' he noted. He acknowledged that he did 'not know what the girls . . . [had since] done in the USA,' but that he nonetheless felt that it had been right to send them. 'We should treat our enemies fairly,' he pronounced magnanimously. 'And I am not sure Mrs. Pandit is an enemy.'[121]

An extensive internal discussion followed. Pilditch brushed off any comparison with Chandralekha and Nayantara. 'They cannot . . . compare with their mother in either political importance or publicity value.' Even so, he noted, the children, in fact, had been quite effective in attracting the spotlight. What would happen if someone of Vijaya Lakshmi Pandit's charismatic abilities took the stage?

Home Department officials unanimously felt that she posed a great danger and opposed her travel. They astutely judged that whatever she said to the contrary, she could be counted on to engage in political activities while abroad. Ultimately, though, they were overruled by the secretary of state for India and the Government of India officially sanctioned the trip.[122]

~

Nehru and Gandhi had been urging Nan to resolve things with Pratap amicably, even if this meant letting go of property and money that should rightfully have come to her. For months, she found herself crippled with doubt. What they were advising was not just. Nehru himself seemed confounded by the issue, constantly reminding her on the one hand that that the behaviour of her brother-in-law was beyond the pale, and on the other, that money was of no real importance.

But it was Nan, and not Nehru, who had to face the consequences of having all that she had earned and owned taken away. She could no longer afford even her newly humbled living arrangements. She embarrassingly informed Oberai that she would have to move out of Mukerjee Road because she could not pay rent and told her downsized staff that they too would have to move on. But none of them would hear of it. Rent was waived, and the staff insisted that they would share whatever little was there without pay if need be. Even shopkeepers and vendors throughout Allahabad extended support and looked after her basic needs. Nan was overcome with emotion, grateful to have such a caring community behind her.[123]

Still, it was obvious that these were but temporary fixes. The matter with Pratap had to be ended one way or another. There were not many options available. The chances of legal victory were remote. And, if she were unable to put the matter behind her, she jeopardized the relationship her children might have with their father's extended family. This, she finally concluded, was an untenable outcome. And so she swallowed the bitter pill.

Over the course of the summer, she moved to settle things with Pratap out of court. After two months of negotiations, he finally withdrew his objections to her succession certificate. Nan gave up claims to the properties she stood to inherit from Ranjit and renounced the right of her heirs to contest the decision. She walked away only with a relatively small sum of cash, enough only for the immediate future. She would henceforth have to make her own way.[124]

~

Nan had wanted for months to turn her attention back to the tragedy in Bengal, but her legal battles and Gandhi's release had waylaid her plans. Once these things looked less pressing in late June, Nan felt freed to return to her work. By July, she was once more fully in the swing of things.

Prior to Ranjit's death, as she was coming to understand the havoc the Bengal famine was wreaking on families and the insidious harm it was especially causing to minors, Nan had realized that her Bengal Relief Fund was simply not enough. A specific mechanism was needed to direct resources to boys and girls whose lives were being ruined. They were the country's future, and harm to them then would have long standing, unacceptable repercussions. So she had launched an initiative through the auspices of the All India Women's Conference to 'save the children', and organized 'a national committee of forty leading men and women from all the provinces and communities' to oversee a fund specifically designed to provide urgently needed welfare assistance for the very young.[125]

In April, Nan had used her outgoing AIWC presidential platform to appeal to women from around the world to support this fund. 'Save the Children' was an all-India effort. While it would serve Bengal with immediate effect, the intention was to create a permanent resource to aid people in any province in India as needs arose.[126]

Money came in, with notable contributions from Madame Chiang, US First Lady Eleanor Roosevelt and Pearl Buck, who together contributed $25,000 (worth just over $448,000 in 2025 terms). With these resources, Nan focused on building up schools and children's homes throughout the state, furthering efforts she had earlier made in these areas. She wanted to create enduring institutions that could re-ground the community in a nurturing environment.[127]

Nan and her colleagues were not the only ones working towards famine relief however. The scope of the problem was simply beyond any one individual or group. She welcomed other efforts though and sought out partnership where possible, even working closely with Shyama Prasad Mukherjee, who was directing the Hindu Mahasabha's famine-related projects. The two got on well, and she appreciated the work he was doing, though they were generally ideologically opposed to one another.[128]

~

In early August, Nan had planned to travel from Calcutta to Bombay to attend to Indira, who was in a late stage of pregnancy. But just as she was about to leave, Rita developed appendicitis and required surgery. It was another moment of stress for Nan, but she managed it. Rita came through it all okay.

Nan was sad to have missed the birth of her nephew. But she was glad that he was born healthy and that her niece was doing fine as well. For a few weeks, she enjoyed the happy distraction of guessing at baby names before the new parents finally settled on Rajiv.[129]

~

Chandralekha was eager to see her mother. 'We are so excited about your coming and are hoping nothing will happen to prevent everything working out according to plan,' she wrote.[130]

Indian conditions had not changed substantively by that point. All anti-colonial efforts had stalled. Gandhi looked at the situation strategically and calculated that the Congress needed to more directly appeal to the United States in the hope that American pressure could finally force Britain to take action. India needed to send someone there who could effectively communicate the Congress position, build new bridges and win people over. And, tactically, it had to be someone able to get travel authorized. There was really only one choice: Vijaya Lakshmi Pandit.[131]

British officials knew this to be true. Internally, they worried that she 'would make [the] ideal Congress propagandist and prejudice . . . [their] own propaganda plans in America'.

Nan by then was in touch with J.J. Singh, who was president of the India League of America, an organization dedicated to advancing India's cause in the United States. Pearl Buck was chair of the League and worked closely with Singh. Chandralekha praised Singh's work, observing that he was an 'excellent public relations man' who had been 'simply wonderful' to her and Nayantara since their arrival. But she nonetheless thought him an 'awful snob' and warned her mother not 'to get too friendly with him' until she could meet him and judge for herself.[132]

Nan had reached out to the India League to inform them that she was hoping to travel the country, and to inquire about opportunities for engagement. They exchanged notes and speculated about speaking arrangements. Singh helpfully informed Nan of another organization that might be helpful, the National Committee for India's Freedom. It had been launched late the previous year, under the chairmanship of one Dr Syud Hossain.[133]

~

Once she received a positive response from the governor of UP, Nan formally applied to the Government of India for a passport in October. British officials in the Home and External Affairs departments sent a series of messages back and forth worrying about political activities that she might engage in abroad. They mulled permitting her to go if she would commit to a strictly personal agenda. But they concluded that none of this was advisable and that her participation in public affairs was a 'foregone conclusion'.[134]

This was assured because her name had also been put forward to represent the Indian Council on World Affairs, which Nan had helped launch the previous year, at an officially sanctioned conference being organized by the Institute for Pacific Affairs in the United States. Nan was to be joined by H.N. Kunzru, B. Shiva Rao, and a few others. The purpose was to discuss the future of Asia in a post-war world.[135]

Nan was granted her passport shortly thereafter and immediately requested priority air transport to the US. She informed the authorities that Rita would make her way by sea. Nan was herself in more of a hurry as she wanted to be with her eldest children in time for their Christmas holidays, so that they could all spend some time together without distractions.[136]

Now that the decision had been made to allow her to travel with no restrictions, British officials hurried to clear her way. Halifax and Bajpai gave their consent, as did all the others who had previously objected. The secretary of the External Affairs Department 'rang up the American mission' to facilitate air passage.[137]

She soon found herself having dinner with George Stratemeyer, the head of Allied Air Command in the Eastern theatre. The general discussed her travel plans with her, and then coordinated with the authorities back home to secure final approval. Sumner Welles, undersecretary of State and advisor to President Roosevelt, personally approved the trip. On 30 November, she at last found herself on a military plane, headed halfway around the world. She looked out her window and surveyed the horizon. A new day was dawning.

CHAPTER NINE

# Americanah

Lights twinkled in shop windows and on street posts. New York, always glittery, was decorated for the Christmas holiday and seemed especially magical.

Nan arrived in the great city in the early hours of 8 December. She had been travelling since late November, first from Allahabad to Bombay, where she had left Rita to begin her own journey, and from there to Karachi, where she had paused to address local Congress workers.[1]

After several days of flying, she deplaned at LaGuardia Field in Queens, where she was met by a member of the Women's Army Corps (WAC), who welcomed her and immediately took charge.[2] The WAC informed her that the US government had assumed responsibility for all of her initial accommodations and basic expenses and escorted her to a waiting military car. A short drive later, she found herself in the *porte-cochère* of the famed Waldorf-Astoria. She collapsed on her bed as soon as she was comfortably settled in her room.

The first thing she did once she awakened the next day was to call her elder daughters. They were so close. For the first time in a long time, she felt 'joy'. She could hardly wait to see them.

Next, she rang Pearl Buck. They had yet to meet but had already developed quite a bond through months of correspondence. Nan was especially grateful for the care she and her husband, Richard Walsh, had given to Chandralekha and Nayantara.

Buck picked her up and took her out shopping. The winter chill easily penetrated Nan's sari, and she felt the cold down to her bones. She needed new clothes and a proper coat first thing. But she only had $20, a parting gift from a friend in Calcutta. Luckily, Nehru had instructed Walsh, who was his publisher, to provide her with $500 from his royalties.

New York was beyond Nan's wildest imagination, and she was wholly unprepared for what she saw: 'tall buildings . . . cars, well-dressed men and women, and signs of affluence everywhere.' Buck had brought her to Saks Fifth Avenue, the flagship location of one of America's most fashionable and expensive department stores. It was such a spectacle. She found herself 'dazzled and bewildered' . . . and tempted.

But images of 'abandoned, diseased babies' flashed before her eyes, along with the 'corpses of men and women who [had] died for want of food'. Nan used the weekend to regain perspective.[3] She moved out of the Waldorf, going five blocks north and one east to the more modest, though still luxurious, Hotel Gotham.[4]

On Sunday, she faced the press corps. She was there on 'an entirely personal visit for a little rest and to see my children'. This was true and reflected what she had told government officials back in India. But her family was unique, and her personal life was wrapped up in larger causes.

She turned to the situation in Bengal. 'The famine was due to mismanagement,' she declared. 'I think the government and its "stooges"—more interested in that they continue in power than that the conditions be cured—were responsible,' she said bluntly.[5]

A few days later, the pioneering journalist and New York heavyweight Dorothy Dunbar Bromley ran a profile in the *Herald Tribune* that proclaimed Vijaya Lakshmi Pandit the 'first outstanding leader of [the] India Congress to visit [the] United States'. Nan noted that she did not see her visit as a 'softening' of Britain's stance on Indian control. At the same time, she clarified that India's opposition to its subjugation did not at all mean that India and the UK were more broadly opposed. To the contrary, she pointed out their overall alignment in the context of the war effort, noting that her brother had consistently spoken out against 'the Fascist danger', and that the Congress 'had passed resolutions' urging more effective action. 'Thinking India,' she insisted, 'has always been anti-Fascist.'[6]

But for this to mean anything, India had to be free. Such 'salvation' had to come from within the country itself, and not through some outside intervention. This was, in fact, a 'very vital part of what the Allies were fighting for, because it involves the definite recognition of the right of four freedoms of the Atlantic Charter to all the peoples of the world'.[7]

~

Nan was the guest of honour at back-to-back receptions, one hosted by the Chinese consulate and the other by Pearl Buck. At the first, a splashy affair with many people she did not know, she felt a little out of place and at one point found herself momentarily isolated off to one side. An elegantly dressed man leaned over and, in typical New York cocktail circuit fashion, said by way of introduction: 'You have chosen wisely, madame. There are only two kinds of people in the world—those who drink martinis and those who don't.' She stared blankly at him for a moment, before confessing that she did not actually know what a martini was, and that she had just grabbed the first drink available from the tray. Only later in the evening did she learn that that her convivial new friend was Somerset Maugham, one of the most popular—and highly paid—authors in the world.[8]

Buck's gathering, by contrast, was more intimate, a 'tea party' of about 125 people, in the reception room of the Hotel Gotham. But the guest list packed a punch. Edward Carter, the head of the Institute for Pacific Relations, the host of the conference she was about to attend, was there, as were 'the first lady of American journalism' Dorothy Thompson, acclaimed biographer Vincent Sheehan, and other notable 'Liberals and Friends of India'.[9]

Nan briefly addressed the gathering, again making the simple and straightforward demand that India should be made free. She asked her American audience what they thought they were fighting for in the war, pointing that that young soldiers were losing their lives in Burma at that moment for the sole purpose 'of keeping India for Britain'. She talked of the grisly situation in Bengal, noting that the government 'having originally engineered the famine ... were further culpable in their deliberate failure to effect a proper distribution of food by way of relief'.

While she was for the most part among a friendly audience, one person in attendance disapproved of what she heard. Frances Pratt, of the Foreign Policy Association, immediately informed the British Information Services of what had been said.[10]

'I am not here to propagandize,' Nan serendipitously pronounced to the *New York Post*, which devoted nearly an entire page to her. 'I am not here to answer cheap propaganda with cheap propaganda.'

'The desire for independence in India is not the result of the work of any political party ... It is the natural result of world conditions ... If only people would realize that India's desire for independence is more than a matter of merely wishing to become a "nation"! What is actually at stake is the whole question of freedom itself.'

She highlighted a point she had made with Dorothy Dunbar Bromley, to appeal directly to her American audience: 'If the Four Freedoms are to have any meaning at all, certainly they must have a meaning for those who are supposed to fight for them. India, after all, represents one-fifth of the human race.'[11]

~

Examinations at Wellesley ended in mid-December, and Chandralekha and Nayantara raced to New York the moment they were free.[12] The reunion at the Gotham was joyful, and the girls were especially happy that they could be there to support their mother after what she had been through over the past year.

Rita and the other delegates to the Pacific Relations conference arrived by sea soon thereafter.[13] Nan celebrated the moment, grateful to be together again with all of her children, and to be surrounded by old friends and new.

~

Nan, her children, and the other newly arrived delegates left New York for their meeting soon thereafter. En route, Nan hoped to have lunch with Eleanor Roosevelt, the First Lady of the United States. Eleanor had been a pioneering force for women in public life in the United States, much as Nan had been in India. Vijaya Lakshmi Pandit felt a kindred spirit.

Nan by then had several major allies working behind the scenes. In addition to the Walshes, the National Association for the

Advancement of Colored People (NAACP) lent its organizational might in support as well. The NAACP had been established in 1909 in New York City as an interracial organization committed to racial justice for people of colour. Its prominent founders included Mary White Ovington, Henry Moskowitz, and W.E.B. Du Bois, who ran the Niagara Movement, a Black activist organization with goals that would be incorporated by the NAACP. Du Bois was the first African American to receive a PhD from Harvard and easily the most important black intellectual in the country at the time. By the 1940s, the NAACP's members included Walter White, who served as secretary, and Thurgood Marshall, who led its legal division.[14]

The organization's interest in India went back to the twenties. Just as Nan had been claiming, they saw the freedom of India as instrumental to a larger, more universal emancipation.

White had been following news of Nan's planned visit to the United States, and in the late fall, he had reached out to Mrs Roosevelt to talk her up. Buck wrote in follow up about a month before Nan's arrival in the country and specifically asked the First Lady to invite Vijaya Lakshmi Pandit to the White House. 'She is one of India's greatest women, a beautiful and cultivated person. She is, as you know, the sister of Jawaharlal Nehru, but she does not need that distinction, for she is distinguished in her own self,' she had written.[15]

The White House did not immediately give a positive reply, leading some to speculate about what political pressure might have been applied. Nan herself did not seem that concerned, focusing her attention on the more immediate matters at hand. Just days before she left New York, she attended yet another reception in her honour, this time organized by the India League of America for the small expatriate community living in the area. The event was held on the evening of 2 January in Caravan Hall, an elegant, intimate space on the third floor of a quirky midtown building that was owned by a member of the Astor family and home to the Bahai community.[16]

J.J. Singh proclaimed that this was the first time anyone able to advance the Indian national point of view had been allowed to counter the constant waves of British propaganda in the country. In her remarks, Nan focused on a key question that had already come up repeatedly: how could Indians be expected to rule themselves when they were so helplessly factionalized along lines of religion and caste? She insisted that this animus was the by-product of British machinations that were insidiously but successfully 'playing one community against another'.[17]

Among the other speakers was Syud Hossain.[18] So much had happened since they had last been together. For his part, Hossain had made a home in the United States and had become a lecturer at the University of Southern California. He regularly spoke throughout the country and used his platform to advocate for the Indian national cause. Together with Anup Singh, a journalist and political scientist who had studied at Harvard, Hossain ran the National Committee of India's Freedom, which was commonly known as the Washington Committee, and which ran parallel advocacy to the League.

Nan was happy to be reconnected. She had been feeling so lonely and isolated over the past year. That her path should once again cross with Hossain's felt fortuitous. While the dynamics of their relationship had changed, the bond they shared with each other was forged anew, and they were glad to have each other's company.[19]

~

The Institute of Pacific Relations was established in Hawaii in 1925. It had a pacifist bent and attempted to foster dialogue, academic study and business interests throughout the region.[20] The conference in Hot Springs, Virginia, which was set to run from the sixth through the seventeenth, had official sanction and so had the patina of a major international event.

The setting was the stately Homestead Hotel, colloquially known as the 'millionaire's holiday house', located in the scenic Shenandoah Valley. The building was made of red brick with a colonnaded ground floor that focused attention on the grand, Ionic portico that served as its entrance. America's wealthiest and most iconic families—'the Morgans, the Vanderbilts, and the Duponts'—had frequented the establishment, as had numerous US presidents.[21]

But the beauty of the place masked a rot that had set in deep. Nan saw it the moment she stepped from the train onto the station platform. There were signs everywhere: 'For Whites' and 'For Coloreds'. This was the Jim Crow South. Nan could 'hardly believe . . . [her] eyes', and grew intensely 'angry'. She thought of European segregation in India and reflected on how racism and imperialism were deeply intertwined. She immediately insisted on using the facilities set aside for black people, embarrassing her hosts (in typical Gandhian fashion) who told her that she should avail herself of the 'finer' facilities.[22]

This matter stuck with her as the conference got underway. First on the agenda was a discussion of the most significant developments of 1944 as they impacted the Allies and on the prospects for peace and economic, social and political progress for the peoples of Asia (the Pacific). Each delegation's leader was to make an opening statement engaging with these issues during the plenary.

Nan represented the Indian team, which also included A.R. Siddiqui, a member of Bengal's Legislative Assembly and a former mayor of Calcutta, and P.S. Lokanathan, an economics professor and editor, along with Kunzru and Shiva Rao. Just before the event got underway, Nan told Reuters that the primary objective of the Indian delegation was to 'work out a way to break the deadlock between Indians and the British, in order that Indians may play a full effective part in the post-war world'.[23]

She immediately attracted the spotlight. The *Baltimore Sun* noted how unique she was, pointing out that she was 'the only woman leader of a national delegation . . . [to appear] at any of the international conferences of the past two years'.[24]

Nan had her remarks ready when her turn came. 'I believe,' she began, 'that we cannot think in terms of national issues; that has been disastrous in the past. In the future we need a wider vision, and international rather than national perspectives.'

'Many nations are being influenced by the fear of their own economic decline,' she continued, 'and therefore of a resulting fall in their standard of living. Which direction their policy will take depends on whether they wish for lasting peace and prosperity or whether they think only of the immediate future.'

As for India, 'she is silent and sullen,' she said. 'In the last few years we have lost millions of lives, partly through the war and partly through hunger. During a long period of depletion of resources, and maladministration by those responsible, conditions of hunger and distress have risen approximating those in occupied Europe. While other nations are given help, India remains a forgotten corner of the world.'

'It is heartening to hear from . . . [the leader of the British delegation (who had spoken before her)] that 99 percent of the British people believe in the Atlantic Charter. As we have been recently told by Prime Minister Churchill that the Atlantic Charter does not apply to India, I presume that the remaining one percent constitutes the governing class. I hope, however, that this small percentage may be won over to the right views so that there may be unanimity regarding applications of the principles of the Atlantic Charter.'

'Therefore I appeal to you to consider matters from a wider view, thinking of the world as one family where each nation can contribute towards the welfare and strength of the other and all may live in equality.' To underscore the point, she ended by quoting the British themselves, but subversively flipped the script: 'Freedom is in peril, defend it with all your might.'[25]

Nan had drawn the needed distinctions, sharply but gently asking the assembled representatives to consider the universalism at the heart of many of their stated ideals and the hypocritical ways they had thus far been applied. This kind of thing was uncommon in the elegant parlours of the world's policymakers, which had long been dominated by men of power and privilege. She had ruffled some feathers—the British were annoyed—but her personal charm and charisma helped smooth things over.

Once opening statements were out of the way, the conference turned to a multiple-point agenda, which they discussed in smaller breakout sessions. The delegates had to consider how to deal with a variety of challenges: the future of a defeated Japan; economic, social, cultural and racial relations throughout the Pacific; dependent peoples and the question of self-government; and a proposed new organization of collective security and the broader idea of a durable peace.[26] Nan and her compatriots commented accordingly, offering their views on the questions at hand.

After sitting through meetings for several days, and chairing the Round Table on security issues, Nan held a press conference, where she spoke out against business as usual. She, after all, represented for the first time the voices of millions of people who had been left out of these kinds of discussions, the ones that decided matters on their behalf. 'Colonies are out of place in the present world order,' she stated categorically, 'because according to the Atlantic Charter, there should be equality of people of all races and all colors. In India we feel the inequality strongly.'[27]

In practical terms, this meant Indian independence first. 'India welcomes participation in any international security organization and would be happy to share responsibility on equal terms, but we realize if there is to be a new world order, all countries must be on the same footing.'[28] A few days later, an op-ed ran in the *Pittsburgh Courier* praising her for being 'brilliant and charming' in advancing her key arguments.[29]

~

Chandralekha and Nayantara were very happy to be reunited with their sister and their beloved mother. But even as gravity started to centre around Nan, the girls continued to attract their fair share of attention, '[t]aking most of the [remaining] spotlight at the Homestead'.[30]

~

Pearl Buck released a statement to the press announcing that Vijaya Lakshmi Pandit was going to be received by the legendary mayor of New York City, Fiorella La Guardia, at City Hall the day after the conference in Virginia ended. 'Mrs. Pandit,' she said, was 'the most distinguished visitor to America from India since Tagore.' So, in addition, the India League, was going to throw a gala reception at the end of the month in her honor to mark India's Independence Day.[31]

~

The Conference at Hot Springs produced a memorandum calling for a new Pacific Charter that would guarantee 'full freedom and equality to all the people of the Far East'. It elaborated, 'The United Nations [the formal name of the Allies and related wartime organizations] emphatically reject the theories of "master races" who claim to have inherently superior qualities entitling them to rule over or act as guardians of other races or peoples. The United Nations proclaim fundamental equality for all peoples . . . They further proclaim the principle of universal international accountability for colonial and dependent people and all peoples or groups within any country who do not enjoy full social, economic and political rights.' It appeared a clear victory for the ideals espoused by the Indian delegation.

But Nan was not at all happy. 'I leave the conference in a curiously dissatisfied state of mind,' she told the press. 'I feel we only expressed old thoughts in new words . . .' She criticized the circular logic and debating tricks common to such fora. It allowed everyone to pat themselves on the back for their pretty words while avoiding tackling any hard problem or making any substantive changes.

'I have heard Allied nations described as peace-loving and right minded, but I would prefer to describe them for the present as power-possessing nations. In their arrogance today they want to decide how to allocate more power to themselves in the hour of victory. I am one of those unhappy people . . . [for] when the war ends it will have been because one group had more men and money and ammunition than another, and peace will therefore not be an indication of the basic rights of humanity.'[32]

She called out the Great Powers directly. Yet in her emotional frankness, she was disarming rather than offensive. As she prepared to head back north, the Indian delegation announced that she would tour the United States 'to speak to and meet Americans interested in the Indian problem'.[33]

~

Nan dashed off a letter to Nehru reflecting her somewhat sour mood. Such conferences, she said, 'do not decide anything important or solve any of the world's problems'. Nehru reassured her that what she was doing would have an impact, even if that would take time to see.

He reminded her of the value in 'meeting earnest and intelligent people representing various viewpoints', which in itself was a welcome challenge to parochialism. 'It is astonishing how narrow-minded and limited in outlook nearly all of us are, whether we live in Asia or Europe or America,' he observed.

'We talk a great deal of international cooperation, and yet that very conception of ours is strictly governed by our national or group outlook. To an American such international cooperation . . . should aim at a kind of Americanization of the world . . . To a Russian the pattern is different . . . To the average Englishman, internationalism is some kind of vague development of the British group of nations allied to others who should . . . fall in line with them.'

'We are all, or nearly all, internationalists today, but for each one of us internationalism has its own particular significance. It is really nationalism in a new garb. Perhaps that is an inevitable phenomenon during the transition stage.'

'We in India, circumstanced as we are, cannot help being rather narrow in outlook in world affairs . . . And yet I do think that basically India is more suited to internationalism than many other countries. The whole essence of the Indian outlook in the past has been one of toleration and peace and live and let live. Once the present distemper is past we ought to be able to adjust ourselves, without too great difficulty, to a new scheme of things.'[34]

~

New York City Hall was a grand structure in the American Federal style, with a façade of white marble. Its double-decker arcades were joined at a tiered centre peaked by a unique spire and cupola.[35] Fiorella LaGuardia was then starting his eleventh year as mayor and remained wildly popular as a New Deal Republican who had taken on the notoriously corrupt Tammany Hall machine while expanding public spaces and services throughout the city.[36]

The mayor welcomed Nan on the eighteenth, telling her of his admiration for her brother, and for the struggle that they both represented. But he could not understand what 'a saint' like the famed Mahatma was doing in politics, or why anyone would follow him. He talked of revolution and wondered aloud about sending India arms. He expressed doubt in India's ability to achieve independence through abstractions like morality. He expressed his sympathy. Nan listened graciously, and expressed her gratitude for LaGuardia's words of support, which she assured him was sufficient. She conveyed this sentiment to Nehru and Gandhi who both 'greatly appreciated' the stand the mayor took.[37]

~

Nan sat down with Clark Getts in late January. He and the Walshes were in regular touch and had been informally discussing possible tour arrangements.[38] The need for a formal speaker's bureau to handle her itinerary had grown increasingly apparent in the short time that Nan had been in the country, as invitations and inquiries seemed to follow her various engagements. After her evening with the regional Indian community in early January had produced 'the finest reports' and a lot of positive behind-the-scenes publicity, representatives of the League of Nations had even reached out to Walsh to ask if she would speak in Toronto. This had to be regretted as she did not have permission to travel to Canada.[39]

Getts had a sterling reputation and his agency had represented many prominent speakers. His interest in Nan was a testament to the magnetic power he believed she had. Even so, he had allowed his vivid imagination to get the better of him. He started to inquire about what kinds of colourful saris she intended to wear and asked where she was keeping her jewels. Americans, he told her channelling P.T. Barnum, would expect to be dazzled by the 'exotic'.

'Please understand,' Nan would later recall she told him, 'that my husband has recently died under tragic circumstances. My brother and the leaders of our freedom movement are all in jail. I have been able to come to this country almost as a refugee to tell people the truth about India. The story of what is happening must be told, and it is so dramatic that it needs no props. I do assure you I am good speaker. I can reach my audience. They won't bother about my clothes or the absence of jewels. Please let me do this my way.'

She had one further stipulation. She would not speak in any forum that excluded African Americans.[40]

There would be six potential topics: what kind of post-war world, the Four Freedoms for Asia, democratic guarantees of peace, the hope for world betterment, why India wants independence, and the coming of Indian democracy. Getts put together a one-page promotional release, which featured a headshot of Nan in a dark sari looking askance.

'One of the most important women of our time,' the brochure read, 'notable for her great ideals and deep personal sacrifices for the benefit of her people, Mrs. Pandit's influence is felt not only throughout India but throughout the world. And her strength will be felt even more widely in the post-war years.'

'Devoted to the general betterment of mankind along with the improvement of political and social conditions in her own country, Mrs. Pandit is an ardent advocate of Democracy. She feels that only Democratic institutions and complete freedom of thought and expression can win the Peace and successfully manage the problems that will follow the war. And that Freedom in the truest sense is the only security against a recurrence of the present catastrophe.'[41]

~

Hotel Commodore was an imposing building adjacent to Grand Central Terminal in the heart of midtown Manhattan. It was named for Cornelius Vanderbilt, a nineteenth-century railroad baron. The entrance alone was considered 'The Most Beautiful Lobby in the World', replete with an indoor waterfall.[42]

The India League had arranged a gala event in the Grand Ballroom there with a thousand guests to mark the occasion of India's Independence Day on 26 January, and Nan was the guest of honour. The Walshes and other organizers conceived of the programme as a vehicle to officially introduce Vijaya Lakshmi Pandit to the American public and to launch her on her new tour. Peral Buck personally wrote letters encouraging people to attend.

The evening's sponsors, numbering well over 400, were New York's rich and powerful. They included noted publisher W.W. Norton; philosopher John Dewey; Alice Gates, whose husband Artemus was in charge of wartime naval aviation; and celebrated writer, artist, and activist Dorothy Norman.

The dinner card quoted parallel passages from the US Declaration of Independence and from its subcontinental cousin. One page was dedicated to India's opposition to fascism, with passages from a 1939 Congress resolution.

'India is, perhaps, the only country in the world that celebrates a day of independence before that independence has been achieved,' Nan began. But such commemorations were symbolically powerful and could rally people from all walks of life to stand up for the larger cause of liberty.

'The world is on the eve of great changes,' she said, 'and is being drawn closer than ever before. It is, therefore, important that a better understanding should be created between the peoples of the world, and that those barriers of prejudice which are the greatest obstacles to progress should be removed . . . thereby hastening the day when a free India can take her rightful place in a Community of Nations and contribute the building of a new order based on justice and equality for all peoples.'[43]

'India's struggle is an experiment in history, for nowhere in the world have people sought to achieve freedom by non-violent means. No other nation either, as far as I can recollect, has fitted in its own aspirations into the framework of the international picture.'

'America and India,' she went on, 'have many points of similarity. You have your freedom from the British—we are striving for ours. You have established the Four Freedoms for your people—we work for their establishment in our own country. You hope to reshape the post-war world in such a way as to make peace and progress possible. It is our earnest desire to help in the creation of this new order.'[44] Her remarks would be broadcast on WABC, a local radio station.[45]

The evening was a huge success. Walsh effusively wrote that Nan had made 'a magnificent impression.' He was sure, he told her, that she was thenceforth 'going to be swamped with invitations to speak.'[46]

~

The next several days were a blur as Nan raced between cities along the Northeast corridor. On Saturday, 27 January, she headed to Washington D.C. for several days of activities arranged in part by the National Committee on India's Freedom. On arrival, she spoke to the press and directly stated that 'India has been greatly disappointed in America'.[47] She hoped her hosts would do more. Despite the criticisms, the very next day she was at the White House having lunch with Mrs Roosevelt, the scheduling at last worked out. She told the press afterwards that America's First Lady had been curious to learn more about her country.[48]

On Monday, reporters who had spoken with Nan over the weekend pressed Undersecretary of State Joseph Grew on the issues she had raised. In the first official comment from the State Department in months, he said that the United States 'would be happy to contribute in any appropriate manner to achievement of a satisfactory solution' since it enjoyed the friendship of both the British and Indian peoples.⁴⁹ Nan was in turn asked to comment on this official position. She replied: 'Of course, the statement does not go very far, but I believe it is helpful in the sense that it shows appreciation of the problem.'⁵⁰

That night, another thousand people gathered to celebrate India's Independence Day, with Nan as the guest of honour, this time at the Washington Press Club. 'India is one large concentration camp,' she declared. Then, parrying a persistent question about internal tensions, she added hyperbolically: 'India has no religious differences; her one religion is [the] religion of freedom.'⁵¹ She pivoted to the broader context of imperialism, reminding her audience that if the objective of war was the promotion of democratic ideals as purported, 'then the oldest notions of empire, vested interests and colonies must go and plans for reshaping the world must be made with vision and courage'. This last point caught the attention of the *Baltimore Afro-American*, one the most distinguished Black-owned papers in the country.⁵²

She was back in New York on Tuesday to attend the annual dinner of the Save the Children Federation. The event took place in Town Hall, a historic forum that had been established by suffragists and was home to legendary performances and pioneering social conversations.⁵³ Nan was one of several featured speakers and used her platform to draw attention to the plight of poor children, especially in light of the famine, in India.⁵⁴

'The poor child in India is the most neglected human being in the world—it is almost as if the child did not exist—while the rich child is terribly pampered and spoiled,' she said. 'When I drew up a scheme of help for these children,' she added referencing her days on the Allahabad Municipal Board, 'the local authorities looked at me as if I was demented.' But the cause was just and she intended to preserve it; so she went on. If everyone pulled together, anything was possible. She saw great hope in the fact that English school children had taken out collections and sent small donations to keep Bengal from starving. These actions, not those of millionaires, she concluded, were the most meaningful and signalled what was truly possible.⁵⁵

Between her travel and her events, she squeezed in a series of press interviews, and the *Christian Science Monitor* ran a lengthy profile on her, highlighting how she was both 'a strong nationalist and a strong internationalist'. Vijaya Lakshmi Pandit 'believes that entry into a new international order can only be made through the portal of a satisfied nationalism and that all must enter as equals,' it clarified. 'It seems to me of vital importance that we should face the reality of the situation,' Nan told them, 'and instead of dividing the world into possessing and dispossessed nations, we should try to bring into being a commonwealth of nations, in which security, justice, and freedom shall be guaranteed to all men, and in which each nation will be able to contribute toward building up a better order for mankind.'[56]

On 3 February, Clare Booth Luce and her husband Henry organized another high-powered reception in Nan's honour. Smaller than the huge production arranged by the India League, the gathering had sixty hand-picked guests, though it packed even more punch because of the circles the Luces moved in. She was a pioneering Republican congresswoman, and he was the publisher of *Time* and *Life* magazines.[57]

The Luces considered themselves friends of India. Clare had travelled there back in 1942 when she had the opportunity to meet Nehru. The two had stayed in touch since then. She quickly concluded that he was the 'greatest and truest friend that the cause of Democracy and the cause of the United Nations [the Allies] has in all of Asia.' She, in turn, had spoken out on India's behalf regularly.

Henry was on the board of the India League. And he also worked closely with the Walshes on Indian famine relief. Nan could hardly have asked for better, or better-connected, allies.

Clare had herself suffered terrible tragedy. Her only child, a teenage daughter, had died accidentally the previous year. Nan had learned of the news through Chandralekha and Nayantara while she was grieving Ranjit's loss.[58] The two women sympathized with one another, and quickly grew attached.

The Luce reception was held in the grand Waldorf-Astoria, where Nan had stayed on her first night in the city. Some of New York's best-known names came out—the Rockefellers, the Sulzbergers, the Trippes—along with the tri-states' governors.

It was another high-flying night. And her lecture tour had not yet begun.[59]

~

Nan's activities flummoxed British officials. Some felt hoodwinked and argued that Nan had gone to the United States on false pretences and deserved censure. But others admitted that she had never explicitly denied that she would speak out while abroad and that nothing could or should be done. They grappled over the impact she was having. Some soothed themselves when told by Sir Girja Shankar Bajpai, the agent general, that American audiences were more won over by her charm than her politics. A few were even convinced that her 'unbridled tongue' would annoy her audiences and that her hosts would see through her 'claptrap'. But others recognized that she had 'calculated [how] to appeal to American emotions' and fretted that she was proving 'successful' and was creating 'a very favourable impression'.[60]

~

Things had happened very quickly since Nan first arrived in the United States, and she had had to adapt accordingly. She had originally planned to be in the country for about three months, but very soon looked into extending her stay to six. Then, as she plotted out her calendar with Getts, and as her invitations began to multiply following each of her appearances, she realized that she would need even longer. By February, she had decided to stay the year, with a break during the summer to spend some time with her family out of the public eye.[61]

Her meetings and speeches made international headlines, and rumours had started right away that she might travel home with a stopover in London. Krishna Menon, who had a reputation as an erudite, accomplished and highly strung man, continued to run what was probably the most successful overseas operation of the India League there. He had developed by then a rapport with Nehru and Nan and was hoping the latter might bring her show to the United Kingdom. She wrote back in a friendly manner, saying that she had been 'wanting to contact' him since her arrival and that she very much hoped to be able to make a trip to England. But her US speaking engagements and her own continuing mental and physical exhaustion made such a trip unlikely at that time. She left unsaid that British officials had discouraged her from doing this for her own safety as wartime passage via this route was not deemed safe. Internally, they had raced to make the real danger as clear as possible for fear of being perceived of having ulterior motives in preventing her travel.[62]

~

The Ritz Carlton was the 'most glamorous edifice in Boston', its very name synonymous with luxury and elegance.[63] Nan was booked to stay there for a few days as the first stop of her national tour.

Things got off to a rocky start. She alighted from her train at Back Bay Station as she had been instructed to do so by her primary hosts, the Coomaraswamys. Ananda Coomaswamy was an intrepid scholar of Indian history and philosophy who had spearheaded efforts to introduce India to Americans. He had by then lived in Boston for thirty years and was a curator at the prestigious Museum of Fine Arts. Nan had tried to coordinate things in advance as best she could, but nonetheless everyone had their wires crossed. A huge welcome had been put together in anticipation of her arrival, but at South Station, which was 10–20 minutes away. The crowd waited for hours. Nan learned of all of this only after the fact and missed the whole thing. Matters only worsened from there.[64]

That evening, as she and the girls settled into their hotel, Nan was visited by the Countess de Pierrefeu, a Boston Brahmin who had acquired a French title by marriage. Elsa Tudor, as she had been previously known, was the daughter of Boston's 'Ice King', Frederic Tudor, who had made his fortune trading frozen water. Count Pierrefeu had been killed during World War I, and the Countess had since gotten drawn into the worldwide pacifist movement and considered herself an admirer of Gandhi.[65]

The Countess was pleasant enough but strangely disdainful at the same time. Pierrefeu brushed aside Nan's questions about her upcoming programme in the city, saying that she had no real interest in the matter. She claimed to have been 'dragged' into involvement in the tour by the India League. But she had nonetheless graciously arranged a press junket in the morning, she continued, and told Nan to supply sherry for the event. Nan did so at personal expense, only to discover the next morning, when she followed up, that the Countess claimed to know nothing of the matter. Nan was not quite sure what to do then but was relieved when reporters from Reuters and the Associated Press drifted in and spent the morning interviewing her.

That evening, the Countess had a letter delivered to Nan reiterating that she had no interest in her personally, but that she had nonetheless put together a 'small, informal' dinner party in her honour at the last minute, set for the following night. Nan was both amused and confused. The letter was tactless, and the hostess seemed out of sorts, but she knew that it served the larger goal, and so decided to oblige.

Before the event began, Serge Koussevitsky, the renowned conductor of the Boston Symphony Orchestra, paid Nan a visit to invite her to that evening's concert. This was a great honour, and personal thrill for her. She loved the arts and was a great admirer of the worldly Russian immigrant. So as soon as she arrived at her party, she informed the Countess and asked if she might be excused a tad early from the evening so that she could attend. Aside from a brusque encounter with the Coomaraswamys, the night unfolded as planned, and she had a marvellous time at the concert.

So she was taken aback when Ananda Coomarswamy wrote her a lengthy note the next day chastising her for her early departure and lecturing her on manners and proper etiquette. Of all the things she had been criticized for in her life thus far, lacking in social graces was not one of them. She second-guessed herself and wrote to the Walshes asking for their advice.[66]

Richard Walsh wrote back empathetically immediately and urged Nan not to bother about the matter. Boston 'was so small a corner of this country that what happens [there] doesn't matter much', he wrote with typical Yankee attitude. He assured her that he continued to repose full faith in her, in her 'thoughtful and gracious attitudes', and in her 'instinct for what to do'. He dismissed Coomaraswamy's letter for 'impertinence'.[67]

Things got back on track from there. She made it out to Wellesley where she had lunch with Mildred McAfee, the president. Heavy snow prevented her from exploring the campus, but she managed to speak to 'several hundred at the International Students' Centre in Cambridge' and then dined with several students back at her hotel.

Back in Boston, she had dinner with a joint committee comprised in part of the Women's International League for Peace and Freedom, and separately with Mr and Mrs William Phillips, he who had been Roosevelt's special representative to India a few years back. Later she addressed a public gathering in New England Mutual Hall.[68]

The *Boston Globe*, the city's leading paper, ran an extensive profile of her, though they garbled her name in the transcription, referring to her as 'Vijaya Kashmi Pundit'. This was a rare mistake. Virtually all coverage of her was carefully precise, errors only occasionally creeping into printed listings announcing her talks or engagements. But the Boston reporter's difficulty with her name was fortuitous for it led in the rest of the story to dubbing her 'Madame Pandit' as shorthand.[69] The use of this title for elite married or widowed women was quite common—not much different from the use of Mrs—but something about its application here seemed special.[70]

Nan spoke at length on various matters, at times appearing overly defensive. She was still fine-tuning her rhetoric and searching for the best calibration. So she emphasized that she had married 'the man of . . . [her] choice' at the age of twenty, an odd thing to highlight, reflecting her sensitivity to the matter. The claim was probably a result of Syud Hossain's re-entry into her orbit.

While she now admitted that 'internal differences' existed in India, she insisted that those were disappearing from inter-religious marriage. Caste too, she said, was 'being eliminated except in a small, conservative section'. These claims were gross exaggerations but stemmed more from her faith in Gandhi's project than any effort to deceive. 'In a free India we see a solution of a problem of all the suppressed races. We shall have our freedom—don't mistake it—and we are paying the price, but we would like to have it without bitterness. That is the wonderful thing that . . . [the Mahatma] has done to our country—he has made us willing to suffer without bitterness.'

Turning back to the war and what was to come after, she again promised that India would throw its 'whole weight' into the effort if only Britain would guarantee freedom. She chastised the deployment of two million Indian men, 'scornfully' claiming these were just 'rice soldiers', people forced to join the Army by their own poverty. Things had to change.

'America has it in her hands to recreate the world,' she said, subversively adding that it was the United States' anti-imperial position that gave it standing. 'The American ideal has given fresh hope to many peoples, but I feel very strongly that there is danger that small self-interests may lead her not only to let down other peoples, but herself.'

'They talk about the affairs of the world being settled by the Big Five . . . [but] who the dickens are the Big Five to determine what is to be done for the world,' she asked piercingly.[71]

~

American forces had landed in Normandy and had begun the long march east in the June prior to Nan's arrival in New York. The Soviets meanwhile had also launched their offensive heading westward. Berlin was square in their sights.

These operations had altered the dynamics of the war and put the Axis on the defence. Within a few months, strategists calculated that the war was nearing an end. The Americans and Soviets joined the British and Chinese at an estate in Washington D.C. called Dumbarton Oaks. There, they hashed out instruments and organizations for future international peace and security. The Hot Springs Conference had been held in follow up to focus on questions specific to the Pacific world.

In February, while Nan was in Boston, FDR, Churchill, and Stalin were meeting at Yalta, in the Crimea. At the end of their conference, they agreed to host an international meeting in San Francisco in late April, together with China and France. Representatives from all the countries who had signed on the United Nations Declaration were to be invited. And the fate of the world was to be decided.

~

Nan's activities did not go unnoticed by Whitehall. The secretary of state for India, Leo Amery, fielded several questions about her comments in the House of Commons. Some MP's found her remarks at the National Press Club, referencing 'concentration camps', the most embarrassing and the most threatening. They pressed Amery on measures that might be taken to counter the 'powerful effect' that such statements could have on public perceptions of Britain in otherwise friendly territory like the United States. The secretary dismissed Nan's 'fantastic assertions', but nonetheless conceded that a concerted propaganda effort was needed to contain the damage.[72]

Frederick Puckle, the director-general of the Central Board of Information of the Government of India, had been in the United States for a few months to advocate on their behalf. The Foreign Office decided to keep him in place there at least through the upcoming United Nations conference to contain the Indian 'firebrands' on the scene. They meant Nan.[73]

~

America's Town Meeting of the Air was one of the country's most popular radio programmes. It took place in New York's Town Hall, where Nan had earlier attended the Save the Children gala.

About seven to eight million people tuned in to the show regularly. *Reader's Digest*, the most widely read magazine in the United States, published transcripts of major events, ensuring widespread reach.

Nan had accepted an invitation to appear live on the show on 1 March, to debate whether colonial empires were a threat to world peace. Nan thought the question absurd, but this was a serious affair. She was going head-to-head with Robert Boothby, a British MP who had served as Winston Churchill's Parliamentary Secretary.

The press saw right away that they had a marquee matchup on their hands. Reuters announced that Vijaya Lakshmi Pandit and Boothby would 'cross swords in a coast-to-coast broadcast' on 'one of the biggest air forums in the United States'.

Two others were scheduled to participate as well. Owen Lattimore, who had advised Chiang Kai-Shek and was a former editor of *Pacific Affairs*, was set to argue in the affirmative with Nan. Confirming the final participant to argue the negative with Boothby proved a bit more of a challenge, with changes taking place up until the last moment, when a radio personality named John W. Vandercook finally agreed to appear.[74]

Anticipation ran high, and a 'seething crowd' gathered early outside the venue clamouring to get a seat to the big fight. Nan was set to speak before 'one of the largest audiences ever assembled in ... Town Hall'.[75]

The debate consisted of three rounds: an opening statement, cross-examination by the speakers, and Q&A with the audience. Nan delivered some of her standard talking points at the outset. She said that political prisoners in India had to be released and that military power alone could not produce or maintain peace. A post-war order had to be built on ideals, and for those ideals to mean anything, they had to be upheld in Asia. Boothby, for his part, talked up the international foundations of empire and the ways in which it bound people together in alliances. He argued that empires were elastic structures and pointed out as an example that India would soon be a dominion. The other two speakers affirmed the points of their teammates, with Lattimore 'emphatically' agreeing with Nan. The audience politely applauded each of the seemingly evenly matched participants.

But things swiftly changed in Round 2. Nan turned the focus to the Indian famine, a subject about which she had complete and unrivalled mastery. She demanded to know how such a thing could unfold if empires were as benevolent as Boothby had claimed. She broadened her attack to ask about Britain's per capita spending on healthcare in the subcontinent. Boothby took the bait and boasted that India was self-sufficient and so required no outside assistance. Nan reeled him in: 'India supports herself *and* England, that is the whole trouble.' Overconfident in his own abilities, Boothby continued, unaware that his struggle was further entangling him in twisted logic from which he had no escape. He argued that the lack of government healthcare spending did not have much to do with anything. 'It is because Mr. Boothby doesn't realize the money is ours and the control is his,' Nan interjected. The mood in the room shifted perceptibly in her favour.

As the evening wore on, it was clear that something dramatic had occurred. She seemed to grow in stature with each quip and every grin and glance. She was funny, charming and devastatingly effective. All the men on the stage had become mere props in a one-woman show.

For all that she had accomplished to that point, she had remained more of a curiosity in the Western imagination. But as she exited the stage that night, she was now a full-fledged national sensation, henceforth known simply as 'Madame Pandit'.[76]

By the next day, Nan was the talk of the town. Ben Gross, the 'dean of American radio and television editors', discussed her performance in his widely read column in the *Daily News*, calling the discussion 'informative' and 'a "must" for every intelligent listener'.[77]

One woman who had been in attendance, Helen Cantor, wrote to a friend in London to say that she 'felt very much in accord with Mme. Pandit', though she was naturally drawn to England. Cantor wrote that Nan and the other participants had tossed 'TNT' at each other. 'Who and why is Robert Boothby,' she wondered. '[H]e is doing harm.' The British Foreign Office blanched.[78]

Nan realized she had had a breakout performance. Richard Walsh and Pearl Buck wrote right away, saying that they felt that she and Lattimore had 'completely defeated' Boothby and Vandercook 'from first to last'.[79] Nan bragged to Padmaja Naidu that she had 'squashed . . . [her] opponents flat'. She told her old friend that she had started to receive 'long distance calls . . . [and] hundreds of letters of appreciation' from all around the vast country. 'America has been good to me,' she gushed.

'I am now beginning to understand the American people and find them charming and lovable,' she added. 'I am also gradually falling in love with New York and in fact with the United States. There is so much variety—such large spaces and a great deal of warmth and hospitality everywhere.'[80]

British intelligence took notice. They admitted that she had strong cards to play, starting with her incredible charm, but convinced themselves that she had 'on balance done herself and her cause more harm than good'. They dismissed her remarks at Town Hall as 'sharp little wisecracks', even though they recognized that the jabs had drawn applause. They were sure that American audiences were 'tired' of her. Her greatest mistake, they erroneously concluded, was that she did not seem concerned with the outcome of the war, missing entirely her demand that the Allies live up to the ideals that they had professed.[81]

~

Just as she was basking in the glow of success following her debate, the National Committee for India's Freedom told Reuters that they intended to send an unofficial delegation to the upcoming United

Nations Conference in San Francisco at the end of April. FDR, Stalin and Churchill were each personally sent a memorandum on the matter.

As it happened, Nan was already scheduled to speak in the Golden City at the same time. Anup Singh told the press mischievously that plans were afoot to add some stops to the visit.

The Committee and the India League were making headlines for other reasons. They were pushing to open US Immigration and expand it more specifically to Indians. Clare Booth Luce had introduced bi-partisan legislation to this effect and all of Nan's new friends were lobbying for it to pass.[82]

For her part, Nan had a more pressing concern. She was to speak at the Book and Author Luncheon at the Hotel Astor in just a few days. The event was hosted by Irita Van Doren, the book review editor of the *New York Herald Tribune*, and co-sponsored by the American Bookseller's Association. Van Doren had been 'very eager' to have Nan as a guest, and she and the Walshes and Getts had been working out the arrangements to make it happen. Richard Walsh thought this was a terrific opportunity for Nan to reach 'many influential people'.[83]

Nan was seated at the Speaker's Table with Pulitzer Prize-winning journalist Leland Stowe and fashion designer Elizabeth Hawes. Van Doren introduced her as 'one of the most notable women of our time'.

Nan talked up the status of women in India, where many had become 'lawyers, doctors, political leaders, business executives, actresses, singers and dancers'. This, she asserted, had historically been true in India, but had been made possible again with the advocacy and encouragement of Mahatma Gandhi. Then she once again subverted the narrative and expressed surprise that women in America still faced so many barriers of their own, keeping them from 'high positions' and the recognition that they deserved.[84]

India's women 'got the jobs ... not because they were women but because they were better than the men'. She paused and then added wryly that 'these are not women whose clothes are described every time they enter the legislative assembly'. The *Tribune* covered the remarks the next day. They highlighted for their American audience her 'statuesque figure', 'black silk sari' and 'smoothly waved gray hair'.[85]

~

Over the rest of March and April, Nan extended her travels to Ohio and Pennsylvania. In Cleveland, she spoke again about decolonization and the freedom of India as necessary preconditions to any kind of a meaningful, lasting peace that might emerge from the war.[86]

The president of the Maternal Health Center arranged her trip to Pittsburgh, where she was welcomed by the mayor. There Nan, recognized as '[i]nternationally famous . . . striking and unusually charming', discussed public health issues in India and attended a dinner reception in her honour.[87] 'We must break down these color barriers, these unfounded prejudices about each other,' she proclaimed.[88]

She gave an extensive interview to Gertrude 'Toki' Schalk, the prominent women's editor of the African American paper, the *Pittsburgh Courier*. Nan highlighted the connection she felt with American Black people and discussed the relationship between race and caste and the possibility that Dalits ('untouchables') in India and people of African descent in the United States had a shared history of oppression. Schalk praised the 'great and beautiful woman . . . whose only interest is the hope for complete equality of all races and all peoples'.[89]

In between these two trips, Nan visited Baltimore, Maryland, where she spoke about the Four Freedoms for Asia at the historic Lyric Theater. In the lead up to her talk, *The Baltimore Sun* called her 'vivacious' and remarked on her 'faultless English with a British accent'. They were also struck by her pink nail polish, white, embroidered sari, and 'American style' haircut. She, in the meantime, urged 'the common people of America' and India to come together to end the belief in war's necessity.[90]

Owen Lattimore introduced her the next day. Nine hundred people had gathered to hear her speak. Among her diverse audience were 'Chinese students and merchants, former missionaries . . . representatives of the British press, and . . . of the British Intelligence Service . . . world travelers . . . [and] a delegation from the local NAACP'. She called for a radical transformation of the world order and demanded that every country be allowed to contribute, based on their ability, to 'the solutions . . . [to] international problems'.

She focused on the upcoming San Francisco Conference and pointed out that India was to be represented there, but not her actual people. 'That is not the way to solve the world's problems,' she asserted. Her message especially resonated with the Black community.

An African American solider asked her during the Q&A how she thought the Four Freedoms should be applied to the race problem in America. It was a penetrating query. 'The rules of hospitality forbid me to discuss this question, which is dear to mine and the heart of the leaders of the Indian Nationalist Movement,' she responded. But she had been 'happiest' in Harlem, she added, 'because the people there understood more fully' what her people were 'struggling for'. 'I am for the complete equality of human beings—whatever their race, caste, or creed,' she declared. She received a 'spontaneous ovation.' The next day, the *Baltimore Afro-American* called her 'The First Lady of India.'[91]

~

The US Immigration Bill to expand access to Indians could not make it through Congress. The Secretary for the Government of India's Ministry of External Affairs, Sir Olaf Caroe, proclaimed this an unfortunate turn of events and audaciously wondered aloud if Vijaya Lakshmi Pandit's activities and speeches had had a detrimental effect on the bill's passage.

Emanuel Celler, the legislation's co-sponsor with Clare Booth Luce, mocked the very idea. 'His observations are utterly absurd and unsupported by facts,' he said. The real culprits, he revealed, were 'reactionary Republicans' and Southern racists who had joined forces to thwart passage. But he predicted that 'liberal forces' would prevail. 'Remember . . . that the side that wins the first battle does not always win the war. The Allies know this and Hitler knows it.'[92]

He would be proved correct. The Luce-Celler Act became law the following year.[93]

~

Just after she had returned from Boston, the National Committee and its allies discussed having Nan travel to San Francisco to raise the profile of the 'India question' while in San Francisco. She immediately cabled Ghanshyam Das Birla and Mahatma Gandhi to request their endorsement. She specifically hoped that Birla would finance such activity. Birla wrote back negatively, indicating he felt that tactically, India had to concentrate on swaying conservative opinion in England and ergo that talking up issues in the United States was a waste of time. Gandhi, for his part, felt his advice was not warranted and that it was best if he simply did not interfere.[94]

British Intelligence intercepted Birla's telegram to Nan but misunderstood it. Some officials concentrated on the request for money and assumed that it must have been for personal needs. Others concluded it was to fund additional anti-colonial activity, such as supporting a follow-up tour by Sarojini Naidu. No one connected the exchange with San Francisco specifically.[95]

By the time Anup Singh had announced after her Town Hall victory that Nan would indeed be travelling to California, plans had essentially been firmed up for her to in fact lead a counter-delegation to the San Francisco conference, and to directly challenge the prerogative of the Great Powers to make decisions on behalf of the rest of the world.

~

Walter White had grown increasingly interested in India since he had been in the room with former Republican presidential candidate Wendell Willkie when they devised plans for what would become his One World tour.[96] In February, just before Nan's duel with Boothby, White published a profile of J.J. Singh and the India League in the *Chicago Defender*, one of the country's leading African American papers. He perceptively called out racism and colourism (the casteism) in the community that he immediately picked up on. 'Most Indians still believe themselves more Aryan than the whitest-skinned, bluest-eyed Nordic,' he wrote. But he argued that white supremacy was a force that should lead Indians to confront their own brown-ness. He praised Singh for his efforts to forge Afro-Asian bonds of unity. And he talked up Nan's visit to the United States and his meetings with her 'charming' daughters.[97]

In April, White took a trip abroad, aiming to visit India as part of his itinerary. While he was travelling, Du Bois organized a meeting at the 135th Street branch of the New York Public Library to discuss the future of colonized people in the post-war world. The parley was attended by representatives from all over the colonized world. Nan was invited but was unable to attend. Prafulla Kumar Goshal, an actor, journalist and activist who had made the United States his home, had recommended her and represented India in her place once she regretted. The group produced four resolutions: 'that colonialism must go,' that there must be an international body to 'oversee the transition', that colonized peoples must be part of this international body, and that this international body must be primarily concerned with the social and economic upliftment of (formerly) colonized peoples.[98]

White, meanwhile, abruptly cut his trip short without making it to India after his plane had a near-miss on landing in the Philippines. He hinted that he might turn up on the West Coast of the United States instead.[99]

He and Du Bois—and Mary McLeod Bethune as well—were heading to San Francisco on behalf of the NAACP to serve as consultants to the official US delegation. There, they planned to present the resolutions from their New York meeting. Du Bois proclaimed that their mission was 'to help save the world'.[100]

~

British officials were keeping close tabs on Nan's activities and those of her friends and allies. Kunzru had visited Yale University, where he had made a poor impression on his hosts. Puckle forwarded to his superiors an observation that British interests might be well served by allowing more such visitors to the United States. Diplomat George Bailey Sansom singled out B. Shiva Rao for making an 'all-around good impression'. Both he and Puckle recognized Nan's popularity and appeal but felt that she may have peaked.[101]

Eleanor Roosevelt, in the meantime, was hearing from women all over the country who wanted to register an opinion on the India matter. She fretted about upsetting the wartime alliance with Britain at that critical juncture and, out of character, reached out to the State Department to see if Nan and the others should be prevented from speaking any further. Edward Stettinius, the secretary of state wrote back negatively, informing the First Lady firstly of the British assessment that the Indian advocates on independence were actually harming their own cause. Since Britain was not worried, he saw no reason for the US to be concerned. Stettinius further argued that the US had to stand for and defend free speech, that they could not be seen as suppressing a freedom movement, and that, in fact, British propaganda in the United States was widespread. He pointed out that the British could withdraw travel privileges if at any point they perceived a true threat.[102]

This was not exactly true of course. Internally, British officials had debated this very point but concluded that, all things considered, it was best to just let Nan and the others carry on. The damage would be much worse, they feared, if they tried to stop her from talking.

~

When the Golden Gate Bridge had been completed less than a decade earlier, it was one of the greatest civil engineering feats the world had ever seen. The massive suspension bridge was, at one-mile long, the longest such structure at the time, connecting the Pacific Ocean and the San Francisco Bay, with the gleaming city of the same name on one side and Marin County the other.[103] As it stretched out over the water, especially when it disappeared into the fog, the Golden Gate could give the impression of stretching out indefinitely, a symbolic connection to other continents, and specifically of the West and East.

The city of San Francisco itself was spectacularly beautiful. Nestled amongst steep, rolling hills in northern California, it had benefited from the gold rush, emerging a wealthy, diverse metropolis, with a prominent Asian population and a Pacific orientation.

Anticipation for the United Nations Conference was high as official and unofficial delegations from all over the world began to make their way to the West Coast. The *United Press of America* recalled the atmosphere and energy of Versailles in 1919. Many groups were hoping to take advantage of the meeting to raise a range of issues and concerns. But none were better organized than Nan and the allies of India, the UPA observed, citing the 'highest and best U.S. Government sources'. They expected her to 'attain worldwide publicity'.[104]

India was officially represented by three men who had been appointed by the British viceroy, Sir Firoz Khan Noon, Sir Ramasawami

Mudaliar, and Sir V.T. Krishnamachari. India had previously been present at Versailles as well, landing as a result a unique position in the League of Nations, the only non-independent power to have a seat at the table. It was India's position at the League that gave it official entry into the UN conference as well. The official delegation talked up India's military contributions during the current war and asserted that perhaps India should hold a seat on the 'world council'.

Anup Singh dismissed all of this as showmanship. Britain, he said, would be dictating terms, and the official Indian delegates would ultimately simply have to toe the line. Only Nan could move things in a new direction.[105]

~

Just before her departure from New York, she announced that she was on her 'way to San Francisco as one who is interested in the establishment of better relations in the world'. Her first formal talk was set for 27 April, two days after the conference was to get underway.

Advance teams blanketed the Bay Area with red and white posters announcing her impending arrival. The National Committee 'issued 1,800 invitations for . . . Pandit's speech to conference delegates and other prominent people . . .'[106] They also released some pamphlets on 'India and the San Francisco Conference', featuring some of India's biggest allies in the United States: Congressman Emanuel Celler, Pearl Buck and Roger Baldwin, a founder of the ACLU. In a related brochure, Nan, Syud Hossain, Anup Singh and others made their case.[107]

Nan 'set off the first fireworks' of the conference as soon as she got into town. She addressed '150 members of the world press at the Mary Hopkins Hotel', a posh facility located in the city's ultra-luxury Nob Hill neighbourhood which served as the temporary residence of the some of the official delegations, including the ones from Britain and India. Nan rebuked Noon, Mudaliar, and Krishnamachari, saying that they simply did not speak for India. Later that same day, in an interview with the *New York Herald Tribune*, she went even further and declared that Hindu and Muslim leaders alike had agreed that India would not be bound by anything that these three fake representatives said or did.

When a heckler, one K.A. Khan who was Noon's stenographer, tried to derail her press conference, she quashed his charges with such ferocity that she drove him out entirely, the crowd shouting that he was 'a British propagandist'. As he was staying at the Mary Hopkins, many concluded this was true. His goateed face was suddenly splashed everywhere, forcing him to try to shave his beard to regain anonymity.

Male reporters covering her trip found her irresistibly attractive, a perfect combination of beauty, grace and gumption. Typical coverage described her 'dazzling white robe . . . [and] alluring curves', her 'Oxonian accents and scrapping American slang'.

Women could also get caught up by such things. Helen Rich, writing for the *Philadelphia Inquirer*, commented on her 'open-toed suede opera pumps' and her 'large, square white lucite compact'. Rich went on to call her the '[u]nofficial First Lady' of India and noted that Nan had 'completely charmed everyone who . . . had the privilege of meeting her'.

Some coverage, often from women, tended to be more substantive, focused on her ideas and her diplomatic skills. Margaret Parton wrote in the *Herald Tribune* that Firoz Khan Noon, on meeting her by chance in the lobby, sheepishly admitted that he shared her political views and now stood ready to 'endorse them from any platform'. But he was simply trying to head off any criticism. Nan declined an invitation to have lunch with him.

Nan clarified that she was not there 'for the purpose of disrupting the conference'. Rather, she had come 'to demand a peace based on justice'. Rich, who helpfully informed her readers that Nan's name was 'pronounced pundit', observed that corridors were 'still ringing with the applause of the press' even after she had exited the hall.[108]

The next night, she delivered a fiery speech to a packed room at the Scottish Rite Auditorium.[109] 'India is the pivot of the whole system of imperialism and colonialism which always breeds war.' She called Indian freedom the 'acid test' of the principles for which the Allies were fighting.[110]

Later, in an interview, she went even further: 'It is not I, coming to you Americans who fought for your independence to tell you India wants her freedom. You should be standing on your street corners, demanding freedom for us. If you acquiesce in denying freedom for others, you end freedom for yourselves.' She called for an end to 'power politics' once and for all. The *Chicago Daily Tribune* reported that she spoke with a 'chill fury'.[111]

India was 'the skeleton at the feast', she provocatively asserted. The *New York Herald Tribune* wryly retorted that it had to be a 'pretty lively skeleton' judging by all of the counter-delegation's activities.[112]

Despite his initial gesture, Firoz Khan Noon had subsequently gone on the attack, charging Nan as being Gandhi's representative and ergo part of a larger group within the Congress Party that were intent on 'sabotaging the Allied war effort.'[113] When rumours began to circulate that a breakthrough might occur, that the British might actually make a gesture to open a path to solving the India problem, he changed his tune once more. He declared his support for Nehru, even as he dismissed Gandhi as being 'half a century out of date'. Nan paused her campaign to assess what was happening.[114]

It became clear almost immediately that no breakthrough was forthcoming. So Nan released a formal memorandum prosecuting her case with renewed vigour. 'The Indian National Congress Party representing the Indian people has always stood uncompromisingly against Fascism, Nazism and Imperialism. Organized Fascism and Nazism have now been liquidated. Imperialism alone remains and is entrenched in a system which implies coercion, domination and exploitation of one country by another.'

'I submit,' she went on, 'that this system should now be renounced in principle and abandoned in practice by an unequivocal acknowledgment and declaration of Free India.' Her demands, she added, were not only for her own country but also for all other countries that were 'under the heels on alien militarists' and unable to 'speak for themselves'. She demanded that the statesmen gathered in San Francisco live up to their grand proclamations.[115]

She formally identified herself for the first time as 'Madame Vijaya Lakshmi Pandit, Spokesman for India', a fact picked up on by the press. Wire services carried news of her memo far and wide, ensuring an international reach.[116]

Her efforts had their effect, forcing the British to respond in a press conference a few days later. Foreign Secretary Anthony Eden, speaking at the Mary Hopkins Hotel, asserted that the Cripps proposals stood and that his country was ready to move forward on them the moment Indians agreed. Additionally, reflecting a larger British strategy to delegitimize the Indian cause, Eden claimed that those who had been arrested since 1942 were primarily sympathizers of the Japanese and the larger Axis cause.

This was a step too far for Nan, who countered it with a harsh press release. She pointed out that Cripps had failed to win anyone over and that his suggestions had been rejected by all sides. Moreover, she wondered how anyone could expect good faith negotiations to occur when one side had authorized the 'wholesale arrest and imprisonment without trial of tens of thousands of leaders and followers alike'.

But what irked her the most was the idea that the Indian National Congress (INC) had somehow vacillated on its position on the war. Eden was not referring to Subhas Chandra Bose and his Indian National Army, which had embedded itself into Japanese forces.

Nan took him to task. Leaders of the INC, and the party as whole, she wrote were 'utterly uncompromising' in denouncing Japanese aggression as far back as 1932, as a matter of public record. India's stand against the Axis, she said with righteous indignation, long predated anything that Eden, Churchill, 'or any other member of the present or the previous British governments had thought it expedient to do'.[117]

The next day, Alger Hiss, an American diplomat serving as the secretary-general of the United Nations Conference (who would be accused of being a Soviet spy a few years later), wrote Nan a letter acknowledging receipt of her memorandum but informing her that it was outside of the purview of the meeting. The Conference was intended only to draft a 'the best possible charter' for a new 'international organization' that would 'maintain peace and security for all people of the world regardless of race, color, creed, or sex'. This meeting was not able, he said, to solve historic problems or to draft a traditional postwar peace settlement.[118]

So she recalibrated. Rather than talk about India's freedom as an additional, outside issue to be resolved, Nan focused on specific negotiations taking place within the conference over language that might be codified in the new institutional charter. She focused on British, French and Dutch efforts to replace calls for the 'independence' of 'dependent peoples' with support for 'self-government'. She savaged these efforts as duplicitous, charging the three European powers with knowingly deploying an 'ancient weasel word'. 'One would have supposed,' she said, that powers that had 'themselves . . . [come] so near to enslavement would have learned better, but, like the Bourbons, they learn nothing and forget nothing.' She tried to sway the United States to act, hoping that 'saner and . . . [and more just] conceptions of the future order of the world' would 'prevail'.[119]

~

Nan was already well-known by the start of the conference. But her high-octane performances and relentless drive now propelled her to true celebrity status. Crowds trailed her wherever she went, hoping to 'get her autograph or snap her picture'. At lunch one day, excited fans swarmed her table, ignoring an actor seated nearby, Hollywood legend James Cagney.

Reuters singled her out. She was a 'one woman' show, a 'fiery' campaigner 'putting in seven days hard work per week'. Typically, her morning started with 'voluminous' mail from admirers and inquirers. Then she spent time talking to individual members of the press in fifteen-minute increments, so she could interact with as many people as possible. Lunch was usually with Syud Hossain or Anup Singh, or both, and occasionally with reporters as well. She could have fun with her meals.[120] One time, she and Hossain took a reservation at a sought-after restaurant and then howled with laughter as they watched the perplexed official (British) Indian delegation, to whom the seats actually belonged, being turned away moments later.[121] K.P.S. Menon, who was serving as chief adviser to Noon and the others, and who met with Nan privately during the conference, watched as she completely 'eclipsed' his team 'in the public eye'.[122]

She took some time for herself every afternoon, strolling, sightseeing and shopping. Then it was back to work. She entertained delegates in her rented apartment, including the foreign ministers of 'Egypt, Iraq, and Saudi Arabia'. Evenings she devoted to working dinners, 'radio or personal appearances, and other public functions'. Despite the heavy schedule, she 'tried never to give the same speech twice'. She turned in at 10 p.m., when she again returned 'messages and letters, and phone calls'. Finally, she read for pleasure before turning out the lights at midnight and doing it all again the next day.[123]

~

Just before she pivoted to focus on specific aspects of the conference negotiations, Nan was invited by Earl Warren, the governor of California, to address the state legislature in Sacramento. People of South Asian descent, particularly from the Punjab, had been settling in California since the late nineteenth century, yet Nan was to be the first Indian accorded this high honour. She told Reuters that she was 'happy to accept' and that she would do her 'best to present the case of India's freedom'.[124]

As soon as word of the speech got out, British officials hurried to have it withdrawn. Lord Halifax, their ambassador to the United States, personally intervened and 'objected strenuously' to Warren. Halifax had just spoken before the legislature and was particularly concerned about being made to look the fool.[125] He was right to be concerned.

The speech went on as planned. Nan aimed her remarks squarely at her American hosts, placing them at the centre of any solution to the world's problems. 'So long as . . . colonial vested interests remain,' she warned, 'there can be no peace, there can be no security. And so long as there is no security or peace, we shall go on destroying all that generations of and centuries of human effort have built up.'[126] 'You cannot rejoice over the end of fascism in Europe when imperialism, its twin brother, is permitted to function in the colonies.'[127]

'We must inevitably consider America and India and all nations of the world as one unity . . . It is necessary to build up a new world with ties of cultural contacts, industrial and commercial contacts and contacts of every sort . . . Before we can talk about interdependence [though], . . . we must realize that it is only through independence that we can achieve [such] interdependence.'[128]

She spoke to a 'full house', but Halifax had succeeded in convincing Warren, Assembly Speaker Charles Lyon, and others to excuse themselves from the event. Ordinary Americans were not amused. One, a resident of Long Beach, California, wrote a scathing letter to the governor demanding to know if 'the spirit of Justice . . .

[was] dead in the breasts of many . . . representatives' or if they were just 'ignorant'. She condemned them for bowing to the British crown and betraying the vision of 'One World' that Wendell Willkie and Franklin Roosevelt had both fought and died for.[129]

~

That evening, Nan threw an elegant cocktail party for three hundred people at the hotel, and 'quite a gang . . . of folks big and little' showed up. Guests included Walter White and Essie Robeson, the gossip columnist and socialite Elsa Maxwell, and Augustus Wilhelm, brother of the Kaiser. Washington State Senator and political pioneer Mary Farquharson also attended, as did Dorothy Detzer of the Women's International League for Peace and Freedom.[130]

The following afternoon, Nan was among several people recognized at a luncheon honouring 'the World's Women of Fame' organized by the San Francisco Women of Achievement. Each honouree was asked to introduce themselves briefly. When her turn came, she stood up and, to much murmuring, said: 'Vijaya Lakshmi Pandit of India—just a rebel against British rule in India.'[131]

~

Nan hoped to dip out of the conference briefly to attend Chandralekha's graduation back at Wellesley. But she was forced to deplane in Los Angeles while en route due to 'military priorities'. Disappointed, she made her way back to San Francisco to continue with her campaign.[132]

She kept up the pressure, dashing off a cable of support to the British Labour Party, which was about to open its conference in Blackpool, Lancashire. 'The Indian people have lost confidence completely in the present British Government . . . British labour can help to save the situation if, true to its own ideals of democracy, it takes steps to end the deadlock by the release of untried political prisoners.'[133]

But by now it was clear that her ability to affect the detailed negotiations on self-government and trusteeship taking place inside the official meeting was limited. Her appearances took on a more ceremonial feel as she marched in a street processional, visited a Sikh temple in Stockton, and spoke with 'hundreds of Indians' who wanted to celebrate her visit.[134]

A statement from US Secretary of State Edward Stettinius gave the first indication that the language in the new charter was not going to be favourable. Nan made a final push: 'Imperialistic powers, even in the last few weeks and months, have used the eternal *alibi* of indefinite unpreparedness of their subject peoples . . . Under British rule, they will never be able to reach that hypothetical preparedness . . . Mr. Stettinius and statesmen who want to achieve a free, peaceful world would do well to address themselves to this matter.'[135]

But it was for naught. The Americans were convinced by British talk of self-government, and Chapters XI and XII of the new charter structured a trusteeship system in terms preferred by the UK. The British Foreign Office was internally gleeful, cheering at language that 'prescribe[d] the principles of Colonial Administration' and that did 'not empower the United Nations organization to intervene in the application of these principles by the Powers concerned'.[136] Nan had lost.

~

Just before she left the Bay Area, Nan spoke again at the Scottish Rite Auditorium. The National Committee for India's Freedom had organized another public meeting. Nan once more called for India's freedom and lambasted the 'discredited and antiquated system of exploitation' that kept people under heel and wrought 'untold human suffering and degradation'. Syud Hossain praised her for all that she had done, but his remarks read like a 'greatest hits' lookback and underscored that the moment was over.[137]

Her charisma was undiminished. One attendee was awed by her 'natural charm, grace and sweetness' and wrote saying that she felt that she had 'met one of God's truly great souls'. But outside the venue, counterpropaganda was distributed raising questions about the Indian National Congress and who and what it represented.[138]

Critics seized the opportunity. One reader cited an Oregon newspaper editorial that charged Nan—bizarrely—with lacking a sense of humour. The quoted columnist had added that they therefore feared being under a government controlled by her.[139] The reader appeared to be J.D. Jenkins, a British partisan given to writing to newspapers and magazines, particularly *The Spectator* in London. In a more detailed missive, Jenkins elaborated Congress shortcomings and focused on the way it failed to represent Muslims properly.[140] Jenkins' comments spurred others to write as well. One Indian writer targeted Nan more directly and tried to undermine her further, broadly claiming that she did not actually represent all of India.[141]

Nan was unfazed by such remarks, but she was profoundly disappointed in herself and in what she felt she had been unable to achieve. In her final remarks to the press before she checked out of her hotel and headed back east, her regret was apparent: 'The compromise that seems likely to be forced on the Conference on the issue of independence is so disingenuous, and the camouflage it embodies so patent, that I fear that the cause of future peace and concord among nations will not be advanced by it.'[142]

~

Jawaharlal Nehru had been moved out of his prison in Ahmadnagar Fort in early April and had subsequently been bounced around from facility to facility, spending short stints in Naini Central Prison, then Bareilly, and then District Jail in Almora. He was finally released in mid-June along with other Congress leaders, just as the San Francisco meeting was ending, and he immediately travelled, via Khali, to the hills of Kashmir for rejuvenation. Asked to comment by the press in the United States, Nan said that she was 'happy' that those 'who should never have been incarcerated' were 'at last' released, and that she felt that this was a step 'in the right direction.'[143]

The siblings exchanged thoughts on their children, gossiped about family and discussed public speaking. Nehru proudly told his sister that he was keeping news clippings about her that he would share on her return. He reviewed Nan's prison diary, which had recently been published, frankly complaining of all kinds of shortcomings he saw in the work. And he wondered about migrant South Asian communities, especially the Sikhs of California and wanted to know about their choices of dress, language and marriage, among other details. She tried to coax him into making a trip to America.[144]

Nehru had kept a close eye on his sister's activities in the United States and had grown increasingly impressed with what she was accomplishing. Initially, he wrote with brotherly encouragement, saying that news about her made him 'very happy', not 'just because . . . [she was] making good and impressing people', but because she was finding herself and 'growing in mind, in outlook, in self-assurance'.[145] His tone shifted noticeably as he learned of her takedown of Robert Boothby. 'How clever you have grown,' he told her, adding that he would have to give up his 'superior elder brother attitude.' He wondered if she would not 'overwhelm' him when next they met and noted that he 'would love to listen' to her deliver one of her lectures.[146]

~

Nan had travelled to Chicago in early June to speak at the elegant Orchestra Hall at an event sponsored by the Civil Liberties committee. There she had made some of her most astute observations about the consequences of the United Nations Conferences. She confessed that she was 'bitterly disappointed' with the outcome and warned of 'war within a few years'. When queried about it further, Nan made clear that she did not mean to suggest that this new war would be the same as previous ones. Rather, imperialism planted the seeds of conflict. She foresaw Great Powers, like Russia, fostering relationships with unfree territories for resources and weapons, and lending backing for proxy war.[147]

~

Nan returned to New York at the end of June. She was weary and weak and needed another operation to address recurring pain. Doctors advised her to have a hysterectomy to gain long-term relief. Nehru encouraged her to get this done right away. He worriedly told her to take proper rest afterwards and warned of 'dire consequences' if she did not.

She was still making the rounds and giving talks, even speaking at the Inter-Cultural Committee of the United Nations Council of Philadelphia, though she was despondent at her perceived lack of success in San Francisco.[148] She welcomed the chance to stay out of the spotlight for a bit. In mid-August, she entered the hospital for a stay of several weeks.¹⁴⁹ Then she took some time to recuperate and enjoy time with her family and new-found friends.¹⁵⁰

~

In England, Winston Churchill and his Tories were defeated in elections and a new Labour government headed by Clement Atlee came to power. Frederick Pethick-Lawrence, whose wife Emmeline had been an early supporter of Nan, was named the new secretary of state for India. Just before her surgery, Nan praised the appointment of 'an old and tried friend of India' and said that she was sure he would 'act in India's best interests'. But, she cautioned, 'the ability or the integrity of the individual' did not matter. Everything was determined by the policy with which everyone was bound. 'India's past experience with the Labour Government was not such as to inspire undue optimism . . . We must . . . not think in terms of a compromise with any British political party on the principle of Indian independence.'¹⁵¹

In a letter to the *Boston Globe*, Mildred Gutterson considered the political developments in the UK. She castigated a 'dying imperialism', and, citing Nan extensively, said that India had 'ties with England that could be made into happy ties—ties of friendship'. It was time for Labour to act without delay.¹⁵²

~

Mary McLeod Bethune returned to Washington D.C. in early June, after spending several weeks in California. She had attended the San Francisco Conference as one of three official consultants to the American delegation, in her capacity as national vice-president of the NAACP. But she was also the founder and president of the National Council of Negro Women, which advocated on behalf of African American women and looked to increase their involvement in all walks of public and private life.

At a press conference, once she was back on the East Coast, Bethune announced that the NCNW was going to take on an 'international character', with an initiative into Liberia. Additionally, 'Mme. Pandit' was announced as a new 'life member' with the promise that the organization would join forces with the All India Women's Conference.[153] Nan's affiliation with Bethune's organization marked her first formal affiliation with a group working on racial, social and economic justice matters that was not specifically concerned with the cause of India.

Several weeks later, Essie Robeson launched her new book, *Journey to Africa*, at the Council of African Affairs. While Nan was still in the hospital, Chandralekha, Nayantara and Rita attended the soiree in their mother's place, their participation underscoring the message of unity.[154]

~

The Attlee government announced in early fall that long-delayed provincial elections in India would take place imminently and scheduled them for January 1946. G.B. Pant, with whom Nan had worked closely while she was a minister in his United Provinces Cabinet, cabled her with the news and requested her to return to India to contest once more from her old Cawnpore (Kanpur) constituency. She contemplated cutting her trip short and heading home early but ultimately decided to stay the course and continue with her US itinerary through the rest of the year.[155]

In October, she set off on tour again, travelling over the next few months throughout the East Coast, Midwest and Southwest of the country. In a prominent interview with the *Washington Post*, she insisted that, moving forward, 'Indian women will work side by side with men in politics as in all phases of life.' She noted that there were more Indian women in elected office than in the United States and chastised American women for not taking public life seriously enough. US women, she added, did seem to care about 'professional advancement' and in this regard were quite successful. When asked about India's starving millions, she talked up distribution problems as the key issue. And when pressed about overpopulation, she responded by talking about her work with Margaret Sanger's methods but acknowledged that much more needed to be done.[156]

It was clear by then that Nan had come to represent the potential of women's achievement in a broad sense, heralded by ordinary folk and those in high positions just the same. One wrote into the *Times of India* lambasting patriarchal stereotypes and historical misogyny, holding up Marie Curie, Sarojini Naidu and Vijaya Lakshmi Pandit as examples of women who were any man's equal, if not better.[157] Maie Casey, the wife of the British governor of Bengal, called Nan a 'great example' to all Indian women, especially for the quality of being 'unboring'.[158]

Chandralekha, relishing her new adulthood, rushed to support her mother in various ways. She signed on to a panel that was to be moderated by Pearl Buck at Town Hall on the 'Search for Common Ground'. Representing India, she spoke on 'Forging a World Bill of Human Rights'.[159] A few weeks later, she participated in a debate on the outlook for India, going head-to-head with Frederick Puckle, Britain's agent-general in the United States.[160]

~

The National Council for Negro Women (NCNW) held their tenth annual workshop over several days in Washington D.C. at the tail end of October. The overall theme of the meeting was 'World Peace through United Action'. Nan participated in several events and headlined the main event, World Community Night.[161] She let 'her hair down' and spoke 'from the heart' to 'loud applause' from the audience, talking up the 'exhilaration' she felt when she first learned of the Four Freedoms and contrasting that with her 'shock' at the reality of things in the US, where 'they had one interpretation for whites and another for colored people'.[162] She warned about the dangers of disunity and called on all people to come together to solve the world's intractable problems. The speaker who followed her, a congresswoman named Helen Douglas, said that she felt 'ashamed' by what she had heard and 'declared "the only way you sell freedom in the world is to live it, and the only way you can sell democracy, you have to live it at home".' 'If we fail this time,' she warned, 'we've left ourselves neither time nor space.'[163]

The NCNW announced that in follow up, they would hold a 'worldwide conference of all women' the following year. 'The proposal not to include only women of the darker races was made after a dramatic plea for unity by India's Mme. Pandit.'[164]

The day after the conclusion of the NCNW gathering, Nan was invited to the White House to meet President Harry Truman, who had assumed leadership in the US after FDR's death. Emanuel Celler had arranged the visit. The three discussed current affairs and the situation in Asia, and Truman pledged his support for Celler's Indian immigration bill, designed to open the US to more people from the subcontinent.[165]

~

Nan wrapped up her US stay with a swing through the Midwest and the South, speaking before large, rapt audiences in Illinois, Louisiana, Oklahoma and Texas.[166] In January, as she began to plan her return to India, she gave several interviews expressing hope that India would soon be independent, setting January 1947 as her preferred target. She suggested that Indians would not accept the status quo ante, warning that the mood appeared to have shifted away from non-violence over the past few years. India, she added, also could count on American sympathy.[167]

Upon her return to India, rapturous crowds received her as a hero on her arrival in Karachi, 10,000 people squeezing into grounds meant to hold no more than 3000. She gave brief remarks expressing gratitude.[168]

Her reception in Allahabad was much the same, 'large crowds' gathering at the airfield itself, even though it was quite far from the city proper. They roared 'Jai Hind' [Long Live India] and 'Inquilab Zindabad' [Vive La Revolution]. Nehru and Indira, Kripalani, and others were there to greet her. Taking the microphone, she said that she had done her best to advocate for India's freedom. But India's freedom was symbolic and stood for something greater. The true goal, she said was 'the struggle for freedom for all nations all over the world from the imperialistic yoke.'[169]

She surveyed the familiar landscape. There was nothing like it. It was good to be home. She just had no idea then how short a time she would be staying.

CHAPTER TEN

# White Teeth

Nan barely had time to get her bearings in Anand Bhawan before she had to dash out the door again to file papers in Cawnpore for the coming election.[1] Before her departure, she met socially with a visiting group of MPs from the UK and more formally with R.M. Deshmukh, the Indian high commissioner in South Africa.[2]

The South African government was about to begin proceedings on the Pegging Act, a temporary measure affecting the status of Indians in the country that was set to expire at the end of March 1946. Jan Smuts, the prime minister, was signalling his hope that a permanent solution to 'the Indian question' would be found soon. Deshmukh discussed the situation with Nan just as he was heading back to Cape Town to follow up.[3]

In the meantime, some of her comments about her experiences abroad caught the attention of the American press. Though she had been, and remained, laudatory overall, Nan had warned that British propaganda was relentless and that in general, the American people had very little understanding of what was happening in India. She had also said that there was a disjuncture in the country between the governing and the governed, suggesting that ordinary people were more gung-ho about India than the country's official position would indicate. The *New York Times*, in the person of their correspondent in the subcontinent, George Jones, got defensive and rejected the suggestion that the US was somehow wilfully 'concealing facts' domestically. Even so, they admitted, albeit begrudgingly, that Nan's observations were largely on point.[4]

Nan was momentarily distracted. She had just been re-elected unopposed to the United Provinces legislature, shortly after formally filing her candidacy.⁵ But once she caught her breath, she doubled down on her observations about British propaganda and American misunderstandings of India. And she again warned that 'the prospect of the post-war world . . . [appeared] dark.' The reason, according to her assessment, was that the 'attitude of the big Powers towards one another . . . [was] one of jealousy, suspicion and selfishness . . . [multiplied by the fact that] [t]heir economic life has been shattered.'⁶

~

In late February, Britain dispatched a team to India—dubbed the Cabinet Mission for the high-level positions members held—to try to move things between colony and metropole to resolution. Patience with the status quo had grown thin throughout the region, with significant, sporadic bouts of violence breaking out in various places, just as Nan had predicted.⁷

Sir Stafford Cripps was hoping for better luck on this round of negotiations. He was joined by A.V. Alexander, Lord of the Admiralty, and Lord Pethick-Lawrence, the Secretary of State for India.⁸ By early April, the emissaries were on the ground and were beginning their various formal and informal meetings. Nan joined Pethick-Lawrence at a silent, Quaker prayer meeting in New Delhi, accompanied by Gandhi and Sarojini Naidu.⁹

Over the next few months, the Cabinet Mission released a plan to move India towards independence in a way that balanced the needs of the Congress, the Muslim League, and the Indian princes, which it saw as the three primary constituencies that had to be brought along. Generally, the British proposed elections for a Constituent Assembly and an interim government to operate in the meantime. The plan was initially accepted by all parties, but the Congress stipulated that the details of what was to follow had to be left to the Assembly, and that the British could no longer expect to dictate terms to an (soon-to-be) independent country.

Nan, for her part, used public pronouncements to signal goodwill. In late January, she declared that she 'would be glad to welcome' Muhammad Ali Jinnah, the leader of the League, 'as head of a new, strong elected Indian government.' She added that the Congress should not 'overwhelmingly dominate all other groups.' She made clear that popular representation was key to legitimate government and therefore was 'more important than party affiliations.'[10] Later, in mid-summer, she declined a Government of India invitation to attend a health conference by politely pointing out that they were now merely 'caretakers' and thus should no longer be taking such initiatives.[11]

But the Muslim League, led by Jinnah, blanched at the Congress notion that the Plan's parameters would not be fully accepted. With a demand for an undefined 'Pakistan' on the table, they withdrew their support for the Plan completely, staying out of the Constituent Assembly and the interim government. In mid-August, the League called for a Direct Action Day to push their agenda and violence subsequently broke out across the country. The city of Calcutta was the hardest hit.

~

Nan took office on the first of April and was once again part of the UP Cabinet. This time around, she added registration to her portfolio of duties, which also included her original assignments in self-government and public health.[12]

Nan got right to work. Within weeks, she had issued a formal appeal to all residents of the state titled 'That we may live,' asking for everyone to do their part to battle plague and cholera. These diseases were once again ravaging the area, taking over 8000 lives in the first few months of 1946 alone.[13]

As the legislative session got under way, Pandit Govind Ballabh Pant, who had taken up his old post as chief minister as well, took the floor and launched into a touching tribute to Ranjit. Nan grew emotional and soon felt overwhelmed as others joined in. This was the first public recognition of her husband's contributions and of her own loss and felt long overdue.[14]

Chandralekha had returned from the United States soon after her mother, and the two had been inseparable ever since. They took up residence together in an official bungalow in Lucknow. Chandralekha boosted her mother's spirits and supported her personally and professionally.[15]

In the summer, Dorothy Dunbar Bromley joined Louis Fisher and several other prominent journalists and academics on a trip to India to examine food and famine conditions in the country and to get a better understanding of ground realities overall. Bromley took the opportunity to reconnect with Nan, who was then in Bombay for an informal meeting of the National Planning Committee.[16] Communal tensions between Hindus and Muslims were at a fevered pitch at that point and Nan reflected on the situation, concluding that the Congress had made a mistake in 1937 by going it alone and steamrolling political opposition. She regretted that they had not then been more sensitive and included the Muslim League in coalition governments, implying that that might have forestalled the developing crisis.[17]

~

Nan was elected to the new Constituent Assembly in mid-July.[18] She had been among the stable of prominent public figures who were immediately considered for a seat. Nan knew how significant this new body was, but she nonetheless felt forlorn, preoccupied with deteriorating conditions in the country. She worried about what exactly could be done. 'India is a difficult place these days—currents + cross-currents + so much bitterness,' she wrote to Nayantara. 'One looks around in vain for someone who will understand.' Nan grew particularly concerned about the 'terrific strain' her brother now bore. 'Heaven knows when + how we shall solve our difficulties.' Gandhi was by then on a 'peace march' through Bengal and she was glad for it. 'Peace, however, seems to be a forgotten word today + we are surrounded by conflict on every side,' she observed.[19]

Nan was cheered to have Chandralekha by her side and thought of her as a 'blessing.' But she did not 'feel happy about the life the poor child' was being subjected to. In the late spring, she sent her eldest daughter off to the UK for several weeks to look into further studies.[20]

Nan's various positions carried professional obligations, so she dashed between cities to attend a variety of receptions and meetings. By far the most interesting was the Science Congress held in Delhi. Nan got a thrill meeting some of the luminaries who attended, including Charles Galton Darwin, the grandson of the famous biologist who himself was a distinguished physicist and Master of Christ's College, Cambridge, and who laid the foundation stone of the Indian National Physical Laboratory while in town.[21]

But Nan anticipated that the Assembly would take up most of her time, or at least whatever remained when she was free of her official duties in Lucknow. So she opened up her schedule, cancelling a trip she had planned to make to Europe in August where she had been hoping to attend the Women's International Conference of Peace and Freedom in Luxembourg.[22]

~

The Asiatic Land Tenure and Indian Representation Bill passed South Africa's Parliament and became law in June.[23] It was popularly known as the Ghetto Act for its rendering of Indians as second-class citizens. The (British) Government of India immediately recalled its high commissioner and cancelled its trade agreement in protest, while the local community in South Africa began a campaign of satyagraha.[24] Nehru had earlier concluded that the South African issue had to be raised 'in the widest context' with a 'demand [for] 100 percent racial equality everywhere in the world.'[25] India thus pressed the first Secretary-General of the United Nations, Trygve Lie, to take up the matter through the General Assembly that fall.[26] As the case gained traction, rumours began to fly as to whom the new interim government would name to lead India's international efforts back in New York.[27]

~

Nan had been working on a village governance bill as part of her local self-government portfolio and had been spending her time preparing for opposition. She had had a particularly rough night and so was especially annoyed to be awakened by a telephone ringing loudly outside of her bedroom door. It was only 6 a.m. on an early September morning and Lucknow was hot and steamy. She was just not ready to face the day. So she tried to turn away and ignore the phone. But her attendant started knocking on her door and informed her that it was an important long-distance call she had to take. Nan reluctantly got out of bed, grumpily made her way to the hallway, and brusquely took the receiver. On the other end was Girja Shankar Bajpai, a career civil servant who had been Britain's agent-general in

D.C. during her American tour and who now served in the Ministry of External Affairs. 'I have been trying to reach you for half an hour,' he told her breathlessly. Nan was startled to her senses.

'You must come to Delhi immediately,' he told her. 'A plane is being sent to fetch you. The Prime Minister [ad interim, Nehru] wishes to see you as soon as you arrive. Mahatma Gandhi will see you at 5 p.m., and you are having dinner with the Viceroy [Wavell] at 8:30 p.m.' A short while later, Nan found herself in a limousine with Sir Girja, where she finally learned what was happening.

Lord Wavell, who had taken a keen interest in the matter at hand, and Gandhi had together chosen a delegation to represent India at the new United Nations, where the South Africa question was going to be taken up. The two men had personally selected Nan to lead the team. 'I can't possibly go,' she weakly protested. Pant was already upset that she was sitting in the capital rather than attending to her big bill. She questioned whether she could handle the task. 'You managed pretty well on your unofficial tour—I personally witnessed that,' Bajpai emphatically told her.

The meetings with the three men, whom she jokingly dubbed the Trinity, went better than expected. She enjoyed breakfast with her brother, who had a good laugh watching her squirm. Gandhi was the most paternal, talking up her abilities but laying down strict parameters in which she was to operate. He told her that the new UN should not be seen as a mere debating society, or as a society gathering. It was, instead, a place to forge 'friendships between nations' and where 'truth and ethics were the guidelines'. 'I want the delegation of my country to set an example. I shall be happy if we get votes, but I shall be most unhappy if these are gained in any manner that is divorced from our guidelines,' he said. Smuts was a friend, though the two disagreed on policy and politics. 'I would not like to lose his friendship and respect for the sake of gaining a majority vote,' he clarified.

Wavell was much less stiff than she had expected. He talked about her American trip, praised her skills, and said that she was the choice that had first come to mind. He added that he had told the prime minister that she would 'make a good Ambassador . . . when the time comes'.[28]

~

Nan landed at La Guardia field to clear skies and pleasant fall weather early in the day in mid-October. The journey had not gone as planned and she was quite exhausted. It had taken nearly a week to get there. Her plane had suffered engine trouble that caused an unexpected layover in Algiers, where she and her companions were served 'omelets for every meal'. She got stuck again in Shannon, Ireland, when the pilots of Trans World Airways (TWA) went on strike. So she and half of the Indian delegation only got to New York the day before the United Nations session was set to begin. She took no questions on landing and went straight to prepare in her rooms in the iconic Hampshire House, a prominent building overlooking Central Park from its south.[29]

In the weeks after it had been announced that she was to lead India's delegation to the UN, Nan had kept a low profile, spending a bit more time with Gandhi where she could, getting ready for her trip and working with her brother and the Ministry of External Affairs to draw up the rest of her team. The 'all-star cast' of delegates and alternates featured India's most savvy, diplomatic, and legal minds, if all men. Among the standouts were M.C. Chagla, a justice of the Bombay High Court, Krishna Menon, who was still head of the India League in London, K.P.S. Menon, India's agent-general in China, and P.N. Sapru, Sir Tej's son.[30]

Just before her departure, she broadcast her analysis of the South African situation and its ramifications and foreshadowed the case she hoped to make in New York. 'Little more than a year ago the organization of the United Nations came into existence ... "to reaffirm faith in fundamental human rights, in the dignity and worth of the human person and in the equal rights of men and women and of nations, large and small["], and the world, grown weary with much bloodshed and suffering, turned hopeful eyes towards the new organization,' she began, citing the preamble to the UNO's charter.

'Today fundamental rights, so recently promised to the peoples of the world, are being denied to Indians living in South Africa, thus raising a question of moral and human issues which contains the gravest implications for the future peace and progress of the world,' she continued. 'The Indian delegation's task will be to claim for Indians in South Africa the removal of all restrictions imposed on them on the grounds of race and colour, and ensure to them the fundamental freedoms to which they are entitled.'

'In fighting for those who share this denial of human rights, and who suffer under foreign control, India stands for equality between peoples and for the independence of all colonial areas. We believe that an enduring peace cannot be achieved so long as there is discrimination against one race by another . . . The Indian case in South Africa becomes, therefore, a test case not only on the question of human rights, but also for the purposes of principles of the charter itself,' she concluded.'[31]

~

The General Assembly opened to much fanfare. As host, New York City rolled out the red carpet, treating the 400-odd delegates and alternates of the fifty-one member states of the new world organization to a motorcade around the city capped by a full ticker tape parade down the legendary Canyon of Heroes, a stretch of Broadway from Battery Park to City Hall. This was followed by a luncheon at the Waldorf-Astoria and then another motorcade to take everyone to Flushing Meadows in the adjacent borough of Queens, where the meetings were to take place. There the delegates were treated to a UN welcoming reception, which in turn was followed by a US Presidential party hosted by Harry Truman back at the Waldorf.

Nan caught the eye almost immediately. The *New York Times* featured a large picture of her and the other Indian delegates along with its coverage.[32] The Associated Press, in a story commenting on everyone's appearance as the first plenary session got under way the next day, observed that the 'handsome, grey-haired' lead Indian delegate struck an 'unusual' sartorial note, 'wearing a graceful, magenta-colored sari'. This they happened to contrast, perhaps in a sign of things to come, with Field Marshal Smuts, whom they chastised for giving up his 'snappy-looking army uniform' in favour of 'anonymous navy blue'.[33]

As the only woman to lead any delegation, Nan automatically garnered attention wherever she went. She welcomed the interest but was glad that in fact there were a few other pioneering women participating as well, if all were not necessarily as out in front as she was. Among them were Eleanor Roosevelt and Helen Gahagan for the United States, Minerva Bernardino of the Dominican Republic, and Agnes McIntosh of New Zealand.[34]

Nan was unafraid to stand out in more meaningful ways. After President Truman opened the meeting with remarks committing the US to the new organization and the larger cause of peace, along with the specific goals of controlling atomic energy and weapons of mass destruction, most delegates applauded. Even the Soviet foreign minister, Vyacheslav Molotov, called it a 'good speech'. Nan, on the other hand, said it was a 'disappointment'. 'We've reached the stage where we are a little tired of hearing phrases and words,' she added, demanding action and implementation to match.[35]

~

Nayantara and Rita were awestruck by the whole affair. The two girls came to New York on weekends to spend time with their mother and to soak in as much as they could.

Nayantara was still at Wellesley and flew in on Fridays from Boston. Rita was by then studying art in New Hope, Pennsylvania and took the train into the city. Like her older sisters, she had matured into a capable, young woman in her own right, with a bubbly, fun-loving personality and unique, heavy-set eyes that vaguely recalled those of Hollywood actress Marlene Dietrich. Rita had graduated earlier that year from the Putney School, a progressive boarding school in Vermont built around the ideas of the philosopher John Dewey and spread across a large farm. Nayantara had been the only member of the family who had made it up for the big event.

The grandeur of the international event in New York City stood in sharp contrast to the serenity of Putney. Yet the girls fit in just as easily, 'colliding with celebrities of all walks of life in the corridors and elevators,' and chatting up 'the best-known political figures' of the age, 'not as great and famous statesmen, but as ordinary friendly people'.

Nayantara looked about idealistically and saw 'the greatest experiment in human relations ever launched'. She felt 'as though the nations had become fellow magicians banded together in a common effort to work the supreme magic—to secure peace for all time through calm discussion and mutual understanding'. Indeed, the overall 'atmosphere was exuberant and optimistic'.

The great hall in Flushing Meadows where the opening session was held was 'beautiful', with a 'giant map . . . sprawled across the wall behind the dais, a constant reminder of the oneness of the world.' It really seemed like the 'days of the Concert of Europe, and rule of the Big Three, or Four, or Five, were over'.

But for all the pomp and circumstance, for Nayantara and Rita, the entire gathering was something deeply personal. They both beamed with pride at the sight of India's first, autonomous delegation to such an event. The fact that it was led by their mother gave everything even more shine. The girls were convinced that their 'Mummie's capacity to work miracles in . . . [their own] lives would be extended to her delegation and to the General Assembly itself'. These were the sentiments of unconditionally loved and loving children for their parent, yet they were sage and prescient ones all the same.[36]

~

Jan Smuts felt well prepared. The UN Charter shielded member states from outside interference under Article 2(7), its domestic jurisdiction clause. As the General Assembly opened, Smuts attempted to deploy this rationale to head the Indians off at the pass, using his position on the agenda-setting General (Steering) Committee to 'block admission . . . [of the] complaint against racial discrimination in South Africa'. The committee comprised fourteen people, the president of the Assembly, the vice presidents, and the chairs of the various committees.[37] Smuts had an extra ace up his sleeve. He had pressured both the United States and Great Britain into supporting his position, using their practices of racial discrimination and fraught internal climates as leverage. So he sat back assuredly, secure in his sense that South Africa would carry the day.[38]

Justice Chagla represented the Indian position in the General Committee, where he mustered a fierce defence in 'the first international clash' within the new world body. The Indians had actually anticipated the domestic jurisdiction defence. In the preceding weeks, their team had meticulously analysed the issue and prepared several confidential memoranda advising on the best steps their delegation could make.

Essentially, they concluded, the matter was one of 'fundamental human rights'. South Africa was thus in contravention of the UN Charter, making the claim of domestic jurisdiction moot. But all of this, they further surmised, was ultimately too legalistic. Everything really depended on the facts of the case itself and the abilities of each of the speakers. The debate raged for 'two supperless hours' before Chagla prevailed. The UN would consider the South African question, in a compromise between the United States, Great Britain, and the Soviet Union, in simultaneous meetings of the Legal and Political Committees. But the 'real decision' was for the General Assembly to take up the matter thereafter and to then decide what action to take. The Indians were ecstatic. Round one belonged to them.[39]

~

Anticipation for Nan's opening remarks was at a fever pitch. She was already in the spotlight because of her wit, charm, oratory, and looks, and for the ceilings she had broken. But now she attracted even more attention as a powerful symbol of the colonized world. And the ruckus over South Africa ensured that she had top billing as one of the featured players at the gathering's main event.

'I stand before this great assembly—unique in the annals of human history where representatives of freedom-loving countries of the world are gathered together, not only to proclaim the adherence of my country to the principles and purposes of the United Nations Organization embodied in its Charter, but the determination of our people to help make it a reality,' she began, becoming the first woman to address the United Nations.[40]

Citing her brother, she said that 'India stands for the independence of all colonial and dependent peoples and their full right to self-determination.' She talked up India's strategic geographic, economic, and cultural significance and advanced the idea that her country deserved to be in the UN's most important administrative positions, including (non-permanently) on the Security Council. 'We believe that peace and freedom are indivisible and the denial of freedom anywhere must lead to conflict and war. We repudiate utterly the Nazi doctrine of racialism wheresoever and in whatever form it may be practised [sic]. We seek no dominion over others—we claim no privileged position over other peoples, but we do claim equal and honorable treatment for our people wherever they may go and we cannot accept any discrimination against them,' she said in a nod to the coming fight over South Africa.

'India firmly believes that imperialism, political economic or social and in whatever part of the world it may exist and by whomsoever it may be established and perpetuated, is totally inconsistent with the objects and purposes of the United Nations, and of its Charter. The sufferings, the frustration, the violation of human dignity and the challenge to world peace, freedom and security that Empire represents must be one of the prime concerns of this parliament of the world's people. Millions look to us to resist and end imperialism in all its forms, even as they rely upon us to crush the last vestiges of fascism and nazism.'

She took a moment to address one of the big controversies that had emerged over the last few days—the issue of the veto in the hands of the world's select, Great Powers. Many smaller countries wanted that power revoked. Nan defended it—with the fate of the League of Nations, which had fallen precisely because of the lack of participation of the Great Powers, informing her views. She warned against the power's abuse but only since any power could be abused.

Then she pivoted to discuss the problem of exclusion more broadly. 'We do not recognize caste, creed or sex as a barrier to progress . . . [And] we earnestly hope that women of all countries will have the occasion to participate more fully with men in all departments of life . . . thus creating a better and more balanced world.'

As she ended, she spoke from the mountaintop. 'We move, in spite of difficulties, toward a closer cooperation and the building of a world commonwealth. Let us do this with more deliberation and speed. The peoples of the world are well aware of our sentiments and look with expectation to their fulfillment. Let us recognize that human emotions and the needs of the world will not wait for an indefinite period. To this end let us direct our energies and remind ourselves that in our unity of purpose and action lies the hope of the world.'[41]

'U.N. Delegates Applaud Attack on Imperialism' blared the *Chicago Daily Tribune* the next day. *The New York Times* observed that Nan had repeatedly been cheered throughout her 'eloquent' remarks, while noting that she possessed the same 'fire and intensity' as 'her famous brother.' The *Christian Science Monitor* wrote that Nan had won 'the most enthusiastic applause to date' while the *Washington Post* gave her front-page coverage.

Nan had met the moment. She had been both fierce and inclusive. Her achievement was underscored when the head of Britain's delegation, Philip Noel-Baker—a Quaker, admirer of Gandhi, and eventual Nobel Peace Prize winner—came over once she was done and shook her hand.[42]

~

As proceedings got underway, Nayantara and Rita would occasionally join their mother, sometimes to sit in on meetings if they were interested and sometimes just to pass the time in the delegates' lounge, which would empty and fill with 'delegates, reporters, photographers, interpreters, and secretaries' in cycles as various sessions began and ended. When Nan was in the room, Nayantara would hover nearby in case her mother needed any assistance. She recalled several years later being called over on one occasion when Nan was in the midst of an interview and being told to tell her sister 'to stop darting to and fro'.

Rita was dashing from one end of the crowded room to the other, weaving between and then around one conversation after another. When Nayantara caught up with her to convey the message, she was wandering around in the hallway. Rita pleaded that her actions could not be helped. She was desperately trying to find a telephone. 'I'm so worried,' she explained. 'Jerry's wife is expecting a baby any moment.' He was desperate for news and she was trying to find out for him. Nayantara looked at her sister 'exasperated' and said reassuringly that Jerry, who was Nan's chauffeur, probably had several children and so could handle himself. At that, Rita broke into a story about Fred, who was driving Chagla around, and talked about his large family. This was to be Jerry's first child—though it was his wife's third since he was her second husband—and so he was understandably worried. Just then, Jerry appeared and asked if there was any word. 'I'll let you know as soon as I have some,' Rita told him soothingly.

They got the news when they finally returned home that evening. 'It's a girl!' Rita exclaimed. 'Just what Jerry wanted. Six pounds, twelve ounces.' Nan let out a sigh of relief. 'Now we can all relax,' she said.

~

Raphael Lemkin was feeling despondent. He had been hoping that the Nuremberg Trials, set up to mete out justice to perpetrators of Nazi atrocities, would establish a precedent for eventually 'bringing up the issue of a Genocide Convention at the U.N.'. He had travelled to the German city in May to witness discussions as they developed. But when the verdict was released in late summer, his 'most modest expectations were thwarted'.

In October, Lemkin was visiting his friend, the Pulitzer-winning *New York Times* reporter Otto Tolischus, and told him of his 'hopes . . . [and] disappointments'. Tolischus listened carefully, then told his friend to pick himself up and '[g]o ahead', assuring him of backing by the press. Newly encouraged, Lemkin raced to take action as the world body convened.

As he strategized on a way forward, he immediately dismissed the idea of approaching the Great Powers, which he felt were committed to certain agendas. He wandered the halls and mingled with people in the Delegates' Lounge and concluded that 'the mood was favorable . . . [with] an accumulation of constructive energies'. He felt there was a 'latent open-mindedness about humanitarian issues'. He only had to 'find the right people'. After some initial consultations, his plan 'in its entirety' was to combine 'the support of a Latin American republic', which came with regional solidarity, 'with that of a nation in Asia, which would attract through its culture and world position many other nations of the East'. Everyone else, he was sure, would then fall in line. He was going to make 'a "marriage" between the West and the East for the sake of this resolution'.

After drafting it and making mimeographed copies, Lemkin set off on his quest. In short order, he secured the support of two tiny states, Panama and Cuba, and through them, the rest of Latin America. As he contemplated what to do next, he struck up a conversation in the lounge with an old friend he happened to see, the feminist and liberal British politician, Dame Margery Corbett Ashby, and raised a 'bold idea'. What about approaching India? Ashby thought this was 'natural'. Together, they hurried to go meet Madame Pandit.

Nan was huddled with her team in a corner. Lemkin could not resist the Orientalist temptation and observed to himself that 'Indians, especially the older ones, always look . . . as if they have just finished a conversation with eternity and are about to begin another'. This, he thought, was because they had 'their feet firmly planted on the ground and use their tremendous intuition to penetrate the present quickly'.

After short introductions, Lemkin laid out his vision for 'the unity of mankind in diversity and the rule of law for the protection of national, racial, and religious groups against destruction. Through this protection,' he added, 'groups are permitted to exist and mankind is enriched—like a universal concert in which every nation plays its part.' Without hesitation, Nan replied that the people of India lived by this principle. 'We are many races and creeds. Still we have the concept of oneness. Our philosophers preached it. Gandhi worked for it.' She signed on as one of the sponsors of the resolution.[43]

Lemkin, elated, rushed the document over to the secretary-general's office and submitted it. From there, the resolution was brought before a plenary session of the General Assembly in early November and approved without comment, sending it on to the Sixth (Legal) Committee for discussion. Over several sessions and with some modifications from various members, including India represented by Chagla, the resolution was approved and sent back to the UNGA where it was eventually unanimously adopted with no further debate, declaring genocide a crime punishable under international law, instructing member states to pass domestic legislation accordingly, and requesting the appropriate arm of the United Nations to draw up a convention on the prevention of genocide.[44]

~

Meanwhile, temperatures inside the Joint Committee room were rising. Smuts and Nan had already directly but politely squared off in committee a few days prior, and she had gotten the better of him then, if by the slightest edge.[45] Where she had been witty and quick on her feet, he had come across as more plodding, reliant on a pre-prepared speech. Now, South African delegate G. Heaton Nicholls chose to take the low road and denigrate 'the social and religious customs' of Indians, and to cast all sorts of aspersions on various beliefs and practices. The committee had only been in session for a few days, but it already looked like it was about to go off the rails.[46]

Nan knew how much was at stake. With lines like, 'Jesus Christ himself, if he were in our midst today, would be a prohibited immigrant', she surgically eviscerated Nicholls. The entire presentation took about thirty minutes, during which members of both the committee and the general audience 'listened attentively'. When at last she was done, 'all parts of the Conference hall' broke into 'cheers', a most unusual occurrence.[47]

~

Nan continued to make waves in New York. The *Christian Science Monitor* singled her out as one of the UN's nine most important 'leading figures', along with Smuts, Eleanor Roosevelt and representatives from the United States, Soviet Union, Belgium, New Zealand and China. While the paper's correspondent criticized various folks for being 'cold', or for not smiling, or for getting a mixed reception, Nan was recognized as the '[c]hampion of women everywhere . . . An international Susan B. Anthony'.[48]

Nan's evenings were filled with glittering receptions and speaking engagements. All of these gatherings only furthered her celebrity. The *China Weekly Review* observed that she was 'very popular in both political and social circles in America'.[49]

Nan harnessed her star power to expand the reach and appeal of her message. She spoke in solidarity at the Abyssinian Baptist Church at the invitation of Paul Robeson and his Council on African Affairs.[50] Robeson had been touring out of the country at that time and had flown in specially to see Nan. When he first arrived back in New York, he came straight to Lake Success, where the UN meetings were being held. Seeing Nan in the lounge, he rushed to embrace her, lifting her off her feet, and loudly gushing 'Good to see you, little sister! I'm so proud of the wonderful job you're doing.' The other delegates 'looked on disapprovingly', though Nan just brushed this off.[51] Earlier, at a reception put on by the India League at the Hotel Gotham, she said her arguments on behalf of Indians in South Africa were meant to speak to 'the struggle of other persecuted people' around the world as well. 'Unless the people forming the world's policy today realize how deep the problem of discrimination is, we will find ourselves overwhelmed by the greatest conflict the world has ever known.'[52]

As much as she made the most of every such opportunity—and was glad to have chances to build partnerships—Nan still found such affairs to be overly 'stiff'. The so-called parties were even worse, each of which she dreaded as 'a deadly bore'. So she decided to throw a few more 'informal' gatherings herself, with hand-picked guests. One evening, she invited Phillipine diplomat Carlos Romulo, Eleanor Roosevelt, British Foreign Secretary Ernest Bevin, Soviet Permanent Representative Andrey Vyshinsky, and several other folks from Burma, Mexico, Denmark, and Great Britain. She was warned ahead of time by protocol minders that such a group did not usually mix and that she was headed for disaster. Instead, everyone drank and laughed the night away while enjoying a catered Indian meal and being entertained by Nan's children. Delegates later commended Nan for the memorable evening.[53]

Nan extended this type of kitchen diplomacy to all sorts of people, but she especially focused her energy on her fiercest opponent, Jan Smuts. He and she would frequently break off from the group at evening soirees and talk together. One such event was hosted by Helen Gahagan Douglas at the Waldorf-Astoria Hotel, where Smuts, Nan, and several others were treated to a World Friendship Dinner sponsored by the World Education Service Council. A group of children from diverse ethnic and national backgrounds performed a program 'dramatizing the concept of One World.'[54]

Nayantara attended quite a few such events and came to observe Smuts closely. She thought that the South African leader was 'impressive-looking, with his soldier's upright carriage and dignified bearing'. When her mother finally introduced her, Smuts gave her a 'sharp look' and said, 'You think I'm a horrible old man, don't you?' With Nan's hand in his, he added 'She is a like a daughter to me. Can you understand that? It grieves me to have to fight with her.' Nayantara, wise beyond her years, thought to herself: 'Then why do you?'[55]

~

South Africa settled on one last Hail Mary pass, a push to have the matter sent for adjudication to the International Court of Justice, where it could argue for domestic jurisdiction on a more legalistic basis. But the Indians outmanoeuvred the South Africans and their allies with some quick negotiations and carried the day.[56] When it was done, Nan magnanimously walked over to Smuts and embraced him. The serious game was racing to a dramatic close, with a head-to-head match-up between Vijaya Lakshmi Pandit and Jan Smuts set before the entire General Assembly.

~

Nan was the featured speaker at a mass meeting of the NAACP at a jazz club in Harlem. A thousand people were in attendance. Walter White introduced her as one of the two 'greatest women in the world' (along with Eleanor Roosevelt).[57]

'[T]he separation of the peoples of the world through suspicion and hatred,' a condition 'far worse than war,' now threatened peaceful human coexistence, she declared. She called for action to match the 'beautiful words' now being heard at the United Nations.

'There is only one problem in the world today, of which all others are merely a part,' she said. 'The name of that problem is the denial of justice. People are being told that they must wait for one thing or another, because of the many problems that must be solved first. But they cannot wait. The time has come when the colored peoples of the world must stand up and claim what is our own.'[58]

~

The plenary session of the General Assembly was scheduled for the evening of 7 December in Flushing Meadows. It was a particularly chilly night but a sizable general public crowd of about 600 turned out, in addition to the delegates, all decked out in their finest. It felt like 'a New York night at the theatre, the opera, or [perhaps most appropriately] a Madison Square Garden boxing bout'.

Observers commented on everyone's appearance as if they were on the celebrity red carpet, focusing on various 'gowns . . . bright scarves, and glistening evening bags'. But, the *New York Times* wrote, the 'center of attraction for fashion was the Indian delegate, Mrs. Vijaya Lakshmi Pandit, who was accompanied by her two young daughters, Rita and Tara, all wearing flowered saris and fur jackets.'[59]

At last, it was time. Smuts came to the podium and defended his country, charging that it would be 'monstrous' for the UN to 'condemn' a member state. He expressed sympathy with the Indian position but resolutely stuck to his claim that there were thorny legal questions involved and that the matter thus had to be sent to the International Court of Justice for adjudication. When he was finished, a US legal advisor, Charles Fahy, leapt up to endorse the South African position, saying that it was 'eminently proper' for the 'World Court' to weigh in.

Then Nan, 'elegant and commanding' in a black, silk sari, strode down the aisle and onto the stage.[60] 'It is too late now to argue that fundamental violations of the Charter are matters of domestic jurisdiction of Members States,' she began. 'If this was the case, the Charter would be a dead letter and our professions about a world free from inequalities of race, free from want and free from fear are empty mockery.'

'I want to carry the Assembly with me in these matters which, I submit, are common ground. If I do, as I must, unless the 54 nations assembled here place on the Charter a meaning and significance far below what its words convey, what its spirit demands, and indeed what we have asked the world to accept . . . then the issue no longer rests with India or South Africa but with us, the nations of the world assembled, who have taken upon themselves the defense of the law of ethics and morality of nations.'

'Therefore, I deliberately refrain from entering into legal and meticulous arguments. The essence of the South African case is, not the denial of the law and practices that we complain of, but on the other hand its assertion that segregation and discrimination is essential to the maintenance of western standards of life, that . . . the presence of Indians and other Asiatics and all non-Europeans is a threat to Western civilization. Western civilization is not confined to any continent and on the theory of the Union Government, its defence essentially demands segregation as part of the world social system. In other words, the Ghetto is to be legalized as part of the world's stable organization and of this Assembly.' These last words echoed across the chamber and stung deeply, the significance not lost on any who had come to grasp the horrors unleashed by the Axis during World War II.[61]

'Mr. President,' she continued, 'let us attempt to realize the tremendous responsibilities that we as members of the United Nations have at this stage. We are trustees of the future, architects of the new world. If we continue to act in accordance with old prejudices and old conceptions which we have so often condemned, we shall betray the trust reposed in us by millions of voiceless people who because of their creed or colour have been relegated to positions of inferiority and are looking up to us for justice, and it is only on the foundation of justice that we can erect a new world order. We have given much thought to the problem arising from the invention of the atom bomb which threatens the future of mankind, and yet we forget that forces generated by maladjustments of human relations are perhaps equally powerful and an equal threat to the future of the world ... Forces and feelings which move the minds of men are often more far-reaching in their effects than material forces.'

'We must create for the United Nations the abounding confidence of the common people in it as the defender of justice, public law and morality. This is what I ask you to do.'

'I ask for no pity, no mercy, no concession for the Indian population of South Africa who have in my humble opinion raised the standard of human dignity by inviting suffering and offering resistance to injustice. Friends, they have not lowered the standard of Western or any civilization.'

'Mine is an appeal to conscience, to the conscience of the world which this Assembly is. I will say no more.'[62]

She had spoken for about fifteen minutes. As she turned to make her way back to her seat, the Assembly roared its approval, with 'loud and prolonged applause' and 'one of the warmest ovations ever accorded a speaker [at any of the international organization's sessions].' Nan acknowledged the support she had won with a smile.[63]

After two additional hours of debate, the meeting was adjourned until the morning. The next evening, a formal vote was scheduled. South Africa and its allies successfully created one more procedural hurdle, arguing that if the matter was truly 'important', as the Indians had claimed, then it required a two-thirds majority to pass. The bar was placed as high as possible, and the Indians grew doubtful. All sound went out of the room as the votes started to roll in around 2 a.m., as everyone held their breath. But the verdict was soon clear. The Indians had triumphed.

Nayantara leapt up from her chair and ran over to her mother, who was still seated at the delegation table. She gave her a joyful kiss which suddenly could be heard in the entire chamber as it was picked up by Nan's live microphone.[64] It was just the spark the crowd needed. The hall broke out into 'tremendous applause'.[65] People from all over the room swarmed forward to congratulate Madame Pandit on her 'great, hard-won . . . victory over racial discrimination'.[66] Emotional delegates started crying for joy, jumping on desks, and embracing one another.[67] Heaton Nicholls looked on glumly from his seat as admirers followed Nan into the lounge next door. Nayantara covered her mother in kisses again.

Nan was overwhelmed by it all. 'At this moment of success I feel utterly humble,' she said. 'I wish to express the deep gratitude of India to all those nations whose support made it possible for the cause we brought before the United Nations to be vindicated. Our faith in the United Nations has been fully justified.'[68]

~

'UN Assembly Cheers Mrs. Pandit, Greets Smuts with Silence.' The prime minister of South Africa was welcomed by such headlines out of Pretoria just as he was touching down in London. He had left New York by plane the night before, skipping out on the big vote.[69]

Before his departure, Nan had walked over to him. 'I hope I have not said anything of a personal nature to hurt you,' she had explained. 'My instructions from Gandhiji before I left home were that I should shake your hand and ask your blessing for my cause.' He looked at her a long time before warning darkly, with her hand in his, 'My child, you may win, but this will be a hollow victory for you.'[70]

This would prove true. South Africa would soon thereafter consolidate its racial policies into apartheid. Nan would continue to spearhead the charge against such engrained discrimination for years, handing off the torch to others when they assumed the leadership roles she once held.

But years later, while acknowledging such setbacks and continuing struggle, she would maintain that what had happened in the assembly chamber was of singular importance. At a personal level, she recalled her landmark achievement at the United Nations as her greatest accomplishment. She selected this episode as 'the time of her life' on an eponymously named BBC program with Mark Tully that asked celebrities and world figures to discuss the defining moments of their careers.[71] She noted that the vote count was particularly satisfying emotionally, just 'the most spectacular thing'. Asked to reflect on how she had managed to pull it all off, she graciously credited her success not only to her rhetorical prowess but to the strength of her whole team. She also confessed that she was aided by her youth and her good looks as well, admitting that she had 'unashamedly' used 'every weapon' in her 'arsenal' to win.[72]

~

The Black press and race justice activists savoured the defeat dealt to white supremacy. The *New York Amsterdam News* wondered on its front page how South Africa would 'save them[selves] from isolation in one world' now that they had been handed such a 'humiliating' setback. The paper noted that 'all comers,' even the 'deceptive and hypocritical . . . Sir Hartley Shawcross . . . and Charles Fahy' were no 'match' for the 'brilliant and silver-tongued' oratory of Vijaya Lakshmi Pandit.[73]

The paper called the victory 'one for our side' in an editorial, evocatively writing that '[r]acial jim crow . . . [had been] blasted as out of line'. They celebrated the stand that the 'diminutive and charming Indian delegate', who they noted had 'broadly identified herself with the struggle of all colored peoples against discrimination,' had taken against 'the full battery of American arrogance, English chicanery, and their bootlicking stooges'. 'It now remains for us,' they wrote, 'and for all who believe in "One World", to work that first step out to its fuller conclusion of justice for all men everywhere.'[74]

The *Atlanta Daily World* headlined a front-page story 'Madam Pandit Leads Fight for Minorities' and noted that she was also urging 'negro unity for independence'. They ended with an observation and a plea: 'Mahatma Gandhi's admonition to his countrymen that freedom is not a cheap commodity may wisely be shared with the American Negro. Rise up, O men of fortune . . .!'[75]

Writing in The *Chicago Defender*, W.E.B. Du Bois declared that '[e]very Negro organization in the United States ought to send an official note of thanks to Madame Vijaya Lakshmi Pandit', adding that she 'should be known to all persons of African descent . . . as the leader of the successful assault upon the color line . . .' He observed that she had not 'confine[d] her attack . . . to the Indian problem. [Rather] [s]he repeatedly spoke of the situation of the Natives and the disabilities under which they labor'. He praised her for her 'unselfish and courageous attitude' and wrote that he hoped that it would spur solidarity and a more united front against racial injustice everywhere moving forward.[76]

~

Nan headed home to India shortly after the UN wrapped up its proceedings. Just before her journey, she was feted at a dinner at the Capitol Hotel put on by the Provisional World Council of Dominated Nations, the West Indies National Council, and the One World Association. Two hundred and fifty people from ten nations attended to recognize Nan along with two other UN colleagues for their 'outstanding advocacy of independence for subject peoples and human rights for all'.[77] Other honours continued to pour in from all corners thereafter as well. She was flooded with telegrams of admiration and congratulations from ordinary Americans as well as from many Indians in South Africa.[78] The *Scotsman* noted that the Indian delegation had been the most successful of the Assembly, having achieved 'virtually all of their objectives,' thanks almost entirely to the 'passionate eloquence' of their 'brilliant and beautiful' leader, whom they also considered 'the chief personal success of the Assembly . . . if Mrs. Roosevelt is excepted'.[79] Grace Lancaster, in India for the annual meeting of the AIWC, told a gathering in Bombay that 'Mrs. Vijaya Lakshmi Pandit has made history and women all over the world are proud of her'.[80] This was echoed by the AP, which singled out Nan, Eleanor Roosevelt and Bodil Begtrup of Denmark, as women who had to be recognized for their 'star roles of world importance'.[81] A short while later, Mary McLeod Bethune named twelve people to the 1946 National Council of Negro Women Honor Roll. Nan joined renowned contralto Marian Anderson and Hollywood legend Ingrid Bergman on the list.[82]

Just before she boarded her flight at La Guardia, she turned to address the waiting press corps. With Nayantara and Rita flanking her side, and wearing some gardenias presented as a parting gift, she said that she was pleased that the United Nations had 'shown itself as a guardian of human rights' and that this 'augur[ed] well for the future of the organization and civilization'. 'To the people of the United States, great and small, who have encouraged us by their affection and support, I send my warmest greetings,' she concluded in farewell.[83]

The Nehru clan in the early twentieth century: (L to R) Swarup Rani, Krishna (Betty), Motilal, Sarup (Vijaya Lakshmi Pandit), Jawaharlal

Swaraj Bhawan (the original Anand Bhawan)

The Nehru clan in the 1920s
Front L to R: Swarup Rani, Motilal, Kamala
Back L to R: Jawaharlal, Vijaya Lakshmi Pandit, Krishna, Indira, Ranjit Pandit

Vijaya Lakshmi Pandit with Subhas Chandra Bose and Jawaharlal, Calcutta, circa 1928

The new Anand Bhawan

Vijaya Lakshmi Pandit walking with Ranjit Pandit, circa 1930s

Vijaya Lakshmi Pandit after becoming a minister in 1937 in Uttar Pradesh

Vijaya Lakshmi Pandit attends a meeting of the Congress Working Committee, with Sardar Patel and Mahatma Gandhi, Anand Bhawan, 1940

Vijaya Lakshmi Pandit at the wedding of Indira and Feroze Gandhi, 1942

Vijaya Lakshmi Pandit at the San Francisco Conference, 1945

Syud Hossain

Vijaya Lakshmi Pandit speaks on the South African question at the United Nations, 1946

Isamu Noguchi, Mrs Vijaya Lakshmi Pandit, 1947. Plaster. 10 1/8 x 7 x 9 5/8 in. (25.7 x 17.8 x 24.4 cm). Collection of The Isamu Noguchi Foundation and Garden Museum, New York. The Noguchi Museum Archives, 00170.

Vijaya Lakshmi Pandit with Albert Einstein, Jawaharlal and Indira, Princeton, 1949

Vijaya Lakshmi Pandit with Mary McLeod Bethune,
Harry Truman and Ralph Bunche

Vijaya Lakshmi Pandit with Minerva Bernardino and Ana Figueroa
at the opening of the fifth session of the UN Human Rights
Commission (1949)

Vijaya Lakshmi Pandit with Dr B.R. Ambedkar at a dinner party

Vijaya Lakshmi Pandit with Jawaharlal in the UK, circa 1950

Vijaya Lakshmi Pandit watches last of US wheat for India donation being funneled aboard Liberty Ship, 1951

Vijaya Lakshmi Pandit with Lester Pearson and Dag Hammarskjöld at the United Nations after being elected President of the UN General Assembly, 1953

Eleanor Roosevelt presenting Madame Pandit with a gavel, 1953

Pandit family circa 1950s, at Teen Murti Bhawan.
(L to R) Vijaya Lakshmi Pandit, Ashok Mehta,
Chandralekha, Gautam Sahgal, Nayantara

Vijaya Lakshmi Pandit with Winston Churchill, Chartwell 1954

UK Queen Mother confers honorary degree on Vijaya Lakshmi Pandit, 1955

Vijaya Lakshmi Pandit with Krishna Menon during the Suez Crisis, 1956

Vijaya Lakshmi Pandit with Jawaharlal and Krishna (Betty)

Vijaya Lakshmi Pandit with Queen Elizabeth II in India, 1961

Vijaya Lakshmi Pandit campaigning in Phulpur in the 1960s

Vijaya Lakshmi Pandit with Rita, Chandralekha, Nayantara, and Padmaja Naidu, 1968

Vijaya Lakshmi Pandit campaigning against Indira Gandhi in 1977

Edmund Halliday 1956 portrait of Vijaya Lakshmi Pandit, hanging in Somerville College, University of Oxford

Commemorative Stamp of Vijaya Lakshmi Pandit, 2000

CHAPTER ELEVEN

# Love of Worker Bees

In December 1946, the British House of Commons opened a debate on the future of India, featuring Sir Stafford Cripps on behalf of the government and Winston Churchill, who now sat in opposition. The latter raised issues related to flaring communal tensions in the country. Nan sat in the gallery listening intently. She was seated next to Muhammad Ali Jinnah.

In London, she had checked into the Savoy for a brief layover. As she made her way around the city, she was suddenly struck by how 'terribly shabby + small' everything seemed after New York. She compared dining at the grand Dorchester to eating at a second-rate restaurant in America's financial capital. She spoke at a meeting of the India League and ran a few errands, immediately regretting seeing a doctor about some skin issues she was having, for she was now on orders to 'cut out tea + coffee, fried food + spices'.

The debate between Cripps and Churchill was held in the House of Lords since the lower house had been 'bombed out of existence' by the Germans during the war. As various members rose to speak, other members put their legs on desks, fell asleep, and otherwise were quite noisy. Nan was struck by the spectacle of it all, likening it to a comic opera. Privately, she thought that Cripps was 'ineffectual' and that Churchill, while 'mischievous', cut 'a pathetic figure' who had 'lost much of his old force'. When asked to offer her thoughts on the former prime minister's comments, she suggested that he ought to 'keep silent about India, for God's sake'. She suggested it was time for Indians to 'fulfill our own destiny'.[1]

~

The interim Indian Government had begun internally discussing exchanging missions with the Soviet Union almost immediately upon assuming office. Throughout that year, Indian representatives had unofficially probed Moscow's ability to provide the subcontinent with much-needed rice and other cereals, to meet the demand caused by wartime shortages and the prospects of yet another major famine. Nehru had even dispatched Krishna Menon to unofficially broach the subject with Soviet Foreign Minister Molotov in September. Officials eventually concluded that reciprocity was a better approach and investigated the possibility of a trade, not just of grains for a desired commodity like jute, but of officials as well.

Indian government officials debated on how best to proceed before settling on the idea of sending representatives to Moscow to negotiate. Krishna Menon was to join the more seasoned K.P.S. Menon (no relation) on a trip to the U.S.S.R. following the conclusion of the UN General Assembly meetings in New York. But there Nan had had the opportunity to discuss matters directly with Molotov and that took care of matters. The follow-up trip would not be required. The Indians and Soviets were going to open formal diplomatic relations with each other.[2]

~

The Constituent Assembly had been meeting for a little over a week. Nan was received by cheers and applause when she entered the chamber for the first time to present her official credentials to Rajendra Prasad, who was presiding as chair.[3]

The scene had been much the same the previous day as she first alighted from her aircraft at Delhi's airport. There she had been received by Sardar Patel, Sarojini Naidu, Govind Vallabh Pant, Hansa Mehta, and, of course, Chandralekha.[4]

Around Christmas, she gave wide-ranging remarks on her experiences at the UN and her hopes for a future Indian foreign policy at a gathering of diplomats in Delhi. Her brother, Khan Abdul Ghaffar Khan (Frontier Gandhi), and Asaf Ali also attended. She praised both the United States and Russia while criticizing Britain for its behaviour in Flushing Meadows and for the anti-India propaganda it had pushed.⁵ She repeated many of these points at the Lucknow City Congress several days later.⁶

~

Nan recalled that she had moved the very first resolution in the United Provinces Assembly following the 'inauguration of Provincial Autonomy' in 1937, calling then for the establishment of a Constituent Assembly that could draft a constitution for a free India. It was thus a full circle moment for her to be standing in the well of just such a chamber in January 1947 speaking on behalf of the Aims and Objects Resolution 'proclaim[ing] India an Independent, Sovereign Republic'. In her first (and what would be only) major remarks, she lamented imperialism's continuing grip on global affairs and noted that Western powers continued to dominate in the new United Nations to the detriment and exclusion of places like Asia. But, to cheers, she added that 'it was perhaps the first time in history that at the last United Nations Assembly, a country, not free itself, was able to raise its voice for the freedom of oppressed and dependent peoples all over the world'. India thus had an important and constructive role to play moving forward, to champion high ideals, and so, she told her colleagues that it was 'not only to ourselves we owe a duty but also to the world which looks to us'.

With strain and mistrust between religious communities, particularly Hindus and Muslims, on the rise, and with the British stoking such passions at various opportunities, she tried to speak reassuringly, highlighting the aim to provide 'the fullest social, economic and cultural justice to individuals and groups'. She emphasized the fact that people had obligations as well as rights and that everyone had to think of their responsibilities to each other and the larger society as well.

Then she reaffirmed India's long-standing commitment to democracy and its intent not only to terminate 'imperialist domination' but also to build up a 'social, democratic State . . . [that would] point the path of lasting peace and progress to the world.' 'In this age of the building up of one world, we cannot talk of separate nations. We have to work in order to build up one world, of which India shall be a worthy partner . . . Our contribution to the future is one of neutralization of political and social discontents and to that end,' she said, 'we must work by the establishment of freedom in our own country and helping all those who strive for freedom in the world . . . A world which is divided into groups cannot be secure.'[7]

~

Nan had a lot on her mind. Just as she was delivering her remarks to the Constituent Assembly in Delhi, John Foster Dulles, a rising US Republican star who had served as a delegate to the General Assembly the previous month, was causing a stir half a world away. He had just a few days earlier warned about Soviet expansionism before the National Publisher's Association, in the process claiming that 'Soviet Communism exert[ed] a strong influence through the interim Hindu government.'[8] This raised hackles in India and both Nan and her brother were called on to respond. Nehru obliquely said that Dulles had a 'lack of knowledge of facts' and left it at that. Nan was more forceful, calling the American's views a 'complete misapprehension'. 'The cause of dependent peoples is one which India has always espoused; and her attitude towards trusteeship is more in accordance with President Roosevelt's own conception than Mr. Dulles's,' she said. 'India, far from blindly following alien influences, Communist or otherwise, will evolve her policy in accordance with her own interests and her own conceptions of right and wrong. Mr. Dulles should know this. His reference to the Government of India, in which Hindus and Muslims are both represented, as the "Hindu Interim Government" is altogether gratuitous.'[9] When asked by American journalists for further comment, Dulles demurred.[10] He may have known better than to get into a war of words with Nan. His brother Allen had spent time with her in Allahabad when she was fourteen and had told his family about his high impressions of her.[11]

Betty, in the meantime, was causing other headaches. She had embarked on a book tour of the United States, with every intention of outshining her sister.[12] Instead, she was called a 'rather modest . . . comely substitute' for 'the vibrant, fascinatingly charming Indian leader, Madam Vijaya Lakshmi Pandit', who was the real attraction everyone 'had been looking forward to with great anticipation'.[13]

And Nan continued to generate news even in her absence, such as when she sent in remarks, along with Albert Einstein, to the World Government News Awards, an event sponsored by the new United World Federalists, and which that year was honouring, among others, the *New Yorker* magazine for a story by E.B. White.[14] Clark Getts in turn tried to coax Nan into returning to the United States for another round of speaking, going so far as to say that he believed it to be of greater importance than anything she could be doing in India.

Betty had picked up on these slights and had started falsely telling friends back home that 'the papers in America' were 'saying the most ghastly things' about Nan. She also said that sales clerks kept telling her that 'Mrs. Pandit [had] bought' this or that in the hopes of enticing her to make similar purchases. Betty held up two obscenely expensive fur coats—worth an eye-popping $3200 together—as examples of things her sibling had supposedly bought.

Nan grimaced at the insinuations about the purchases, since they appeared to be figments of her sister's imagination. But she laughed it all off, joking that Getts' persistence was probably so that he could get his wife, the famous actress Osa Johnson, some new clothing. More generally, she privately wrote to Rita, she was glad for any happiness or success that came Betty's way.[15]

There were things of greater importance to worry about in any event. Communal violence between religious communities had broken out all over the country and various parts of the northwest already lay 'in ruins' from it. Nan fretted over every 'ghastly' and 'tragic' detail and especially the terrible toll the 'great tention [sic] + suspicion' was taking on her brother.[16]

Closer to home, she had to tend to Rita, who needed to undergo a procedure in the United States for a narrow pelvis. Nan coordinated the 'adjustment' with Nayantara and the Walshes, who promised to look after everything. But the doctor undertook a full operation when he went in, scaring Rita with 'a lot of irrelevant' information before and after. Nan had to comfort her daughter from afar, reassuring her that 'a narrow pelvis is a nuisance but thats [sic] about all'. She confided that Indira and she herself had the same issue with 'no trouble at all. She encouragingly wrote in typical good humor that Rita would be 'ever so fit now', so she had to 'hurry up + get strong', so that she could compete with Padmaja Naidu in alluring posturing.[17]

Through all of this, Nan found joy in Indira's two young sons, Rajiva and Sanjaya, who always enthralled her with their respective charms and 'laughs + kicks + talks'.[18] Together with a house that was always full of guests, she was constantly occupied. She also fussed over Chandralekha, who had started to accompany her mother on various matters. 'Whatever else may happen to us as a family,' Nan wrote to Nayantara, 'we certainly shall not die of boredom'.[19]

~

The United Nations had begun broadcasting basic reports about its activities around the world and had found a particularly receptive audience in the Soviet Union. The officially sanctioned Moscow Radio Committee supplemented the reporting with more elaborate programming of its own, featuring government recordings of UN affairs and interviews with various representatives on international matters. These popular broadcasts were then sent out to the entire country. Among those featured was a 'special talk in English' by Vijaya Lakshmi Pandit.[20]

~

The Indian Council on World Affairs had spent weeks putting together a massive, first-of-its-kind gathering of Eastern countries to foster dialogue between them and to lay the groundwork for 'closer cooperation'. The Asian Relations Conference, as it was called, was scheduled to be held in Delhi in late March, with about 250 representatives from twenty-five countries meeting on the grounds of the city's majestic Purana Qila (Old Fort). Nan was a delegate, together with an all-star cast that included the likes of Maulana Azad, Dr B.R. Ambedkar, G.D. Birla, Rajkumari Amrit Kaur, and Sarojini Naidu, who served as leader.[21]

The event stemmed from the experiences of India's unofficial counter-delegation to the San Francisco conference. There, Nan, Syud Hossain, Shiva Rao, Shridharani, J.J. Singh and Anup Singh had all felt that 'Asia and Africa were grossly under-represented'. As they discussed the topic, the idea for a meeting of nations exclusively from these otherwise neglected parts of the world, sponsored by India, gradually took shape. Shiva Rao had then brought the proposal formally before the Executive Council of the ICWA, which green-lit the project. Nehru was enthusiastic and 'enlarged its scope.'[22]

While the focus remained on Asia, people from all over the world, including observers from the United States, United Kingdom, Australia, and New Zealand, attended. At a personal level, Nan found the Tibetan delegation the most 'picturesque.'[23]

Unity was the overriding theme of the event—Gandhi used his brief remarks to talk of his belief in One World. So it was surprising when Nan struck a slightly discordant note, albeit one that was discreetly supported by her brother. A committee working on migration issues and racial problems proposed several measures for participating governments to take up. Leelamani Naidu, one of Sarojini's daughters, wanted official recommendations to be made. Nan immediately seconded the idea, causing an uproar by saying that the 'whole purpose' of the gathering was 'to make specific recommendations to our governments'. When organizers from the ICWA rushed to the microphone to remind everyone that the conference was unofficial and thus unable to put forward resolutions, Nan defended the need to act forcefully, declaring any inability to do so would be shameful, particularly if Asian countries wanted to champion equity and justice—essential for true unity—in larger fora like the UN.[24]

But Nan did not let her determination to stand for principle, or her defeat on the issue of the formal resolution, keep her from adhering to the primary message of the conference. When Jewish and Palestinian delegates looked close to clashing, she 'persuaded them to drop the matter and shake hands'.[25]

~

The Attlee government had announced in late February its intention to transfer power formally to India by the summer of 1948. Lord Louis Mountbatten arrived in India as the new Viceroy on the same day that the Asian Relations Conference opened.[26]

Nan's mood swung up and down with the shifting winds, as the news in the air alternately brought hope and despair. She was happy that the end of the status quo was near.[27] But she also felt despondent about the 'bloodshed + terror' stalking the land, as religious communities tore each other apart. By June, she knew the Congress had accepted the partition of the subcontinent in principle, though it went against their previous pledges and filled everyone with 'great sorrow.' What exactly any of this meant was still 'very complicated', with some even entertaining the notion of India gaining independence while Pakistan remained within the Empire.[28]

~

Nan had two bills to shepherd through the UP Legislative Assembly under her ministerial portfolios in public health and local self-government. The first one, regarding the provincialization of hospitals, was essentially a carry forward of earlier legislation that coordinated administration and ownership between the state government and local bodies, and it sailed through with 'negligible opposition'.[29] The second, the Gaon Hukumat Bill, empowered local village panchayats (councils) with the aim of revitalizing local communities and giving them control over their own lives, but this faced opposition from the Muslim League over representation.[30] Nan had to put in a 'great deal of time' and personally intervene on several occasions to push the bill through to its eventual successful passage.[31] She breathed a sigh of relief when it was done.[32]

~

It was no small matter for an as-yet still colonized country like India to open mutual diplomatic relations with other countries, for it also signalled recognition of the legitimacy of their interim and soon to be independent government. And all of this had to be simultaneously approved and facilitated by the outgoing power—Great Britain—which inevitably was informed by its perspectives. But many officials on both sides worked in good faith to get everything done.

Among the first foreign affairs choices India faced was where to open embassies. They did not have the resources, either in terms of 'expert staff' or financial resources to build a presence in every major capital at once, let alone one in every country. So strategic choices had to be made, each a signal about India's estimation of a selected partner's place in the global hierarchy of powers. To get around this as much as possible, India could economically maximize the use of its limited resources, using a popularly replicated American precedent with Tehran and Kabul to have one head of mission accredited for multiple countries at the same time, with lower-level consular offices handling day-to-day matters in the countries where the head envoy was not resident. Only the world's largest, most complex and most significant powers—like the United States, the USSR, and China—would have unique ambassadors dedicated solely to them.[33]

Opening each new mission required attention to the smallest detail. This was especially true for Moscow, which had many unique circumstances. Although Russia had long been a major power, its diplomatic relationships with many countries had been altered by the Revolution and the secrecy that Stalinism thereafter further imposed. The situation had somewhat improved over the course of World War II but many peculiarities still remained, and paranoia was tightening its already strong hold. Many powers, including important ones, for instance, were forced to work out of hotels in the country rather than being accorded permanent facilities.

A British officer at their Moscow Embassy provided a detailed note on what diplomatic life was like there and urged the Indians to prioritize certain needs, foremost among them acquiring an actual facility for a proper embassy. The officer also commented on everything from supplies and petrol to security and newspapers and highlighted especially the need to think about things like furniture, recommending Sweden as the best source for such acquisitions.[34]

After internal deliberations, the Indians decided to finalize an agreement to establish relations through an informal conversation conducted by their new Chinese Ambassador, K.P.S. Menon, in Nanking. Menon reported back in early April with urgency, saying that 'no further time should be lost' in moving forward at the highest levels as tensions between the Soviets and the Americans were on the rise and that any delay could be interpreted as a slight. The very next day, the interim government drafted a carefully worded communique.[35]

This was released to the press shortly thereafter, a little under two weeks after the Asian conference came to an end. Nan's name immediately started circulating as the rumoured choice for ambassador.³⁶ But it was not until a month later that the decision was formally made and announced. Vijaya Lakshmi Pandit would be India's first ambassador to the Soviet Union.³⁷

~

Isamu Noguchi felt the stars aligning. The accomplished artist and architect had just done the set designs that spring for an elaborate new performance by his frequent collaborator, the pioneering dancer, Martha Graham.³⁸ Weeks later, he publicly premiered what would become his most iconic creation, an elegant glass coffee table balanced on three points of overlaid wooden legs.³⁹ Now he hoped his streak would extend into matters of the heart. He wanted to marry his love, a young woman twenty-three years his junior: Nayantara Pandit.

The two had met back in 1943 but had kindled a romance only the year previous in 1946. They saw reflections of themselves in each other, sharing Asian and American origins and influences, and a passion for the art world and all that it had to offer.

Nayantara said later that he had swept her off her feet. Noguchi too was head over heels. He had proposed marriage, but she had turned him down, firstly because of the age difference but also because she thought her family simply would disapprove. But Noguchi was determined to prevail.

Nan, in the meantime, was preparing for her move to Moscow. She wrote frantically to her children, informing them of her imminent departure and of her desire for them to join her once again. But she was unsure what advice exactly to offer since so much of her own life was up in the air. In the interim before the announcement of her appointment was made public, she felt she could be made to go at a moment's notice. Meanwhile, the political situation on the ground was tense and tenuous and she continued to worry about her brother's burdens. Finally, she told her children to come to India to see her, then stay with Nehru for a while, and then eventually join her in the Soviet Union. But Nayantara protested and asked to remain with Rita in the United States for the remainder of the summer. Telegrams and letters between mother and daughter flew back and forth before Nan eventually relented.⁴⁰

'In public,' Nayantara would later observe, Nan 'projected a serenity people sometimes described as spiritual. In private life, she was embroiled in a hectic daily activity . . . laden with an almost unceasing aura of crisis . . . The lightning speed with which she made and unmade decisions sometimes left us dazed'. Even so, there was never a question of motive. Behind her every action was 'a continuous and lavish generosity associated with love and warmth and plenty'.[41]

~

The Metropol was one of the grandest hotels in Moscow, designed in Art Nouveau style by varying teams of architects during the twilight of the Tsar's rule in the early twentieth century. Its iconic façade was so well designed that it had withstood artillery during the Russian Revolution with relatively little damage. The elegant main dining hall inside was located under a magnificent glass canopy and glittered with crystal chandeliers from the imperial era. The building was situated in the heart of the city, adjacent to Red Square on one side and the world-renowned Bolshoi Theater on the other. It served as the centre of diplomatic life in the country and was the base of operations for most foreign delegations.[42] Nan and her team of officials and staff were put up there upon their arrival in the Soviet Union in early August 1947.

It had been an eventful journey. She had left New Delhi on the third, making pitstops in Karachi, Basra, and Baghdad before taking a longer break in Tehran. There she had been greeted by a 'big reception' where the local 'enthusiastic' Indian community, comprised entirely of Sikhs, had 'turned out in full force'. Reza Hekmat, who would later that year become prime minister for several days, oversaw the visit.

Accommodations were provided at a hotel just beyond the city limits where Nan and the others were treated to a magnificent seven-course lunch that included caviar, vodka, saffron chicken, and rice pilaf. Nan thought the food simply divine though she and the others were unable to 'appreciate the caviar + vodka', much to the chagrin of her hosts. The foreign minister met her for tea afterwards and then later that evening entertained the whole group at their hotel over an elaborate dinner. There, he and Hekmat discussed with Nan a proposal she had brought from Nehru for the two countries to formally exchange high-level emissaries. The next day, she met with the Shah's sister, Princess Pahlavi, attended another reception, and was hosted by the British ambassador for dinner on a lawn, which was momentarily interrupted when some guests briefly called out in support of Mohammed Ali Jinnah and Pakistan. Nan took it all in stride.

From Iran, Nan made stopovers in Baku and Stalingrad before arriving exhausted in Moscow. She was greeted on the tarmac by the Soviet protocol officer as well as representatives from Britain and the other Commonwealth nations. The Egyptian ambassador honoured her by bringing his entire family.[43]

India had been awarded an individual facility to serve as their embassy, a special honour by the Soviet government. List House had previously been the home of none other than Serge Koussevitzky, the conductor of the Boston Symphony Orchestra who had personally invited Nan to attend his concert several years earlier during her American tour. After 1917, the house had been nationalized and operated as a school for a while.[44] Nan and her team were asked to stay at the Metropol while their new space was made ready.

~

Assisted by Isamu Noguchi, the Pandit sisters had spent their summer vacation in Mexico, a country they had visited before and enjoyed. This time, the illustrator and artist Miguel Covarubbias and Rosa, his wife and noted photographer, welcomed the girls into their Mexico City home. Noguchi saw to it that Nayantara also had the opportunity to spend time with his former lover, Frida Kahlo. The young women had terrific fun in La Casa Azul (the Blue House, where Frida lived then), dressing the celebrated painter up in one of their saris, taking pictures with her, and forging a near-instantaneous bond of friendship.[45]

~

The date of India's much-anticipated independence was fast approaching. Nan was a jumble of emotions. She felt excitement and jubilation, but also guilt for being away from her home just then, and a light undercurrent of resentment at those, including her brother, who had put her at such distance. But more than anything, she felt the great weight of the responsibility placed on her to represent her country abroad at that moment and the privilege of having that honour.[46]

Nan had hoped to throw a reception in Moscow to mark the occasion, but it quickly became apparent that this would not be possible. She simply did not have enough staff to manage such an event. Even more seriously, the costs of goods and services in Russia were prohibitive. So instead, Nan decided to hold a small ceremony for her officials and staff.[47]

On the night of the fourteenth, everyone gathered around the radio to listen to the proceedings of the Constituent Assembly. As she listened to her brother speak of India's 'tryst with destiny', of its calling to put an end to the enduring suffering of poverty and social injustice, and to build a better world of peace and freedom built on trust and cooperation, Nan burst into tears and 'wept copiously and unashamed'. This was a release of both joy and sorrow, as she reflected on the struggle of millions, some known but most not, and of the terrible toll that had been exacted for their collective efforts.

On the fifteenth, Nan hoisted the Tricolor flag on the balcony of their Metropol rooms, using a pole tipped with a gold spearhead procured by the hotel management. Later that morning, they assembled at List House and sang Bande Mataram, a popular Bengali poem by Bankim Chandra Chattopadhyay that had been named the national song by the 1937 Congress. Nan had the flag hoisted outside there as well, then read a message from her brother and delivered her brief remarks, before wrapping up with a chorus of Jana Gana Mana, the beautiful song by Rabindranath Tagore that would later become India's national anthem.

In the afternoon, she took calls from her new diplomatic colleagues in other delegations and received formal 'felicitations' from the Soviets. The British Embassy held a luncheon to honour the occasion and also raised both the new Indian and Pakistani flags next to their own. That evening, Nan capped everything off by hosting 'a little party' for her embassy team.[48]

~

The Soviets were gracious and supportive of the Indian delegation's celebrations. But there was a widespread feeling—held by everyone from government officials and local guards to the local hotel staff—that the credulous Indians were being hoodwinked by the British 'into a false sense of security.' When Nan requested the flagpole to use on her balcony, the director of the Metropol laughed loudly and asked 'How can you be independent while the British army is in control of your country and a British viceroy and other British officials remain there? That isn't what we call independence!'[49]

About two weeks after this exchange, an article appeared in the popular local trade unionist paper *Trud* denouncing the 'Mountbatten plan' transferring power as nothing more than traditional colonial 'divide and rule' tactics. In the paper's analysis, the British had 'artificially stirred up . . . religious friction,' leading to the partition of the subcontinent and the creation of the new states of India and Pakistan. The creation of these two countries would only feed notional religious differences and lead to bloody clashes, the paper predicted. Ultimately, land reform and an end to feudalistic structures were necessary to bring true liberation to India's hungry and poor, it concluded.

Nan reported all of this to New Delhi. For the most part, she thought that the Russians were missing the momentousness of unfolding events. Yet in ways she could not quite put into words, she also found their observations a bit unsettling.[50]

~

Nan had realized that List House was going to pose all sorts of challenges as an embassy from the moment she first saw it, when she had been escorted by the chief of protocol directly from the airport upon her arrival for tea there. The Soviets had gone all out, richly appointing the residence, and providing an official staff as well. But right away Nan saw that the building, while 'very charming and nice to live in' for an individual, was 'far too small + badly situated' for a diplomatic mission. It immediately became clear that most personnel would have to remain in the Metropol, where most business would also have to be conducted. Only Nan and Chandralekha, who had accompanied her mother and was volunteering in the press department, would be able to live in List and use it for basic work and tiny gatherings.[51] Worse still, the Indians were being charged rent beyond their wildest imaginings for the fancy furniture. There were also telephones placed throughout the house which rang at all hours of the day and quickly proved an unbearable nuisance.

On top of all this, the US Ambassador, Walter Bedell Smith, warned with dark humour that the Soviets were sure to bug the house to gain access to sensitive, private discussions. The Americans had discovered such devices in their quarters just days earlier. Nan thought a moment before retorting that, as followers of Gandhi, Indians behaved the same behind closed doors and in front of open ones. Bedell Smith said with a snort that he simply did not believe in Santa Claus.[52]

Nan had moved into List House the day before independence. Just days later she was sure that India would need a different facility. She observed that the Chinese, British, American, and French delegations had not only been allotted proper diplomatic quarters but 'palatially' sized ones as well. At the very least, she was intent on ensuring that India's embassy 'be made equally beautiful and attractive.'

The Russians agreed to her request several weeks later. But they warned that other delegations were already whispering about favoured treatment and so offered to make a new facility available a few months later.[53]

~

The first few weeks in Moscow were a hurried haze of procedural obligations and introductory meetings. The most pressing matter involved the formal presentation of Nan's credentials to the Soviet government, which she did on the thirteenth. She coordinated this with Deputy Foreign Minister Andrey Vyshinsky, whom she had met earlier in New York and with whom she had developed a warm relationship. So she was quite surprised when she received a call from the Foreign Office soon after informing her that there had been a mistake in her documents. What was shocking was not that there was an error—the material had been addressed to Stalin when it should have been made out to Nikolai Shvernik, the chairman of the Supreme Soviet—but that the Soviets had caught it. The papers were written in Hindi, translated from English by Purshottamdas Tandon, one of Nan's Congress colleagues. Right away it was clear that the Soviets were taking India seriously. This became even more apparent within a few more days, as Nan met other officials who came very prepared with incredibly detailed knowledge about the situation in the subcontinent. In this context, she brought up the dire food situation in India. Vyshinsky responded positively but made no commitments.[54]

As she gauged her hosts, Nan quickly determined 'that the Russians attach[ed] great importance to the rank and standing of the men . . . sent out with Embassies', as they viewed this as a reflection of the respect their country was accorded. She wrote to her brother asking that well-known figures be dispatched as scientific and military attachés and that India elevate and develop the Press department further. She noted that Moscow disapproved of 'publicity in the ordinary sense' but did value 'information correctly presented'.[55]

Aside from engaging with Kremlin officials, Nan also had to meet formally with each of the forty-six other ambassadors and their legations. This she found tedious but necessary. She much preferred informal encounters and get-togethers.

On the seventeenth, Nan attended a meeting of Commonwealth nations at the British Embassy, where countries were to talk about their joint assessment of Russian affairs. The priority was a film in development on the Battle of Stalingrad (eventually released in 1949) that irked everyone for downplaying Allied war efforts. Nan simply observed the conversation that followed but other matters caught her attention. The ongoing revolution in Indonesia against Dutch colonial control was also discussed, immediately revealing different worldviews and providing the first inkling of the changed dynamic that India's independence had rendered. Nan saw an opportunity to challenge long-held assumptions of Western supremacy but realized she had to tread carefully because of the circumstances.[56]

Nan was disappointed to learn that, for the most part, such debate was the exception. Essentially, all delegations had concluded that the Soviets had restricted diplomatic mobility and access to such a degree that they had made themselves essentially inscrutable. Rather than continually trying to break through such barriers, the ambassadors in Moscow had given up and focused instead on what they were allowed to do: constantly mixing with one another in a never-ending swirl of luncheons, dinners, and dance parties. Nan found all this a dreadful bore.

One of the issues that arose from all of this involved the etiquette of placing Nan in various social gatherings. Generally, the political appointees, all men, gathered in one room, while their spouses, all women, gathered in another. Madame Catroux, the wife of the French ambassador, handled such matters in an unofficial capacity and was especially perplexed and requested guidance from the Soviet Foreign Office. They responded unambiguously: Vijaya Lakshmi Pandit was the ambassador and was 'to be treated as such'. Nan was delighted by the directness of this statement, while the astonished wives took pity on her. 'Isn't she wonderful,' one said, 'she never gets tired of politics.'[57]

In early September, Nan attended her first diplomatic reception, held at the Embassy of the Netherlands. She was reluctant to go but was told by colleagues that this would have been inopportune to do given her views on Indonesia. It was a grand affair. Everyone wore 'their best clothes + jewels' and were treated to '[w]hole hams, turkeys, fish, + even suckling pigs' and endless drinks. It was Nan's first public appearance, so she arrived 'late wearing a plain black sari + blouse, no ornaments,' but carrying a 'very beautiful' Kashmiri, jamavar shawl. Her simple elegance contrasted with the glitter of other guests, ironically making her stand out more. The event started at 9.30 and, like all such events there, ran until 3 or 4 in the morning. Nan stayed until 11.[58]

~

Moscow proved a very expensive city. Nan wrote home that the 'design of living' was 'bewildering and complex'. She asked her brother for raises in staff allowances to help with costs while reassuring him that everyone was mindful of the tight resources. Entertainment was to be kept at a minimum per protocol requirements. Nan clarified that she had no intention of competing 'on the social plane with other Embassies.'[59]

So for a few days in early September, she flew over to Stockholm to try to secure some food supplies and basic embassy furniture. As strange as it seemed, such a trip was necessary to save money and was the norm followed by other delegations, just as India's internal memos had indicated earlier.[60]

Almost immediately, a firestorm arose back in India, seeing her actions as part of a larger pattern of various officials. The *Bombay Chronicle*, somehow catching wind of her proposed trip, had produced a story in late August that made it seem like she was demanding fancy foreign furniture, exactly the opposite of the actual situation. Nehru wrote to Gandhi clarifying the matter, but rumours continued for months thereafter, leading to further recriminations.[61]

Nan was blissfully unaware of all of this as she made her way through the city, which she thought was 'very beautiful'. The Swedish government and press gave her an enthusiastic welcome, the former discussing the opening of diplomatic channels and informally suggesting that she might expand her existing portfolio to include them as well.[62]

Over the course of her conversations, one name was brought up repeatedly: Alexandra Kollontai, a pioneering Russian who had been the first woman diplomat in the world, representing her country in several places, including Sweden. During the war, she had briefly held the title of ambassador. The Swedes spoke 'very highly' of her and with great affection. Nan had had the opportunity to meet with her just before embarking on her trip. While she still advised the Ministry of Foreign Affairs, Kollontai by then had been debilitated by a stroke and was confined to her 'beautiful flat' back in Moscow. Nan, who had read her work and admired her 'brilliant career', found her gracious and helpful, and indeed one of the only Russians who would open their home to her and speak somewhat freely.[63]

~

Moscow was abuzz with excitement as Nan returned home. It was the eighth centennial of the city, which looked especially 'beautiful with flags + buntings + very spectacular illuminations at night.'

Guests were coming in from all over to mark the occasion. On her way back, Nan encountered one particularly unfortunate visitor, the mayor of Bangkok. He had been abandoned en route by his travelling secretary, did not have his papers in order, and was completely flummoxed as he had never been outside of Siam (Thailand) before, but managed to get through with her assistance.

On the evening of 6 September, the city hosted a grand reception at the Bolshoi. All of the foreign delegations and visitors were invited to attend, and ambassadors were given special box seats. As was by now common, Nan attracted a great deal of attention as she entered.

At one point, various messages were read out. The Indian Embassy had sent a brief, official note of congratulations, believing it to be proper etiquette, but it turned out that no other delegation had done so. So when the mayor announced what India had done, the audience broke out into prolonged, sustained applause. The mayor turned towards her and bowed in appreciation. While the spectacle was 'thrilling', Nan was deeply embarrassed by the whole thing.

On stage was an enormous 'bronze bust of Lenin draped with flags + flowers'. Soviet flags were the primary decoration everywhere, but Nan thought it was all tastefully done and 'pleasing to the eye'. The mayor and various city officials sat on stage backed by four men made to look like statues. The evening included a variety of speeches and performances, including a ballet. Nan found herself enthralled and 'tremendously impressed' by the entire affair.

For all the glamour, Nan noticed that ordinary people were also able to attend. All special guests, including diplomats, were asked to be mindful of this and to be wary of ostentation.

The day after, Nan was invited to an event at a 100,000-seat athletic stadium and seated just above Vyshinsky and the president. Thousands of boys and girls participated in a beautiful show. In the evening, there were fireworks and various other forms of entertainment on almost every street corner, and everything was well attended by farmers who had come in from the surrounding villages. Nan was just overcome by the 'wonderful + heartening spectacle' she witnessed.[64]

~

Nan had informed her Soviet hosts on the day of her arrival of her intention to lead India's delegation to the United Nations again that year. Vyshinsky informed her that he and his government fully and enthusiastically supported her going. So just days after the citywide celebrations tapered off, she headed back to New York, via Stockholm.

Once again, Nan received glowing coverage in the international press in the lead-up to the opening of the new session. A local paper in Allentown, Pennsylvania recalled that she was one of the 'outstanding personalities' from the year before.[65] The *New York Herald Tribune* covered her arrival at La Guardia field.[66] And the *New York Times* reported that Nan (along with Eleanor Roosevelt) was 'besieged' by 'well-wishers' and was the primary focus of 'delegates, guests, and visitors' alike.[67]

Stories began to circulate that she could become the president of the UN General Assembly.[68] US officials discussing the matter internally concluded that there was some substance to the rumour as China, in particular, was pushing for her consideration. But the consensus for the time being was for other candidates, particularly the Brazilian diplomat Oswaldo Aranha, who would go on to secure the post.[69]

As she spoke out publicly, Nan acknowledged that India, while now free, was facing many challenges. Among the greatest was the deadly 'fratricidal strife' that had gripped the country. She looked to Mahatma Gandhi, through the 'magic of his sincerity' to help pacify the situation, as he had just miraculously done in Calcutta.[70]

These were domestic matters, though, and so she signalled her intention not to raise such things at the UN. Her focus, instead, was on pushing South Africa to abide by agreements previously made and to move forward with the agenda of equality that she had secured earlier. On this, she thought Pakistan and India would be in complete agreement though she clarified they were independent delegations and each would vote according to their own needs. At the broadest level, she also said that she hoped that the Great Powers would wield their authority judiciously while promising that India would do everything in its hands 'to help other nations towards freedom'.[71]

But things at the UN were very different this time. Tensions between the Soviet Union and the West were much more apparent and everyone else was essentially forced to pick a side. Nan did her best to avoid doing so but straddling the two was a precarious business. In one instance, she got caught between the United States, which wanted to scale back the veto, a power limited to the Great Powers on the Security Council, and the USSR, which wanted to keep things as they were as a way to force the rich and powerful to compromise and work in unanimity, acting as a shield against aggression by any one of them.[72] To loud and sustained applause, she agreed that the veto could easily be abused but also argued that changing it would involve opening the Charter up to revisions, which she thought too dangerous to allow.[73] She warned that the world was in 'tense suspense' and urged all sides to tone down their rhetoric and try to resolve their differences amicably.[74] She tried to put her words into practice by engaging in 'conciliatory discussions' with South Africa as well.[75] Despite her best efforts—she was singled out as the only 'serene' and 'temperate' speaker—the first week's meetings were widely seen as 'depressing', the openly rancorous tone a far cry from the year before and one that ominously foretold a 'hopeless' future.[76]

~

Struck by the animus bedevilling the proceedings, Nan decided to throw a reception for fellow delegates at the Waldorf-Astoria, hoping the less formal setting and her charms would facilitate better relations, as had happened before. The event was 'the most elaborate' thus far at the UN and was attended by numerous high-powered guests, including Eleanor Roosevelt, John Foster Dulles, and US Ambassador to the UN Warren Austin.[77] She followed this up with a small dinner for Mrs Roosevelt and seventeen other guests.[78]

While the evenings went off well, they ultimately did little to address the problems inside the official chambers, where the emergence of showboating, bare-knuckle politics, and arm-twisting deal-making had made idealistic dialogue much more difficult. Nan had come face to face with this reality when she tried to work with the Soviets on elections to the Security Council.

The Council comprised five permanent members and six non-permanent ones. Three countries—Brazil, Australia, and Poland were stepping off and new members had to be named. Nan decided to have India stand. She spoke to US Secretary of State George Marshall, who expressed his support and indicated that the US would vote in favour if their previously committed choices did not survive the first ballot. Nan then got support from Hector McNeil, the British representative who was also serving as vice president of the General Assembly. Finally, she turned to Vyshinsky, with whom she had so far had such a warm relationship. He told her that the Soviets 'warmly welcomed' India's service on the council and that they had decided to support such an action before they had left home. In return, they asked only that Nan support their efforts to keep out Argentina, then led by the Peróns, on the grounds that it remained fertile ground for fascism. Nan agreed to this deal and, thinking she now had the support of the major players, put her country's name forward. So she was surprised when it was soon revealed that the Soviets and Argentina had struck a deal supporting each other and that the USSR had therefore put up Ukraine for the same seat that India wanted. Over multiple secret ballots, both sides failed to win the majority required. Vyshinsky fully expected Nan to stand down and so was utterly shocked when instead she stood up and pushed India's candidacy forward, with the backing of the United States.[79] Vyshinsky flew into a rage at the podium when Nan forcefully (and truthfully) stated that India was standing to represent a geographic region otherwise under-represented on the council and that India would not be 'party either to the barter of votes or the subordination of principles to the expediences of policy'.[80] In the end though, when neither side could defeat the other, Nan cabled New Delhi for instructions on what they wished to do and eventually pulled India's name from the floor, feeling that the stalemate was holding up other important business in the Assembly.[81]

The entire affair left Nan with a bitter taste in her mouth. When asked for her thoughts on Moscow by American officials at a reception thrown by them just before her own, Nan admitted that she was 'disturbed' that the Soviets did not allow her to meet with people freely. And she made it clear that Vyshinsky had angered her here at the UN by his behaviour and the backroom shenanigans over Argentina. She confessed that she was feeling 'disillusioned'.[82]

~

Nan in the meantime waded into two other highly charged subjects. Just before the fight over the Security Council seat got underway, Nan spoke before a gathering at the Hotel McAlpin in midtown Manhattan at an event jointly put on by the Committee for the Celebration of Vietnam Independence and the Vietnam American Friendship Association. Among the other invited speakers was Pearl Buck.

The revolutionary Ho Chi Minh had declared independence from France in 1945 shortly after World War II had ended. France and the nationalist Vietminh had been in conflict until early 1947 and were at that moment in an uneasy state of tension. Nan and the other guests adopted a resolution calling on the United Nations to intervene in Indochina and to bring an end to aid to France which was being funnelled into the colonial fight against Vietnam.[83] Several days later, Ho Chi Minh's Democratic Republic of Vietnam made public its efforts to have India sponsor its case before the Security Council. Such appeals had been going on behind the scenes for several months. Nan could not answer as such a decision had to be made by the government, but she went out of her way to express 'complete sympathy' for the Vietnamese cause, adding that India supported 'all colonial peoples' struggle for independence.'[84]

Simultaneously, Nan had gotten involved with the work of the Ad Hoc Committee on Palestine. This group was tasked with considering the work of the United Nations Special Committee on Palestine, known as UNSCOP, which had been composed of eleven member states and established back in April. UNSCOP had published a unanimous report before the start of the new UN session calling for the end of the mandate of Palestine and the granting of independence. But the committee had disagreed on the way forward beyond that, with the majority prescribing partition of the territory into Jewish and Arab states. India, one of the members of UNSCOP, had disagreed strongly with this advice and instead supported a federalized bi-national solution, which it put forward as a minority report supported only by Iran and Yugoslavia.[85] As the General Assembly moved to accept the majority report, with the support of the United States and the opposition of Arabs, Nan spoke forcefully in favour of the minority position. She urged her fellow delegates to see the matters of European Jews harmed by the war and Palestinian independence as separate and argued that Jews in Palestine should be given maximum autonomy under a majority Arab-led state.[86]

Over the next few weeks, despite life-threatening pressure to back off, Nan worked religiously to try to revive the Indian position, eventually gaining Arab support for it. But by that point, partition had been sealed and the Indian alternative was no longer considered.

For her efforts, nonetheless, she won widespread admiration within the Arab world while still keeping the door open to overall good relations with Jewish representatives as well.[87]

~

New York kept Nan busy in other ways. She was glad to have the company of all three of her daughters once more. Rita, Nayantara and Chandralekha often accompanied their mother and supported her in various ways.

In mid-October, even as she was getting involved in thorny issues at the world body, Nan made time to attend a gala at the Waldorf on behalf of Wellesley College. It was the institution's seventy-fifth year, and to mark the occasion, President Mildred McAfee Horton launched a campaign to raise $7.5 million for the school's endowment. One thousand guests, each paying $10, were invited to the formal celebration. Some of 'the most famous relatives' of 'Wellesley girls' were asked to make remarks. Nan was among the roster of speakers, which also included Clare Booth Luce and Herbert Hoover, though the former President fell ill beforehand and was unable to make the event.[88]

Over the next few weeks, Nan's calendar was filled with meetings, dinners, and cocktail parties, where she was a featured guest. She spoke at each gathering about racism, hunger, and public health.

At the same time, Nan had to keep up social appearances. She had dinner at the home of John Foster Dulles, lunched with Clare Booth Luce, and met an editor of the *New York Times*, who relentlessly told her that she was 'most beautiful'.[89]

Meanwhile, the accolades again started to roll in. Nan was named the honorary president of the Indian division of the Asia Institute. The National Association of Colored Graduate Nurses in the United States awarded her a bouquet of roses in recognition of her work 'for international peace and health' and for efforts to increase the recruitment of new nurses.[90] And her life story was featured as that of 'the brilliant Indian diplomat' on *Headliners*, a popular Canadian programme broadcast on the CFRB radio station.[91]

Between all of this and numerous media appearances and smaller meetings, Nan somehow managed to squeeze in a trip to D.C. to serve as one of the two lead speakers, along with Eleanor Roosevelt, of the twelfth annual convention of the National Council of Negro Women. But her schedule was so tightly packed that she had to turn down a tea reception put on by the US First Lady, Bess Truman, at the White House.[92]

~

Nan was happy with India's overall performance—the *Manchester Guardian* lauded the country's 'success overseas' and credited Nan for the achievement—but was nonetheless growing increasingly dissatisfied with her team's organization and direction.[93] She felt like she was expected to captain a ship without a sail or rudder. From her point of view, India did not have a clearly defined foreign policy in a practical sense. The general admonition to avoid alliances and to judge each situation on its merits, she thought, was of little help, since doing so still led to the choosing of sides in individual instances. She urged her government to carefully consider their interests and to determine delineated goals, warning that India otherwise risked being drawn unwittingly into serious conflicts.

She also felt that Asaf Ali, India's representative in Washington DC, was unfit for his position. He did not follow diplomatic protocols and was out of his depth as ambassador.

On top of this, she felt that New Delhi simply did not have realistic understanding of international requirements, setting allowance standards far too low for various environments, though she was sympathetic to cost-consciousness. She lived by the idea that India had to prioritize maximal effectiveness and minimalist expenditures, with elegance wedded to the economy.

Nan joked with Sir Girja Shankar Bajpai, now the Secretary-General of the Ministry of External Affairs and her formal point of contact, with whom she was developing a close relationship, that her response to all of these headaches was to 'immediately retire to the highest peak of the Himalayas.' He wrote back soothingly, while adding that it was unlikely anything could be done on any of these fronts. In the meantime, he had some other news he thought might interest her. Syud Hossain had been appointed ambassador to Egypt.[94]

~

Nan briefed reporters before she entered her plane to begin her journey back east. 'I would be lacking in candour if I were to say that the session of the United Nations General Assembly which has just ended has gone entirely to our satisfaction,' she admitted. 'It revealed deep differences between two leading Powers, and a disturbing tendency for votes of member States to be frozen into solid blocs which could not always be dissolved by reason and argument.'

Even so, she found it 'heartening to find that America . . . [was] alive to her responsibilities to the world beyond her frontier'. 'I trust that the generosity of the American people, which is proverbial' she added in a nod to her hosts, 'will, as time goes on, be equalled [sic] by the wisdom of their statesmanship'. But for now, she said, India could hold its head up high confident that it had done everything it could 'to maintain an unswerving adherence to the principles of the United Nations'.[95]

~

As soon as she deplaned in Bombay, Nan repeated her views in a more direct fashion. Americans had a 'growing suspicion of Russia . . . more intense than before'. At the same time, she felt that they were conversely 'less concerned with the rest of the world. There is a greater tendency now, than at any time I can remember, to mind their own business'. On the whole, her view of the second session of the General Assembly was 'negative'. She ruefully concluded that 'there was no affirmation of anything worthwhile'.[96]

Shortly thereafter, she gave a detailed accounting of her experience to the Congress. And then she took some much-needed personal time to relax and unwind.[97]

During this time, the Soviets sent advance officials to begin preparations for their new Embassy in India. New Delhi reciprocated conditions in Moscow by providing accommodations in the Hotel Imperial, the city's best.[98]

~

Nan settled back into List House and life in the Soviet capital once she returned on New Year's Eve. Chandralekha had arrived beforehand, coming straight from the United States and bringing along for a visit an American friend named Nancy, the daughter of acclaimed photographer and writer Dorothy Norman. Rita and Nayantara stayed back in India with the intent of travelling a bit later. The newly redone embassy now felt cosy and comfortable, and Nan suddenly preferred it to a larger facility.[99] But the new building had already been allotted and preparations were underway to make it ready for a move-in within a few more months.[100]

Nan quickly fell into a routine, working from 11–6 daily on official business. She spent much of that time reading relevant analyses, handling paperwork, and meeting with various colleagues. She also dedicated herself to learning Russian and improving her French. By that point, her children and staff had already surpassed her in their command of the local language, each also having developed a tremendous affinity for the local people and their way of life. Nan was determined to acquit herself well.[101]

Nan's evenings were filled with dinners and cocktail parties, with time carved out for her reading and writing. One issue she struggled with involved the serving of alcohol. New Delhi started suggesting that Indian representatives should not serve such beverages when entertaining. Nan sought clarity if this was meant only as a domestic directive or if it applied abroad as well. Such an edict put Nan in a funny position since everyone drank copiously whenever they went out, raising questions about Indian hypocrisy and tight-fisted-ness. In Russia, where drinking was culturally equated with entertainment, and as something necessary for health in such a climate, this posed a special challenge.[102]

Nan at that time did not drink or smoke and had informed her hosts of this upon her initial arrival. This was considered entirely acceptable since Russian women generally did not drink in public. Even so, Nan had been instructed by the foreign office to sip a glass of wine if certain kinds of toasts to Soviet leadership were made.[103]

The response from the Ministry of External Affairs, when it finally came, was unhelpful. The directive had come from the Cabinet and therefore external affairs was bound by it, they informed her. At the same time, they realized the need to align with certain customs to facilitate diplomacy. Their advice was not to serve alcohol at 'official or semi-official parties,' but that it was okay to do so at private ones, leaving it to Nan's discretion to determine which was which.[104]

In her spare time, meanwhile, Nan attended a range of performances and concerts. Her favourite was *Swan Lake*, the world-renowned Russian ballet production.[105] She also enjoyed a visit to the famous Tchaikovsky Theater, where she watched 'a program of national dances'.[106]

Politically, she smoothed things over with Vyshinsky and carried on as before.[107] She pursued excellent relations with almost everyone. The Swedish foreign minister, Östen Undén, for instance, wrote in his diary following dinner with her one evening that she was an 'alert observer and a handsome lady'. He concluded that 'Women as diplomats is probably not a bad idea.'[108]

There were only one or two who oddly took exception with her. The British ambassador, who had been away when she had arrived in August, confided in another ambassador that he thought her 'a very dangerous woman' who was so 'complex within' that she was 'not to be trusted'. This found its way back to Nan's ear almost immediately.[109] Her only other problem was the wandering eye of the Egyptian ambassador, who, despite having a family, appeared to be making moves on both Chandralekha and her.[110]

The only other excitement involved bizarre scandals from the other embassies. In one instance, some Argentinians were trying to pass over to Poland when some boxes they were carrying fell at the border checkpoint. When they made an odd sound, the patrol forced them open and discovered an operation to smuggle Russians out of the country. The Russians were all captured and sent off to Siberia as punishment. In another episode, a British official was found to have been importing cloth through his diplomatic bag and disseminating it on the black market for a hefty profit with the assistance of a Russian woman. When she was discovered and arrested, the Briton disavowed any knowledge of the operation and claimed the woman was merely his mistress. He was soon sacked.[111]

At the end of the month, Nan received some startling news. Nayantara had met someone, a dashing businessman named Gautam Sahgal, and had been swept off her feet. She was so head over heels that she immediately decided to get engaged. Nan took the news, delivered by her brother, rather well. Nayantara had mentioned Sahgal in her letters, though it had not appeared serious. Nan had wanted her daughter to spend some time in India getting to know the country and its people before rushing into things. But she nonetheless was supportive and hoped only that the two young people—Nayantara was only twenty—would take some time to get to know one another before rushing into an actual marriage.[112]

~

Mahatma Gandhi was assassinated on 30 January 1948. He had been greatly pained by the growing animus between religious communities in India and had done everything in his power to prevent such wounds from getting any deeper. From October 1946, when the city of Calcutta had descended into brutal violence, he had toured throughout the region, unarmed and fearless, talking to affected groups and preaching forgiveness and tolerance. Shortly after partition, Gandhi began a fast that forced the warring elements to stand down. He then replicated his efforts in Delhi, culminating in the declaration of an 'indefinite fast' on 13 January. Death, he said, would keep him from having to witness 'the destruction of India', the world's great religions, and all he held dear. But if there was value in his life, he hoped that an 'awakened sense of duty' would lead to a 'reunion of hearts'. The Great Soul lent courage to those who needed it, repaired the breach, and brought pledges of peace from all over. The whole of India was moved. He called off his fast five days after he had begun. It was his 'finest hour'.

Less than two weeks later, Nathuram Godse, a Hindu nationalist who felt that the Mahatma had betrayed the nation and his own faith, and who had found sympathy and support for this position among fellow right-wing travellers, shot Gandhi three times while the old man was on his way to prayers. Gandhi died with the words 'Hai Ram' on his lips.[113]

Nan could not believe the news when she heard it. She had been extremely anxious about the last fast, fearing the direction things were headed. Now she was in shell shock.

As soon as she confirmed what had happened, Nan informed the Soviet Protocol Department and Dr Fu, the Chinese ambassador who was also the doyen of the diplomatic corps. Fu, in turn, informed the other delegations, though most had already heard through the radio. Nan took many condolence calls though otherwise kept her ear glued to broadcasts for each new update.

Each embassy flew its flag at half-staff in honour of India's fallen icon. On the thirty-first, Nan fixed a two-hour period for guests to come and pay their respects and sign a book of mourning. Leaders from every mission visited and sent official letters of tribute that Nan thought were 'moving and beautiful'. The only country that did not respond or show any personal interest was the Soviet Union. *Pravda* announced the death that morning in a most perfunctory manner. It was only several days later that Nan received any acknowledgement at all of what had happened from the Russians, in the form of cards from the heads of departments in the Foreign Office as well as from the foreign minister himself. The behaviour, she thought, was peculiar and inexplicable.[114]

~

The Communist Party of India (CPI) had been established in 1926, with antecedents going back several years earlier. For most of the late colonial period, it was banned, and communists operated instead within the Congress Socialist Party and local peasant organizations. After the Soviets joined the Alliance against Nazism, the British Government of India lifted its restrictions against the communists. Though they formally opposed the Quit India movement in exchange, and received opprobrium for it, they gradually found their footing working for famine relief in Bengal. Between 1946 and late 1947, the party had difficulty settling on a clear course of action, supporting a doomed farmer's agitation in the Northeast while also futilely seeking to unite the Congress and Muslim League in a front against communal violence. Following independence, they moved to work with the Congress on containing the continuing bloodshed.

Moscow, in the meantime, had been concerned with the Marshall Plan, a US initiative named after the US secretary of state to rebuild the economies of European countries hurt by the war. The Soviets saw the move as a duplicitous effort to expand American influence and power. They rejected aid in territories under their control and instead sought to counter it with the Zhdanov Doctrine. Through the Cominform, an organization designed to coordinate international communism, the Soviets greenlit local communist parties to act against anything deemed enemies of true democracy.

By December 1947, the CPI and the state Congress government in West Bengal were at odds over growing unrest, the latter blaming the communists for anti-state activities. The communists, with the blessings of Moscow, responded by declaring independence a lie. The national government, led by Nehru, had to be overthrown, they declared. By January, West Bengal had passed a heavy-handed ordinance built off previous legislation put forward by its preceding Muslim League government, meant to crush the communists with repressive power.

In March, the state, against Nehru's express wishes, declared the CPI illegal and started to arrest its leaders. This in turn led to the breakout of a regional insurgency that would last for another two years. The Soviet press amplified these activities by denouncing the Indian national government as 'reactionary,' much to Nan's consternation. Eventually, the CPI realized that its methods were not actually all that popular. In the early 1950s, it would do an abrupt about-face, give up its commitment to revolutionary violence and accept constitutional electoral politics as the practical way forward.[115]

~

Nan had been able to meet Gandhi briefly during her visit to Delhi in December 1947. The old man told her then that a big change was imminent. She was soon to take up a new position in the West.

The two of them discussed the matter for a while, before Gandhi cut their conversation short. 'I would like to talk more but I am very tired,' he said, and they parted. These were his last words to her.[116]

~

It took a few months to finalize the details of her new assignment. By May, the former occupant of the post, Asaf Ali, was, to his great unhappiness, relieved of his duties and brought home to New Delhi.

A few weeks later, it was announced. Vijaya Lakshmi Pandit would be India's next Ambassador to the United States of America.[117]

CHAPTER TWELVE

# Raw Silk

Nan arrived in Washington to a rapturous welcome. An enthusiastic group of well-wishers greeted her right on the tarmac as she deplaned, 'one of the largest crowds of United States officials, foreign diplomats, and countrymen ever to meet an arriving Ambassador'.[1]

The contrast with the remainder of her time in Moscow was sharp. She had stayed on in her position there for nearly a year after internally accepting the Washington portfolio, keeping the news of her new appointment secret to avoid offending the Soviets, by order of the Ministry of External Affairs.[2]

Nan had tried to make the most of her opportunities in the Soviet Union, looking to tour local hospitals and collective farms, visit some of the Asian republics, and otherwise interact with a range of people.[3] But she found herself continuously stymied by inexplicable Russian stonewalling.

Soviet officials by that point had drawn up a formal assessment of her. They acknowledged her extensive career and achievements and recognized the roles she had played in advocating for peace and friendship with their country, deciding that she ultimately had indeed been a 'loyal' friend 'without negative remarks'. Even so, they took exception to her joust in the UN over Ukraine's inclusion on the Security Council, as well as to some observations she had made shortly thereafter on the food situation in the Soviet Union. Even worse in their view, she had the previous year praised the United States and offered to work with them in furthering freedom and democracy in Asia. 'In reality', the Soviets had concluded, 'she is pro-American'.[4] Media speculation that she could soon take over the American Embassy did not help matters.[5]

But Nan did not feel especially singled out. She observed that 'priorities and privileges' for diplomats across the board were 'being withdrawn; outside contacts . . . reduced and the surveillance inside Embassies tightened'. The Soviet Government, she and her colleagues determined, wanted 'to make the isolation of the [entire] Foreign Colony in Moscow complete'.[6]

She pressed on undeterred as much as she could, managing to engage in some soft power cultural diplomacy, bringing in some Indian performers to mark the one-year occasion of Indian independence.[7] In the months prior, she held meetings with Molotov and Vyshinsky, and negotiated, at Russian urging, a wheat-for-tea deal with India that was concluded by July. The Russians expressed an urgency for the pact that surprised her and seemed to suggest an effort to woo India back into their orbit and away from the West. Yet they expected reciprocity from India that it was simply unable and unwilling to deliver. Nehru and Nan concurred that India could not and would not march lockstep 'in international affairs with the Soviets,' though they were happy to lend support wherever there was agreement. This only soured the Soviets further, even though the siblings made clear that their policy extended universally and applied to the West as well. A few weeks after the wheat deal was concluded, Nan was invited to an official meeting with Alexandra Kollontai, with whom she had been in regular if informal contact. It was immediately clear that this time the pioneering Russian diplomat was there to 'convey a message'. The Soviets wanted the Nehrus to be more pro-communist and were disappointed that both were proving more reactionary than it had been presumed they would be. Nan was taken aback and critical of her inability to improve the situation.[8]

Back in India, Russian ambassador K.V. Novikov met with Girja Shankar Bajpai to discuss various matters related to Indo-Soviet relations. Among the topics of conversation was the possibility of Nan meeting privately with Joseph Stalin, the iron-fisted premier of the Soviet Union. This stemmed from a slight misunderstanding. In informal conversation, Nan had politely said earlier that she looked 'forward to an opportunity of paying . . . [her]respects' to the Soviet leader. This then got represented by Bajpai as a request that had been denied by the Soviets and taken as a personal slight by the Indians. Novikov stressed that the Soviets knew of no such application. Nan later clarified to Bajpai what had actually occurred, and he decided it best to interpret that as 'a polite request' and let the matter stand. In the event of it, Nan was not in the Soviet Union for long enough thereafter—she left in August and stayed abroad through the top of the following year—for anything really to be done about the matter.[9]

The issue, however, dogged her for many years thereafter as critics raised questions as to why she could not get an audience. All of this was made even worse by the showy visit of a communist couple from India, whom Stalin did meet contemporaneously. But the civilians were government critics whose views hewed to the Soviet line and elevating them was in keeping with the overall Soviet position towards India at that time. Moreover, Stalin rarely saw foreign dignitaries. The first one he met during Nan's tenure was just as it came to an end: the American ambassador regarding the Berlin blockade. Years later, a public relations official from the Soviet Embassy in Delhi claimed to her that Stalin had been dealing with illness—his chronic ailments included 'typhus, smallpox, tuberculosis . . . irritable colon syndrome, acute appendicitis with complications, and hypertension'—and that that was the primary reason for lack of a meeting.[10] Still, the overarching situational context meant that it was impossible not to conclude that Stalin's evasion sent some kind of purposeful signal.

Nan had entered the Soviet Union with great hopes and had often thought admiringly of the people and what they had accomplished. These setbacks left her feeling disillusioned, though she remained as committed as ever to continuing friendship and dialogue. So she settled for small victories. In late April or early May, she received sanction to visit a girls' school in Moscow. The institution she picked served over 1400 children and was one of several hundred such facilities in the city. Nan observed that the education was free, but that students had to pay a small fee for food, which many could not afford, significant since many were also 'definitely undernourished.' Uniforms too were no longer provided at no cost, a casualty of the war. Nan was impressed with the methods of teaching subjects like math and psychology, but it was her visit to an English class that particularly stuck out in her mind. There in the classroom was a list of reasons why the students should study such a foreign language. The last one read: 'So that we may know our enemies.'[11]

She gave up on her desire to tour the outer Soviet republics and instead visited Leningrad (St Petersburg). She spent a week there in July enjoying sights that included Peter the Great's Summer Palace and the renowned Hermitage Museum. But the real highlight was a visit to the State University that had been established by Peter in the early eighteenth century and was the country's oldest. She was presented with a copy of the first Russian translation of the Indian epic, the Ramayana, and was treated to a special tour of manuscripts in the school's vast library. Above all, she was grateful to have an opportunity to speak freely with local professors, among the only informal and unofficial conversations she was allowed.[12]

Between her local diplomatic outings, Nan oversaw her mission's long-pending move to new quarters. In anticipation, she had again travelled to Stockholm to acquire furniture and some decorative necessities. List House was temporarily transferred to Pakistan, which had just opened formal relations of its own. India moved into its new building in late May. While the new facility was much more spacious, it had an unexpected downside. It was located on a busy street and so was inundated with noise at all hours, a problem that was worse in the warmer months when windows had to be kept open because of the heat. Nan suddenly found herself missing the quiet, little garden she had back at List. But she was sure that things would 'settle down' and that, ultimately, the move had been a necessary one. To compensate for the shortcomings of the new facility, she facilitated her country's purchase of a small dacha (country house) about an hour away, an amenity common to most officials there. It was bare bones—bathing was in a nearby stream and sanitation was a hole in the ground—but the serenity offered by the getaway felt priceless.[13]

~

These small accomplishments were significant in their way, but the overarching dramatic change in tone remained unchanged. Gone was the euphoria of the immediate postwar moment. Increasingly cold relations between the Soviet Union and the West, and particularly the United States, started to creep over every proceeding. The threat of the apocalyptic end to humanity suddenly took on a new and more terrifying form, and loomed ever larger over the horizon, casting a dread pall over global affairs.

Nan saw it as ever more her purpose, and that of her country, to resist the forces of doom. In one instance, as she attended a parade to commemorate May Day that Stalin himself presided over. She was struck by the endless display of weapons that snaked down the road in such synchrony as to give the impression of some kind of grotesque, mechanical monster. 'Every invention known to Science for the destruction of the human race' was there. Suddenly the Italian ambassador turned to her and asked, 'Where is Gandhi now?' Without missing a beat, she replied, 'In your heart Excellency, only his voice cannot compete to-day [sic] with the loud noise of the military bands.' But, she reassured him, 'Tomorrow it will rise above the din.'[14]

Nan left Moscow at the end of August 1948 to take up leadership of India's delegation to the United Nations once more. She had been surprised to learn just two months prior that she was again being tasked with this job. It was a full-time position in its own right and difficult to juggle along with any other position. But she understood why she was selected all the same and agreed to go.[15] This time the annual meeting was taking place in Paris instead of New York, as construction was simultaneously beginning on the organization's new Gotham headquarters in east midtown.

Once in the City of Light, Nan used her opening remarks to warn against taking the path the world found itself on and to offer instead an alternative way forward. 'Every field of international endeavour,' she said, 'is threatened by the ever-widening gulf between the major Powers . . . The disappearance of that harmony among the 'Big Five' which, while it lasted, was the single greatest factor in winning the most deadly war in human history, now endangers the peace of the world.'

'India has . . . in the past, avoided alignment with this bloc or that, an attitude which has often been misunderstood,' she said in a nod to the diplomatic difficulties she faced in Moscow. 'We are, however, convinced that this is a correct stand even if means some temporary disadvantage, it is not based on any weakness, but on the result of our conviction that by avoiding grouping with any Power bloc, we are, in howsoever small a fashion, helping toward maintenance of peace.'

She then tried to offer specific steps that the international community could take to further this objective. Colonialism was pernicious and persistent and effective measures had to be taken to facilitate the freedom of all remaining subjugated peoples. In conjunction with decolonization efforts, Nan also spoke forcefully in favour of the rights of minorities in all sovereign states, focusing on South Africa, a throwback to the stands she had taken in previous sessions, but now with new urgency and meaning.[16] Only universal protections and rights would guarantee the safety of all peoples everywhere.

Nan's task was made more difficult this round, though, since India was now a concretely operating independent state, with a record of its own to defend. Critics immediately raised questions about the country's actions in two territories, Hyderabad and Kashmir, and charged hypocrisy.

The colonial subcontinent had been home not only to the directly administered regions of British India but also to the indirectly ruled 'princely states', roughly 600 odd principalities of various sizes that made up about 2/5ths of the region, governed by a wide assortment of hereditary monarchs and wealthy landlords. At the time of independence, most chose to join with either India or Pakistan depending on their location. But these two states (along with Junagadh, a smaller third one) chose differently, one declaring itself independent while the other found itself contested by both the partitioned siblings. In the case of Hyderabad, New Delhi moved in in the face of rising violence and took over the territory, absorbing it into the Union. The situation in Kashmir was brought before the UN in the hopes that neutral arbitration would bring a lasting, peaceful solution. Nan held her tongue on the latter situation but vociferously defended the Indian position on the former.

This time she was met with a much more muted reaction. The crowd merely smiled at her as she returned to her seat, though individuals still congratulated her on her eloquent presentation.[17] This seemed set to be the tone for the coming meetings. Nan was undeterred and pushed on relentlessly, again winning plaudits for her presentations and intervening where she could to ease tensions between the Soviets and the West.[18] Her efforts were helped along when her brother arrived in Paris to much fanfare, coming in via

London. Nehru's presence drew the spotlight and electrified the crowds, giving the entire Indian delegation a boost in public relations. Together, he and Nan threw a splashy reception for 'hundreds of guests' and 'an impressive assembly of world diplomatic figures' that included Vyshinsky, Prince Faisal of Saudi Arabia, and notably Pakistani Prime Minister Liaquat Ali Khan and his wife.[19]

Before she left France, Nan signed India onto the 1948 Paris Protocol for international drug control, becoming the first woman ever to sign a treaty on behalf of India. She signed in Hindi, also the first time in the modern era that an agreement was made in a native Indian language.[20]

Later, an international gathering was held to recognize the contributions of women in international affairs, particularly at the United Nations. Nan, who was not even present, was once more singled out as 'the most outstanding delegate'.[21]

All of Nan's actions were almost overshadowed, though, when speculation began to appear in the press that she was soon to become the ambassador to the United States.[22] She pointedly denied these claims, just as she had earlier rumour-mongering, and insisted that she planned to return to Moscow shortly, though she admitted that as a member of the foreign service, she could be called on to travel anywhere at any time.[23]

~

Both of her eldest children and her soon-to-be son-in-law Gautam had travelled to England and France early on in Nan's trip, and they all had made sure to spend quality time together during the weeks of their stay. Nan for her part had also made time to familiarize herself with the 'fascinating city' of Paris, which she concluded was 'wonderful'. As she walked around, she also kept her eye out for potential properties that India could acquire for an embassy once her country was able to add new diplomatic posts. In between her formal and familial obligations, Nan squeezed in a trip to Cairo to visit Syud Hossain, with whom she had maintained a close relationship.[24]

Towards the tail end of her European stay, Nan began to coordinate wedding arrangements with Nayantara, her fiancé, his family, and Indira, as well as Chandralekha and Nehru. By that point, news of planned nuptials had made gossip columns around the world. The ceremony was fixed for early January.[25]

~

The wedding took place in Anand Bhawan. Things were kept simple and muted, with no reception, in recognition of the many struggles the country was facing. Gautam's family had lost their home in Lahore due to Partition and now found themselves as refugees. The family made the best of it. Nayantara wore a plain khadi sari, adorned with flowers as jewellery. The event still received media coverage all over the world. Once it was over, Nayantara and her new husband went off to Shimla for their honeymoon, while Nan and the others were left to get things back in order.[26] Chandralekha, in the meantime, had found someone for herself as well, a member of the Foreign Service named Ashok Mehta. The two would also marry a few months later to a bit more fanfare in a civil ceremony at Teen Murti (Nehru's formal residence in Delhi), and a Hindu one thereafter. Pratap Pandit sat in for his late brother during the rituals. A 1000-person reception ended the celebration.[27]

Nan wanted to do something extra special for her children to mark the momentous occasion of their unions. A few weeks after the guests had all gone, she went out and purchased a set of crystal glasses with matching ice cream plates. It was an extravagance. She was 'absolutely financially broke' as she jokingly put it to her children. But the things were beautiful, and she relished the chance to dote on her family.[28]

~

Syud Hossain had died of a sudden heart attack in Cairo in February 1949, in between the wedding celebrations. Nan had taken the shocking news hard and felt 'very depressed'. Hossain had been ill on her last visit, but she had heard that he had improved a bit and 'was looking years younger'. She had consoled herself that his end was at least 'merciful & swift.' As she was grieving, she learned that Sarojini Naidu had also passed away. As she thought about her old friends, she ruminated on the meaning of life and the inevitability of death.[29]

~

The atmosphere was much the same as it had been in Moscow when Nan returned to her post the following month. The press continued to hammer her country for what was perceived to be a broad-based anti-communist campaign. Bureaucratic hurdles hampered the daily functioning of the embassy and made life generally difficult. And the Chinese ambassador, Fu Bingchang, who had paternally looked after all the other foreign delegations, was now withdrawn and forlorn, completely 'broken down' by the ongoing Communist Revolution in his country. Nan invited Fu to dinner to try to console him on a personal level, though she had 'great doubts' about his interpretation of events in his country.[30]

There was a notable bit of excitement when Vyacheslav Molotov, the long-serving foreign minister, was removed from his position and replaced by Vyshinsky. Molotov had fallen out of favour after his wife, Polina, was arrested the previous December for spending time with her old classmate, the recently arrived second woman ambassador to the country, Golda Myerson (Meir) of the just-created country of Israel. Nan and the other ambassadors were not privy to these details regarding Molotov and speculation was rife as to what might have happened to him.[31]

In the midst of this, more definitive news broke in the media of her imminent appointment to the United States.[32] Nan steadfastly refused to confirm this, but the spreading story further hemmed in her diplomatic manoeuvrability.

So she decided to request permission to travel to the home and museum of one of Russia's most celebrated writers, Leo Tolstoy, who had special resonance with India for the influence he had had on Gandhi. The Mahatma was very much on her mind as she made the emotional visit. Nan hoped her acknowledgement of Tolstoy would highlight Indo-Russian bonds. But though her journey had all been approved, her party was stopped and carded at multiple checkpoints along the way. Nan felt 'absolutely suffocated' by these actions.

On the other side of her trip, her car stopped at a little village tea shop as it made its way back to Moscow. After Nan and the others had finished their refreshment and started to make their way out of the establishment, 'a group of eight or ten women . . . came near and stared . . .' Each was 'very poor and shabbily dressed.' In a hurried moment, one turned and confided to the Indians, 'We are worked to death, our souls are sick and tired—it does us good to see that some people in the world live differently.' Nan glanced around and noticed a policeman nearby, and she suddenly grew fearful that the women might come to harm for their candidness. She left things there and hurried away but carried the 'bitter memory' of the encounter with her, concluding that it was now 'obvious why contacts between foreigners and the people of the country . . . [were] forbidden.'[33]

Nonetheless, she believed in the need to continue building trust, determining that this was the only way to defeat the dangerous forces of fear and paranoia. When Alexandra Kollontai wrote her a gracious note of farewell in anticipation of her as yet unannounced departure, highlighting the wheat treaty she had negotiated and wishing her well in her efforts to 'maintain peace in the world', Nan responded in kind. She thanked the pioneering Russian diplomat for her thoughtful gesture and all of her 'kindness and friendship', and wrote that she left 'with feelings of goodwill for the people of this great country and for the courageous manner in which they are facing the gigantic tasks' that lay before them.[34]

In her exit interview with Vyshinsky, she leaned into the personal connection the two of them had forged over the past few years. Her meeting, scheduled for ten minutes per the custom, lasted for about half an hour. She congratulated him on his promotion, and Vyshinsky in turn called her the 'soul of the General Assembly.' When she indicated that she had no plans to lead her country's delegation to the UN again, he praised her efforts in Moscow, saying that she had 'endeared' herself to Soviet officials. As she hesitantly confessed that she expected to be transferred out of her post shortly, he said reassuringly that he hoped she would leave with the 'same feelings of goodwill and friendship' that she had brought with her. Nan admitted that there were things about the country that had 'confused and baffled' her during her stay, but she very much hoped that things would be cleared up and that a 'happy relationship' between the USSR and India would soon ensue.³⁵

~

The American press made much of Nan's appointment to the United States. The *New York Herald Tribune* called her 'India's most notable woman,' while analysis in the *Daily Boston Globe* went further, saying that she was 'without question one of the three or four most influential women in the world.' The *Washington Post* pointed to her 'remarkable record' and called her a person of 'great charm and unusual ability'. Gossip columnists fixated on how 'strikingly handsome' she was. Some journalists, like those in Black media, heralded her as 'one of the world's great enemies of racial discrimination,' and a true champion of justice. But others were especially interested in her transfer from the Soviet Union, with several highlighting reports of her disappointment and disillusionment with life there. The Cold War jaundiced their view and they saw a hopeful opportunity to swing India fully to the American side.³⁶ The *Baltimore Sun* inversely observed that Nan's commission already reflected the increasing importance that India placed on its relationship with the U.S. and discussed the imperatives of capital investment in the subcontinent.³⁷ The United Press reported that '[d]iplomatic and official quarters' in the US all 'reacted favorably to the appointment', and that 'Washington [was] [p]leased'.³⁸

Just before she began her journey West, she spoke to The *New York Times* to clarify matters. She acknowledged her frustrations while she had been in Russia but insisted that her interest, and that of her country, was 'to avoid entanglement in the "cold war"', and to 'be friends with everybody'.

The *Times*' Robert Trumbull wrote a lengthy feature on her, ostensibly devoted to talking up India's aims for world peace. But a substantial portion of the piece devolved into a discussion of clothing choices. Nan, he titillatingly told his readers, was 'a beautiful woman' with 'youthful complexion'. 'She looks as good in a sari,' he emphasized, 'as a sari looks on her.'³⁹

Nan days later told the Indian press that she had several primary objectives while in the US, aside from furthering mutual understanding. She was hoping to increase US capital investment and technical aid, particularly as it related to 'food self-sufficiency' and 'accelerating industrialization'.[40] In a formal editorial, the *Washington Post* dubbed her the 'hope of the East' and India the 'real bridge between the east and west'.[41]

~

Nan hit an unpleasant bump on her journey to the US when she stopped over in London. V.K. Krishna Menon, who was by then the high commissioner there, slighted her in minor but visible ways. In one instance after an official function, he 'dashed off in the car which had brought' her there, leaving her 'stranded high and dry'. Eyewitnesses were left stunned by what seemed like inexplicable behaviour. The next day, as he was escorting her to the airport for her departure, he suggested in a 'very sarcastic manner' that she was poaching his staff. Nan was put off by these episodes, less by the idea that there was some tension between the two and more by the passive-aggressive way Menon was choosing to express his resentment.

What lay behind the apparently sudden fissure involved the Russian wheat deal that had been negotiated the year before. Nan had been at the centre of those discussions in Moscow when she got word of alternate channels being opened and run by the high commissioner in London. When she confronted Menon about this, he offered a strangely worded apology denying his involvement and suggesting that it was all a misunderstanding caused by a news report that had come from his Public Relations Department but which he had not seen until after publication. Nan bemusedly saw this as a version of Soviet denialism, where things would appear in the press that officials would immediately distance themselves from. Everyone knew that the government itself was responsible for such stories, but they nonetheless played along with the farce. Here, Nan understood very well that Menon was involved. She informed the Ministry of External Affairs that this in itself was not a problem, but that one or the other mission should pursue such matters, but not both. In the end, she would bring the matter to a conclusion, leaving Menon's ever-expanding ego feeling considerably bruised.

By the time of Nan's stopover en route to her American post, Menon's churlishness was well known in the Ministry. Officials had gently tried to suggest some reorganization of his office to bring some method to the way it functioned. They had been met rather typically with a theatrical reaction, the thin-skinned Menon threatening his immediate resignation over the mere suggestion that he might benefit from some changes.

For the moment, Nan could not be bothered by any of this. She had more important, and exciting, matters to tend to.[42]

~

An agreement to end the Berlin Blockade—a Soviet siege of the former German capital that was an attempt to keep the Western powers out of the city, but that had been outmanoeuvred by an ongoing massive Western airlift—was reached just as Nan arrived in New York. She acknowledged the importance of this breakthrough as she faced '[b]atteries of movie cameras and photographers,' adding that she hoped that it would be a 'good sign for world peace.'[43]

Within days, she was in a meeting with President Truman, where she formally presented her credentials. The White House took the occasion to announce that Prime Minister Nehru had accepted an invitation to visit the United States later that year.[44]

~

Washington was abuzz with the news of Nan's arrival, as people clamoured to know about her comings and goings, which parties were thrown in her honour, and what shows she was headed to see.[45] The adulation she received was equal to that of any celebrity. But underlying it all was a recognition of the immensity of her achievement, and the potent possibilities she symbolized for so many. One writer, Malvina Lindsay, wrote 'that women are getting restive again. This publicity about Mrs. Pandit . . . has started them asking questions.' In a remarkable essay, she asserted that women would no longer settle for being 'an adviser, a consultant, an observer . . .' 'Mrs. Pandit,' she said, 'didn't come here to do research or to smirk at committee meetings.' She was a political leader with the ability to effect real change. Women everywhere were inspired to demand this for themselves now.[46]

The very evening that Lindsay's column was published, Nan attended the annual dinner of the Women's National Press Club. The President and Mrs Truman presided over a meal and a series of comedic skits, while also presenting a 'Woman of the Year' award to Eleanor Roosevelt. The evening was good fun and facilitated Nan's introduction to some of Washington's powerbrokers. Among the most significant attendees was Perle Mesta, who immediately took special notice of Nan.[47] Mesta had only just been featured on the cover of *Time Magazine* a few weeks previous. A few years later, she would be known as 'the hostess with the mostest,' when Irving Berlin penned a song about her for the musical about her life, 'Call me Madam.' Mesta threw the hottest parties in town and was considered one of DC's most influential socialites.[48]

Several weeks after the Press Club get-together, Attorney General Thomas Clark arranged a programme for charity, headlined by contributions from Bob Hope and Bing Crosby, the country's top talent. Mesta invited Nan to 'join her party' at the event and then to join her for a private supper party thereafter 'at a fashionable club'. Nan agreed and stood waiting at the appointed time. She was taken aback when Mesta arrived not in a simple car, but in a full motorcade, complete with a police escort. The night only grew more elaborate from there. 'The gowns + jewels + food + drinks were all fantastic,' Nan observed. She admired the exquisite taste and elegance of it all, but suddenly grew uneasy. It just seemed too much, especially given all that was happening in the world at that time. Her feelings recalled her initial reaction to New York when she could not help but compare the glitz she saw there to the misery of those she had just witnessed starving from the Bengal famine. 'Vijaya Lakshmi Pandit—where exactly are you heading for,' she asked as she chided herself to remember who she was, where she came from, and what she stood for.[49]

Nan knew that she had a special responsibility to speak out on all of this. 'I think that [it] is very pleasant to attend so many official functions and dinners and cocktail parties and so on, but I think they might easily impair one's health and also get in the way of objectives which one wants to carry out,' she announced in a radio interview.[50] In another engagement, she grew specific about one issue she cared about deeply. 'Too many sugar things are said in the world today, and I am surfeited with them,' she declared. There was 'discrimination against women' in the United States, as elsewhere. Women needed things to change and deserved the positions of leadership to make it happen, she said.[51]

About a month after the big charity event, Perle Mesta was appointed Ambassador to Luxemburg, becoming only the third woman in United States history to hold such a position. Madame Pandit was credited as the catalyst.[52]

~

Ralph Bunche, an acclaimed African American intellectual who had studied at Harvard and taught at Howard University, had known Nan for several years through their mutual work at the United Nations. Bunche had achieved prominence there first by running the Trusteeship Department and second by serving as a mediator for the Israel/Palestine crisis, both building on prior work he had done for the US Government. He was subsequently offered the post of Assistant Secretary of State but declined. He privately confided to Nan that he simply could not 'expose his family to the humiliation of life in Washington' again. He told her bitterly that, despite his renown, he was still prevented from dining in the city's premier hotels and restaurants, while his children were not allowed to attend certain schools or visit various movie theatres. Such 'restrictions and indignities' were suffered by all Black people in the capital, 'a life of the Ghetto' that had to change.[53]

At their eighty-first commencement, Howard, a prestigious historically Black university founded shortly after the American Civil War, voted to award Nan an honorary law doctorate, along with three others that included Bunche. Nan told the massive audience of 10,000 people that India, while independent, was not fully free. This was, she said, because freedom was indivisible and that no one could have 'lasting freedom . . . until liberty is assured to all races, peoples, and communities.' She called on the graduates to fight for this goal with pure motivation and high ideals. The *Baltimore Afro-American* called her speech 'moving' and 'filled with wisdom, friendliness, and understanding.'[54]

The NAACP by then had decided to award Bunche with the Spingarn Medal, its highest honour, given annually in recognition of outstanding Black achievement. Bunche was being recognized for his work with Israelis and the Arab world. The ceremony was to be held at the Hollywood Bowl in Los Angeles, which declared the day of the awarding Ralph Bunche Day. Nan was asked to present the medal, the first time that distinction had ever gone to someone from outside the country.[55] Nan used her remarks to highlight the 'universal desire for an enduring peace' and said that the current moment demanded 'a fresh approach to human relations . . . established on a recognition of the dignity and worth of the human person and the need for a balanced development of all the peoples of the world . . .'[56]

A few days later, Nan and Bunche shared the stage again, this time at the grand Beverly Hills Hotel, where she received the primary honour from forty 'major' women's organizations. About 600 guests attended what was 'one of the largest luncheons of the summer season'. Nan used the occasion to call on women, especially American women, to work selflessly and with 'simplicity and renunciation' towards world peace.[57]

Observing these varied events, writers in the Black Press adopted Nan as one of their own. The *Atlanta Daily World* included her in a list of fourteen 'top personalities,' that included Bunche, Walter White, Channing Tobias, Lena Horne, Eleanor Roosevelt, Adam Clayton Powell, and Paul Robeson. They declared her a 'gracious lady' and the 'best orator in the public's eye.'[58]

~

Nan's stay in LA was the second stop in the first national speaking tour she arranged in her capacity as ambassador.[59] She had by that point already given several major addresses in the capital, including one to the Women's National Democratic Club, a forum Eleanor Roosevelt had been using to advance many of her key ideas for reform. Speaking to the 'largest ever' audience at the club's celebrated luncheons, Nan explained the early stands she, her brother, and the Congress had taken in opposing fascism and the invasions of Manchuria and Ethiopia by Japan and Italy respectively, and the strong aversion they all felt to the appeasement of the Munich Pact. All of this was to reassure those gathered that India's commitment to democracy was unwavering. Even so, the West, she told them, was far from perfect and had made many mistakes in judgement. India's policy of nonalignment and nonviolence offered the world something new, and she hoped everyone in the United States would see the potential benefit of it. The overflow crowd of guests and members gave her a 'spontaneous [standing] ovation.'[60]

Nan began her tour soon thereafter by participating in Mt. Holyoke College's second annual Institute on the United Nations, which was focused on how 'We, the People' could effect a just peace. About 100 people attended events over the course of four weeks. Nan proved one of the biggest draws of the entire event, speaking to about 1300 people.[61] There she asserted that the United States had an obligation to join India in opposing colonial domination. She talked about enduring oppression and the essential interconnectedness of liberty. The US, she said 'had to feed and clothe the souls of human beings . . .'[62]

In LA, aside from her events with Bunche, she met with the Los Angeles Chamber of Commerce and the World Trade Association of Southern California. She spoke to about 300 business leaders and pressed for capital investment and government loans, pointing to her country's plans to expand industries like 'steel works, textile mills, [and] shipbuilding yards'. 'India may well be the last great area in the world where American trade can expand on mutually advantageous terms as well as in terms of a new hope for millions of people in Asia.'[63] The Los Angeles *Mirror* lavished praise on her: 'You can say that she is one of the most beautiful women in the world. That is true, but unimportant,' they wrote. 'You can say that few women before her, and few men too, ever held such responsibility . . . She is distinguished by more than great beauty and great ability, however. Say that she has the nobility of great compassion and great courage, and you will come closer to the real truth.'[64]

Afterwards, Nan spoke to students at the University of Southern California and worked with women's organizations. In Hollywood, the Association of Motion Picture Producers threw a reception for her. Among those she met was an up-and-coming actress named Ava Gardner.

The remainder of her three-week tour was spent in San Francisco, where she continued in the same vein. Her broad goal was to improve Indo-American understanding and to foster US economic policies that might assist India.⁶⁵ When she left, the acting mayor presented her with a commendation expressing the 'pride and gratification' of his city and the 'high esteem and the deep affection' with which she was held there.⁶⁶

She ended her tour in New York City with a speech at Columbia University. There she called on Americans to live up to the ideals of Thomas Jefferson and Abraham Lincoln. 'Your atom bombs and your skyscrapers will stand you in little stead unless that message is taken to heart and put into practice,' she warned.⁶⁷

By the time Nan had returned to the East Coast, she had been named to a list of the '10 most attractive women' in the American capital, a frivolous ranking that followed a similar one for men made just a few weeks previous. Nan, at number 2, was recognized for her 'hard, tough-disciplined mind' and her 'enormous sex appeal.' But she was especially praised for being 'smarter than any man' anyone could think of.⁶⁸

~

The endless cycle of travel and news left Nan breathless and fatigued. She made an appointment to see her doctor. After examining her, he said that she simply needed some rest and relaxation and prescribed two tickets to see 'South Pacific' on Broadway, which he then promptly gave to her. Her doctor, it turned out, was Mortimer Rodgers, brother of Richard, who worked with Oscar Hammerstein to create the famed musical.⁶⁹

~

For the first time since its creation, Nan was not going to serve as leader of the Indian delegation to the United Nations. She nonetheless remained highly sought after at the international gathering and was asked to give one of the event's marquee speeches, an address to the closing session of its scientific conference on the conservation and utilization of resources.

Nan used the platform to stand up for science, even as she acknowledged that the dangers the world was now facing stemmed in large measure from technological change and innovation. 'The fear of war is the single most dominating characteristic of our time,' she averred in reference to the looming threat of nuclear weapons.

'Looking upon the history of scientific achievement, my faith in its service to humanity, notwithstanding recent doubts and scepticisms [sic], is not diminished. When dogmas bound the intellect of man, science fought valiantly and suffered nobly to secure for us the precious heritage of free thought and now, when the heart of man is frozen with fear, fear of want, of insecurity, of death swooping upon him suddenly and swiftly in ways that may be fantastic and unpredictable—science must once again lead the crusade, not only because it has the means and the ability to do so, but also because many of the spectres which haunt us today have unfortunately emanated from its own creations.'

'The most important job that lies ahead of us,' she added, 'is that of human emancipation—the chance of full development to every human being. The lack of this is the reason for the unrest in Asia and Africa.' The solution, she concluded, was for the world community 'to redress the existing world unbalance in the distribution of material goods, services, and skills.'[70]

~

India was a founding member of the World Bank, one of two major institutions born of the Bretton Woods Conference held in 1945. The bank was originally established to assist with post-war reconstruction in affected countries, and it made its first loan to France in 1947 in this regard. With the Marshall Plan in 1948, the bank began to shift its focus to the financing of development projects in targeted countries. India was seen as especially worthy of assistance because of its planning and credit. Discussions for an aid package, originally broached as early as 1947, had been going on for some time before Nan arrived in the US.[71]

Soon after she assumed her post, she had a 'cordial' conversation with John Snyder, the US Treasury Secretary. It was an out-of-the-ordinary meeting, since it was 'not necessary or usual to call personally on members of the Cabinet', but Nan felt it important since he was knowledgeable and involved in relevant matters. The two discussed the proposed Bank loan and Snyder ended with an offer to speak directly with her moving forward if any additional assistance were needed.[72]

By the time Nan had had this meeting, the US Secretary of State, Dean Acheson, had been growing increasingly concerned with the inability of India and Pakistan to resolve their dispute over Kashmir. The two countries had just fought a brief war over the princely state, which had ended in a ceasefire at the outset of 1949. Bajpai had tried to reassure US Ambassador to India Loy Henderson that all was under control. But Acheson concluded in May that the State Department had to be prepared to use the leverage of the Bank loan and other assistance to pressure India to accept a workable long-term solution.[73]

Several weeks after her visit with Snyder, Nan met directly with Acheson. She was interested in probing the possibility of India taking a non-permanent seat on the Security Council. Acheson hedged but indicated general support for this possibility.[74] In turn, he pushed on Kashmir.

By this point, he and Henderson had decided that Nehru was simply undecided on what he wanted to do with respect to the northern territory, torn 'between a desire for world acclaim as [a] great political figure willing to resort to peaceful methods in finding solution[s] [to international disputes and desire for popularity in India as a strongman who will not permit foreign pressure to [to] persuade him [to] sacrifice national interests'. He was, additionally, facing pressure from his right. The Americans concluded that it was best that they 'exercise caution' in attempting to bring pressure and that whatever they did had to be 'couched in lofty language which would appeal to Nehru's *amour propre* [his sense of himself/his vanity]'.[75]

Nan and Bajpai had already anticipated the Kashmir issue would act as a temporary drag on India's Security Council seat ambition and felt the time was not right to pursue that strategic objective then. Nonetheless, they both had decided to make preliminary inquiries about a Council seat, hoping that such efforts could lay the foundation for success in the future.[76] Nan was thus not at all surprised when the Secretary of State looped back to the princely state in the meeting. She used the change in topic to inquire about the status of India's pending loan inquiries, expressing concerns about the holdup.[77] Acheson tried to alleviate her concerns, but, whatever his intentions, by the end of the day Nan was upset by what she perceived to be an effort to strongarm India using its financial needs as leverage. Specifically, it was understood that the Americans were tying the World Bank loan to the satisfactory resolution of the Kashmir conflict, exactly the message Acheson had indicated back in May that he wanted to get across. A flurry of messages between Nan and Delhi followed. Nehru indicated that he found the American attitude and constant sermonizing 'rather irritating.' He and Bajpai both told Nan that India would stand firm on their position and not back down.[78]

A little over a month later, Nehru met with Henderson and expressed his displeasure at American behaviour. He conveyed his commitment to the Kashmiri people and his promise that India would abide by their will. But he also believed strongly that Pakistan had not acted appropriately and that, in the context of that bilateral conflict, India was in the right. Acheson followed up shortly thereafter with another meeting with Nan in Washington. Again he brought up Kashmir but this time conveyed an offer from President Truman to intervene and broker a truce, while laying on the flattery, calling Nehru a 'world figure of great influence' whom 'the entire world now had a claim upon . . . as one of its great statesmen'. Nan expressed her appreciation for the American view of her brother but brushed off persistent US criticism even as she promised to convey the President's message.[79] Shortly thereafter, she communicated India's rejection of US arbitration, saying that her country would instead honour the terms proposed by the United Nations.[80] By that point, India had successfully secured the loan from the World Bank.

Amounting to $34 million, the money was formally to go towards the improvement of India's railways, but because of the high regard with which the country's leaders and civil servants were held, latitude was built in.[81] It was the country's first dollar loan and the Bank's first loan to Asia. Nan signed the loan agreement on behalf of her country, becoming the first woman to do so.[82] Bank President Eugene Black broke with house rules to celebrate the moment over sherry.[83]

About a month and a half later, Nan and Black sat down together again, this time to sign an agreement for $10 million for agricultural production, the first of many follow-up loans. Over the next seventy years, India would become the Bank's top loan recipient.[84]

~

Jawaharlal Nehru arrived in the United States on 11 October. Nan had been working on the arrangements for the visit for months, coordinating with State Department officials, while at the same time fending off inappropriate interference from the India League. League President J.J. Singh, in particular, had been used to being involved in high-profile Indian visits to the United States, and he had expected things to carry on in much the same fashion even with the new post-independence government. He insisted on offering all sorts of unsolicited advice, oblivious to the change in circumstances. When Nan politely declined his various prescriptions, he grew surprisingly resentful and lashed out at her perceived ingratitude. She said nothing publicly, but privately she grimaced at his impertinence. She continued planning all the same, finalizing a multi-faceted schedule that would allow her brother to see many parts of the country and engage with all kinds of communities.

Harry Truman himself formally received Nehru at the airport with full military honours, after sending the official presidential plane, the Independence, to fly the prime minister from London to D.C. Nan was on hand at the airport as well and drove back in an open car seated between her brother and the American leader.[85]

The following three weeks were a blizzard of dinners, parties, and meetings. Everyone from Dean Acheson and Eugene Black to Supreme Court Justice Felix Frankfurter, General George C. Marshall, and Admiral Chester Nimitz attended various events.[86] Nehru was warmly received at speeches at the US Congress and was given a ticker tape parade in New York City.[87] Other highlights of the packed trip included a visit with Albert Einstein in Princeton, a stopover at Wellesley, and a meeting to discuss racial justice with Ralph Bunche, Mary McLeod Bethune, and other Black leaders.[88] Nan for the most part stayed in the background, though she accompanied her brother on most of his engagements.

Nehru hit the right notes with the public and walked away from the tour with a 'personal triumph'.[89] Press coverage was largely laudatory and popular opinion was very favourable. Still, some political circles were disappointed that he had not been more committed to a Western alliance. Such an outcome, however, had never really been on the table. Nehru saw Cold War animosity as a threat to world stability, and he saw India's role as that of a diplomatic mediator bent on warding off catastrophe.

Americans, for the most part, grasped this. They saw Nan in particular, and her brother as well, as great champions for justice and the cause of peace. As Nehru's visit came to an end, Nan was again showered with honours that recognized her abilities and her efforts to put them to use for the greater good. The Alpha Kappa Alpha sorority, the first historically African American Greek society for women and creator of the American Council of Human Rights, with members that included legendary singer Marian Anderson and nursing pioneer Estelle Massey Osborne, recognized her for her contributions towards 'human freedom' and hailed her as 'one of the truly great women of all time'.[90] Several days later, she was given a medallion 'for achievement' by the Women's International Exposition, joining US Senator Margaret Chase Smith and Israel's Golda Meir (Myerson) among a few others.[91] The *Washington Post*, meanwhile, ran another flattering story, this time giving her a full-page spread, highlighting the beauty of her embassy, her speeches that sounded 'like poetry', and her incredible eloquence. 'Sending her as ambassador,' they wrote, was like 'scattering rose petals of good will'.[92] At year's end, *The Book of Knowledge*, a highly regarded encyclopaedia, named her, along with the likes of anthropologist Margaret Mead and actress Bette Davis, one of 'the world's 12 smartest women'.[93]

~

Despite the crowds and adulation, the constant visitors and hurried activity, Nan felt twinges of homesickness. Betty came for a visit and brought along her children. This helped, but she missed her elder children and thought of them often. She worried intensely over Rita's future and was especially concerned that she did not seem particularly concerned about her education. In the fall, Rita left to take up a course of study in Geneva for a time.[94]

In the meantime, Nan grew anxious about her old family property, the Khali estate and the Edmonstone Road house. Khali had deteriorated from lack of use and the thought of the place in shambles made Nan upset. She put both properties up for sale.[95]

~

Everything again took their toll, and Nan admitted herself to a hospital for several days. She finally confessed to her brother that the cause was an inexplicable, persistent pain in her right breast that often left her feeling 'sick and exhausted'. Her doctor in Moscow had previously suggested that she see a specialist about it, but she had let it go as the pains were transient and not long lasting. But as they had returned with some ferocity in the US, she felt she ought to have it all examined thoroughly.

She was relieved to learn that there was nothing serious going on. She had some minor gastric irritability and low pressure, the latter of which was diagnosed as the source of her frequent fatigue. She joked that she was 'disgustingly healthy'.[96]

~

The Constituent Assembly wrapped up its work and voted to adopt its newly drafted Constitution in late November. It was set to take effect in late January of 1950.

Nan was adamant that she had to be in India for that historic moment. She still resented having been away from home at Independence and informed the Ministry of External Affairs that she intended to make up for that sense of loss by being present on this occasion at all costs. As this was not official ambassadorial business, she made clear that she would use leave and cover the expenses of her trip out of pocket.[97]

India officially became a Republic on the twenty-sixth. Delhi was awash in tricolour as various ceremonies and festivities were held throughout the city.

For her part, Nan spoke to the members of Parliament about American attitudes towards India. She answered questions and tried to put various misunderstandings and rumours to rest. But she hedged when pressed on her stance on American racism, saying that she would be unable to earn goodwill if she spoke out directly against the country's internal policies.[98]

~

Nan returned to the United States accompanied by Chandralekha. En route, they stopped over in Geneva to see Rita.

Nan had enjoyed the few weeks of relaxation at home reconnecting with friends and family out of the public eye. But she was especially happy that both of her eldest daughters were now expecting. She was about to become a grandmother.

Chandralekha, who by then was living in Goa where Ashok had been placed, stayed with Nan for several months. By the end of the year, both she and Nayantara had given birth. Nan was thrilled to welcome Arjun Mehta and Nonika Sahgal into the world.[99]

~

Other good news awaited Nan immediately on her return. Wellesley had voted to award her an honorary doctorate of law. Among her fellow recipients were two Pulitzer winners and the 'chief of the medical clinic of the New York Hospital-Cornell University Medical Center.' Nan was self-effacing on stage. 'When my daughter heard that I had been invited to receive an honorary degree, she raised her eyebrows and said, "Well, mother, for a gal who's practically illiterate you're doing pretty well!"'[100]

~

Senator Joseph McCarthy was on the rampage. The Midwestern Republican from the state of Wisconsin had grabbed headlines by charging that known Communists were active in the State Department and elsewhere in prominent positions throughout the United States. He fanned the flames of fear, scaring people into believing that a Red Menace was upon them.

The U.S. Congress decided to investigate. They empanelled a special subcommittee to look into the matter. It was known as the Tydings Committee after its chair, Maryland Senator Millard Tydings. McCarthy preened through the proceedings, flamboyantly subjecting witnesses to harsh but theatrical interrogations.

Nan was horrified by the 'rising tide of hate'. She had been tracking the activities of the House Un-American Activities Committee, a forum in the US House of Representatives that had been fostering an atmosphere of suspicion for about a year, questioning the patriotism even of folks like Pearl Buck and Eleanor Roosevelt.[101] Now, as she returned to her embassy, Nan discerned a sudden change in the climate, with the Tydings Committee having a chilling effect on the country. More of her old friends were being dragged through the mud, among them Owen Lattimore, who had been on her team during her famous Town Hall takedown of Robert Boothby during her first tour of the country. She likened the smear campaign to the Spanish Inquisition, writing that 'nothing [was] more terrifying than this so-called democratic procedure of attacking those with whom you disagree'. She feared the consequences of such reckless political behaviour. 'There is a real danger,' she told her brother, 'of its overflowing the banks + inundating the rest of the world'.[102]

Nan knew she had to do something, to leverage her popularity and prestige in defence of those being threatened unfairly. The matter was delicate though and not one she could easily speak on given the nature of her position. But she found a way.

One of McCarthy's targets was Judge Dorothy Kenyon, a feminist who was outspoken in her support for broadening rights. Nan decided to show her support for Kenyon, and by extension all the others, by taking a prominent seat in the gallery of the Tydings Committee. She brought Chandralekha along for good measure. Sure enough, the cameras followed. When asked by the press what she thought, she responded diplomatically by saying that Judge Kenyon's 'side of the story' had to be heard. Then she went further, criticizing McCarthyism itself, if only obliquely, framed as a reflection on things back in India. She said that similar charges were being leveled against some members of her own Congress Party in her country. This, she made clear, she found 'troublesome'.[103]

~

Nan had another problem on her mind. The Prime Minister of Pakistan, Liaquat Ali Khan, and his wife, Begum Ra'ana, were visiting the United States. Nan followed developments closely. She had maintained cordial relations with her DC counterpart, Mirza Abul Hassan Ispahani, and even extended an invitation to host a meal for the visiting couple, though this ultimately could not be worked into their schedule. There was a relative thaw in relations between the two sibling subcontinental states then, with diplomatic efforts at rapprochement underway.

Still, the Pakistani PM was coming close on the heels of her brother's recent tour, and Nan grew defensive of what she and Nehru had accomplished. Her hackles were further raised when she learned that Khan's team and the State Department were working hard to ensure an identical itinerary for the sake of treating to the two rival nations on equal terms.

When the Pakistanis finally arrived, Nan had to face something she had never had to before: a true competitor. Begum Ra'ana proved up to the challenge, attracting attention and positive reviews.

The prime minister and his wife invited Nan over for drinks soon after they arrived. They spoke graciously of her brother and the recent diplomatic efforts. Nan appreciated this but blanched when they said they had no interest in discovering America and instead wanted America to discover Pakistan. This rubbed against her sensibilities. She found it a rather tasteless thing to say and felt sure that it was not the best approach to foreign relations.

For Nan etiquette and elegance went hand in hand. She was comfortable amongst any kind of crowd, from ordinary people to celebrities, from students to experts in their fields. Yet there was no doubt that she, like her brother, always gave off an aristocratic air, stemming in part from her commitment to propriety.

Her eloquence and brilliance, as well as her good looks, had won her many plaudits and made her tremendously popular in the United States, reinforcing her certainty in her values. So she was taken aback when Liaquat Ali and the Begum made traction despite taking a very different approach.

Neither had the rhetorical flourish that Nan and Nehru wielded with ease. Yet Khan was named by the *New York Times* as the premier leader of Asia. And Begum Ra'ana was called 'vivacious and charming'. One senator confessed that he found her 'quite a gal'. The secret to the Pakistani couple's success was that they behaved as 'plain people talking plain language', a surefire way to win over vast parts of America.

Nan had a difficult time accepting the inroads Khan and his wife were making. She downplayed their accomplishments in her assessments, only grudgingly acknowledging the praise they were receiving. She felt sure that, in any event, the impression they were making would not be lasting, at least in intellectual terms.

Yet at the same time she was alarmed that the prime minister and the begum had used every opportunity to press Pakistani claims on Kashmir. She worried about what the consequences of all of this would be.[104]

~

India was facing an acute food shortage and faced the grim prospect of a possible famine. The country had already spent its foreign exchange reserves as well as its sterling balance to procure grains. Now they decided to reach out to the superpowers for assistance, albeit somewhat reluctantly for fear of unwanted strings being attached. Nan and her team were tasked with sounding out the prospects for an American package. She met with State Department officials in December, generally receiving a 'sympathetic' response. The Americans had already assessed that India was going to fall short of about 40–5,000,000 tons of needed grain in total. Nan hoped that a portion of this requirement could be met by the United States and put in a request for 2,000,000 tons.

Things started well enough. Aside from positive diplomatic signals, various private organizations reached out to see if they could help. Dorothy Norman also got involved, putting together the American Emergency Food Committee for India, to coordinate some of the efforts and to advocate on behalf of the cause.

Just as the effort got underway, Nan had to dash off to London for a short time. Nehru was flying in for the Commonwealth Prime Minister's Conference, and she wanted to see him. The Americans believed that she was going to help foster Indo-US understanding. On her return to Washington, she encountered some unexpected headwinds.[105]

Just before her departure, she had given a short press briefing in which she urged people to consider war a greater looming threat than something as amorphous as 'communism', stressing that preventing the former was India's top priority. She talked up Indo-US relations, somewhat jokingly adding that she would be very happy to help interpret America to the East.[106] For the most part, it was all in keeping with things she said regularly. But for whatever reason, commentators back in India reacted sharply. The *Times of India* ran a harsh editorial charging that her indiscretion was 'no way of winning friends and influencing people'.[107] The backlash then became news in the United States.[108]

Nan was surprised. It all seemed so perfectly upside down, for if she had been successful at one thing, it had been winning friends and influencing people. The Indian press, however, did not see it this way and negative coverage continued for months afterwards. While she said nothing for the most part publicly, she grew defensive with Bajpai and Nehru, offering even to resign if the people back in India were so apparently unhappy with her service. Her brother dismissed the whole thing as a tempest in a teapot and urged Nan just to continue as she had been.[109]

It was good advice, for US–India relations were entering a period of severe turbulence. The Americans had grown unhappy with India's aloof posturing and its unwillingness to take a stricter anti-communist stand. They were particularly bedevilled by Nehru, who was not easily pushed around, giving the appearance of recalcitrance to them. Pakistani public relations added to all of this, making for the perfect storm.[110]

India's neighbour had once again dispatched a formidable woman to advocate in the United States on its behalf. This time it was Begum Ikramullah, a pioneer in her own right, the first Muslim woman to receive a doctorate from the University of London.[111] The begum generated positive publicity on a tour of the US, helping in part to counter the message and methods of Madame Pandit. Nan for her part concluded that this was all the handiwork of the American Ambassador to Pakistan, who was keen to undercut her work in the advancement of his own. She grudgingly admitted to the Begum's talents and the relative success of her efforts.[112]

Together, all of this made for a difficult diplomatic moment. Yet the food situation in India was so dire that Nan knew she simply could not fail.

~

Robert Oppenheimer was at his wits' end. The famed nuclear scientist, who had helped develop atomic weapons as part of the Manhattan Project, had grown increasingly alarmed by US efforts to develop the hydrogen bomb, a program authorized by Truman the previous year in 1950. Fearing what such power unleashed might do, he reached out in extreme secrecy to Nan, telephoning her first to say that he was sending an emissary to discretely 'communicate something of a very urgent nature'.

Oppenheimer begged 'India in the name of humanity' to maintain her present foreign policy and not be swayed by any pressure national or international to depart from it. He told her of the arms race underway and indicated that India was being eyed for a potentially big role, since it had vast reserves of thorium, an element with nuclear potential. Oppenheimer specifically asked Nan to ensure that India did not share its thorium.[113]

Nan immediately alerted Nehru to the conversation. He responded by saying that he would take the information under advisement. He also asked his sister to follow up with Oppenheimer casually and in person at her discretion.[114]

~

The Americans were convinced that they were misunderstood in India and that relations between the two countries were decidedly off track. They blamed Nehru in large measure for this but felt sure of the solution: Vijaya Lakshmi Pandit. Her credibility and popularity in the United States remained undiminished and unmatched.

One evening in late February, Nan attended a dinner party with Ambassador William Bullitt, who shared with her the distinction of having been his country's first ambassador to the Soviet Union. After the meal, a senator in attendance came up to her and said: 'my dear, you know we love you in this country—Anyone of our States would be honoured to accept you as a citizen. You are the only foreign woman who commands the affection and respect of the American people as a whole—but we cannot forget that you are Nehru's sister!'

News of this story quickly made the rounds. Albert Einstein was especially 'tickled'. 'These are strange times where the Americans and Russians are setting the tone for the "court ceremonial" in the official world,' he wrote with a wink. 'Somebody ought to write a book collecting all those flowers of courtesy.'[115]

But the American establishment generally and genuinely believed these things. For the next several weeks, they pushed Nan to return home for 'consultations' with her government. They were sure that she could clear the air and persuade New Delhi of the integrity of the American position. While flattered, Nan quickly dismissed the idea. Still, American faith in her abilities helped strengthen her overall position.

Efforts to secure food assistance had by then stalled in the US Congress, where frustration at Indian policy had boiled over. This in turn had only inflamed tensions in India, enraging people and further turning them against the United States. Things seemed to be quickly spiralling out of control.

Indian advocacy had until then been largely handled by bureaucrats within various departments under their purview, each very protective of their respective fiefdom. After Nan pointed out the inefficiencies of such methods, Nehru reorganized things. The food deal was above all a political negotiation, so Nan was now given full control.[116]

Within just a few weeks, 'a quite remarkable situation' developed. Ordinary people throughout the United States, led by local farmers, began to organize small, private donations. Some even undertook symbolic fasts of sympathy, a few lasting several days. One group drove in from Chicago to hand deliver one ton of wheat to Nan to much fanfare. 'We were convinced that there was a pronounced feeling that the dawdling action of Congress on the wheat for India legislation was neither characteristic nor representative of the American people,' they said. The Indian ambassador graciously accepted the small but substantive gift on behalf of her country, gaining prominent press coverage in the process.[117]

Nan, in the meantime, worked her more elite connections. She reached out to Robert Hutchins, a former president of the University of Chicago and dean of Yale Law School, who was then an associate director at the Ford Foundation. Hutchins had also been involved with efforts to draft a world constitution. He was keen to foster a better relationship with India and had asked Nan what might be done about it. She thought the time was right for a high-level visit to her country by a team of prominent Americans, and she quickly made all the arrangements with her government to facilitate such a visit.

Hutchins coordinated with the likes of US Supreme Court Justice William Douglas to get the trip off the ground.[118]

Vocal public opinion and such behind-the-scenes manoeuvrings—along with a rapid Soviet approval and delivery of their own grain package—seemed to turn the tide. The US aid loan was finally approved by the Congress in early summer. As soon as President Truman signed the India Emergency Assistance Act into law, Nan in turn signed the loan agreement, thanking everyone involved for their support, but especially highlighting the role that the regular, American people had played. She hailed the agreement as 'historic', with 'far-reaching consequences'.[119]

~

Despite all the acclaim and success of the past two years, Nan was restless by 1951. She had already once delicately raised the subject of her future with her brother, though had left the matter open-ended at the time. At the top of the year, shortly after the two of them had returned from their meeting in London, Nehru asked her what her wishes were. He wanted her to stay in Washington but accepted that she might have different compunctions.

Nan was not hesitant. She listed several reasons why she felt the time was right for her to step down as ambassador. She acknowledged that she had made many friends in the United States, and that she had found happiness there in her work. But she had been hurt by the criticism from home and she began to doubt whether she still represented 'India'? She wanted to reconnect with her homeland and its people. She additionally but no less importantly worried about managing her expenses with her limited government salary. Most of all, though, she longed to be near her brother again. She also wanted to experience once more the joys of living with her loved ones again.

Still, she went back and forth, and discussion of the matter went on for several months before it was finally decided. Vijaya Lakshmi Pandit resigned as ambassador to the United States at the end of the year.[120]

CHAPTER THIRTEEN

# Milk and Honey

India was gearing up for its first national elections. The new Constitution had gone into effect in 1950, laying the foundation for democracy and representative government to take shape in the country. Voting was to begin in mid-January 1952.

Nan was keen to stand for a seat. She had grown increasingly uneasy in her diplomatic posts, fearing that foreign living had put too much distance, physical as well as spiritual, between herself and the people she intended to represent. She believed that running for Parliament would allow her to grow more intimate with local constituencies, allowing her to reforge her connection with her communities.

Nehru was at first reluctant to see his sister get involved with politics. Primarily this stemmed from his belief that the country was best served with her as one of its premier ambassadors. But additionally, he worried about the business of elections. They appeared rough and messy. The jostling for positions he felt was unseemly, some appearing more to seek power than to serve the people.

Nan was a little startled by her brother's concerns. She offered to stand down out of respect for his wishes.

But Nehru came around quickly. He felt his sister's rationale made sense. And he did not want to come in the way of her own choices.

Her nomination faced some additional initial challenges when some questioned her ability to run on various technicalities. These matters were decided in her favour relatively quickly. Nan was named an official candidate for the lower house representing Lucknow in UP.

When the results were announced in early February, the verdict was overwhelming. Vijaya Lakshmi Pandit won 68.5 per cent of the votes cast, defeating three other rivals to become a member of independent India's first-ever elected class of parliamentarians.[1]

~

Though now an MP, diplomacy was too much in Nan's blood to simply leave behind. Shortly after the election was called, Mrs Roosevelt arrived in India for a month-long visit. Nan played tacit host, greeting Eleanor Roosevelt on arrival and then accompanying her to various events on her tour.[2] Among the highlights was a meeting at the Bombay Presidency Women's Council, where Nan had just assumed leadership.[3] The two of them spoke about child welfare issues, Mrs Roosevelt emphasizing that young people were 'future citizens' of the country and so paying attention to their needs was a matter of national importance. Nan for her part easily fell back on her older roles and spoke about illiteracy, inequality, and population control issues.[4]

A little over a week later, Nan interviewed Mrs Roosevelt on All India Radio. The two covered many topics, including India's village communities, agricultural matters, and the idea of peace. When Nan asked her what, if any, 'significant contribution to the world' India had made in the recent past, Mrs Roosevelt singled out its commitment to three things: electoral democracy, secularism, and egalitarianism.[5]

~

War had broken out in the Korean peninsula in 1950 when communist Northern forces crossed the 38th Parallel to politically unite the region. The United Nations responded militarily, bolstered primarily by US forces, led by General Douglas MacArthur, repulsing the Northern advance. Late that year, the UN launched a massive counter-offensive, itself crossing the 38th Parallel and now trying to unite the region under Southern, non-communist leadership.

China, by then under the new leadership of Mao Tse-tung and Chou En-Lai, warned the UN against such incursion, seeing it as a more direct threat to their position. When MacArthur pushed ahead, China entered the conflict on the side of the North, halting the Southern advance and returning to offence. By the middle of 1951, battle lines had coalesced around the 38th Parallel and essentially remained there for the remainder of the conflict.

India had watched these events unfold with growing alarm. Nehru for his part was insistent that the country should not get directly involved other than to use all its resources to push for peace. US officials quickly grew very angry at this stance, arguing that it betrayed India's avowed commitment to democracy and, for all intents and purposes, aligned instead with the communists. To make matters worse, the Indians maintained a strong defence of the Chinese, insisting that the new government be recognized and allowed to assume the country's seat at the United Nations.

These issues helped alter the atmosphere in the United States during the last year of Nan's term as ambassador and drove much of the negative sentiment in official circles. It had taken all her charisma and personal popularity to mitigate the situation, which made the criticism she received from the Indian press at the time all the more galling.

Nan was horrified as American officials worked themselves into a frenzy over the situation in Korea. She had used opportunities large and small to try to calm things down right from mid-1950, but to little effect initially. US representatives for the most part saw Nan as eminently reasonable and someone who understood the American point of view very well, erroneously concluding that any fault in India's policy related to the crisis was only because New Delhi did not heed her counsel enough.[6] This held true even as things took a turn for the worse once China entered the theatre of war.

For their part, Nan and her brother had been discussing changing circumstances in their northern neighbour since her days in Moscow. The siblings gathered new information over this time and grew unsettled when they learned about numerous allegations of corruption levelled against Generalissimo and Madame Chiang. The Chinese first family had been steadfast allies of India through the Second World War, so it was painful in a sense to consider a change in assessment. But both Nan and Nehru approached the subject matter-of-factly, separating any residual, personal warmth from necessary political decisions involving their two countries.[7] The Chiangs had made many mistakes, they concluded, and the Communists had won as a result, in addition to their increasing strength. India had to deal with the

Chinese leadership as it was not as they had perhaps once believed it would be. Nan departed soon thereafter on a goodwill mission to India's large, northern neighbour.[8]

~

The fourteen-member Indian delegation arrived in China on 27 April for a six-week visit.[9] The Americans hoped that the trip might afford an opportunity for back-channel communications. Acheson had written to Nan asking her to convey certain points to Peking (Beijing): the US wanted to avoid a larger war and had no intentions of dominating other people, but they were reacting to an unjust invasion in Korea. They hoped for better relations once the present matter was settled.

Nan had several meetings with Chou En-lai and one with Mao early on. She and Nehru kept in constant communication about it and, while insisting publicly and privately that India could not mediate between the warring parties, concluded that India had to leverage its 'good offices to bring about a settlement fair' to both sides. The Indians hoped to work with the UK to help resolve the conflict. The first part of Nan's tour was dedicated to this high-stakes, delicate diplomacy.

She conveyed the essence of the American message and seemed to make some headway, but when British Prime Minister Anthony Eden came out forcefully in support of Truman's positions, Nan and Nehru were forced to abort their peace initiatives and default to making pleas for moderation.[10]

While their hope to bring the Korean War to a quick end suffered a setback because of changing global political circumstances, the Indians pressed ahead with their more limited but no less important efforts to engage with the new People's Republic and to foster better relations between the two giants of Asia. One important issue involved the imprisonment of Western missionaries, which was seen as an action taken by the state in the context of the war. Nan carefully pushed for their release, directly bringing the matter up with Chou. The Indian ambassador to China, K.M. Pannikar, picked up the matter in the days after the delegation returned home and soon thereafter the Indian efforts paid off with the release of prisoners.

Nan had built a warm rapport with Chou. Her only meeting with Mao was briefer and more perfunctory, but nonetheless positive. She and Mao had a smoke together when he pressed her to join him.

Nan immediately sized up both men in her official assessments. Chou had talent and polish, an 'infectious' sense of humour, and the makings of 'a great statesman'. Mao, meanwhile, gave 'the impression of being kind and tolerant and very wise.' But, she stressed, one had to be careful of appearances. She astutely likened what she saw to poses taken by 'Russian leaders, particularly Stalin'.[11]

As she and the team travelled around the country over the next few weeks, Nan made a series of similarly discerning observations. She found Madame Chiang's estranged sister, Madame Sun Yat-sen, the widow of the founder of modern China and current Vice President of the country, 'friendly and gracious'. Yet, while she parroted widely held anti-American beliefs, she surrounded herself with American things. And though she was much revered, Madame Sun seemed almost a prisoner of sorts, by her admission confined mostly to her home and forced primarily to speak through an official interpreter though she was fluent in English, having attended Wellesley. Nan passed on a letter from Eleanor Roosevelt, which was meant as a humanitarian appeal aimed at getting the missionaries released.[12]

When she met with former labourers and now 'reformed' landlords, she was struck that both praised the extensive land reform policies that had been in place, though the reformed landlords were penalized beyond property loss with temporary disenfranchisement and isolation. She found the policies themselves, at least in terms of redistribution, to be a general success. She was moved by peasants' 'genuine and spontaneous enthusiasm' in talking about it. By contrast, she found the landlords' praise 'mechanical and meaningless' and impossible to digest.

At universities, where she was received repeatedly with rapturous welcomes, she was impressed by the 'extraordinary personal discipline' of the students. She felt their eagerness and excitement for their new government and way of life to be authentic and 'not regimented by force or fear'. And while she was especially pleased that as a group they were 'genuinely friendly to India,' she worried they were consumed by an 'unrelenting hatred' for the United States, which she concluded would ultimately not do anyone any good.

She was favourably impressed with other things, including the progress of women's liberation and the Huai River development project, but she was struck by the suppression and 'liquidation' of 'counter-revolutionaries' and by the public trials and mass executions of those charged with corruption.[13] Yet despite all of these reservations, Nan remained impeccably on message throughout her visit, talking up Sino-Indian partnership, posing for photos, and generally winning friends wherever she went.

At one point, a picture that was part of a travelling Indian art exhibition was stolen, embarrassing local officials. They immediately launched an investigation, redoubled security, offered to compensate the Indian artist for the loss of their work, and formally apologized to the embassy. Nan was gracious. She thanked them for all actions 'already taken' and added that 'such accidents' were 'unavoidable'. She assured her hosts that they were of 'no blame'. Instead of taking any payment, she assumed 'personal responsibility' and promised to see that the painter in question would receive their due.[14]

The trip, which had received extensive international press coverage, came to an end in early June. Nan and her team had travelled by special train to multiple cities, including Nanking and Shanghai, sightseeing along the way, and taking in many cultural programs while being wined and dined.[15]

It was exhausting, but by all accounts, a big success. Nan's primary takeaway was that China was a country on the move. There was much to admire, but with an underside that warranted some concern.

~

Nan briefed Parliament on her return, then spent the next few months trying to settle back into life in India. She busied herself once more with ceremonies and conferences, receiving 500 tons of private food and medical aid sent to India by US churches.[16] She delivered a convocation address at a conference on native languages and talked of the importance of a national language like Hindi even as she also recommended that people also learn their various regional and local languages as well.[17] And she was scheduled to chair the reception committee of the Third International Conference on

Planned Parenthood, which was co-organized by Margaret Sanger in Bombay (Mumbai). This was to be an important meeting as it was to launch the International Planned Parenthood Association. In the event of it, Nan could not attend, though her future participation in the birth control movement was announced.[18] Her absence was thought understandable. Vijaya Lakshmi Pandit had once more been sent to New York as the leader of India's United Nations delegation.

~

Nan received quite a shock at the outset of the 1952 meetings. Voting for the president of the UN General Assembly was held by secret ballot. Canada's Lester Pearson was standing for election and as expected, received an overwhelming majority of votes. But Nan came in second though she was not a candidate.

She brushed the matter off quickly for she had more important things to worry about. The Indians planned a major peace offensive.[19] Joining Nan as a member of her delegation this time was Krishna Menon, who had spent the previous months trying to hammer out an armistice agreement to end the Korean conflict. The war on the Asian peninsula remained the biggest issue of the day. But the Indians had additional concerns as well. Tunisia was beginning to pull away from the colonial control of France and support for this and the broader movement towards decolonization was also seen as a priority. And South Africa's new policy of apartheid was concerning as well.

Menon's Korea plan had hit a roadblock over disagreements regarding prisoners of war and other issues. The team hoped to use the UN meetings to try to resolve the matter.

The Americans continued to hold Nan in the highest esteem, the State Department placing her internally in an elevated category of prestige essentially on par with that of foreign ministers.[20] Dean Acheson initiated conversations with her to see what headway could be made regarding Korea.[21] While she discussed such things privately, she also used her public speech to the assembly to try to rally everyone to action.[22]

Behind the scenes, however, all was not well. The long-simmering tensions between Nan and Krishna Menon were starting to surface. British officials, led by Minister of State for Foreign Affairs Selwyn

Lloyd, seemed growingly impressed by Menon, who had also been India's envoy to the UK since independence. Lloyd was convinced that 'a possible attitude of jealousy' seemed to be developing between him and Pandit. The Americans were not sure what to make of all of this. They admitted that Menon seemed to be 'carrying the ball on the Korean issue,' at least for the moment. Nonetheless, they concluded they ought to lean in and 'stay in the closest possible touch' with Nan.[23]

After Nan and her team had held many formal and informal conversations with various parties, the Indians felt they had a deal. Dean Acheson internally heralded India's efforts as nothing short of 'historic' and noted the country was on the cusp of achieving a 'remarkable success'.[24] British Prime Minister Anthony Eden, having been informed of New Delhi's plan by Nan, was cautiously optimistic.[25] The rival Labour Party, in the meantime, cabled Nan to express their 'appreciation' for the efforts she and her country had made towards peace.[26]

In December, the deal came up for a vote in the General Assembly Political Committee, winning by an overwhelming margin of fifty-three to five. China, which was still represented at the UN by the ousted Nationalist camp, abstained, knowing that Mao's government remained opposed. Only the Soviets and their allies voted against the bill. Though Nan had tried to connect with Vyshinsky, he lashed out against the Indian plan, calling it a 'meek and emaciated copy' of what the Americans wanted. Krishna Menon clashed directly with the Russians in debate, arguing that the plan was fair and balanced, took all views into account, and was urgently needed to restore stability to Asia, but they remained unconvinced. The vote by the full Assembly a few days later closely mirrored the one taken in committee, the Indians winning fifty-four to five. But the Soviet and Communist Chinese opposition meant that the armistice could not take effect or have any immediate impact. Even so, India's plan was still seen as the best way forward for ultimate peace. The press correctly credited Menon as the architect of the plan, while Nan's role as delegation leader and the overall shepherd was also recognized.[27]

~

Despite its significance, Korea had not been the only thing on the UN's docket that year. Questions concerning decolonization in places like Tunisia and Morocco and apartheid in South Africa had also been front and centre. The situation in Kashmir had come up as well. Nan and her team had stepped out front of every issue, even while also contributing to important decisions on 'U.N. Trusteeship . . . self-determination . . . political rights for women . . . freedom of information and U.N. sponsored funds for economic development.' India had been such a key force that Nan thought the entire meeting could 'justifiably' be called the 'India session'.[28]

As the session went into recess for the holidays with much still on its plate, Nan was singled out for a major honour. She was named one of seven to win that year's batch of One World Awards. These prizes were named in memory of Wendell Willkie. The selection committee overlapped with the one for the American Nobel and the awards were fashioned as a peer to their prestigious Swedish cousins. Nan won 'in the field of international statesmanship and humanity'. Other winners in that category that year were US Supreme Court Justice William Douglas and the renowned philosopher and physician Albert Schweitzer, who would go on to win the Nobel Peace Prize as well.[29]

~

The Americans had quickly taken a disliking to Menon. In the days leading up to the vote, he had taken some mysterious delays, and they feared that he would upend the fragile compromise by accepting additional Soviet emendations, though this had not come to pass. They had confessed their concerns to Nan, who had to navigate many such minefields as she oversaw the entire process. Shortly after the vote, Menon delivered remarks critical of American behaviour and blamed them for the setbacks faced by his plan. This cemented the Americans' earlier judgement.[30]

~

Nan arrived back in New Delhi in January. En route, she had stopped over in London, Cairo and Damascus. In Egypt, she was received and feted by General Mohamed Naguib, who along with Gamal Abdel

Nasser had led the Free Officers Movement and who now served as prime minister of the country.[31] In Syria, she met with the de facto head of state, Adib Shishakly. All her visits were given high priority and seen as important diplomatic steps towards fostering good relations between each country and India.

But the biggest concern remained Korea. Nan bristled at accusations at home and abroad that India had simply kowtowed to the 'Anglo-American bloc.' She acknowledged irritation at the Chinese and Soviet reception of the Indian plan, but nonetheless expressed hope that the parties would still come together. She underscored India's good intentions and praised her country's leadership on the issue.[32]

~

In February, despite hinting that she planned to stay in India, she once again headed back to New York to lead India's delegation to the UN as the General Assembly resumed, aiming to resolve the Korean conflict. This time, the only other member of her delegation was Menon.[33]

Almost immediately upon arrival, news broke that Stalin had suffered a life-threatening stroke. Speculation was rife as to what impact this would have. Nan put the Indian response delicately, saying that they were 'very sad, as . . . [they] would be for any one suffering from serious illness.' Though this was transparently merely a polite expression of condolence, Nan's was considered the 'most frankly sympathetic' reaction of any major official.[34]

But even as this story made the rounds, Nan found herself in the middle of another frenzy, as her name was suddenly floated as a possible successor to UN Secretary-General Trygve Lie. Canada was keen to have Lester Pearson, then the president of the UN General Assembly, take the position. Pearson had almost been the UN's first secretary-general instead of Lie, but he had been opposed by the Soviets and there was fear they would torpedo him again.

Nan was flattered by the support she received but indicated that she was not running as India was supporting Pearson. She did, however, agree to take the job if she was nonetheless elected. Just as the election was getting underway, Stalin was pronounced dead, sending shockwaves through the diplomatic corps, as everyone tried to find a new equilibrium. Lie then revealed that he had felt the Russians had been improperly pressuring him over Korea and was stepping down to protect the integrity of the office. Rumours began to fly that Vijaya Lakshmi Pandit was the only person capable of winning support from all parties in such a fraught moment.[35]

When the vote finally came, the Soviets predictably vetoed Pearson, while all other first-round candidates failed to get enough votes to advance. The Soviets then formally proposed that Nan be named secretary-general, or alternatively her countryman Sir B.N. Rau, a jurist on the International Court of Justice. It was the Americans especially who were not keen on allowing this to happen, though their issue had mostly to do with Nehru's supposed neutralism, and to a lesser degree the lack of executive experience from either Indian candidate.[36] When the time came, Nan was rejected by the Security Council, garnering only two votes in favour and one against, with the rest abstaining.[37] The lone vote against came from Nationalist China, taken because India recognized its communist successor, though it took this stand only in consultation with the US.[38] Nan did not take the result too personally or hold it against anyone, laughing it up at the White House with President Eisenhower and John Foster Dulles just days later.[39] For their part, US and Nationalist Chinese officials had hoped to avoid taking any kind of negative stand against Nan and regretted that the matter had required a formal vote.[40]

Sweden's Dag Hammarskjöld emerged as a surprise consensus choice for secretary-general. Within just a few short days, his nomination raced through, receiving no substantive opposition and helping to end the acrimony of the previous few weeks.[41]

While the matter seemed officially closed, Nan's nomination triggered excitement in certain circles that had decided to push for it further. The Crusade for World Government, led by notable figures from the British left like MP Fenner Brockway, Labourite Lord Farringdon, and the great philosopher Bertrand Russell and poet Cecil Day-Lewis, created a petition to support her cause, arguing that she presented an 'outstanding opportunity to establish a bridge between East and West'.[42] Ordinary Britons too had expressed their support for Nan and bewilderment at the West's actions. They wondered aloud if the West had missed a unique opportunity to break the deadlock in international relations and agree to what they felt was a reasonable offer from the Soviet Union.⁴³

~

Even as the debate over UN leadership was ongoing, Chou En-lai suddenly offered a set of peace proposals on Korea that closely mirrored what had been in the India proposal. Since the Chinese had never given any indication beforehand that they had had any issues with what India had been planning, many analysts had concluded that opposition had come from primarily at Soviet direction. With changes taking place in Moscow, a new wind seemed to be blowing. Nan called Chou's moves 'very encouraging.' She added that she hoped that this would mark the 'beginning of the peace in Korea'.⁴⁴

~

Nan arrived back in India in early April and reiterated her long-standing claim that she hoped now to spend more time in the country. Her reputation did not appear to have taken any serious hit from her loss at the UN.⁴⁵ In May, a US poll named her among the ten greatest living women in the world, along with Queen Elizabeth II, Helen Keller, Senator Margaret Chase Smith, and Eleanor Roosevelt.⁴⁶ Shortly after, she helped host US Secretary of State Dulles during his visit to New Delhi.⁴⁷

Just weeks later, a peace settlement for Korea was reached, with the armistice that Menon had crafted, and Nan had steered through, as the basis. *Newsweek* hailed Nehru as the savvy Korean middleman.⁴⁸

With such a huge weight lifted from her shoulders, Nan was able to turn her attention to other important matters. She joined her brother on a trip to Pakistan, to engage in talks with her country's neighbour.⁴⁹ The Pakistanis would reciprocate later that summer, when Prime Minister Mohammed Ali would visit New Delhi, where Nan would help to host him.

~

As the race for secretary-general was underway, some people floated the idea of Nan serving as president of the General Assembly as an alternative. Nan had brought both possibilities up with her brother, who had indicated that she let matters take their course since she had not raised the question and was not herself seeking anything. He had at the time dismissed the role in the UNGA, though star diplomat Lester Pearson, who would go on to win a Nobel Peace Prize several years later, held the position of president that year.[50]

In early summer, the United States began internal discussions on whom to support to replace Pearson. Henry Cabot Lodge, Jr, the US ambassador to the UN and future running mate to presidential candidate Richard Nixon, came out swinging in favour of Madame Pandit. He quickly dismissed potential competitors, including Thailand's Prince Wan, who had been campaigning for quite some time and who had garnered preliminary US backing, as well as Lebanon's legendary diplomat Charles Malik, and possibilities from Western Europe. The Indians by that point were sounding out potential interest for Nan to run. Lodge argued that the US had to 'take some initiative' and lead, rather than either opposing her candidacy later or appearing to jump 'on the bandwagon'.[51] US officials at that point believed that Nan might also become India's next minister of external affairs.

The Indians reached out with their feeler two days after Lodge's push had begun. When the Americans probed about Nan taking a leading role in her country's government, they received a categorical response: there was no chance of Vijaya Lakshmi Pandit taking over the Ministry of External Affairs (MEA) as 'the Prime Minister did not wish to favour his own family too much . . . and . . . would not wish to have his sister in the cabinet.'[52]

Western governments, particularly Britain and Canada, were notably cool to Nan's UNGA candidacy. Lower-ranking State Department officials shared this assessment, claiming that Nan was simply too 'unstable' of a US ally, highlighting her positions on Korea as an example. Secretary of State Dulles eventually agreed with the critique. But Lodge held his ground and issued a forceful rejoinder that won over several other officials. Dulles took the issue to President Eisenhower, who weighed in in Nan's favour, saying that the US 'should appeal to world opinion by supporting an intelligent woman like Madame Pandit'.⁵³ Lodge triumphantly sent Nan a personal telegram informing her of the decision.⁵⁴ Just weeks later, the entire Western bloc followed the American lead, making Nan the public frontrunner for the position.⁵⁵ In announcing the news, the *Christian Science Monitor* hailed her as the 'Indian Mrs. Roosevelt'.⁵⁶

~

The United States opposed India's participation at the political conference meant to formally end hostilities in Korea. It was a bizarre position to take considering all that the Indians had done to successfully broker an armistice. The Commonwealth and NATO broke with their nuclear-armed partner and either voted in favour or abstained. India won a majority vote but not the two-thirds needed to secure a seat and was thus excluded from the conference. Nonetheless, the results were seen as a symbolic rejection of the US position and support for India's. The media observed increased strain between the two countries. But both privately and publicly, officials on both sides minimized the issue. India recognized the *realpolitik* at play. And US backing for Nan's UN candidacy was seen as an effort to compensate.⁵⁷

~

Rita was married to A.K. Dar, an MEA official, in early September. The venue in New Delhi was 'tastefully decorated'. The occasion was graced by many of the city's elite, including President Rajendra Prasad, members of Parliament, and Prime Minister Nehru.⁵⁸ Nan could not linger for long. Within days, she was off to New York as leader once more of India's delegation to the United Nations.

~

Vijaya Lakshmi Pandit was elected president of the UN General Assembly on 15 September 1953. The event was not a foregone conclusion as Prince Wan stayed in the race and fought it out, trying to rally enough support for his cause. But Nan proved the popular choice, winning thirty-seven to twenty-two with the support of all major powers. Pakistan also voted in favour.[59]

The international press celebrated her victory. The *Globe and Mail* thought her election a moment of 'sweetness and light', a rare moment of unanimity prefacing an acrimonious session filled with fireworks.[60] The *Austin Statesman* lionized her as an 'aristocratic rebel' who spoke 'with a ring of prophecy.'[61] The *Christian Science Monitor*, calling Nan 'flashing and forthright', recognized the significance of what she had achieved, writing that for 'the first time in history, a woman heads a great diplomatic assemblage'. They added that her new role was a sign of 'emancipation, not only of Asia but of the rest of the world'.[62] Playing off the translation of her name, the *Los Angeles Times* reported that 'India's 'goddess of victory' had chalked up 'another first'.[63]

Nan immediately assumed her new office. 'I regard your choice,' she said, 'as a tribute to my country and a recognition of her profound desire to serve the purposes of the United Nations and through them the paramount interests of world peace. It is also recognition of the part that women have played and are playing in furthering the aims and purposes of this great organization'.[64]

~

Not everyone was thrilled by Nan's elevation. The *Daily Express* editorialized that Britain should quit the UN as a result, claiming that Nan had sometimes shown 'more sympathy for the enemies of Britain . . .' They warned that she could make the international body 'downright dangerous' to the island kingdom's interests.[65] In the same vein, US anti-communists warned that Madame Pandit, 'a Marxian Socialist', would end up lending aid to communism.[66]

Nan put a good deal of this concern to rest shortly after taking office. She tried her best to be even-handed and fair, but also firm. The Americans noticed right away, commenting internally that she in fact had proven to be more surefooted in her approach even than Lester Pearson had been.[67] US Vice President Richard Nixon noted that he 'was very much impressed by the way in which she presided' over a session he witnessed, adding that he thought she conducted the meeting 'in a very dignified way'.[68]

Allen Dulles, John Foster's brother who was the Director of the Central Intelligence Agency (CIA), in the meantime, sent her a private note of 'felicitation' that read simply 'Allahabad 1914.' It was a nod to the time they had spent together decades earlier, when he had grown both very impressed and very fond of her.[69]

~

Nan saw her position as president of the General Assembly as one beyond any one country, including her own. She vowed to be as impartial as possible, as she felt her position demanded. She immediately stepped down as leader of India's delegation, handing the reigns over to Krishna Menon, and further tried to distance herself from the group's actions.

When the nationalist Chinese delegation was seated, Menon threatened to challenge their credentials. Nan, who had long been on record supporting the right of Communist China to be accredited at the UN, quickly intervened, ruling her countryman out of order. Knowing that she was correct on the rules, she offered a chance for appeal, but neither Menon nor those supporting his position took it. While the press noted the confrontation, they also recognized the high-mindedness behind her actions. 'This was the first time Mrs Pandit had been forced because of the duties of her high office to make a ruling opposed to the policies she championed before election.'[70]

Menon's challenge was news, however, because, by that point, the personal rivalry and outright bitterness between the two South Asian foreign affairs stalwarts was public knowledge. The *Daily Boston Globe* joked that the relationship between the two made 'India's relations with Pakistan one of brotherly love by comparison'.[71]

Menon immediately distinguished himself at the UN by being far different from Nan. While both shared a love of sharp barbs, she had always laced hers with grace, charm, and wit. Menon, by contrast, looked down on most of his opponents and was unafraid to take more ideologically driven stands.[72] He was particularly known to try to act independently, keeping information from colleagues, including Nan, and acting as if he was Nehru's personal representative.[73] Within just a few weeks, he had ruffled many Western feathers as officials saw his positions as less neutral and more pro-Soviet than either of the Nehrus had ever indicated.[74] Nan noted privately that Menon spent all his time rushing about and sending 'long telegrams home' but the result was 'a muddle all round'. 'There is no doubt at all,' she wrote, 'that he is largely responsible for . . . [Nehru's] unpopularity. His [Menon's] way of doing even the most innocent things is so open to suspicion + questioning.' 'And yet,' she astutely bemoaned, 'one can't make . . . [Nehru] see this'.[75]

~

Nan's election, a brief moment of 'East-West accord', was seen as a big breakthrough for women.[76] While Nan accepted this latter point in principle, she quickly demanded that she not simply be seen as a woman who had accomplished something, but as a person who had done so. She had no hesitation in speaking up for women's empowerment, but she felt that a focus on her gender most often brought the conversation to sexist lows. At the press conference soon after she officially took office, a reporter retread a tired narrative and asked after her sari. She curdled immediately and sourly retorted that she 'never had time to consider clothes'.[77]

Writers could not seem to help themselves. Each new profile seemed to further emphasize her feminine allure. London's *Observer* began a story by calling her 'handsome, well dressed, and noble in manner', before concluding more seriously that there was 'probably no one better able to deal with the spokesmen of the great Powers than this determined and gifted lady, whose life has taught her to understand the politics of revolution, the responsibilities of administration, and the possibilities and impossibilities of modern diplomacy'.[78]

*Newsweek* highlighted her criticism of the fascination with her appearance, but nonetheless pointed out 'the lengthy eye-lashes around her deep, dark, almond-shaped eyes' and the fact that she wore 'a faint trace of lipstick and high heels'. 'Her wavy, silvery hair always looks as if she has just been to her Fifth Avenue coiffeuse' they added for good measure before turning to a discussion of her temper.[79] The *Times of India* noted that she had 'mastered another art rare in most women—the art of growing old gracefully', clarifying that she still looked so 'young'.[80]

~

Nan's powers as president were procedural but nonetheless substantial. She enforced the body's rules, determined who could speak and for how long, directed all plenary discussions, ruled on points of order, and generally had 'complete control of the proceedings at any meeting.'[81] Popularly she was understood to be the 'UN President', 'the First Lady of the World' and a major world leader.[82]

Among the highlights of her session, she oversaw Turkey's election to a two-year term on the Security Council, in the process ruling against and cutting off the Soviet Union's Vyshinsky, who wanted to speak out in opposition.[83] She also facilitated a rare unanimous vote in the Assembly, to make permanent the highly successful UN International Children's Emergency Fund, known by its acronym UNICEF.[84] On UN Day, she heralded the work of the fund, which by then had 'fed six million hungry children in 13 countries', as 'one of the most vivid examples within the U.N. framework of international cooperation and peaceful purposes'.[85]

But the headline-making issue remained Korea. India by then had placed Custodian Forces in the DMZ (the demilitarized zone at the 38th Parallel, separating North and South Korea) and was busy overseeing the transfer of prisoners of war, one of the thorniest issues involved in the brokering of an end to the conflict. South Korean President Syngman Rhee was angry at the Indians for having remained a 'neutral' nation during the war, and he looked upon all of their activities with suspicion. In October, he threatened to upend the peace process by militarily forcing the release of tens of thousands of anti-communist prisoners then held in Indian custody. The Custodian Force felt that they needed better cooperation from the UN, and by implication the US as well, to be able to carry out the mission. It fell to Nan to manage all of this behind the scenes, shoring up the needed support and pushing peace talks through delicate conversations with various officials, including Henry Cabot Lodge, John Foster Dulles, and President Eisenhower.[86]

~

Just a few months into her new job, mysterious men showed up in Nan's office and queried her secretary about some recent activity. As soon as they left, a secretary raced over to Nan to warn her that the US Federal Bureau of Investigations had been there asking questions.

Nan reported the incident to Dag Hammarskjöld but stressed that she did not want to make much of it. The secretary-general understood her wishes but, as another similar incident had just occurred in Washington D.C., he nonetheless conveyed the matter first to the State Department as a courtesy, and then formally to Lodge, who raised the matter with the attorney-general. Herbert Brownell, in turn, wrote immediately to the legendary FBI director, J. Edgar Hoover, warning that the matter was 'serious [and] unwarranted' and demanding 'prompt attention'. Hoover, by then, had created a massive surveillance operation and kept extensive files on almost all figures of influence.

The FBI had received complaints about Nan's activities dating back to her first major tour of the United States in the mid-forties. Yet Hoover had essentially dismissed such concerns, choosing not to investigate her activities in any detail.

The Bureau now took the matter seriously and launched an internal investigation but came up empty. They could find nothing linked to anything at the agency.

Hammarskjöld in the meantime looked into things further. He discovered to his surprise that the men in question were from the UN Security Office and were following up on some invitations that had accidentally been misdirected.

The whole affair was a simple misunderstanding. Not one to miss an opportunity, however, Hoover feigned a broader innocence, protesting to Brownell that 'this is but one of several instances wherein the FBI has been unjustly charged with activity for which it was in no way responsible'.[87]

~

Nan reached the apogee of her fame in the United States. She had been popular there since making waves during her first tour. By the time she had returned as ambassador, ordinary working Americans such as taxi drivers knew who she was and deeply admired her.[88] Now she was even the subject of middle-school assemblies where she was always held up as an outstanding woman to be admired.[89]

Her many media appearances, sometimes in serious conversation with newscasters and sometimes interacting more playfully with young people, had made her a household name.[90] A group of men approached her in the fall following one of her appearances and said 'Mrs. Pandit, we missed watching our usual Saturday football game on television so that we might listen to you. It was worth it'.[91] It was the same everywhere she went, from washroom attendants and bellboys to little girls who thought of her as the 'elected mother of the world's children'.[92] Nan found all the spontaneous expressions of affection 'overwhelming . . . embarrassing . . . unbelievable . . . [and] quite terrifying'.[93]

At the end of 1953, she was named by the Fashion Division of the Federation of Jewish Philanthropies of New York as 'Woman of the Year', while a New Year's Gallup poll declared her the third, after Eleanor Roosevelt and First Lady 'Mamie' Eisenhower, most admired woman in the world.[94]

~

In December, President Eisenhower travelled to the United Nations to speak about nuclear arms. Nan presided over what would later be called the 'Atoms for Peace' speech, one of the most significant of the Cold War. She 'received and introduced' the US president, who pushed a new perspective, framing weapons, rather than atomic power, as the real threat. Eisenhower called on the UN to establish a regulatory agency to monitor and strictly control the use of nuclear energy for a range of peaceful purposes, what would become the International Atomic Energy Agency. Nan told reporters afterwards that the 'very fine speech . . . has in it the seeds of great opportunity for the world'.[95] As she closed the session for recess the next day, she said of the president and his remarks, 'Here was a man who is recognized as one of the greatest soldiers of our time picturing the certain destruction of mankind if it cannot pull away resolutely and at once from the edge of the abyss . . . It is my hope,' she added with a flourish, 'that this Assembly will have the opportunity of similarly listening to the counsel of other personalities equally concerned with the great issues that concern us—more particularly of peace and disarmament.'[96] Just before departing the next day, with reports of pushback against

Eisenhower's plan circulating, she threw the full weight of her office, and her personal prestige, behind his initiative. 'The proposal was of the highest importance,' she told the press, 'and deserves the careful consideration of all the governments of the world.'[97]

~

Nan had hoped to reconvene the General Assembly to help resolve the Korean crisis at the top of the new year. India made the formal request in early January. A majority of polled member states needed to assent for everyone to be called back into session. The US, however, strongly opposed this move and ultimately prevailed, bringing Nan's formal role as president to an end, save for the one final task in September of opening the new UN session where her successor would be chosen.[98] Disappointed, she devoted the remaining months of her presidency to the ceremonial functions she was left with.[99]

In India, while awaiting the decision, she spent time with her family and busied herself with leadership of a fundraising campaign for the Kamala Nehru Hospital in Allahabad and of a UN association.[100] Later, she spoke at a convocation at Nagpur University, where she received an honorary doctorate.[101] In the months that followed, she made trips to Ceylon (Sri Lanka), Burma, Yugoslavia, Malaya (Malaysia), Singapore, Switzerland and Indonesia.[102] In these places, she was hosted and honoured by the highest officials, among them Prime Minister John Kotalawala, President Soekarno, and Marshal Tito.[103] She also was a guest at a number of important functions, such as the ceremony commemorating the 2500th birthday of the Buddha in Rangoon. She used every occasion to speak up for peace, to warn against the dangers of arms, blocs, and militarism, and generally to promote goodwill.[104]

~

Nayantara Sahgal published her first book in early 1954. *Prison and Chocolate Cake* was a memoir of her childhood and early adulthood. While it revealed many interesting anecdotes about her family, the well-received book also brought into dramatic relief her talents as a writer. Her poetic sensibilities made words on the page sing. The book heralded the beginning of her much-celebrated career.[105]

~

By the early summer of 1954, rumours began to swirl that Nan would soon take another important assignment, that of high commissioner to the United Kingdom.[106] She had actually just been offered the position and understood the news to be part of a larger campaign to pressure her to accept and quickly take charge. She thought the post to be a good one, but privately wondered if she would be a good fit since all of her 'ties were with the U.S.'. She admitted that her 'basic sympathies ... [lay] there [America] ... no matter how their policies' irritated her 'from time to time'.[107]

Her children nonetheless encouraged her to take on the new job. Only Nehru seemed strangely ambivalent. Though she loved and admired him as much as ever, an unmistakable distance had emerged between them. Their outlooks seemed increasingly divergent. He felt she was a bit too flashy for his tastes while she grew vocally critical of what she saw as his anti-American outlook, which was fed, it seemed, by whispers from Krishna Menon.[108] Nan thought it important to distinguish between the people and their country and the decisions sometimes taken in their name.

The question of the high commissionership lent a mid-summer visit to Britain added significance. Just as she arrived, she received joyous news, which added a little bounce to her step. Rita had given birth to a seven-pound baby boy named Gopal.

Nan's trip was an official visit. She had been invited by Prime Minister Churchill, but he had had a stroke just before her arrival and was recovering near Kent. Foreign Minister Selwyn Lloyd took over hosting duties while Queen Elizabeth received her at Buckingham Palace.[109] A few days into her trip, as she was staying with her friend, Conservative MP Evelyn Emmet in Amberley Castle, she was surprised to learn that she had been invited to spend the afternoon at Churchill's country house, Chartwell. Lady 'Clemmie' (Clementine) Churchill phoned Nan apologetically to say that the PM had wished to have her stay over for the whole weekend but had been forbidden from doing so by his doctors.

When Nan arrived, Clemmie hurriedly whispered that Sir Winston was very unwell and that Nan was to try to keep him from talking too much, from walking, and from heading over to the nearby pond. Tea was served as soon as he entered. 'I don't want this,' Churchill responded. 'I want some brandy.' When Nan tried to change the subject by mentioning her newborn grandson, he immediately demanded that everyone have champagne. It took a serendipitous announcement about his own soon-to-be-born grandchild to make him forget his quest for alcohol.

A bit later, he insisted that Nan had to see his fish and, when no reason could be found to stop him, the two of them went off to the pond on their own. He erupted angrily when his eye caught his Secret Service hovering nearby. Nan suppressed a smile as she reflected on the similarity between her old nemesis and her father. Churchill suddenly turned to her and asked what she knew about English history. 'A great deal,' she said confidently. Then, after a brief pause, she added mischievously 'you never let me learn anything else'. Churchill looked at her sternly before erupting in laughter. The two relaxed and spent the rest of the afternoon in playful banter. 'I hope you don't hold it against us for putting you in prison,' he told her. 'Not at all,' she replied sincerely. Churchill confessed that the British had made mistakes during their time in India.

He stuck to his guns on other matters, saying he did not believe that women had a place in politics. 'I have accepted you,' he said, 'but don't start trying to incite anyone here.' Nan talked about the many qualified women of Britain and asked how long he hoped 'to keep them out'. 'As long as he could' came the roguishly truthful reply.

As she readied herself to leave, Churchill paid her a high compliment. She had conquered 'two of man's greatest enemies—hate and fear,' the same as her brother, he told her.

Churchill had caused India many heartaches. And he remained irascibly committed to the Old World until the end. But at a personal level, he and Nan forged a friendly and respectful bond that, in true Gandhian fashion, eschewed any bitterness about the past.[110]

Nan's visit, and her overall trip, received the usual positive press. David Eccles, who had just overseen the Queen's coronation and who served as a minister in Churchill's Conservative government, singled her out as 'the most distinguished lady politician in the world'.[111]

~

Nan's appointment as India's next high commissioner to the United Kingdom and ambassador to Ireland was announced in September 1954 soon after the next president of the General Assembly was named.[112] Before she moved to London, however, she scheduled a personal visit to Tokyo to see Rita and her family. As she prepared to depart New York, she delivered a bevvy of talks around town, including a prominent one to a group called Women United for the United Nations, where she remarked on the recently decided US school segregation Supreme Court case, Brown v. Board of Education, saying 'a wave—not a ripple, but a wave—of emotion swept [India] . . . I must have had . . . a hundred or more letters from all parts of the country asking me for more details about this, saying that . . . if this can still happen in America, everything is all right'.[113] She added: 'It was quite amazing and to me, who loves America, the most heartening thing that has happened in the last decade.'[114]

Nan arrived in Japan a few days later, after first stopping over at Pearl Harbor in Hawaii. Though she was there unofficially, the country nonetheless accorded her diplomatic honours. She was received by the prime minister and met Empress Kojun and Emperor Hirohito at their autumn imperial garden party.[115] She was made an honorary citizen of Tokyo, the first Indian so named, and given the key to the city, the twenty-first person ever to receive one.[116]

After a stay of several weeks and a brief visit back home, Nan made her way to London by the end of the year and presented her credentials to Queen Elizabeth, once again breaking barriers to become the first woman high commissioner ever accredited to the UK.[117] The *Manchester Guardian* claimed that she by then 'had more diplomatic experience than any woman in history'.[118] As happened in America, she was greeted with enthusiastic press coverage so over the top that a summary concluded that 'no Envoy to Britain from any country . . . [had ever] found so much popular acclaim at the beginning of an assignment'.[119]

~

Despite all the recognition, Nan suddenly felt her stature diminish back home. Krishna Menon had been steadily undermining her for years. But he had increased his efforts over the past few months. He had long exercised a mysterious hold on the prime minister, one that even Nan could not break. Nehru saw in Menon a kindred spirit and admired his commitment to hard work. So he unendingly overlooked the exasperating personality quirks and questionable behaviours. One of the additional secrets to Menon's uninhibited ascent was his close friendship with M.O. Mathai, Nehru's powerful personal secretary, who was only half-jokingly referred to by Delhi's elite as 'the "joint" or "deputy prime minister"'.

Menon was driven by ambition and an extraordinarily high impression of himself and his abilities, which he believed to be near unequalled. He had disdain for Nan, whom he saw simultaneously as his rival for position and as someone far beneath him in intellect and ability. Ironically, he had gotten a big break when she had become president of the UNGA and he became the head of India's UN delegation in her place. With this much larger international platform, and his success with the Korean negotiations, he had gotten a taste of true global fame. He became more convinced that Nehru, and indeed the whole world, needed his unique wisdom, over and beyond any other. He made his move.

Just as Nan was taking office in London, Mathai sent a warning to Subimal Dutt, who was just then taking a position as Commonwealth Secretary (and would soon become Foreign Secretary). Keep your distance from Vijaya Lakshmi Pandit, he was told. For she was in the process of 'falling from grace'.[120]

CHAPTER FOURTEEN

# Brick Lane

The Indian mission in London was of a scale quite different from what Nan had previously experienced. The facilities this time were split between two locations. The office of the High Commission was located off Aldwych, situated proximate to the Strand and the river Thames in the centre of the city. India House, as it was known, had been opened by King George V in 1930 to serve the British high commissioner for India and had been transferred to Indian control at independence. The residence for the ambassador, which had been purchased on a long lease by Sir Girja Shankar Bajpai in the late forties, was several miles away located at 9 Kensington Palace Gardens. The gilded mansion, decked out with a French wood-panelled drawing room and Italian and Adam marble fireplaces, was located on one of the city's most exclusive streets, which was also home to other foreign envoys.

Krishna Menon wanted to project austerity during his original run in the post and so had avoided Kensington Palace Gardens by staying on-site at India House. At the same time, he had somewhat inexplicably maintained a 'fleet of staff cars—and a custom-built Rolls Royce' for his use.

By the time Nan had arrived, both opulent buildings and all the vehicles had suffered from years of neglect and were in states of disrepair. She immediately set about having things cleaned, polished, and revived.

Diplomacy, classically the purview of rich and powerful men, remained an expensive affair. But the Ministry of External Affairs as well as the Indian Parliament were reluctant to sanction most work and any upgrades, worried about frugality and the appearance of reckless spending in a country still reeling from the devastating impoverishing consequences of colonialism.

Nan sympathized with the demands of her countrymen while also understanding the needs of elite diplomacy. She had always had to straddle these two worlds and had been more or less successful at effectively blending simplicity with style. To work around her current problem, she chose to supplement or replace the embassy's worn-out things with her personal materials to avoid unnecessary costs. Yet everything she did seemed to raise someone's eyebrow, and she faced increasing criticism back home for her 'luxurious living and extravagance'.[1]

~

Nan knew soon after her arrival that something was amiss. One of her first tasks was to prepare for a visit by Nehru, who was to attend a conference of the Commonwealth heads of state in late January 1955. The prime minister was being accompanied by Mathai, his Personal Secretary, N.R. Pillai, the secretary-general of the Ministry of External Affairs, and Krishna Menon. But tongues began to wag when Menon arrived several days in advance of the rest of the party. Speculation was rife as to what he was doing there and why whatever he was tasked with was not being entrusted to the high commissioner.[2]

Nan had been warned as she was still unpacking that India House had been the source of unending intrigue in the years prior. She was set to be India's third envoy to the UK. The low-key B.G. Kher had preceded her, serving unhappily in the position for the two years before her, following Menon's departure. When Nan had spoken with the soon-to-be Tory PM, Anthony Eden, as well as his earlier Labour predecessor Clement Attlee, for her entry interviews, both had painted a picture of a sorry state of affairs. They indicated that Menon had repeatedly gone around Kher and engaged in direct talks with various officials, leaving the British to fill in the high commissioner after the fact. Even worse, everyone in and out of the Indian Embassy was divided into pro or anti-Krishna Menon camps, resulting in a generally poisonous and distrustful atmosphere.

Nan likened the situation to the Cold War. Eden and Attlee expressed hope that she would quickly put things in order and streamline the official channel of communication, the latter explicitly asking her to spend time 'cleaning up the mess'.

So Menon's actions just weeks later were seen by all as a direct challenge to her authority and legitimacy. Nan tried to get control of the situation internally thereafter but was simply outmanoeuvred by the wily Menon. Over the next few months, he repeatedly flew in and out of London backed by special requests from the Ministry or from Nehru himself to arrange for meetings with various high-ranking officials. On each occasion, he pushed Nan aside both directly and indirectly, excluding her from most of his conversations. Beyond this, Nan was also kept in the dark about Menon's other international meetings, which she only learned about second-hand from other countries' ambassadors. All of this she found acutely 'embarrassing'.[3]

But the sabotage went deeper even than this. As Nan tried to straighten things out at India House by shuffling her staff and bringing in high-quality officers, she ran into one mysterious roadblock after another. She warned the MEA that there was an urgent need to 'live down the past and set standards for the future' there, but her pleas went largely unanswered. Many posts, including ones 'already sanctioned' were kept pending for extended periods, while Mathai sometimes engineered transfers for others, all kneecapping her further.[4]

Within just six months, Nan appeared smaller. It was widely felt, and by her especially, that her purpose had been reduced to social affairs and that anything of importance to international affairs was being 'bypassed' around her.[5]

~

Tensions between India and the United Kingdom flared through Nan's first year as high commissioner. Several issues seemed to particularly draw the ire of the conservative British press. The first involved the Afro-Asian Conference that was taking place in Bandung, Indonesia.[6] The West was excluded from the meetup and there was consternation about what was taking place there because of the context of the broader Cold War. Nan addressed the concern in meetings with groups of Labour and Tory MPs that ranged from thirty-five to 100 people at a time, most notably to the Conservative Commonwealth Group in the House of Commons. Her reassurances proved effective, and things righted themselves, but only temporarily.[7]

Portugal by this point had declared its intent to hold onto its territories in the subcontinent, chiefly the coastal region of Goa. By 1955, it faced growing resistance to its continued rule even as it rejected any dialogue over the matter. The issue rose to dominate other concerns in India, as opposition parties and the government sought to address the situation in various ways. Right around then, the Portuguese President visited the United Kingdom. Nan and her team stayed away from all official functions. The decision drew fierce condemnation from the likes of the *Daily Express*, which chastised Nan for being discourteous to the Portuguese head of state.[8]

Just as that firestorm began to die down, another one flared up when Soviet Premier Nikita Khrushchev and President Nicolai Bulganin visited India to much fanfare. British papers ran relentlessly hostile coverage criticizing Nehru for opening the door to communism, inflaming public opinion. When Nan discussed the problem with UK Foreign Secretary Harold Macmillan, he dismissed the complaint saying the stories were 'not so bad'. The Soviet leaders, he went on, were putting on a 'twin music hall act', and he pleaded helplessness regarding public reaction, saying that the government was 'powerless to do anything about it'.[9]

The Indian public, for its part, grew increasingly angry at persistent British efforts to press for movement on the Kashmir question. Both Nan and Nehru reacted indignantly as well, defending India's actions and its efforts at coming to an agreeable solution. They pointed to various statements coming from Pakistan's leaders and to the situation in the state to argue that conditions were not suitable for any further Indian conciliation. In a meeting with Lord Home, the Secretary of State for Commonwealth Relations, Nan charged Britain with having a lingering 'old imperialist attitude,' adding that its clumsy and ineffective approach 'to delicate and complicated problems' was only serving to make matters worse.[10]

By the start of 1956, Macmillan's replacement, Selwyn Lloyd, paid a visit to 9 Kensington Palace Gardens to try to steady the India–UK relationship, which had become 'a bit shaky'. When he asked Nan to distil the source of unhappiness to just one thing, she replied that it all boiled down to the Baghdad Pact, a military alliance that had involved Britain, Turkey, Iraq, Iran and Pakistan, to the exclusion of India. When Lloyd tried to minimize the impact of the group, saying that it posed no threat to India, Nan strongly disagreed. The two argued and left things inconclusively.[11]

~

Nan faced several problems on the home front as well. Relations with Betty, which had been fraught for years, became especially bumpy. By this point, Krishna Hutheesing had grown increasingly resentful of her older siblings and dissatisfied with her relative anonymity. Nan was hurt when her sister had not sent a word of congratulations as she took up the high commissionership. But things were made much worse when Betty published a tell-all essay in *The Ladies Home Journal* that claimed to reveal the real Nehru and Madame Pandit. While the article shared some family history and lore and embellished her own contributions, Betty was generally ungenerous and mean-spirited throughout, writing that Nehru had lost his charm and warmth and that Nan's 'greatest concern' was her figure, adding that even a few extra pounds made her look 'dumpy' because of her short stature. She went on to say that Nayantara, Chandralekha and Rita were not 'ambitious' like their mother. The unflattering portrait was harmful and hurtful.

Tellingly, Betty had begun her story with an anecdote of how she had been mistaken for Nan on the steps of the landmark Taj Mahal Hotel in Bombay. 'No, I am not Madame Pandit,' she had responded 'with a sigh of resignation.' 'How many times I had been asked the same question,' she wrote, before confessing that she sometimes wished that she did not 'belong to a family that is so much in the limelight'.[12]

Nan tried her best to sympathize with Betty's point of view. Whatever their differences, Nan valued family. Eventually, she invited her sister for a visit. It went so well that Betty stayed for over a month. Nan half-jokingly told Nehru that it appeared their sibling had no plans of leaving, adding that she hoped that she was not 'unconsciously supplying material for another article!'[13]

In the meantime, Betty was anxious about the future of her two sons, Harsha and Ajit, who wanted to settle in the West after completing their studies abroad. She reached out to Nan to ask for her assistance in helping the boys adjust, going so far as to suggest that one of them live with her permanently. Nan for her part was equally concerned about her nephews and did her best to help them find their way, though taking on wards did not seem to her or Nehru a particularly good idea. Betty never saw it that way however, and in due course wrote Nan a letter attacking her for being disloyal to the family, for lacking integrity, for being greedy and more.[14] She had also involved other family members in her squabbles.

Raja Hutheesing in truth worried about his wife's mental health. Nehru concluded that Betty was not 'mentally quite stable' and prone to 'delusions,' with a tendency to exaggerate everything.[15]

These matters were troubling enough, but in the middle of all of this, Nan had to face an even more intimate crisis. Nayantara's marriage was on the rocks. Gautam Sahgal never got over his wife's earlier relationship with Isamu Noguchi and still burned with jealousy. Nayantara was singularly beautiful and brilliant, and generally magnetic to men, and Gautam had grown ever more insecure through the first few years of marriage. The situation was exacerbated by a brief relationship Nayantara had had with Nicolas Wyrouboff, a noble of Russian origin who had migrated to France. The two had met when Nan was at the United Nations meeting in Paris in 1948. Gautam, while deeply in love with his wife, became suspicious of her activity and desperately tried to control her every move, his suffocating grip serving to push her further away. Gautam could not handle the irresolvable tension and flew into violent rages, physically abusing Nayantara in the process.

By 1959, the Sahgals had made close friends with the Danish trade commissioner, Kjeld Packness and his wife. Nayantara and Kjeld found each other's company interesting and one day planned to meet over lunch. Gautam found this unacceptable, and this led to much back and forth between the two, drawing in both Nan and Nehru. Nehru brokered a temporary peace while Nayantara travelled to London to be with her mother to sort through things. Gautam had threatened divorce and she needed to figure out what she wanted to do.

Nan did not know all the details of what was going on. She wanted to support and protect her daughter and initially thought that salvaging the marriage was the best way forward. But as it became clear that a breakup was necessary, she threw her full weight behind Nayantara. Nonetheless, it would be several more years before the marriage officially ended.[16]

One of the few bright spots amidst all of this was Nan's relationship with her niece, Indira Gandhi. She frequently inquired after her in correspondence with her brother, and he in turn shared news about his daughter's various activities, and his worries about what she was getting into. Nan called for Indira to visit and even planned parties in her honour. And late in her tenure in the UK, she arranged for Indira's eldest son, Rajiv, to stand for entrance to Cambridge University, where he was soon accepted. She doted on the boy and treated him and his mother with the utmost affection. Indira sent her a 'brief note' expressing her love and thanking her aunt for all that she had done for Rajiv and her.[17]

~

As her role in international affairs narrowed, Nan recalibrated to focus primarily on dinner diplomacy, using entertainment and social affairs to build relationships and burnish larger Indian foreign policy objectives. It was a subtle art for which she was especially adept. Throughout her high commissionership, she attended many parties, threw a few notorious ones herself, and had numerous important conversations over food and drink, including notable interactions with the likes of Ghanian President Kwame Nkrumah, French Ambassador to India Count Stanislas Ostrorog, Labour leader and former Secretary of State for India Lord Stansgate, American journalist Walter Lippmann, Chief Justice of the English and Welsh courts Hubert Parker, and NATO's Deputy Supreme Allied Commander for Europe Field Marshal Bernard Montgomery.[18]

Among those with whom she had an immediate rapport was Winston Churchill. She met him again at 10 Downing Street a few months into her term. In that meeting, the British PM inquired as to why Nan was called 'Madame Pandit'. 'It's pure affectation,' he chided before insisting that she go by 'Mrs. Pandit' while in the UK.[19] He called Nehru the 'light of Asia' and told Nan that he expected her to be 'the conductor through which this light from the East could be spread to the West'. These views he repeated in a letter he sent directly to Nehru shortly thereafter, in which he specifically added that he was 'so glad . . . [Nehru's] Sister . . . [was] in so important a position over here'. As she left her meeting with the prime minister, Nan was especially struck when he walked her to her car in the rain and saw her off himself, standing alone outside to the shock of the policeman on duty.[20]

Churchill retired just a few weeks later but he maintained his contact with Nan, inviting her to his home at Hyde Park Gate and back to his Chartwell estate. The two developed quite a close bond, with Churchill often making a 'fuss' over her. Churchill's daughters also spoke regularly with Nan, reinforcing their father's admiration for the Nehrus and India and indirectly suggesting that he very much wanted to come to 9 Kensington Palace Gardens for a meal, a request that Nan obliged.[21]

She quickly became similarly familiar with the Royal Family. The Windsors found her gracious and interesting and generally enjoyed her company.[22] When the Queen Mother, Elizabeth, was named chancellor of the University of London in early 1955, she made the unusual move of hand-selecting several people she wanted to receive an honorary degree at her installation later that year. Nan was one of her choices. At the ceremony that November, broadcast on BBC television, Queen Elizabeth I noted the University had been the first in the country to confer degrees to women, the first to appoint a woman as a professor, and the first to elect a woman as vice chancellor. The Queen's appointment as the first woman Chancellor was in keeping with this tradition. All this lent Nan's selection for a Doctor of Laws a special significance.[23] Reuters observed that the public orator called her 'this great world figure, this great lady of the Commonwealth' as she was hooded by the Queen Mother to 'thunderous applause'.[24]

The closest friendship that Nan nurtured in the UK was with an extended royal, Lord Louis Mountbatten, the uncle of Prince Phillip and second cousin to Queen Elizabeth II. Dickie, as he was known to those close to him, had been the last viceroy to India and had overseen independence and the Partition. He and his wife Edwina developed a unique bond with Nan and Nehru and essentially considered them members of the clan. The Mountbattens frequently had the siblings over to Broadlands, their estate in south-eastern

England, where they acted as counsel and confidantes. Their younger daughter, Pamela, then in her upper twenties, looked on both Indian guests with fondness, and considered Nan someone who was 'very intelligent . . . very cosmopolitan, civilized, and sophisticated . . . and very clever'. She was in 'awe of her beauty' and 'very impressed with her'. Nan, to her, was simply 'one of the most distinguished people of the times', someone who was 'always in the light if she was in a gathering of people'. Whatever was going on behind the scenes in Indian politics, the Mountbattens, with their ear to the ground, never heard any criticism of Nan, and were struck by how universally she was admired.[25]

~

Perle Mesta, the 'hostess with the mostest', completed a seventeen-country tour in 1955, with visits to India and the UK as part of the itinerary. She had by then completed her stint as US ambassador to Luxembourg. In New Delhi, she met with Nehru for an hour, saying only one 'impertinent' thing. She demanded to know why he would not send his sister back to the US once more as ambassador. 'We like her,' she declared. When she related this story to the High Commissioner in London, Nan practically fell off her chair, summoning her children into the room 'to hear "'what Mrs. Mesta [had] said to . . . [their] uncle"'.[26]

Nan indeed remained a beloved figure in the United States, the frequent subject of newspaper puzzles, quizzes, and games.[27] The American Federation of Soroptimist Clubs honoured her as one of seventeen women of achievement, along with several writers, a cancer specialist, and psychoanalyst Anna Freud, daughter of Sigmund.[28] Even young beauty contestants selected her as the most outstanding woman in the world.[29] When Marlon Brando, atop Hollywood with A Streetcar Named Desire, Julius Caesar, On the Waterfront, and Guys and Dolls, was asked to name one woman 'he particularly admired,' he was quick with his answer: 'Mrs. Pandit'.[30]

~

Bertrand Russell was growing increasingly worried about the safety of the planet, fearing the true cost of nuclear war. As part of the

Parliamentary Group for World Government, he helped devise a plan to safeguard everyone's future. In its first incarnation, broadcast a year before in 1954, he had sketched out an idea for 'neutral nations' to draw up a fair-minded 'assessment of the effects of atomic warfare'. By the top of 1955, he told the House of Commons with much enthusiasm that he had concluded that the best path forward was simply 'to invite India alone to make the assessment' since the Indian prime minister had already laid out a similar vision in 1954 as well. He had already discussed the matter with both Nan and Nehru when the latter had been in London for the Commonwealth Conference.[31]

In February, just five days after an official announcement that Britain would take steps to develop hydrogen weapons, a delegation came to see Nan to take their case forward. Their original plan was to send a '"large and representative" deputation' to speak with her, but in the end they decided on a much smaller group. They submitted a proposal and asked for approval to launch an educational campaign around the matter. She consulted with her brother, and he indicated that he indeed planned to do something about this soon, though he wanted no publicity about it.[32]

Dag Hammarskjöld had in the meantime convened a panel of nuclear scientists as well, to lay the groundwork for an international atomic energy conference to be held later in 1955 in Geneva, the evolution of the proposal made by Eisenhower in late 1953. By the end of the follow-up UN discussion, Homi Bhabha, India's preeminent expert in the field, was asked to lead the Swiss event as president.[33]

Nehru brought Russell's idea, a variation of his own, before his Cabinet and received authorization to go ahead. Nehru then discussed the matter with Bhabha, who endorsed the concept in principle but thought that the international conference he was heading might be directly relevant. Nehru ultimately created a private commission to look into the atomic question without any fanfare.[34]

Russell in the meantime was pursuing a separate track, reaching out to Albert Einstein to see if prominent scientists could put out a statement warning against the dangers posed by super destructive arms and urging the peaceful resolution of all conflicts. Einstein signed onto the Russell Declaration just before he died in 1955. The Russell-Einstein manifesto was released in the middle of the summer, with additional signatories that included Linus Pauling, Max Born, Joseph Rotblat, and Herman Muller.[35]

A few months later, the Nobel-prize-winning nuclear scientist Arthur Compton, who was the chair of the Organization for World Brotherhood, an outgrowth of the US National Conference of Christians and Jews, announced that several high-powered figures would be joining his group to help take it forward. Konrad Adenauer, West German Chancellor, Paul Henri-Spaak, the Belgian foreign minister, Carlos Romulo, the Philippine ambassador to the US, and Vijaya Lakshmi Pandit were named the new co-chairs of the organization, dedicated to fostering 'friendship, mutual respect, and co-operation among people of different religions, races, countries, and cultures'.[36] That April, Nan published an essay in *Foreign Affairs* in which she linked India's foreign policy to the project of peace, promoting coexistence over fear, and poetically claiming that her country's objective was to 'hold a hand uplifted over hate'.[37]

~

The British Museum, founded in 1753, had gained a reputation for having one of the best collections in the world. This was in no small part due to acquisitions that had taken place over centuries of imperial activity.[38] Among its priceless artefacts were Buddhist relics that had been found in 1851 in a stupa in Sanchi, a town with ancient Mauryan origins in the Indian state of Madhya Pradesh. The Museum had taken possession of these materials in 1887.

Buddhists had been lobbying British officials for the return of various relics for decades, and they had an initial success soon after independence when a set housed at the Victoria and Albert Museum was sent back to India via Ceylon (Sri Lanka). The objects continued to be of religious value but were meant to be experienced through internment in a stupa and not displayed.[39]

In 1956, one trustee of the British Museum pushed for the institution to return a second set of relics in its possessions, which were from the same source as those already given back by the V&A. Buddhists around the world were commemorating the 2500th death anniversary of the Buddha. The Museum consulted with the Indian government which in turn sent Nan to handle the matter. In February, she hand-delivered the relics to her government in a 'solemn ceremony', which in turn transferred them to the Buddhist Mahabodhi Society, which shared the artefacts with Ceylon and Burma as well.[40]

~

The Duke of Wellington was keen to make a trade. He was descended from a rather famous relative, Arthur Wellesley, the first Duke of Wellington, known as the Iron Duke. Wellesley had fought in the Battle of Srirangapatnam (Seringapatam) which saw the defeat of the legendary Tiger of Mysore, Tipu Sultan, one of the last major holdouts against the British takeover of the subcontinent. The Iron Duke had then become Governor of the region for a short period.

The current Duke as a result had in his possession several things that once belonged to Tipu. Inversely, India possessed a rather fancy portrait of Wellesley. The Duke was interested in making a bargain and approached the Government of India. Nan met with him at his townhouse and was impressed with the assortment of fine 'books, china, glass, portraits, and furniture' he had on display. She carefully reviewed the Tipu material and immediately 'strongly recommend[ed] the exchange'. She told Nehru that 'Pictures of English Generals and Viceroys will inevitably perish in the years to come if they remain in India. If they are returned, they will be preserved in the families to which they belong. On the other hand,' she concluded, 'we shall get something of greater value and interest to us in exchange.'[41]

The oil portrait of Wellesley was in the Government House in Madras. Since it had been in rather poor condition, the Governor of Madras had had it restored. He had proudly provided the Government of India with a detailed description of the work and its history. After some quick negotiations, the Duke agreed to hand over additional items in exchange for two portraits, the original he had inquired about and one more of Marquess Wellesley, Arthur's brother and the fifth Governor-General of India.[42]

Sometime later, Nan met the Duke at a party. He was 'very sad' and dejectedly told her that the two paintings he had received were 'fakes'. The Duke had had the art reviewed by experts and had learned that the works had been 'retouched' some sixty years prior and had practically been 'repainted'. The original paintings had 'disappeared'.

The Duke held nothing against Nan or the Indian Government, for they had delivered as promised, but he felt very foolish nonetheless.

London society, however, found the story altogether amusing. Nan came away looking rather brilliant, having gotten the better of 'a man who . . . [had] always had the better of everyone else'.[43]

~

Nan continued to be an inspiration to women everywhere. Months into her term, she was invited to be the first honorary member of the new University Women's Union, a counterpart to their male predecessor. Nan formally opened the new debating society, before sharing the evening with Lady Violet Bonham Carter, 'the best woman orator in England'.

But for all the recognition of her achievement, she still had to face down everyday misogyny. Even after all this time, certain diplomats would make remarks behind her back that were just short of catcalls, saying for instance that her best feature was her 'nice arms'.[44] Nan despised such attitudes, and it was one of the main reasons that she disliked too much media or professional focus on her womanhood, even as she always advocated for women's rights.

One episode illustrated some of the regular indignities she had to suffer, flattering though they may have been. In late 1958, Brazil sent a new ambassador to the Court of St James. He was a 'warm hearted' gentleman of wealth. When he first met Nan on a protocol visit, he brought her 'dozens of red roses,' then kissed her hand, embraced her, and kissed her on both cheeks. He then announced that 'for many years there had been only three women in his life', Margot Fonteyn of the Royal Ballet, Queen Elizabeth, and Nan herself. He immediately invited Nan to fly back to Brazil the following weekend on his private plane where she would be overwhelmed by the love of the people. Nan politely declined and took the whole thing in good humour, but this treatment from 'another planet unhampered by rules or codes of conduct' persisted.[45]

~

Nan visited Ireland to much fanfare in April 1956. This was her second visit, after she had made an earlier protocol trip the year before to present her credentials. The Irish generally had a fondness for India and were especially pleased to have her as their envoy. A profile in the *Irish Times* at the outset described her as 'The Remarkable Mrs. Pandit'.[46]

Her first stay had lasted a week and was extraordinarily jam-packed with events as the Irish wished to show their tremendous affection and admiration for her. British officials had monitored the trip closely, internally observing that 'Dublin had expected great things from this distinguished lady, and had laid itself out to welcome not only the first woman Ambassador ever accredited to the Republic, but also one of the most celebrated women of the day. It felt greatly honoured and did its best to show it'. Nan, they observed, 'of course [had] made an impression of charm, grace and ability wherever she went'.[47]

The first tour had not been without a snafu, however. Nan had been pressed to give her views on Partition. This was an extremely delicate topic, because it not only involved India's relations with Pakistan, but also with Great Britain, as well as the UK's association with Ireland, which had been partitioned in the early twentieth century to the chagrin of the majority Catholic, nationalist population. Southern Ireland had broken away to form an independent Republic as a result, while Northern Ireland remained within the United Kingdom. Irish Republicans remained fiercely opposed to all of this. Nan had made a carefully worded statement, both in London before her departure and again in Dublin, saying that 'partition was not a happy solution [to] the problems of any country' but that India 'had accepted Partition as a solution of the problem there, recognized Pakistan as a separate State, [and] had opportunities for discussion on common problems and looked forward to closer co-operation with it'. The British, for their part, were extremely satisfied with this response. But her words somehow got twisted around in press reports, which had her saying that the 'partitioning of my country is a very bad thing'.[48]

~

In the summer of 1956, Gamal Abdel Nasser nationalized the Suez Canal Company, which had been operated by Britain and France since the nineteenth century. Nasser wanted to raise funds to help with his Aswan Dam project, an effort to modernize hydropower and irrigation on the Nile and only took this action when previous funding promises from the West had fallen through. He offered to compensate the old colonial powers for the worth of their seized assets. Britain and France found all this unacceptable and conspired with Israel to retake the canal militarily. The US in the meantime coordinated with India to try to resolve the matter diplomatically.

Nehru had been visiting London in the month before all these events began to unfold. Nan had carefully planned the itinerary in consultation with Louis Mountbatten.[49] Within a few days, the prime minister came to better understand his sister's prowess. Writing to her earlier boss, Govind Ballabh Pant, the former chief minister of UP who was then home minister, he observed that 'Vijayalakshmi has got a very great reputation here in all circles. She is very popular with the public and is often cheered when she is on the streets. She is also popular with the Government as well as with the Buckingham Palace.' He added that an 'important person' spoke 'very highly about her' to him. This person thought Nan's high commissionership was 'magnificent'. Nehru noted that they had also felt similarly about Krishna Menon as well, though they had been less enamoured of Kher.[50] A few days later, Nehru was awarded the Honorary Freedom of the City of London, a high distinction. In accepting, Nehru spoke about One World, his long-standing foreign policy objective, where 'national cultures and interests are intermingled in the culture and interest of the human race'. Citing the ancient Indian emperor Ashoka, he added 'that persons of other faiths should be suitably honoured. Acting in this manner, one certainly exalts one's own faith and helps persons of other faiths. Acting in a contrary manner,' he warned, 'one injures one's own faith and also does disservice to others.'[51]

Nasser took over the canal just a few weeks later. Nehru, who had a close relationship with the Egyptian leader, was taken by surprise, but tried to see all sides and positioned India as the peacemaker.[52] Nan's days were filled with meetings with British officials and consultations with her government.[53] She assessed that Nasser had been 'crude' in his announcement and had miscalculated in explicitly linking the takeover with the dam, but that he was otherwise 'fully within his rights' to do so. The Canal in any event would have reverted to Egyptian control in 1968 according to an agreement signed in 1954.

She feared the war hysteria she saw being whipped up in Britain and thought that both the UK and France were 'living in the past' with a colonial mindset. At the same time, she knew that the maintenance of the Canal was a complicated operation that required internationally skilled operators. She worried about Egypt's ability to carry the burden on its own.[54]

In late summer, a conference was held in London to try to figure out a way forward. Twenty-two countries were invited to participate, with India playing a leading role, and representing Egypt on behalf of Nasser.[55] Nehru appointed Krishna Menon his team's lead negotiator and asked Nan to participate as well. She would once again be the only woman in the room. The British public, whatever else their concerns, remained sympathetic to her.[56] The PM explained that he felt there might be diplomatic issues with her there, however, since India planned to oppose the UK on some points, and he felt she might be put into 'an embarrassing position of conflict with the country to which . . . [she was] accredited'.[57] Nan, of course, further worried about dealing with Menon, whom she found impossible to bear, but felt that she 'could not discharge . . . [her] duties effectively later unless . . . [she was] in the picture' at that moment.[58]

The internal dynamics of her group turned out to be as bad as she had feared they might be. She wondered how much longer she could continue in her position, admitting that things were now personally harmful to her and were doing 'little good to the Govt' either.[59] The conference ultimately proved to be little more than a diversion, as Britain, France, and Israel used it as cover to prepare for a military strike shortly thereafter.

In the uneasy weeks that followed the conference, Nan tried to focus on more enjoyable matters, continuing with her regular outreach programmes.[60] Nan took some time off shortly afterwards and flew home to spend time with her family.[61] She had hoped to spend a full month in India, but a dramatic turn in international affairs brought her hurriedly back to London.[62]

~

The Soviets invaded Hungary in early November to quash a revolution led by Imre Nagy, who had been declared the people's prime minister.

In the meantime, Britain, France, and Israel had invaded Egypt over the Suez, giving cover and legitimacy to Russian actions. India, working closely with the United States, came out strongly against the West's actions over the Canal. But when it came to Hungary, Krishna Menon, then the head of the country's UN delegation, prevaricated, obliquely defending Russian actions. He voted against one critical resolution and then, more shockingly, had India abstain on another sponsored by the United States that called for food and medical supplies to be sent to the Hungarian people.[63] The effects of this on India's reputation were devastating, as many came to question whether Nehru was truly the moral giant they had presumed.

Nan returned to England in the middle of this firestorm. Right away she saw the damage that Menon had done. She was further bewildered by what appeared to be her brother's silence on the matter and was glad that the Indian press had started calling for action. She saw the matter clear eyed and felt strongly that her government 'should have come out long ago + condemned the terrible things happening in Budapest'.[64] She knew that she was in for a challenging few weeks.

She sent a telegram to Nehru admonishing him and urging him to come out forcefully with a statement.[65] Subimal Dutt too was deeply disturbed by Menon's actions, which had been contra the official Ministry position, and threatened resignation over the matter.[66] Nehru was initially quite defensive, saying that both Menon and the country were being misunderstood. Nan wrote again in a more personal fashion shortly thereafter warning that charges of India's 'double-standard' were gaining traction. Something had to be done.

As he learned more about the revolution, Nehru grew more explicit in linking Egypt and Hungary, taking similar stands against the invasions of both. He then made a trip to the United States to confer with President Eisenhower. Nan swung into action in the UK trying to salvage the situation and repair India's tattered image.

Anthony Eden in the meantime felt the effects of the past few months and announced that he was going on holiday.[67] Though he clung onto office for a little over another month, his time in leadership was at an end. The UK, it soon became apparent, had suffered a serious blow from its actions in Suez and saw its influence start to wane.

A group of Labour leaders visited Nan to ask that she work with her brother to take charge of international affairs, which they feared 'had gone beyond the moral resources of the British Government'.[68] Respected journalist Alistair Cooke proclaimed that Nehru was 'now seen to be as just and lofty as he always claimed to be'.[69] On his journey back, Nehru met up with Nan in London, and both lunched with Eden and discussed things informally.[70] From there, they travelled to Ireland together, where Nan delivered remarks that explained India's actions broadcast on Radio Eireann on New Year's Day. 'Our attitude towards Egypt and the Suez problem was understood and even shared by other nations, but this understanding was not extended to our stand on Hungary,' she admitted frankly. 'Some of you may have thought that we were unmindful of the human tragedy enacted in Budapest, but this was not so. The Indian Government wished to make a real contribution to the basic issue, which is the withdrawal of Soviet troops and the right of the Hungarian people to freedom; merely joining in a chorus of condemnation would not have been of much assistance,' she said, truthfully articulating the government's position, but artfully eliding over Menon's gaffe.[71] In lesser hands, this might have come across as unconvincing, but she managed to convey the message with sincerity, backed by the fact that her statement reflected her own core beliefs.

The following year, Nan was at a birthday party celebrating Queen Elizabeth. Nan was the centre of attention at one point when the Commonwealth Relations Secretary, Lord Home, said in a toast that she was 'the woman in his official life'. As the alcohol flowed freely, an intoxicated Philippine ambassador, Leon Guerrero, came up to her, grabbed her by the arm, and 'dragged' her over to the smiling Soviet representative, Yakov Malik and said, 'look here Mally tell me in front of Madame Pandit why you murdered Nagy?' It was a shocking moment and Malik exploded in anger at Guerrero while Nan slipped away before apologizing the next day.[72] Nehru found the episode 'significant'. This 'does indicate how very touchy the Russians are about this Imre Nagy execution . . . I am afraid the Russians have got a guilty conscience in this matter,' he wrote. He worried about what had happened and how India could deal with it without increasing global tensions. 'For my part,' he said, 'I have been deeply distressed by these Hungarian executions and the inevitable consequences . . . I shall try to exercise restraint, though at the same time I cannot be untrue to myself.'⁷³

~

Nan admitted to Nayantara in April 1956 that Krishna Menon had become 'the heaviest . . . [of her] burdens'. Just a few months before Suez, she had become convinced that she had 'been reduced to . . . a clerk'. There was 'no incentive left', she went on, since she was being excluded from 'the higher types of diplomatic negotiations'. She knew that she had nonetheless already won over 'public sympathy', but wondered what good that would do if she could not effectively translate that at the High Table.⁷⁴ Although rumours of these tensions were widely circulating amongst foreign officials, Nan assured her own ministry that she would do everything she possibly could to support Menon. The virtual smile she signalled through her missive was, however, transparently through gritted teeth.⁷⁵

A few weeks after her admission to her daughter, she subtly tried to ask her brother to address the situation. 'I am rather upset,' she put it, 'to think our Government does not take more advantage of my presence here', pointing out how successful she had already been in working with 'all parties and groups' in the UK.⁷⁶

Meanwhile, the crafty campaign against her continued. She learned that the Queen of Greece had invited her to visit but that the Ministry had never forwarded her the message. The Mediterranean monarch had expressed her distress to Queen Elizabeth, who in turn shared the news with Nan, who was terrifically embarrassed. When she raised the matter with her brother, he dismissed the issue by suggesting that the invitation had been informal and that 'this . . . [was] no time to go there' in any event.⁷⁷

After the Hungary debacle, Nan could no longer hold her tongue for Menon appeared to be misfiring in other ways as well. Selwyn Lloyd, for instance, had worriedly approached her to say that Menon appeared to have misunderstood a conversation they had had about the Suez and now was further mischaracterizing it to the press. Lloyd hoped that Nan could set the record straight.⁷⁸ The next thing she knew, Menon was telling diplomats in New York that Nan had forbid him from meeting with Lloyd because the British Foreign Secretary 'was antagonistic to India and disliked India'. Nan was livid that Menon was spreading such things. Lloyd reassured her that he knew this was 'just another of Krishna's tactics.'[79]

By then she had hesitantly sent her brother a formal 'S.O.S.' in which she frankly told him about what had been happening. 'I have several times tried to point out that there are forces at work here which are constantly trying to discredit me—but you have thought I was imagining this,' she wrote. 'You only know Krishna's great ability—you know nothing of that other side of his character which is in complete contrast to the one you see,' she added, warning that Menon's 'twisted approach to problems and his manner of dealing with them' was causing his 'growing unpopularity' and costing India. She truthfully pointed out that she, unlike Menon, had been able to speak openly with British officials and the broader public about international affairs while remaining enormously popular. It was a singular feat managed by the sheer force of her personality.[80]

Nehru seemed to acknowledge the problem, saying that he was 'well aware of . . . the forces . . . trying to discredit you' and that he 'strongly disapprove[d] of it.' Nehru further agreed that though Menon was a person with 'considerable . . . abilities, virtues and failings,' it was possible that his shortcomings could not be mitigated. He reassured his sister that he had not been 'swept away by Krishna' just as he hoped that his 'affection' for her had never been allowed to 'influence . . . [his] judgement' of her professional work, even as this very affection itself was rightly a marker of her good nature.

'Krishna has often embarrassed me and put me in considerable difficulties,' he went on. 'He is always on the verge of some such nervous collapse.' Yet for all this he also noted Menon's capacity for 'hard work' and his willingness to ultimately change his mind when he learned he was wrong.[81]

Nan was buoyed by her brother's words. A few months later, Menon was given a new assignment. He was named India's defence minister.

While the shift took Menon out of direct competition with Nan, and her mood lightened a little, things did not change substantially. When Chester Bowles, the former US ambassador to India wrote at the end of 1957 to ask her for her assistance with something, she told him candidly that, while she would do her best, he well knew that 'for some years' her brother no longer 'attach[ed] much importance to . . . [her] advice on international affairs'.[82]

Menon in the meantime held onto his position as leader of India's UN delegation. Just a few weeks after Nan had written to Bowles, she visited New York on a brief trip and was astonished, on speaking to her nemesis by telephone, to find him out of sorts and talking somewhat incoherently. When she saw him in person at the UN a few days later, he was even worse off than she had suspected. One of his staffers whispered to her in advance of Menon's arrival that he was 'very ill'. Just the previous night, they went on, he had been 'lying in bed looking dazed—the saliva running out of his mouth + the [unscrupulous] doctor giving him an injection'. He was shouting delusionally that 'the Prime Minister . . . [was] trying to speak to . . . [him] . . . Let the P.M. speak'. When Menon finally walked into the room, Nan was shocked. 'He was obviously under the influence of drugs—his eyes were glazed, his hair + clothes somewhat disarrayed + he could not walk straight.' In the Security Council soon after, he behaved so erratically and mumbled his words to such a degree that the whole meeting was adjourned. The press caught wind of the incident, but chalked up his actions to 'tension, exhaustion, and intestinal troubles'.[83]

The news reports prompted Nan to write to her brother in dismay, saying that her analysis was 'no longer something . . . [he could] afford to brush away as inspired by ill will or jealousy'. Nan told Nehru that Menon was 'extremely insecure + unhappy' and was in desperate need of an 'expert psychiatrist + then some rest.' She begged her brother not to see an 'ulterior motive' in her letter, saying that the truth was being hidden from him and that only she dared tell it to him straight.[84] Nehru responded by telling her that he was glad that she had written and that he had 'suspected as much'. He concluded that Menon had 'slipped' and was now 'in a bad mental and emotional state.'[85]

The exchange marked something of a turning point. Nan seemed to let her grievances with her rival go, and she grew more willing to re-engage on international issues with Nehru. The damage to her reputation in certain Indian official circles, however, could not be undone. Weird slights and protocol breaches continued for the remainder of her term, as when one of India's UN advisors bypassed

India House completely while on an official visit to England, instead coordinating directly with the British UN delegation and the Commonwealth Relations Office.[86]

~

The 'atmosphere of frustration', 'abnormal' conditions, and constant behind-the-scenes jousting finally had by then taken 'its toll' on Nan's health. She had started to have 'constant and recurring colds and influenza' along with a nagging sense of 'listlessness and general fatigue' between 1957 and 1958. Doctors warned her that something was amiss and that she needed to be careful.[87] She entered into the care of a cardiologist who monitored her carefully. This got her worrying about every ache and pain, fearing a heart attack or stroke. She was right to be concerned. She had developed hypertension, which had largely gone untreated over the years. Miraculously, though she received the diagnosis only as she was about to leave her post in 1961, the high blood pressure did not do any lasting harm. She would require no special treatment but would nonetheless have to be more careful going forward.[88]

~

Morarji Desai was the sixty-two-year-old newly appointed finance minister in Nehru's cabinet. While he agreed with the PM on issues like international peace, he approached his portfolio from the right and advocated for a more free-market position. The BBC described him as an 'upright Tory Gentleman'. In 1958, he visited London on his first tour outside of India.

It was an 'important mission'. India was facing a foreign exchange shortage, and he needed to shore up the country's finances.

Nan played host throughout. She threw several parties for him, including a glittering affair where 'about 300 people' attended. The nearly weeklong visit turned out to be 'an unqualified success' with Desai leaving 'a very good impression with all those who met him'.[89] He returned to India having secured a £40-million loan.[90]

~

Nan was concurrently assigned to Spain late during her term in the UK. This position proved substantially more challenging and much less productive than her Irish mission. The post had been authorized after 'pressure from the Spanish Ambassador in Delhi'. Nan immediately felt that her appointment was 'an error in judgement' and wrote a strongly worded memo to the Ministry of External Affairs warning them of the misstep. The Indians had sided with the pro-democracy Republicans during the Spanish Civil War, and the victorious Nationalists had never really forgiven them. Moreover, Nan herself had taken firm stands against them during her time at the United Nations. She considered herself 'perhaps the worst choice' for the position.'[91]

When she finally met General Franco in October 1958 to present her credentials, she was surprised to find him 'impressive . . . courteous but direct'. The two exchanged pleasantries and hope for better relations. Nan toured a bit of the country and met other members of the diplomatic corps.

The doyen of the group in Spain was the emissary from the Vatican, who acknowledged that Franco was a dictator but argued that he had nonetheless 'managed to give the country peace and prosperity for the . . . [previous] twenty years'. The British ambassador conversely suggested that her preliminary assessment was, in fact, the correct one. He told her that the Spanish were very annoyed that she had been chosen to represent India and were further bothered by the history shared by the two countries. Nan ultimately decided that the British assessment was an overstatement. She felt confident that things could be made better.

Over the next several years, she oversaw the deputation of officers to Spain and made an additional visit, as well as committed to learning Spanish. The countries were put on a 'friendly' course even as both acknowledged the divergence in their 'approach'.[92]

~

The Dalai Lama fled to India in March 1959, after a full-scale uprising against Chinese repression in Tibet had led to a brutal crackdown. India and China by then had an ongoing dispute over the exact lines of demarcation marking the border between the two countries.

The Chinese takeover of Tibet once again sent India House into crisis mode. Nan fielded endless media requests even as she simultaneously was speaking to British officials—up to the PM himself—about the situation. She likened the circumstances to what had happened in Hungary and was determined to strike the right balance.[93] 'India will do everything possible, within reason, to help Tibet,' she announced. Though her country had signed the Panchsheel Agreement (Five Principles of Peaceful Coexistence) with its large, Asian neighbour, stipulating mutual respect and non-intervention, Nan made clear that India's policy had always been to speak truthfully to countries that it considered its friends. 'Our view is that no country should be dominated by another foreign country . . . I am interested in the ability of Tibet, India, and other countries to stand up to the country that tries to dominate,' she concluded.[94]

Things grew very tense a few months later when India sent its army to the border to prevent any incursion. President Eisenhower, who was in London at the time, met informally with Nan to discuss what was happening.[95] Immediately after, Nan flew to India, where she listened intently to debates in Parliament about the aggression.[96]

She returned to London to find the Chinese apparently involved in an attempted espionage operation. The Ministry of External Affairs had requested India House to provide a historical map from 1851 of Ladakh and its eastern borders. Staff reached out to the India Office Library to supply the necessary materials. After some back and forth over what was needed, a clerk named Madan was sent to fetch the correct map and to make a copy of it. While he was returning by bus, he was approached by a Chinese man who asked him if his name was 'Banerji'. Madan grew suspicious right away but engaged in conversation to determine what exactly was going on. The mysterious man told him that he wanted the map that he was holding and that he was willing to pay £100 each to all of the India House workers who had been involved in acquiring the map. Madan was appalled, replying that he was 'not a cheap person to be purchased . . .'. He quickly got off the bus, returned to the embassy and had the entire incident reported to Nan. India House, in turn, informed British officials and asked the India Office Library to remain vigilant and not allow any 'unauthorized person to remove maps and relevant documents pertaining to India's borders with China, more particularly those of

Tibet with Ladakh, Gharwal District, Sikkim, Bhutan and the whole of the MacMahon [sic] Line'.[97] When he learned what had happened, Nehru put London and Delhi 'on . . . guard'. He was right to do so. Just weeks later, China initiated skirmishes on the Ladakh border.[98]

Nan had in the meantime told reporters that 'the Indian border dispute with China had "shaken the people of India deeply"'. Her country 'felt "a very deep sorrow" for the people of Tibet', she had said. '"But, ultimately, what is the action one can take?" . . . "It is condemnation—and the whole of India has been ringing with it".'

She had said that she hoped an 'amicable settlement' with China could still be found regarding the border. Small adjustments here and there were possible. 'But, naturally, that does not mean that we would allow large portions of our territory to be taken over.' When pressed on whether her government was prepared to use force if necessary, she had responded that India 'would fight to defend itself' but that, should it be compelled to do so, 'would involve a great break with all the things we have stood for'.[99]

~

Nan delivered her remarks about the border dispute from New York, where she had come for one last major US tour. She had journeyed back to the country two times previously, once in 1957 and again earlier in 1959. The first of those trips involved visits to Ohio and San Francisco as a guest of the US State Department. In the first city, she was treated to 'the World of Tomorrow', where the US Airforce was training young recruits for future military craft. She found the whole thing 'frightening' and 'incredible'. In San Francisco, she spoke before the US National Commission for UNESCO where she blasted the growing inequality in the world. 'What we must all understand is that half the world cannot move around in oxcarts, while the other half rides in Cadillacs,' she had told her audience. 'And it is equally important to understand that the gifts of Cadillacs [to those that don't have them] . . . will not solve our problems.'[100]

Her second visit was a quick one—just a few days—to participate in Eleanor Roosevelt's birthday. While she was there, she was invited to the state funeral for John Foster Dulles, who had passed away right before her arrival. As she was committed to being with Mrs

Roosevelt in Chicago, she had to decline, though she sent a personal letter of condolence to Mrs Dulles.[101] Before her departure, she also participated in a National Conference of Christians and Jews Dinner, where she conferred a Pioneer in Brotherhood medal on Arthur Compton.[102]

The contract for a more extended lecture tour had been signed in between her other two trips. While New York was her first destination, this time she had arranged to see the 'deep South', a part of the country with which she had never engaged substantially.

She announced as she began that she felt that relations between the US and India were now 'extremely good' and saw no reason for any deterioration going forward.[103] At Columbia, she pushed for China's inclusion in the United Nations, despite all that was going on with the country at that time, since the government there represented a very large portion of humanity and since the UN 'stood for the universality of membership.' She chalked up India's seemingly paradoxical stand on its large Asian neighbour to 'that little bit of Gandhi in our hearts'.[104]

Nan's travels through North Carolina, Virginia, and Georgia shocked her, however. She had never before come face to face with American racism in such a blatant way. She stayed with wealthy white families whose homes were attended by numerous Black staff. She grew alarmed by aspects of American consumerism, with rich, teenage children seemly focused only on leisure and pleasure, some being given their own cars and access to private planes. She was amazed that the 'fantastic increase in prosperity' went hand in hand with a growing detachment from any sense of social responsibility.

In contrast, the Black workers she met lived in 'the meanest imaginable shantys—broken down, letting in the elements and all huddled together'.[105] She likened what she saw to something out of Dickens. The South, she felt, was stuck in a time that had otherwise passed, or at least should have.

The one bright spot was a visit to the Atlanta University Center, which brought together several historic Black colleges and universities (HBCUs), including Spelman College, Morehouse College and Clark Atlanta University.[106] A choir performance by students descended from enslaved families moved her to tears.

These experiences opened her eyes to another side of the country. Though she had come to love it very much, and though she had previously been aware of its racial history, she felt sickened by the gross disparity and discrimination that she realized remained deeply ingrained in some parts of American society. She cancelled the second half of her tour and returned to the UK.[107]

~

Queen Elizabeth arrived in India in early 1961. Nan had been coordinating the trip for several months and flew to Delhi in advance to finalize arrangements. She and the British high commissioner for India put together a programme on the 'Personality of the Queen' for All India Radio to help acquaint the Indian audience with their royal visitor.[108] Nan received the Queen at the airport, along with her brother and other dignitaries.[109]

As preparations were underway, Nan admonished the British not to try to build relations with India based on nostalgia for a flawed and now dead past. Rather, they had to forge ties anew, in partnership.[110]

Nan accompanied Elizabeth and her husband, Prince Phillip, on their tour, which included Calcutta and Bombay (Mumbai) as well as parts of Rajasthan.[111] In Delhi, the Queen participated in Republic Day celebrations, a symbolic gesture received warmly by her hosts.[112] The entire tour was widely hailed as a rousing success.

On their return to London, Nan hosted the Queen at a 'glittering reception' at 9 Kensington Palace Gardens. The event turned into an international sensation when Elizabeth showed up in an open-shouldered, form-fitting sequined dress. Reporters immediately fixated on the clothes that she and Nan were wearing that evening and splashed pictures of the two of them across their newspaper pages.[113]

~

Nan had been considering retirement for several years.[114] The constant struggle with the Ministry and the strain on her health were heavy burdens. In 1958, she had actually made a formal attempt to step down, but she was ultimately persuaded to stay.[115] She held on for a bit longer but finally decided in late 1960 that India House was 'depleted' and that she had had enough. She announced that she would be leaving her post as high commissioner following the Queen's visit.[116]

~

She had one last official act she wanted to complete. She had overseen the acquisition of some significant military equipment during her time as envoy, most notably an aircraft carrier called the Hercules.[117] She had also accepted a warship dubbed the INS Mysore and launched a modernized frigate called the INS Brahmaputra.[118]

The Hercules was 'a [British] Majestic-class aircraft carrier' originally intended for use during the Second World War. The war ended before the ship was completed however, so its final construction was put on hold. India purchased the ship in 1957 and sent it to be modernized in Belfast.[119] Nan in the meantime commissioned a squadron of Seahawk aircraft, the Indian Navy's first combat aircraft, for use on the ship once ready.[120] In March 1961, among her last major, official functions in the UK, Nan commissioned India's first aircraft carrier, the Hercules now renamed the INS Vikrant.[121]

~

Nan left Great Britain in triumph. She had successfully pushed India's views even against Western opposition while nonetheless winning over people wherever she went. Indo-British ties were undoubtedly in a much stronger position than they were on her arrival. She had become a much-beloved figure throughout the UK and Ireland, much as she had been in the United States.

Nan found herself amidst a 'flurry of goodwill' as she began her formal exit. Thirty-five women's organizations came together to throw her a farewell reception in the House of Commons. Among those who participated were Lady Nancy Astor, the first woman ever seated in the British Parliament, and Dame Irene Ward, 'the longest-serving female Conservative MP in history'.[122] Later, the Queen herself threw a farewell luncheon for her.[123]

Nan's friend, the Tory MP Baroness Evelyn Emmet, in the meantime, echoed popular feelings when she determined that something should be done to keep Nan connected to Britain. She came up with 'a remarkable proposal'. She wanted Madame Pandit to become a Life Peer of the United Kingdom, granting her the same title of Baroness and a permanent seat in the House of Lords.[124] Life peerage was open to citizens from the Commonwealth and was often given to those retiring from public office. Emmet repeatedly pressed Nehru during a weeklong visit to India to allow this to happen. While it was all very flattering, it was also out of the question, as India's Constitution prevented its citizens from pledging allegiance to the British crown, something required of a life peer.[125]

As she ended her term in mid-summer 1961, Indira Gandhi sent her a note saying how thrilled she and everyone at home were reading about the wide range of tributes paid to her. She added that all of this was 'richly deserved' because Nan had earned it 'not only because of . . . [her] personality', but also because of her 'hard work, struggle + long years of lovely effort'.[126] Nehru congratulated her for leaving 'at the top of . . . [her] fame'.[127]

CHAPTER FIFTEEN

Home Fire

Nan returned to an unexpected scene in India. As she deplaned at Santa Cruz Airport in Bombay (Mumbai), reporters rushed forward with questions. Among the din, someone suddenly asked if she would accept the vice presidency if offered to her. Nan grimaced at the hypothetical suggestion. She was not the right person, she replied, but 'added that obviously it would be a tremendous honor'.

Over the next few months, the idea of her becoming vice president gained traction. The scholarly Sarvepalli Radhakrishnan was currently in that position, having been elected twice and serving the previous ten years. He was about to stand for president and wanted Nan to be his running mate. Radhakrishnan had already talked with Nehru to press the point. At dinner the next night, the prime minister confirmed to Nan that she was being considered for VP. She responded with humility and clarified that her brother should do nothing that might raise eyebrows. Rumours circulated for a while as Nehru mulled over the matter, fielding appeals for and against Nan's nomination. In the end, although support was actually in her favour, Nehru decided against her selection, choosing instead the Gandhian economist Zakir Husain. Nan kissed her brother on his head, her usual signal of reassurance, and told him that he had done the 'right thing', adding that he 'could not have made a better choice.'[1]

~

Dag Hammarskjöld had been killed in a suspicious plane crash shortly before Nan had come back home. Media reports at the time suggested his plane was fired upon and rumors persisted of a larger, unknown conspiracy.² Nan had been vacationing in Greece and Egypt and detoured to attend the funeral of her old friend and colleague in Uppsala, Sweden.³

Once back in India, Nan busied herself presiding over a social education week in Bombay, inaugurating a book exhibition, and participating in a convocation at Visva Bharati University in Calcutta.⁴ In January 1962, she was awarded the Padma Vibushan, one of India's highest honours, for 'exceptional and distinguished service.'⁵

~

Jackie Kennedy arrived in New Delhi in March 1962. The fashionable and wildly popular American First Lady was there to help foster goodwill between the two democracies. Nan, Nehru, and Indira Gandhi welcomed her at the airport.⁶ Nan helped host over the next few days.⁷

The following month, Nan was back in the United States to deliver several lectures. One of the organizers of a talk before the National Council on Women described her as 'a great human being—brilliant, resourceful'.⁸ After Eleanor Roosevelt introduced her, Nan called for more women to enter politics around the world.⁹ She also told her audience that the 'conquest of prejudice can be as enriching an experience for mankind as the conquest of space'.¹⁰ Coinciding with her trip, the American journalist Anne Guthrie brought out a short biography of Nan.¹¹ Meanwhile, soon-to-be American broadcasting legend Barbara Walters, who had accompanied Mrs Kennedy on her trip, conducted a lengthy interview with Nan comparing Jackie's trip to Queen Elizabeth's. She dubbed the piece 'a look at the two First Ladies of the West through the eyes of the First Lady of the East'.¹² Eleanor Roosevelt, deflecting a title often given to her, suggested that Nan was in fact 'the First Lady of the World'.¹³

~

Nan mulled her next move over the summer of 1962. She somewhat hesitantly accepted an offer to become the next Governor of Mysore, a prominent state in South India. She accompanied her brother on a tour of several cities there and the press made a preliminary announcement.[14] But before she occupied her seat, the sitting governor of the western state of Maharashtra suddenly passed away in office in early October. This state was where she had already been living at the time and was an adopted home through Ranjit. So when given the option, she chose instead to become the next Governor of Maharashtra.[15]

~

China invaded India in late October. Tensions between the two countries had been building for several years and border skirmishes had occurred several times. Krishna Menon, then the minister of defence, was caught flat-footed. The Chinese army marched virtually unopposed into the country.

Nan was abroad at the time, with engagements in London and West Germany. Her trip was unofficial, to open a hostel at London University and to participate in some functions at the University of Heidelberg.[16] But her trip suddenly turned into a diplomatic emergency.

The visit to West Germany was already a delicate one. Nan had to avoid discussing Berlin, where the infamous wall had divided the city in half at the direction of the communists in charge of the East the previous year. There was also some controversy over the extent to which she could acknowledge East Germany.[17]

Nan arrived in Bonn for an eleven-day visit just a few days after China had begun its operation. Every high-ranking German official from Chancellor Adenauer and President Lubke on down treated her visit with the utmost importance and met with her personally.

Adenauer had a fearsome reputation and a no-nonsense personality. He was staunchly anti-communist. But he and Nan had known each other for years, working together as co-chairs of the World Brotherhood since the mid-fifties. They got on very well. Adenauer had until then paid India little attention in foreign affairs and, in fact, had been quite 'apprehensive' of the country. 'From all accounts, Mrs Pandit's conversation with him seems to have [single-handedly] assuaged these misconceptions,' noted Indian officials.[18] Now he offered her 'the highest degree of sympathy' for India's situation and an immediate 'readiness to help'.[19] '[A]fter the conversation with Mrs. Pandit . . . [the Chancellor] sent a directive down to all Departments that every effort should be made to meet Indian requests both in the military plane and in . . . [the] economic relationship.' Nan's other meetings with the leading 'personalities in the political, economic and cultural life of the Federal Republic' all produced similar results. And as usual, she 'received spectacular attention from the Press throughout her stay'. Indian officials, astounded by Nan's abilities, wrote in their report that 'the visit proved to be in every way a significant event in Indo-German relations'.[20]

Nehru, in the meantime, had reached out to US President Kennedy, who also agreed to support India. Nan joined in discussions of various aspects of international defensive assistance.[21] Then, suddenly, the Chinese unilaterally withdrew their forces, while holding onto several pieces of captured territory.

Krishna Menon was sacked as defence minister in the fallout.[22] But it was Nehru on whom the toll taken was the heaviest. He felt personally betrayed by the Chinese attack and grew disillusioned.

Critics in India, sensing blood, attacked the government from all sides, challenging some of the country's long-held policies. Nehru only half-heartedly addressed any of this.

Nan, by contrast, gave a rousing defence of the country's cherished ideals and called on young people to stand their ground against their neighbour's illegitimate aggression. India, 'which shook a powerful empire would not succumb to totalitarianism,' she declared.[23] She called on people to once again be ready to make sacrifices to save the country and especially appealed to women 'joining the special technical classes for the defence to do their task with "grit, strength and enthusiasm".'[24] She also rallied the citizens of Bombay (Mumbai) to participate in a 'vote for victory' campaign, to express 'solidarity with the rest of the country in its determination to fight the Chinese . . . and to preserve their freedom and . . . [the] democratic way of life'.[25]

Nan took her message abroad as well. In January, she appeared on the 'well received' CBS News special program, 'War at the Top of the World', which was broadcast in the United States.[26]

~

Nan was formally inaugurated as governor shortly after the Chinese withdrawal. As she took office, she promised 'no walls' between herself and the people.[27] Aside from her defence activities, she spent her first few weeks attending to ceremonial duties and continuing with her social work.

Among the first things she did was launch a mobile clinic in Bombay 'donated by the people of America' to the Missionaries of Charity.[28] Mother Teresa, a saintly Catholic nun who had devoted herself to supporting and treating India's poor, sick, and marginalized, had asked Nan to participate.

The two had first met while Nan was in London. The Vatican ambassador (the Papal Nuncio) had asked the high commissioner if she would have an informal dinner with his special guest in the evening, and Nan readily agreed. When she entered the room to greet her, Nan had what she would later describe as a 'cleansing experience'. As she first looked at the nun, the room receded, and the tiny Mother suddenly seemed to loom large. As they touched hands, Nan emerged from her trance and told her visitor that she 'had made . . . [her] see truth and *maya* [illusion]'.[29]

After the Bombay launch, Mother Teresa would remain in touch. She even visited Nan in her home in later years.[30]

~

Nan needed to clear the air with her brother. The gap between them had grown considerable over the past decade or so. The 'love was there, of course, but the earlier comradeship [had] ended'. After the China debacle, she felt she no longer had the luxury of letting things lie. She wrote him a long confessional.

She reassured Nehru of her enduring faith in him and generously credited him for encouraging her and showing 'trust and confidence' in her decisions. 'There has been no other person in my life whose approval meant so much to me as yours,' she told him, 'because your whole life has been a dedication to the values by which men live . . .' 'Everything I have learned of truth and ethics and the yardstick by which to measure men and events in political life,' she went on, 'has come from you, and I have tried in my small way to follow the examples you have set.'

'After a long period of sharing the same wavelength we suddenly ceased to synchronize.' Finally, she got to the heart of the matter. 'I do not know why this happened, but part of it was certainly due to Krishna Menon and Mac Mathai during the period of their close friendship. Both in their own ways subtly misinterpreted my actions and quite deliberately gave you a wrong idea of me and my relationship with our own people. The trust you had in me was damaged.'

'This has been one of the reasons for my antagonism with Krishna Menon,' she admitted. 'The other, as I have perhaps told you, is his habit of telling half-truths in order to present only the kind of picture he wishes to get across.'

She ended by telling the prime minister not to respond to her letter. Rather, she just wanted him to mull over what she had said, and they could discuss things later.[31]

~

Nan quickly realized that she had made a mistake in accepting the Governorship. The post was 'even more useless than . . . [she had first] imagined.' She likened working in Raj Bhavan (the Governor's house) to running 'a sort of second-class hotel'. Her only function, it seemed, was entertaining VIPs.[32]

To make matters worse, she had approached her position with the same gusto as all her others and had set about trying to get her house and staff in order. This had once again brought not entirely unfounded charges of her extravagance.[33]

She begged to be relieved of her position. As this request was being considered, she asked her brother if she could once again be sent to the United Nations as leader of India's delegation. She felt that she was nearing the age of total retirement and wanted to spend the last vestiges of her energy doing as much as she could to help the country.[34] Nehru approved her request.

~

The reaction in the Ministry of External Affairs was profoundly different this time from what it had been for the past several years. The new foreign secretary, M.J. Desai, appeared genuinely courteous, helpful, and friendly. Staff prepared detailed briefing materials on the issues they felt would be on her agenda: relations with China and Pakistan, and the unresolved questions over Kashmir. The MEA also asked her to stop over in Ghana and Nigeria while en route to New York.

Nan had been on friendly terms with Kwame Nkrumah since her days as high commissioner. But the situation was much changed since the time they spent together in London. Nkrumah had gone from a wildly popular figure with mass appeal to an anti-democratic leader of a one-party state living in fear of his people. He was insisting on trying to help negotiate a settlement between China and India. Ghana had at the same time grown more distant from India, as well as from Nasser and some other African states, according to an internal MEA assessment. Nan spoke frankly with Nkrumah, challenging some of his points of view, but in her inimitable way. The two emerged on friendly terms.

Nan's trip to Nigeria was less eventful as relations between it and India were fairly stable and friendly. But while there, she made news by calling for 'universal equal rights and status for men and women.'[35]

The MEA's assessment of both missions was positive. Rajeshwar Dayal, who was then the Ministry's Special Secretary, concluded that her 'timely' trips had 'an excellent effect'.[36]

~

Nan's return to the United Nations in 1963 once more as leader of India's delegation was widely seen as a moment of personal triumph, her ultimate victory over her defeated foe, Krishna Menon. The *New York Times* sighed with relief, describing her predecessor's tenure as '10 uninterrupted [years of] . . . unpleasant . . . [and] antagonizing' hectoring. They noted that Nan, in contrast, had 'managed to follow India's nonalignment policy and remain friendly with both camps in the cold war.' 'If for no other reason,' they concluded, 'she is regarded as more Western than Mr. Menon.'[37]

Nan held a press conference shortly after her arrival and immediately threw herself into the thick of things, addressing a variety of hot-button topics, including prospects for another Chinese attack and India's relations with Pakistan. She also sounded off on the situation in Vietnam, roundly criticizing President Diem's anti-

Buddhist bias.³⁸ Reporters, in the meantime, noted that she had lost none of her magic, leaving her audience 'enchanted' by the time she wrapped things up.³⁹

But as the meeting got underway, Nan discerned a change in the atmosphere. India, she realized, had lost much of its significance since she was last there. She attributed this only in part to Menon's 'temper . . . [and] misinterpretation of policies'. The country had made other missteps that had a larger impact—it had never really engaged effectively outside of the Assembly sessions, and it had never provided delegation continuity over the years, outside of its leaders. Meanwhile, UN membership had expanded considerably, with representation from African countries dramatically increased.⁴⁰ Nan was happy about this, even as she observed the new diplomatic complexities that had to be navigated. She stressed in her report back to the ministry that India had for too long conflated personal goodwill with an 'acceptance of one's policies'. Both were important, she argued, but the former alone was insufficient and could not replace the effective advancement of the latter. Her country, she said frankly, had work to do.⁴¹

~

Nan's most significant accomplishment this time around involved a presentation before the UN Security Council.⁴² The situation in South Africa had only grown worse since Nan's original victory in the General Assembly. The Ghetto Act had metastasized into the cancerous policy of apartheid, the formal separation of races based on white supremacy and the brutal suppression of the native black population. The UN had continued its criticisms of the country, but to no avail. In August, the Security Council passed, with several abstentions, Resolution 181, calling for a voluntary arms boycott. But South Africa had rebuffed even this, informing the organization formally of its refusal to comply.

Coming full circle, Nan once again delivered an impassioned, eloquent plea for action against South Africa's heinous policies. She was at her most stirring.

'The struggle for racial equality in South Africa,' she began, 'is associated with the name of Mahatma Gandhi, and India had come at that time to the United Nations in a spirit of humility. We were and are conscious of our shortcomings, our failures. We are in no position to condemn. But like our sister nations, we believe that there is a moral law which must be recognized and obeyed if mankind is to continue its onward march towards a brave new world. Because of this belief, our Government seeks to implement the promise of justice and equality enshrined in all democratic constitutions into the life of every citizen. The pace may sometimes be slower than we would wish but, nevertheless, we move on and strive for the elimination of discrimination and the breaking down of all artificial barriers which separate man for each other . . .

'We believe that apartheid is bad not only for those who are its victims,' she continued, 'but also for those who preach and practice it. No group of human beings can, for any length of time, act unjustly and inhumanly towards their fellows without disastrous consequences for themselves . . .

'For years many of us have repeated the warning that there can be no double standards in the world. Freedom and justice must have the same meaning for all men and women or the values by which decent people live and, indeed, civilization itself stands in jeopardy. What use is it for us to talk of one world, to speak about freedom from want and from fear if, side by side, we contribute, actively or by our silent acquiescence, to the building up of a situation which must erupt and, erupting, lead to horrible consequences . . .

'Many things are important to human beings. Freedom is important; security is important; food is important; but nothing—nothing—can take the place of the feeling of equality between man and man which must exist if the world is to survive in peace . . . While the smallest shadow of discrimination remains between people on ground of race and colour, other benefits will be meaningless for all else stems from this feeling of oneness, the knowledge that we are equal and are equally entitled to all the rights and privileges which man has made possible for man . . .

'From one murderous tyranny to another . . . [the South African] Government has gone on denying freedom, suffocating justice and perpetuating racism of the worst kind. One lawless law after another is enacted and brave sons of South Africa like Nelson Mandela, Walter Sisulu, and Ahmed Kathrada, to name only a few, are condemned to long terms of imprisonment and solitary confinement for daring to ask that the ideals of the Charter of the United Nations be put into practice . . .'

Nan blasted South Africa's unyielding commitment to white domination. 'That is the brutal mandate which the South African racists have awarded themselves. They are determined to convert that land into a valley of death. The comparison with Nazi Germany is inescapable. To destroy the house that Hitler built, a terrible world war had to be fought. Must another war be fought before South Africa mends its ways . . .'?

Echoing the words of the African National Congress President Arthur Luthuli, Nan proceeded to call for an economic boycott of South Africa, particularly targeting trade that benefited the country's defence capabilities. 'The United Nations cannot ignore and is rightly concerned with the growing military strength of South Africa . . . The total security budget, namely, the expenditure on armed and police forces, has increased in the past four years by nearly 300 per cent. Even more revealing and alarming is the spectacular rise in the government expenditure on the manufacture of ammunition. In the same four-year period, it has jumped up nearly seventy fold. Against whom is this piling of arms being done . . .? All this increase in the defence budget is for the sole purpose of crushing the brave patriots who are fighting against the apartheid policies . . .'

'Let us not forget,' she ended, 'that "Except the Lord build the house they labour in vain who build it". Beneath the poetic imagery of these words lies a hard scientific truth: unless people live in amity and have a sense of higher purpose, nothing of enduring values can be constructed or reconstructed.'[43]

Just a few days later, the Security Council unanimously passed Resolution 182, authored by Norway, reiterating its calls in 181 and further explicitly calling on 'all States to cease forthwith the sale and shipment of equipment and materials for the manufacture and maintenance of arms and ammunition in South Africa.'[44] Nan's words had had their effect, and she was credited with helping to persuade all members of the Council, including a hesitant France and Britain, to act.[45] It would, nonetheless, be years longer before the boycott became mandatory and later still for apartheid finally to crumble.

~

The biggest highlight of the UN session was a speech by John F. Kennedy. The young US president's remarks came just after his country, the UK, and the Soviet Union had concluded the Treaty of Moscow, banning certain kinds of nuclear tests.

The issue had been close to Nan's heart for some time. The world's leading nuclear scientists had long seen her and her brother as humanity's great hope against further weaponization.[46] She had by then spent years advocating for peace and arms reduction.[47] And when Nehru had set off to meet with Kennedy back in 1961, she had teamed up with J.J. Singh to launch a million-signature drive to petition for 'a ban on nuclear tests', closely following the UN's adoption of an Indian resolution on the same subject.[48] Just two days after the Limited Nuclear Test Ban Treaty had been signed, and right before her travel to Ghana, Nan had sent personal letters of congratulation to Khrushchev and Harold Macmillan, extolling them for their historic action and setting humankind on a path of 'hope ... and a future free from fear'.[49] Later in New York, she met separately with Soviet Foreign Minister Andrei Gromyko and Secretary of State Dean Rusk and discussed disarmament along with other issues.[50] And when the UN adopted by acclamation an Indian-inspired proposal to designate 1965 the International Year of Cooperation, to mark the twentieth anniversary of the signing of the UN Charter, she repeated her wish that humanity finally be freed from the burden of terror under which it had found itself these past decades.[51]

President Kennedy's speech came about a year after the near catastrophe of the Cuban Missile Crisis when the US and USSR stood 'eyeball to eyeball', with Armageddon a mere miscalculation away. With the treaty under his belt, JFK was able to project a renewed optimism, saying that he was there 'not [as] a sign of crisis, but of confidence'.[52] A nascent bonhomie seemed visible throughout the Secretariat building.

Nan had an opportunity to speak directly with the American president before he left. But when her moment came, what was on her mind was a story that Adlai Stevenson had recounted to her. Stevenson was then the US ambassador to the UN, but Nan had known him for many years. He had only just returned from a trip to Dallas, Texas, where he had been 'manhandled and spat upon'. Stevenson had immediately urged JFK to postpone his upcoming trip to the southern city, but the President had rebuffed him saying that the visit was a necessity before the upcoming election. Nan took her chance to stress the feelings of anxiety and suggest that the President reconsider. 'I have to go,' he told her.[53]

~

Nan was shellshocked when she learned of JFK's assassination in Dallas a few weeks later. After the General Assembly held a moment of silence for the slain leader, she hand-wrote a letter to her brother informing him of what had happened. 'It seems incredible that a young + promising life should have been cut short by the hand of a fanatic,' she said. 'We haven't moved so far from the jungle with its laws of hatred and violence.'

Hours later, she and Nehru released a tribute to JFK on All India Radio. The prime minister, who also had to address the deaths of several service members in a helicopter crash, called November 22, 1963 'a day of ill omen . . . full of disasters'. Nan spoke to the tragedy of the situation, that such a 'young man, so full of vigor and life and the desire to serve should be . . . denied a normal span of life which was his due.' She added, 'America has lost a leader of very high quality, a man who upheld the things by which men live through justice and equality and freedom for people. And the world also has lost in President Kennedy a champion of noble causes. It is not only America that mourns his death today but . . . a great portion of the world . . .'[54]

Nan then travelled to D.C. to pay her respects at the President's funeral. Afterwards, at a reception at the White House, she spoke with Jackie briefly and offered her condolences.[55]

~

Nan returned to more troubling news in India. Jawaharlal Nehru was in decline. He suffered a stroke in January. Speculation about his successor was rife. Indira Gandhi, his daughter, was among a small group believed to be in contention. Nan's name, in the meantime, did the rounds as a potential foreign minister, possibly taking over as soon as Nehru gave his formal consent. Indira too, it was said, was in contention for this position. It was not long before reports began to emerge that the two women were antagonists and that Indira, taking advantage of her position as her father's primary nurse and gatekeeper, was going to all lengths to prevent her aunt from spending time alone with the ailing prime minister.[56] Nan, for her part, dismissed such gossip, chalking up her short visits to her brother's admonition that she should immediately get back to work.[57]

~

Nehru died of a heart attack in late May 1964, on the day he had wished, Buddha Jayanti, the day it was believed the Buddha was born, received enlightenment and died.[58] He had earlier recovered briefly from his stroke, and Nan had gotten to spend a bit of time with him as he resumed some of his political activities.[59] But he was in New Delhi and she in Bombay when he was struck this second time.[60] Indira had telephoned to say that he was fading, and that both Nan and Betty should hurry to get there. The sisters made haste but just could not reach soon enough.[61] On arrival, Nan embraced Indira, who was sobbing, and then sat down on the bed next to her fallen brother and kissed him on the forehead.[62]

The two sisters rode with Indira and her younger son Sanjay in the car behind the body during the funeral. After Rajiv arrived, he and his brother performed the last rites as Nan, Betty and Indira observed.[63] Subsequently, the family travelled with the ashes by train to Allahabad, where they immersed the remains of India's first prime minister, mixed in with some belonging to his departed wife Kamala, in the Sangam, the confluence of the Ganga (Ganges), Yamuna (Jamuna), and (mythical) Saraswati rivers, and to which Nehru had always held special personal—though not religious—attachment.[64]

~

Nan resigned from her position as governor in October.[65] She had remained in office much longer than she had anticipated, having tried to leave since early 1963. While she had been at the UN, Nehru had finally consented to her resignation but had recommended that she resume her duties on her return to India for a few months before finally stepping down.⁶⁶ Among the very last things she had written to her brother just days before his death was a letter informing him that the Maharashtra chief minister had reluctantly agreed to her departure later that year.⁶⁷

In the days and weeks following Nehru's death, press reports suggested that she might take up a position in the new government led by Lal Bahadur Shastri or become the governor of Mysore. The correct story broke just as she was set to leave her position: Vijaya Lakshmi Pandit was going to run for her brother's old seat in Parliament.⁶⁸

~

Oxford University had been considering awarding Nan an honorary degree for nearly two years. The registrar of the university had informed her of the university's intentions in early 1964 and asked if she would accept and be willing to make a trip to the UK if so. Nan considered this to be 'a high honour.'. She had heard through friends that this had been in the offing since her time as high commissioner.⁶⁹

The ceremony finally took place in October, presided over by former British P.M. Harold Macmillan, then the chancellor. Nan said in accepting: 'I do not see the statesmen of the world, or governments, or even the orators of the United Nations, bringing about the concept of one world; but I do see that it can only come about if the people can come together—a thing they can do only if they know one another'. As part of her visit, she opened a new graduate house at Somerville College, which shortly thereafter named her a lifetime Honorary Fellow. Nan praised the new facility as such a place where 'young people from all over the world would come together', the ultimate key, she felt, to better understanding and more unified humanity.⁷⁰

~

'Please forget . . . that I am Nehru's sister,' Nan told a gathering of farmers as she campaigned for election in Nehru's constituency of Phulpur. 'Judge me on my own record for whatever it is worth and on that of the Congress Party,' she added for clarity. She made no further mention of her sibling on the road.

Standing for the seat was risky. It was rumoured that Indira Gandhi had turned down the chance to run for fear of losing, given the general economic unrest in the country and a party in some disarray. Informed commentators noted that Nan's entire 'political future' was on the line, even as they called her 'India's most talented woman leader'.[71] She faced fierce competition from left- and right-wing competitors. Reports suggested that no one candidate would be able to win a majority.[72] But when the votes were tallied, Nan came out on top with a thumping majority, winning nearly 60 per cent of the ballots cast.[73]

~

Nan's victorious entry into politics sent the press into overdrive. Stories flew in every direction suggesting that she might join Shastri's Cabinet, that she could become the next speaker of the House, and even that she potentially could become India's prime minister in the future.[74] This went to such ridiculous lengths that the *Canberra Times* got in on the act, somewhat facetiously proposing that she become Australia's next Governor General. 'Mrs. Pandit,' they wrote, was 'a woman of outstanding personality'. And as 'a woman and an Indian her appointment would infuriate all the reactionary forces in Australia until she actually arrived, when she would immediately charm them'.[75]

A common thread running through many such narratives involved Nan's relationship with Indira, which was said to have blossomed into a full-fledged rivalry. Nehru's daughter was then the minister for information and broadcasting. Newspapers wrote that if Nan joined the government, she would immediately outrank her niece, resulting in Indira most likely quitting and going abroad on a diplomatic post. So breathless were such reports from wagging tongues that Indira was forced to issue a denial.[76]

~

Nan had felt for some time that India had lost its way. The country was beset with problems, and there seemed to be no political will to address them. This had brought Nan to the unusual place of agreeing with Krishna Menon, who had taken to using his sharp tongue to eviscerate the government. The press had immediately taken notice of the startling, oddball alliance.[77]

In March, soon after her return from the United States, Nan made her maiden speech to the Lok Sabha (the People's House/Lower House of Parliament) as an MP. There she lamented the 'demoralization and decadence and deterioration' that had overtaken the land. She blasted the normalization of corruption. She cited poetry from Oliver Goldsmith to capture the state of affairs:

'Ill fares the land to hastening ills a prey
Where wealth accumu'ates but men decay'

Nan ripped into tax cheaters and evaders and all others who put their stock in 'personal aggrandizement'. 'This is one of the reasons why things are slipping so badly,' she said plainly, 'and Government is coming into disrepute.' She called on officials to see clearly between right and wrong and to act.

'I do not refer to speeches. We have had enough speeches,' she said, calling the government 'prisoners of indecision.' She turned her attention to a recent food crisis, recalling her earlier work against famine. She wondered how those in the capital had become so soulless as to party endlessly while the people they were meant to serve starved.

The country was stuck, she concluded, in the grip of outdated thinking. 'We are always called back from any attempt to move forward,' she noted, 'by saying that our grandfathers did not do it—*Parampara*—and we must go on that line. But *Parampara* did not have science; there was no space age, no atom bombs, no nuclear weapons.' Her solution, which she had been pushing for some time, was to demand principled and ethical leadership that was driven towards the common good, real socialism. 'It is true we have accepted a socialist pattern of society. I do not know exactly what that means . . . but there is such a thing in the world as co-operation / and understanding and co-ordinating one's activities. It is a world in which we must all share. It is a world in which me must give and take, and unless we do that we are going to find ourselves not only not leading anybody, [but also] possibly not even able to lead our own country.'[78]

Other members of the House were riveted by her remarks and sat 'in rapt attention.' When she was finished, they called what she had to say 'a breath of fresh air'.[79] It quickly became the talk of the town, The *Times of India* calling it a 'brutally frank appraisal of the state of the nation'.[80] The next day, Krishna Menon cited her in his remarks to the House, calling her his 'colleague' in a way that suggested that they were on the same side.[81]

Some Congress officials took umbrage at the attacks. And while she did not necessarily see herself in the kind of contest with Nan the press reported, Indira bristled nonetheless at her aunt's comments.[82]

~

Shastri seemed to take things in stride. The press portrayed him as a gallant Gandhian who saw some merit in Nan's criticism, even if he thought she was out of line in the manner of her delivery. Going further, they described him as making it his 'first concern to protect her from excessive harassment and even from self-reproach'.[83] Nan for her part parried attacks on her character by talking up her commitment to Congress ideals and reiterating her loyalty to Shastri.[84] Even so, some concluded that she was making a move to become the prime minister.[85]

~

While this political dust-up was taking place, Pakistan and India were engaged in small-scale confrontations along their northwestern border in the Rann of Kutch. Nan, specially attuned to India's defence following the debacle with China, now predicted that the subcontinent was hurtling towards yet another conflict. She called on the country to prepare its defences and to stand on the principle of democracy. On that basis, she argued, the West might yet be prepared to act together. She clarified that she wanted peace and friendship with Pakistan, but that that had to be done based on 'honour'. She saw the hand of China acting invisibly in the background and called them out for being the 'master mind' pulling the strings to 'humiliate' India.[86]

She went further a few days later, after the countries exchanged artillery fire. This time, India had photographic evidence that Pakistan was using American military weapons, including tanks, to advance its aims, something the US had promised would never occur. Once again, Nan found herself on tag team with Krishna Menon, the two joining forces to demand action. She claimed the matter had now driven 'a deep wedge' between her country and the United States.[87]

She closed ranks with Shastri, saying that 'decency, patriotism and civilized behaviour "demands that we join up as one, sink our differences, and give a reply to Pakistan in no uncertain terms".'

'I would suggest that we all support the Prime Minister in exploring every civilized method in order to show Pakistan that we wish to have peace in a civilized way,' she added. 'But if that is not possible, even though we are pledged to policies other than violence, there comes a time in the history of every nation when policies have to be reversed.'[88]

~

Nan put in papers to run for deputy leader of the Congress Parliamentary Party for the Lok Sabha in May, contesting against B. Gopala Reddy, a minister in Shastri's government. Despite her professed commitment to the government, it was difficult to see her move as anything but a further challenge to the prime minister, though Nan did her best to convince everyone that her intention was only to strengthen the overall hand of the Congress. Before the time came, in any event, Nan withdrew her challenge at the personal request of Shastri.[89]

While the deal saved the party some embarrassment, the press criticized such covert manoeuvres as bad for democracy and argued in favour of open contests as the healthy alternative. Nan, they added, would have been the better choice.[90]

~

Nan doubled down on her frank assessments of the Congress party. In June, she warned that the organization was growing increasingly disconnected from the masses it claimed to speak for and could soon find itself with no base of support. Echoing the earlier observations in the press about backroom dealmaking, she chastised the Congress for not being open to 'new blood'.[91]

She then called on 'the people' to have a more participatory role in affairs, calling on them to raise 'the standards of society', to make 'democracy an established pattern of government as well as a way of life', and to unite the world 'for the common benefit of mankind'.[92] She announced plans to build a small, modernized hut in a village outside of Allahabad, where she intended to live when Parliament was not in session.[93] It was impossible now not to see her political ambitions. The press in the meantime had recalled something she had once said: 'I always aspire high . . . and there is no sin in that—is there?'[94]

~

Shastri appeared to have survived the various challenges to his leadership by July and declared his intention to try to solve some of India's intractable problems, including its relationship with China. Nan, coincidentally, was heading out at just that moment to Hong Kong and Japan, to speak about 'international cooperation'.[95]

But just as the domestic scene appeared ready to achieve a new equilibrium, external affairs again destabilized the situation. By midsummer, Pakistani elites had concluded that India's defences at the Rann of Kutch had once again proven weak, and they convinced themselves that the time was ripe to force the issue of Kashmir by trying to foment an uprising there. The popular Kashmiri leader Sheikh Abdullah, who had been imprisoned from 1953 to 1964, had just been re-arrested and held in detention in south India for some foreign conversations he had engaged in.

When the efforts to mobilize the Kashmiris fizzled, Pakistan opted for an outright military incursion. Battles raged for two weeks in September. While India initially had some setbacks, the net effect of the attack was to deliver the widespread unity the political class had been hoping for. Indians of all stripes rallied to the country's defence.[96] In the middle of the month, the United Nations intervened, with Secretary-General U. Thant personally pushing a ceasefire.[97]

In the days that followed, Nan praised Shastri's 'bold leadership'. She redirected all her verbal fire at Pakistan, calling its actions 'shameful', and China, saying that it had been given 'a fitting reply'. But her harshest words were reserved for the United Kingdom and other Great Powers which had, she felt, not only left India stranded and alone, but which had even tilted in Pakistan's direction.[98]

Shastri recognized the delicacy of the moment. While direct hostilities with Pakistan had ceased, a war for global, popular opinion was still underway. The prime minister assembled India's diplomatic A-Team, which included Foreign Minister Swaran Singh, former president Sarvepalli Radhakrishnan, Krishna Menon, and Nan, and dispatched them around the world to make India's case.

Nan spoke plainly on British television, saying that the isles' 'stock in India had never been so low'. She expressed disappointment that the UK did not seem to show India any 'understanding'. Things were so grim, she went on, that even she thought that it was perhaps time for India to 'reassess . . . [its] relationship with the Commonwealth'.[99]

But France was really her focus. Her meeting with Charles De Gaulle especially was considered 'one of the most delicate' of missions. She had to speak to the French president not only regarding Pakistan, but China as well. And France appeared to be moving closer to Peking (Beijing), following Paris' recognition of the People's Republic and the resumption of diplomatic relations the previous year.

In an internal assessment prepared for De Gaulle just before the meeting, the French Ministry of Foreign Affairs characterized Nan as 'very experienced in foreign policy' and someone who had 'often shown great courage and a real sense of the possible'. They believed that she feared 'India might take too marked a shift to the left' and that she saw 'in a certain socialism the means of warding off this danger'. They concluded that, in all her time as a 'confidante and advisor' to her brother, she had played 'a moderating role with him . . . counterbalancing the anti-Westernism' of Krishna Menon and others.[100]

Throughout their one-hour discussion, Nan delicately but repeatedly pointed out India's existential need to protect itself from threats of dissolution. She reiterated her country's commitment to the ceasefire while also asking for support in preventing any further outside intervention. And she noted that the one upshot of the recent encounter had been the wave of centripetal forces that rippled throughout India, helping to bring the people and territory together.

De Gaulle for his part was adamant that the first order of business was the cessation of hostilities. He then insisted repeatedly that the relations between India and Pakistan and the fate of Kashmir could only be decided by the Great Powers, and with the inclusion of China. This ultimately meant that China would have to be included in the UN and take its seat on the Security Council.

Nan restated India's longstanding commitment to peaceful coexistence and its overall rejection of war. Nonetheless, she insisted on her country's unquestionable right to defend itself from aggression and promised that it had it within its power, if necessary to do so. Then, with the opening De Gaulle had given her, she launched into a conversation about China's strategic motives, arguing that China saw the success of a democratic India as a threat. Nan stressed that India was a diverse, 'multi-lingual, multi-racial, multi-religious' state. This was its strength and so any talk of secession was particularly risky not just to the union, but to the larger dream that it represented.

De Gaulle concurred with this point, saying that he fully understood the need for India's cohesion and admitting that the country was necessary for 'peace in Asia' and for its contributions to the 'international concert'. He praised the friendship France and India shared and recalled 'the work of Nehru'.

Having succeeded in getting the President to agree on these core matters, Nan then circled back to the Chinese invasion of 1962 and asked De Gaulle for his insights as to why this might have occurred. She confessed that the Indians generally were mystified by the whole thing and that their only conclusion was that the Chinese wanted to distract their southern neighbour to keep them from focusing on their economic and social development on their terms.

De Gaulle's answer was at once astonishing and enlightening. While admitting that the Chinese could be difficult to read, he argued that China was a 'big state' and that that big states frequently caused problems for others. So, he chalked up China's earlier actions, firstly, to the need for internal propaganda.

But the bigger reason, he surmised, was that China above all was against outside intervention in Asia. It was opposed to the United States and the Soviet Union operating in the region. Since India was close to both the superpowers, it was in a most 'disagreeable position vis-à-vis China', and so could not be 'spared'. He ended by saying that it was undoubtedly true that India should continue to be helped from the outside, as all countries were.[101]

Nan was satisfied with her meetings, which included one with the Interim French Foreign Minister. The rest of her time was spent with radio and television engagements, and with personal diplomacy. She announced to the press that she had been treated with 'great warmth' and that she considered 'her mission . . . to be complete and successful'.[102] Once back in India, she said that she hoped that India would pay more attention to France moving forward and that relations between the two could be strengthened.[103] De Gaulle, for his part, followed up with a letter to Shastri carrying forward the topics raised by Nan.[104]

~

Nan returned to India with some happy news. The acclaimed writer and activist Vera Brittain, her old friend, had just completed a biography about her. Excerpts from *Envoy Extraordinary* were published in the *Times of India* in regular instalments.[105]

~

After a short stay, Nan headed back to Europe, this time for talks in Amsterdam, Bonn, and London.[106] She hoped, she announced, 'to sow new seeds of understanding'.[107]

In the Netherlands, Nan met with Prime Minister Joseph Cals, and his foreign and finance ministers, as well as with Queen Juliana.[108] Later, she had lunch with British Prime Minister Harold Wilson at 10 Downing Street and tea with the Queen at Buckingham Palace.[109] She followed all of this up with another visit to the United States at year's end as well.[110]

In Bonn, she had discussions with Chancellor Ludwig Erhard and other government officials.[111] A few days afterwards, she visited Berlin and conferred with President Lubke, whom she knew from previous occasions.

The German internal assessment prepared ahead of time was, if anything, even more adulatory than the French one. Nan, they felt, was 'highly respected . . . [and] world famous . . . by virtue of her own achievements, diplomatic experience and wide-ranging connections.' They concluded that she was 'a sophisticated, accomplished and highly educated' woman who impressed everyone she encountered because of 'the cleverness of her political judgment, the sincerity of her nature, and the magic of her cultivated personality'. They were, moreover, convinced that she was sympathetic to the West German point of view since Ranjit had long ago attended Heidelberg University.[112]

Nan again used her conversations to press the idea that India was not interested in continuing to fight with Pakistan and reiterated that she hoped that the two could come to a solution, though this was something that both would have to do on their terms and without outside brokerage. The bigger matter, she stressed, was China, which was coordinating efforts against India. This was because what India represented posed a threat to the Chinese authoritarian experiment and its hopes for extended influence around the world.[113] What was at stake was plain: democracy itself.

~

While Nan was trying to repair India's relations abroad, her own with Indira was deteriorating. Just before she departed for the West, her niece wrote to her expressing concerns about renovations taking place at Anand Bhawan. Nan was staying downstairs in the grand old house until her new hut was completed. The home had fallen into disrepair. Nan and Padmaja Naidu (Sarojini's daughter and her long-time close friend) had previously offered to help with the costs of upkeep, but Indira, whose property it now was, had declined. While she was making use of some of the rooms, Nan had undertaken a refurbishing, as she usually did in any place she stayed. Indira had not taken kindly to this. Betty had only made matters worse by spreading false gossip that Nan was allowing others to pay for the changes.

While setting the record straight on such matters, Nan took the opportunity to try to clear the air about other matters. She had heard rumours that Indira was unhappy with her holding the Phulpur seat. Nan offered to step aside if her niece so desired, hastening to add that she felt that she was at 'the end of . . . [her] career' and 'in the evening of . . . [her] life' and was not interested in competing with those younger to her. Indira assured her aunt that she was not at all interested in serving in the Lok Sabha in any capacity, feigning disinterest in political life altogether.

While both women chalked up their disagreements to loose tongues and misunderstanding and wrapped up their missives in affectionate language, Indira made clear that she had, in fact, been annoyed by the speeches that Nan had given both inside and outside of Parliament and had taken personal offence to them.[114]

~

The India-Pakistan War finally came to an end with the signing of the Tashkent Agreement. The Indian prime minister had personally travelled to the Soviet Union to see the settlement through.

Lal Bahadur Shastri died shortly after signing the agreement. Nan, who was in the United States, was staggered by the news. Terming him a 'younger brother', she called his loss 'a terrible blow' and praised his 'dedication to his country' and his 'concern for the welfare of the world' which 'came above all else'. She cut her travels short and raced back home.[115]

India descended into a few days of political tumult before Indira Gandhi emerged as the new prime minister. A picture of Nan jovially embracing her niece accompanied announcements of the results in the global press.[116]

~

Things started on the wrong foot when Nan was misquoted as saying that she felt her niece 'needs experience' and that she was 'in very frail health indeed'. The papers repeatedly framed the relationship of the two women as one of competition.[117] Worse, her critics soon took to calling Indira a 'prisoner of indecision', the now famous phrase Nan had used the year before referring to the previous government.[118]

Nan kept her head down for the most part, focusing on her work in the Lok Sabha and attending various functions. In May, she toured Australia and Hong Kong.[119] She again spoke about the imperatives of democracy.[120]

As the months went by, Nan worried about the 'tragic' direction her country was taking even as it grew increasingly clear that something had definitively shifted in her relationship with Indira, who had decided to sideline her aunt. As Nan busied herself with family matters, she held out hope that she could at least mend the personal bond with her niece. But visits with the prime minister were spent in 'stony silence'. Nan felt frustrated, sad, and helpless. She was simply unable 'to make a breakthrough' despite her repeated efforts.[121]

~

In January 1967, the Congress Party suffered a political setback when it lost seats in Parliament, though it maintained enough to continue in the majority. Indira Gandhi comfortably won the election contesting from the Rae Bareilly constituency in UP, while Nan coasted to re-election in Phulpur as well.[122]

But Nan's heart just was not in it. She found herself 'tired + unhappy'. Campaigning had descended into violence, name-calling and dirty tricks. She found herself sympathizing with Indira, who was subjected to similar kinds of antics, though the prime minister was also the cause of much of her aunt's distress.[123]

Indira Gandhi in the meantime had not hesitated to send further signals that Nan was now *persona non grata*. Nan was purposely left out of an official roster of candidates for the Executive Committee of the Congress Parliamentary Party. But the move backfired when Nan and other critics won anyway, at the expense of most of the government's choices.[124] To add insult to injury, Nan and some other MPs then formed a 'study group' to improve the functioning of the party in Parliament. They had wanted to ensure transparency and fight against 'unhealthy' antidemocratic tendencies that had emerged. So they tried to approach the matter delicately, by not announcing their intentions publicly and saying that their aim was ultimately to strengthen the Congress against the Opposition.[125] But Indira clearly did not see it this way.

Lord Mountbatten took that moment to suggest to the prime minister that Vijaya Lakshmi Pandit once again be sent to the United Kingdom as high commissioner, a proposition he had discussed directly with Nan as well.[126] When Indira finally brought the matter up in a private meeting in her office, Nan asked what she thought of the idea. 'Well, Puphi [Aunty], I don't really trust you.' Nan let out a sigh of relief as the honesty released some of the tension in the room. She walked around the table and kissed her niece on the forehead, thanking her for at last speaking to her frankly. Indira proposed that

Nan go to Paris for a year instead, a potentially productive position since Nan had forged a good relationship with De Gaulle during her last visit. But Nan declined, sure that she no longer wished to pursue her diplomatic career.[127]

~

Nan spent good parts of the rest of the year travelling internationally. She represented India at the funeral of Konrad Adenauer and then flew to the Philippines at the invitation of the relatively new president, Ferdinand Marcos.[128] She found herself in the news when Robert Hardy Andrews, a former Chicago newspaper reporter, published another biography of her, this one a more idealizing, anecdote-driven account.[129]

At the end of the year, she was once more in New York City, this time to receive a citation of recognition from the sponsors committee of the Margaret Sanger Institute for her contributions towards planned parenthood. Other honorees included opera singer Marian Anderson and anthropologist Margaret Mead.[130] The Institute was being established at New York University (NYU) to honour the legacy of Sanger, who had passed away the year before.[131]

This was not the only death on Nan's mind at the moment. Just before she left for the United States, Betty passed away in London while returning from a lecture tour of the US. Nan, Nayantara, and Indira Gandhi all attended the cremation in Bombay when the body had been brought back.[132]

~

In February 1968, Indira's eldest son, Rajiv, married his fellow Cambridge University student Sonia Maino, at the home of the prime minister. Nan, in whom Indira had confided about the relationship early on, was among a close circle of witnesses to the occasion.[133]

~

But there was no serious reproachment between aunt and niece. If anything, the chasm between them was only growing larger. In July,

Nan finally decided that she had had enough. She could no longer be effective without a bare minimum of the prime minister's confidence. She resigned from Parliament.

The explanation she gave publicly was that she felt 'out of tune' with what was happening in the government. MPs were taken by surprise by her decision, which they interpreted to have been taken out of disgust and disillusionment with the state of political affairs in the country. Some expressed a wish that she had stayed to try to make things better from within.[134] The Canadian *Globe and Mail* bemoaned her decision, arguing that India had lost a 'respected . . . aristocratic watchdog' who had the 'calibre' needed to hold the country to its ideals.[135]

~

After initially vowing to stay active in other forms, Nan made the 'hard decision' to 'retire from public life' at the age of sixty-eight.[136] At the time she formally ended her career, Nan remained among the Top 20 most admired women in the world, according to the American Gallup Poll. She had held a spot on this list almost from its inception.[137]

As she made ready to leave the public eye, Nan received the unexpected news that another woman, Angie Brooks of Liberia, had at last again been elected president of the United Nations General Assembly. She travelled to New York to congratulate her and symbolically pass the baton.[138]

~

Indira Gandhi fought off the remaining challenge to her power by forcing a split in the Congress Party, the original becoming the Congress (O) and the branch loyal to her the Congress (R). She subsequently called a midterm parliamentary election. The Congress (O) joined forces with left and right opposition parties to try to stop her, organizing under the slogan 'Indira Hatao' (Get Rid of Indira). But Mrs Gandhi had proved herself a savvy politician. She twisted the expression to her advantage, calling instead for 'Garibi Hatao' (Get Rid of Poverty). The Congress (R) stomped to victory.

The situation in Pakistan had deteriorated in the meantime, with its western and eastern wings at odds. This led to civil conflict that began to spiral out of control by mid-year, sending waves of refugees into India. Mrs Gandhi rallied support for the East Pakistanis, who were then mobilizing based on their regional identity for an independent country of their own. By the end of the year, India was involved in a full-scale war with Pakistan again. It lasted two weeks. Bangladesh (Land of the Bengalis) was born. And Indira emerged triumphant.

Through this period, Nan watched warily at what was happening. Indira was at the height of her fortunes and was being compared to a Hindu Goddess (Durga).[139] Such sanctification was dangerous for anyone but was especially so given the tendencies her niece had displayed earlier. As placards magnified her personality further, Nan found Indira's actions analogous to outright Fascism.

But her tightening vice belied a weakening grip on the situation in the country, which faced numerous crises. Political opposition to her gained traction. In 1974, an old activist named Jayaprakash Narayan (JP), Nan's long-time acquaintance, whom many thought had the moral stature of Mahatma Gandhi, joined a student movement in his home state of Bihar calling for a better government. By mid-summer, he was calling for 'total revolution'. A year of unrest and protest followed.

In June 1975, things got even worse for Mrs Gandhi. Her 1971 challenger in Rae Bareilly had gone to court accusing her of using inappropriate tactics during the campaign. After winding its way through the system for years, the case was finally decided in early summer. The judgment, though acquitting her of most charges, was nonetheless against Mrs Gandhi on two minor counts. The penalty was severe. Her election to the Parliament was overturned, and with it her right to be prime minister, and she was further debarred from running again for another six years. The judge—who was seated in Motilal's old home, the Allahabad High Court—gave Mrs Gandhi twenty days to file an appeal. As the Supreme Court considered her case, she faced growing calls for her resignation. Her son Sanjay pressed her to hold onto office.

Believing that she was the subject of a conspiracy and that malign forces were out to destroy India, Mrs Gandhi declared a state of emergency, which took effect on 26 June. All fundamental rights were suspended. The press was censored. The political opposition, including leaders J.P. and Morarji Desai, were put in prison. Mrs Gandhi was now, for all intents and purposes, a dictator.[140]

~

Nan was in London for Nayantara's son's wedding at the time the Emergency was declared. As she was mobbed by reporters, Nan declined to comment saying that she had been caught unawares and 'knew nothing'. She and her daughter dashed over to India House to learn what was going on only to find the staff eerily acting as though all was normal. Horrified, they left and then hurriedly headed back to India.

Nan returned to her home, now in Dehra Dun by the foothills of the Himalayas, to find her phone tapped, her mail censored, and her house under surveillance.[141] Things had come full circle, as she recalled her days holding fort in Anand Bhawan against the colonial power.

As she looked around, she saw a man comically receding into the hedges in a vain attempt to avoid being seen. She had her long-time family retainer, her cook Budhilal, invite her spy into her garden, where he could cool down with a drink and carry on his 'dirty work'. The man was withdrawn a few weeks later.[142]

As the weeks turned to months, and the months into more than a year, Nan became despondent at the situation, feeling helpless to do anything. She tried to focus her energies on her family and wrote regularly to Nayantara, who had temporarily taken up residence in the United States on a research scholarship at the Radcliffe Institute in Cambridge, Massachusetts. The two found underground ways of discussing the ongoing crackdown.[143]

By the summer of 1976, neither of the two women could contain their dissatisfaction at the terrible conditions under which the people were living. In one letter, Nan told her daughter that 'nothing changes except for the worse'. 'You see,' she wrote, 'lack of news leads to rumors but in between there are glimpses of the truth + the truth is ugly. What seems so dangerous . . . is the growing apathy—there is plenty of discontent but to accept the fait accompli is more and more the pattern.' She railed against government doublespeak. 'We are constantly reminded that what is happening is a great mobilization of material + moral forces—[but] my generation has heard this in several languages several times before + some of us are afraid of the consequences.' She saw a special menace in the actions of Sanjay, who was enacting policy and centralizing power with tremendous speed.[144]

Earlier that same month, Nayantara had daringly broken the dread pall of public silence that hung over Indian affairs by writing in the *New Republic* under the pseudonym 'Azad' (Freedom). Her assessment was brutal 'When Mrs. Gandhi declared an emergency,' she wrote, 'she acted in character. Having become increasingly authoritarian over the past six years she finally took the plunge . . . Once it was launched, the dictatorship was easy to perpetuate.' In coldly precise detail, she took a scalpel to her cousin's lies, eviscerating one false claim after another and revealing the true horrors Indira Gandhi's government had been unleashing on the people. She warned that India would now find it difficult to turn from the dark path on which it found itself. 'Lifting the emergency will [still] leave intact the vast police force, as big as the army and inflated with powers. Law and order is a state subject but the Border Security Force, used for defense, is far better armed than the normal police force, and has been freely used along with the powerful Central Reserve Police against citizens.'[145]

A few weeks later, Nayantara shed the shield of anonymity and announced that she had authored the piece. The *New York Times* highlighted her story and those of several other dissidents, declaring the United States to be 'the main center of dissent against the authoritarian Indian Government of Prime Minister Indira Gandhi'.[146]

In October, roused to action by her daughter's bravery, Nan spoke out to a reporter from the *Times* herself, announcing that she was 'profoundly troubled' at the direction the Government was taking.' 'If there are no civil liberties and no dissent, then where is the democracy we fought for,' she demanded to know. Then, devastatingly, she added: 'It is far more repressive today, in many ways, than it was under the British.'

'The essence of democracy has always been the right to dissent . . . And it was working in India, though slowly and perhaps awkwardly. One can't govern simply by clapping into jail everyone who disagrees.'

'Please understand that I'm very proud of Indira,' she hastened to add. 'But the good career she had begun is being threatened by all this sorry business of muzzling people and stifling dissent.'

Mahatma 'Gandhi made us Indians into big people. But when a man loses his ability to speak out, he becomes a littler person, and we are now becoming a little people.'[147]

The interview was an act of courage at India's most desperate hour. While her daughter and others had heroically broken through the wall of secrecy surrounding the Emergency, they had done so from the relative safety of a foreign country. Nan was square in the middle of things. But though she was no longer the household name she had once been, the words of Madame Pandit still carried a mighty weight.

The *Christian Science Monitor* latched onto her remarks, calling them 'much-needed'. They called on 'freedom loving people everywhere' to wish India well as it re-engaged with the 'continuous striving' that true self-government demanded.[148]

The floodgates opened. Withering criticism of Indira Gandhi came in from all international directions.

~

In January 1977, Indira Gandhi called off the Emergency just as suddenly as she had announced it. Political prisoners were released. Elections were to be held immediately.

What motivated Mrs Gandhi to act in this way was a mystery. Some attributed her decision to the criticism she received, especially from the West. Others felt that she felt assured of winning the elections she was calling, and that she intended to lay the groundwork for her son Sanjay to take over.[149]

Whatever it was, Nan for the moment was simply awash in euphoria. India had come out of the other end of a 'dark tunnel', and the light felt good. Newly released activists and politicians met to exchange news of their experiences and to find their voices again.

But the extent of the terror that the country had been subjected to soon became apparent: torture, abductions, missing people. And the threat that Mrs Gandhi's re-election now posed grew clearer.[150]

Opposition forces united across all lines to try to coordinate their efforts to bring her down. The lifting of the curtain helped some who had been working with Mrs Gandhi to flee her stage-managed political theatre, including her powerful agriculture minister, Jagjivan Ram.

Nan knew what had to be done. She had gotten Morarji Desai's blessings to work with the umbrella Janata (People's) front, with which J.P. was now affiliated as well. She coordinated with Jagjivan Ram on how best to move forward. In early February, they made the big announcement. Vijaya Lakshmi Pandit was coming out of retirement to join one last fight, the most important of her life.[151]

'I have remained a passive spectator far too long,' she said, 'but I cannot live at peace with myself if, by my silence, I seem to agree with the destruction of all I have been taught to hold dear.'

'It is of the highest importance to put an end to the authoritarian trend which has grown to vast proportions and is destroying cherished values—values which have guided us through the freedom struggle, values which uphold the dignity and worth of the individual.'[152]

The 'institutions which we had built up through years of independence were smothered and destroyed one after another . . . The rule of law was undermined and the independence of the judiciary ended. Press censorship was imposed'.[153]

'Now courage, moral and physical, are at their lowest ebb and the shadow of fear has reduced us [to mere shells] . . . People are afraid to speak and . . . have acquiesced in the denial of the very freedoms for which an earlier generation fought and laid down their lives.'

'The essence of democracy is the right to dissent. This does not imply disloyalty to the country. Exchange of views and discussions are a democratic way towards a solid base on which the future progress and prosperity of the nation should be built.'[154]

'The corrosion of democracy must stop,' Nan declared, noting that she had been unable to 'see a single reason' for the Emergency. She pledged to work actively for opposition candidates wherever she could be helpful, clarifying that she sought no seat for herself and would not join any political party. Rather, she pledged only to 'campaign for principles'.[155]

Her remarks were excerpted into the 'Quotation of the Day' by the *New York Times*, which further observed that Madame Pandit remained 'one of the best-known women in India' with a mystique that made her special.[156] She was, once again, 'without exception, front-page news'.[157] The *Chicago Tribune* lauded her announcement, warning Mrs Gandhi that her aunt was 'tough . . . and surprisingly fair . . . [and had] lost none of her vigor'. In Vijaya Lakshmi Pandit, they wrote, Mrs Gandhi had found her match.[158]

Within just one week, they were proved right. The Congress, which had been posed for a dominant victory, suddenly saw its lead over the opposition cut in half. Opinion pollsters attributed this dramatic change to Nan's entry into the field.[159]

People around the world sat up and took notice. One paper in the US attentive to Madame Pandit's effect felt that 'the Third World's future [as well as America's] may hang on the example India now sets by accepting or rejecting political freedom'.[160]

Nan crisscrossed the country addressing massive rallies, receiving 'rapturous ovations' wherever she went. Desai, J.P., and Jagjivan Ram were popular among the crowds as well. The Congress proved unable to muster anything 'even remotely comparable'.[161]

Together with Atal Bihari Vajpayee, the head of the Hindu-oriented Jana Sangh, Nan tried to forge a real spirit of solidarity across ideological lines. She and Vajpayee worked closely with the Imam of the Jama Masjid (Friday Mosque) in Delhi to restoke cross-religious alliances that had existed during the quest for independence.[162] She further summoned the spirit of Mahatma Gandhi to call on the enormous number of students now mobilized to remain non-violent and not give the government any kind of pretext to reimpose restrictions.[163]

At the tail end of the campaign, Nan had proved so popular that the press started to lean into a new idea. The President of India, Fakhruddin Ahmed, died just as the elections were announced. An Interim President was then in place but was one the Opposition did not entirely trust.[164] Reporters started to probe if Nan might consider becoming the President of India. 'I would not like another funeral so soon,' she retorted with her characteristic wit, before insisting that she had only plans to return to private life once the campaign was over. She told the press to focus on the real issue at hand. Referencing a famous slogan her brother had used for the *National Herald*, a newspaper he had established, she said 'Freedom is in peril, defend it with all your might.'[165]

That Mrs Gandhi saw her aunt as the prime threat was soon made clear when acolytes like the All-India Congress Committee General Secretary, V.B. Raju, started personally attacking Nan, saying that she had never even really been in the Congress.[166] Congress MPs joined in once the signal had been given.[167] Such behaviour was in marked contrast to Nan's vow at the outset not to directly campaign against Indira, whom she loved dearly, or to do anything that might hurt her niece personally.[168]

Nan did not back down. She continued to draw 'mammoth' audiences. On the eve of the election, she summoned the people to action. 'Treat next week's poll as a pilgrimage . . .', she thundered. 'Recapture the spirit of the freedom struggle and vote fearlessly as taught by Mahatma Gandhi.'[169] The people repeatedly broke into cheers.[170]

As the campaign drew to a close, the Young Democrats Society, a Bombay-based non-political organization committed to high standards in political affairs, announced 'the most Ideal campaigner' of the season. They named Nan.[171]

When the results came in, the people's verdict was unambiguous. The Opposition had won a stunning victory, securing an absolute majority in Parliament. Everywhere there was jubilation and amazement at the rapid and remarkable turn of events.

The Congress went down to ignominious defeat. Mrs Gandhi and her son Sanjay both lost their seats in Parliament. It was over. The darkness was lifted.[172]

Democracy had prevailed.

# Coda

## Fireflies in the Mist

Nan had led a long and distinguished career. She had capped it off by coming to her country's aid when it needed her most. Now, it was time for her to retreat from the scene.

She turned to completing her memoirs. As she recalled the events that had just occurred, she wrote:

> 'Indira and I belong by upbringing and education on the same side, that of human rights, the need to work for freedom from oppressions that continue to crush humanity in so many parts of the world. When she strayed from that concept, it was my duty to oppose her. Love for an individual must be kept separate from one's deep convictions and beliefs, and this I did with all the strength and faith I possessed. When I went to meet her several weeks after the elections, I embraced her and wept. Why had my child erred so grievously when she had reached a pinnacle and could have left a mark of greatness on the world? I cried for an opportunity lost, the creation of a situation which had made nonsense of her pledge to serve the people of India and had belittled us all. Her greatest mistake was in trying to build up her younger son, Sanjay, in allowing him to imagine he was some kind of crown prince.'[1]

Nan always tried to keep her personal and professional judgements of her niece separate, just as she had done in international affairs to great effect. She repeatedly spoke of her affection for Indira, even as she had drawn ever sharper lines of criticism around her political proclivities in later years. But Indira by this point did not see things the same way at all. She harboured terrible anger and resentment against her aunt. Slights she recalled from her childhood were amplified in her recollections. In subsequent accounts, she cast Nan as her longstanding bête noire, a Machiavellian villain who had always operated behind the scenes to undermine her.[2] When Mrs Gandhi was re-elected prime minister in 1980—which Nan had tried to prevent—she did everything she could to erase Nan from the past, marginalizing her in every way possible and even eliminating her from the accounts of the history of Anand Bhawan.[3]

~

Nan spent the remainder of her days trying to focus on her family and enjoying what life had to offer. She had had one last hurrah in political affairs with the Janata Government. As soon as they had come to power, she briefly entertained the idea of becoming President of India, campaigning for the post for a bit.[4] When that did not go anywhere, she accepted an offer to represent India on the Human Rights Commission and return to the United Nations in an official capacity one final time between 1978 and 1979. In this capacity, she was unanimously elected the first Chairman-Rapporteur of the Commission's Working Group on drafting a convention against torture, which would evolve over the coming years, culminating in its adoption by the UN in 1984.[5]

Even as she was in the middle of that work, she completed her autobiography, titling it *The Scope of Happiness*. Louis Mountbatten, her old friend, wrote the foreword. The book was released to positive reviews in 1979. The *New York Times* hailed it 'a wise and fascinating book'.[6]

~

Nan kept active into her eighties. In 1982, she even returned once more to New York City to attend a celebration honouring FDR's role in the creation of the United Nations.[7] Two years later, one of her old friends, the writer Fleur Cowles asked her to contribute to a book featuring over 100 celebrities explaining what animal they would like to be reincarnated as. In her short piece, Nan mused about being an elephant, playfully talking about karma and *samsara* (the cycle of rebirth), and about elephants in the wild, in relation to humans, and in mythology. She also wistfully imagined a better balance between the modern world and nature.[8]

In 1985, she received an invitation from Diane Feinstein, then the mayor of San Francisco, to commemorate the signing of the UN Charter. Nan was unable to make the trip due to illness but released a message instead. 'In today's climate of violence, I would like to remind you of what Mahatma Gandhi said after the explosion of the first atomic bomb—that the only deterrent was the mind of man,' she wrote. 'Four decades later it is evident that moral values are necessary not only for peace but to avoid the threat of total extinction. While celebrating the anniversary of the Charter, it is my earnest hope that mature leadership will be able to translate rhetoric into action, to save our planet and ensure a more meaningful life for its inhabitants. This would be a fitting tribute to those who framed the Charter and sought to provide a just foundation for a safe and civilized world.'[9]

~

Indira Gandhi had been assassinated in 1984 by her bodyguards following her authorization of a military assault on the Sikh Golden Temple in Amritsar. Her elder son, Rajiv, had come to power on a wave of sympathy, pledging to clean up Indian politics and set the country back on the right path. But just a few years later, he was mired in a controversy over a Swedish arms deal.

Nan was by then eighty-seven years old but remained as lucid as ever. As it was the fortieth anniversary of Indian independence, she was approached for a round of interviews. She told one reporter that she felt Rajiv should 'either resign or make a full statement' to clear the air.[10]

On a popular television programme, she admitted to despair over the state of things, and the lack of meaningful progress for the poor and opportunities for the young. 'I'm happy, but in many ways, I am a frustrated woman,' she said. 'When I think of twenty years when I did nothing when I should have been doing something . . . it was my weakness, undoubtedly. I should have fought against all the things that were coming in the way. I didn't, and now I feel it, but too late, at 87.'[11] The critical self-assessment was unduly harsh, for few indeed had as consistently stood up for their values as she.[12]

Moreover, Rajiv in temperament and outlook was not his mother. He loved Nan as much as she did him and called her his grandmother. This brought her tremendous joy.

To the end of her days, she remained devoted to her family, immediate and extended, never allowing public disagreements to cloud her affection for everyone. On her ninetieth birthday, the entire clan—Rajiv, Sonia, Maneka (Sanjay's widow), and her children and grandchildren—gathered in her cosy home in Dehra Dun to celebrate. From an armchair in the corner, she glanced around, keeping an eye on all, ever the watchful guardian.[13]

~

Vijaya Lakshmi Pandit died on 1 December 1990. She had lived through a tumultuous century of war and grief, witness to the worst humanity had to offer. She tackled such matters with an indomitable spirit, embodying a cosmopolitan vision of a brighter future. She thought of herself a global citizen, a woman comfortable with all kinds of people, from any background. Yet she remained quintessentially Indian, devoted to the larger ideals for which she believed her country stood.

In its obituary, the *New York Times* quoted India's President to say that Madame Pandit had been 'a luminous strand in the tapestry of India's freedom struggle . . . [d]istinctive in her elegance, courage, and dedication . . .'[14] The *Times of India* wryly observed that she was 'an individual who had the distinction of living before her time, during her time and after her time.'[15] For the *Guardian*, she represented something even more, 'the last grand lady of a great family'.[16]

# Notes

## Preface

1. Her name was Swarup. To distinguish between her mother, Swarup Rani, and herself, she was often referred to as Sarup, a convention she followed in her memoir and which I follow throughout this book.
2. 'Most Remarkable Woman Named by Mrs. Roosevelt', *New York Times* (hereafter *NYT*), 9/6/1950, 8.
3. Quoted from Manu Bhagavan, *The Peacemakers: India and the Quest for One World* (Delhi: HarperCollins, 2012), 163.
4. Longines-Wittnauer Interview with Mme. Vijaya Lakshmi Pandit. https://www.youtube.com/watch?v=IoXfXzlE_oA&t=113s, 29/3/2023. Hereafter dates that follow URLs indicate date of last access.
5. I am indebted to Khushi Singh Rathore for her extensive efforts to help me track down this alternative version of the photograph. We were not successful and are thus left only with my fleeting memory of what I once saw.
6. See Ann Stoler, *Along the Archival Grain* (Princeton: Princeton University Press, 2009); Antoinette Burton, *Dwelling in the Archive* (New York, Oxford University Press, 2003) and as ed., *Archive Stories* (Durham: Duke University Press, 2005).
7. See for example, the forthcoming work of Khushi Singh Rathore, including 'Women in Early Years of India's Foreign Policy', PhD dissertation, Jawaharlal Nehru University, 2023.

## Chapter 1: Little Woman

1. Vijaya Lakshmi Pandit, *The Scope of Happiness: A Personal Memoir* (New York: Crown, 1979), 56–57; Vera Brittain, *Envoy Extraordinary: A Study of Vijaya Lakshmi Pandit and Her Contribution to Modern India* (New York: A.S. Barnes, 1965), 37–38. Brittain credits a soothsayer seeking alms with the prophecy, but Pandit's own account years later specifies that it was her mother who made it. Brittain's source is Krishna Hutheesing, Pandit's sister. Hereafter, Vijaya Lakshmi Pandit, aka Sarup 'Nan' Nehru, is referred to in the notes as VLP.
2. According to B.R. Nanda, Pandit Raj Kaul was persuaded to move to Delhi by the Mughals. There he took up a house by a canal, called a nahar. Kashmiris then began calling the clan that descended from it, the Kaul-Nehrus, the Kauls

of the Canal, or sometimes just 'the Nehrus' for short. See B.R. Nanda, *The Nehrus: Motilal and Jawaharlal* (London: George Allen & Unwin, 1962), 18. https://en.wikipedia.org/wiki/Achabal_Gardens, 2 April 2023.
3   Ibid., 22–25.
4   Ibid., 26–31.
5   Ibid., 41, 62–63.
6   Ibid., 63.
7   Ibid., 27–28.
8   Ibid., 30, 63.
9   Ibid., 36–40. Motilal made them change their name to the Satya Sabha, Community of Truth.
10  Gitanjali Surendran, *Anand Bhawan* (Delhi: Jawaharlal Nehru Memorial Fund, 2018), ix, 8. Nanda, 31, claims Motilal paid Rs. 19,000. Cf. David Lelyveld, 'The Mystery Mansion', in 'Ghosts', *The Little Magazine* IV:4, http://www.littlemag.com/ghosts/davidlelyveld.html, 21/2/2023. See also 'Swaraj Bhavan,' https://en.wikipedia.org/wiki/Swaraj_Bhavan, 21/7/2023. Hereafter all dates follow DD/MM/Year format.
11  *Scope of Happiness*, 43. Hereafter referred to as *SoH*.
12  Lelyveld, 'The Mystery Mansion.'
13  Nanda, 31
14  *SoH*, 24. Krishna Hutheesing claims that VLP was born 'while a storm was raging outside' and for this reason was nicknamed 'The Tempest'. Krishna Hutheesing, 'Nehru and Madame Pandit, By their Sister,' *Ladies Home Journal* 72 (1), January 1955, 34. VLP writes that 'Tempest' was the 'code word' for her birth, but says she is unclear what its deeper meaning might have been. She notes with a touch of humor that the name fit well with her personality. There was 'a lot of rainfall' during the twenty-four hours of her birthday, so Betty's account seems accurate. I am grateful to Mark Beswick of the Met Office National Meteorological Archive of the United Kingdom for checking on my behalf a register of monthly rainfall records produced by the Meteorological Office of the Government of India.
15  For more on Tipu, see Kate Brittlebank, *Tipu Sultan's Search for Legitimacy* (Delhi: Oxford University Press, 1997).
16  Hume, quoted in Anil Seal, *The Emergence of Indian Nationalism* (Cambridge: Cambridge University Press, 1971), 268.
17  At its core, theosophy preached an appreciation for all religions, and to see value in India's heritage. To his father's skeptical bemusement, the young Jawaharlal found this all alluring, and got involved during the years he was under Brooks' care.
18  *SoH*, 51–52. I replicate the spelling of Nanhi that VLP uses in her memoir, but Motilal refers to her as Nanni and other variants in his letters.
19  Physical description based on my interpretation of childhood photographs. Quote from Motilal to Jawaharlal, 30/7/1905, in Ravinder Kumar and D.N. Panigrahi, *Selected Works of Motilal Nehru*, Volume I (Delhi: Vikas Publishing, 1982), 63.
20  Motilal to Jawaharlal letter, quoted in Nanda, 67. Cf. Letters from 23, 27/8/1905, *Selected Works of Motilal Nehru (hereafter SWMN)*, Volume I, 70–72.
21  Nanda, 67. Motilal to Jawaharlal, 20/9/1905, *SWMN*, Volume I, 72–73.
22  Nanda, 68.

23 *SoH*, 51–52.
24 Ibid., 59. Addressing the issue of her education late in her life, VLP pointed out that there were no good Indian governesses available, as this was not a profession Indian women really chose, and 'that there were no good English schools for girls', either, reinforcing the former situation. But she did in fact have the finest of tutors, including professors from Allahabad University, who worked with her on advanced material. Vijaya Lakshmi Pandit, 'We Nehrus', *The Illustrated Weekly of India*, 17 April 1988, 10. When she rose to prominence, these facts did not go entirely unnoticed, with some even amusedly picking up on the fact that she purposefully downplayed her educational training to disarm those she encountered. 'Madame Ambassador—The First', 1948, 2, Poppy Cannon White Correspondence, Series I, Correspondence: Vijaya Lakshmi Pandit, Walter Francis White and Poppy Cannon White Papers, JWJ MSS 38, Box 11, Folder 75, Beinecke Rare Book and Manuscript Library, Yale University.
25 *SoH*, 59-60. VLP's fiancée was Dewan Anand Kumar, who was nineteen at the time of engagement and just about to go off to Cambridge. His father was Narendranath and, most importantly, his sister was none other than Rameshwari Nehru. I am grateful to Arjun Raina for sharing this information with me. More information about Anand Kumar and his family is available on the Panjab University Oral History Project: https://oralhistory.puchd.ac.in/panjab-university-early-history/, 23/2/2023.
26 *SoH*, 60.
27 As quoted in Robert Hardy Andrews, *A Lamp for India: The Story of Madame Pandit* (Englewood Cliffs, NJ: Prentice-Hall, 1967), 42. Nanda, 78, indicates that Jawaharlal came home for three weeks in the summer of 1906, and spent the time with his family in Mussoorie.
28 *SoH*, 59-62.
29 *Lamp for India*, 44–51. VLP's version is, in fact, the correct one. See Sugata Bose and Ayesha Jalal, *Modern South Asia*, 59. The story of the Black Hole of Calcutta as told by Hooper continued to circulate around the world for generations, even entering popular Western lexicon as a hellish environment in which to stay. The American cartoon television serial, *The Flintstones*, refers to the Black Hole of Calcutta in Season 5, Episode 20, which originally aired 29/1/1965.
30 Motilal Nehru's letters to his son, as quoted in Nanda, 75.
31 *Lamp for India*, 40; *SoH*, 50–52. Hutheesing, *We Nehrus*, 3. Nanda (42) incorrectly inverts the story to claim that Hooper came up with Betty on her own, and that the family went along with it because it sounded like *beti*.
32 *SoH*, 38.
33 *SoH*, 54–55.
34 Hume, quoted in Nanda, 49.
35 Nanda, 50–51.
36 Bose and Jalal, 94.
37 Ibid., 95.
38 Ibid., 95–96, citing Sumit Sarkar.
39 Nanda, 86.
40 Ibid., 86.
41 *SoH*, 62.
42 Nanda, 115–116.

43  Ibid., 116. Cf. 'The Maharaja Who Chose to Insult the King Emperor', 11/12/2011, https://www.indiatoday.in/india/north/story/baroda-maharaja-sayajirao-iii-gaekwad-insulted-the-emperor-148448-2011-12-11.
44  For a full analysis of the Gaekwad Incident, please see Manu Bhagavan, *Sovereign Spheres* (Delhi: Oxford University Press, 2003), 47–69.
45  https://www.indiatoday.in/india/north/story/baroda-maharaja-sayajirao-iii-gaekwad-insulted-the-emperor-148448-2011-12-11
46  Nanda, 122–124. *SoH*, 55.
47  *SoH*, 55.
48  Ibid., 55-56.
49  Ibid., 56-57.
50  Ibid., 60.
51  Bose and Jalal, 104.
52  *SoH*, 62.
53  Ibid., 62, 64.
54  Ibid., 61.
55  See Elena Borghi, 'Forgotten Feminisms: Gender and the Nehru Household in Early-Twentieth-Century India', *Gender & History* 29(2), August 2017, 254–272.
56  Ibid., 266.
57  The material in this section largely summarizes Borghi, 263–267.
58  For more on Cousins, see Purnima Bose, *Organizing Empire* (Durham: Duke University Press, 2003), 74–127.
59  *SoH*, 61–62.
60  When she was fourteen, VLP met Allen Dulles, the future head of the American Central Intelligence Agency (CIA). The two spent hours talking and arguing passionately over politics and other matters. Dulles had recently graduated from Princeton University and was in India for a year to teach English at a missionary school. According to Dulles, biographers, Allen found VLP engaging and enthralling and 'did not treat her like' the fourteen-year-old she was. Their time together was so memorable that he would recall it decades later when the two would meet again. Leonard Mosley, *Dulles: A Biography of Eleanor, Allen, and John Foster Dulles and their Family Network* (New York: The Dial Press/James Wade, 1978), 33–34. James Srodes, *Allen Dulles* (Washington DC, Regnery Publishing, 1999, 36–38. VLP confided to her granddaughter, Nonika: 'I was in + out of love several times always with what my parents considered the wrong man.' VLP to Nonika Sahgal, September 1970, private collection of Nonika Sahgal.
61  Milton Israel, *Communications and Power* (Cambridge: Cambridge University Press, 1994), 218–219.
62  Nanda, 182–183.
63  Ibid., 187.
64  Motilal writes to Jawaharlal on 10/2/1920: 'I am thoroughly dissatisfied with Ranga Iyer, and cannot give him a free hand to put in any nonsense he likes . . . For the last nine months we have been playing at this stupid game.' Nanda, 188. Motilal is writing about who should serve as editor of the *Independent*. C.S. Ranga Iyer had taken over from Syud Hossain. Based on this letter, it is clear that Hossain was forced out a mere three months after taking the reigns of the paper, on account of his relationship with VLP.

65 *SoH*, 65; https://maddy06.blogspot.com/2013/03/dr-syud-hossain-true-patriot.html, 29/3/2023.

66 The exact details of VLP's early relationship to Hossain are hazy, apparently purposefully scrubbed from the record. M.O. Mathai, Nehru's one-time private secretary, claims in his vindictive, sensational, and not-entirely-trustworthy memoir, that Nehru was given a file by Rajkumari Amrit Kaur shortly after Gandhi's assassination. Nehru in turn handed the papers over to Mathai and said 'These are the papers about young Vijaya Lakshmi's elopement with Syed Hussain [sic]. You had better burn them'. Mathai then had them 'reduced to ashes' in the kitchen. M.O. Mathai, *Reminiscences of the Nehru Age* (New Delhi: Vikas Publishing, 1978), 134. According to an account by Pakistani journalist H.M. Abbasi, cited by N.S. Vinodh in his excellent biography of Syud Hossain, the two were married by Hazrat Maulana Rashid Fakhri, 'a well-respected Congress leader'. Vinodh notes that Abbasi's account is filled with errors and so serves more to underscore the idea that the marriage was 'informal.' He also cites K.L. Gauba, a lawyer to support the idea that the two were in fact married. It is also possible that the ceremony was officiated by Maulana Mohammad Fakhir, a Sufi pir from the Daira Shah Ajmal. See also: Sheela Reddy, *Mr and Mrs Jinnah* (Delhi: Penguin/Viking, 2017), 57; Francis Robinson, *Separatism Among Indian Muslims* (Cambridge: Cambridge University Press, 2008, first published 1974), 375; Nandini Gooptu, *The Politics of the Urban Poor in Early Twentieth-century India* (Cambridge: Cambridge University Press, 2004. first published 2001), 275. I am grateful to N.S. Vinodh, Francis Robinson and Nayantara Sahgal, and others as well, for conversations and exchanges related to this matter. Whatever the nature of the ceremony, she definitely married Syud Hossain. Once the two of them reconnected in the United States in the forties (see later chapters), she revealed her story to some of their close associates, such as Walter and Poppy White, and in fact let the news go public. A publication calling her 'India's First Lady' released in early 1947 said, 'Against her family's wishes, the young lady eloped with a young Moslem student, a member of the Congress Party. Her Brahmin family persuaded her to abandon her husband and . . . she was married to a member of her own faith and caste.' 'World Personalities: Mrs. Pandit: India's "First Lady", in 'Hon. Mrs. Vijayalakshmi Pandit, Minister of Public Health and Local Self-Government of U.P.', IOR L/I/1/1482, F. No. 8, The British Library. In a document promoting her imminent arrival to the US as ambassador, the Whites note: 'Her first was a rebel marriage to a charming young man of whom everyone seems to have disapproved. This marriage was quickly annulled. Her second marriage could not have been more suitable—or happier.' 'Madame Ambassador—The First', 3, undated but written in 1948 by context, Poppy Cannon White Papers, JWJ MSS 38, Box 11, Folder 75, Beinecke Library, Yale. She also confided to her granddaughter, Nonika: 'I was married a few months before I was 20 + though I was considered rather sophisticated for my day + age, I was innocent beyond words of the real meaning of life. I don't mean the facts of life . . .! In marriage I looked for a handsome husband, also rich, who would be so enamored of me that from that day forth he would look at no other woman--+ and an easy life of pleasant things.' VLP to Nonika Sahgal, September 1970, shared from the private collection of Nonika Sahgal. As she reflected on relationships at the very end of her life, VLP wrote: 'When I look back on it now, I laugh; because when one of my granddaughters married a

Muslim some time ago, nobody even raised an eyebrow.' Vijaya Lakshmi Pandit, 'We Nehrus', *Illustrated Weekly of India*, 17 April 1988, 11.
67  *SoH*, 65.
68  *SoH*, 65.
69  VLP to Padmaja Naidu, 13 March. Correspondence with VLP, Padmaja Naidu papers, NMML, 51–56. (Hereafter PNaidu papers.) The year is not given but it can be inferred to be 1920, by its place in the paper collection and by various references made in the letter. Vinodh comes to the same conclusion in his Hossain biography.
70  Krishna Hutheesing, *We Nehrus*, 46. *SoH*, 63–70, especially 65–66. See also D.K. Palit, *Major General AA Rudra* (New Delhi: Reliance Publishing House), 1997, 67. This book is an autobiographical narrative of Rudra, as told to Palit, who then told the story in his own words, though in Rudra's voice. According to this account, VLP, Hossain, Jawaharlal, and even Gandhi stayed for a time in Rudra's house in Delhi. Hossain and VLP were not allowed to see one another and instead were made to pass notes via the children of the house. VLP was visibly 'sad, disillusioned'. When this exactly takes place is not clear, though the book claims that it is after the two were separated. In his biography of his grandfather, for whom he was named, George Joseph writes that his grandmother, Susannah 'acted as a peace-maker' between the Nehru family members. His grandfather was asked by Motilal to run *The Independent* for a short while after Hossain's departure. George Gheverghese Joseph, *George Joseph: The Life and Times of a Kerala Christian Nationalist* (New Delhi: Orient Longman, 2003), 103–104.

## Chapter 2: The Portrait of a Lady

1  Interview with Arjun Raina, 25/2/2021, and subsequent exchanges, February 2023.
2  VLP confided to Nonika that her 'darling mother [Swarup Rani] had made up her mind no one would marry . . . [her/VLP] because, according to the times . . . [she/VLP] was "fast" . . .' VLP to Nonika Sahgal, September 1970.
3  *SoH*, 25–26. In a later essay, VLP confesses that she and Ranjit had actually met 'years before . . . [their] marriage' in Bombay. But their 'courtship', by this account as well, followed what is charted here. Vijaya Lakshmi Pandit, 'We Nehrus', 11. Cf. Irene Jensen, 'The Men Behind the Woman: A Case Study of the Political Career of Madame Vijaya Lakshmi Pandit', *Contributions to Asian Studies*, Volume X, 1 January 1977, 76–93.
4  See Gail Minault, *The Khilafat Movement* (Delhi: Oxford University Press, 1981).
5  Secretary of State for India Edwin Montagu and the Viceroy Lord Chelmsford agreed on a package of reforms that expanded voting rights and granted more power to the central and local legislative councils. While these were positive steps, the reforms adopted the policy of Dyarchy, which allowed Indians to hold lower-tier portfolios while the British maintained control of all important ones, including those with power of the purse and the sword. Dyarchy was seen as a betrayal, and as evidence of duplicity. But to make matters worse, the British passed the Rowlatt Bills, which continued wartime ordinances into peacetime, and essentially restricted Indians' rights to free assembly and denied them due process or fair trials. Resentment over all of this rose throughout the region. In April

1919, a large group of predominately Sikh men, women, and children gathered in Jallianwala Bagh, an enclosed public garden in the Punjabi city of Amritsar, for celebrations and to discuss and protest local political matters, including the Rowlatt Acts. General Reginal Dyer marched troops into the garden, supported by a tank that could not access the small entry tunnels, and without warning fired upon the crowd, resulting in a horrific, largescale massacre. See Kim Wagner, *Amritsar 1919* (New Haven: Yale University Press, 2019).
6   *SoH*, 71–72.
7   *SoH*, 77–78.
8   Jai Bhandarkar, ed. *A Royal Palette: The Portraits of Vamanrao S. Pandit, 1882-1941* (Mumbai: Turtle Books, 2010), 18-19.
9   Brittain, 39.
10  *SoH*, 76. Brittain, 38.
11  *SoH*, 73–74.
12  This and the previous two sections from *SoH*, 74–84.
13  Gandhi, Young India, 29/12/1920 and 12/3/1925.
14  The material so far in the section is from *SoH*, 86–88.
15  *New York Herald*, European Edition, 19/3/1922.
16  'Gandhi Thanks British Jurist for 6 Year Term,' *Chicago Daily Tribune*, 20/3/1922, 11.
17  *SoH*, 86.
18  *SoH*, 87–90.
19  *SoH*, also 89.
20  Gandhi to Sarojini Naidu, 20/12/1925, https://www.mkgandhi.org/Selected%20Letters/Sarojini/letter29.htm, 5/5/2018.
21  Naravane, 42.
22  Jawaharlal Nehru, *Towards Freedom* (New York: The John Day Company, 1941), 120–121. Hereafter JNTF.
23  *SoH*, 89–90.
24  http://www.italianliners.com/lloyd-triestino-en, 7/5/2018.
25  Andrews, 109.
26  Postcard from Vijaya Lakshmi Pandit to Miss D. Dove, 6/10/1926, in Small Collections, Vijaya Lakshmi Pandit Correspondence, 190 (XXXIX), NMML.
27  JNTF, 121–127. Cf. Michele Louro, *Comrades Against Imperialism: Nehru, India, and Interwar Internationalism* (Cambridge: Cambridge University Press, 2018).
28  Andrews, 109. Andrews does not provide proper citations in his book, and is confused in places, making his narrative somewhat unreliable. But he knew Vijaya Lakshmi Pandit personally, and the quotes appear to be drawn from his conversations with her. His description of the European trip mixes a number of things up, claiming, for instance, that the Nehrus began their excursion with a visit to Moscow. This actually occurred in October 1927, to commemorate the ten-year anniversary of the Russian Revolution. I am fairly certain that he drew on Nehru's autobiography for these claims, confusing Betty for Nan and muddling the story.
29  Frances Stonor Saunders, *The Woman Who Shot Mussolini* (New York: Metropolitan Books, 2010).
30  VLP recounts the European trip in *SoH*, 89–90.
31  *SoH*, 94.

32  https://archive.org/stream/govtofindiaact19029669mbp/govtofindia act19029669mbp_djvu.txt, 10/5/2018.
33  '"Boycott Simon": Nehru's Open Letter to LU Students', *Times of India* (hereafter *TOI*), 14/112014. https://timesofindia.indiatimes.com/city/lucknow/Boycott-Simon-Nehrus-Open-Letter-To-LU-students/articleshow/45140692.cms, 10/5/2018. JNTF, 135.
34  JNTF, 140.
35  http://nehrumemorial.nic.in/en/digital-archives/category/72-towards-purna-swaraj-the-lahore-congress-1929.html, 14/5/2018.
36  http://www.satyagrahafoundation.org/purna-swaraj-the-declaration-of-the-independence-of-india/, 14/5/2018.
37  Irfan Habib, '*Civil Disobedience 1930–31*', *Social Scientist*, 25 (9–10): 43–66.
38  *SoH*, 96–97. And VLP to Ranjit Pandit, 25/6/1930, V.L. Pandit Papers, Ist Inst. (Ranjit Pandit), 1930-38, Correspondence with V.L. Pandit, Part I (hereafter PPCRP), 2. Cf. Taylor Sherman, *State Violence and Punishment in India* (London: Routledge, 2010), 69–71.
39  VLP to Ranjit Pandit (hereafter VLPtoRP), 26/6/1930, PPCRP, 3–6.
40  *SoH*, 95–97.
41  Nayantara Sahgal, *Prison and Chocolate Cake* (New York: Alfred A. Knopf, 1954), 21–22. Hereafter *PandCC*.
42  Letters from Gandhi and Ranjit Pandit from late 1930, quoted in *SoH*, 98–99.
43  VLPtoRP, multi-dated omnibus letter, 19-22/9/1930, PPCRP, p 14.
44  VLPtoRP, 22/9/1930, PPCRP, 15.
45  Ibid., 22/9/1930, 12–13.
46  Ibid., 28/91930, 19–25.
47  JNTF, 176-77.
48  VLPtoRP, 7/11/1930, PPCRP, 27–34.
49  Ibid., 16/11/1930, 40.
50  Ibid., 7/11/1930, 27–34.
51  Ibid., 16/11/1930, 35–36.
52  Ibid., 16/11/1930, 36–44.
53  Ibid., 19/11/1930, 45–48; 16/11/1930, 36–44.
54  Ibid., 19/11/1930, 51. Much has been made of VLP's relationship with Kamala Nehru. Some, like Katherine Frank, have claimed that Indira Gandhi was always angry at her aunt because of the way she felt her mother was treated, and VLP comes across as one of the key villains in Frank's account. Bertil Falk makes similar assertions, going even further to say that 'nobody never ever' liked VLP, with the exception of P.D. Tandon. Katherine Frank, *Indira* (London, HarperCollins, 2002, first published 2001). Bertil Falk, *Feroze* (Delhi: Roli Books, 2016), Kindle edition, 633. Neither of these portrayals match the picture that emerges from my reading of the historical record. As with many families, there were moments of anger and dispute but also of love and adoration. It is fair to say that Kamala was uncomfortable and somewhat out of place in the Nehru household, and that slights did sometimes occur, though these for the most part seem much less intentional than described. Nayantara Sahgal, recalling her mother's own reflections on the matter, wrote that VLP had a special, adoring relationship with her brother. In continuing with that, she was 'insensitive' to Kamala's feelings, and that, rather than purposeful barbs or bitterness, is what often led to unhappiness. VLP regretted such behavior later in her life. (Email

from Nayantara Sahgal to me, 20/1/2019.) She flatly and forcefully denied ever purposefully mistreating her sister-in-law in one interview. See 'The Forgotten Nehru,' VLP interview with Shailaja Bajpai, *Gentleman*, August 1986, 40–41. Another Indira biographer, Inder Malhotra, claims that 'too many' witnessed what had happened to Kamala to completely believe VLP's denials, yet provides no direct corroboration of this assertion as proof while his own personal contact with Indira Gandhi only began in the late fifties. Inder Malhotra, *Indira Gandhi* (London, Hodder & Staughton, 1989), 29–30. In 1988, VLP wrote of Kamala: 'I never had a close relationship with her. She came from an orthodox family which was quite different in terms of values from the environment we grew up in. She was hard in judging people and had strong likes and dislikes. She really came into her own after the national movement gained ground and she joined Gandhi.' 'Indira had a feeling that her mother had not been treated properly by the Nehrus. I cannot say how justifiable this is but all I can say is that her mother was unhappy until Gandhiji came along. And then she threw herself into the movement and did a great job, sick as she was. [But] I don't think that Indu [Indira] was ever close to her mother, whatever she may have said later.' Vijaya Lakshmi Pandit, 'We Nehrus', 12-14. This characterization, at least of her relationship with Kamala, comports with the one presented by Betty in a book released after her death. Krishna Hutheesing, *Dear to Behold* (New York: Macmillan, 1969), 28–29.
55  Ibid., 11/12/1930, 63–64.
56  JNTF, 181-185; *SoH*, 99–100.
57  VLPtoRP, 5/5/1931 and 8/7/1931, PPCRP, 71–81.
58  *SoH*, 101–102.

## Chapter 3: Knowing Why the Caged Bird Sings

1  This section is a summary of *SoH*, 101–104.
2  *SoH*, 103–109. For broader analysis of prisons and colonial India, see Mushirul Hasan, *Roads to Freedom* (Delhi: Oxford University Press, 2016), and specific to VLP and the Nehrus, Mushirul Hasan, *When Stone Walls Cry: The Nehrus in Prison* (Delhi: Oxford University Press, 2016).
3  VLPtoRP, 25/5/1932, PPCRP, 83, 85.
4  Ibid., 25/5/1932, 84. The Alhambra is a renown fortress-palace in the south of Spain that combines Moorish base architecture with Renaissance additions. It was once home to Ferdinand and Isabella and is now recognized as a UNESCO World Heritage Site. https://en.wikipedia.org/wiki/Alhambra, 30/3/2023.
5  *PandCC*, 22–23.
6  *SoH*, p. 110.
7  VLP to Ranjit Pandit, 5/5/1932, PPCRP, 247.
8  *SoH*, 110; VLP to Ranjit Pandit, 25/5/1932, PPCRP, 91.
9  VLPtoRP, 10/9/1932, PPCRP, postscript 11/9, PPCRP, 103.
10  Ibid., 10/9/1932, 100.
11  *SoH*, 110–111.
12  VLPtoRP, 10/9/1932, PPCRP, 100.
13  *SoH*, 111-113.
14  VLPtoRP, 25/5/1932, PPCRP, 85.
15  Ibid., 5/5and 20/6 1932, 89, 246.

16  *SoH*, 113.
17  VLPtoRP, 20/6/1932, PPCRP, 90.
18  Ibid., 10/9/1932, 94–96.
19  Ibid., 7/10/1932, 108.
20  Ibid., 10/9/1932, 95.
21  Ibid., 10/9/1932, 101–102.
22  This and above quotations from letter from Ibid., 7/10/1932, 105–107; 22/10/1932, 114.
23  VLP asserts in her memoir that she was sentenced to 'one year's rigorous imprisonment'. 'In addition,' she adds, 'I was fined fifteen hundred rupees or six month's imprisonment in lieu of the fine. Congress policy forbade the payment of fines, so my sentence amounted to eighteen months' imprisonment.' *SoH*, 103. Elsewhere, she contradicts herself and refers to her sentence as 'a year (109),' though in context this passes off as literary licence. Circling back in conclusion, she states that she 'was released two months before my sentence ended because I had earned marks for 'good conduct',' and that she was pleased to see her children after 'sixteen months (113-114).' In fact, she was in prison from the end of January 1932 until mid-December that same year, about eleven months. She is brutally honest about her difficulties transitioning from her life of privilege to one of sacrifices and services, and freely discusses various times she fell short of Congress ideals, as when she confesses that she acquired and accepted reading material in prison through payments made by outside friends. Though this was 'conduct unbecoming a true satyagrahi', she 'indulged in it with a clear conscience (111)'. It is unclear, therefore, why she misstates the length of her sentence. Perhaps she paid the fine and felt ashamed of doing so. Perhaps she just misremembered the events. The sources do not make this clear.
24  VLPtoRP, 7/10/1932, PPCRP, 109.
25  Ibid., 7/10/1932, 110.
26  Ibid., 22/10/1932, 122.
27  *SoH*, 109, 113.
28  VLPtoRP, 31/12/1932, PPCRP, 126-128.
29  Ibid., 31/12/1932, 130. SoH, 114.
30  Chandralekha Pandit to Ranjit Pandit, 31/12/1932, PPCRP, 137.
31  VLPtoRP, 31/12/1932, PPCRP, 133.
32  Ibid., 2, 14/2/1933, 142, 144.
33  Ibid., 2/2/1933, 138-139.
34  Details on Kshama Row, Rajkumari Amrit Kaur, and Leela Row are from Sidin Vadukut, 'The Remarkable Life of Leela Row Dayal,' 30/6/2018, *LiveMint*, https://www.livemint.com/Leisure/hL3EjZctOHVopSB5TCOQUK/The-remarkable-life-of-Leela-Row-Dayal.html, 27/7/2018.
35  VLPtoRP, 2/2/1933, PPCRP, 139–140.
36  Ibid., 14/2/1933, 146–147; 23/2/1933, 157.
37  Ibid., 14/2/1933, 153.
38  Ibid., 2/2/1933, 140. For more on the Pasis, see Ramnarayan Rawat, *Reconsidering Untouchability* (Bloomington: Indiana University Press, 2011).
39  VLPtoRP, 2/2/1933, PPCRP, 140.
40  Ibid., 14/2/1933, 145.
41  Ibid., 23/2/1933, 154–165.
42  Ibid., 23/2/1933, 166.

43  Ibid., 23/2/1933, 164.
44  'Poona Pact', n.d., http://www.ambedkar.org/impdocs/poonapact.htm., 27/7/2018.
45  VLPtoRP, 7/5/1933, PPCRP, 180.
46  Ibid., 5/5/1933, 170–171.
47  Ibid., 10/5/1933, 188-189. Cf. JNTF, 236–240.
48  Telegram, VLP to Ranjit Pandit, 12/5/1933, PPCRP, 194.
49  VLPtoRP., 18/5/1933, PPCRP, 201.
50  Ibid., 10/5/1933, 192.
51  Ibid., 16/5/1933, 195.
52  Ibid., 20/5/1933, 204–205.
53  Ibid., 27/5/1933, 215–216.
54  Ibid., 2/3 June 1933, 219.
55  Ibid., 4/6/1933, 223–224.
56  Ibid., 4/6/1933, 227.
57  Jawaharlal JNtoVLP (hereafter JNtoVLP), 11/7/1933, in Nayantara Sahgal, ed., *Before Freedom* (Delhi: HarperCollins, 2000), 118. Hereafter *BF*.
58  Krishna Hutheesing, *With No Regrets: An Autobiography* (New York: John Day, no date given, reproduction from Andesite Press), 96.
59  VLPtoRP, 8/5/1933, PPCRP, 183-184. As near as I can tell, VLP is writing to Ranjit about Raja Hutheesing, but she never actually refers to him specifically, only calling him 'M'. It is possible this is someone else, though nothing I have found would indicate that it was.
60  Hutheesing, *With No Regrets*, 97–100. Betty claims that the wedding was fixed so soon because that is what she and Raja wanted, and because Swarup Rani wanted to see her (Betty) settled before she (Swarup Rani) died, which she feared would be very soon. VLP privately implies to Ranjit that the marriage is hurried because of Betty's state of mind, to help her stabilize and find happiness. Jawaharlal writes that the timeframe was impacted by the fear that he might be re-imprisoned at any moment, as well as worry for Swarup Rani's health. JNTF, 286.
61  *SoH*, 115; Brittain, 40. Brittain, following Nehru's own claims, notes that the ceremony was a civil one because a Brahmin was marrying a non-Brahmin, non-Hindu Jain, and 'under present British Indian law no religious ceremony had validity for such a marriage.' But 'a recently passed Civil Marriage Act' gave them a way out. JNTF, 286. Both VLP and Jawaharlal agree that the ceremony was simple because of the ongoing freedom struggle and because of their mother's frail health.
62  JNTF, 293–302.
63  JNtoVLP, 12/9/1934, *BF*, 123. Ranjit Pandit in this period was also under the watchful eye of the British government, which labeled him a communist revolutionary. 'Report on the political activities of Ranjit Sitraram Pandit, brother-in-law of Jawahir [sic] Lal Nehru,' Government of India, Home Department, Political section, F. No. 7/12/34, 1934, Secret, NAI.
64  VLP to Jawaharlal Nehru (hereafter VLPtoJN), 23/2/1935, *BF*, 125-126.
65  VLPtoRP, 5/5/1933, PPCRP, 170-171.
66  JNtoVLP and VLPtoJN, 23/2/and 1, 10, 15, 27 March and 2 April 1935, *BF*, 125-148.
67  VLPtoJN, 10/3/1935, in *BF*, 133.

68  Navnit Parekh, *Himalayan Memoirs* (Bombay: Popular Prakashan, 1986), 92-94. Cf. http://www.khaliestate.com/history.htm, 6/8/2018. https://www.telegraph.co.uk/travel/destinations/asia/india/hotels/mountain-resort-khali-estate-hotel/, 6/8/2018.
69  According to local guides, the property acquired this name supposedly because the area was originally barren of trees. But the emptiness it embodied was more of the spiritual, Buddhist-Zen quality, the kind associated with peace and solitude. Ravi Wazir, 'Seeking Genuine Hospitality and Contact with Wilderness? Welcome to Khali Estate', DNAInfo, 29/4/2011, http://www.dnaindia.com/business/report-seeking-genuine-hospitality-and-contact-with-wilderness-welcome-to-khali-estate-1537250, 6/8/2018.
70  *PandCC*, 35-38.
71  VLPtoJN, 26/4/1935, *BF*, 152.
72  JNTF, 354-355; JNtoVLP, 10/9/1935, *BF*, 160.
73  *PandCC*, 48.
74  JNTF, 306-307.
75  JNtoVLP, 5/10/1935, *BF*, 178.
76  VLPtoRP, 29/9/1936, PPCRP, 232–233.
77  JNTF, 355

## Chapter 4: The Awakening

1  See Chapter 1.
2  For details, see Sumita Mukherjee, 'The All-Asian Women's Conference 1931: Indian Women and their Leadership of a Pan-Asian Feminist Organization', *Women's History Review* 26:3 (2017), 363–381.
3  VLP, speech before the AIWC, in *Proceedings of the All-India' Women's Conference*, Twelfth Session, 28–31 December 1937, 24.
4  JNtoVLP, 15/11/1935, *BF*, 192. The acronym stood for the All India Women's Association, a variant of the name.
5  Sanger's letter to Gandhi has 'not been found' according to the editors of the Sanger's papers. Gandhi's letter to Sanger does not appear in his Collected Works but is found in her papers. In his letter, he refers to her original. Gandhi to Sanger, 8/7/1925. Esther Katz, *Selected Papers of Margaret Sanger*, Vol. 4 (hereafter SPMS) (Urbana: University of Illinois Press, 2016), 83–84.
6  Sanger had been thinking of a trip to India shortly after she had heard from Tagore in 1925. Tagore to Sanger, 30/9/1925, in SPMS, 90–91. She informs Tagore of her intention to make the trip in 1926 in a response to his letter. Sanger to Tagore, 11/11/1925, in SPMS, 91–92. Cf. Barbara Ramusack, 'Embattled Advocates: The Debate over Birth Control in India, 1920–1940', *Journal of Women's History* 1:2 (Fall 1989), 36. I am grateful to Barbara Ramusack and Ellen Chesler for their insights.
7  Sanger to Cousins, 10/05/1935, LCM:17, 743. SPMS, 277.
8  Karve, the son of Maharishi Dhondo Keshav Karve, was India's first and most vocal advocate for birth control. The elder Karve was the founder in 1916 of S.N.D.T. Women's University, the establishment of which had been dependent on the financial support and partnership of Sir Vithaldas Thackersay. Nan and the late Sir Vithaldas' wife Lady Premilla were friends and associates, as seen

in Chapter 3. Agnes Smedley to Margaret Sanger, April or May 1925, SPMS, 82–83. Cf. Ramusack, 'Embattled Advocates', 41–43.
9   Sanger to Cousins, in Sanger, SPMS, 277–279. See also accompanying editors' notes, which clarify that even organizations in the US and elsewhere that might have supported things like 'birth control legislation', they fundamentally had very little to do with birth control itself (n3, 278).
10  Sanger, Journal Entry, 1/11/1935, n11, in SPMS, 284.
11  Pandit recalls in her memoir that she invited Sanger to visit India. It is possible that she meant this in the aggregate sense since the invitation came from the AIWC collectively. The official invitation letter came from another prominent member of the AIWC, Charulata Mukerjee, on 2/8/1935. *SoH*, 116–117. Sanger to Marian Paschal, 13/8/1935, SPMS, 279–281. Library of Congress Microfilm, Papers of Margaret Sanger (LCM, MS) Reel 135. Mukerjee was then the organizing secretary and the incoming chair of the standing committee, on which Pandit sat, and on the authority of which the invitation was sent. Mukerjee was married to Satish Chandra Mukerjee, a close associate of Gandhi and J.B. Kripalani. Nehru wrote to VLP in on 15 November saying that 'She [Sanger] is going soon to India in response to an invitation from the All India Women's Association of which you [VLP] are now a shining light.' *BF*, 192. VLP and Sanger wrote to each other shortly after the latter met Jawaharlal in London, their letters dispatched at around the same moment in November. VLP invited Sanger to be her guest in Allahabad, and to speak to women in the city. She stated clearly that she was writing in her capacity as one of the AIWC Vice-Presidents and that she [Sanger] should thus consider this an official invitation from the organization. VLP to Sanger, 26/11/1935, LCM, MS 135. Sanger's letter arrives shortly after Nan's is posted, so VLP writes again on 30 November indicating her receipt of the missive and directing Sanger to her letter of a few days prior. LCM, MS 135.
12  Sanger to Marian Paschal, 13/8/1935, in SPMS, 279–281.
13  Sanger, Journal Entry, 1/11/1935, SPMS, 282–284.
14  JNtoVLP, 15/11/1935, *BF*, 191–192. In this and in letters from 28 October and 2 November, Nehru informs his sister that he is traveling to London, Oxford, Birmingham, and Cambridge with Indira. No specific reason for the trip is given. See 185–190.
15  Sanger, Journal Entry, 2/12/1935, SPMS, 297.
16  Sanger to J. Noah Slee, 9/12/1935, SPMS, 309–311.
17  Margaret Sanger, *An Autobiography* (New York: W.W. Norton & Co, 1938), 479.
18  For a Western woman's description of the 'Purdah Club,' see Muriel Caswall, 'The 'New Woman' who Rules Bhopal,' *World Outlook* 3:1 (January 1917), 13–14.
19  Sanger, *An Autobiography*, 479.
20  VLP to Sanger, 26/11/1936, LCM, MS 135.
21  All-India Women's Conference, *Tenth Session* (Trivandrum, Government Press, 1936), 36–37.
22  Sanger, *An Autobiography*, 481–483. https://archive.org/stream/margaretsangerau1938sang/margaretsangerau1938sang_djvu.txt. See also Sanger to Intimate Friends and Family, 2/1/1936, SPMS, 316–322. Sanger wrapped up her Indian tour over the few weeks that followed the AIWC meeting with visits to Madras,

Mysore, and Hyderabad, and from there headed home to the United States via Hong Kong and Japan. See Sanger, *An Autobiography*, 483–492. But just before she left the subcontinent, Mahadev Desai released the essay of her interview with Gandhi to the press. She had been coordinating with him and her own assistant, Anna Phillips, and had hoped that the interview would first appear in the American press rather than, as it did, in the *Illustrated Weekly of India* on 19 January. The piece was hard hitting, roasting the Mahatma for claiming he 'knew women'. Sanger exclaimed that he hadn't 'the faintest glimmering of either the "experiences and aspirations" or the inner workings of a woman's mind, heart, or being'. Mahadev Desai responded angrily in the 25 January issue of *Harijan*, saying, 'She utters not one word about the points of agreement sought at the interview, and the extent to which Gandhiji said he was prepared to go with her.' Sanger was disappointed in all of this and dashed off a letter to Gandhi hoping to reinforce a positive takeaway: 'Perhaps you saw my challenge to your knowledge of women in the Illustrated Weekly. It was rather sketchy and abrupt and badly done. Please forgive the scolding tone it seems to have taken on in print. I meant it to be humorous and laughing and to get you to laugh too. It was too hurriedly done to get that over . . .,' she conceded. She ended by wishing him good health and 'success in your great struggle for the liberation of India'. 'What He Told Me at Wardha,' 19/1/1936, and Sanger to Gandhi 30/1/1936, SPMS, 325–331. For more on VLP's take on Sanger's visit and additional, varied perspective on related issues, see Sanjay Srivastava, *Passionate Modernity* (Delhi: Routledge, 2007).

23  JNtoVLP, 15/3/1935, 136, and 15/2/1936, 218–219, BF. Motilal's letter cited by Nayantara Sahgal in the preface to Part IV, where she also provides further description, 225. *SoH*, 128–129.
24  JNtoVLP, 15/11/1935, BF, 192.
25  'Nine Congressites Elected: Allahabad Municipality', *NYT*, 6/12/1935, 26.
26  JNtoVLP, 28 and 31/12/1935, 204–209.
27  Quotes in this paragraph taken from *SoH*, 120–121.
28  The United Provinces Government launched specialized clinics on an experimental basis in 5 cities, including Allahabad, in August 1934. Students, with some exemptions, were asked to contribute one anna per month towards the clinics, which was to be collected by schools and then submitted to the government. The clinics were to provide 'milk and spectacles to poor boys.' It is unclear if the medical checkups that students were receiving according to VLP's account were through these clinics or some other means, though the clinics seem the likely option. Milk distribution also seems likely through these outlets, meaning that students were actually paying directly for the milk and other things that they were being denied. 'Medical Clinics for Schoolboys,' *TOI*, 13/8/1934, 3.
29  *SoH*, 121–124.
30  Ibid., 124.
31  Ibid., 124–125. By comparison, Scottish teachers launched an effort to provide local children with 'one-third of a pint of milk for a halfpenny' in November 1934, so U.P. was at the forefront of linking nutrition to childhood learning. 'Summary of the News', *Scotsman*, 30/10/1934, 8. VLP was on the cutting edge, reforming her program to make it truly work.
32  Quotations from *SoH*, 124–125.
33  *SoH*, 126.

34  VLP, *So I Became a Minister* (Allahabad: Kitabistan, 1939), 11–12.
35  Her husband was Sir Jwala Prasad Srivastava, who had served on the Simon Commission and in the UP government from 1931 until the 1937 elections. He would eventually go on to sit in the Constituent Assembly and to serve as a Member of Parliament. https://en.wikipedia.org/wiki/Jwala_Prasad_Srivastava, 18/9/2018.
36  Summary of *SoH*, 126–128.
37  Jawaharlal Nehru, 'Presidential Address to the Indian National Congress at Faizpur', *Labour Monthly* 19:2 (February 1937), 98–107. Online at the Marxist Internet Archive, https://www.marxists.org/history/international/comintern/sections/britain/periodicals/labour_monthly/1937/02/x01.htm, 19/9/2018. Nehru delivered the remarks reproduced here in December 1936.
38  'Keen Contest for Legislatures: U.P. Candidates', *TOI*, 28/12/1936, 4.
39  'Council of State Elections: Unopposed Results from U.P.', *NYT*, 22/12/1936, 12. The objection was that she was the wife of someone who was a resident of a 'native state' and therefore not really part of British India. 'Objection against Candidature', *NYT*, 23/12/1936, 17.
40  'Polling Begins', *TOI*, 20/1/1937, 8; 'The Indian Elections', *Spectator* 158:5665 (January 22, 1937), 112.
41  *SoH*, 130.
42  *PandCC*, 64.
43  *SoH*, 130. Cf. 'What Next?', *TOI*, 20/2/1937, 12; 'Through Nationalist Eyes: Aftermath of the Elections', *TOI*, 24/2/1937, 10.
44  'Congress Committees Discuss Office Issue', *TOI*, 22/2/1937, 8.
45  'Acceptance of Office: Mr. Gandhi's Views', *TOI*, 1/3/1937, 11. The CWC meetings took place in Wardha on the 27 and 28 of February.
46  'Congressmen and Office Acceptance: U.P. Opposition', *TOI*, 8/3/1937, 10.
47  'Congress Terms for Office Acceptance: Working Committee Decision', *TOI*, 17/3/1937, 11. VLP moved a resolution in U.P. several months later, on 4/9/1937, 'demanding the repeal and replacement of the Act of 1935 "by a Constitution for a free India framed by a Constituent Assembly elected on the basis of adult franchise".' It passed on 2 October. B.R. Nanda, ed., *Selected Works of Govind Ballabh Pant*, Volume 9 (Delhi: Oxford University Press, 1997), n. 30, 148–149.
48  *SoH*, 132.
49  The text is blurry, and it is unclear if the vote in favor was 135, 165, 185, 195 or some other slight variation. My reading of 135 is my best assessment of what the text says.
50  'A.I.C.C. Votes for Office Acceptance', *TOI*, 19/3/1937, 13. The Working Committee's resolution was passed with a minor but not insignificant change to a line rejecting interference by Governors, removing a clause about abiding by the Constitution, which was felt to place too much faith in the British.
51  'Relief at Wardha Decision', *TOI*, 9/7/1937, 11.
52  'Congress Ministry in U.P.: Invitation Accepted', *TOI*, 13/7/1937, 9.
53  '2 Women Members in the U.P. Cabinet?', *TOI*, 15/7/1937, 12.
54  'India's First Cabinet Minister', Reuters Correspondent, *Irish Times*, 17/7/1937, 10; 'Woman Cabinet Minister', the *Manchester Guardian* (hereafter TMG), 17/7/1937, 13; 'First in India,' 17/7/1937, 14; 'Woman Minister in U.P.', *TOI*, 17/7/1937, 11; 'Congress Accepts: A Woman Minister', 19/7/1937, 14 (story dated July 17).

55 The first was Constance Markiewicz, who served as Minister for Labour in the revolutionary government of Ireland from 1919 to 1922. https://www.britannica.com/biography/Constance-Markievicz, 3/11/2018. She was followed by Mary Ellen Smith, who held a position in British Columbia for eight months in 1921. https://www.collectionscanada.gc.ca/women/030001-1326-e.html, 24/9/2018. The next was Margaret Bondfield, who served as Minister of Labour in the UK from 1928–1931. https://www.britannica.com/biography/Margaret-Bondfield, 24/9/2018. The very first woman to hold a post of substance appears to have been Yevgenia Bosch in revolutionary Russia. https://en.wikipedia.org/wiki/Yevgenia_Bosch. Francis Perkins had also been named to the U.S. Cabinet by Franklin Roosevelt in 1933. Kristen Downey, *The Woman Behind the New* Deal (New York: Anchor Books, 2010). For the larger transnational context of women's suffrage in India, and the place of VLP in the imagination of that movement, see Sumita Mukherjee, *Indian Suffragettes* (Delhi, Oxford University Press, 2018). Cf. Shoba Sharad Rajgopal, '"Fiery Sparks of Change": A Comparison Between First Wave Feminists of India and the U.S.', *Journal of International Women's Studies* 24(2), June 2022, https://vc.bridgew.edu/cgi/viewcontent.cgi?article=2888&context=jiws, 11/3/2023.
56 *So I Became a Minister* (SIBAM), 141–142.
57 *SoH*, 133.
58 SIBAM, 13–16.
59 *SoH*, 134.
60 Ibid.
61 *PandCC*, 64–65. *SoH*, 135.
62 *SoH*, 135–136.
63 Ibid., 136–137.
64 *SoH*, 137–138.
65 'Minister to Tour in a Cart', *TOI*, 16/9/1937.
66 'Literacy Drive in Lucknow', *TOI*, 25/5/1938, 17.
67 SIBAM, 22.
68 *SoH*, 137.
69 *SoH*, 138.
70 *SoH*, 138–139. SIBAM, 17–23.
71 *PandCC*, 66. For broader analysis of VLP's work in UP, and that of other women as well, see Visalakshi Menon, *Indian Women and Nationalism: The U.P. Story* (Delhi: Shakti Books, 2003).
72 *SoH*, 140–141
73 VLP, 'Women as Nation Builders', broadcast on All India Radio and reproduced in *The Listener: The Official Organ of All India Radio*, Volume III, No. 9, 22 April 1938, 571. As she reflected on her own experiences in the very late stages of her life, VLP repeated this assessment almost word for word. 'It is very sad but a Hindu woman is tied to a man all through her life. To her father during her youth, to her husband during her marriage, and finally to her son during her old age. And, of course, all through her life she is tied to a priest too, as she has to observe innumerable vows for the well-being of the family.' VLP, 'We Nehrus', 14.
74 VLP speech to AIWC, *Proceedings of the 1937 meeting*, 34–36.
75 Mrs. Naidu to AIWC, 1937 Proceedings, 42.
76 Discussion of Education Resolutions, 1937 Proceedings, 45–46.

77 'Woman's Career in India Typifies Changing Times,' *Christian Science Monitor* (hereafter *CSM*), 7/1/1938.
78 'Mrs. Motilal Nehru Dead', *TOI*, 11/1/1938, 19.
79 'Mrs. Motilal Nehru is Stricken in Delhi', *NYT*, 11/1/1938, 23.
80 'Allahabad Tribute to Mrs Nehru', *TOI*, 12/1/1938, 3. *SoH*, 145.
81 'Darbhanga Maharaja', *TOI*, 13/4/2018, 6.
82 SIBAM, 54–61.
83 'Cow Protection Conference', *TOI*, 12/4/1938, 17.
84 *SoH*, 141–143.
85 SIBAM, 34–41.
86 SIBAM, 63–77, quotes from 65–66.
87 SIBAM, 63–64, 67–69.
88 SIBAM, 79–87.
89 SIBAM, 31–33.
90 'Cholera at Hardwar,' *TOI*, 20/4/1938, 15.
91 '132 Deaths from Cholera,' *TOI*, 26/4/1938, 5.
92 'Cholera Outbreak in India Kills Many', *NYT*, 1/5/1938, 39.
93 'Over 15,000 Deaths from Cholera', *TOI*, 15/6/1938, 9.
94 'Cholera Plague Spreads in India; Thousands Die,' *CDT*, 18/6/1938, 2.
95 'Cholera in U.P.', *TOI*, 4/7/1938, 10.
96 'Mrs. Vijaya Lakshmi Pandit', *TOI*, 30/7/1938, 11. She refers to the person who accompanied her as 'my Director-General'; I could find no further information on this person or whom she meant. It's likely it was her subordinate Director of Public Health mentioned earlier. It could also have been the Director-General of the Indian Medical Service, who was following the epidemic and discharging advice. See 'State of Cholera Epidemics', *TOI*, 12/5/1938, 13.
97 JNtoVLP, 23/6/1938, *BF*, 253. The exact ailment is not specified here, but years later VLP would have a hysterectomy, so this very likely involved fibroids, cysts, or something of that nature. This was apart from her mental health, which needed attending at that point as well.
98 JNtoVLP, 25/6/1938, *BF*, 256. Nehru and Cripps were joined by Clement Atlee. The Labour Government of the future would largely try to abide by the terms the men agreed to at this retreat. Michael Jago, *Clement Atlee* (Biteback Publishers, 2014), 109.
99 JNtoVLP, 4 and 5/7/1938, *BF*, 259.
100 JNtoVLP, 9/7/1938, *BF*, 261.
101 JNtoVLP, 22–24/7/1938, *BF*, 264–265.
102 JNtoVLP, 26/7/1938, *BF*, 266.
103 'Hon. Mrs. Pandit's Departure,' *TOI*, 20/8/1938, 12.

## Chapter 5: The West with the Night

1 JNtoVLP, 4–5, 9, 22, 26, 27, 29, 31/7/1938, *BF*, 259–272.
2 'Hon. Mrs. Pandit's Departure: Portfolios Distributed', *TOI*, 20/8/1938, 12. 'Mrs. Vijayalakshmi Pandit: Arrival at Budapest', *TOI*, 22/8/1938, 9.
3 VLP erroneously claims in her memoir that she was in Prague when 'the German army marched into the Sudetenland and the war moved closer', but she had actually already left the country by the time this occurred a month later.

4   'London—Day by Day', 7/9/1938, *TOI*, 8. The account is dated 29 August, but VLP was already in Prague by then. VLP erroneously states in her memoir that she began her trip in Prague and proceeded from there to Hungary, when in fact it was the reverse.
5   Mark Mazower, 'The Strange Triumph of Human Rights, 1933–1950', *The Historical Journal* 47, no. 2 (2004); Benjamin Hett, *The Death of Democracy* (New York: Henry Holt, 2018); Manu Bhagavan, 'Minority Report: Illiberalism, Intolerance, and the Threat to International Society,' in Harsh Pant and Ritika Passi, eds., *Raisina Files 2018*, 44–46.
6   VLPtoRP, 1/9/1938, PPCRP, 236. *SoH*, 146.
7   VLPtoRP, 1/9/1938, PPCRP, 236–237.
8   Stanislava Vavrouskova, 'Ways to Understand India: the Czech Experience', *Acta Orientalia Vilnensia* 9:2, 2008, 128–129. VLPtoRP, 1/9/1938, PPCRP, 236.
9   VLPtoRP, 1/9/1938, PPCRP, 237–238. *SoH*, 146.
10  'London—Day by Day: Mrs Vijialakshmi Pandit', *TOI*, 19/9/1938, 9.
11  VLPtoRP, 20/9/1938, PPCRP, 239. 'Mrs. Pandit's Visit: India's First Woman Cabinet Minister,' *TMG*, 2/9/1938, 13.
12  'A Woman Cabinet Minister', *TMG*. 3/9/1938, 14. On 8/7/1938, VLP had formally proposed that the 'Agra Medical School for Women should be converted into a nursing centre in order to make more nurses available for improving the standard of health care for women. She had also proposed . . . stipends to cover all expenses of a maximum of 25 trainees be given annually. As regards lady doctors . . . they could be recruited from the medical colleges in the Punjab, Madras, and Bengal.' Pant expressed his agreement on the 17th, noting that the school in Agra produced a startlingly low number of female medical graduates. He expressed willingness to provide stipends to support women at other medical colleges in Lucknow and Delhi, as well as his support for classes of thirty nurses. 'On the recommendation of the U.P. Medical Reorganization Committee, which submitted its report in September 1939, the Agra Medical School for Women was finally closed in April 1941 and training of 10–15 nurses every year started.' By that point, the Congress ministries had been dissolved, so Nan was unable to follow through on the implementation of her idea. *Selected Works of Govind Ballabh Pant*, Vol 8, 374–375.
13  'London—Day by Day: Mrs Vijialakshmi Pandit', *TOI*, 19/9/1938, 9.
14  'India's Freedom: Mrs. Vijayalakshmi Pandit on Congress Aim', *TOI*, 7/9/1938. The press conference was held on the 6th. Despite her efforts, she continued to be covered by global media as a glamorous celebrity. *The Toronto Daily Star* carried a picture of her a week later, sitting in a Hollywood starlet pose, wearing a leopard-print sari with a sleeveless, plunging neckline blouse. *Toronto Daily Star*, 14/9/1938, 25. The caption noted that India's first woman cabinet minister was 'spending a holiday in Great Britain.'
15  Whether or not this is true remains a matter of contention.
16  VLPtoRP, 20/9/1938, PPCRP, 239–240.
17  'Pandit Nehru', *TOI*, 15/9/1938, 12. Nehru left London on the 15th. VLP again gets the sequence of events muddled in her memoir, saying that Indira was sent to Geneva prior to she and her brother coming to London. *SoH*, 146. The number of mistakes in this section of her book is unusual, and probably reflective of her health issues during the trip.

18   https://houseandheritage.org/2018/11/15/new-lodge/, 10/1/2019.
19   https://gut.bmj.com/content/gutjnl/20/6/463.full.pdf, 10/1/2019.
20   Undated letter, VLP to Ranjit Pandit. By context, I place it very late September, but prior to actual signing of the Munich Pact. Pandit papers 260.
21   Ibid., 260–261
22   Neville Chamberlain returns from Germany with the Munich Agreement. https://www.youtube.com/watch?v=SetNFqcayeA, 11/1/2019.
23   'Premier Appears on Palace Balcony: London's Tumultuous Welcome: Address from Window: "Peace with Honour",' *TMG*, 1/10/1938.
24   *SoH*, 146. VLP conflates several different episodes in her description, writing of Chamberlain's return for Berchtesgaden (which occurred on the sixteenth), of his 'infamous' waving of the White Paper (which occurred at the Heston Aerodome upon his arrival on the thirtieth), and of his window at 10 Downing Street (which occurred in the evening of the thirtieth). As she makes no mention of Chamberlain or Czechoslovakia in her letter to Ranjit on the twentieth, despite filling in all kinds of other details from the previous week, I think it safe to conclude that she was not in the crowds on Downing Street on the sixteenth. Moreover, her letter explicitly states that she traveled directly to Windsor Forest from Broadstairs, and that she arrived at New Lodge on the twentith. Putting this together, I place her and Nehru outside 10 Downing Street on the evening of the 30$^{th}$, the night of the 'peace for our time' speech, which is also referenced in her memoir.
25   'The Coming Week', *New Statesman and Nation*, 1/10/1938, 493. See also Matt Perry, *'Red Ellen' Wilkinson: Her Ideas, Movements, and World* (New York: Manchester University Press, 2014).
26   '"India's Rasputin"? V.K. Krishna Menon and Anglo-American Misperceptions of Indian Foreign Policymaking, 1947-1964,' *Diplomacy and Statecraft* 22: 239–260, 2011, 240; Manu S. Pillai, 'The Complicated V.K. Krishna Menon,' *LiveMint*, 5/5/2018, https://www.livemint.com/Leisure/KBOvkvrqms6FQtImfyxUvM/The-complicated-VK-Krishna-Menon.html (last accessed 14/1/2019).
27   Sarvepalli Gopal, *Jawaharlal Nehru: A Biography, Volume I, 1889–1947*, 202.
28   Soon after meeting Menon and being introduced to the latter's circle of friends, Nehru wrote to VLP asking her to send Menon, Laski, and several others copies of his books. 2/11/1935, *BF*, 187-188.
29   http://www.open.ac.uk/researchprojects/makingbritain/content/india-league, 14/1/2019. http://www.bl.uk/learning/timeline/item124205.html, 15/1/2019.
30   'British Sympathy for India: Mrs. Pandit's Views', *TOI*, 5/10/1938, 11. See also Janet Clark, *The National Council for Civil Liberties and the Policing of Interwar Politics* (Manchester: Manchester University Press, 2012). Just prior to the event at Friend's House, VLP joined her brother at the Indian Student's Union (aka the Indian Students' Hostel) for a celebration of Gandhi's seventieth birthday. Nehru, Agatha Harrison, Menon, and the scholar and novelist Edward John Thompson all made brief remarks. 'Cult of "Lathi" in Europe: Mr. Nehru on the Recent Crisis', via Reuters, *TOI*, 4/10/1938, 12; 'The Generation of Gandhi', *TOI*, 15/10/1938, 19. Lord Pethick-Lawrence, Emmeline's husband, would later go on to become Secretary of State for India.
31   'Friends House, Euston Road, London', n.d., http://manchesterhistory.net/architecture/1920/friendshouse.html., 15/1/2019.
32   Description of the event and details of VLP speech from three sources: 'British Sympathy for India: Mrs. Pandit's Views', *TOI*, 5/10/1938, 11; 'The Shame

of England', *TMG*, 5/10/1938, 17; and 'The Generation of Gandhi', *TOI*, 15/10/1938, 19. In his memoir, Dr. M.R. Vyas recalls that VLP was a good speaker, though he also recalls that she could occasionally flash her temper. He writes that in other instances during the 1938 visit, such as one at Royal Albert Hall, 'most of . . . [those present] felt that' she, more than Nehru, made the more compelling case. M.R. Vyas, *Passage Through a Turbulent Era: Historical Reminisces of the Fateful Years, 1937–47* (Bombay: Indo-Foreign Publications and Publicity, 1982, 91–93.

33 'Winston Churchill's Speech in the Munich Debate', House of Commons, 5/10/1938, *Hansard*, Column 365, https://hansard.parliament.uk/Commons/1938-10-05/debates/25851755-dbcd-4704-9334-fdf2574d6453/PolicyOfHisMajestySGovernment?highlight=munich%20debate%20churchill#contribution-16a0a7f5-cc48-4b61-b31c-11e7fb172f32, 30/3/2023.

34 'Indian Political Notes: Reactions to European Happenings', *TOI*, 12/10/1938, 10; 'Indian Press and the "Peace": Sharp Criticism: Surrender to Force', *TMG*, 13/10/1938, 13. Both stories discuss the coverage from a range of Indian newspapers, including the *Amrita Bazar Patrika*, the *Hindusthan Standard*, the *National Herald*, the *Tribune*, and the *Statesman*, aside from those mentioned in-text.

35 'U.P. Minister in England', *TOI*, 15/10/1938, 19.

36 'India's Woman Cabinet Minister: Says Women Now May Rise Through Gradual Promotion', *CSM*, 14/10/1938, 6.

37 Historic England, 'FINSBURY TOWN HALL, Non Civil Parish - 1293112 | Historic England', n.d., https://historicengland.org.uk/listing/the-list/list-entry/1293112., 16/1/2019.

38 https://www.theoldfiSPBUrytownhall.co.uk/about/. Last accessed 16/1/2019.

39 'London—Day by Day', *TOI*, 20/10/1938, p. 8.

40 'U.P. Minister in England', *TOI*, 15/10/1938, 19; 'First Indian Mayor in England: Dr. Katial's Work for FiSPBUry,' *TOI*, 19/11/1938, 24; http://www.bl.uk/learning/timeline/item124211.html, last accessed 16/1/2019.

41 'London—Day by Day', *TOI*, 20/10/1938, 8.

42 'U.P. Parliamentary Secretary Dead: Mr. S.P. Shah', *TOI*, 4 October, 12. Shah had gotten a fever and gone to Juhu in Bombay to heal but suffered a heart attack and collapsed.

43 VLPtoRP, 14/10/1938, PPCRP, 242.

44 'Mrs. Vijayalaxmi Pandit', *TOI*, 14/11/1938, 10. She was looked after by Dr. and Mrs. Lancaster (alt. Lankester) (Nehru uses both spellings to refer to them.) JNtoVLP, 27, 31/10/1938, *BF*, 273–276. VLP appears to have had a physical ailment in addition to her stress and mental fatigue. According to Nayantara Sahgal, VLP had some chronic issues common to many women, involving 'stomach cramps' 'to do with uterus, maybe fibroids' though the exact nature of the condition is unknown. VLP would eventually require a hysterectomy while in the United States. Nayantara Sahgal to Manu Bhagavan, email, 20/1/2019.

45 G.P. Pant to Jawaharlal Nehru, 20/10/1938, Cables and previous correspondence referenced in the notes as well, *Selected Works of Govind Ballabh Pant*, Volume 8), 313–314.

46 JNtoVLP, 27/10/1938, *BF*, 273.

47 JNtoVLP, 28, 31 October 1938, *BF*, 275–276.

48  JNtoVLP, 11/11/1938, *BF*, 277.
49  'Hon. Mrs. V. Pandit', *TOI*, 7/11/1938, 10; Untitled, *TOI*, 11/11/1938, 14; 'Hon. Mrs. V. Pandit', *TOI*, 12/11/1938, 12.
50  'Mrs. Vijayalaxmi Pandit', *TOI*, 14/11/1938, 10.
51  'Mrs. Pandit back in Lucknow: Charge of Portfolio Assumed', *TOI*, 17/11/1938, 14.
52  'Mrs. Pandit at Allahabad', *TOI*, 15/11/1938, 12.
53  'Mrs. Pandit back in Lucknow: Charge of Portfolio Assumed', *TOI*, 17/11/1938, 14.
54  'Mrs. Pandit back in Lucknow: Charge of Portfolio Assumed', *TOI*, 17/11/1938, 14. JNtoVLP, 27 October and 11 November 1938, *BF*, 273, 277.
55  'Women's Part in World Peace: Mrs. Pandit's Message to Agra Conference', *TOI*, 21/11/1938, 12.
56  'Debate on the U.P. Tenancy Bill', *TOI*, 20/12/1938, 10.
57  'Sunnis and Shias Sentenced; Statement in the U.P. Council', *TOI*, 6/7/1939, 11. 'Extracts from the proceedings of the United Provinces Legislative Assembly', May–July 1939, and the United Provinces Indian Medicine Bill, 1939, in Legislative, F. 439, Box 101, UP State Archives, Lucknow. Cf. Shamshad Khan, 'Systems of Medicine and Nationalist Discourse in India', *Social Science & Medicine* 62(11), June 2006, 2786–2797.
58  Speech by VLP inaugurating the 15th All-India Medical Conference, 'Indian Doctors' Difficulties: Lack of Government Support', *TOI*, 28/12/1938, 11. See also n. 15.
59  'Purdah System', *TOI*, 20/12/1938, 18; 'Constructive Politics' for Women,' *TOI*, 29/12/1938, 4. Cf. Gail Minault, 'Coming Out', *India International Centre Quarterly*, 23(3/4), Winter 1996, 93–105.
60  'Epidemics in the U.P.: Government to Appoint Board', *TOI*, 18/7/1939, 4.
61  'Mobile Hospitals for U.P.: Capitalists' Offer', *TOI*, 13/1/1939, 14.
62  'Custom of Purdah Breaking Down: More Women Attend Hospitals', *TOI*, 22/6/1939, 2. While she and the fund shared priorities, VLP was much more effective and attentive to the needs of the local population.
63  'Delhi Swadeshi Exhibition: Women's Conference', *TOI*, 27/12/1938, 8.
64  'Women to Combat Evil of War', *TOI*, 30/12/1938, 10.
65  'Indian Women Abhor War: Appeal for Non-Violence', *Scotsman*, 18/1/1939, 13.
66  'Indian Women's Conference: Independence as Goal: Declaration on Non Violence', *TMG*, 11/1/1939, 5. VLP's performance was so well received, and her reputation was now so sterling, that she was nominated to become President of the AIWC the following year, but she withdrew her name from consideration in June of 1939. 'Women's Conference', *TOI*, 26/6/1939, 15.
67  'National Planning Committee: Work Reviewed', *TOI*, 15/8/1939, 12.
68  Girish Mishra, 'Nehru and Planning in India', *Mainstream Weekly*, 16/11/2014, http://www.mainstreamweekly.net/article5320.html, 24/1/2019. See also http://krishikosh.egranth.ac.in/bitstream/1/19117/1/BPT7825.pdf, 24/1/2019.
69  *National Planning Committee No. 2: Being an Abstract of the Proceedings and other Particulars relating to the National Planning Committee* (Bombay: National Planning Committee, 1940), https://dspace.gipe.ac.in/xmlui/bitstream/handle/10973/38760/GIPE-069009-03.pdf?sequence=3&isAllowed=y, 24/1/2019. See also JNtoVLP, 20/6/1939, *BF*, 279. VLP's name was suggested

as chair of the status of women committee, but Nehru felt that it would be an unfair added burden.
70 'Indian Political Notes: Universal Condemnation of Hitlerism', *TOI*, 6/9/1939, 6. Gandhi famously wrote to Hitler in July 1939 in respectful, almost friendly terms, asking him to stand for the larger cause of peace. He revealed what he had done in a press conference on 5 September, shortly after the war had begun. 'But even as I wrote it ... I realized how little was the chance that Herr Hitler would heed what I had to say to him,' he announced, saying that 'India's deliverance ... will come. But what will it be worth if England and France fall?' 'Mr. Gandhi on War Horrors,' *TOI*, 6/9/1939, 7.
71 '"A Democratic India will join in Opposing Aggression"', *TOI*, 15/9/1939, 8.
72 '"War Resolution" in U.P. Ssembly [sic]', 25/10/1939, 9. 'War Debate in U.P. Assembly,' 28/10/1939, 9. 'Resolution on War Passed, U.P. Assembly', 31/10/1939, 8. All in *TOI*. See also *SoH*, 147.

## Chapter 6: The Time in Between

1 'National Planning: Women's Sub-Committee Meeting in Bombay', *TOI*, 16/12/1939, 17.
2 *National Planning Committee No. 2: Being an Abstract of the Proceedings and other Particulars relating to the National Planning Committee* (Bombay: National Planning Committee, 1940), 83. https://dspace.gipe.ac.in/xmlui/bitstream/handle/10973/38760/GIPE-069009-03.pdf?sequence=3&isAllowed=y, 24/1/2019.
3 *National Planning Committee No. 2*, 18. 'Need to Plan for Future: Pandit Nehru's Plea', *TOI*, 2/5/1940, 11. 'National Planning: Women's Sub-Committee Meeting in Bombay', *TOI*, 16/12/1939, 17. JNtoVLP, 25/6/1938, *BF*, 255–256.
4 'Women's Rights Still Minus Quantity: Duty by Masses', *TOI*, 29/1/1940, 5.
5 Ayesha Jalal, *The Sole Spokesman* (Cambridge: Cambridge University Press, 1991), 43–47.
6 'Mrs Pandit at Agra', 1/8/1939, 13; 'Cancellation of Minister's Visit', *TOI*, 31/8/1939, 10.
7 Pant to Nehru, 13/4/1938, in *Selected Works of Govind Ballabh Pant*, Vol 8, (Delhi: Oxford University Press, 1997), 286.
8 'Communal Problem', *TOI*, 22/12/1939, 10.
9 'Vijaya Lakshmi Pandit: So I Became a Minister', *Modern Librarian* 10:2, January 1940, 103. I make extensive reference to this book in the previous chapter.
10 'First Woman Minister', *TOI*, 3/2/1940, 14.
11 Nayantara Pandit to Ranjit Pandit, 11/9/1939, and Ranjit Pandit to Nayantara Pandit, 19 September, 1939, cited in full in *PandCC*, 88–91. Ranjit couches his appeal to his daughter in the language of caste, talking of traditional Brahmin serenity.
12 'India's Bid for Recognition', *Baltimore Sun*, 11/2/1940, 11.
13 'No Civil Resistance at Present', *TOI*, 12/2/1940.
14 'Allahabad Congress Talks', Photo by Nehru, *TOI*, 20/12/1939, 9. 'Mr. Patel Foreshadows Final Struggle for Independence', *TOI*, 20/1/1940, 1. 'Congress Executive Meets at Wardha: Discussion about "Next Struggle"', *TOI*, 16/4/1940, 8. 'Congress Leaders Leave Wardha', 19/4/1940, 12.

15  'Winston Churchill: We Shall Fight on the Beaches', https://www.youtube.com/watch?v=MkTw3_PmKtc, 8/2/2019.
16  'Congress to Organize People for Self-Defense', *TOI*, 22/6/1940, 10.
17  'How to Combat Hitlerism', written on 18/6/1940 and published in *Harijan* on 22 June, *Collected Works of Mahatma Gandhi*, Volume 78, 343–345. http://www.gandhiashramsevagram.org/gandhi-literature/mahatma-gandhi-collected-works-volume-78.pdf. Last accessed, 8/2/2019.
18  'Congress to Organize People for Self-Defense', *TOI*, 22/6/1940, 10.
19  'Congress to Organize People for Self-Defense', *TOI*, 22/6/1940, 10; 'Congress and Mr. Gandhi 'Agree to Differ' on Non-Violence', *TOI*, 23/8/1940, 7.
20  'Official Reaction Awaited: Congress Demand', *TOI*, 26/7/1940, 7.
21  Ranjit Pandit to Nayantara Pandit, 1/7/1940, cited in full in *PandCC*, 91–92.
22  'Congress Offer Spurned,' 'Wardha Meeting', *TOI*, 5/9/1940, 7.
23  'Mr. Gandhi Urged to Assume Congress Leadership', 14/9/1940, 5. 'Mr. Gandhi's Come-Back: Scenes at A.I.C.C. Meeting', 17/9/1940, 3; B. Shiva Rao, 'India's Change of Heart', *The Baltimore Sun*, 11.
24  'Congress to Obey the Law for the Present', *TOI*, 19/9/1940, 7.
25  'Individual Satyagraha by Congress mooted', *TOI*, 16/9/1940, 1.
26  'Mr. Gandhi to Act in his Own Way', *TOI*, 3/10/1940, 7; 'Mr. Gandhi Against Satyagraha', *TOI*, 3/10/1940, 1; 'India Leaders Forecast: Individual Disobedience', *New York Herald Tribune* (hereafter *NYHT*), 13/10/1940, 8.
27  'Two Indians to Seek Arrest', *Irish Times*, 14/10/1940, 5; 'Two Gandhi Aides to Defy India Law', 14/10/1940, 3.
28  'Defiance of Law, Mr Gandhi's Plan', and 'Direct Civil Disobedience by One Man', *TOI*, 16/10/1940, 1, 7.
29  'Congress Speaker Arrested: Anti-War Meeting', *TMG*, 18/10/1940, 7.
30  'Pandit Nehru's Talks with Mr. Gandhi', *TOI*, 31/10/1940, 7.
31  'Gandhi Aid Arrested in India for Making Antiwar Speeches', *CDT*, 1/11/1940, 2.
32  'Nehru Seized in India for Pacifist Speech', *NYT*, 1/11/1940, 4.
33  'Congress Executive Summoned', *TOI*, 2/11/1940, 9.
34  *SoH*, 149. 'Nehru's Trial Concluded', *NYT*, 5/11/1940, 6.
35  'Gandhi Anti-war Speaker Sentenced to 4 Year Term', *CDT*, 6/11/1940, 8. *SoH*, 150.
36  'Nationalist Bloc in India Invites Arrest of 1500', *CSM*, 13/11/1940, 5.
37  'More Indian Arrests', via Reuter, *SCMP*, 6/12/1940, 7.
38  Nayantara Sahgal, *PandCC*, 93–94.
39  Jawaharlal Nehru to Chandralekha Pandit, 26/12/1940, *BF*, 285–289.
40  For instance: 'More Indian Arrests,' *SCMP*, 6/12/1940, 7. 'Cables in Brief: Disobedients', *Palestine Post (The Jerusalem Post)*, 6/12/1940, 3.
41  'Our London Correspondence', *TMG*, 6/12/1940, 4
42  'Mrs. Pandit Sent to Prison', *TMG*, 10/12/1940, 4. 'Mrs. Pandit is Sentenced Under India Defense Act', *NYHT*, 10/12/1940, 10. 'Nehru's Sister Jailed', *NYT*, 10/12/1940, 21. VLP's was a lighter sentence than Nehru's, but this was in keeping with widely disparate punishment terms. Mrs. Naidu, for instance, was released from prison early after just a few weeks, while Vinoba Bhave was sentenced to only three months. 'Mrs. Sarojini Naidu', *TOI*, 14/12/1940, 11. 'Mr. Vinoba Bhave Released', *TOI*, 16/1/1941, 7.
43  'Fresh Approach to Indian Situation', via Reuter, *TOI*, 1/1/1941, p 1.
44  *SoH*, 150–151. This is the only source I could find with any details about VLP's second prison term.

45 'If Mr Gandhi is Arrested: No Successor to Guide Congressmen', *TOI*, 29/1/1941, 7.
46 'Mr. Bose Suddenly Disappears', *TOI*, 28/1/1941, 7.
47 'Congress not Self-Seeking', *TOI*, 7/3/1941, 1.
48 'Mrs. V. Pandit Released', *TOI*, 3/4/1941, 7; 'Mrs. Pandit at Wardha', *TOI*, 22/4/1941, 7.
49 Mrs. V. Pandit', *TOI*, 14/5/1941, 4. 'Congress Press Told to Close Down', *TOI*, 15/5/1941, 7.
50 *SoH*, 151–152.
51 *SoH*, 155.
52 Jawaharlal JNtoVLP, 28/8/1939, 18/5/1940 *BF*, 282–284.
53 'India and China', *SCMP*, 17/10/1940, 10. The news of the mission was first broken in the London press.
54 'Communist View', *South China Morning Post* (hereafter *SCMP*), 5/11/1940, 12.
55 'Mrs. V. Pandit', *TOI*, 4/4/1941, 10. 'China and India', via Reuters, *SCMP*, 7/4/1941, 14. 'Madame Chiang Invites Nehru's Sister to China', via Reuters, *North-China Herald and Supreme Court & Consular Gazette*, 8/4/1941, 42. 'Men and Events', *China Weekly Review*, 12/4/1941, 204.
56 'Mrs. Vijay Laxmi Pandit', *TOI*, 10/5/1941, 4. VLP to Ranjit Pandit, 4/5/1941, Pandit papers, 274.
57 VLPtoRP, 8/6/1941, PPCRP, 288.
58 Ibid., 26/5/1941, 277–278.
59 Ibid., 3/6/1941, 288.
60 'Realise India's Peril & Join War Effort: Message to Women', *TOI*, 12/6/1941, 7.
61 VLPtoRP, 24/6/1941, PPCRP, 309.
62 'Women's Reply to British Plea: Lack of Realism', *TOI*, 24/6/1941, 2. These last lines echoed language that VLP used in her original response. For details, see Rosalind Parr, *Citizens of Everywhere* (Cambridge: Cambridge University Press, 2021), 73–74. This book locates VLP's activities in the context of those of other members of the All India Women's Conference, and in the larger, international(-ist) women's movement. It has a chapter specifically devoted to VLP's early experiences in the United States.
63 VLPtoRP, 24/6/1941, PPCRP, 309.
64 'Miss Nehru Returns from Europe', 18/4/1941, 10. VLPtoRP, 4/5/1941, PPCRP, 276.
65 'Mrs. V. Pandit', *TOI*, 4/4/1941, 10.
66 VLPtoRP, 4/5/1941, PPCRP, 273.
67 Ibid., 4/5/1941, 276.
68 Ibid., 4/5/1941, 276.
69 Ranjit Sitaram Pandit, *Mudra-Rakshasa or The Signet Ring: A Play in Seven Acts* (Bombay: New Book Company, 1944). https://archive.org/details/in.ernet.dli.2015.528550/page/n21, 26/2/2019.
70 VLPtoRP, 4/5/1941, PPCRP, 272–273.
71 Ibid., 26/5/1941, 281–282.
72 Ibid., 3/6/1941, especially 285–286.
73 Ibid., 3, 24/6/1941, 283–292, 311–312.
74 Ibid., 12/6/1941, 293–296.
75 Ibid., 12/6/1941, 298–299.
76 Ibid., 12/6/1941, 296–297.

77  Ibid., 24/6/1941, 305–306.
78  Ibid., 12/9/1941, 300–301, 324.
79  Ibid., 3/6/1941, 287–288.
80  Ibid., 24/6/1941, 310
81  Ibid., 4/8/1941, 315.
82  Ibid., 4/8/1941, 316.
83  Ibid., 19/8/1941, 317–320.
84  Ibid., 26/9/1941, 330.
85  Ibid., 19/8/1941, 317–318.
86  Ibid., 12/9/1941, 321–324. The 'other guest' was Raihana Tyabji, who came from a distinguished Muslim family that had made their mark in the legal profession and in the Indian National Congress.
87  Ibid., 26/9/1941, 331–332.
88  Ibid., 4/10/1941, 333–334.
89  Ibid., 13/11/1941, 336.
90  Vera Brittain had been fighting for the cause of India for some time and had developed a close friendship with VLP. She would go on to write one of the three major biographies of VLP produced during her lifetime, and easily the best one. Another of the biographies was written by the American Anne Guthrie, who actually was in attendance at the conference. For more on the WILPF, see Linda K. Schott, *Reconstructing Women's Thoughts: The Women's International League for Peace and Freedom Before World War II* (Stanford: Stanford University Press, 1997). See also https://wilpf.org/ Last accessed 19/3/2019.
91  Descriptions of events and selections of speeches from the meeting taken from: *All-India Women's Conference*, Sixteenth Session, Cocanada, 29/12/1941–1 January 1942, 3–19.
92  Ibid., 12–13. For more on Kamaladevi, see: Vinay Lal and Ellen Du Bois, eds., *A Passionate Life: Writings by and on Kamaladevi Chattopadhyay* (Delhi: Zubaan, 2017).

## Chapter 7: The Night Watch

1  'Decision by Mr. Gandhi: Anti-war Policy: Disagreement with Congress', *TMG*, 31/12/1941, 5.
2  Mahatma Gandhi to Abul Kalam Azad, 30/12/1941, *CWMG*, Volume 81, 397–398. https://www.gandhiashramsevagram.org/gandhi-literature/mahatma-gandhi-collected-works-volume-81.pdf, 6/6/2019.
3  'Congress for Armed Defence of India?: Conditional Aid in War Effort: Parting with Mr. Gandhi', *TOI*, 30/12/1941, 1.
4  'Mr. Gandhi on Congress Policy', Associated Press, *Irish Times*, 16/1/1942, 1.
5  'Gandhi would "die for Britain"' Harbours no Enmity', *TMG*, 16/1/1942, 5.
6  *Proceedings of the All-India Women's Conference: Sixteenth Session* (Cocanada, 29/12/1941–1/1/1942), 111-112.
7  'Indian Women's Conference: Resolutions on Post-War Reconstruction', *TOI*, 3/1/1942, 9. See also *Proceedings of the All-India Women's Conference: Sixteenth Session*, 112–113. The conference passed several other resolutions as well, condoling the death of Rabindranath Tagore, calling for communal harmony, and praising the girl scout movement. But the three related to the war received the most fanfare.

8 *Proceedings of the All-India Women's Conference: Sixteenth Session*, 113. See also 'Indian Women's Conference: Attitude to the War', TMG, 14/1/1942, 6.
9 'Marshal and Madame Chiang in Delhi', TOI, 10/2/1942, 1.
10 'Chiang Kaishek visiting India', The Globe and Mail (hereafter GandM), 10/2/1942, 13.
11 SoH, 155.
12 'Chiang Kaishek visiting India', GandM, 10/2/1942, 13.
13 'Chiang confers with Indian leaders to map aid for Britain', CDT, 11/2/1942, 3.
14 'Pandit Nehru meets Marshal Chiang', TOI, 11/2/1942, 1. The later head of the Rashtriya Swayamsevak Sangh (RSS), Rajendra Singh, would have a brief encounter with VLP in this period (in late January, just a few weeks prior) that he would recall unhappily. As a young student, he was part of a group of students that approached her for her autograph while she was seated in a second-class train compartment with Padmaja, Indira, and Ranjit. She snapped at them for intruding on her private conversation and had to be calmed down by Ranjit. Arun Anand, *Biography of Prof. Rajendra Singh (Raju Bhaiyya)* (Delhi: Prabhat Prakashan, 2020). Others affiliated with the RSS write about VLP with a certain level of admiration. See for instance, Prashant Pole, *Those Fifteen Days* (Delhi: Prabhat Prakashan, 2022), who notes that she was 'a very intelligent woman' with 'her own achievements', (no page number available).
15 'Parade in Honour of Marshal Chiang: India's Welcome', TOI, 12/2/1942, 7.
16 'Another busy day for Chiang', TOI, 13/2/1942, 7.
17 'War at India's Doorstep: Madame Chiang asks people to prepare', TOI, 13/2/1942, 1.
18 'Role of Press in Wartime', TOI, 16/2/1942, 1.
19 'Two small men, leaders of big nations of little people, find their roles in war', *Austin Statesmen*, 19/2/1942, 12.
20 'Madame Chiang visits Agra', TOI, 14/2/1942, 7; 'Chinese visitors to India', *Palestine Post*, 15/3/1942, 4; 'The Chiangs of China on their recent visit to India', NYT, 8/4/1942, 3.
21 SoH, 156.
22 JNtoVLP, 2/4/1935, BF, 142–146.
23 Feroze Gandhi to VLP, 8/11/1938, BF, 234–235. Cf. Bertil Falk, *Feroze*.
24 Details of the wedding in PandCC, 95–104. See also 'Miss Indira Nehru Weds,' TOI, 27/3/1942, 7; Betty Graham, 'The Wedding of Indira Nehru,' *Harper's Bazaar* 75:2768: August 1942, 74–75, 134. Krishna Hutheesing, in *Dear to Behold* (90), explains that Nehru was especially concerned that Indira had been very sheltered and perhaps had not yet had a chance to meet other men before she committed to such a long-term relationship. He also felt that Feroze and Indira came from different backgrounds and may have trouble adjusting to each other, perhaps a reflection of his own experiences with Kamala.
25 Arthur Herman, *Gandhi and Churchill* (New York: Bantam, 2008), 482–485. Gopal, *Jawaharlal Nehru*, 140. Nehru to Mahadev Desai, 9/12/1939, in Jawaharlal Nehru, *A Bunch of Old Letters* (Delhi: Oxford University Press, 1988), 412–413.
26 SoH, 154.
27 'Louis Johnson to be first U.S. Minister to India', *Washington Post*, 16/3/1942, 1. 'Johnson unofficial minister to India', *The Hartford Courant*, 11. Gopal, *Jawaharlal Nehru*, 142; Herman, *Gandhi and Churchill*, 486.

28  Drafted but unsent letter, FDR to Churchill, 25/2/1942, cited in Herman, 484.
29  'FDR may mediate in India', *Austin Statesman*, 3/4/1942, 1.
30  'Congress Executive', *TOI*, 17/4/1942, 7.
31  'Nehru says India must resist invasion, won't hinder allies,' *NYHT*, 13/4/1942, 1. Johnson was quite pleased that the Indians did not accept Britain's half-hearted efforts, writing to FDR that the official Congress rejection of Cripps was 'a masterpiece . . . [that would] appeal to free men everywhere.' Telegram from Johnson to FDR, 11/4/1942, Papers of the Franklin Roosevelt Library Related to Indian Affairs, NMML, F. No. 4, 11. The cables reveal that Johnson was rather dazzled by Nehru, calling him 'magnificent' and someone that the president would like. He saw the failure of the Cripps' mission as entirely intentional, the blame falling squarely on the shoulders of the Viceroy, Wavell, and Lord Halifax (15–16).
32  'Congress fissures deepen: Move for Mr. Gandhi's leadership', *TMG*, 4/5/1942, 4. Gandhi had submitted a draft 'Quit India' resolution on 27 April, but it was not adopted at that time. http://cw.routledge.com/textbooks/9780415485432/31.asp, 21/6/2019. 'Text of Resolution Drafted by Gandhi,' *NYT*, 5/8/1942, 6.
33  This section a summary of *PandCC*, 105–114.
34  'Congress Working Committee', *TOI*, 15/7/1942, 7.
35  *SoH*, 156–157. Two weeks before, Gandhi had written directly to FDR asking him to facilitate the liberation of India: 'I venture to think that the Allied declaration that the Allies are fighting to make the world safe for freedom of the individual and for democracy sounds hollow, so long as India and, for that matter, Africa are exploited by Great Britain, and America has the Negro problem in her own home . . . If India becomes free, the rest must follow, if it does not happen simultaneously.' He noted that while he himself 'hate[d] all war,' he knew that not all felt as he did, and he pledged a free India to helping the Allied war effort, at least by allowing Allied troops to freely use the country as a base of operations. Gandhi to FDR, via Louis Fischer, 1/7/1942, Papers of the Franklin Roosevelt Library Related to Indian Affairs, NMML, F. No. 12, 11–12.
36  'Britain and India', *TMG*, 15/7/1942, 5. Nehru had kept Madame Chiang informed of the rapid developments, and she in turn kept the American government abreast of his analysis with secret cables, writing of Gandhi's upcoming campaign and the need now for Indian independence or self-determination. Telegram from Madame Chiang to Lauchlin Currie, 31/5/1942, Papers of the Franklin Roosevelt Library Related to Indian Affairs, NMML, F. No. 4, 19–20.
37  'Demand for free India again: An ally of the United Nations', *Irish Times*, 6/8/1942, 1. The full resolution in Arun Chandra Guha, *India's Struggle Quarter of a Century, 1921–1946*, Part II (Publications Division, 2017).
38  Bhagavan, *The Peacemakers*, 14–17.
39  'British charge Gandhi sought deal with Japs', *Chicago Daily Tribune* (hereafter CDT), 5/8/1942, 1. 'All India group and Gandhi hit as "appeasers"', *Daily Boston Globe*, 5/8/1942, 1.
40  'Gandhi's reply', *Scotsman*, 5/8/1942, 6. Gandhi had privately tried to resolve the situation, hoping the British would bend just enough for him to agree to back down. He asked FDR, via Louis Fischer, to 'dissuade' him for launching a campaign, as he knew just how precarious the world situation was. Louis Fischer

to FDR, 7/8/1942, Papers of the Franklin Roosevelt Library Related to Indian Affairs, NMML, F. No. 12, 40. FDR had in the meantime tried to get a letter to Gandhi, but the latter had been arrested before it arrived. Cordell Hull to FDR, 9/9/1942, informing the president of the diplomatic headache the undelivered letter posed, 46–51. Fischer had telegrammed FDR immediately on his arrival back in the US on 5 August, stating that he had Gandhi's letter and that he wanted to speak urgently. FDR replied on 11 August saying that he was 'trying to keep in very close touch with the situation'. 38–39.

41 Arun Chandra Guha, *India's Struggle Quarter of a Century, 1921–1946*, Part II (Publications Division, 2017). *SoH*, 156.
42 *PandCC*, 115. Author exchange with Nayantara Sahgal, 26–27 June 2019.
43 *SoH*, 159.
44 *PandCC*, 116.
45 *SoH*, 159.
46 *SoH*, 160.
47 *PandCC*, 116.
48 Vijaya Lakshmi Pandit, *Prison Days* (VLPPD) (Calcutta: The Signet Press, 3rd edition 1946), 1; *SoH*, 160.
49 , *PandCC*, 117.
50 *SoH*, 161.
51 VLPPD, 1–2.
52 Ibid., 2.
53 Ibid., 2–3.
54 Ibid., 3.
55 The narrative in this section is based on *SoH*, 157–162; *PandCC*, 113–119; VLPPD, 1–5; and author exchange with Nayantara Sahgal, 26–27 June 2019. There are some discrepancies between the various sources that I discussed and clarified through the exchange.
56 VLP published the diary as *Prison Days*. The account she provides in *SoH* appears to be primarily drawn from this source. My account draws directly from her diary entries, supplemented by *SoH*. Where there is a discrepancy between the two, I take the information in the diary to be the more accurate, unless it has to do with a broader context of which she would not have been aware while in prison.
57 VLPPD, 20/8/1942, 24. Dates refer to entries.
58 Ibid., 13/8/1942, 5–7.
59 Ibid., 17/8/1942, 13–14.
60 *SoH*, 164.
61 VLPPD, 19/8/1942, 21.
62 Ibid., 29/8/1942, 39.
63 Ibid., 20/8/1942, 24.
64 Ibid., 19/8/1942, 18–19.
65 Ibid., 13/8/1942, 7.
66 Ibid., 17/8/1942, 13.
67 Ibid., 19/8/1942, 19–20.
68 Ibid., 21/8/1942, pp 28–29.
69 Ibid., 20/8/1942, 25.
70 Ibid. 20/8/1942, 26. Cf. Mary Leland Hunt, 'Geffray Mynshul and Thomas Dekker', *The Journal of English and Germanic Philology* (11:2, 1912), 231–243.

71  VLPPD, 20/8/1942, 25.
72  Ibid., 21/8/1942, 26–27.
73  Ibid., 24–26 August 1942, 32–35.
74  For some context and background, see Banerji to Nehru, 7 May and 8 November 1941, in *A Bunch of Old Letters*, 457–458, 466–467.
75  VLPPD, 24/8/1942, 33.
76  Ibid., 30/8/1942, 40–43.
77  Ibid., 30/8/1942, 42–43.
78  Ibid., 11/9/1942, 50.
79  Ibid., entries for 11, 19 September 1942, 50, 55.
80  *SoH*, 166.
81  *SoH*, 166.
82  *VLPPD*, 13/9/1942, 53.
83  Ibid., 27/11/1942, 82–83 and SoH, 166.
84  Ibid., 11, 25·26, 29, 31/10/1942, 67, 73–75.
85  Ibid., 25/10/1942, 73.
86  Ibid., 18/11/1942, 78–80.
87  Ibid., 8/10/1942, 66.
88  Ibid., 31/12/1942, 88.
89  Ibid., 8/9/1942, 50.
90  Ibid., 5/9/1942, 46.
91  Ibid., 1, 13 September, 7, 14, 15, 16 October 1942, 1/1/1943 44, 53, 65, 68, 70, 92.
92  Ibid., 15/9/1942, 1/1/1943 53–54, 92.
93  Ibid., 1/1/1943, 92–94. *Prison Days* incorrectly uses the word 'it's' in the last line of the poem, and I have corrected in text to 'its'. Chaplin was also famous for writing 'Solidarity Forever.' Cf. https://blogs.baylor.edu/robert_darden/2010/06/03/mourn-not-the-dead/, 7/1/2020.

## Chapter 8: The Good Earth

1  VLPPD, entry for 14/10/1942, 68.
2  Ibid., 16/10/1942, 70.
3  Ibid., for 23–28 September 1942, 56–58
4  Ibid., 15/10/1942, 69.
5  'Gandhi, Interned by the British, will Punish his Skinny Frame by New Fast of Protest', *Austin-American Statesman*, 10/2/1943, p.1.
6  VLPPD, 9, 14 February, 17/3/1943, 94–95.
7  VLPPD, 17–21/3/1943, 96.
8  Jawaharlal Nehru to Nayantara Pandit, 24/11/1942, *BF*, 304–306.
9  VNtoVLP, 21/3/1943, *BF*, 313–317.
10  Jawaharlal Nehru to Nayantara Pandit, 29/1/1943, *BF*, 3307–311. Nayantara would eventually receive the letter in September 1945, when Nehru re-sent it to her along with a new letter.
11  *PandCC*, 118–119.
12  Jawaharlal Nehru to President Franklin Roosevelt, 12/4/1942, *A Bunch of Old Letters*, 479–480.
13  Letters and documents from February–April 1942, including some marked 'Secret and (Strictly) Confidential,' declassified by the US State Department in

1995. Europe files: India, 1942; Sumner Welles Papers; Franklin D. Roosevelt Library, Hyde Park, New York. Cf. Bhagavan, *The Peacemakers*, n6, 175–176.

14 Herbert Matthews, 'Indians Lose Hope of Early Self-Rule', *NYT*, 1/4/1943, 9. British intelligence intercepted Matthews' wire back home and reviewed it over the next two months. VLP's interview was specifically flagged for possible sedition, but officials instead concluded that the interview was acceptable. Indeed, it appeared to them that VLP's comments were 'positively useful'. 'Cable to America by Herbert Matthews regarding his interview with Mrs. Vijay Lakshmi Pandit during her release on parole, and his views on public feelings towards Gandhi and the Civil Disobedience Movement,' Government of India, Home Department, Political (Internal) Sec, F. No. 3/63/43–Poll (I), 1943, NAI. Quote from page 2.
15 JNtoVLP, 9/4/1943, *BF*, 319.
16 JNtoVLP, 21/3/1943, *BF*, 316–317.
17 Nehru to Chandralekha Pandit, 26/3/and 23/4/1943, *BF*, 318, 324.
18 JNtoVLP, 21/3/and 9 April, 1943, *BF*, 313–317, 319–323.
19 *PandCC*, x.
20 VLPPD, entry for 20/4/1943, 96; *SoH*, 167.
21 'Copy of the Express Letter No.26OPP/VIII–From the Secy. to Govt. U.P. to the Secy. Govt. of India, External Affairs Dept. New Delhi, 16/4/1943,' in 'Mrs. Vijaya Lakshmi Pandit a.) Release on Parole, b.) Grant of passports to her daughters, Misses Chandralekha and Nayantara Pandits, to proceed to the U.S.A. Their admission to the Wellesley College sponsored by Madame Chiang and Mrs. Gunther,' Government of India, Home Department, Political Branch, F. No. 44/11, 1943, 10, NAI.
22 Cf. Kenton Clymer, *Quest for Freedom* (New York: Columbia University Press, 1995), 48, 300.
23 'Mrs. Vijaya Lakshmi Pandit a.) Release on Parole, b.) Grant of passports to her daughters, Misses Chandralekha and Nayantara Pandits, to proceed to the U.S.A. Their admission to the Wellesley College sponsored by Madame Chiang and Mrs. Gunther,' Government of India, Home Department, Political Branch, F. No. 44/11, 1943, 12, NAI.
24 'Mrs. Vijaya Lakshmi Pandit a.) Release on Parole, b.) Grant of passports to her daughters, Misses Chandralekha and Nayantara Pandits, to proceed to the U.S.A. Their admission to the Wellesley College sponsored by Madame Chiang and Mrs. Gunther,' Government of India, Home Department, Political Branch, F. No. 44/11, 1943, 10–13, NAI. The Indian Agency-General in Washington, once they got word of the impending arrival of the girls, thought there was some mistake, and they wrote hurriedly warning of the political risks involved with letting the Pandits into the country, but the Home Office rebuffed these concerns, along with erroneous rumors that Chandralekha had been shot and killed by police during the encounter in Allahabad.
25 Krishna Hutheesing and Alden Hatch, *We Nehrus* (New York: Holt, Rinehart and Winston, 1967), 167.
26 *PandCC*, xi–xiii.
27 Jawaharlal Nehru to Chandralekha Pandit, 23/4/1943, *BF*, 325–326. Cf. Hutheesing and Hatch, *We Nehrus*, 167–168, which includes reproduction of the contents of a letter Nehru had sent to Betty.
28 VLPPD 20, 21, 25/4/1943, 96–100.

29  Ibid., 27 April, 3, 11/5/1943, 100–102, 104–106.
30  Ibid., 3/5/1943, 101–102.
31  Ibid., 3/5/1943, 101–102.
32  https://www.italianliners.com/conte-biancamano-en, 27/1/2020. Cf. Chapter 2. The Biancamano had a sister ship, the Conte Grande.
33  Memorandum on the Polish Refugee Camp in Mexico, from Grace W. Tellier to James G. Johnson, Jr., 5/1/1944, 1–5. 'Polish Refugee Project in Mexico' folder. http://www.fdrlibrary.marist.edu/_resources/images/wrb/wrb0474.pdf, 29/1/2020.
34  This section is a summary of *PandCC*, 3–7.
35  'Mrs. Vijayalaxmi Pandit: Refusal to Submit to Surveillance', in *TOI*, 24/5/1943, 7.
36  'Mr. Gandhi—Nehru's Sister Rearrested', *TMG*, 27/5/1943, 5.
37  VLPPD, entries for 13, 27 May and 4/6/1943, 107–109. See also: 'Mrs. Vijayalaxmi Pandit: Refusal to Submit to Surveillance,' in *TOI*, 24/5/1943, 7.
38  'Mrs. V.L. Pandit Released,' *TOI*, 14/6/1943, 7. And VLPPD 7, 11/6/1943, 110–111.
39  Resolutions passed by the Standing Committee of the All India Women's Conference at its meetings on the 29th and 30th of May 1943, Home Department, Poll (I) Section, F. No. 96/43–Poll(I), 1943, 3, NAI.
40  JNtoVLP, 29/6/1943, *BF*, 330–333.
41  'Mrs. Vijaya Lakshmi Pandit a.) Release on Parole, b.) Grant of passports to her daughters, Misses Chandralekha and Nayantara Pandits, to proceed to the U.S.A. Their admission to the Wellesley College sponsored by Madame Chiang and Mrs. Gunther,' Government of India, Home Department, Political Branch, F. No. 44/11, 1943, 6–10, some marked Secret, NAI.
42  JNtoVLP, 29/6/1943, *BF*, 330–333.
43  Krishna Nehru Hutheesing, *With No Regrets*.
44  JNtoVLP, 29/6/1943, *BF*, 330–333.
45  VLP to Padmaja Naidu, 30/7/1943, PNaiduPapers, 91–94.
46  JNtoVLP, 29/6/1943, *BF*, 332.
47  VLP to Padmaja Naidu, 30/7/1943, PNaiduPapers, 91–94.
48  VLP to Padmaja Naidu, 30/7/1943, PNaiduPapers, 91–94; second quotation from 'Mr. R.S. Pandit Released', *TOI*, 25/9/1943, 5. Cf. JNtoVLP, 13/7/1943, *BF*, 334. Nehru is hopeful about the care he will receive but expresses anxiety about his condition.
49  JNtoVLP, 3/8/1943, *BF*, 336.
50  VLP to Padmaja Naidu, 30/7/1943, PNaiduPapers, 91.
51  VLP to Padmaja Naidu, 30/7/1943, PNaiduPapers, 91–94.
52  VLPtoRP, 18/8/1943, PPCRP, 341–343. JNtoVLP, 24/8/1943, *BF*, 340.
53  VLP to Colonel G.R. Oberai, 11/8/1943, secretly intercepted by the Intelligence Bureau. 'Mrs. Vijaya Lakshmi Pandit a.) Release on Parole, b.) Grant of passports to her daughters, Misses Chandralekha and Nayantara Pandits, to proceed to the U.S.A. Their admission to the Wellesley College sponsored by Madame Chiang and Mrs. Gunther,' Government of India, Home Department, Political Branch, F. No. 44/11, 1943, 9, NAI.
54  VLPtoRP, 18/8/1943, PPCRP, 341–343.
55  Vimal Mishra et.al., 'Drought and Famine in India, 1870–2016', *Geophysical Research Letters* 46(4), 28/2/2019, 2075–2083. Cf. 'New Soil Study Confirms 1943 Bengal Famine was caused by Winston's Churchill's Policies, not Draught', *Scroll*, 30/3/2019, https://scroll.in/article/918373/new-soil-study-

confirms-1943-bengal-famine-was-caused-by-winston-churchills-policies-not-drought, 6/2/2020. Michael Safi, 'Churchill's Policies Contributed to 1943 Bengal Famine—Study', *Guardian*, 29/3/2019, https://www.theguardian.com/world/2019/mar/29/winston-churchill-policies-contributed-to-1943-bengal-famine-study, 6/2/2020.

56  Madhusree Mukherjee, *Churchill's Secret War* (New York: Basic Books, 2010), 67.
57  Amartya Sen, *Poverty and Famines: An Essay on Entitlement and Deprivation*, New Delhi: Oxford University Press, 1999. First published 1981. For additional context, see Benjamin Siegel, *Hungry Nation* (Cambridge: Cambridge University Press, 2018), 21–49.
58  Mukherjee, *Churchill's Secret War*, 106-109.
59  'Free Food Served in Bengal', *Irish Times*, 25/9/1943, 1.
60  'Australia to Held Indians in Distress', *TOI*, 30/9/1943, 5
61  'Australia to Held Indians in Distress', *TOI*, 30/9/1943, 5. The AIWC got 50 *bigahs* of land for the home. A bigah was standardized in colonial Bengal at about 1/3 of an acre. https://en.wikipedia.org/wiki/Bigha. Last accessed 6/2/2020. 'The Famine Tragedy in Bengal: Congress Workers Helping in Relief', *TMG*, 7/10/1943.
62  'Rationing Plan: Introduction in a Few Weeks' Time', *TOI*, 11/10/1943, 5.
63  Sonia Tomara, 'Relief Work in Starving Bengal gives India Women a New Job', *NYHT*, 17/10/1943, C9. The sub-header spelled her name 'Vijawa,' but as it was spelled correctly as 'Vijaya' in the rest of the story, this appears to simply have been a typographical error. I have used the corrected spelling in the narrative.
64  'Mr. R.S. Pandit Released', *TOI*, 25/9/1943, 5.
65  'Pandit Released, is Ill at his Home', *Daily News*, 28/9/1943, 5.
66  JNtoVLP, 19/10/1943, *BF*, 349.
67  JNtoVLP, 24 August, 7/9/1943, *BF*, 340–344.
68  Norma Buchanan, 'In Enfield, Communist Sympathies and a knife by the bedside', *The Hartford Courant*, 22/9/2019. https://www.courant.com/opinion/op-ed/hc-op-buchanan-taking-note-robeson-house-0922-20190922-4rxjj52vubhkfijioojzt5v5fm-story.html, 10/2/2020. https://en.wikipedia.org/wiki/Eslanda_Goode_Robeson and https://en.wikipedia.org/wiki/Paul_Robeson, 10/2/2020. The Robesons had had some ups and downs in their marriage by that point but had pulled together.
69  For more on Essie Robeson and some additional context for her relationship with VLP, see Barbara Ransby. *Eslanda* (Chicago: Haymarket Books, 2022, first published 2013), esp. 217–221. Quoted phrase from 218. Ransby describes VLP as one of Essie's three 'political sisters', along with Shirley Graham Du Bois and Janet Jagan (216).
70  'Seminary Foundation to Entertain Guests', *Hartford Courant*, 15/10/1943, 17; James Moore, 'Indian Girls Guests at Foundation', *Hartford Courant*, 16/10/1943, 16.
71  'Conditions Worse: Mrs. Pandit's Observations', *TMG*, via Reuters, 26/10/1943, 6; 'Medical Supplies for Bengal', *TOI*, 27/10/1943, 4.
72  Tillman Durdin, 'Epidemic Stalks Famine in Bengal', *NYT*, 28/10/1943, 10.
73  'Bengal Famine: Wavell begins his Tour', *TMG*, 27/10/1943, 5.
74  'The Calcutta Destitutes', *TMG* 9/11/1943, 5.
75  '25 Per Cent Increase Bengal Monsoon Crop', *TOI*, 21/10/1943, 4.
76  'Calcutta Returning to Normal', *TOI*, 17/11/1943, 4.

77 'Indian Council of World Affairs', *TOI*, 22/11/1943, 5.
78 'Starvations in Bengal Put at 100,000 a Week', *NYHT*, 25/11/1943, 3. 'Women's Relief Plans', *TOI*, 26/11/1943, 5. 'Future Critical in Bengal—Mrs. Pandit', *TMG*, 27/11/1943, 6. 'No Food Shortage in Major Famine Areas', *TOI*, 6/12/1943, 5.
79 JNtoVLP, 9/11/1943, *BF*, 356–361.
80 Krishna Hutheesing, *We Nehrus*, 169. JNtoVLP, 30/11/1943, *BF*, 362.
81 JNtoVLP, 30/11/1943, *BF*, 362–364.
82 JNtoVLP, 28/12/1943, *BF*, 367–370.
83 JNtoVLP, 11/1/1944, *BF*, 376–378.
84 *BF*, 373. His death made headlines around the world, some chalking his death up to 'heart attacks' while underplaying the role of prison itself in contributing to his sickness. See for instance, 'R.S. Pandit, 50, Brother-in-law of Nehru, Dies: Interned in 1942 Roundup, He was Freed 6 Months ago because of illness', *NYHT*, 15/1/1944, 8A. 'Mr. R.S. Pandit Dead,' *TOI*, 15/1/1944, 4.
85 *SoH*, 176-177. Email exchanges between Nayantara Sahgal, Gita Sahgal, and Manu Bhagavan, 5/3/2020, 29/5/2020.
86 *SoH*, 176. Email from Nayantara Sahgal to Manu Bhagavan, 29/5/2020.
87 JNtoVLP, 29/1/1944, *BF*, 386–387.
88 JNtoVLP, 29/1/1944, *BF*, 386.
89 VLP to Nayantara Pandit, 4/3/1944, Letters between VLP and her daughter, Nayantara Sahgal Archives, Boston University.
90 'Mrs. Vijaya Lakshmi Pandit's complaint regarding the withholding of messages from her daughters studying in America,' Home Department, Political (Internal), F. No. 20/2/44-Poll, 1944, NAI. Quotation is from VLP to Sir Reginald Maxwell, 21/3/1944, 4. Her suspicions were not at all unwarranted. The government was indeed watching her every move. While they were not, in fact, holding up any letters from her daughters, even so small a thing as a condolence message from fellow political leader and friend Jayaprakash Narayan drew their attention. Officials internally investigated how and why he could have written such a letter, and argued whether it breached protocol, resulting in an investigative file on the matter. See GOI, Home Department, Poll(I) Sec., F. No. 44/29/44–Poll(I), 1944, NAI.
91 *SoH*, 177–178.
92 JNtoVLP, 13/3/1944, *BF*, 390–396.
93 *SoH*, 178.
94 JNtoVLP, 13/3/1944, *BF*, 390–396.
95 Walsh to VLP, 21/7/1943, Pearl S. Buck Archives.
96 Walsh to VLP, 6/10/1943, Pearl S. Buck Archives. Walsh and Buck collectively called themselves the Walshes. They also handled all the basic finances for the girls.
97 'Reception Honors Nieces of Nehru, Indian Leader', *The Chicago Defender*, 15/1/1944, 15.
98 'Vanity Fair Features: In the News', *Vogue* 103 (4), 15/2/1944, 78.
99 Email exchange between Nayantara Sahgal and Manu Bhagavan, 29/5/2020.
100 'Kasturba Gandhi Memorial Fund', 15/3/1944, *TOI*, 7.
101 http://kgnmthyd.org, 5/3/2020.
102 'Bombay Red Cross Week', *TOI*, 1/4/1944; 'Exhibition of Arts and Handicrafts', *TOI*, 6/4/1944, 9.

103 'Exhibition of Arts and Handicrafts', *TOI*, 6/4/1944, 9.
104 'Bills Affecting Women's Rights', *TOI*, 10/4/1944, 5.
105 'Appeal to Women of India', *TOI*, 11/4/1944, 5.
106 JNtoVLP, 4/4/1944, *BF*, 397–399.
107 JNtoVLP, 18 April, 6, 17/5/1944, *BF*, 400–410.
108 'British Release Gandhi due to Failing Health', *The Atlanta Constitution*, 6/5/1944, p.1.
109 'Mr. Gandhi Spends Quiet Day', *TOI*, 8/5/1944, 1.
110 'Appeal to Britain', *TOI*, 11/5/1944, 5.
111 'Fortnight's Silence to Recoup Health,' *TOI*, 15/5/1944, 1.
112 Gene Overstreet and Marshall Windmiller, *Communism in India* (Berkeley: University of California Press, 1959), 406–407.
113 'Russian Heroism: Tributes at Bombay Conference', *TOI*, 5/6/1944, 3.
114 VLP to Frances Gunther, 26/4/1944, reproduced in GOI, Home Department, Political Section, F. No. 61/44–Pol and K.W. I and II, 1944, 4, NAI.
115 Clark Getts to VLP, 8/11/1943, reproduced in, F. No. 61/44–Pol, 12, NAI.
116 Richard Walsh to VLP, 1/5/1944, reproduced in, F. No. 61/44–Pol, 5, NAI.
117 The initial opposition by Halifax and Bajpai led an internal British assessment to conclude that, since it was a presidential election year, Roosevelt's opponents might somehow make hay of VLP's activities to undermine the US president and spoil his bid for reelection. See also the assessment of J. Sahay, the Secretary of the . . ., 8–9. E. Conran Smith, 18/7/1944, 10. F. No. 61/44–Pol, 70, NAI.
118 Secret telegram from Halifax and Bajpai to Government of India, 23/24/4/1944, F. No. 61/44–Pol 64, NAI.
119 VLP to the Chief Secretary to the Government, U.P., 7/7/1944, F. No. 61/44–Pol, 68, NAI.
120 Assessment of the Director of the Intelligence Bureau of the Home Department, 22/7/1944, F. No. 61/44–Pol, 13, NAI.
121 Confidential, Maurice Hallett, Governor of the United Provinces, to Sir John Thorne, House Member of the Council, 13/7/1944, F. No. 61/44–Pol, 65–67, NAI.
122 Summary of correspondence and assessments, July–October 1944, in F. No. 61/44–Pol, 8–23, 69–70, NAI. Quotes from Pilditch taken from 12–13.
123 *SoH*, 178–179.
124 Letters from JNtoVLP, 22 May, 27 June, 2/9/1944, *BF*, 411–418, 421–423, 428–431. *SoH*, 179–181.
125 'Future Critical in Bengal—Mrs. Pandit,' *TMG*, 27/11/1943, 6.
126 'All-India Women's Conference,' 4/4/1944, 5.
127 *SoH*, 185. Letters from JNtoVLP, 20 July and 1/8/1944, *BF*, 424–427. VLP claims in her memoir that she issued an appeal to women around the world for contributions for her Save the Children fund. I was unable to find anything other than the appeal she made at the AIWC meeting in April, so I presume that is what she is referring to. Current value of the donation calculated at https://www.dollartimes.com/inflation/inflation.php?amount=25000&year=1944.
128 *SoH*, 184. Mukherjee's campaigns nonetheless had the effect of broadening the appeal of religiously inflected Hindu nationalism, and legitimizing the famously communal organization with which he was then associated. For more, see Abhijit Sarkar, 'Fed by Famine: The Hindu Mahasabha's Politics of Religion,

Caste, and Relief, in Response to the Great Bengal Famine, 1943–1944,' *Modern Asian Studies*, published online 14/2/2020.
129  *SoH*, 185. JNtoVLP, 1 August, 2, 26/9/1944, *BF*, 426–434.
130  Chandralekha Pandit to VLP, 9/10/1944, F. No. 61/44–Pol, 26–27, NAI.
131  United Provinces Police Report, 29/9/1944, in F. No. 61/44–Pol, p 22, NAI.
132  Chandralekha Pandit to VLP, 9/10/1944, F. No. 61/44–Pol, 26–27, NAI. Singh had gotten in touch with Chandralekha and Nayantara immediately upon their arrival to the United States. He, Frances Gunther, and Richard Walsh all coordinated aspects of the girls' public relations early on. J.J. Singh to Chandralekha and Nayantara Pandit, 30/6/1943, J.J. Singh Papers I–II, Sub-file 34, NMML, 10–11, and other correspondence, 12–25.
133  J.J. Singh to VLP, 6/9/1944, F. No. 61/44–Pol, 28–30.
134  Short exchanges, 21 October-1 November 1944, F. No. 61/44–Pol, 23–24, NAI.
135  Note by O.K. Caroe, 29/10/1944, F. No. 61/44–Pol, 24, NAI.
136  Confidential telegram from the Governor of UP to Foreign, New Delhi, 6/7 November 1944, F. No. 61/44–Pol, 79, NAI. 'Mrs. Vijayalakshmi Pandit', *TOI*, 6/11/1944, 5.
137  Handwritten note from O.K. Caroe, November 1944, F. No. 61/44–Pol, 81, NAI.

## Chapter 9: Americanah

1  'League and Assembly Election in Sind', *TOI*, 20/11/1944, 5. 'Mrs. Vijayalakshmi Pandit,' *TOI*, via Reuters, 25/11/1944, 6. 'Mrs. Vijayalakshmi Pandit', *TOI*, via the Associated Press, 1/12/1944, 4. 'Mrs. Vijayalakshmi Pandit', *TOI*, 2/12/1944, 7. 'Weather-2,' *TOI*, 4/12/1944, 4. 'Indian Delegate on Way Here', *NYT*, 3/12/1944, 5. 'Indian Prince Arrives by Air', *NYT*, 9/12/1944, 7. For additional perspectives on the material in this chapter, cf. Julie Laut, 'The Woman who Swayed America,' *Deportate, esuli, profughe*, no, 37, 2018, 26–47. https://www.unive.it/pag/fileadmin/user_upload/dipartimenti/DSLCC/documenti/DEP/numeri/n37/05_Laut.pdf, 9/3/2023.
2  New York Municipal Airport-LaGuardia Field had opened in 1939. It was colloquially called LaGuardia Airport right from the start but was not officially named that until 1953. https://portfolio.panynj.gov/2016/06/17/laguardia-airport-flashback-to-the-past/, 16/6/2020. Nan flew to New York from Karachi via Cairo and Casablanca, spending two nights in the former and one in the latter. She was alone on the first leg of her journey, and the relative youth of her two pilots, 23 and 24, made her nervous, though she managed. VLP to Indira Gandhi, 4/1/1945, 'Visit to the United States of America of Mrs Vijaylakshmi [sic] Pandit', 44.
3  *SoH*, 188–189.
4  https://www.hospitalitynet.org/opinion/4096859.html, 16/6/2020. She stayed in what is today known as The Peninsula Hotel at 5th Avenue and 55th Street. Nan noted that it 'is to the Waldorf what Claridges in London is to the Dorcester.' VLP to Indira Gandhi, 4/1/1945, F. No. 61/44–Pol, 44, NAI. A countryman warned her shortly after she moved in that the hotel 'was in the service of the British.' She brushed this off, laughingly saying that she would then feel 'really at home.' VLP to Indira Gandhi, 4/1/1945, F. No. 61/44–Pol, 44, NAI.

468                                   NOTES

5   Interview given on December 10. 'Noted Indian Woman Here to Visit Daughters in Wellesley', *Daily Boston Globe*, 11/12/1944, 6.
6   'Mrs. V.L. Pandit says India keeps a Grim Silence', *NYHT*, 17/12/1944, A6.
7   'No propaganda tour', *Hindustan Times*, 13/12/1944, reproduced in F. No. 61/44–Pol, 98, NAI. The quotation and this story come from her Sunday conference, which preceded her interview with Bromley.
8   *SoH*, 190.
9   'New York Reception to Mrs. Pandit', *The Hindu*, 17/12/1944, in F. No. 61/44–Pol, 105, NAI. The reception was held on 14 December at 4:30p.m. Letter of invitation from Pearl Buck, 11/12/1944, in Record Group 5, Records of the East West Association, Box 3, Archives of the Pearl S. Buck House, Pearl S. Buck International. The file contains various letters to and from guests related to the reception.
10  Report from the Director, Intelligence Bureau, 18/12/1944, F. No. 61/44–Pol, 103–104, NAI. Pratt also claimed the people at the party numbered 75.
11  'Britain's Policies in India: Mrs. V.L. Pandit's attack', *The Hindu*, 21/12/1944, F. No. 61/44–Pol, 99, NAI. This story uses Reuters to reproduce parts of her interview with *The New York Post*.
12  *Wellesley College News*, 2/11/1944, https://repository.wellesley.edu/cgi/viewcontent.cgi?article=2208&context=news, 22/6/2020.
13  Email from Nayantara Sahgal to me, 19, 23 June 2020.
14  'Founding and Early Years - NAACP: A Century in the Fight for Freedom | Exhibitions - Library of Congress', n.d., https://www.loc.gov/exhibits/naacp/founding-and-early-years.html, Last accessed 29/3/2023.
15  Pearl Buck to Eleanor Roosevelt, 9/11/1944, Record Group 1, Papers of Pearl S. Buck, Serial Group 2: Correspondence, Box 20, Archives of the Pearl S. Buck House, Pearl S. Buck International. For additional discussion of White's relationship with VLP, and broader context, see Gerald Horne, *African Americans and India* (Philadelphia: Temple University Press, 2008). Correspondence between Walter and Poppy White and VLP, available at the Beinecke Rare Book and Manuscript Library at Yale University, indicates that they maintained a close friendship through Walter's death and after.
16  'About New York: Quaint Caravan Hall in Midtown Mixes Bahai, Irish Dances and Tales of Old New York', *NYT*, 22/7/1957, 17. Cf. http://fancyclopedia.org/Caravan_Hall, 25/6/2020.
17  'White House's 'No' to Mrs. Pandit: Please Turned Down by Mrs. Roosevelt', *TOI*, 4/1/1945, 5. The claims about the White House decision were made by G.L. Mehta who had been deputy leader of an Indian delegation to an international business conference in the United States. He had returned to India just a few days before and spoke at a press conference there. 'Indian Opposition to Export Subsidies', *TOI*, 2/1/1945, 3.
18  *India Today*, the monthly newsletter of the India League of America, Volume V, No. 10,/1/1945, 4. In Record Group 5, Records of the East and West Association, Box 3, Archives of the Pearl S. Buck House, Pearl S. Buck International.
19  This assessment is based on interviews with Nayantara Sahgal, N.S. Vinodh (Syud Hossain's biographer), and K. Shankar Bajpai (who served as VLP's Private Secretary in the fifties), as well as my reading of a broad survey of records.
20  Sean Phillips, 'A Pacific Precedent: The Institute of Pacific Relations in the Emergence of Asia-Pacific Studies', https://theasiadialogue.com/2018/06/27/a-

pacific-precedent-the-institute-of-pacific-relations-in-the-emergence-of-asia-pacific-studies/, 24/6/2020.
21  https://www.historichotels.org/us/hotels-resorts/the-omni-homestead-resort/history.php. Last accessed 24/6/2020. https://www.hotelnewsresource.com/article83999.html, 24/6/2020. 'Pacific Relations Conference: Talks on India Likely', *TOI*, 6/1/1945, 8.
22  *SoH*, 191.
23  'Pacific Relations Conference: Talks on India Likely', *TOI*, via Reuters, 6/1/1945, 8.
24  'Jap Emperor to be Topic', *The Sun*, 7/1/1945, 7.
25  Opening statement of V.L. Pandit, Leader of the Indian delegation, *Security in the Pacific: A Preliminary Report of the Ninth Conference of the Institute of Pacific Relations* (New York: International Secretariat of the Institute of Pacific Relations, 1945), 11-12. Cf. 'Post-war Treatment of Japan', *TOI*, 9/1/1945, 5.
26  *Security in the Pacific*, v.
27  'India and New World Order', *TOI*, 11/1/1945, 5; 'European Dependencies in Far East,' 15/1/1945, 5.
28  'Date must be set for Indian Freedom', *The Hindu*, 10/1/1945, in F. No. 61/44–Pol, 93, NAI.
29  'As an Indian sees it', *The Pittsburgh Courier*, 13/1/1945, 7.
30  Carolyn Bell, 'Town Talk', *WaPo* (hereafter WaPo), 16/1/1945, 7.
31  'Mrs. V. Pandit', *TOI*, 17/1/1945, 7.
32  'Pacific Charter for Far East', *TOI*, 23/1/1945, 6.
33  'Mrs. Pandit to Tour U.S.', *TOI*, 17/1/1945, 7.
34  JNtoVLP, 27/2/1945, *BF*, 453–457.
35  https://www.nyc–architecture.com/SCC/SCC026.htm. Last accessed 29/6/2020. The Commodore is today the Hyatt Hotel.
36  https://www.britannica.com/biography/Fiorello-H-La-Guardia, 29/6/2020.
37  *SoH*, 197–198.
38  *SoH*, 192.
39  Walsh to VLP, 11/1/1945, RG2, Papers of Richard J. Walsh, S2: Correspondence, Box 25, Archives of the Pearl S. Buck House, Pearl S. Buck International.
40  *SoH*, 192.
41  Clark Getts promotional brochure, RG2, Papers of Richard J. Walsh, S2: Correspondence, Box 25, Archives of the Pearl S. Buck House, Pearl S. Buck International.
42  https://www.nyc-architecture.com/GON/GON061.htm, 30/6/2020.
43  (Generic) Letter of invitation from Pearl Buck to 'Friend,' 12/1/1945; Program of Indian Independence Day Dinner; and *India Today*, Vol V, No. 10, January 1945, p.1, in Records of the East and West Association, RG5, Box 3, Archives of the Pearl S. Buck House, Pearl S. Buck International.
44  'U.S. Attitude to India', *TOI*, 30/1/1945, 7.
45  'On the Air', *Daily Home News* (New Brunswick), 28/1/1945, 6.
46  Walsh to VLP, 29/1/1945, RG2, Papers of Richard J. Walsh, S2: Correspondence, Box 25, Archives of the Pearl S. Buck House, Pearl S. Buck International. See also: Kumar Ghoshal, 'As an Indian sees it', *Pittsburgh Courier*, 10/2/1945, 7.
47  'U.S. Attitude To India', *TOI*, 30/1/1945, 7. This story claimed that she specifically chastised FDR for his silence. She refuted these claims when she learned of them. 'Mrs. Pandit's Complaints', *TOI*, 26/3/1945, p.1.

48 'Mrs. Pandit at White House', *Hindustan Times*, 29/1/1945, F. No. 61/44–Pol, 100, NAI.
49 'Gives Assurances on India,' *NYT*, 30/1/1945, 8.
50 *The Indian Annual Register*, ed. Nripendra Nath Mitra, Volume II, July–December 1945 (Calcutta: The Annual Register Office, 1945), 74. One report indicates that she also was the guest of honor at a reception organized by the National Woman's Party and that she also addressed 'an "off the record" meeting at which Congressmen were present.' But the dates provided are vague and do not comport with established elements of her itinerary. This likely just has to do with the way the story was recorded and reported. 'Dinner in Honour of Mrs. Pandit', *TOI*, 5/2/1945, 8.
51 *The Indian Annual Register*, 74; 'India has no religious differences,' *The Statesman*, 1/2/1945, 'Visit to the United States of America of Mrs Vijaylakshmi [sic] Pandit', 108; '"Independence Day" in Washington', *TOI*, 2/2/1945, 5.
52 'Indian seeks end of Empire notion', *BAA*, 17/2/1945, 12. Cf. Louis Bromfield, 'Importance of India,' *The Atlanta Constitution*, 22/2/1945, 9.
53 http://thetownhall.org/history, 2/7/2020.
54 'Nehru's Sister to Speak Here', *NYT*, 29/1/1945, 8; 'Events Today', *NYT*, 30/1/1945, 15; '$1,915,309 Donated to Assist Children', *NYT*, 31/1/1945, 23.
55 'Plight of Indian village children', *TOI*, 1/2/1945, 7. VLP was invited to follow up on her remarks by addressing the Harlem chapter of Save the Children a little under a month later. 'Mrs. Pandit, Indian Leader's Sister to Speak at save the Children Meet', *NYAN*, 10/2/1945, A10 (hereafter *NYAN*). 'Vijaya Lakshmi Pandit to Speak Here/2/23', *NYAN*, 24/2/1945, 7A. In that meeting, she spoke again about the famine and added: 'There is no promised land unless one travels the broad road of suffering and sacrifice.' 'I fear the future,' she went on. 'There is so much hate, suspicion, and injustice in the world about us.' 'Indian Children Impoverished: Madame Pandit', *NYAN*, 3/3/1945, 1A.
56 C.K. Cumming, 'Mrs. Pandit Urges Leaders on to Keener Work for Peace', *CSM*, 2/2/1945, 12. See also: 'Hindu-Muslim Objectives', being a report of an interview she gave to *The Washington Star* via Reuters, *TOI*, 7/2/1945, 7; 'Mrs. Pandit's Daughters', being a reproduction of an interview she gave to *Globe*, *TOI*, 7/2/1945, 4.
57 'Dinner in Honour of Mrs. Pandit', *TOI*, 5/2/1945, 8.
58 JNtoVLP, 6/5/1944, *BF*, 403–404.
59 *The Peacemakers*, 37–38. Illustrative of the mark she was making, the popular gossip columnist Elsa Maxwell wrote about the India League and Luce events and described VLP as the 'most distinguished of all women from India . . . [a] great feminine intellectual and eloquent speaker'. Maxwell had introduced VLP at the former event and was pro Indian independence. Still, her reaction was indicative of the delicate line VLP had to walk. Maxwell felt that it was 'bad timing' to 'embarrass an ally' that was fighting so heroically against a larger menace. Elsa Maxwell, 'Party Line', *Pittsburgh Post-Gazette*, 21/2/1945, 9.
60 Handwritten and typed commentary on VLP's activities, from 26 January–15/3/1945. Quotation from assessment of her January 26$^{th}$ Indian Independence Day speech (43), 'Visit to the United States of America of Mrs Vijaylakshmi [sic] Pandit', 35–43.
61 JNtoVLP, 20/3/1945, *BF*, 463–466; Telegram and letter, F. No. 61/44–Pol, 86–88, NAI; 'Visit of Mrs. Pandit to the United States', TNAUK: FO 371/44560 C437369.

62  VLP to V.K. Krishna Menon (hereafter VKKM), 7/2/1945, F. No. 61/44–Pol, 42, NAI. See also correspondence on 86–88. Cf. VLP to VKKM, 4, 8/2/1939, 27 (possibly 24, handwriting unclear)/3/1946. The affection the two have for each other, or at least she for him, is clear. Correspondence with Vijayalakshmi Pandit, VKKM papers, NMML, 1–9. While there were some dangers in her travel, the reality was that the India Committee of the British War Cabinet had engineered these conversations to dissuade her from coming to the country, apparently for fear of the trouble she could cause. 'Visit of Nehru's Sister and Nieces to the U.S.A.', Memorandum by the Secretary of State for India, India Committee, War Cabinet, Secret, 3/1/1945, and other documents in IOR L/I/1/1482, F. No. 8, The British Library.
63  Christopher Muther, 'Don't call her the Ritz', *Boston Globe*, 1/11/2019, https://www.bostonglobe.com/lifestyle/travel/2019/11/01/don-call-her-ritz-she-taj-more-say-hello-newbury-boston-grand-dame-hotels/UfbCkM6aJUd5B7mh4LnkLM/story.html, 3/7/2020.
64  VLP to Richard Walsh, 13/2/1945, RG2, Papers of Richard J. Walsh, S2: Correspondence, Box 25, Archives of the Pearl S. Buck House, Pearl S. Buck International.
65  'Becomes a Countess', *Cincinnati Inquirer*, 17/11/1945, 9; http://findingaids.library.umass.edu/ead/mums815, 6/7/2020. 'Count de Pierrefeu is Killed in France', *Boston Globe*, 24/5/1915, 1.
66  VLP to Richard Walsh, 13/2/1945, and Ananda Coomaraswamy to VLP, 11/2/1945, RG2, Papers of Richard J. Walsh, S2: Correspondence, Box 25, Archives of the Pearl S. Buck House, Pearl S. Buck International.
67  Walsh to VLP, 17/2/1945, RG2, Papers of Richard J. Walsh, S2: Correspondence, Box 25, Archives of the Pearl S. Buck House, Pearl S. Buck International.
68  VLP to Richard Walsh, 13/2/1945, RG2, Papers of Richard J. Walsh, S2: Correspondence, Box 25, Archives of the Pearl S. Buck House, Pearl S. Buck International. For more on Ambassador Phillips, see William Phillips, *Ventures in Diplomacy* (Boston: The Beacon Press, 1953. 1$^{st}$ published 1952). See also 'Mrs. Pandit', in *India Today* Vol. V, No. 11, 2/1945, 3. https://credo.library.umass.edu/view/pageturn/mums312-b106-i207/#page/3/mode/1up, 14/9/2020. VLP had earlier met Madame Chiang in her New York apartment, building on her personal rapport with her and grateful for the opportunity to thank her for her support of her children, the eldest of which the Chinese First Lady had grown particularly attached to. JNtoVLP, 20/3/1945, *BF*, 465.
69  Frances Burns, 'India Offers Britain Aid for Freedom, Says Leader', *The Boston Globe*, 11/2/1945, D1.
70  Alexandra Buxton, 'When "Mistress" meant "Mrs." and "Miss" Meant "Prostitute"', *New Republic*, 12/9/2014, https://newrepublic.com/article/119432/history-female-titles-mistress-miss-mrs-or-ms, 7/7/2020.
71  Frances Burns, 'India Offers Britain Aid for Freedom, Says Leader', The *Boston Globe*, 11/2/1945, D1.
72  'Indian Propaganda in the US: Commons Questions', *TOI*, 23/2/1945, 5; TNAUK: FO 371/44560 C437369, National Archives, UK. The Commons also talked about generosity due British troops in India, with one questioner specifically demanding to know if VLP had been encouraged to extend this courtesy as well. 'Hospitality to Troops in India', 23/2/1945, 5. Some also took offense at her comments about 'rice soldiers', deflecting it by defending the honor

of all Indians in the army. 'Rice Soldiers', *TOI*, 28/2/1945, 6; 'Propaganda', *TOI*, 6/3/1945.
73   Clymer, *Quest for Freedom*, 183–184; TNAUK: FO 371/44560 C437369.
74   'U.S. Broadcast Debate,' *TOI*, 27/2/1945, 5.
75   'Britain and India: A New York Debate', *Scotsman*, 3/3/1945, 6.
76   Summary of *The Peacemakers*, 38–41. Boothby's real claim to fame had been his early assessment of Hitler. He had considered himself a Germanophile and had the opportunity to meet the Fuhrer in the 1930's. But as soon as he made the trip, he sensed menace and grew alarmed. It was he who had convinced Churchill of the danger Germany posed. There was thus irony in the choice of competitor, since VLP and her brother had actually been the earliest and most consistent public figures to warn of rising Fascism in Europe. Regarding her title: Examining the public record, the Boston story is the first major usage I can find of the term 'Madame Pandit.' But this is how she is referred to throughout the Town Hall debate. The immediate coverage thereafter mixes in the title with her full name and with 'Mrs.' But as the press begins to write about events and activities thereafter, it grows increasingly common to simply refer to her as 'Madame Pandit'. For the duration of her international career, and at the peak of her worldwide fame, this was how she was known.
77   Ben Gross, 'Listening In', *Daily News*, 2/3/1945, 24, Ben Gross, *I Looked and I Listened* (New York: Random House, 1954).
78   'American attitude towards the Indian problem: criticism of Mr. Robert Boothby', TNAUK: FO 371/44561 C437369.
79   Walsh to VLP, 2/3/1945, RG2, Papers of Richard J. Walsh, S2: Correspondence, Box 25, Archives of the Pearl S. Buck House, Pearl S. Buck International.
80   VLP to Padmaja Naidu, 22/3/1945; F. No. 61/44–Pol, 57, NAI.
81   Report of the Intelligence Bureau of the Home Department, 5/3/1945, F. No. 61/44–Pol, 53–55, NAI.
82   'US Citizenship for Indians', 5/3/1945, *TOI*, 10.
83   Walsh to VLP, 29/1/1945,
84   'India's Women are called free by Mrs. Pandit', *NYHT*, 7/3/1945, 19.
85   Leonard Lyons, 'The Lyons Den,' *Pittsburgh Post-Gazette*, 9/3/1945, 21; Leonard Lyons, 'Broadway Bulletins', *WaPo*, 10/3/1945, 5.
86   'India can weather Civil Wars: Mrs. Pandit's Views', *TOI*, 13/3/1945, 4.
87   'Social Leader of India to Speak Here', *Pittsburgh Press*, 23/3/1945, 5. 'Dinner for Indian Visitor', *Pittsburgh Post-Gazette*, 3/4/1945, 12.
88   'We Must Break Down Color Barriers, Warns Mme. Pandit', *Pittsburgh Courier*, 14/4/1945, 1.
89   Toki Schalk, 'Madame Pandit, Indian Leader, Found Happiest Hour in Harlem,' *Pittsburgh Courier*, 14/4/1945, 5. Cf. Isabel Wilkerson, *Caste* (New York: Random House, 2020).
90   'Skeptic Mood Seen in India', *Sun*, 5/4/1945, 15.
91   'India's Stand on War Cited', *Sun*, 6/4/1945, 10; 'India Stands for Equality, Leader Tells Baltimoreans', *BAA*, 7/4/1945, 1.
92   'Current Topics: U.S. Immigration Bill', *TOI*, 24/3/1945, 6. 'U.S. and Indian Immigration', *TOI*, 5/4/1945, 4.
93   https://www.saada.org/news/20140702-3609. Last accessed 15/3/2023.
94   Telegrams between VLP and Gandhi, 22 and 26/2/1945, in *The Collected Works of Mahatma Gandhi*, Volume 85, 422. https://www.gandhiashramsevagram.

org/gandhi-literature/mahatma-gandhi-collected-works-volume-85.pdf, 10/7/2020.
95  Telegram from G.D. Birla to VLP, 25/2/1945, and follow up intelligence assessment, F. No. 61/44–Pol, 45–48, NAI.
96  See Bhagavan, *The Peacemakers*
97  Walter White, 'People, Politics, and Places: The Work of the India League', *Chicago Defender*, 24/2/1945, 11.
98  'Instant Freedom Planned at NAACP Colonial Parley', *BAA*, 21/4/1945, 16. For more on Kumar Goshal, see Leonard Gordon, 'Bridging India and America: The Art and Politics of Kumar Goshal', *Amerasia* 15:2 (1989), 66–88. See also correspondence between Kumar Goshal and W.E.B. Du Bois in February–March 1945. https://credo.library.umass.edu/search?q=goshal+du+bois, 14/9/2020. The meeting's resolution can be found here: https://credo.library.umass.edu/view/pageturn/mums312-b107-i141/#page/1/mode/1up.
99  'Walter White will return Home Soon', *Atlanta Daily World*, 5/4/1945, p.1.
100 Jonathan Rosenberg, *How Far the Promised* Land (Princeton: Princeton University Press, 2006), 161. Cf. Brenda Plummer, *Rising Wind: Black Americans and U.S. Foreign Affairs* (Chapel Hill: University of North Carolina Press, 1996).
101 Copy of a Secret Letter from India Office, Whitehall, London, to Sir Olaf Caroe, Secy, E.A. Department, New Delhi, 30/3/1945, in F. No. 61/44–Pol, 112–113, NAI.
102 *The Peacemakers*, 49–50.
103 https://en.wikipedia.org/wiki/Golden_Gate_Bridge, 29/3/2023.
104 'India Question & San Francisco', *TOI*, 17/4/1945, 5.
105 '"Foreign Ministers" Talks in Washington', *TOI*, 24/4/1945, 5.
106 'India not Willing Participant in War: Mrs. V. Pandit's Criticism', *TOI*, 25/4/1945, 5.
107 Pamphlets in VKKM papers, Sub file 118, NMML, 1–31.
108 K.P.S. Menon explains the heckler episode and provides other insights into the San Francisco conference in his memoir. K.P.S. Menon, *Many Worlds* (London: Oxford University Press, 1965), 216–217. William Moore, 'Challenger: Indian Woman Twists the Tale of the British Lion', *CDT*, 27/4/1945, 6; Margaret Parton, 'India Delegates Challenged by Nehru's Sister', *NYHT*, 27/4/1945, 13; Helen Rich, 'Unofficial First Lady of India in Spotlight', *The Philadelphia Inquirer*, 28/4/1945, 5; 'British Policy in India', *TOI*, 28/4/1945, 9. See also Irene West, 'San Franciscans Reveal Concern over Conference', *BAA*, 5/5/1945, 15; P.L. Prattis, 'Mme. Pandit makes Stirring Plea for Freedom of India at San Francisco', *The Pittsburgh Courier*, 5/5/1945, 5. Cf. Raphaëlle Khan, 'India as a Norm Claimer', in Mischa Hansel et. al., *Theorizing Indian Foreign Policy* (New York: Routledge, 2017), 69–90. For more on the heckling episode and the broader British evaluation of VLP's U.S. activities, see: 'Hon. Mrs. Vijayalakshmi Pandit, Minister of Public Health and Local Self-Government of U.P.', IOR L/I/1/1482, F. No. 8, The British Library.
109 https://digitalcollections.hoover.org/objects/41307, 14/9/2020. For some views inside the old Scottish Rite building, see: https://www.sfgate.com/realestate/article/Regency-Ballroom-history-freemasons-6790950.php#photo-9319091, 14/9/2020. Cf. http://freemasonsfordummies.blogspot.com/2016/02/the-old-san-francisco-scottish-rite.html.
110 'Leaders speak for Colored Peoples', *Atlanta Daily* World, 3/5/1945, 1.

111 William Moore, 'Two Spokesmen Denounce Reds and British; Indian asks U.S. Aid', *CDT*, 29/4/1945, 10.
112 A.T. Steele, 'India Congress Spokesman Stir San Francisco', *NYHT*, 29/4/1945, 32.
113 'India Honored at San Francisco', *TOI*, 3/5/1945, 5.
114 William Moore, 'Report India Settlement is Growing Near', *CDT*, 3/5/1945, 10.
115 'Memorandum submitted by Vijaya Lakshmi Pandit', 2/5/1945, Pandit papers, II Inst., Subject File I, 9–10. Cf. William Moore, 'India Self-Rule Issue Pressed by Mrs. Pandit', *CDT*, 5/5/1945, 8.
116 'Declare India Independent at Once', *TOI*, 7/5/1945, 6; 'Asks Independence of India at Once', *GandM*, 5/5/1945, 3.
117 'Statement by Mrs. Vijaya Lakshmi Pandit', 10/5/1945, Pandit papers, II Inst., Subject File I, 12. Cf. 'Full Dominion Status for India', *TOI*, 12/5/1945, 7. See also 'Madame Pandit: Raps Eden's India Alibi', *Pittsburgh* Courier, 19/5/1945, 12. J.J. Singh and Anup Singh were both in Eden's audience and pressed him on his positions on India. For more on Bose and the INA, see Yasmin Khan, *India at War* (Oxford: Oxford University Press, 2015).
118 Alger Hiss to VLP, 11/5/1945, Pandit papers, II Inst., Subject File I, 13.
119 'Statement by Mrs. Vijaya Lakshmi Pandit', 20/5/1945, Pandit papers, II Inst., Subject File I, 17.
120 '"One Woman" Campaign by Mrs. Pandit"', via Serge Fliegers, *Reuters*, *TOI*, 14/5/1945, 7.
121 VLP Interview with Mark Tully, 'The Time of My Life', Broadcast 11/7/1969, BBC, The British Library Recording Room.
122 Menon, *Many Worlds*, 216.
123 '"One Woman" Campaign by Mrs. Pandit"', via Serge Fliegers, *TOI*, 14/5/1945, 7. VLP was staying in the home of Mrs. Dorothy Mills, who offered up her space saying that she was a fan of Gandhi and Nehru. Mills' husband Ogden had been Secretary of the Treasury under President Hoover. *SoH*, 196.
124 'California invites Mrs. Pandit', *TOI*, 14/5/1945, 7.
125 'Charge Halifax Effort to "Gag" Indian's Speech', *CDT*, 15/5/1945, 2.
126 'Colonies in Way of World Peace', *Times of* India, 16/5/1945, 7.
127 'Charge Halifax Effort to "Gag" Indian's Speech', *CDT*, 15/5/1945, 2.
128 'Anglo-American Opposition to Soviet "Independence" Plan', 17/5/1945, 9.
129 Ibid. See also: 'Irene Rochester to Governor Earl Warren', 26/5/1945, PP(II)I, 19.
130 P.L. Prattie, 'Conference Confetti', *Pittsburgh Courier*, 26/5/1945, 12. The hotel referenced in this story is the Mark Hopkins. The house which is core of the famous hotel is the Mark and Mary Hopkins House. For more on Mary Farquharson, see: http://web.leg.wa.gov/WomenInTheLegislature/Members/FarquharsonM.htm. Cf. *The Voice of India*, June 1945, 153.
131 *The Voice of India*, June 1945, 149.
132 'Mrs. Pandit returns to San Francisco', *TOI*, 19/5/1945, 9.
133 'Mrs. Pandit's Plea to Labour', *TOI*, 19/5/1945, 6.
134 'Future of Dependent & Colonial Nations', *TOI*, 17/5/1945, 1. The processional took place on May 13, the day before she addressed the California legislature. See 'Mrs. Pandit at San Francisco', *The Voice of India*, Volume I, No. 10, June 1945, 152, https://www.saada.org/item/20130123-1235, 13/10/2020.
135 'Problem of Pacific Strategic Islands', *TOI*, 19/5/1945, 9.
136 As cited in *The Peacemakers*, 58.

137 'Excerpts from speeches delivered at the Scottish Rite Auditorium Meeting for Mrs. Vijaya Lakshmi Pandit, held under the auspices of the Naional [sic] Committee for India's Freedom, Washington, D.C.', 28/5/1945, Pandit papers, II Inst., Subject File I, 20. See also 'Shackled India called Bar to Lasting Peace', 29/5/1945, *CDT*, 6.
138 Frida Huge to VLP, 29/5/1945, Pandit papers, II Inst., Subject File I, 21.
139 J.D.J. (from Poona), 'Reader's Views: Freedom from Fear', *TOI*, 29/5/1945, 4.
140 J.D. Jenkins (from Poona), 'India and the U.S.A.', *The Spectator* Vol 174 (6101), 1/6/1945, 501. This piece also talks of 'freedom from fear'. It's clear that this is the same writer as the person who wrote to *TOI*.
141 Ramprakash Roy (Bombay), 'Readers' Views: Mrs. Pandit,' *TOI*, 5/6/1945, 4.
142 *The Voice of India*, June 1945, 155. More details of her remarks may be found at 'Formation of World Organization', *TOI*, 20/6/1945, 5.
143 'New Round Table Conference', *TOI*, 18/6/1945, 7; 'Look Ahead not Back', *TOI*, 18/6/1945, 7.
144 'Next meeting of A.-I.C.C.', *TOI* 19/7/1945, 5.
145 JNtoVLP, 10/4/1945, *BF*, 469.
146 JNtoVLP, 25/4/1945, *BF*, 473. Generally, see letters 20 March–24 July, 463–491.
147 'Peace Parley Called Spur to War in the East', 5/6/1945, 3.
148 E. Washington Rhodes, 'Under the Microscope', *Philadelphia Tribune*, 28/7/1945, 4.
149 'Mrs. Pandit in Hospital', *TOI*, via Reuters, 13/8/1945, 6; 'Mrs. Pandit Improving', *TOI*, 18/8/1945, 5.
150 Email, Nayantara Sahgal to Manu Bhagavan, 21/10/2020. JNtoVLP, 24/7/1945, *BF*, 491. The siblings had been corresponding and cabling on this matter for some time previous. Cf. 'Mrs. Vijayalaxmi Pandit,' *The Times of* India, 26/7/1945, 4.
151 'Views of Indians in the US', *TOI*, via Reuters, 6/8/1945, 8.
152 Mildred Gutterson, 'What People Talk About: Labor and India', *Boston Globe*, 13/8/1945, 10.
153 'Indian Women Join Council', *BAA* 09/6/1945, p.12. Cf. 'Mrs. Bethune Launches $55,000 Campaign and Discusses World Conference at Meeting,' *The Pittsburgh Courier*, 9/6/1945, 9. According to one account, Bethune and VLP had a 'connection' and grew to be 'close friends.' Ashley Robertson, *Mary Mcleod Bethune in Florida* (Charleston, SC: The History Press, 2015), 44–46.
154 'Society, Literary Crowd Gathers to Discuss Eslande Robeson's New Book', *NYAN*, 18/8/1945, 8.
155 'Mrs. V. Pandit for India', *TOI*, 26/9/1945, 4. See also 'Mrs. Pandit on New Plan,' 24/9/1945, 4. Cf. 'Mrs. Pandit's Plans in U.S.', 8/10/1945, 11.
156 Genevieve Reynolds, 'There's no 'Battle of the Sexes', in India, Mrs. Pandit Declares,' *WaPo*, S2.
157 'Letter to the Editor: Women by a Woman', *TOI*, 4/9/1945, 4.
158 'Are Women Key', *SCMP*, 10/10/1945, 3.
159 'Town Hall Calls Current Issues Popular Topics', *NYHT*, 7/10/1945, A7.
160 'Debate on India in U.S.', *TOI*, 1/11/1945, 9.
161 'NCNW Convene in Annual Workshop Discussing Peace', *NYAN*, 13/10/1945, 10.
162 Edelle Webster, 'Capital Chatter', *The Baltimore Afro American*, 10/11/1945, 11.
163 'Mme. Pandit warns U.S. of Disunity Dangers', *Chicago Defender*, 10/11/1945, 10.

164 'Negro Women call Internat'l Meet for 1946', *Cleveland Call and Post*, 10/11/1945, 10b.
165 'Mrs. Pandit greets Mr. Truman', *TOI*, 2/11/1945, 6. See also Harry Truman Papers, Sub file-1, NMML.
166 'Mrs Pandit of India will talk today in Morgan Park High', *CDT*, 4/11/1945, SW3; 'Success of World Organization', *TOI*, 8/11/1945, 3; 'India's Champion', *SCMP*, 16/11/1945, 4; 'Weary of Promises: Indian Advocate Assails British Labour', *SCMP*, 17/11/1945, 2; 'Groups to Hold Joint Meeting in Kenilworth,' *CDT*, 2/12/1945, n3.
167 'Mrs. Pandit urges Change in Policy', *TOI*, 26/1/1945, 5; 'Independence for India before 1947', *TOI*, 28/1/1945, 8.
168 'Independence for India before 1947', *TOI*, 28/1/1945, 8; 'American Interest in India's Case: Mrs. Pandit's View', *TOI*, 29/1/1945, 5.
169 'Mrs V. Pandit: Rousing Reception in Allahabad', 30/1/1946, 5. For another version of the material in this chapter, and a general introduction to VLP's life and views, see R.L. Khipple, *The Woman Who Swayed America: Vijaya Lakshmi Pandit* (Lahore: Lion Press, 1946). Khipple's aim is to 'eulogise' VLP in his book, in his words (vii).

## Chapter 10: White Teeth

1 'Mrs. Vijayalaxmi Pandit', *TOI*, 6/2/1946, 7.
2 'Good-will Mission to India: M.P.'s to see ordinary life of people,' *Scotsman*, 3/1/1946, 5; 'M.P. Delegation Meets Pandit Nehru', *TOI*, 1/2/1946, 3; 'Sincerity of M.P. Delegation', *TOI*, 2/2/1946, 5.
3 'Mr. R.M. Deshmukh leaves for Durban', *TOI*, 31/1/1946, 5; 'Solution of Indian Problem in Natal', *TOI*, 11/2/1946, 4.
4 George Jones, 'Views on America are Issue in India', 6/2/1946, 16.
5 'Indian Provincial Elections', *TMG*, 9/2/1946, 6.
6 'Major Powers' Attitude', *TOI*, 12/2/1946, 5. Ironically underscoring her point, the *Austin Statesman* referred to her as 'Mrs. Pandit Nehru, wife of Indian leader,' when quoting her comments. 'So They Say,' *The Austin Statesman*, 1/3/1946, 4.
7 'Violence Condemned', *TOI*, 28/2/1946, 6; George Jones, 'Violent Methods are Issue in India', *NYT*, 9/3/1946, 7.
8 'Three British Cabinet Heads Going to India', *NYHT*, 20/2/1946, 1.
9 'Quaker Prayer Meeting', *TOI*, 8/4/1946, 5.
10 'Mrs. Pandit urges change in Policy', *TOI*, 26/1/1946, 5.
11 'Invitation Declined', *TOI*, 20/7/1946, 6.
12 'U.P. Ministry Formed', *TOI*, 1/4/1946, 8. When taking the oath of office, she flubbed her lines, possibly deliberately, giving the appearance of resistance to a loyalty pledge to the British monarch. See Sir F. Wylie (United Provinces) to Field Marshal Viscount Wavell (Extract), L/P&J/5/275: ff 142–3, 151–2, Secret, No. U.P.-19, 30/4/1946, in Nicholas Mansergh, ed., *The Transfer of Power, 1942–1947*, Vol. VII, 391–392.
13 'Plague Havoc in U.P.', *TOI*, 24/4/1946, 5.
14 'U.P. Speaker', *TOI*, 29/4/1946, 10.
15 VLP to Nayantara Pandit, 6/6/1946, VLP to Sahgal letters 1944–1951, Nayantara Sahgal papers, Boston University. *PandCC*, 187.

16 'National Planning Essential', *TOI*, 10/7/1946, 5. The Committee criticized the government's moves to eliminate their planning department in anticipation of what was by then perceived to be an imminent transfer of power. The Committee passed a resolution on the importance of planning a country like India and asserted that such work needed to go on continually to help raise the standard of living for all people.
17 'Famine Mission from America', *TOI*, 25/6/1946, 5; Dorothy Dunbar Bromley, 'Visit to India Gives Writer Insight into Nation's Hopes', *NYHT*, 11/8/1946, A5.
18 'U.P. Nominees', *TOI*, 17/7/1946, 9; 'Sir J.P. Srivastava Elected from U.P.', *TOI*, 23/7/1946, 7.
19 VLP to Nayantara Pandit (hereafter VLPtoTara), 6/6/1946, Nayantara Sahgal papers.
20 'Miss C. Pandit for India', *TOI*, 1/5/1946, 8; 'Miss Pandit', *TOI*, 2/5/1946, 10.
21 VLPtoTara, 6/6/1946, Sahgal papers. George P. Thomson, 'Charles Galton Darwin: 1887–1962', *Biographical Memoirs of Members of the Royal Society*, November 1963 (Vol. 9), 69–85.
22 'Mrs. V. Pandit', *TOI*, 13/7/1946, 6.
23 'S. African Asiatic Bill Now Law', *TOI*, 4/6/1946, 1.
24 'Recall of High Commissioner in S. Africa', *TOI*, 12/6/1946, 1; 'Indian Leaders Jailed in S.A.', *BAA*, 13/7/1946, 20.
25 'Support to Union Indians', *TOI*, 10/4/1946, 7. 'Miss Pandit', *TOI*, 2/5/1946, 10.
26 'India Asks UNO Action on S. Africa', *Atlanta Constitution*, 24/6/1946, 1.
27 'India to Carry Plaint Against S. Africa to U.N.', *CDT*, 31/8/1946, 5.
28 The material in this section is a synopsis of *SoH*, 204–206. See also, 'Mrs. Pandit', *TOI*, 2/9/1946, 7. 'Mr. Gandhi's Visitors,' *TOI*, 2/9/1946, 7; 'To Present India's Case', *NYT*, 2/9/1946, 2. For an analysis of VLP's self-representation through her autobiography, in the context of other women like Kamaladevi Chattopadhyay, see Annie Devenish, 'Performing the Political Self', in Katie Barclay and Sarah Richardson, eds., *Performing the Self* (London: Routledge, 2015), 104–118.
29 In *SoH*, 207, VLP says that she was stranded in Casablanca, but news reports from the time say Algiers. Since her memoir was written many years later, I've gone with the contemporary record. One press account quotes VLP as saying of her delayed travels that 'on arrival at Cairo in an Indian air service plane, which had for the first time left India with an Indian crew, we had a delay and then two and half hours' delay at Algiers owing to maintenance trouble. We had a further delay of several hours at Madrid due to engine trouble'. This was all followed by the delay in Shannon caused by the strike. 'India-South Africa Dispute', *TOI*, 23/10/1946, 1. On Hampshire House, see https://www.elliman.com/insider/hampshire-house-penthouse/, 7/12/2020. 'Plane Trouble Delays India's U.N. Delegation', *NYHT*, 20/10/1946, 30. 'TWA Planes Halt in U.S. Overseas as Pilots Strike', *NYT*, 22/10/1946, 1. 'UN Groups Polish Ideas for Opening', *Austin Statesmen*, 22/10/1946, 1. 'Woman Flies in at Head of India U.N. Delegation', *NYHT*, 23/10/1946, 2. Frank Adams, 'Ticker-Tape War Tests U.N. Today', *NYT*, 23/10/1946, 2.
30 Percy Wood, 'Hindu, Moslem Groups Gather for Vital Talks', *Chicago Daily Tribune*, 22/9/1946, 11. K.P.S. Menon by this point had taken a disliking to Krishna Menon. Menon, *Many Worlds*, 220–222. Cf. Entry for 25/10/1946, Diary-29, Menon papers, NMML, 148. VKKM, however, appears to have been

included in the delegation at the personal behest of VLP herself. VKKM to VLP, 8/10/1946, VKKM papers, Sub-file 250, NMML, 17.
31  'Indian Delegates Leave for U.S.', *TOI*, 14/10/1946, 1. K.P.S. Menon had met with VLP shortly after she had been assigned to handle the South Africa case, and while he had thought her 'charming', he had wondered to himself how well she comprehended the issues involved. By the time she departed India, it was clear that she had done her homework. Entry for 5/9/1946, Diary-29, K.P.S. Menon papers, NMML, 123.
32  Frank Adams, 'Ticker-Tape War Tests U.N. Today', *NYT*, 23/10/1946, 2.
33  'Molotov, Byrnes Share Assembly's Spotlight', *GandM*, 24/10/1946, 29.
34  'Four Women Sit as Delegates at U.N. Assembly', *NYHT*, 24/10/1946, 6.
35  'Fears of War not Justified, Truman Tells U.N. Assembly', *Los Angeles Times*, 24/10/1946, 1. '"Good Speech", Most of World Delegates Agree', *Los Angeles Times*, 24/10/1946, 4. 'Truman Speech Fails to Impress India's Delegate', *NYHT*, 24/10/1946, 5.
36  The material in this section is a summary of *PandCC*, 187–198.
37  Peter Kihss, 'Small Nations Urge End of Veto, Scold Big U.N. Powers for Rivalry', *NYHT*, 25/10/1946, p.1.
38  *The Peacemakers*, 75–76.
39  Peter Kihss, 'Small Nations Urge End of Veto, Scold Big U.N. Powers for Rivalry', *NYHT*, 25/10/1946, p.1; Pandit Papers, II Inst., Subject File II, *Confidential Memorandum*, 99, 106, NMML; Ministry of External Affairs, India, no. 6(22)-CC/46, Copy of Cable, Jawaharlal Nehru Comrel New Delhi, 83, NAI; *The Peacemakers*, 75–76.
40  'Distinction', *The Irish Times*, 1/11/1946, 6.
41  VLP, speech to General Assembly of the United Nations, full text, Pandit Papers, Ist Inst, Speeches/Writings by Her, F. No. 4, NMML.
42  Joseph Hearst, 'U.N. Delegates Applaud Attack on Imperialism', *CDT*, 26/10/1946, 3. 'Colonial Freedom is Urged by India: The United Nations General Assembly hears from the Argentine Delegate', *NYT*, 26/10/1946, 3. 'Good Reception in Press', *TOI*, 28/10/1946, 8. 'Woman Delegate Draws Applause', *CSM*, 31/10/1946, 7. For additional analysis contextualizing India's actions, see Carol Anderson, *Bourgeois Radicals* (New York: Cambridge University Press, 2015), esp 66–132. See also Ria Kapoor, *Making Refugees in India* (Oxford: Oxford University Press, 2022), esp 76–77. And Susan Pennybacker, '"Fire by Night, Cloud by Day": Exile and Refuge in Postwar London', *The Journal of British Studies* 59(1),/1/2020, 1–31. Cf. Rahila Gupta, 'Trustee of the Future: Vijaya Lakshmi Pandit', https://mediadiversified.org/2016/10/29/trustee-of-the-future-vijaya-lakshmi-pandit/, 11/3/2023.
43  Donna Lee-Frieze, ed., *Totally Unofficial: The Autobiography of Raphael Lemkin* (New Haven: Yale University Press, 2013), 120–123.
44  *Yearbook of the United Nations*, 1946–1947 (New York: Department of Public Information, 1947), 'The General Assembly', 255–256. UN documents: A/PV.47 (November 9 plenary meeting), A/C.6/SR. 22, 23, 24, and 32 (Sixth Committee meetings), A/PV.55 (December 11 plenary meeting). I'm grateful to Maricela Martinez at Dag Hammarskjöld Library for her assistance. PV47 indicates that the matter was referred to the Second Committee (Economic and Financial) but this appears a typographical error and is contradicted by the Yearbook and by

the Sixth Committee records. If the second committee considered it, it sent it right along to the Sixth Committee.
45  'Mrs. Pandit & Marshal Smuts Present Rival Cases', *TOI*, 23/11/1946, 8. '8 Lands Back India on African Issues', *NYT*, 22/11/1946, 17.
46  VLP speech before the Joint Committee, 26/11/1946, 74-86, PP(II)II.
47  VLP speech before the Joint Committee, 26/27 November 1946, Press Information Bureau, Government of India, Ministry of External Affairs, D-2915-CC/46, 11, NAI. This is the same speech as appears in the NMML file, but this adds a small description of the reception that VLP received after her remarks. 'South African Delegate Flayed by Mrs. Pandit', *Atlanta Daily World*, 8/12/1946, 1.
48  Homer Metz, 'Little Nations Wait Big-Power Declarations; Molotov, Smuts & Co.: What are they like?,' *CSM*, 29/10/1946, 9.
49  'People in the News', *The China Weekly Review*, 16/11/1946, 341.
50  'Only Woman Delegate at UN Heard in Protest Meeting', *New Journal and Guide*, 23/11/1946, A7. 'African Plan Assailed', *NYT*, 4.
51  *SoH*, 217.
52  'Indian Delegate Speaks', *NYT*, 18/11/1946, 3.
53  *SoH*, 215–216. *PandCC*, 197–198.
54  'Schools will Honor U.N.', *NYT*, 26/11/1946, 14.
55  *PandCC*, 203.
56  Ministry of External Affairs, India, no. 6(22)-CC/46, Telegrams, some secret, between VLP and team and Jawaharlal Nehru, 28–30 November 1946, 2/3 December, 120–124, 148. December telegram listed as 'Secret 12548, D3059-CC/46', no formal page number provided, NAI. See also: 'India Gains UN Backing', *Pittsburgh Courier*, 30/11/1946, 1. 'Moral Victory Won by India on African Issue,' *NYHT*, 1/12/1946, 26. 'India Wins Point on South Africa,' *NYT*, 1/12/1946, 5. 'Success for India,' *TOI*, 3/12/1946, 6. VLP magnanimously walked over and shook Smuts' hands after the vote was taken.
57  'Crowd Hears Indian Leader at New York Mass Meeting', *New Journal and Guide*, 4/1/1947, 11.
58  'Mrs. Pandit Talks at Harlem Meeting', *NYHT*, 2/12/1946, 18. 'Madam Pandit Tells Meet Way to Peace', *NYAN*, 7/12/1946, 22. 'The Social Swirl', *NYAN*, 7/12/1946, 8.
59  'U.N. Night Session like Opera Scene', *NYT*, 8/12/1946, 8.
60  Alistair Cooke, 'Mrs. Pandit's Clash with Gen. Smuts', *TMG*, 9/12/1946, 6. 'U.N. Assembly Hears Debate on Africa Dispute', *NYHT*, 8/12/1946, 29.
61  Alistair Cooke, 'Mrs. Pandit's Clash with Gen. Smuts', *TMG*, 9/12/1946, 6.
62  Full text of Mrs. Pandit's speech, in 'Press Information Bureau, Government of India: Red Letter Day for India', Ministry of External Affairs, PS 833(50) D3408cc, 3–7 of the file, contained within a larger file on India and South Africa, 248–252, NAI.
63  A.M. Rosenthal, 'Smuts Fights Test on Indians' Issue', *NYT*, 8/12/1946, 19. 'U.N. Assembly Hears Debate on Africa Dispute', *NYHT*, 8/12/1946, 29. 'Big Ovation for Mrs. Pandit', *TOI*, 9/12/1946, p.1. K.P.S. Menon adds: 'While delivering her final speech, Mrs. Pandit developed a twitch in the eye, and many people thought she was in tears.' Menon, *Many Worlds*, 220.
64  *PandCC*, 204.
65  *New York Daily News*, 9/12/1946, 315.

66 Henry S. Hayward, 'U.N. to Consider India's So. Africa Plea', *CSM*, 9/12/1946, 6. *SoH*, 210.
67 VLP interview with Mark Tully, The Time of my Life', BBC, 11/7/1969.
68 'India Scores over South Africa', *TOI*, 10/12/1946, 1. For additional analysis and perspective on VLP and the South Africa question, see Khushi Singh Rathore, 'Excavating Hidden Histories', in Rebecca Adami and Dan Plesch, eds., *Women and the UN* (New York: Routledge, 2022), DOI: 10.4324/9781003036708-3. And Alexander Davis, *India and the Anglosphere* (New York, Routledge, 2019).
69 G.H. Archambault, 'U.N. Voted Weighed by South Africans', *NYT*, 10/12/1946, 3.
70 This conversation between VLP and Smuts is recounted in *SoH*, 211, and *PandCC*, 202–203, and in an interview with Mark Tully on the BBC, 'The Time of My Life', aired 11/7/1969. In her memoir, VLP incorrectly claims that this conversation takes place after the vote. Sahgal says in her memoir that it took place after the debate but before Smuts departed by plane. VLP specifies in her interview with Tully that it took place the night before the vote, when both she and he had delivered their final remarks.
71 Mark Tully interviewed VLP for 'The Time of My Life', a programme that featured celebrities talking about the most defining moments of their career. The interview, which aired on 11/7/1969, was wide ranging and covered many aspects of her life. But she particularly highlighted her role at the San Francisco conference and her great debate with Smuts, choosing the latter as 'the time of her life', the singular moment of her career. The show required such she make one such selection.
72 For analysis of VLP's self-representation, and the performative aspects of her work, see Julie Laut, 'India at the United Nations: A Post-colonial Nation-State on the Global Stage, 1945–1955', Ph.D. dissertation (University of Illinois at Urbana-Champaign, 2016).
73 A.M. Wendell Malliet, 'Little Nations Deal Blow to Ambition of Gen. Smuts', *NYAN*, 14/12/1946, 1. Cf. Vinay Lal, 'Gandhi, "The Coloured Races", and the Future of Satyagraha: The View from the African American Press', *Social Change* 51(1), https://journals.sagepub.com/doi/10.1177/0049085721991573, 11/3/2023.
74 'One for 'Our Side,' *NYAN*, 14/12/1946, 10. Cf. Annie Devenish, *Debating Women's Citizenship in India* (Delhi: Bloomsbury, 2019), esp. 227–250.
75 Lawrence Burr, 'Madam Pandit Leads Fight for Minorities', *The Atlanta Daily World*, 21/12/1946, 1.
76 W.E.B. Du Bois, 'The Winds of Time', *The Chicago Defender*, 18/1/1947, 15. VLP granted the *Baltimore Afro-American* (hereafter *BAA*) three exclusive interviews while she was in New York, meeting with reporters in her hotel suite, in the limousine ride to her meetings, and at Lake Success, all on the condition that they be published after she returned to India. They were released in mid-February. In them, she discussed the possibility of African Americans using nonviolence to fight for their own freedom. She seemed skeptical, framing the method as something that fit the Indian ethos and had a unique effect on the British conscience. But then she added that they had a Gandhi who had spurred everyone to action. '[A]s yet you have no Gandhi,' she added, suddenly opening the door to the future possibility. The interview also touched on a range of other topics, including her rejection of the caste system (though she demurred when asked about her daughter's marriage choices). Michael Carter, 'Head of Indian Delegation to UN is Colored Too,' *BAA*, 15/2/1947, M_9.

NOTES 481

77  'People of 10 Nations Honor Pro-Freedom UNO Delegates', *Chicago Defender*, 21/12/1946, 4.
78  'Mrs. Pandit Flying Home', *NYT*, 11/12/1946, 16.
79  Martin Wright, 'Indian Delegates' Success at U.N. Assembly', *Scotsman*, 19/12/1946, 4.
80  'Bombay "At Home"', *TOI*, 19/12/1946, 7.
81  Adelaide Kerr, 'Women Score in First Year of United Nations Program', *Austin Statesman*, via the AP, 27/12/1946, 3. See also 'Women's Achievements for 1946 are Brilliant', *Pittsburgh Courier*, 4/1/1947, 8.
82  'Marian Anderson Heads NCNW'47 Honor Roll; Ingrid Bergman, Mme. Pandit Among Twelve Named', *Pittsburgh Courier*, 8/2/1947, 9. 'Defender Washington Bureau Head 12 Others on NCNW Honor Roll', *The Chicago Defender*, 8/2/1947, 3.
83  Richard Newcomb, 'Mrs. Pandit Leaves for India', *TOI*, 12/12/1946, 1.

## Chapter 11: Love of Worker Bees

1  'India Debate in Lords', *TOI*, 14/12/1946, 5. 'Be Quiet About India, Plea to Mr. Churchill', 13/12/1946, 17. The broader material from this section comes from VLPtoTara, 12/12/1946, Sahgal papers, Boston University (SPBU).
2  'Exchange of Diplomatic Missions Between India and the USSR/Appointment of Mrs. Vijay [sic] Lakshmi Pandit as Ambassador for India in Russia', F. No. 20(4)-EUR/47, Ministry of External Affairs and Commonwealth Relations, Secret (Downgraded), 1947, NAI, summary of documents on 1–48. Telegram from VLPtoJN, 8/9 December 1946, 135.
3  Constituent Assembly of India Debates, 17/12/1946, Volume I, https://www.constitutionofindia.net/constitution_assembly_debates/volume/1/1946-12-17, 12/1/2021. Nan arrived in Delhi via Karachi. While she was still en route, a mysterious kerfuffle arose when papers asserted that she claimed while in Karachi that she had been shadowed in United States because of warm relations with the Soviet delegation. 'Mrs. Pandit Complains', *NYT*, 16/12/1946, 5. This story is illustrative of the general coverage, which received widespread attention. 'That statement is something I never said and never implied,' she said in a formal denial when learned of the stories the next day. 'There was nothing in my Karachi speech to convey that impression.' 'Hindu UNO Delegate Denies Reported Charge', *The Atlanta Constitution*, via the AP, 18/12/1946, 21.
4  'Mrs. V. Pandit in Delhi', *TOI*, 16/12/1946, 7. See also 'Hindu-Moslem Differences', *Scotsman*, 28/12/1946, 4.
5  'India's Success at U.N.', *TOI*, 25/12/1946, 5.
6  'Mrs. Pandit's Views', *TOI*, 27/12/1946, 4. She had stayed in Delhi for a week or so after her arrival before traveling to Lucknow for the first time. She met up with friends and had discussions about family thereafter.
7  VLP's speech before the Constituent Assembly of India, CAD, 20/1/1947. https://www.constitutionofindia.net/constitution_assembly_debates/volume/2/1947-01-20, 15/2/2021. This speech was broadcast on All India Radio and Prasar Bharati Central Archives has made a portion of the recording public. While the speaker on the audio has certain intonations and tones that sound like VLP, the accent is slightly different. I was unable to confirm if the speaker in the recording is VLP or is of someone reading parts of the speech that VLP delivered

in the Constituent Assembly. VLP making the speech in the Assembly is not in question, but Nayantara Sahgal does not believe that the woman on AIR is her mother (correspondence between Sahgal and Bhagavan, 22–29 November 2020). I am grateful to Rohit De for bringing the recording to my attention and for several helpful conversations on the matter. Thinking about this late in her life, VLP felt that she had not 'contributed anything particularly remarkable' to the Constituent Assembly, save for this speech and perhaps a few others. Vijaya Lakshmi Pandit, 'We Nehrus', *The Illustrated Weekly of India*, 17/4/1988, 15.

8 'Text of Dulles Address on Foreign Policy to National Publishers Association', *NYHT*, 18/1/1947, p.4.
9 'No Alignment with Power Grouping', *TOI*, 21/1/1947.
10 'Dulles Draw Reply from Nehru and Mrs. Pandit', *NYHT*, 23/1/1947, 6A. Emmanuel Celler quoted VLP and Nehru on the floor of the US House of Representatives in formally protesting Dulles' claims as well. '"No Communist Grip on India"', *TOI*, 23/1/1947, 5.
11 Mosley, *Dulles*, 33–34. See also Chapter 1.
12 'Miss Nehru Tells of Women's Fight,' *NYHT*, 14/1/1947, 16A
13 Marian F. Downer, 'Speaker of Famed India Leader Speaks to Chicago Audiences', *Chicago Defender*, 15/2/1947, 17. The 'famed leader' in the headline was a reference to VLP, not Nehru. In text, the phrase 'had been looked' was used in error; I have corrected to 'had been looking' here.
14 'Stronger U.N. Held Only Key to Peace', *NYT*, 13/3/1947, 9.
15 Letters from VLP to Rita Pandit, 11/1/1947 and 21/3/1947, SPBU. While VLP downplayed her sister's actions, the false stories planted by Betty generated a whisper campaign about VLP's profligate spending that would endure for the rest of her career. There was, though, a measure of truth to the claims. VLP had 'a taste for luxury and an appreciation for beauty and comfort ingrained in her' from her early childhood, Nayantara later wrote. These impulses VLP sublimated to the larger anti-colonial cause and Gandhi's directions. But Ranjit's death and the losses that followed depressed her. She finally felt liberated once she got to the United States and started earning money on her own for the first time. Free in a new and profound sense, she doted on her daughters every chance she had, ordering up out-of-season strawberries and early violets every so often to sweeten and brighten their day as well as hers. She rearranged every hotel she stayed in on the premise that it was her home if she was in it, more so since she had none that she could actually call her own. And she bought her daughters fine things, like cashmere sweaters, 'lacy lingerie', and Russeks beaver fur coats. Her daughters would comment good naturedly about her 'extravagance'. Nayantara Sahgal, *From Fear Set Free* (New York: Norton, 1962/63), 15–18.
16 VLP to Rita Pandit, 11/1/1947 and 21/3/1947, SPBU.
17 VLP to Rita Pandit, 21/3/1947 and 5/5/1947, SPBU.
18 VLP to Rita Pandit, 21/3/1947 and 5/5/1947, SPBU.
19 VLPtoTara, 24/2/1947, SPBU. VLP writes in the letter that Chandralekha had an opportunity to visit Madame Chiang in China and was excited to make the trip. But Nayantara Sahgal tells me that the trip 'didn't come off.' Email from Nayantara Sahgal to me, 24/2/2021. I am grateful to Ambassador Nirupama Rao, in consultation with the family of K.P.S. Menon, and to Arunabh Ghosh and Tansen Sen for their assistance in confirming that Chandralekha did not make the trip.

20  Kenyon Kilbon, 'Moscow Hails 4 Months of U.N. on Radio', *NYHT*, 9/3/1941, A1.
21  'First Effort to Bring Asian Countries Together', *TOI*, 17/3/1947, 7. Margaret Parton, '25 Asia Nations Open Assembly in India Capital', *NYHT*, 24/3/1947, 10.
22  Speeches and Writings of B. Shiva Rao (II)–12, 16–18, 28, 96, 98, 124–137, NMML.
23  VLP to Rita Pandit, 21/3/1947, SPBU.
24  Margaret Parton, 'Equality for all is Goal as Asian Leaders Confer', *NYHT*, 27/3/1947, 11. Iqbal Singh, 'All Asia at Delhi', *Spectator* 178 (6199) 18/4/1947, 424. Parton asserts that VLP had broken with Nehru over the issue of resolutions, but Singh suggests that they were on the same side.
25  R. Gopala Krishna, 'Colored Races Ask Peace and Self-Rule', *Pittsburgh Courier*, 12/4/1947, 1.
26  'Renascent Asia', *TOI*, 25/3/1947, 6.
27  VLPtoTara, 24/2/1947, SPBU.
28  VLP to Rita Pandit, 8/6/1947, SPBU.
29  'Five U.P. Bills Passed', *TOI*, 12/2/1947, 7. The legislation can be found at: https://www.indiacode.nic.in/bitstream/123456789/11635/1/provincialization_hosp.pdf, 25/2/2021.
30  Shri Gopal Tiwari, 'Panchayat Raj in the United Provinces', *The Economic and Political Weekly* (then just *Economic Weekly*), 30/4/1949, https://www.epw.in/system/files/pdf/1949_1/18/panchayat_raj_in_the_united_provinces.pdf, 1/3/2021. 'The U.P. Panchayat Raj Act, 1947', https://www.panchayat.gov.in/documents/20126/0/Uttar+Pradesh_Panchayat+Raj+Act_1947_english+%281%29.pdf/bd46f02e-f570-4af9-aa66-f5d7c6a7b922?t=1554884193141, 1/3/2021. Cf. Venkat Dhulipala, *Creating a New Medina* (Cambridge: Cambridge University Press, 2016), 464. 'U.P. Gaon Hukumat Bill', *TOI*, 4/6/1947, 6. 'Minorities', *TOI*, 2/7/1947, 4.
31  'Making Villages Autonomous', *TOI*, 27/5/1947, 3. VLP to Rita Pandit, 8/6/1947, SPBU.
32  VLP to Rita Pandit, 8/6/1947, SPBU.
33  Note by External Affairs Secretary Weightman, 30/10/1946, F. No. 20(4)-EUR/47, Ministry of External Affairs and Commonwealth Relations, Secret (Downgraded), 1947, NAI, 26–27.
34  Mr. Watson, British Embassy official in Moscow, 'Opening of an Indian Embassy in Moscow: Points for Prior Discission with Soviet Government', in F. No. 20(4)-EUR/47, 34–38. The Indians got a second opinion on all of this from the Canadian ambassador to Moscow, who verified the general points being made, 142–144.
35  F. No. 20(4)-EUR/47, documents and notes on 55–58, 150–157.
36  'India and U.S.S.R. to Exchange Envoys', *Irish Times*, 14/4/1947, 1.
37  F. No. 20(4)-EUR/47, documents and notes on 64, 158–162. Moscow went out of its way to express its pleasure at the choice. Their ambassador to China, through whom all preliminary communication was being carried out by KPS Menon, specifically added to his official agreement to accept VLP as ambassador that his Government was 'very happy to welcome' her, 161. The United States Central Intelligence Agency (CIA) had its ear to the ground on all of these matters and produced a secret report over February and March on the rumor that VLP

was headed to Moscow. Their information suggested that VLP preferred to stay in India rather than go abroad, and that she was not particularly keen on a Moscow posting. They concluded she had a 'liberal' character and was open-minded about Americans, though against 'reactionary circles'. 'Vijaya Lakshmi Pandit', CIA Intelligence Report, 2/4/1947, SO-3697 56649 (illegible: could also be 3897 58649), access granted through FOIA. The British, for their part, included in their own assessment a Reuters report that claimed VLP was the 'Foremost woman in the Indian Independence Movement'. 'India Appoints Ambassador to Russia,' in 'Hon. Mrs. Vijayalakshmi Pandit, Minister of Public Health and Local Self-Government of U.P.,' IOR L/I/1/1482, F. No. 8, The British Library.

38  Walter Terry, 'The Dance: Martha Graham', *NYHT*, 5/5/1947, 14. Cf. https://magazine.artland.com/artistic-collaborations-martha-graham-isamu-noguchi/, 12/4/2021. See also Victoria Phillips, *Martha Graham's Cold War* (New York: Oxford University Press, 2020).

39  'Noguchi Designs a New Coffee Table', *NYHT*, 29/5/1947, 14. The table would not appear in the Herman Miller catalogue until the following year. https://www.noguchi.org/isamu-noguchi/biography/chronology/, 12/4/2021.

40  Letters from VLP to Rita and Nayantara Pandit, 5, 19, 23 May and 8, 10/6/1947, SPBU.

41  Sahgal, *From Fear Set Free*, 15–17.

42  Francesca Ebel, 'Moscow's Metropol: Elegance to Revolution and Back Again', *Associate Press*, 23/7/2019, https://apnews.com/article/67996f7815054a8fa1825557b9fb9d59, 22/4/2021. Yulia Shamporova, 'Legends of the Metropol', *Russia Beyond*, 5/3/2018, https://www.rbth.com/arts/327738-legends-of-metropol-hotel, 22/4/2021.

43  VLPtoJN, 8/8/1947, *V.L. Pandit in Moscow: Correspondence*, NMML.

44  'List House', *Wikipedia*, https://en.wikipedia.org/wiki/List_House, 22/4/2021. And *SoH*, 236. The Bolsheviks had seized his property, but Koussevitzky had remained supportive of the Soviet Union, and especially its people, through the war. For more, see Jonathan Rosenberg, *Dangerous Melodies* (New York: W.W. Norton, 2020), 196–197. For broader context and further analysis, see Arun Mohanty, *Tracing Indo-Russian Diplomatic History* (New York: Routledge, 2020), especially 113–194.

45  The material in this section related to Noguchi is a summary of Hayden Herrera, *Listening to Stone* (New York: Farrar, Strauss, and Giroux, 2015), 230–234. I am grateful to Ram Rahman and Zette Emmons for discussing various details with me. Cf. Vijay Prashad, 'Flashback: How Mexican Artist Frida Kahlo Came to be Photographed in a Sari', Scroll.in, 11/5/2017, https://scroll.in/article/837352/flashback-how-mexican-artist-frida-kahlo-came-to-photographed-in-a-sari, 12/4/2021.

46  VLPtoJN, marked 'confidential', 18/8/1947, *V.L. Pandit in Moscow: Correspondence*, 21, NMML (VLPMoscow). Page numbers reflect those provided in the file, not the letter itself.

47  *Ibid.*, 8/8/1947, 3.

48  *Ibid.*, 18/8/1947, 20–21.

49  *SoH*, 237–238.

50  VLPtoJN, 31/8/1947, includes story by G. Stylyarov in *Trud*, VLPMoscow, 20–21, 22–29.

NOTES 485

51 VLPtoJN, 8/8/1947, VLPMoscow, 1–2. Nehru to Gandhi, 22/8/1947, *Selected Works of Jawaharlal Nehru*, Second Series, Volume 4, 14.
52 *SoH*, 236.
53 VLPtoJN, 8, 18, 31 August and 6, 8/9/1947, VLPMoscow, 1–48.
54 VLPtoJN, 8, 18 August 1947, VLPMoscow, 8, 17–18. *SoH*, 236–237. 'Mrs. Pandit at Kremlin', *NYT*, 14/8/1947, 3.
55 VLPtoJN, 18/8/1947, VLPMoscow, 18–19.
56 *Ibid.*, 18/8/1947, 15–17.
57 Ibid., 31/8/1947, 22–23. SoH, 238–239.
58 VLPtoJN, 6/9/1947, VLPMoscow, 39–40.
59 Ibid., 31/8/1947, 22–23.
60 Ibid., 18/8/1947, 19–20.
61 Nehru to Gandhi, 22/8/1947, in *SWJN*, Second Series, Volume 4, 15–16. https://nehruselectedworks.com/pdfviewer.php?style=UI_Zine_Material.xml&su*B*Folder=&doc=s2v4.pdf|10|724#page=39, 1/7/2021. I am using page numbers as they appear on the printed, scanned pages. See also: Nehru to Patel, 27 October (514–515), where he took issue with a scurrilous story in the right-wing *Hindu Outlook* along the same lines. And Nehru's reply on foreign policy in the Constituent Assembly, 4/12/1947, 602–603. Cf. *SoH*, 242–243. 'Mrs. Pandit in Stockholm: Furnishings for Embassy', *TOI*, 6/9/1947, 6. VLP to Sir Girja Shankar Bajpai, confidential, 9/10/1947, in V.L. Pandit (I Installment) Subject I-55, pp.15–16, NMML. And Girja Bajpai to VLP, Secret & Personal, 24/10/1947, VLP and GS Bajpai Correspondence, 16, digital download, NMML.
62 VLPtoJN, 6, 8 September 1947, VLPMoscow, 43–44, 47–48.
63 Ibid., 6/9/1947, 42–43. *SoH*, 241.
64 VLPtoJN, 6, 8 September 1947, VLPMoscow, 37–38, 47–48.
65 'Woman Diplomat from India Sirs U.N.', *The Morning Call*, 10/9/1947, 8.
66 'Mrs. Pandit Here', *NYHT*, 13/9/1947, 6.
67 'Women Delegates win the Spotlight', *NYT*, 17/9/1947, 3.
68 'U.N. General Assembly: Mrs. Pandit Tipped for Presidency', *TOI*, 5/9/1947, 1.
69 15/9/1947, *FRUS*, Volume I: General: United Nations, Document 71, https://history.state.gov/historicaldocuments/frus1947v01/d71. And 16/9/1947, *FRUS*, Vol. 1, Document 73, https://history.state.gov/historicaldocuments/frus1947v01/d73, 8/7/2021.
70 'Objectivity Asked in India's Strife', *NYT*, 19/9/1947, 8.
71 Quote is from 'Women Delegates win the Spotlight', *NYT*, 17/9/1947, 3. See also: 'Mrs. Pandit Here', *NYHT*, 13/9/1947, 6. 'Pakistan's View on South African Issue', *TOI*, 15/9/1947, 6. *The Austin Statesman*, 20/9/1947, p.1.
72 'Gromyko says Change Peril to Big 5 Unity', *Daily Boston Globe*, 20/9/1947, 1.
73 'Mrs. Pandit warns Assembly', *TOI*, 20 September, 1.
74 Thomas Hamilton, 'Tension Eased in Assembly Despite New Soviet Attack,' *NYT*, 20/9/1947, 1.
75 Nancy MacLennan, 'India, South Africa Seek Settlement', *New York* Times, 20/9/1947, 3.
76 Alistair Cooke, 'End of Depressing Week at U.N. Assembly', *TMG*, 22/9/1947, 6.
77 Gladys Graham, 'Mrs. Pandit and Indian Delegate Fete UN Guests', *Atlanta Daily World*, 8/10/1947, 3.
78 VLP to Sir Girja Shankar Bajpai, confidential, 9/10/1947, in PP(I)I55, 10.

79 'Security Council Elections,' *TOI*, 29/9/1947, p.1. 'UN Assembly Fails to Break Deadlock on Council Seat,' *Austin Statesman*, 1/10/1947, p.1. Alistair Cooke, 'Struggle for a Seat', *TMG*, 1/10/1947, 5. Paul W. Ward, 'Russia Wins Latin Group in U.N. Vote', *Sun*, 1/10/1947, 1. Carlyle Holt, 'Russia Says Ukraine has Right to Seat', *Daily Boston Globe*, 2/10/1947, p.1. John Rogers, 'Vishinsky Fails Again to Win Ukraine a Seat', *NYHT*, 2/10/1947, 11. VLP to Sir Girja Shankar Bajpai, confidential, 9/10/1947, in PP(I)I55, 11–12.
80 'Vyshinsky in Another U.N. "Scene"', *Irish Times*, 2/10/1947, 1.
81 12/11/1947, *FRUS*, Volume I, Document 110, https://history.state.gov/historicaldocuments/frus1947v01/d110, 8/7/2021.
82 8/11/1947, *FRUS*, Volume I, Document 109, https://history.state.gov/historicaldocuments/frus1947v01/d109, 8/7/2021.
83 'U.N.'s Intervention on Indo-China Asked', *New York Times*, 24/9/1947, 4.
84 'Vietnam Urges India to Bring Case to U.N.', *NYT*, 10/10/1947, 14.
85 'U.S. States Palestine Stand Today', *The Austin Statesman*, 11/10/1947, p.1.
86 John G. Rogers, 'U.S. Backs Palestine Partitioning', *NYHT*, 12/10/1947, 1.
87 'India, China Too', *Palestine Post*, 12/10/1947, 1. P.C. Gordon-Walker's Report of Talk with Nehru, *SWJN*, Second Series, Volume 5, 205. https://nehruselectedworks.com/pdfviewer.php?style=UI_Zine_Material.xml&su*B*Folder=&doc=s2v5.pdfl9l628#page=240, 9/7/2021. Rami Ginat, 'India and the Palestine Question', *Middle Eastern Studies* 40(6) 2004, 189–218. General review of relevant UN records available at un.org: https://www.un.org/unispal/. And The Israeli-Palestinian Conflict: An Interactive Database. https://ecf.org.il/issues/issue/454, 12/7/2021. Cf. Meron Medzini, 'Zionist Federations and Zionist Diplomacy in Asia to Ensure United Nations Support for the 1947 Partition Plan', in Manfred Hutter, ed., *Between Mumbai and Manila* (Bonn: Bonn University Press, 2013), 117–118. And P.R. Kumaraswamy, *India's Israel Policy* (New York: Columbia University Press, 2010), 104–107.
88 'Wellesley Fund Drive is Opened at the Waldorf', *New York Herald Tribune*, 16/10/1947, 25. 'Wellesley Opens $7,500,000 Drive', *NYT*, 16/10/1947, 2.
89 VLPtoTara, 23/10/1947, SPBU.
90 'Nurses Hail Mrs. Pandit', *NYT*, 25/11/1947, 35. 'Photo Standalone', *Atlanta Daily World*, 2/12/1947, 1.
91 Advertisement for the CFRB program featured in *Toronto Daily Star*, 24/10/1947, 22. 'Mme. Pandit is Honored', *NYT*, 31/10/1947, 25.
92 'Negro Women's National Group Convenes Here', *WaPo*, 8/11/1947, B4. 'Mrs. Truman Hostess to 550 at Tea at White House', *BAA*, 22/11/1947, 11.
93 'Indian Foreign Policy', *TMG*, 26/11/1947, 4.
94 VLP to Sir Girja Shankar Bajpai, confidential, 9/10/1947, in PP(I)I55, 7–17. Delivered by Nayantara Pandit. And Bajpai to VLP, Secret & Personal, 24/10/1947, V.L. Pandit: G.S. Bajpai Correspondence, 13–16, NMML. VLP had supported Bajpai during the transition from colonial rule to independence. For more on this and a broader analysis of postcolonial Indian foreign policy, see Vineet Thakur, *Postscripts on Independence* (Delhi: Oxford University Press, 2018).
95 'India's Unswerving Support to U.N. Principles', *TOI*, 2/12/1947, 9.
96 'Mrs. Pandit Returns from U.S.', *TOI*, 5/12/1947, 1.
97 'Union Ministers' Salaries', *TOI*, 8/12/1947, 6.
98 'First of Russian Embassy Officials Arrive in New Delhi', *CDT*, 11/12/1947, 10.

99   VLPtoJN, 1/1/1948, VLPMoscow, 63.
100  VLPtoTara, 18/1/1948, SPBU.
101  Ibid., 1/1/1948. VLPtoJN, 12/1/1948, VLPMoscow, 72.
102  VLP to Bajpai, 26/1/1948, V.L. Pandit: G.S. Bajpai Correspondence, 19–20, NMML.
103  VLPtoJN, 19/1/1948, VLPMoscow, 54.
104  HVR Iengar to VLP, 22/3/1948, DO No. 325.PA/48, V.L. Pandit: G.S. Bajpai Correspondence, 24, NMML.
105  VLP to Rita Pandit, 8/1/1948, SPBU.
106  VLPtoTara, 18/1/1948, SPBU.
107  VLPtoJN, 19/1/1948, VLPtoJN, 9/1/1948, VLPMoscow, 52–53.
108  Quoted in Susanna Erlandsson, *Personal Politics in the Postwar World* (London: Bloomsbury, 2022), 139.
109  VLPtoJN, 9/1/1948, VLPMoscow, 69.
110  VLP to Rita and Nayantara Pandit, 12/1/1948, SPBU.
111  VLPtoJN, 12, 26/1/1948, VLPMoscow, 79–80, 81–82.
112  VLPtoJN, 23/1/1948, VLPMoscow, 56–58.
113  The previous two paragraphs are a summary of David Hardiman, *Gandhi in His Time and Ours* (New York: Columbia University Press, 2003), 184–191. All quotations taken from here.
114  VLP to Bajpai, 2/2/1948, V.L. Pandit: G.S. Bajpai Correspondence, 21–22, NMML. And *SoH*, 245–247. In *SoH*, VLP says that it was Fu who first informed her of Gandhi's death, but in her letters from that time she writes that she informed him. See also Confidential letter of the British Embassy, Moscow, 19/2/1948, TNAUK: DO 35/2912, F2920/44, 1948.
115  The material in this section is a synopsis of Sekhar Bandyopadhyay's insightful article, 'The Story of an Aborted Revolution: Communist Insurgency in Post-independence West Bengal, 1948-50', *Journal of South Asian Development* 3:1 (2008), 1–32. Cf. Nehru, 'The Advent of a New Era,' *SWJN*, Second Series, Volume 5, 85–88. VLP to Iengar, 22/4/1948, V.L. Pandit: G.S. Bajpai Correspondence, 28–29, NMML.
116  *SoH*, 248.
117  Bajpai to Pandit, 11 May, 4 June, 1948, V.L. Pandit: G.S. Bajpai Correspondence, 32–35, NMML. Benegal Rama Rau served as India's ambassador to the United States in the interim. See 'Letters of Credence + Commission of appointment of Shrimati Vijaylakshmi Pandit as Ambassador of India in the U.S.A.; Letters of Recall for Shri B. Rama Rau,' GOI Ministry of External Affairs, Protocol Branch, F. No. 1(28)-PH49, 1949, Secret, NAI. And 'Appointment of Shrimati Vijaya Lakshmi Pandit as Ambassador in U.S.A . . .', GOI Ministry of External Affairs and Commonwealth Relations, ESH: Branch II, F. No. 33(50)-EII/48, NAI.

## Chapter 12: Raw Silk

1  'Mrs. Pandit in Capital', *NYT*, 10/5/1949, 23.
2  Girja Shankar Bajpai to VLP (GSBtoVLP), 4/6/1948, 35, Correspondence with G.S. Bajpai, Pandit Papers, NMML.
3  Letters from VLPtoJN, 3, 20 May 1948, 50, 54, V.L. Pandit Papers (Ist Installment), Sub. File no-57, NMML. Hereafter referred to as PP followed by file number.

4   Personal file of Vijaya Lakshmi Pandit, Fond 495, Opis 213, del 67, list (page) 60, 2/6/1948, RGASPI (Russian State Archives. I am grateful to my research assistant, Andrey Edemskiy, for all of his help. He helped collect relevant material which is generally reflected in my depiction of VLP's time in the Soviet Union. I thank Swapna Kona Nayudu for her assistance as well, and my friend and former colleague, Iryna Vushko, for her help with translations.
5   'May be India's Envoy to U.S.', *Pittsburgh Post-Gazette*, 18/6/1948, 2. The news was reported by the Associated Press and widely reported. Cf. 'Nehru's Sister may become Envoy to U.S.', *The Los Angeles Times*, 18/6/1948, 8.
6   Secret, VLPtoJN, 30/3/1948, 36, File no-57, Pandit papers.
7   '"India Evening" in Moscow', *TOI*, 14/8/1948, p.1.
8   For further details on the information in this section, and wider analysis of Indo-Soviet relations in this period, see: Rakesh Ankit, 'India-USSR, 1946-1949: A False Start', in Madhavan K. Palat, ed., *India and the World in the First Half of the Twentieth Century* (New York: Routledge, 2018), 160–188. The precise quote cited was 'conveying a message'. The Soviet press had been going on about the 'reactionary Indian government' for several months; Kollontai's message made clear that this was no coincidence. VLP to Iyengar, 22/4/1948, Papers of Vijaya Lakshmi Pandit, Correspondence with G.S. Bajpai, 28, NMML.
9   Letters from G.S. Bajpai to VLP, 27 June, 22/7/1948, Papers of Vijaya Lakshmi Pandit, Correspondence with G.S. Bajpai, 42–46, 57–58, NMML. VLP to G.S. Bajpai, 10/7/1948, 43, PP(I)I55. Triloki Nath (T.N.) Kaul, who worked closely with VLP, later recalled in his memoirs that 'Mrs. Pandit never asked for a meeting with Stalin—not even when she was about to leave Moscow in/4/1949 . . . 'Why should I? He can send for me if she wants to' [she told Kaul] . . .' T.N. Kaul, *Diplomacy in Peace and War* (New Delhi: Vikas, 1979), 15. This book also provides additional perspective on VLP's stints in Moscow and Washington as well as her trip to China in the fifties. Kaul's assessment of VLP was that she 'was a great lady . . . [who] could get away with a lot of minor lapses'. (17)
10  Francois Retief, Andre Wessels, 'Was Stalin Mad?,' *South African Medical Journal* 98(7), 2008, http://www.scielo.org.za/scielo.php?script=sci_arttext& pid=S0256-95742008000700016. Last accessed 24/9/2021. VLP, *SoH*, 245. Letters from VLPtoJN, 3 May, 1/6/1948, 50, 56 V.L. Pandit Papers (Ist Installment), Sub. File no-57, NMML. Record of the meeting between K.V. Novikov and G.S. Bajpai, 43–46, Correspondence with G.S. Bajpai, NMML. Cf. David Engerman, *The Price of Aid* (Cambridge: Harvard University Press, 2018), 43.
11  VLPtoJN, 3/5/1948, 49–50, Pandit papers. VLP gave an interview to the *Manchester Guardian*'s special correspondent in May in which she discussed her feelings about her treatment in Russia in light of the overall context of decolonization and the emergent Cold War. 'Indian Embassy in Moscow', *TMG*, 25/5/1948, 6. By June, stories about her predicament were widely circulating, especially in the West. For instance: '. . . Mrs Pandit's Embassy to Moscow on behalf of Pandit Nehru has proved a bitter disappointment—for she has been cold-shouldered where she innocently expected a warm welcome . . .' Patrick Maitland, 'Pattern for the Conquest of S.E. Asia', *Scotsman*, 18/6/1948, 6.

12  VLPtoJN, 1/6/1948, 57, Pandit Papers; *SoH*, 241–242; 'Cultural Contact with Russia', *TOI*, 14/7/1948, 6.
13  VLPtoJN, 20 May, 1/6/1948, 55–58, Pandit papers.
14  VLPtoJN, 3/5/1948, 47, Pandit papers.
15  VLPtoGSB, 28/6/1948, 40, PP(I)I55.
16  Camille Cianfarra, 'India to Champion South Asian Lands', *NYT*, 26/9/1948, 3. 'Mrs. Pandit's Replies to Critics in U.N.', *TOI*, 26/9/1948, 1.
17  'Mrs. Pandit's Replies to Critics in U.N.', *TOI*, 26/9/1948, 1. VLP would continue to defend India's position on Kashmir during her various stints at the UN.
18  'Future Status of South-West Africa', *TOI*, 11/11/1948, 1. 'Vyshinsky Again Turns Down Western Plan for Atom Curb', *CSM*, 4/11/1948, 11.
19  'India's Reception to Diplomats', *TOI*, 1/11/1948, 1.
20  'Mrs. Pandit Sets up Precedent', *TOI*, 21/11/1948, 9.
21  'Reception Honors UN Women Leaders', 11/2/1949, C2.
22  'India's Woman Envoy', *WaPo*, 14/10/1948, 11.
23  'Berlin Dispute will Drag on', *TOI*, 22/11/1948, 7. VLP to G.S. Bajpai, 10/7/1948, 44, PP(I)I55.
24  For details, see Vinodh, *A Forgotten Ambassador in Cairo*, 259–261.
25  Letters from VLPtoTara, 31 August, 1 September, 27/11/1948, SPBU. 'Mrs. Pandit Leaves for India', *TOI*, 31/8/1948, 7. Walter Winchell, 'Gossip of the Nation,' *The Philadelphia Inquirer*, 6/9/1948, 13.
26  'Miss Pandit Weds', *TOI*, 3/1/1949, 6. 'Miss Pandit's Wedding', *TOI*, 6/1/1949, 5. 'Daughter of Mrs. Pandit weds in India', *NYHT*, 14/1/1949, 10. 'Indian Marital Rites', *WaPo*, via the AP, 14/1/1949, 14.
27  Manu Bhagavan correspondence with Nayantara Sahgal and Manjari Mehta, 13–16 October 2021. Day Price, 'Mrs. Pandit in London', *New York* Times, 3/4/1949, 29. Chandralekha's wedding took place on 14 April, a little less than two weeks after VLP had left the Soviet Union. 'Ambassador's Daughter', *TOI*, 17/4/1949, 3.
28  VLPtoTara, 16/2/1949, SPBU.
29  VLPtoTara, 28/2/1949, SPBU. Woman Second to Gandhi in India's Affection Dies,' *The Baltimore Sun*, 4/3/1949, 18.
30  VLPtoJN, 17 February, 1 March, 1949, 67–76, PP57.
31  VLPtoJN, 15 March, 1949, 78–79, PP57. 'First Israel Envoy Arrives in Moscow,' *NYHT*, 5/9/1948, 16.
32  'U.S. Post for Mrs. Pandit,' *NYT*, 21/2/1949, 3.
33  VLPtoJN, 15 March, 1949, 82–84, PP57, NMML.
34  VLP and Alexandra Kollontai (spelled Kollontay), 26, 27/3/1949, 64, PPI55.
35  VLPtoJN, 15 March, 1949, 80–81, PP57.
36  'Mrs. Pandit, Nehru's Sister, is India's New Ambassador to U.S.,' *NYHT*, 17/3/1949, 7. 'Mme. Ambassador', *WaPo*, 28/3/1949, 8. Elizabeth McGuire, 'Washington Society to Fete Pact Signers', *WaPo*, 27/3/1949, S1. 'Mrs. Pandit named to U.S. Post', *Chicago Defender*, 26/3/1949, 2. 'Good Omen', *Daily Boston Globe*, 18/3/1949, 28. 'Mrs. Pandit in London', *NYT*, 3/4/1949, 29. 'Mrs. V.L. Pandit', *SCMP*, 4/4/1949, 5.
37  'India Tightens Ties with U.S.', *The Sun*, 1/4/1949, 19.
38  'Mrs. V. Lakshmi', *SCMP*, 26/3/1949, 7.
39  Robert Trumbull, 'Mrs. Pandit Urges U.S.-Indian Links', *NYT*, 24/4/1949, 7.

40 'Fostering Amity with U.S.', *TOI*, 28/4/1949, 7.
41 'Hope of the East', *WaPo*, 9/5/1949, 6.
42 VLPtoGSB, 10/7/1948, 6/5/1949 and from Sir Girja to VLP 12/5/1949, 42–43, 52–53, 124, 126, PPT55. The person who evaluated the High Commissioner's office and who drafted the report was Subimal Dutt. The story of his experiences with Menon during this process, and the means by which Menon escaped making any substantive changes, are told in the meticulously researched and detailed biography by Amit Das Gupta. See *Serving India* (Delhi: Manohar, 2017), 124–131.
43 'Mrs. Pandit Hails Lifting of Blockade', *WaPo*, 6/5/1949, B3. 'Friendly Ties with U.S.', *TOI*, 6/5/1946, 7.
44 'Two Foreign Envoys Call on the President', 13/5/1949, 12.
45 Elizabeth McGuire, 'Big Indian Embassy Fete to Welcome Mme. Pandit', *Washington Post*, 8/5/1949, S3. 'Mme. Pandit to see Presentation of "Medea" Wednesday', *WaPo*, 12/5/1949, B5. 'On the Capital Party Front', *WaPo*, 14/5/1949, B4. Gladys Graham, 'Ambassador Pandit Feted with Dinner', 3/6/1949, 7.
46 Malvina Lindsay, 'Top Job Monopoly', *WaPo*, 14/5/1949, 6.
47 'Women Press Writers Rib World's Great', *Los Angeles Times*, 15/5/1949, B23.
48 Alden Whitman, 'Reigned for Thirty Years', *NYT*, 17/3/1975, https://www.nytimes.com/1975/03/17/archives/reigned-for-30-years-perle-mesta-hostess-to-the-politically-famous.html, 1/11/2021.
49 VLPtoTara, 8/6/1949, SPBU. See also 'Mrs. Mesta to Entertain after Godfrey Show', *WaPo*, 3/6/1949, C3.
50 'Parties Pleasant—but Secondary, says Mme. Pandit', *WaPo*, 31/5/1949, B6.
51 'Mrs. Pandit Holds Women Shirk Role', *NYT*, 28/5/1949, 12.
52 Elizabeth McGuire, 'Diplomatic Circling', *WaPo*, 29/5/1949, S2. 'Truman may name Woman Envoy', *WaPo*, 4/6/1949, B5. Doris Lockerman, 'Perle Mesta may become Diplomat', *Atlanta Constitution*, 20/6/1949, 14. 'Woman takes Oath as Envoy to Luxembourg', *The Los Angeles Times*, 9/7/1949, 2. 'Americans Like Women Diplomats', *The Los Angeles* Times, 1/8/1949, 28. Ruth Bryan Owen Rohde and Mrs. J. Borden Harriman had been appointed US Ambassadors to Denmark and Norway in the thirties. 'Women Ambassadors', Reader's Letters, *TOI*, 24/7/1949, 10.
53 VLPtoJN, 17/6/1949, 20, 22, PP59.
54 '900 get Degrees; Mme. Pandit, Bunche Honored', *WaPo*, 4/6/1949, 2. 'Degrees given 917 in Howard's Largest Commencement', *BAA*, 11/6/1949, 6.
55 'Indian Ambassador to Present Bunche Medal,' 4/6/1949, 2B. 'Californians Plan Ralph Bunche Day', *Philadelphia Tribune*, 21/6/1949, 3.
56 George Streator, 'Bunche Receives Spingarn Award', *NYT*, 18/7/1949, 10.
57 Bess Wilson, '600 Honor Mme. Pandit at Luncheon', *Los Angeles Times*, 20/7/1949, B1.
58 James Hicks, 'Hicks Uncovers Top Personalities', *Atlanta Daily World*, 24/7/1949, 2.
59 'Mrs. Pandit's Tour of U.S. Cities', *Times of* India, 7/7/1949, 9.
60 Genevieve Reynolds, 'India to Keep Free from Power Blocs in Aiding Democracy', *WaPo*, 14/6/1949, B4. VLP repeated this theme in another luncheon given in her honor by the Overseas Press Club in New York. 'India's Status: Democratic Force in Asia', *SCMP*, 24/6/1949, 10.

61 '2ⁿᵈ Mt. Holyoke Institute Forges Ahead', *NYHT*, 24/7/1949, A4.
62 'Freedom of Asian Countries', *TOI*, 13/7/1949, 3.
63 'U.S. Loan for India', *TOI*, 16/7/1949, 1.
64 Editorial, 'A Great Woman who Serves Greatly', Los Angeles *Mirror*, 16/7/1949, PP59, 33, 35. Nan by then had taken note of the press' general habit of commenting on her 'hair and clothes as if [she were] . . . a film star.' It annoyed her.
65 'Mrs. Pandit's Tour of U.S. Cities', *Times of* India, 7/7/1949, 9. 'Mrs. Pandit's Hollywood Visit', *TOI*, 6/8/1949, 5.
66 George J. Christopher to VLP, 26/7/1949, 31, PP59.
67 'America's Responsibility for World Peace', *TOI*, 4/8/1949, 7.
68 Elise Morrow, 'Mrs. Longworth heads 'Most Attractive' List', *Philadelphia Inquirer*, 27/7/1949, 27.
69 Leonard Lyons, 'The Lyon's Den', *WaPo*, 4/8/1949, B13.
70 'Cure World's Fear of War, Science Told', *CDT*, 7/9/1949, 16. 'Use Science to Enrich Life', *TOI*, 8/9/1949, 5. Cf. S. Rajen Singh, 'India's Response to Nuclear Non-Proliferation Measures', *India Quarterly* 58(3–4),/7/2022, 31–92. VLP felt bad about attracting a lot of attention during her visit, pulling away from that year's delegation. She decided to minimize her time at the UN moving forward to keep that from happening again. VLPtoJN, 23/9/1949, 58, PP59.
71 B.R. Shenoy, 'Aid to India from World Bank Group', *Il Politico* 36:3 (1971), 523–549. Jochen Kraske, 'India and the World Bank', https://documents1.worldbank.org/curated/en/216261468267877421/pdf/768330WP0India01B00PUBLIC00aug01997.pdf, 1/12/2021. Dennis Merrill, 'Indo-American Relations 1947-50', *Diplomatic History* 11: 3 (Summer 1987), 207. Merrill argues that the British were working behind the scenes to support financial assistance to India, but I think he overstates the case. I am very grateful to Vijayendra Rao, Syed Akbar Hyder, Karna Basu, Rupal Oza, and especially Vikram Raghavan for their assistance with this section.
72 VLPtoJN, 2/6/1949, Secret, MEA, F.45-73/49-AMS D.2312/49-AMS, 4, NAI.
73 Document 1189, 29/5/1949, Secret, FRUS, 1949, Volume VI. https://history.state.gov/historicaldocuments/frus1949v06/d1189, 29/11/2021. For additional analysis, see Francine Frankel, *When Nehru Looked East* (New York: Oxford University Press, 2020).
74 Document 157, 29/6/1949, Secret, FRUS, 1949, Volume II. https://history.state.gov/historicaldocuments/frus1949v02/d157, 29/11/2021.
75 Document 1194, 11/6/1949, Secret, FRUS, 1949, Volume VI. https://history.state.gov/historicaldocuments/frus1949v06/d1194. Last accessed 29/11/2021.
76 VLP and Bajpai, 15 June (Secret) and 25 June 1949, 74–75, PPT55. And PPGSB, 85.
77 'Memorandum of Conversation with Madame Vijayalakshmi Pandit, Ambassador of India, and Mr. Joseph S. Sparks, June 29, 1949', Dean G. Acheson Papers, The Harry S. Truman Library, https://www.trumanlibrary.gov/library/personal-papers/memoranda-conversations-file-1949-1953/may-june-1949-0?documentid=41&pagenumber=1, 3/12/1949. I am grateful to David Clark, archivist, for his assistance.
78 JNtoVLP, 1/7/1949, SWJN, Second Series, Volume 12, 408. https://nehruselectedworks.com/pdfviewer.php?style=UI_Zine_Material.xml&su*B*Folder=&doc=s2v12.pdf|12|524#page=446, 29/11/2021.
79 Document 1207, 30/8/1949, Secret, FRUS, 1949, Volume VI. https://history.state.gov/historicaldocuments/frus1949v06/d1207, 1/12/2021.

80 'India Bars U.S. Plan in Kashmir Dispute', *NYHT*, 16/9/1949, 7.
81 For details, see Jason Kirk, *India and the World Bank* (New York: Anthem Press, 2011), 4-9.
82 'World Bank lends $34,000,000 to India', *NYT*, 19/8/2021, 5. 'World Bank Group Exhibit Series: President Eugene Robert Black, No. 16, January 2016, 1st pub. April 2003. https://documents1.worldbank.org/curated/en/759741467740019396/pdf/104640-WP-PUBLIC-2003-04-President-Eugene-Robert-Black.pdf, 1/12/2021. 'Celebrating 75 Years of World Bank-India Partnership', 19/10/2021, https://www.worldbank.org/en/country/india/brief/75-years-of-world-bank-in-india, 1/12/2021. *WaPo* wrote that Madame Pandit became 'the first woman to negotiate a loan from the World Bank'. Bank records indicate that she was not involved in the formal negotiations over the loan in any way. She may have been credited thus for her political diplomacy over the issue. 'World Bank lends 34 Million to India', *WaPo*, 19/8/1949, 3.
83 'Banking: Good Risk', *Time Magazine*, 29/8/1949, http://content.time.com/time/subscriber/article/0,33009,855011,00.html, 1/12/2021.
84 '10 Million Dollar Loan for India,' *TOI*, 30/9/1949, p.1. Chaitanya Mallapur, 'India Largest Recipient of World Bank Loans over 70 Years,' *The Business Standard*, 13/1/2016, https://www.business-standard.com/article/specials/india-largest-recipient-of-world-bank-loans-over-70-years-116011300637_1.html, 1/12/2021. See also Harry Truman Papers, Sub file-4, NMML, 190–200.
85 'India's Nehru gets Welcome from Truman', *CDT*, 12/10/1949, 28. Nehru had taken exception to J.J. Singh as well, perturbed especially by his harsh criticism of Sardar Patel, the Deputy Prime Minister who was considerably to the right of the PM on many issues. Nehru made clear that Singh could speak and think as he wished, even if it was disagreeable, but that his posing as some kind of representative of the Government of India was unacceptable. Nehru to Richard Walsh, 27/6/1949, pg. 31, PP60. See also, Harry Truman Papers, Sub file-5, NMML.
86 'India Heads Brilliant Group at Achesons' Dinner', *WaPo*, 13/10/1949, B6.
87 D.R. Mankekar, 'Nehru-Acheson Talks in Washington', *TOI*, 15/10/1949, 1. 'Nehru Due Today on 6-Day Visit; Ticker-Tape Welcome Monday', *NYHT*, 15/10/1949, p.1.
88 'Nehru Honored by N.A.A.C.P., Gets Life Card', *NYHT*, 6/11/1949, p.2. Theodore Cook, 'Nehru gets Wellesley Ovation', *CSM*, 21/10/1949, 1. 'Prime Minister Nehru gets First Hand Briefing on Problem', *Atlanta Daily World*, 9/11/1949, 1.
89 D.R. Mankekar, 'Verdict on Pandit Nehru's U.S. Tour', *TOI*, 9/11/1949, 1. Nan's assessment was the same. She reported being 'thrilled' by the 'repercussions' of the trip, writing that 'his personality . . . captured all sections'. VLPtoTara, 17/11/1949, SPBU.
90 'A.K.A.'s to Cite Mme Pandit's Contributions to Humanity,' *The Chicago Defender*, 5/11/1949, 8. Fannie Keene, 'Mme. Pandit is Lauded in Only Boro Appearance,' *NYAN*, 19/11/1949, 9.
91 'Romulo Presents Medals at Women's Exposition', *NYHT*, 12/11/1949, 7.
92 Elizabeth McGuire, 'Eloquent Mme Pandit Proves the Proposition', *WaPo*, 13/11/1949, S1.
93 'Smartest Women', *South China Sunday Post*, 1/1/1950, 7.
94 VLPtoTara, 3 July, 7 October, 9 November, and 18/12/1949, SPBU.
95 VLP to Gautam Sahgal, 4/9/1949, and to Nayantara, 19/9/1949, SPBU.

NOTES 493

96 VLPtoJN, 18/12/1949, 76, PP59.
97 Bajpai to VLP, 28/11/1949, 112, PPGSB. VLPtoTara, 17/11/1949, SPBU.
98 'India's Relationship with the United States', *TOI*, 1/2/1949, 7.
99 VLPtoJN, 113–114, PP59. Letters from VLPtoTara, 22/12/1949, 17/10/1950, SPBU. 'Mrs. Pandit in U.S.', *TOI*, 6/3/1950, 7.
100 Frances Burns, 'Wellesley Inaugurates Miss Clapp', 18/3/1950, *Boston Globe*, 1. John Fenton, 'Dr. Clapp assumes Wellesley Office, 18/3/1950, *NYT*, 15.
101 VLPtoJN, 17/6/1949, 20–23, PP59.
102 VLPtoJN, 27/3/1950, 85–86, PP59.
103 Doris Fleeson, 'Judge Kenyon Stands Up', *Boston Globe*, 16/3/1950, 7. Kenyon would go on to have a lasting influence on American jurisprudence, serving as inspiration for Supreme Court Justice Ruth Bader GiSPBUrg.
104 Letters from VLPtoJN, 20/5/1949, 17 April, 2, 4, 22/5/1950, 13–16, 91–95, 97–108, PP59. VLP to Bajpai, 7, 15, 20, 22, 27 May 1950, 147–173 and Bajpai to VLP, 30/5/1950, 174–177. PPGSB.
105 'U.S. Studying Plan to Give Food to India', *WaPo*, 4/1/1951, 5; 'Premiers Meet Today', *TMG*, 4/1/1951, 5. 'U.S. is Said to Study Food Help for India', *NYT*, 5/1/1951, 4. For broader context, see Siegel, *Hungry Nation*, 50–118.
106 'Chinese Intervention in Korea out of Fear', *TOI*, 2/1/1951, 5.
107 'Less Talk', *TOI*, 3/1/1951, 4.
108 'India Paper hits at Mrs. Pandit for her TV Interview', *WaPo*, 4/1/1951, 6.
109 VLPtoJN, 1/3/1951, 180, PP59. JNtoVLP, 21/3/1951, 186, PP60. VLPtoGSB, 1, 10/3/1951, GSBtoVLP 13/3/1951, 302–305, 312, PPI55. 'Another Faux Pas?' *TOI*, 12 April 1951, 6.
110 VLPtoJN, 29 January, 5/2/1951, 149–155, PPI59. JNtoVLP, 8 March1951, 185, PP(I)60.
111 Francis Robinson, *Islam in South Asia* (Oxford Bibliographies Online, 2010), 30.
112 VLPtoGSB, 14, 18 June, 2/8/1951, 374–383, 405–409, PP(I)55.
113 'Thorium', World Nuclear Association, https://world-nuclear.org/information-library/current-and-future-generation/thorium.aspx, 8/3/2022. For more on Oppenheimer, see Kai Bird and Martin J. Sherwin, *American Prometheus* (New York: Vintage Books, 2006).
114 VLPtoJN, 21/2/1951, 166–167, PP(I)59. JNtoVLP, 8/3/1951, 184, PP(I)60.
115 Albert Einstein to VLP, 27/2/1951 and VLPtoJN, 1/3/1951, 177–179, PP(I)59.
116 VLPtoJN 22 February, 21 April, 23 May Statement from the Prime Minister's Secretariat, 3/5/1951, Official cable, Prime Minister to US Ambassador, undated, 165–169, 191–194, NMML. JNtoVLP, 22 March, 2/6/1951, V.L. Pandit papers (Ist Inst.), Sub-file no, 60, 189, 198, PP(I)59. VLP to Bajpai, and Bajpai to VLP 24 May, 11 June 1951, 349–352, 356–358, 371–373, PPCGSB. It was in this period that VLP met Edward Bernays, nephew of Sigmund Freud and the so-called 'father of public relations'. The two got along well, and she arranged for him to formally work for the Government of India in assisting the ambassador (her) in bringing India and the United States closer together. Bernays received encouragement and unofficial sanction from the State Department and US Ambassador to India Chester Bowles to promote India's cause, saying that they very much felt closer relations with the country were a top priority. Bernays concluded that VLP was just as billed, 'a woman of intelligence, experience and ability'. So he was surprised to hear from Louis Fischer, the famed biographer

of Mahatma Gandhi, that VLP, in Fischer's judgement, was 'stupid, knew nothing about economics and politics and had made many errors because of her ignorance and arrogance'. (1151) These views did not comport with any other. Bernays would gain notoriety a few years later for his involvement with the United Fruit Company and the American–backed coup of the democratically elected government of Guatemala. See Edward Bernays, *Biography of an Idea* (New York: Open Road Media, 2015, first published 1965), Chapters 63, 66.

117   'Mme. Pandit gets a Grain Gift,' *WaPo*, 25/4/1951, 2. VLPtoJN, 21, 26 April, 14 June 1951, 195-201, 221, PP(I)59.
118   VLP to Ray Hutchins, 5/6/1951, and related correspondence with the Ford Foundation. Rockefeller Archive Center. Cf. https://www.lib.uchicago.edu/e/scrc/findingaids/view.php?eadid=ICU.SPCL.HUTCHINSRM, 11/3/2022.
119   'President Truman Signs Grain for India Bill', *TOI*, 16/6/1951, 1. 'Truman Signs Bill Providing India 2 Million Tons of Grain', *WaPo*, 16/6/1951, 3. See also Harry Truman Papers, Sub file-3, NMML.
120   VLPtoJN, 1 March, 23 May, 4, 11 June, 6 August, 29/10/1951, 180-186, 213-220, 223, 233, PP(I)59. JNtoVLP, 20 February, 21/3/1951, PP(I)60, 100, 186. VLP to Bajpai, and Bajpai to VLP 10, 26 March, 4 April, 28 May, 11 June, 5, 23 July, 2/8/1951, 305, 320-322, 324-325, 353, 369-373, 389-390, 399-401, 410-411, PPCGSB. K.P.S. Menon makes an unusual notation in his diary on 20/8/1951, saying that VLP is 'Most agreeable. Most ingratiating.' And that 'Butter will not melt in her mouth' (which he means as a compliment). But then he adds that she is 'utterly unreliable'. No further context is provided for this comment, and I was unable to find any further such suggestion. Given the period, Menon may have been reflecting on VLP's uncertainty about herself and her future, despite all of the successes she had had. Diary-32, Menon papers, NMML, 49. Cf. Srinath Raghavan, *War and Peace in Modern India* (London: Palgrave Macmillan, 2010), 23. Raghavan chalks Menon's entry up to general inter–personal rivalries within India's foreign policy establishment. On announcement of her departure, the renowned journalist Walter Lippmann, who was someone taken very seriously in policy circles, wrote her privately: 'Never doubt that your mission to Washington in these extraordinarily trying times has been a success. As you know, I am one of those who thinks that the main lines of India's foreign policy are right—identical with American foreign policy when we were in a similar position, and in the best interests now not only of India but also of the United States. There are not many Americans who would really deny this, though there are a great many who do not understand it. Your great role has been to make it impossible for those who did not understand your government's policy to doubt its motives. Nobody, I think, but you could have done that so well'. Walter Lippmann to VLP, 9/11/1951, Walter Lippmann Papers, Box 94, Folder 1661, Vijaya Lakshmi Pandit, Microfilmed from Series III, Part 2, Section I Correspondence, Manuscript and Archives Division, Sterling Memorial Library, Yale University.

## Chapter 13: Milk and Honey

1   'Four Central Ministers Elected to Parliament', *TOI*, 7/2/1952, 7. JNtoVLP, 13, 15, 21 October, 7/11/1951, 231–234, PP(I)60.
2   'Bowles Helps Welcome Mrs. Roosevelt to India', *Hartford Courant*, 3/3/1952, 1.

## NOTES

3 'Warm Reception at Airport', *TOI*, 3/3/1952, 5.
4 'International Cooperation in Social Welfare', *TOI*, 5/3/1952, 7.
5 VLP interview with Eleanor Roosevelt, All India Radio, 22/3/1952, Eleanor Roosevelt Papers Project, The George Washington University, https://erpapers.columbian.gwu.edu/radio-interview-vijaya-lakshmi-pandit-march-22-1952, 9/6/2022. 'Egalitarianism' refers to Roosevelt's support for anti-caste legislation.
6 VLPtoJN 29 June, 20, 24/7/1950, 109–11, 115–117,119–121, PP(I)59. Document 123, 27/6/1950, Secret, FRUS, 1950, Volume VII. Document 132, 28/6/1950, Secret, FRUS, 1950, Volume VII. Document 298, 16/7/1950, Top Secret, FRUS, 1950, Volume VII. Document 325, 19/7/1950, Confidential, FRUS, 1950, Volume VII. Document 359, 27/7/1950, Top Secret, FRUS, 1950, Volume VII. Document 471, 24/8/1950, Secret, FRUS, 1950, Volume VII. For a broader analysis of India's role in the Korean conflict within the context of larger Commonwealth relations, and with additional study of the roles played by VLP, Krishna Menon, and Nehru, see Robert Barnes, *The US, the UN, and the Korean War* (London: Bloomsbury, 2020, first published 2014).
7 VLPtoJN, 17/2/1949, 68A–69, PP(I)57. VLPtoJN 23/9/1949, 27 July, 24/8/1950, 61, 122–124, 132–135, PP(I)59. JNtoVLP, 1/7/1949, 14, 19/9/1950, 32–33, 143–146, PP(I)60.
8 'To Lead India Mission', *WaPo*, 14/3/1952, 2.
9 July 1952, 22, PP(II)18.
10 Telegram from Bajpai to VLP, and VLP and Nehru, 1/2, 6, 8, 10, 14 May 1952, 6–16, 20, PP(II)23. See also: Document 123, 17/5/1952, Top Secret, FRUS, 1952–1954, Volume XV, Part I, https://history.state.gov/historicaldocuments/frus1952-54v15p1/d123, 21/4/2022.
11 VLPtoJN, with formal assessment of Mao and Chou, 16/5/1952, 17–19, PP(II)23.
12 This letter was pushed by the U.S. Department, which saw India as facilitator for such an initiative. Document 12, 28/3/1952, Confidential, FRUS, 1952–1954, Volume XIV, Part I, https://history.state.gov/historicaldocuments/frus1952-54v14p1/d12, 19/4/2022. VLP delivered most of her official remarks during her trip in Hindi.
13 Summary of Official report of Vijaya Lakshmi Pandit, on the Indian delegation's visit to China, July 1952, 3, 9–11, 13–17, 19–22, PP(II)18. Cf. V.L. PP(II)23, 9.
14 PP(II)23, 21–22.
15 July 1952, PP(II)18. Cf. *SoH*, 265–274. Her account in her memoir mistakenly dates her trip to the fall and also erroneously claims that the river project they visited occurred on the Yangtze river.
16 'India Receives U.S. Gift', *NYT*, 11/8/1952, 2.
17 'Need to Learn Hindi', *TOI*, 5/8/1952, 8.
18 'Planned Parenthood', *Times of* India, 28/8/1952, 5; Robert Trumbull, 'World Unit Set up for Birth Control', *NYT*, 30/11/1952, p.1.
19 Aran Moore, 'India Plans 'Peace Offensive', *The Jerusalem Post*, 28/9/1952, 4.
20 Document 20, 24 September 1952, FRUS, 1952–1954, Volume III, https://history.state.gov/historicaldocuments/frus1952-54v03/d20, 21/4/2022.
21 Document 293, October 1952, Secret, FRUS, 1952–1954, Volume XV, Part I, https://history.state.gov/historicaldocuments/frus1952-54v15p1/d293, 21/4/2022.
22 'Korea is Biggest Problem Before U.N.,' *TOI*, 11/11/1952, 7.

23  Document 295, 1/11/1952, Secret, FRUS, 1952–1954, Volume XV, Part I, https://history.state.gov/historicaldocuments/frus1952-54v15p1/d295, 21/4/2022. Khushwant Singh recalled an episode in this period when Krishna Menon's detractors reached out to VLP to try to air their grievances to her in person when she visited London. The wily Menon packed her itinerary with all sorts of events and entertainment so that she was unable to meet with those opposed to him. She was livid when she later found out. For more, see Khushwant Singh, *Not A Nice Man to Know* (Delhi: Penguin, 1993), 74–75.
24  Document 354, 28/11/1952, Top Secret, FRUS, 1952–1954, Volume XV, Part I, https://history.state.gov/historicaldocuments/frus1952-54v15p1/d354, 11/5/2022. 'Mrs. Pandit says U.N. Holds Secret Talks on Korea', *Daily Boston Globe*, 25/10/1952, 8. 'Mrs. Pandit to meet Mr. Vyshinsky: Korean & Tunisian Issues to be Discussed', *TOI*, 30/10/1952, 7.
25  'Whitehall Caution on Korea Truce', *South China Sunday Post-Herald*, 16/11/1952, 13. See also Papers of V.K. Krishna Menon, S-file 858, NMML.
26  'Labourites Message to Mrs. Pandit', *SCMP*, 20/11/1952, 1.
27  John G. Rogers, 'India Formula for Truce wins U.N. Test, 53-5', *NYHT*, 2/12/1952, 1. 'India's Proposal on Korea Voted by U.N., 54-5', *Daily Boston Globe*, 4/12/1952, 1.
28  'India's Prominent Role in U.N. Assembly Session', *TOI*, 24/12/1952, 7.
29  'Seven are Given One World Awards', *NYHT*, 11/12/1952, 3. Schweitzer won the Nobel for 1952, but the award was named and given retroactively in 1953. 'Nobel Peace Prize is Withheld', *Hartford Courant*, 4/10/1952, 15b. 'Gen. Marshall, Dr. Schweitzer Nobel Winners', *CDT*, 31/10/1953, 20. For more on the One World Awards, see Michael Keith and Mary Ann Watson, eds. *Norman Corwin's One World Flight* (New York: Continuum, 2009), 1–3.
30  Document 354, 28/11/1952, Top Secret, FRUS, 1952–1954, Volume XV, Part I, https://history.state.gov/historicaldocuments/frus1952-54v15p1/d354, 13 May 2022.
31  'Mrs. Pandit to see Gen. Neguib', *TOI*, 30/12/1952, 1.
32  'Charge against India "Outrageous"', *TOI*, 28/12/1952, 1. 'Korea Proposals not Dictated by Western Powers', *TOI*, 17/2/1953, 1.
33  Marie McNair, 'Mme. Pandit may not return to U.S.', *WaPo*, 15/12/1952, 19. 'Mrs. Pandit Heads Unit', *WaPo*, 18/2/1953, 8.
34  John Rogers, 'U.N. Delegates Preoccupied by Stalin's Stroke', *NYHT*, 5/3/1953, 8. Alistair Cooke, 'Useless U.N. Debate on Korea', *TMG*, 6/3/1953, 14.
35  'Mme. Pandit Mentioned for Top UN Post', *The Atlanta Journal and the Atlanta Constitution*, 8/3/1953, 8A. 'Successor to Mr. Lie', *TOI*, 7/3/1953, 1. 'U.N. Secretary-General', *SCMP*, 9/3/1953, 10. John Rogers, 'Lie tells U.N. Soviet Pressure made Him quit', *NYHT*, 11/3/1953, 1. Cf. JNtoVLP, 6/3/1953, SWJN, Series 2, Volume 21, 562.
36  'Soviet would agree to Rau or Mrs. Pandit as Lie's Successor', *Daily Boston Globe*, 18/3/1953, 17. 'Indian to Succeed Mr. Lie', *TMG*, 18/3/1953, 1.
37  'Reject Indian Woman as U.N. Chief', *CDT*, 20/3/1953, 1.
38  Paul Ward, 'Soviet Move for Mme. Pandit as Lie Successor Defeated', *Baltimore Sun*, 20/3/1953, 1.
39  Murrey Marder, 'Probers are Warned on Blunt Propaganda', *WaPo*, 24/3/1953, 3.
40  Document 208, 19/3/1953, Secret, FRUS, 1952–1954, Volume III, https://history.state.gov/historicaldocuments/frus1952-54v03/d208, 3/6/2022. Ibid., Document

209, Confidential, 19/3/1953, https://history.state.gov/historicaldocuments/frus1952-54v03/d209.
41 'Swedish Economist Surprise Choice of East and West as UN Secretary', *Austin Statesman*, 1/4/1953, A1.
42 'Our London Correspondence', *TMG*, 27/3/1953, 6.
43 Gerald Bailey, 'Mr. Lie's Successor', Letters to the Editor, *TMG*, 30/3/1953, 4.
44 Sir Francis Low, 'Repatriation of Korean Prisoners', *TOI*, 1/4/1953, 7.
45 'Mrs. Pandit to Stay in India', *TOI*, 13/4/1953, 1.
46 'Ten Greatest Women Listed by Students', *WaPo*, 19/5/1953, 11.
47 'Shoeless Dulles Pays Honor at Gandhi Shrine', *CDT*, 21/5/1953, b2.
48 'Nehru of India: Korea Middleman', *Newsweek* 41 (25), 22/6/1953, 38–39. The armistice would officially take effect on 27 July.
49 'Nehru arrives in Karachi', *South China Sunday Post-Herald*, 26/7/1953, 1.
50 JNtoVLP, cable, 6/3/1953, SWJN, Series 2, Volume 21, 562–563. VLP's name had in fact been in circulation as a possible president of the UN General Assembly from as early as 1948, when the US State Department and Eleanor Roosevelt internally supported India generally, and she specifically, for the position, though they saw this as a tactical trade in exchange for other seats of authority. See 'Conferring with the State Department,' Secret Memorandum of Conversation, 24/8/1948, in Allida Black, ed., *The Eleanor Roosevelt Papers*, Volume I (New York: Charles Scribners and Sons, 2007), 887–891.
51 Document 227, 7/7/1953, Confidential, FRUS, 1952–1954, Volume III, https://history.state.gov/historicaldocuments/frus1952-54v03/d227, 6/6/2022
52 Document 229, 9/7/1953, Confidential, FRUS, 1952–1954, Volume III, United Nations Affairs, h https://history.state.gov/historicaldocuments/frus1952-54v03/d229, 6/6/2022.
53 Document 238, 1/8/1953, Confidential, FRUS, 1952–1954, Volume III, https://history.state.gov/historicaldocuments/frus1952-54v03/d238, 6/6/2022. The rest of this paragraph is a summary of various documents from this volume, July 1953. Also, Dulles Telephone Conversation with President Eisenhower, 1/8/1953, John Foster Dulles Papers; Telephone Conversations Series; Box 10; White House Telephone Conversations, May–December 31, 1953 (2), Eisenhower Presidential Library.
54 Document 240, 3/8/1953, Confidential, FRUS, 1952–1954, Volume III, https://history.state.gov/historicaldocuments/frus1952-54v03/d240, 6/6/2022. Document 241, 3/8/1953, Confidential, FRUS, 1952–1954, Volume III, United Nations Affairs, https://history.state.gov/historicaldocuments/frus1952-54v03/d241, 6/6/2022.
55 'Mrs. Pandit as U.N. Assembly President', *TOI*, 31/7/1953, 5. 'US May Back Nehru's Sister,' *Austin Statesman*, 13/8/1953, A12.
56 William Frye, 'Mme Pandit leads Race to head UN Assembly,' *CSM*, 13/8/1953, 14.
57 Chesly Manly, 'India Fails in Bid for Parley Seat,' *CDT*, 28/8/1953, 1. Robert Trumbull, 'U.S.-India Relations Strained by U.N. Debate over Korea,' *NYT*, 30/8/1953, E5.
58 'Dar-Pandit Wedding', *TOI*, 4/9/1953, 3.
59 'Pak Vote for Mrs. Pandit', *TOI*, 2/9/1953, 1.
60 'UN Assembly May Open with Sweetness and Light', *GandM*, 14/9/1953, 15.

61 A.L. Goldberg, 'Aristocratic Rebel, Mrs. Pandit, wins Top General Assembly Post', *Austin Statesman*, 16/9/1953, 24.
62 Erwin Canham, 'The Time for Leadership', *CSM*, 16/9/1953, 20.
63 'India's Victory Goddess Marks up Another First', *Los Angeles Times*, 16/9/1953, 10.
64 Paul Ward, 'U.N. Votes Down Soviet Move to seat Red China', *Baltimore Sun*, 16/9/1953, 1.
65 'Britain is Urged to Quit the UN', *The Baltimore Sun*, 17/9/1953, 1.
66 'Pandit Election seen as Red Aid', *The Los Angeles Times*, 17/9/1953, 13.
67 Document 473, 29/9/1953, Confidential, FRUS, 1952–1954, Volume III, https://history.state.gov/historicaldocuments/frus1952-54v03/d473. Last accessed 7/6/2022.
68 'Mrs. Pandit Impresses', *TOI*, 23/9/1953, 1.
69 Mosley, *Dulles*, 34. Allen Dulles had only just overseen the coup d'etat in Iran that had removed the democratically elected Prime Minister, Mohammed Mosaddegh, from office and returned the brutal monarch, Shah Reza Pahlavi, to power. For more, see Ervand Abrahamian, *The Coup* (New York: The New Press, 2013).
70 Chesly Manly, 'India Delegate in U.N. Silenced by Mrs. Pandit', *CDT*, 30/9/1953, 5. 'Mrs. Pandit Rules Russ China Move Out of Order', *Los Angeles Times*, 30/9/1953, 6.
71 Henry Hars, 'First Woman President of the U.N. Knows How to Call Angry Men to Order: Are her Tears Real?,' *Daily Boston Globe*, 20/9/1953, C1.
72 'Mr. Menon, the Diplomat', *TOI*, 22/10/1954, 11.
73 *SoH*, 286–287.
74 Alistair Cooke, 'Icy Ballet of Despair at the UN', *TMG*, 1/10/1953, 1. Paul Ward, 'India's U.N. Delegate Chides U.S.', *Baltimore Sun*, 29/9/1953, 1.
75 VLPtoTara, 21/10/1953, SPBU.
76 'The World', *NYT*, 20/9/1953, E1.
77 Elizabeth Toomey, 'Mrs. Vijaya L. Pandit', *Jerusalem Post*, 18/9/1953, 4.
78 'Profile: Mrs. Pandit', *Observer*, 20/9/1953, 3.
79 'The U.N. "Goddess of Victory",' *Newsweek*, 42(13, 28/9/1953, 51.
80 'Ariel's Men, Matters and Memories', *TOI*, 20/9/1953, 8.
81 UN Rules of Procedure, 30–37. https://www.un.org/en/ga/about/ropga/prez.shtml, 13/6/2022. VLP prepared thoroughly for her job, 'reading + re-reading the Rules of Procedure' and acquainting herself with Parliamentary Law. VLPtoTara, 23–25/9/1953, SPBU.
82 Cynthia Lowry, 'Mantle of World Leadership Suits Nan Pandit Like a Sari,' *The Atlanta Journal and the Atlanta Constitution*, 18/10/1953, 1F. Joseph Cerutti, 'U.N. President Calls on U.S. President,' *CDT*, 13/10/1953, 3.
83 Jesse Zel Lurie, 'Turkey wins Coveted Security Council Seat', *Jerusalem Post*, 6/10/1953, 1. 'Mrs Pandit Reprimands Vyshinsky', *SCMP*, 6/10/1953, 1.
84 'U.N. Yesterday: UNICEF is backed by all 60 nations', *NYHT*, 7/10/1953, 8.
85 'Vivid Example of Cooperation: UNICEF Praised', *TOI*, 23/10/1953, 8.
86 '"Consequences Serious" if Rhee Frees Captives as He Plans, Reds Warn', *Toronto Daily Star*, 7/10/1953, 1. Neha Banka, '70 Years of the Korean War', India's Lesser-Known Role in Halting It,' *Indian Express*, 1/7/2020, https://indianexpress.com/article/research/70-years-of-korean-war-indias-lesser-known-role-in-halting-it-6476030/, 13/6/2022. 'UN to Back Guards',

*CSM*, 8/10/1953, 1. 'Reds in Angry Protest at Panmunjom Meeting', *WaPo*, 8/10/1953, 3. '"Korea Impasse can be Solved": "Ike" Expresses View to Mrs. Pandit', *TOI*, 13/10/1953, 1. 'Suggested Date for Korea Talks', *Irish Times*, 13/10/1953, 1. Record of meeting between Madame Pandit and President Eisenhower, Eisenhower's Records as President; Official File Series; Box 290; OF-85-B General Assembly (1), Eisenhower Presidential Library. See also TNAUK: FO 371/105530, Fk1076/310, 1953.

87 The material in this section is a summary of documents contained in FBI files related to VLP that I acquired via a Freedom of Information Law (FOIL) request. The quote from Hoover is a declassified secret, personal and confidential memo for the Attorney General, dated 13/11/1953. Cf. Document 138, '*Memorandum of Conversation, by William O. Hall of the Mission at the United Nations*', 23/10/1953,, FRUS, 1952–1954, Volume III, United Nations Affairs, https://history.state.gov/historicaldocuments/frus1952-54v03/d138. Last accessed 9/6/2022.

88 VLP was in the city of Chicago early on in her days as US ambassador and was riding in a taxi. The driver noticed she was an Indian woman and began to speak highly of Gandhi and Nehru, before bursting out 'But that sister of his, Madame Pandit! She is the greatest!' VLP, flattered and bemused, asked if he had ever met her. When he said no, she introduced himself to his great shock and delight. As recalled by missionary and writer Anna Mow. Nayantara Sahgal, Chandralekha Mehta, and Rita Dar, eds., *Sunlight Surround You* (New Delhi: Orient Longmans, 1970), 147. On another occasion in September, shortly after she had taken up her post as president, she was returning home from an evening with Dorothy Norman. The taxi driver in New York City told her as he picked her up 'how thrilled he was to see [her] . . . standing on the pavement'. He said that 'all the right people in the country' were backing her and her brother'. He refused payment from her saying, 'Don't spoil the happiest day in my life. God bless.' The doorman at her building was flabbergasted and told her he had never heard of such a thing happening. VLPtoTara, 23–25/9/1953, SPBU.

89 Rosemary Whitaker, 'Activities at . . . Ruffner Junior High', *New Journal and Guide*, 24/10/1953, C13. The CIA produced a secret report on VLP in 1954, summarizing the 'considerable information' it had collected on her over the years. It concluded that the 'bulk' of their data was 'non-derogatory' in nature. Other than that, it noted the outreach she had made to the communist and 'Arab-Islamic' worlds, saying of these that they might be either derogatory or of intelligence interest to the US, but also that such accounts as they had were only fragmentary. There was nothing in the report that might be characterized as negative. 'Vijaya Lakshmi Pandit,' CIA Secret Report, 2/4/1954, 105-HQ-8802-3 FDPS, 9–10, access given through FOIA.

90 'Mrs. Pandit Stresses Atrocity Proof Need,' *WaPo*, 2/11/1953, 3. Longines Chronoscope interview with VLP, CBS, 1953, https://search.alexanderstreet.com/preview/work/bibliographic_entity%7Cvideo_work%7C1786729, 14/6/2022.

91 'Duties Carried out with Tact and Intelligence': Tribute to Mrs. Pandit as U.N. President,' *TOI*, 11/12/1953, 8.

92 VLPtoTara, 28/10/1953, SPBU.

93 VLPtoTara, 11/10/1953, SPBU.

94 'Honor Mme. Pandit as "Woman of Year"', *Women's Wear Daily*, 87(113), 8/12/1953, 6. George Gallup, 'Mrs Roosevelt Voted Most Admired Woman',

*Los Angeles Times*, 06/1/1954. An Associated Press poll named VLP runner up for its Woman of the Year, which went to Queen Elizabeth. 'Woman of the Year', *SCMP*, 16/12/1953, 10. Long-serving Indian Foreign Service officer Maharajakrishna Rasgotra, who would eventually rise to become India's Foreign Secretary, got to know VLP from the early fifties and worked closely with her while she was the UNGA President. He writes that she 'had a great capacity to laugh and to make others laugh' and observes that she 'was a natural master of the art of diplomacy' (27–28). He classifies her as one of India's 'star-quartet' of top diplomats, which also included Krishna Menon, Radhakrishnan, and K.M. Pannikar. He writes that she and the others were 'heroes' and 'good teachers' to the younger members of the I.F.S. MEA top brass freely criticized all the others, but not VLP, which he says was, while of course because she was Nehru's sister, but primarily 'because of her undoubted diplomatic skills' (39). Maharajakrishna Rasgotra, *A Life in Diplomacy* (Delhi: Penguin/Viking, 2019).

95 'Eisenhower urges Pooling Atom Resources', *Hartford Courant*, 9/12/1953, 1. '60 Years of 'Atoms for Peace', https://www.iaea.org/newscenter/news/60-years-atoms-peace, 14/6/2022. 'Atoms for Peace' speech, President Dwight D. Eisenhower, 8/12/1953, https://www.atomicarchive.com/resources/documents/deterrence/atoms-for-peace.html, 14/6/2022. 'Ike the Gallante', *Newsday*, 9/12/1953, 64.

96 Thomas Hamilton, 'State Heads Urged to Speak at U.N.', *NYT*, 10/12/1953, 8.

97 'Mrs. Pandit Doubts Soviet Rejection', *Los Angeles Times*, 11/12/1953, 22. Cf. Phillip Merriweather, 'Atom-Moulded World of Tomorrow', *TOI*, 5/12/1954, 8.

98 'Peaceful Co-Existence of East-West Important', *TOI*, 21/9/1954, 5. 'Van Kleffens New Assembly President', *Jerusalem Post*, 22/9/1954, p.1. 'Excerpts from Addresses at the Opening of the U.N. Assembly', *NYT*, 22/9/1954, 6. Technically, she would have to reconvene the 8th Session and bring it to a close, and then open the 9th Session. See also Erlandsson, *Personal Politics in the Postwar World*, 50–52.

99 'Mrs. Pandit Hopeful of U.N. Session Next Month', *Times of* India, 21/1/1954, 6. Francis W. Carpenter, 'West Stand Seen Dooming U.N. Session on Korea', *Hartford Courant*, 29/1/1954, 7. Alistair Cooke, 'No U.N. Debate on Korea', *TMG*, 30/1/1954, 5. Document 856, 20/1/1954, Confidential, FRUS, 1952-1954, Volume XV Part 2, https://history.state.gov/historicaldocuments/frus1952-54v15p2/d856. Last accessed 15/6/2022. And Document 863, 28/1/1954, Confidential, Ibid., https://history.state.gov/historicaldocuments/frus1952-54v15p2/d863, 15/6/2022.

100 'Kamala Nehru Hospital', *TOI*, 3/1/1954, 2. 'Mrs. Pandit', *TOI*, 6/1/1954, 8. VLPtoTara, 9, 11/1/1954, SPBU.

101 'U.N.'s Success Depends on Loyalty of Individual', *TOI*, 30/1/1953, 11.

102 'Great Welcome for Mrs. Pandit', *TOI*, 16/3/1954, 7. 'Great Buddhist Council Opens', *TMG*, 18/5/1954, 16. 'Mrs. Pandit Tours', *GandM*, 16/6/1954, 10. 'The Queen to receive Mrs. Pandit on July 5', *TOI*, 28/6/1954, 5. 'Malaya Tour of Mrs. Pandit', *TOI*, 11/8/1954, 11.

103 *SoH*, 278–282.

104 'Declaration of "No War",' *Times of* India, 30/3/1954, 7. 'Women M.P.s Condemn H-Bomb Tests', *TOI*, 8/4/1954, 7. 'Ending Arms Race', *TOI*, 15/4/1954, 9. 'Only Gandhian Way to Peace', *TOI*, 21/4/1954, 7. 'Work to

Create Climate for Peace to Thrive', *TOI*, 8/7/1954, 7. 'Women's Role in Peace', *TOI*, 13/8/1954, 8.
105 Dorothy Bowles, 'A Lovely Take of Childhood During India's Revolution', *NYHT*, 9/5/1954, E4.
106 'Mrs. V.L. Pandit', *SCMP*, 12/6/1954, 10. Envoys within the Commonwealth were designated 'High Commissioners' instead of 'Ambassadors', but the meaning was the same.
107 VLPtoTara, 10/6/1954, SPBU.
108 VLPtoTara, 14/6/1954, SPBU.
109 'The Queen to receive Mrs. Pandit on/7/5', *TOI*, 28/6/1954, 5. 'Mrs. Pandit's Visit', *TMG*, 6/7/1954, 16. I wrote to Queen Elizabeth to inquire if she had any recollections of VLP she might share and received the courtesy of a response from Buckingham Palace. Her Majesty could not possibly comment, I was told, but she wished me well with this book.
110 Manu Bhagavan interview with K. Shankar Bajpai, personal secretary to VLP in 1954. Cf. Nayantara Sahgal, *The Political Imagination* (Delhi: HarperCollins, 2014).
111 'Mrs. Pandit calls for Tolerance', *TOI*, 14/7/1954, 7. Cf. Stella Alexander, 'Mrs. Pandit feted at Big Receptions', *TOI*, 25/7/1954, 10.
112 'Embassy Post for Mrs Pandit', *SCMP*, 24/9/1954, 8. 'Mrs. Pandit Named', *Jerusalem Post*, 26/9/1954, p.1. 'New Envoy to Ireland', *The Hartford Courant*, 5/10/1954, 7.
113 'Mme. Pandit Bid U.S. Bolster Asians' Hopes', *NYHT*, 7/10/1954, 3.
114 'Mme. Pandit says India hailed School Decision', *NYT*, 7/10/1954, 26. By this point, Menon had undertaken serious efforts to undermine VLP. The Ministry of External Affairs wanted her to return to India immediately after her term as president ended because, they claimed, she might otherwise embarrass the Indian delegation. They also expressly rejected allowing her to travel to Japan in an official capacity. Nehru had also been reluctant to commit to making VLP High Commissioner through August, ostensibly because Menon was making hints that he wanted the position again for himself. These matters had really angered her. VLPtoTara, 5/8/1954, SPBU.
115 *SoH*, 285. 'Royal Family Attends Autumn Garden Party', 29/10/1954, Getty Photos, https://www.gettyimages.co.nz/detail/news-photo/emperor-hirohito-greets-guests-during-the-autumn-garden-news-photo/1262031895, 20/6/2022.
116 'Mrs. Pandit Honoured', *TOI*, 29/10/1954, 5. 'Mrs. Pandit Honoured', *TOI*, 7/11/1954, 9. Cf. TNAUK, FO 371/112223, DL1903/41, 1954.
117 'India's Woman Envoy', *TOI*, 28/12/1954, 7.
118 'Our London Correspondence', *TMG*, 22/1/1955, 4.
119 S. Mulgaokar, 'U.K. Press Warmly Hails Mrs. Pandit as Envoy', *TOI*, 22/12/1954, p.1. See also John Mason, 'Madame Ambassador: The Remarkable Mrs. Pandit,' *The Irish Times*, 18/1/1955, 6.
120 Quoted material is from Amit Das Gupta, *Serving India* (Delhi: Manohar, 2017), 195, 198–199, 231. Jairam Ramesh, *A Chequered Brilliance* (Delhi: Penguin/Viking, 397–398, 400–401, 406–407, 411–412, 414–415. These works are very detailed biographies of Subimal Dutt and VKKM respectively. Ramesh (305–306) notes that VKKM and Mathai were 'thick as thieves' in this period (1945–1955/56) and that they routinely shared information and documents. (Ramesh to me, email, 20/2/2023.) These included even 'secret' and 'personal'

material sent to the Prime Minister (perhaps explaining how all sorts of files are among VKKM's papers at NMML). (See, for instance, Radhakrishnan to Nehru, 31/8/1951, with personal notation from Mathai (12/9/1951), VKKM papers, S-file 695-II, NMML, 513.) Menon made the most of this special intelligence, deploying it for his own ends as needed. (One illustration of his maneuverings against VLP can be found in Telegram from VKKM to Mathai, 16/8/1951, Immediate, Top Secret, Priority, VKKM papers, S-file 695-II, NMML, 964. Here he prods Mathai to keep VLP from her brother to prevent the P.M. from being over-burdened.) But privy to confidential whispers while bereft of broader context and other private communications also fed his paranoia and sense of self-pity.

## Chapter 14: Brick Lane

1 *SoH*, 286–289. See also: India House (Offices of the Indian Embassy), Making Britain, The Open University, https://www.open.ac.uk/researchprojects/makingbritain/content/india-house-offices-indian-embassy, 4/7/2022. 'Kensington Palace Gardens', Wikipedia, https://en.wikipedia.org/wiki/Kensington_Palace_Gardens, 4/7/2022. Cf. Dipankar De Sarkar, 'No Plush Residence for Indian High Commissioner in London', *India Today*, https://www.indiatoday.in/magazine/international/story/19900531-no-plush-residence-for-indian-high-commissioner-in-london-812634-1990-05-31, 4/7/2022. 'The Crown Estate in Kensington Palace Gardens', British History Online, https://www.british-history.ac.uk/survey-london/vol37/pp162-193#h2-0004, 4/7/2022. 'Kensington Palace Gardens: London's Most Expensive Street', 21/3/2022, https://www.homeviews.com/blog/kensington-palace-gardens-londons-most-expensive-street/, 4/7/2022.

2 'Mr. N.R. Pillai in Premier's Party', *TOI*, 18/1/1955, 11. VLPtoJN, Confidential Note, 8/7/1955, Pandit Papers (Ist Inst.), Sub File 62, 17.

3 VLPtoJN, Confidential Note, 8/7/1955, 17–20, PP(I)62. 'Mrs. Pandit', *TOI*, 25/12/1954, 10. The British internally were keenly aware of VKKM's deleterious nature, noting that he had done everything in his power to obstruct VLP's appointment as High Commissioner. Alec Clutterbuck, the UK's High Commissioner to India wrote that VKKM had many flaws: 'His tortuous mind . . . his total incapacity to express himself in any straight-forward way; his light regard for the truth; and his inordinate ambition and self-conceit.' He added that the 'utterly unscrupulous' Menon was universally mistrusted, except by Nehru (and Mathai), even revealing that Mahatma Gandhi had so been informed earlier. He mocked the view, frequently touted by Nehru, that VKKM was well-respected in Western quarters. TNAUK, FO 371/112223, DL1903/40, 1954, Secret.

4 VLP to Subimal Dutt, Personal and Confidential, 29/3/1955, 13–14, PP(II)17(I). These problems would persist for the duration of her London stay. See letter to N.R. Pillai, 18/12/1959, 327–328, PP(II)17(ii). In one instance, she had to facilitate the departure of P.N. Haksar, whom she thought very highly of and with whom she developed 'a warm, personal relationship'. (62). Haksar had been with the High Commissioner's Office for five years by that point and was keen to move on, his decision not reflective of VLP or MEA related issues. Haksar would go on to become a close advisor to Prime Minister Indira Gandhi. For details, see Jairam Ramesh, *Intertwined Lives* (New Delhi: Simon & Shuster, 2018).

5   VLPtoJN, Confidential Note, 8/7/1955, 20, PP(I)62.
6   For a good overview of diplomatic relations during VLP's High Commissionership, see Rakesh Ankit, 'Between Vanity and Sensitiveness', *Contemporary British History* 30(1): 2016, 20–39. For an analysis of VLP's contributions to international law and to the development of intellectual thought on non-alignment in the years leading into Bandung, see Parvathi Menon, 'Vijayalakshmi Pandit: Gendering and Racing against the Postcolonial Predicament', in Immi Tallgren, ed. *Portraits of Women in International Law* (New York: Oxford University Press, forthcoming), 244-252. I am grateful to Menon for sharing advance proofs of her chapter with me.
7   VLPtoJN, 13/5/1955, 13–14, PP(I)62. I tried to cross check VLP's parliamentary discussions in Hansard's but was unable to locate any relevant record. Across the pond, despite critical press accounts, Western officials in the United States concluded that the Bandung Conference 'was highly constructive' and they credited Nehru almost entirely for serving as a moderating influence, which they felt could yield new diplomatic fruit—a means to discuss and resolve other matters of tension in the world. Communication of this was done through back-channels via VLP. Chester Bowles to VLP, 2/5/1955, VLP to Bowles, 3/5/1955, Chester Bowles Papers, Part 4, Correspondence: Vijaya Lakshmi Pandit, 150 0506, Group No. 628, Series No. I, Box No. 150, Part IV: 1953 Apr–1958 Dec, Manuscript Collections, Yale University Library.
8   JNtoVLP, 22 August, 12/10/1955, 59–60, 66, PP(I)61. VLPtoJN, 1/12/1955, 33, PP(I)62.
9   VLPtoJN, 1, 21 December 1955, 33–36, 49–50, PP(I)62. JNtoVLP, 5/12/1955, 72-72a, PP(I)61.
10  Secret Memorandum of VLP talk with Lord Home, 9/12/1955, 39–43, PP(I)62. JNtoVLP, 15/12/1955, 73, PP(I)61.
11  Secret Summary of conversation between VLP and Selwyn Lloyd, 22/1/1956, 54–55, PP(I)62. See also S. Mulgaokar, 'A Letter from London: British-Indian Relations', *TOI*, 11/2/1956, 6. And Pallavi Raghavan, 'Journeys of Discovery,' in Manu Bhagavan, ed. *India and the Cold War* (Delhi: Penguin, 2019), 32).
12  Hutheesing, 'Nehru and Madame Pandit, By their Sister', 34–35, 76–83.
13  VLPtoJN, 15/5/1956, 75–76, PP(I)62.
14  VLPtoJN, 21/12/1955, 28/8/1958, 26/10/1959, 52, 220, 294, PP(I)62. JNtoVLP, 1/8/1957, 15/9/1958, 160, 224, PP(I)61.
15  JNtoVLP, 1/9/1958, 219, PP(I)61. Cf. K. Natwar Singh, *Treasured Epistles* (Delhi: Rupa, 2018). The sisters continued to 'quarrel' regularly through the rest of Betty's life (Kindle page 2234).
16  For details, see Ritu Menon, *Out of Line* (New Delhi: Fourth Estate, 2014), esp. 33–37, 82–85, 322–323. JNtoVLP, 8/11/1958, 4, 12, 15 January, 18/6/1959, 231, 237–239, 255, PP(I)61. 'Nicolas Wyrouboff', *Wikipedia*, https://fr.wikipedia.org/wiki/Nicolas_Wyrouboff, 18/7/2022.
17  VLPtoJN, 13/5/1955, 5 March, 15/5/1956, 1/7/1958, 6/3/1959, 6/11/1960, 9 April (jointly to Indira Gandhi), 26 May, 3/6/1961, 13, 70, 77, 201, 254, 355, 371-372, 391-393, PP(I)62. Indira Gandhi to VLP, 7/8/1961, Pandit papers (Ist Inst.), Correspondence with Indira Gandhi, 27-28, NMML. Email from Nayantara Sahgal to me, 16/7/2022.
18  VLPtoJN, 28 March, 17/11/1955, 30 March, 15 August, 29/9/1ssss959, 14/4/1961,10, 25, 257, 273-274, 280, 376, PP(I)62. VLPtoTara, 21/1/1956, SPBU.

19 *SoH*, 290.
20 Top Secret Memo of Interview with Winston Churchill, VLPtoJN, 28/23/3/1955, 6-9, PP(I)62. Churchill to Nehru, 21/2/1955, 7, PP(I)61.
21 Secret and Personal, VLPtoJN, 15/5/1956, 79, PP(I)62. JNtoVLP, 22/5/1956, 84, PP(I)61.
22 Personal and Secret, VLPtoJN, 28 June, 22/10/1958, 23/3/1959, 196-197, 235, 255, PP(I)62.
23 'L.L.D. for Mrs. Pandit,' *TOI*, 20/5/1955, 7. 'Voice Only,' *TMG*, 9/11/1955, 5
24 'U.K. Honour for Mrs. Pandit,' *TOI*, 25/11/1955, 7. The ceremony and VLP's recognition can be seen in several videos: 'UK: London University: Queen Mother as Chancellor (1955)', https://www.youtube.com/watch?v=tZ-IePszTJE, 19/7/2022. 'Queen Mother as Chancellor of London University (1955), https://www.youtube.com/watch?v=k_SDW3CAKTU, 19/7/2022. Selected Originals - Queen Mother As Chancellor Of London University (1955), https://www.youtube.com/watch?v=0slKhWnF5G4, 19/7/2022.
25 Manu Bhagavan interview with Lady Pamela Hicks, 14/6/2019. VLPtoJN, 15/5/1956, 4 March, 22/10/1958, 29/9/1959, 73-74, 190, 235, 280-282 (PPI)62. Edwina had grown close to both Nehrus while her husband was serving as Viceroy in India. For details, see Alex Von Tunzelmann, *Indian Summer* (New York: Picador, 2007), 176-177.
26 Josephine Ripley, 'Mrs. Mesta Relates Asian Adventures', *CSM*, 21/10/1955, 5. Marie McNair, 'Perle Mesta says the Far East "is Sizzling",' *WaPo and Times Herald*, 20/10/1955, 17.
27 See for instance: 'How Many of these 16 'Great Ladies' can you name?' *NYT*, 5/10/1955, 22.
28 'Honors for 17 Women', *NYT*, 20/7/1956, 30.
29 'Green eyed, 5-foot-5 Brunette (36-23-36)—That's Miss Nassau', *Newsday*, 16/5/1955, 4.
30 'Brando Goes for Warmth', *Picturegoer* 32 (1124), 17/11/1976, 29.
31 'Effects of Atomic Warfare: Lord Russell's Plan', *TMG*, 10/2/1955, 16. 'Mr. Nehru Appeals', *The Times of* India, 3/4/1954, 6.
32 'Russell's Move on H-Bomb', *TOI*, 20/2/1955, 9. VLPtoJN, 22/2/1955, 2-3, PP(I)62. JNtoVLP, 28/2/1955, 6, PP(I)61. *The Collected Works of Bertrand Russell, Volume 28: Man's Peril (1954-1955)*, 464-469.
33 'World Atom Experts End Week of Talks', *The Baltimore Sun*, 23/1/1955, 3. 'Indian is asked to head Atoms-for-Peace Parley', *NYT*, 29/1/1955, 7.
34 'Consequences of Nuclear Warfare', 2/3/1955, Letter to Homi Bhabha, 11/3/1955, 'Appointment of an Investigatory Committee,' 21/3/1955, 'International Control of Atomic Energy', 18/4/1955, 'Peaceful Uses of Atomic Energy', 18/4/1955, 'Banning the Use of Nuclear Weapons,' 18/4/1955, *SWJN*, Series 2, Volume 28, 199-210. https://nehruselectedworks.com/pdfviewer.php?style=UI_Zine_Material.xml&su*B*Folder=&doc=February_1955-May_1955-Series2-Vol28.pdfl24l662#page=4, 20/7/2022. Cf. Bakhtiar Dadabhoy, *Homi Bhabha: A Life* (Delhi: Rupa, 2023), esp. 490-500.
35 Russell, Man's Peril, 466; 'Russell-Einstein Manifesto', https://www.atomicheritage.org/key-documents/russell-einstein-manifesto, 20/7/2022; https://pugwash.org, 20/7/2022. The Manifesto would serve as the basis of the Pugwash Conferences, which would begin in 1957 and carry forward Russell's mission, leading to a Nobel Peace Prize in 1995.

36 'World Brotherhood', *SCMP*, 6/2/1956, 7. 'World Brotherhood Organization Formed in Paris; Religious Groups Meet to Expand It', 13/6/1950, https://www.jta.org/archive/world-brotherhood-organization-formed-in-paris-religious-groups-meet-to-expand-it, 20/7/2022.
37 VLP, 'India's Foreign Policy', *Foreign Affairs* 34(3), April 1956 (no page numbers available).
38 'Collecting and Empire', https://blog.britishmuseum.org/collecting-and-empire/, 20/7/2022.
39 Shashank Shekhar Sinha, 'The Lesser Known Journey of Buddhist Relics—from India to UK and Back', *Wire*, https://thewire.in/history/the-lesser-known-journey-of-buddhist-relics-from-india-to-uk-and-back, 20/7/2022. Information about the value and meaning of Buddhist relics quoted from Vidya Dehejia.
40 Himanshu Prabha Ray, *The Return of the Buddha* (Delhi: Routledge, 2014), 122-123. 'Helping Foreign Objects', *TOI*, 2/2/1956, 5. 'Mrs. Pandit on Indo-British Relations,' *TOI*, 4/2/1956, 5. 'Buddhist Relics Given to Society,' *TOI*, 6/2/1956, 1. 'Buddha's Message Alone Can Save the World', *TOI*, 7/2/1956, 8. 'Claiming Indian Art Treasures from Other Countries', 3/2/1956, *SWJN*, Series 2, Volume 32, 90-92. https://nehruselectedworks.com/pdfviewer.php?style=UI_Zine_Material.xml&su*B*Folder=&doc=February_1956-April_1956-Series2-Vol32.pdf|16|642#page=126, 20/7/2022. VLPtoTara, 21/1/1956, SPBU.
41 VLPtoJN, 15/9/1956, 93-95, PP(I)62.
42 JNtoVLP, 24/7/1956, 19/9/1957, 92-97, 173-175, PP(I)61.
43 VLPtoJN, 19/8/1957, 132-134, PP(I)62.
44 Manu Bhagavan interview with K. Shankar Bajpai.
45 VLPtoJN, 14/10/1958, 231-232, PP(I)62.
46 'Madame Ambassador', *Irish Times*, 18/1/1955, 6.
47 'Irish Republic: Visit by Mrs. Pandit', 22/3/1955, in 'Visits of Mrs Vijaya Lakshmi Pandit (to present her credentials as the new Ambassador of India) to "Ireland" in/3/1955 and April 1956', TNAUK: DO 35/5038.
48 '"Partition is bad", says Mrs. Pandit', *Irish Times*, 25/2/1955, 9. See also extract of private Gilbert Laithwaite to Alexander Clutterbuck, 9/5/1956, in TNAUK: DO 35/5038.
49 VLPtoJN, 1, 29 June 1956, 84-87, PP(I)62. The 29 June letter appears erroneously dated by context and was likely written on the 19th.
50 Nehru to GB Pant, 26/6/1956, *SWJN*, Volume 34, 262. https://nehruselectedworks.com/pdfviewer.php?style=UI_Zine_Material.xml&su*B*Folder=&doc=June_1956-August_1956-Series2-Vol34.pdf|16|516#page=300, 25/7/2022. In truth, there were many who were unhappy with VKKM, and who desperately tried to convey this message to the Indian government, but Menon had consistently outmaneuvered them, preventing such news from reaching Nehru's ears. I could not find similar discontent with VLP. See Khushwant Singh, *Not A Nice Man to Know*, 74–75.
51 'Towards One-World', 3/7/1956, *SWJN*, Volume 34, 265-266. https://nehruselectedworks.com/pdfviewer.php?style=UI_Zine_Material.xml&su*B*Folder=&doc=June_1956-August_1956-Series2-Vol34.pdf|16|516#page=306, 25/7/2022.
52 'Cable to Vijayalakshmi Pandit', 27/7/1956, *SWJN*, Series 2, Volume 34, 318-319. https://nehruselectedworks.com/pdfviewer.php?style=UI_Zine_

Material.xml&suBFolder=&doc=June_1956-August_1956-Series2-Vol34. pdf|16|516#page=358, 26/7/2022.
53 VLPtoJN, 28/7/1956, 89, PP(I)62. JNtoVLP, 4/8/1956, 100-101, PP(I)61.
54 VLPtoTara, 7/8/1956, SPBU.
55 'Iraq Backs Egypt on Suez', 6/8/1956, *Courier* Post, 6/8/1956, 1, 3. S. Mulgaukar, 'No Commitment is Implied', *TOI*, 7/8/1956, p.1. 'India Seen Likely Mediator on Suez,' *The Jerusalem Post*, 8/8/1956, 1. JNtoVLP, 8/8/1956, 102-104, PP(I)61. Dulles asked Nehru to attend the conference personally, but the Indian PM decided against this. 'Our London Correspondence', *TMG*, 9/8/1956, 4. The British leaned on VLP to persuade Nasser not to reject the conference outright. Secret minute by the Foreign Secretary, seen by the Prime Minister, 24/8/1956, TNAUK: FO 371/119122, JE14211/1279, 1956.
56 'Our London Correspondence', *TMG*, 17/8/1956, 6.
57 'Cable to Vijayalakshmi Pandit', *SWJN*, Series 2, Volume 34, 359-360. https://nehruselectedworks.com/pdfviewer.php?style=UI_Zine_Material.xml&suBFolder=&doc=June_1956-August_1956-Series2-Vol34.pdf|16|516#page=402. Last accessed 26/7/2022. One of the other Indian delegates was Jagat Mehta, my teacher at the University of Texas at Austin.
58 VLPtoTara, 11/8/1956, SPBU.
59 VLPtoTara, 23/8/1956, SPBU.
60 'Our London Correspondence', *TMG*, 3/10/1956, 6.
61 VLPtoTara, 16/8/1956, SPBU. 'Mrs. Pandit flies Home', *WaPo*, 10/10/1956, 4.
62 'Mrs. Vijaya Pandit,' *SCMP*, 13/11/1956, 7.
63 Francine Frankel, *When Nehru Looked East* (New York: Oxford University Press, 2020), 239.
64 VLPtoTara, 12/11/1956, SPBU.
65 Cable to G.L. Mehta and Vijaya Lakshmi Pandit, 15/11/1956, *SWJN*, Series 2, Volume 35, 27/7/2022.
66 Amit Das Gupta, *Serving India*, 248–266. In his review of the book, TCA Raghavan points out that there was a substantial section within the MEA that contorted themselves into believing Suez to be an inappropriate colonial intervention and Hungary to be an event where a Great Power was somewhat legitimately acting in its interests in its own neighborhood. TCA Raghavan review of Amit Das Gupta, *Serving India*, https://networks.h-net.org/node/22055/reviews/1486995/raghavan-das-gupta-serving-india-political-biography-subimal-dutt, 27/7/2022.
67 VLPtoJN, 26/11/1956, 99-101, PP(I)62.
68 'Lead Sought from Mr Nehru', *TMG*, 20/12/1956, 2.
69 Alistair Cooke, 'A Lesson from Pandit Chips', *TMG*, 22/12/1956, 1.
70 'Nehru Sees Signs of World Peace', *NYT*, 25/12/1956, 3.
71 'Indian Envoy finds Ireland "Soothing",' *Irish Times*, 2/1/1957, 7.
72 Personal and Secret, VLPtoJN, 28/6/1958, 198-199, PP(I)62.
73 JNtoVLP, 1/7/1958, 213, PP(I)61.
74 VLPtoTara, 4/4/1956, SPBU.
75 Personal and confidential, VLP to Subimal Dutt, 9/1/1956, 30-31, PP(II)17(I).
76 VLPtoJN, 15/5/1956, 79, PP(I)62.
77 VLPtoJN, 15/5/1956, 80, PP(I)62. JNtoVLP, 26/5/1956, 85, PP(I)61.
78 TNAUK: FO 371/125505.
79 Top Secret and Personal, VLP to N.R. Pillai, 28/2/1957, 90, PP(II)17(I).
80 VLPtoJN, 4/2/1957, 108-110, PP(I)62.

NOTES 507

81  Secret and Personal, JNtoVLP, 13/2/1957, 121-123, PP(I)61.
82  VLP to Chester Bowles, 31/10/1957, 144-145, PP(I)62. VLP had known Bowles for quite some time and had developed a close friendship with him. In 1952, she had sent him a *rakhi* for the festival of Raksha Bandhan, saying that this made him her 'bracelet bound brother'. VLP to Chester Bowles, 5/8/1952, Chester Bowles Papers, Part 3, Series 2, 099 0326, General Correspondence: Government of India, Vijaya Lakshmi Pandit, Group No. 628, Series No. 11, Box No. 99, Part III: 1951–1953, India and Nepal Correspondence, Manuscript Collections, Yale University Library. For his part, Bowles credited VLP with kindling his interest in India, tracing it to a dinner she threw for him in October 1951. Bowles to VLP, 16/4/1969, Chester Bowles Papers, Part 7, Series 1, 335 0167, Correspondence: Vijaya Lakshmi Pandit, Group No. 628, Series No. I, Box No. 335, Part VII: 1963 July–1969 May, Manuscript Collections, Yale University Library.
83  Kathleen Teltsch, 'Exhaustion Stops Indian's U.N. Talk', *NYT*, 12/11/1957, 4. See also 'Mr. Menon Ill', *TOI*, 12/11/1957, 1. 'Menon Halts Kashmir Talk in Exhaustion', *NYHT*, 12/11/1957, 4. British officials were also taken aback by 'the Menon exhibition' in New York. See conversation between VLP and the Secretary of State for Commonwealth Relations, 20/11/1957, TNAUK: FO 371/129782, DY1041/425, 1957, Secret. See also 'Conversation with Mrs. Pandit', FO 371/129780, DY1041/393, 1957. Officials note on the file cover that 'Mrs. P and Mr. Menon hate each other like poison!'
84  Handwritten letter from VLPtoJN, 20/11/1957, Pandit Papers (Ist Inst.), Sub File 62, 160-169.
85  Handwritten response from JNtoVLP, 27/11/1957, 193, PP(I)61.
86  VLPtoJN, 24/12/1958, 251-252, PP(I)62.
87  VLPtoJN, 2/11/1957, 10/1/1958, 149-150, 170-172, PP(I)62.
88  VLPtoJN, 28/6/1958, 8,17, 20, 26 May, 4/8/1961, 195, 379, 381-384, 390, 408, PP(I)62. Restricted telegram VLPtoJN, Dr. Pratool Bhandari to Nehru, 24/4/1961, 334, 342-343, PP(I)61.
89  VLPtoJN, 3, 6 September 1958, 221-226, PP(I)62. 'Mrs. Pandit's Reception,' *TOI*, 5/9/1958, 7.
90  'India wants Loans not Grants,' *TOI*, 6/9/1958, 9.
91  Secret Memo, VLP to Ministry of External Affairs, 24/10/1958, pp, 199-200, PP(II)17(ii).
92  Secret Report on Visit to Spain, VLPtoJN, 13/11/1958, VLPtoJN, 28/6/1958, 19/2/1960, and Dutt to VLP, 19/11/1958, 199, 239–250, 319-321, PP(I)62. VLP to Ministry of External Affairs, 3 November, 19/12/1958, pp, 209–212, 216–218, PP(II)17(ii).
93  VLPtoJN, 9/4/1959, 266-270, PP(I)62.
94  'Help by India', *SCMP*, 6/4/1959, 18.
95  'India Send Army to Tibet Border to Block Chinese', 30/8/1959, 1. VLPtoJN, 30/8/1959, 275, PP(I)62. 'Eisenhower, Macmillan Confer on World Issues', *Baltimore Sun*, 30/8/1959. VLP met with Eisenhower in the home of America's ambassador, John Hay Whitney.
96  'China indicted for going back on Assurances', *TOI*, 11/9/1959.
97  Top Secret, VLPtoJN, 1/10/1959, 286-290, PP(I)62. Includes a secret report from M.A. Husain.
98  JNtoVLP, 6/10/1959, Telegrams to VKKM, 23, 24 October 1959, *SWJN*, Series 2, Volume 53, 488, 491-493. https://nehruselectedworks.com/pdfviewer.

php?style=UI_Zine_Material.xml&su*B*Folder=&doc=October_1959-Series2-Vol53.pdf|5|588#page=514, 31/7/2022.
99  'India upset by Dispute with China', *Irish Times*, 6/10/1959, 1. VLP repeated these claims a bit more forcefully a few weeks later at Washington University of St. Louis. 'India May Have to Resort to Force', *TOI*, 20/11/1959, 8.
100 'Mrs. Pandit Scores Attitudes of U.S.', *NYT*, 10/11/1957, 55. VLPtoJN, 9/4/1959, Pandit Papers (Ist Inst.), Sub File 62, 153-158. This was the same trip where she grew deeply concerned about VKKM's physical and mental health.
101 VLPtoJN, 4/6/1959, 271-272, PP(I)62.
102 Paul Tobenkin, 'Stevenson in Warning Against U.S. "Despair",' *NYHT*, 1.
103 Mary Hornaday, 'Mrs. Pandit chats about U.S.-India Relations', *CSM*, 6/10/1959, 5.
104 'Mrs. Pandit asks Peiping U.N. Seat', *NYT*, 6/10/1959, p.1.
105 VLPtoJN, 26/10/1959, 297, PP(I)62.
106 https://aucenter.edu/history/, 1/8/2022.
107 VLPtoJN, 26/10/1959, 295–300, PP(I)62.
108 'Queen's Visit of Great Significance', *TOI*, 21/1/1961, p.7.
109 P. Das Gupta, 'Great Delhi Welcome to Elizabeth II', *TOI*, 22/1/1961, 1.
110 Henry Hayward, 'State of the Nation', *CSM*, 23/1/1961, 1.
111 Punyapriya Dasgupta, 'Visit to Village in Rajasthan', *TOI*, 23/1/1961, p.1. Punyapriya Dasgupta, 'Calcutta's Massive Welcome to Queen', *TOI*, 18/2/1961, 1. 'Two-day Visit to City', *TOI*, 23/2/1961, 1.
112 'Queen Joins in Celebrations', *TOI*, 28/1/1951, 8.
113 The *LA Times* was among the worst of the coverage, practically catcalling through its entire story, using words like 'knockout . . . wow . . . a doll . . . [and] wolf whistles'. 'Queen a Knockout in New, Slinky Gown', *Los Angeles Times*, 20/3/1961, 2.
114 Emma Harrison, 'Bridge to Peace Held India's Aim', *NYT*, 15/1/1957, 6.
115 VLPtoJN, 13/10/1958, 229-230, PP(I)62.
116 VLPtoJN, 22/11/1960, 357, PP(I)62.
117 VLP had also received non-military equipment, as when she accepted papers for a small fleet of airliners on behalf of Indian Airlines. 'India Receives first of Fleet of "Viscounts",' *SCMP*, 17/8/1957, 22. 'Viscount Brings the Jet Age to India', *TOI*, 4/10/1957, 10. She also signed an agreement between her government and Rolls Royce to build aircraft engines for the Indian Airforce. 'India to Build Aircraft Engines', *SCMP*, 31/12/1959, 14.
118 'Proposal to Purchase Three Destroyers', *TOI*, 25/4/1957, 1. 'British Cruiser Transferred to the Indian Navy', *SCMP*, 30/8/1957, 1. The Mysore had been acquired in 1954. 'Second Cruiser for Navy', *TOI*, 29/8/1957, 4. 'Another U.K. Cruiser Acquired', *TOI*, 31/8/1957, 4. 'Anti-Aircraft Frigate', *TOI*, 1/4/1958, 5.
119 https://en.wikipedia.org/wiki/INS_Vikrant_(R11), 2/8/2022.
120 'India's First Naval Air Squadron', *SCMP*, 8/7/1960, 9.
121 VLPtoJN, 5/12/1960, 367, PP(I)62. JNtoVLP, 7, 15/12/1960, 321, 327, PP(I)61. *The Observer*, 5/3/1961, 8. 'India Gets her first Carrier', *SCMP*, 5/3/1961, p.1.
122 https://en.wikipedia.org/wiki/Irene_Ward. https://en.wikipedia.org/wiki/Nancy_Astor,_Viscountess_Astor, 2/8/2022. Soon after this event, VLP was one of seven individuals awarded a medal by the Integral Union for Human Rights in Mexico, an organization dedicated to promoting the values of the Universal Declaration. Winston Churchill was among the other recipients. I was unable to track down

any additional information about this Union. VLP was unable to attend the ceremony, so a local Indian official accepted on her behalf. P.L. Bhandari to S.K. Banerji, 408, 412, PP(II)17(ii).
123 'Farewell Luncheon', *The Hartford Courant*, 18/7/1961, 16.
124 https://www.thegazette.co.uk/awards-and-accreditation/content/103823, 2/8/2022.
125 JNtoVLP, 21/10/1960, 311-312, PP(I)61. Although India was a member of the Commonwealth, it did not accept the suzerainty of the crown, something that had been explicitly worked out by VKKM. *A Chequered Brilliance*, 346-350.
126 Indira Gandhi to VLP, 7/8/1961, Pandit papers (Ist Inst.), Correspondence with Indira Gandhi, 27-28, NMML.
127 JNtoVLP, 23/7/1961, 351, PP(I)61.

## Chapter 15: Home Fire

1   This section as recounted in *SoH*, 308–310. The exact timeframe of these discussions is muddled in the memoir. VLP returned to India after Hammarskjöld's funeral and was in the country by October 1961. In *SoH*, she suggests that all vice-presidential conversations took place shortly after her arrival. But she says that Nehru's final decision came on Holi, which in 1961 took place in March. Nehru's decision was actually made on Holi in March 1962. This is made clear in Nehru to Padmaja Naidu on 19/3/1962, *SWJN*, Series 2, Volume 76, 220. https://nehruselectedworks.com/pdfviewer.php?style=UI_Zine_Material.xml&suBFolder=&doc=March_1962-May_1962-Series2-Vol76.pdfl5l693#page=252, 5/8/2022. He admitted to Naidu that VLP would 'undoubtedly be a popular Vice-President . . .' The announcements of presidential and vice-presidential selections were then made the following month, So VLP's description of all of this being resolved within just a few days of her arrival back in India is overdrawn. 'Radhakrishnan is nominated,' *TOI*, 15/4/1962, 9. At the end of her life, VLP was more forthcoming, writing that in fact it was none other than VKKM who 'spiked' her candidacy. 'He advised Jawaharlal Nehru that if I were nominated as vice-president . . . it would be setting an unhealthy precedent.' This was, in truth, quite a valid assessment, however much it might have been painful to VLP. She further admitted that she was 'quite hurt' by the rejection and churlishly told her brother that she then wanted no job. Nehru chastised her for this behavior. She accepted that he was correct, ultimately leading her to accept the position of Governor of Maharashtra. This entire characterization of events is different than what is portrayed in *SoH*. See Vijaya Lakshmi Pandit, 'We Nehrus', *Illustrated Weekly of India*, 17/4/1988, p, 16.
2   'Was Dag Shot Down?,' *Austin Statesman*, 19/9/1961, 4. Susan Williams, *Who Killed Hammarskjöld?* (New York: Oxford University Press, 2014). Cf. Nehru to Harold Macmillan, 23/9/1961, *SWJN*, Series 2, Volume 71, 705-709. https://nehruselectedworks.com/pdfviewer.php?style=UI_Zine_Material.xml&suBFolder=&doc=August_1961-October_1961-Series2-Vol71.pdfl5l869#page=738, 4/8/2022.
3   JNtoVLP, 29 August, 20/9/1961, Pandit papers (II Inst), Correspondence with Jawaharlal Nehru, NMML (PPIICJN). Arthur Veysey, 'Dag is Buried Beside Father in Elm Grove', *CDT*, 30/9/1961, C10. 'India to Pay Homage', *NYT*, 24/9/1961, 16. Before his death, Hammarskjöld had come under criticism from

the Soviet Union and about his efforts to resolve the Congo crisis. He had reached out to Nan to ask for her help. Hammarskjöld's idea had been to convene a small, high-powered group of advisers consisting of VLP, Canada's Lester Pearson, and Peru's Victor Belaúnde to advise him on how to navigate the geopolitical situation. VLP had thought about it but was counseled against it by her brother, who argued that the plan seemed designed only to invite further controversy. JNtoVLP, 21/10/1960, 311-314, PP(I)61. VLP later continued to honor the UN Secretary-General's memory by joining the Board of the Foundation created in his name and delivering one of the first Dag Hammarskjöld Memorial Lectures at Columbia University. Henning Melber, ed., '50 Years Dag Hammarskjöld Foundation,' *Development Dialogue*, no. 60 (August 2012), 18-19. Andrew Cordier and Wilder Foote, eds., *The Quest for Peace* (New York: Columbia University Press, 1965).

4  'Eradication of Illiteracy', *TOI*, 17/12/1971, 7. 'A.K. Gopalan', *TOI*, 21/12/1971, 11. 'Books Exhibition', *TOI*, 7/2/1962, 8. 'Best Links of Friendship', *TOI*, 7/2/1962, 8.

5  https://www.padmaawards.gov.in/AboutAwards.aspx, 5/8/2022. 'Mrs. Pandit, Miss Naidu & Mr. Iengar Honoured', *TOI*, 26/1/1962, 1. VLP received the actual award in April 1962. 'State Award to Mrs. Pandit', *TOI*, 30/4/1962, 1.

6  Gwen Morgan, 'Mrs. Kennedy in New Delhi', *CDT*, 12/3/1962, 1. 'Indians Jam Streets to Greet First Lady', *Los Angeles Times*, 12/3/1962, 1.

7  'Lunch with the President', *TOI*, 14/3/1962, 7. Frances Lewine, 'Taj Mahal Awes Travelling Jackie', *Austin Statesman*, 15/3/1962, B15. Paul Grimes, 'India Gives Jackie a Glowing Goodby', *Atlanta Constitution*, 21/3/1962, 2.

8  Philip Dougherty, 'Mrs. Jacobs Measures Work by Golden Rule', *NYT*, 25/3/1962, 92.

9  Anna Petersen, 'Mrs. Pandit Cites Need for Women in World Politics', 6/4/1962, 22.

10 Howard Jackson, 'Make Prejudice Conquest Great as Space Conquest—Mme. Pandit', *Philadelphia Tribune*, 17/4/1962, 3.

11 'Teen-Age: Men and Events', *NYT*, 13/5/1962, BR27.

12 Barbara Walters, 'Comparison of Excellence', *Town and Country* 116 (4476: July 1962), 44-46-95-96.

13 Mary Hornaday, 'Mrs. Roosevelt: A Career for Peace', *CSM*, 8/11/1962, 3. The original reads with no caps 'first lady of the world'. When Eleanor Roosevelt died, Poppy Cannon White (who had been married to the late Walter White) wrote a column endorsing the title for VLP. Poppy Cannon White, 'First Lady of the World', *NYAN*, 14/12/1963, 13.

14 JNtoVLP, President Radhakrishnan, and Home Minister Lal Bahadur Shastri, and Mysore Chief Minister Nijalingappa to Nehru, 31 August, 2, 4 September 1962, *SWJN*, Series 2, Volume 78, 192-194, 818. https://nehruselectedworks.com/pdfviewer.php?style=UI_Zine_Material.xml&suBFolder=&doc=July_1962-September_1962-Series2-Vol78.pdf|5|883#page=852, 6/8/2022. 'Mrs. Pandit may be Next Mysore Governor', *TOI*, 16/7/1961, p.1. 'Cake Model of Museum', *TOI*, 19/7/1962, 9. Letters from VLPtoJN, Mysore Chief Minister Nijalingappa, and President Radhakirishnan, 23, 24 August 1962, 12-14, PPIICJN.

15 'Subbarayan Passes Away in Madras', *TOI*, 7/10/1962, 1. 'Mrs. Pandit', *TOI*, 21/10/1962, 9. 'Mrs. Pandit is to be our New Governor', 15/11/1962, 1. VLPtoJN, 28/11/1962, 4-5, PP(I)71. Nehru to Radhakrishnan, 10/11/1962, *SWJN*, Series 2, Volume 79, 36. https://nehruselectedworks.com/pdfviewer.

php?style=UI_Zine_Material.xml&suBFolder=&doc=October_1962-November_1962-Series2-Vol79.pdfl5|876#page=66, 6/8/2022.
16  'Nations Must Live Together', *Guardian*, 24/10/1962, 5.
17  JNtoVLP, 3, 4/10/1962, 60, 63-64, PP(II)43.
18  'Visit of Smt. Vijaya Lakshmi Pandit to Federal Republic of Germany', 104-105, PP(II)43.
19  'Mrs. Pandit Happy about Assurances from Chancellor Adenauer', 31/10/1962, PP(II)28. 'Bonn Eager to Help India', *TOI*, 31/10/1962, 7.
20  'Visit of Smt. Vijaya Lakshmi Pandit to Federal Republic of Germany', 104-105, PP(II)43. See also 107-116.
21  'U.K. & U.S. Generals Fly to Assam', *TOI*, 26/11/1962, 1. 'Reception to Dr. Luebke', *TOI*, 5/12/1962, 1. 'Warm Welcome to Dr. Luebke', *TOI*, 5/12/1962, 9.
22  'The Fall of Menon', *NYHT*, 4/11/1962, A2.
23  '"Chinese Attack is on our Way of Life"', *TOI*, 10/12/1962, 6. VLP picked up another honorary degree, this time in absentia from Andhra Pradesh University, where these remarks were delivered.
24  'Governor asks Business Men to back War Effort', *TOI*, 12/12/1962, 7. 'Governor was told She was "No Good",' *TOI*, 16/12/1962, 1. 'Women Urged to Take to Defense Work', *TOI*, 16/12/1962, 9. Jyotsna Sheth, 'Indian Women Aid in Crisis', *CSM*, 8/1/1963, 14.
25  'Victory Poll Today: City is Keyed Up', *TOI*, 16/12/1962, 1.
26  CBS News Producer David Lowe to VLP, 30/1/1963, 13, PP(II)42. https://www.imdb.com/title/tt1638030/, 7/8/2022.
27  'Mrs. Pandit takes over Office', *TOI*, 28/11/1962, 1.
28  'Governor Lauds work of Catholic Nuns', *TOI*, 27/2/1962, 9.
29  *SoH*, 313-314.
30  Nayantara Sahgal to me, 6/8/2022.
31  Strictly personal and confidential, VLPtoJN, May/9 June1963, 40-45, PP(I)71.
32  Strictly personal and confidential VLPtoJN, May/9 June 1963, 40-45, PP(I)71. Cf. Kuldip Nayar, *Beyond the Lines* (Delhi: The Lotus Collection/Roli, 2012), and VLP to Natwar Singh, 18/5/1964, in K. Natwar Singh, *Treasured Epistles*, Kindle 1380-1406. 'I was not cut out to be 'The Hostess with the Mostess', she bemoaned, referencing her friend Perle Mesta.
33  *SoH*, 310-312.
34  VLPtoJN, 15/6/1963, 56-57, PP(I)71.
35  'Pandit Calls for Equality', PP(II)30.
36  Rajeshwar Dayal to VLP, 28/9/1963, 31, PP(II)5.
37  Thomas Brady, 'Kashmir Debate in U.N. Foreseen', *NYT*, 19/8/1963, 2. See also Prem Bhatia, 'Mrs. Pandit to lead U.N. Delegation', *Irish Times*, 13/8/1963, 1. 'Mrs. Pandit Gets Menon's U.N. Post,' *NYT*, 18/8/1963, 15. 'Aristocratic Rebel', *NYT*, 19/8/1963, 2. H.R. Vohra, 'U.S. Relief at Mrs. Pandit's U.N. Assignment', *TOI*, 20/8/1963, 1.
38  Mary Hornaday, 'India's Mrs. Pandit Jumps into Debate on Vietnam', *CSM*, 16/9/1963, 5. 'Mrs. Pandit Rules Out Concessions to Pakistan, *TOI*, 15/9/1963, 7. 'Mrs. Pandit sees India still in Peril of Attack', *NYT*, 14/9/1963, 2.
39  'Press Disarmed', *TOI*, 13/9/1963, 9.
40  Secret and Personal, VLP to Foreign Secretary M.J. Desai, 21/9/1963, 17-18, PP(II)5.
41  Secret report from VLP on her experience as UN Delegation Leader, 30/12/1963, 5-19, PP(II)7.

42  'India to Address Council', *TOI*, 23/11/1963, 4.
43  Security Council Official Records, 1074th meeting, 29/11/1963, VLP speech on 10-17, UN ODS S/PV.1074, https://documents-dds-ny.un.org/doc/UNDOC/GEN/N65/195/50/PDF/N6519550.pdf?OpenElement, 29/8/2022. VLP's presentation and the Security Council vote takes place after JFK's assassination, discussed in the next section. I have reversed the order here for the sake of narrative flow.
44  UN Security Council Resolution 182, 4/12/1963, S/RES/182 (1963), United Nations Digital Library System, https://digitallibrary.un.org/record/112182?ln=en, 29/8/2022.
45  Thomas Hamilton, 'U.N. Urges Denial of Arms Material to South Africa', *NYT*, 5/12/1963, 1. Poppy Cannon White, 'First Lady of the World', *NYAN*, 14/12/1963, 13.
46  H-bomb Commission, *TOI*, 19/2/1955, 9.
47  'The Disarmament Approach', *TMG*, 20/2/1958, 1. See also TNAUK: FO 371/117371, UN1192/97, 1955 and FO 371/117382, UN1192/367, 1955.d
48  'Indians to Petition for Test Ban', *NYT*, 12/11/1961, 32. 'Nehru Looks forward to Meeting Kennedy', *TOI*, 4/11/1961, 7. For additional analysis and context, see N.M. Ghatate *India's Disarmament Policy* (New Delhi: Ocean Books, 2016).
49  VLP to Khrushchev and Harold Macmillan, 7/8/1963, 40-41, PP(II)42. https://www.jfklibrary.org/learn/about-jfk/jfk-in-history/nuclear-test-ban-treaty, 24/8/2022. See also TNAUK: PREM 11/4298.
50  Records of meetings between VLP and Gromyko and Dean Rusk, 22, 25 September 1963,, 13-16, 23-25, PP(II)5.
51  '1965 Designated Co-operation Year', *TOI*, 23/11/1963, 4. The UN acted on November 21st, the night before the Kennedy assassination.
52  JFK Address at 18th UN General Assembly, 20/9/1963, JFKPOF-046-041-p0001, John F. Kennedy Presidential Library and Museum. https://www.jfklibrary.org/asset-viewer/archives/JFKPOF/046/JFKPOF-046-041, 24/8/2022. See also 'UN marks 50th Anniversary of JFK's Final Address to General Assembly', 12/9/2013, https://news.un.org/en/story/2013/09/448772, 25/8/2022.
53  Secret report from VLP on her experience as UN Delegation Leader, 30/12/1963, 5-19, PP(II)7. *SoH*, 262. Bill Minutaglio and Steven Davis, 'A Month Before JFK's Assassination, Dallas Right Wingers Attack Adlai Stevenson,' 18/11/2013, *The New Republic*, https://newrepublic.com/article/115601/jfk-dallas-right-wingers-attack-adlai-stevenson, 24/8/2022.
54  Tribute to John F. Kennedy, Broadcast by All India Radio Network, 23/11/1963, Sound Recording, USIAAU-078, John F. Kennedy Presidential Library and Museum. https://www.jfklibrary.org/asset-viewer/archives/USIAAU/USIAAU-078/USIAAU-078, 25/8/2022.
55  'Jacqueline Kennedy with Chief Delegate to the United Nations from India, Vijaya Lakshmi Pandit, at Reception Following Funeral of President John F. Kennedy, Acc number ST-C422-43-63, John F. Kennedy Presidential Library and Museum. https://www.jfklibrary.org/asset-viewer/archives/JFKWHP/1963/Month%2011/Day%2025/JFKWHP-1963-11-25-C?image_identifier=JFKWHP-ST-C422-43-63. See also Acc number KN-C30687, https://www.jfklibrary.org/asset-viewer/archives/JFKWHP/1963/Month%2011/Day%2025/JFKWHP-1963-11-25-C?image_identifier=JFKWHP-KN-C30687, 25/8/2022.

56 Sharokh Sabavala, 'The Tenacious Prime Minister,' *New Leader* 47(3), 3/2/1964, 6. Thomas Brady, 'India's Big Question: Who After Nehru?' *NYT*, 19/1/1964, E5. Thomas Brady, 'Nehru and the Future,' *NYT*, 11/1/1964, 8.
57 *SoH*, 315. By this point, Indira had served for 'barely a year' of a two-year term as Congress President. Nayantara Sahgal writes that Nehru was unhappy that she had sought out and taken the post, concerned about her health and what he saw as the inappropriateness of his own daughter serving in serving in such a position while he was Prime Minister, as he told G.B. Pant at the time. He, however, also felt he should not interfere in his daughter's choices and so her do as she saw fit. She left the position early, complaining that she felt she did not have a free hand to do as she wished. Soon thereafter, she had a procedure to remove a kidney stone. For further details, see Nayantara Sahgal, *Indira Gandhi* (Delhi: Penguin 2012, 1st published 1982), 2-5.
58 *SoH*, 317.
59 Photo, VLP and Nehru at AICC Meeting, *TOI*, 16/5/1964, 1.
60 Conrad Fink, 'India's Nehru Dies After Heart Attack', *Austin Statesman*, 27/5/1964, 1.
61 *SoH*, 315-316.
62 'Jawaharlal Nehru is Dead', *TOI*, 28/5/1964, 1. Cf. I.K. Gujral, *Matters of Discretion* (Delhi: Penguin/Hay House, 2011).
63 'Grandsons Collect Ashes', *TOI*, 31/5/1964, 1.
64 'India Bids Nehru a Last Farewell', *NYT*, 8/6/1964, 4. 'Rivers Receive Nehru's Ashes to the Chanting of Scripture', *NYT*, 9/6/1964, 3. Louis Rukeyser, 'Nehru Asked No Funeral', *Baltimore Sun*, 4/6/1964, 6.
65 'Mrs. Pandit Resigns as Governor,' *TOI*, 19/10/1964, 1.
66 JNtoVLP, 17/11/1963, 51, PP(II)5.
67 VLPtoJN, 8/5/1964, 100, PP(I)71.
68 'Mrs Pandit May Seek Nehru Seat,' *NYT*, 16/11/1964, 7.
69 VLPtoJN, 19/2/1963, 5/2/1964, 25-27, 85-87, PP(I)71.
70 'Hon. D.C.L. for Mrs. Pandit,' *TOI*, 16/10/1964, 6. Cf. Janet Vaughn to VLP, 3/12/1964 and VLP to Vaughn 3/1/1965; and 'President's Report, Oxford Letter,' Somerville College Association of Senior Members, Thirty-Ninth Annual Supplement to the Report to the College, 1964, 21-25, Archives of Somerville College, University of Oxford. See also 'Visit of Shrimati Vijaya Lakshmi Pandit, former Governor of Maharashtra, to London to receive the Honorary Degree of D.C.L. from the Oxford University . . .,' GOI Ministry of External Affairs, GA Section, Part file Q(GA) 122/25/65, NAI.
71 Sundar Rajan, 'A Successor to Nehru?' *GandM*, 12/11/1964, 7.
72 'No Party may score Majority in Phulpur', *TOI*, 18/11/1964, 1. See also Maya Shaw, 'Dynamic Mrs. Pandit Fights to Follow Nehru's Footsteps', *Atlanta Constitution*, 24/11/1964, 16.
73 'Mrs. Pandit wins Phulpur Poll by Big Majority', *TOI*, 24/11/1964, 1.
74 'Sister of Nehru may be Speaker of Indian House', *NYT*, 25/11/1964, 7. 'Mrs. Pandit Sworn in', *TOI*, 28/11/1964, 5. Maya Shaw, 'Dynamic Mrs. Pandit Fights to Follow Nehru's Footsteps', *Atlanta Constitution*, 24/11/1964, 16. Prem Bhatia, 'A Cabinet Post for Mrs Pandit?' *Guardian*, 24/11/1964, 7. Dan Coggin, 'Indian Saris are Swishing in Politics', *WaPo, Times Herald*, 25/1/1965, B5. Dan Coggin, 'Women in India', *Baltimore Sun*, 1/3/2022, 12.
75 'Mrs. Pandit as Australian G.-G.', *TOI*, 8/2/1965, 5.

76 'Party's Faith in Nehru Legend Restored by Mrs. Pandit's Win', *GandM*, 17/12/1964, 16. 'Reports Untrue, says Indira', *TOI*, 29/11/1964, 11.
77 Trevor Drieberg, 'Testing Times ahead for Shastri', *The Jerusalem Post*, 10/2/1965, 3. Just weeks after Nehru had died, VLP had written to Walter Lippmann: 'I fear, + this is a fear shared by many, that in the next few years the image of India will undergo considerable change. It will become more + more Indian India—a going backwards, a rejection of things which in one ignorance [sic] we will think of as harmful to national growth. We shall become insular . . . Unless we can understand the West + make it possible for the West to remain close to us we shall find ourselves in many difficulties. The forces of reaction are very strong + are interwoven in the lives of the present leadership. The only man who stood above all this + challenged it has gone. If we should again depend on the stars + not on ourselves to shape our destiny the future will be dark . . . I have asked for a seat in Parliament as I believe some plain speaking will now be required.' VLP to Walter Lippmann, 19/6/1964, Walter Lippmann Papers, Box 94, Folder 1661, Vijaya Lakshmi Pandit, Microfilmed from Series III, Part 2, Section I Correspondence, Manuscript and Archives Division, Sterling Memorial Library, Yale University. The U.K. Solicitor General told VLP of VKKM's striking turn towards her that 'time brought its revenges.' 'Mirable dictu,' he added. Top Secret Report of Dingle Foot, Solicitor General, 26/11/1965, The National Archives of the UK: PREM 13/386.
78 VLP speech before the Lok Sabha, 24/3/1965, *Lok Sabha Debates*, Third Series, XXXVIII, No. 24, 5548-5558. 'Prisoners of Indecision' was the phrase used to encapsulate her message. The exact wording in the speech read 'We are becoming the prisoners of our indecision.' Cf. *SoH*, 4.
79 Dr Karni Singh, Maharaja of Bikaner, 24/3/1965, *Lok Sabha Debates*, Third Series, XXXVIII, No. 24, 5636.
80 '"Ministers are now Prisoners of Indecision",' *TOI*, 25/3/1965, 10.
81 speech to the Lok Sabha, 25/3/1965, *Lok Sabha Debates*, Third Series, XXXVIII, No. 27, 5938.
82 Sharokh Sabavala, 'Indian Government Buffeted', *CSM*, 29/3/1965, 2. 'There are Many Peep-holes in Ruling Party's Armour', *TOI*, 29/3/1965, 6. *SoH*, 4.
83 Cyril Dunn, 'Congress Barons Ride against Shastri', *Observer*, 25/4/1965, 13.
84 'P.M. Refutes Charge of "Indecision",' *TOI*, 3/4/1965, 1.
85 Dan Coggin, 'Nehru Sister Seeks Helm', *Atlanta Constitution*, 4/4/1965, 5B.
86 'Prompt Action to Guard Borders', *TOI*, 27/4/1965, 11. 'Pakistan Must Be Taught a Proper Lesson, Say MPs', *TOI*, 29/4/1965, 9.
87 'Pakistan Uses U.S. Tanks Against Her, India says', *The Hartford Courant*, 29/4/1965, 8. The U.K. Solicitor General
88 'Pakistan Must Be Taught a Proper Lesson, Say MPs,' *TOI*, 29/4/1965, 9.
89 'Poll for Congress Party Posts', *TOI*, 8/5/1965, 9. 'Efforts to Avoid Contest Fail', *TOI*, 10/5/1965, 1. 'Reddy is Elected Deputy Leader', *TOI*, 11/5/1965, 1.
90 'A Soporific?' *TOI*, 11/5/1965, 8.
91 '"Congress Losing Hold on Masses"', *TOI*, 14/6/1965, 5.
92 '"People Must Help Tackle Problems', *TOI*, 23/6/1965, 6.
93 'Mrs. Pandit's Hut', *TOI*, 6/6/1965, 6.
94 Dan Coggin, 'Nehru Sister Seeks Helm', *Atlanta Constitution*, 4/4/1965, 5B.
95 'Post Secure, Shastri Goes on the Offensive', *Chicago Tribune*, 18/7/1965, A1. 'India will not Mediate in Vietnam Situation, Madame Pandit says', *SCMP*,

7/8/1965, 7. 'Cordial Ties with Japan', *TOI*, 10/8/1965, 8. 'Betrayal of U.N. Charter,' *TOI*, 11/8/1965, 7. See also 'Information Bulletin, Embassy of Japan,' Vol XII, No. 15, 1/8/1965, marked V/252, NAI. No additional identifying information available.

96 Ramachandra Guha, *India After Gandhi* (New York: Echo, 2007), 397-402.
97 'Thant Proposes Cease-Fire from this Evening,' *TOI*, 14/9/1965, 1.
98 'Defects in U.N. Resolution,' *TOI*, 25/9/1965, 5. 'Fitting Reply to China,' *TOI*, 18/9/1965, 5.
99 'Mrs. Pandit Flays U.K.,' *TOI*, 29/9/1965, 11. There had been growing calls in India for the country to leave the Commonwealth altogether. VLP was not among them, but the U.K.'s actions during the 1965 war provoked her into calling for some kind of reassessment. VLP did not actually visit London on this trip, declining invitations from the Government to do so for fear of receiving 'hostile criticism' in India, such was the climate against Britain there. She would make the trip just a few weeks later, reflecting how fast things had cooled back down. For more, see Confidential Brief for the [U.K.] Prime Minister, on the visit of Mrs. Pandit, 21–24 November 1965, TNAUK: PREM 13/386.
100 French Ministry of Foreign Affairs, Note on VLP, 30/9/1965, 1–2, in 'Entretien avec le Général De Gaulle: Audience de Madame Vijayalakshmi Pandit, Membre du Parliament indien,' 1/10/1965, French National Archives, Paris. Originals in French.
101 'Entretien du Général De Gaulle et de Madame Pandit', 1-9, in 'Entretien avec le Général De Gaulle: Audience de Madame Vijayalakshmi Pandit, Membre du Parliament indien', 1/10/1965, French National Archives, Paris. Originals in French.
102 'West is Inclined to Pakistan', *TOI*, 3/10/1965, 11. 'Mrs. Pandit Satisfied with her Talks in Paris', *TOI*, 6/10/1965, 12. These views and assessments were corroborated in the official, reports to the MEA and correspondence with government officials. See PP(II)31.
103 'French Well Informed of Our Stand', *TOI*, 8/10/1965, 1.
104 'Letter from De Gaulle', *TOI*, 12/10/1965, 10.
105 'Envoy Extraordinary', *TOI*, 24/10/1965, 1.
106 'Mrs. Pandit for Bonn', 1/11/1965, 1.
107 '"Sowing Seeds of Understanding"', *TOI*, 9/11/1965, 6.
108 'Mrs. Pandit Sees Luns,' *TOI*, 12/11/1965, 9.
109 K.C. Khanna, 'Expect no Dramatic Results: Mrs. Pandit', *TOI*, 26/11/1965, 8. She and Shastri coordinated her London appointments. PP(II)45, 117. She had a private meeting with the UK's Solicitor General; VLP was asked about her own political future. She said that she felt she was 'extremely unpopular' at that time, but British officials walked away feeling she harbored a hope of one day becoming the Prime Minister. Top Secret Report of Dingle Foot, Solicitor General, 26/11/1965, TNAUK: PREM 13/386: PREM 13/386. See this file for more on her UK trip.
110 'Mrs. Pandit Here to Lecture', *NYT*, 23/12/1965, 16.
111 'Mrs. Pandit in Bonn', *TOI*, 15/11/1965, 8.
112 'Persönlichkeitsbeschreibung Mrs. Vijaya Lakshmi Pandit', 10/11/1965, B 122/5464, fol. 1-394, 164–165, German Bundesarchiv (Federal Archives). I am grateful to my colleague Benjamin Carter Hett for his help with the translations from the German. For India's internal briefing materials and other documents related to the trip to Germany, see PP(II)32.

113 Aufzeichnung, between the Federal President of Germany and VLP, 19/11/1965 (meeting held on the seventeenth), B 122/5464, fol. 1–394, 135–151, German Bundesarchiv (Federal Archives).
114 Correspondence between Indira Gandhi and VLP, 6 November, 6, 7/12/1965, Pandit papers (Ist Inst), Correspondence with Indira Gandhi, 33–38, NMML. Cf. Coomi Kapoor, *The Emergency* (Delhi: Penguin, 2022).
115 '"A Terrible Blow', Mrs. Pandit Asserts"', *Baltimore Sun*, 11/1/1966, A2. 'Mrs. Pandit Shocked', *TOI*, 12/1/1966, 13. 'Shastri's Work at Tashkent: Mrs. Pandit's Praise', *TOI*, 17/1/1966, 7.
116 Sharokh Sabavala, '"First Lady" Leads India', *CSM*, 20/1/1966, 1. 'Mrs. Gandhi Chosen as India's New Leader', *Irish Times*, 20/1/1966, 1.
117 Warren Unna, 'Mrs. Gandhi Voted India Premier', *WaPo*, 20/1/1966, A1. According to her own account, VLP had said when Indira became Prime Minister that she 'hoped the task laid upon her 'would not prove too heavy for her frail hands'. *SoH*, 22. The difference in meaning between this phrasing and the one quoted is subtle and perhaps easily missed. VLP identifies this quote, and Indira's reading of it, as the pivotal moment in which their relationship declined into one of total distrust. Vijaya Lakshmi Pandit, 'We Nehrus', *Illustrated Weekly of India*, 17/4/1988, 17.
118 Trevor Driberg, '"Prisoner of Indecision"', *The Jerusalem Post*, 15/8/1966, 5.
119 'Mrs. Pandit's Tour', *TOI*, 11/5/1966, 5. 'Mrs. V.L. Pandit', *TOI*, 30/5/1966, 7. As usual, VLP made a deep impression wherever she went. See, PP(II)33, 25-27.
120 'Public Needs Must be Met', *TOI*, 26/5/1966, 10.
121 VLPtoTara, 10/9/1966, SPBU.
122 'Congress Party has Setback', *Hartford Courant*, 26/2/1967, 15A.
123 VLPtoTara, 27/1/1967, SPBU. 'Candidates face wave of violence', *SCMP*, 23/1/1967, 20.
124 'Official Candidates Routed: Party Poll', *TOI*, 8/4/1967, 1.
125 'Congress MPs Set Up Study Group to Pep Up Party', *TOI*, 18/4/1967, 9.
126 Rakesh Ankit, 'Mountbatten and India, 1964-1979: After Nehru', *Contemporary British History* 35:4 (2021), 576.
127 *SoH*, 5.
128 'Adenauer's Funeral', *TOI*, 23/4/1967, 7. Norman Crossland, 'World Leaders Mourn Adenauer', *Guardian*, 26/4/1967, 1. 'Mrs. Pandit Explains Absence at Poll', *TOI*, 22/5/1967, 7. For her official report on the funeral, see PP(II)34, 22-25.
129 Eileen O'Brien, 'Madame Pandit', *Irish Times*, 22/11/1967, 9. Robert Hardy Andrews, *A Lamp for India* (Englewood Cliffs, NJ: Prentice Hall, 1967).
130 'Birth-control Group Honors 4 at Start of $1-million Drive', *NYT*, 16/11/1967, 26.
131 'Lunch to be in Aid of Sanger Institute', *NYT*, 12/11/1967, 105.
132 'Mrs. Krishna Hutheesingh is Cremated,' *TOI*, 12/11/1967, 1.
133 'Sonia and Rajiv Wed', *TOI*, 26/2/1968, 1. 'Mrs. Gandhi's Elder Son Weds Italian in New Delhi', *NYT*, 26/2/1968, 14. *SoH*, 21.
134 'Mrs. Pandit Resigns Lok Sabha Seat', *TOI*, 17/7/1968, 1.
135 'A Watchdog Leaves Her Post and Unrest Spreads Across the Land', 20/7/1968, 9. VLP suffered an additional personal loss for her opposition to her niece, when Padmaja Naidu sided with Indira over her old friend. VLP could not understand and was deeply wounded. She considered Padmaja her deepest and truest— her only—friend, and she never understood why she had felt forced to choose

between herself and the Prime Minister. Shailaja Bajpai, *Gentleman*, August 1986, 44. Padmaja died before the Emergency was announced.
136 *SoH*, 6.
137 George Gallup, 'Ethel Kennedy Tops List of Most Admired', *Los Angeles Times*, 2/2/1969, G5. The poll was launched in 1946, but only asked about 'most admired woman' starting in 1948. VLP started featuring in responses in 1950. https://en.wikipedia.org/wiki/Gallup%27s_most_admired_man_and_woman_poll#cite_note-17. Last accessed 28/9/2022.
138 Zena Cherry, 'After a Fashion', *GandM*, 16/9/1969, 10. 'Women with Much in Common', *SCMP*, 29/10/1969, 15. VLP would travel back to the United Nations in the spring of 1970 to participate in the Conference on Human Survival, with U. Thant, Lester Pearson, and select other experts. The primary points of discussion focused on ways of strengthening the UN and the international system, and going beyond 'national interest' for the sake of human survival. For details, see V.L. Pandit papers (II Inst), Sub-file 49. Cf. 'Existence on Planet in Jeopardy', But Pearson Letter Offers Ideas', *GandM*, 29/5/1970, 9.
139 'No Poll in U.P. Now', *TOI*, 9/1/1972, 1.
140 This section is a summary of Guha, *India after Gandhi*, 438–490. *SoH*, 1–8. Cf. Gyan Prakash, *Emergency Chronicles* (Delhi: Penguin/Hamish Hamilton, 2018).
141 Paraphrase of a sentence from *SoH*, 9.
142 *SoH*, 9–10.
143 *SoH*, 14. VLP had signaled her resistance to the Emergency right from the outset, but just as quickly realized that she herself was a target. See Central Foreign Policy Records of the U.S. State Department, Case No. F-2016-06100, Doc. Nos. C06049337, C06049325, and C06049341, confidential, accessed by FOIA.
144 VLPtoTara, 29/8/1976, SPBU. In reminisces at the very end of her life, VLP was blunt in her assessment about Sanjay's maliciousness: 'I didn't get on with him at all. I did not like his attitudes to life. I did not approve of him. Even as a child, he was self-willed. I was always struck by the influence that Sanjay had over his mother. It was not the usual influence that a child could have over his parent. It was a sort of hold he had over her—it was uncanny. He had her completely under his thumb . . . I never liked Sanjay . . . Sanjay was stubborn and wanted things done his own way. The Emergency was in a sense typical of his attitude to life.' Vijaya Lakshmi Pandit, 'We Nehrus', *Illustrated Weekly of India*, 17/4/1988, 15, 17.
145 Azad, 'A Letter from Mrs. Gandhi's India', *New Republic*, 7 and 16/8/1976, 19-23, in PP(II)50, 1–5.
146 Paul Grimes, 'U.S. Emerging as a Center of Emigre Resistance to Gandhi Regime', 3/10/1976, 14.
147 William Borders, 'Indira Gandhi's Aunt Says She is "Profoundly Troubled" at Direction India is Taking', *NYT*, 31/10/1976, 11.
148 'Recalling India's Ideals', *CSM*, 2/11/1976, 28.
149 Prakash, *Emergency Chronicles*, 342. As Prakash notes, her motivations have remained the subject of speculation to this day. We await new records, perhaps hidden in her papers, to see if anything further might be known.
150 'More Repression if Cong. Wins Says Mrs. Pandit', *TOI*, 4/3/1977, 9.
151 'Gandhi's Aunt Joins Foes', *Austin American Statesman*, 14/2/1977, A10. William Borders, 'Mrs. Gandhi's Aunt is Joining Foes', *NYT*, 14/2/1977, 2.
152 VLP's Statement to the Press, 11/2/1977, 1-5, PP(II)51.

153 William Borders, 'Indira Gandhi's Aunt Joined Foes to "Live at Peace with Myself"', *NYT*, 15/2/1977, 3.
154 VLP's Statement to the Press, 11/2/1977, 1-5, PP(II)51. *SoH* gets various details regarding this moment incorrect, mistitling Jagjivan Ram the finance minister and incorrectly suggesting that her statement to the press was made on the 12$^{th}$, when in fact it was a few days later.
155 'Nehru's Sister Joins Campaign to Unseat Her Niece, Mrs. Gandhi', *GandM*, 15/2/1977, 10. 'Indira's Aunt Comes Out for India's Opposition', *Jerusalem Post*, 15/2/1977, 4. 'Nehru's Sister Opposes Gandhi', *Irish Times*, 15/2/1977, 5. William Borders, 'Indira Gandhi's Aunt Joined Foes to "Live at Peace with Myself",' *NYT*, 15/2/1977, 3.
156 'Quotation of the Day', *NYT*, 15/2/1977, 33. William Borders, 'Indira Gandhi's Aunt Joined Foes to "Live at Peace with Myself"', *NYT*, 15/2/1977, 3.
157 'Big Welcome to Mrs. Pandit's Step', *India West*, 1/3/1977, 2.
158 'Mrs. Gandhi's Aunt Speaks Out', *Chicago Tribune*, 18/2/1977, B2.
159 'Congress Lead Severely Cut Say Pollsters', *SCMP*, 20/2/1977, 3.
160 Herbert Brucker, 'India Tries Once Again', *Hartford Courant*, 23/2/1977, 19.
161 Inder Malhotra, 'Opposition Has Edge Over Cong. In Bihar', *TOI*, 28/2/1977, 1. See also Martin Woollacott, 'Gandhi Up Against New Solidarity', *Guardian*, 2/3/1977, 2. And Inder Malhotra, 'Decorum in Poll Campaigning', *TOI*, 7/3/1977, 1.
162 Martin Woollacott, 'Gandhi Up Against New Solidarity', *Guardian*, 2/3/1977, 2. 'Imam Launching "Hindu-Muslim Unity Wave"', *TOI*, 3/3/1977, 7.
163 'Students Urged to Remain Peaceful', *TOI*, 2/3/1977, 9.
164 'Congress Lead Severely Cut Say Pollsters', *SCMP*, 19/2/1977, 3.
165 'I am Not Looking for Any Office: Mrs. Pandit', *TOI*, 6/3/1977, 1.
166 'Mrs. Pandit was Never in Cong.: Raju', *TOI*, 7/3/1977, 9.
167 'Mrs. Pandit's Stand Flayed by Cong. MP's', *TOI*, 8/3/1977, 13.
168 William Borders, 'Indira Gandhi's Aunt Joined Foes to "Live at Peace with Myself"', *NYT*, 15/2/1977, 3. 'Nehru's Sister Opposes Gandhi,' *Irish Times*, 15/2/1977, 5.
169 'Give Clear Verdict Against Congress: Mrs. Pandit', *TOI*, 9/3/1977, 9.
170 'Poll Has Aroused Hope: Mrs. Pandit', *TOI*, 13/3/1977, 4.
171 'Most Ideal Campaigner', *TOI*, 17/3/1977, 3.
172 William Borders, 'India Returns to Democracy', *NYT*, 22/3/1977, 1. VLP later wrote that Indira held her responsible for the loss of her seat. Vijaya Lakshmi Pandit, 'We Nehrus', *Illustrated Weekly of India*, 17/4/1988, 13.

## Coda: Fireflies in the Mist

1 *SoH*, 23.
2 Pupul Jayakar, Indira Gandhi's noted friend and biographer, wrote in 1985 that Indira considered VLP a dark fairy in the Motilal household. She added that Indira never forgave her aunt for saying when Indira was young that she was 'ugly and stupid'. Pupul Jayakar, *Indira Gandhi: An Intimate Biography* (New York: Pantheon Books, 1988), 17, 33. Nowhere in any record from VLP could I find anything even remotely approaching such views. Instead, there are repeated assertions of affection and concern. Nayantara Sahgal too recalls that she and her family had a very warm, loving relationship with Indira and that things only began to change very late in life, as Indira began to rise in power. It's of course

entirely possible, even likely, that VLP did make some passing remark or two and that Indira harbored secret wounds from such comments. But the broad tenor of their relationship was much more positive than has been portrayed. VLP says as much in an essay she penned late in life. Here she tried to be as candid as possible, arguing that Indira was a very 'insecure' person, which she thought justifiable given the national turmoil during her upbringing. While she believed that Indira was not very close to either her mother or father, 'whatever she may have said later,' VLP regretfully accepted that there 'could have been something in . . . [her/VLP's] approach which must have put her [Indira] off or prevented her from coming too close.' Vijaya Lakshmi Pandit, 'We Nehrus', *Illustrated Weekly of India*, 17/4/1988, 12-13. See also See Krishna Hutheesing, *Dear to Behold*, which seems for the most part to corroborate the accounts presented by VLP and Nayantara.

3   'Attack on Gandhi', *Guardian*, 14/12/1979, 6. 'Indian Voter Group Seeks to Keep Mrs. Gandhi Out,' *NYT*, 23/12/1979, 6. Anand Bhawan is today a museum. VLP hardly appears as much more than a ghost.
4   William Borders, 'Nehru's Sister Campaigning for Presidency of India', *NYT*, 27/5/1977, 8.
5   https://legal.un.org/avl/ha/catcidtp/catcidtp.html, 3/10/2022. And Reports of the Thirty-Fourth and Thirty-Fifth Sessions of the Commission on Human Rights, E 1978 34 E CN.4 1292-EN and E 1979 36 E CN.4 1347-EN. https://digitallibrary.un.org/record/220211?ln=en, https://digitallibrary.un.org/record/2607?ln=en, 3/10/2022. See also Central Foreign Policy Records of the U.S. Department of State, Case No. F-2016-06100, Doc Nos. C06049338, C06049340, C06049328, C06049323, C06049329, C06049324, C06049326, C06049334, and C06049336, confidential, accessed through FOIA.
6   Emily Hahn, 'Passage Through India', *NYT*, 19/8/1979, BR4. Margaret Thatcher had just been elected the first woman Prime Minister of the United Kingdom. VLP sent her a note of congratulations recalling her time as ambassador. British officials internally noted that VLP was a 'distinguished person' and so deserved a reply directly from Thatcher herself. The letter was drafted by staff, but Thatcher added a handwritten note commending VLP for paving the way for her. Their politics, of course, went in very different directions. TNAUK: FCO 37/2156, secret.
7   'U.N. Luminaries of Past and Present Honor Roosevelt', *NYT*, 17/6/1982, A3.
8   PP(II)46. See also Fleur Cowles, *If I Were an Animal* (New York: Morrow, 1987).
9   PP(II)8.
10  Colin Smith, 'Dream That Became a Dynasty', *Observer*, 16/8/1987, 8.
11  Television interview with Rajiv Mehrotra. Exact date unknown, but when she was eighty-seven years old. https://www.youtube.com/watch?v=LmFZoGSPi6o, 3/10/2022.
12  VLP continued giving interviews and making news after this. At 88 and after a stroke, she sat down with *The Times* Barbara Crossette to talk about things, causing a bit of a flutter when she responded, when asked whether brother might have had an affair with Lady Edwina Mountbatten, 'If there was a relationship, I'm glad for him . . . If it brought a little joy into his life, good for him. And good for her!' Barbara Crossette, 'Sister Burnishes Nehru's Image, Lest India Forget,' *NYT*, 22/5/1989, A4. The month before, she released a coda to her

autobiography in *the Illustrated Weekly of India*. There she held no punches and attempted to set the record straight on various matters, talking frankly about Sanjay and Indira Gandhi, Krishna Menon, and Kamala Nehru, among others. Vijaya Lakshmi Pandit, 'We Nehrus', *Illustrated Weekly of India*, 17/4/1988, 9-17. She called Rajiv her grandson and wrote of the affection they shared. She remained critical of political errors he had made but placed most of the blame on the advisers he had surrounded himself with (17).

13 Nayantara Sahgal, 'Reflections on a Death', *TOI*, 16/12/1990, 11. And conversation with Manu Bhagavan.
14 Sanjoy Hazarika, 'Vijay Lakshmi Pandit, Politician and Nehru's Sister, is Dead at 90', *NYT*, 2/12/1990, 53.
15 'Vijayalakshmi Pandit', *TOI*, 3/12/1990, 12.
16 Taya Zinkin, 'India, silk or steel', *Guardian*, 4/12/1990.

# Archives Consulted

Archives Nationale (Paris, France)
Adam Matthew Digital Research
Archives of the Pearl S. Buck House
Archives of the United Nations
Archives of Wellesley College
Beinecke Library, Yale University
Bodleian Special Collections, Bodleian Library, University of Oxford
Cadbury Research Library, University of Birmingham
Columbia University Libraries
Cork City and County Archives, Ireland
Dag Hammarskjöld Library, United Nations
Dwight D. Eisenhower Presidential Library
Federal Archives (Bundesarchiv), Germany
Federal Foreign Office, Political Archive (Berlin, Germany)
Franklin Delano Roosevelt Presidential Library
Harry S. Truman Library and Archives
India Office Library and Record Room, The British Library
John F. Kennedy Presidential Library and Museum
Libraries of the City University of New York
Library and Archives, Canada
Manuscripts and Archives, Yale University
National Archives of the Netherlands
National Meteorological Library & Archive, UK
Nayantara Sahgal Collection, Howard Gotlieb Archival Research Center, Boston University
New York Public Library

Prasar Bharati Archives
Private Collection of Aryan D'Rozario
Private Collection of Nayantara Sahgal
Private Collection of Nonika Sahgal
Rockefeller Archive Center
Rossiyskii Gosudarstvennyi Archive of Social'no Politicheskoi Istorii (RGASPI) (Moscow, Russia)
The Library of Congress
The National Archives of India
The National Archives of the United Kingdom
The National Archives of the United States of America
The Nehru Memorial Museum and Library, New Delhi
The Putney School
Save the Children
Somerville College Archives, University of Oxford
Swarthmore College Peace Collection
U.P. State Archives, Lucknow
Vera Brittain Literary Estate

# Acknowledgements

I first grew interested in Vijaya Lakshmi Pandit while working on my last book, *The Peacemakers*. She emerged as a key actor in shaping India's foreign policy. She seemed to sparkle with personality and was involved in many things, yet I knew little about her. Her mention is missing from many accounts of modern India's past—there are perhaps only a handful of superficial references. I was sure there was something there worth exploring. Little did I know then how much I had underestimated her and her story. As I started to work my way through her letters, diaries and notes, I very quickly felt overwhelmed by the scale of her life and the mountain of material related to it.

I was only able to move forward with the generous assistance of my family, friends, colleagues, and students and strangers to boot. They talked me through one neurotic crisis after another, pointing me to leads, giving me books to read, connecting me with contacts, thinking through thorny problems with me, and just generally filling me with good cheer. This book is as much theirs as it is mine.

I am so grateful to Ranjana Sengupta for allowing me to tell this story, and for nudging me along the way. Ramachandra Guha, David Nasaw, Kai Bird and Blanche Wiesen Cook all gave me invaluable feedback that got me started and saw me through.

My research was facilitated by many dedicated librarians and archivists, whose expertise makes work like this possible. I especially thank Dr N. Balakrishnan, Anumita Banerjee, Kristen Carter, Wendy Chmielewski, David Clark, Eric Diouris, Helen Fisher, Natalia Gutiérrez-Jones, Oliver House, Michelle Kopfer, David Langbart, Brian McGee, Santos, Amitabh Pandey, Yuthika Mishra, Kate

O'Donnell, Sara Powell, Jaya Ravindran, Fleur Smith, Marie Toner, and Michael Weins, as well as all other staff at the repositories I consulted. I also had outstanding research assistants: Akhtar Hussain, Victoria Apostol-Marius, Alexander Poulakis, Andre Edemskiy, Shivani Bajpai, Abhinand Siddharth, Gaurav Garg, Rashmi (who wishes to be identified by her first name only) and Khushi Singh Rathore. In India, my work was additionally supported by the Centre for Policy Research, New Delhi, to which I also extend thanks.

Many people provided me with useful information, and some with formal interviews. I am indebted to Lady Pamela Hicks, Ambassador K. Shankar Bajpai, United Nations General Assembly President Maria Fernanda Espinosa Garcés, Ambassador Dan Mulhall, Ambassador Nirupama Rao and Sudhakar Rao, Ambassador T.C.A. Raghavan, Ram Rahman, Kiran Desai, Navina Haidar, Ruchira Gupta, Manira Alva, Stacy-Marie Ishmael, Suketu Mehta, R.S. Gill, Jairam Ramesh, Aryan D'Rozario, Arjun Raina, Uday Singh Mehta, Akeel Bilgrami, Francis Robinson, Durdana Ansari, David Lelyveld, David Ludden, Dina Siddiqui, Dilip Menon, Meena Alexander, Sumathi Ramasawamy, Vijayendra Rao, Vikram Raghavan, Lisa Trivedi, Sven Beckert, Mark Kramer, Stephen Kotkin, David Engerman, Gail Minault, Pratap Bhanu Mehta, Sidin Vadukut, Kirin Hutheesing, Nikhil Hutheesing, Ellen Chesler, Mrinalini Sinha, Manisha Sinha, Syed Akbar Hyder, Sumita Mukherjee, Barbara Ramusack, Pallavi Raghavan, Swapna Kona Nayudu, Srinath Raghavan, Rahul Sagar, WPS Sidhu, Anton Harder, Janaki Ram, C. Raja Mohan, Sunil Khilnani, Beena Kamlani, Leonard Gordon, N.S. Vinodh, Rohit De, Jessica Neuwirth, Robert Jenkins, Jonathan Fanton, Jai Bhandarkar, Rupal Oza, Ash Rao, Karna Basu, Sangeeta Pratap, Purvi Sevak, Anurima Bhargava, Aseem Chhabra, Mallika Dutt, Dev Benegal, and Zette Emmons. Her Majesty Queen Elizabeth II declined to share her recollections, but Buckingham Palace did extend the courtesy of an encouraging reply.

No one has been more generous with their time, more open and transparent, and more supportive than Vijaya Lakshmi Pandit's family: Nayantara Sahgal, Gita Sahgal, Manjari Mehta, and Nonika Sahgal. They endured many hours of questioning, provided endless testimony and opened their home and private collections to me. They unfailingly prompted me to tell the Pandit story with unvarnished truth, 'warts and all' and never once sought any kind of oversight of my project.

I had the opportunity to share some preliminary pieces of this book at the Global Thinkers Project at the University of Oxford and as the inaugural speaker of the GloBio Working Group at the London School of Economics. For their invitations, hospitality and critical engagement, I thank Sharinee Jagtiani, Marina Perez de Arcos, Baroness Janet Royall, Carol Souter, Kate Sullivan de Estrada, Victoria Phillips, Haakon Ikonomou, Laura Almagor, Taylor Sherman, Shruti Sinha and Eugenia Zinovieva, as well as all attendees. I also participated on a stimulating American Historical Society panel on radical biography, co-sponsored by the Leon Levy Center for Biography, and learned so much from Theresa Meade, Benjamin Talton and Brian Peterson. Many undergraduate and graduate students also workshopped various elements of this book.

This book was initially edited by the team at Penguin Random House India, which included Manasi Subramaniam, Shubhi Surana, and Ahana Singh, as well as Tarini Uppal, Anushree Kaushal, and Meru Gokhale at earlier stages. My agent, Matthew Carnicelli, was an important sounding board.

Caelyn Cobb, Emily Simon, Zachary Friedman, Leslie Kriesel, and the rest at Columbia University Press have expertly shepherded the international edition. Their careful guidance, along with the supportive feedback from anonymous reviewers, have helped shape the book's contours.

This work has been supported by a sabbatical from Hunter College and by other small grants and awards. I am so lucky to have had the constant backing of President Jennifer Raab, Provosts Lon Kaufman, Valeda Dent and Manoj Pardasani, Dean Andy Polsky, and my chairs (and good friends) Mary Roldán and Donna Haverty-Stacke. My departmental colleagues have never failed to make my work better. For that, and for generally being an amiable, humorous, and fun little group, I am especially thankful to Jonathan Rosenberg, Benjamin Hett, Elidor Mëhilli and Jill Rosenthal. Ben and my former colleague Iryna Vushko both helped me with translations as well.

My little village has been a noisy, feisty, zany bunch that I would not trade for anything. S. Mitra Kalita and Nitin, Naya and Riya Mukul, Meera Nair and Arun and Anokha Venugopal, Sucheta

Sachdev and Avyan, Aakash and Hari Sreenivasan, Sumathi Reddy, Jonathan Rockoff, and Nikhil and Priya Reddy-Rockoff, Vikas, Molly, Zawadi, and Xander Bajaj and Shobana Ram, Sandeep Junnarkar and Krithi and Sulekha Ram-Junnarkar are some crazy, fine people.

My family has been behind me all the way (often pushing me to finish my work). I thank all my extended aunts and uncles and cousins, and especially B.S. Haritsa and Roopa for the care and affection they always show. Minni, Ajei, Prajit, and Rohit Gopal, Sharad, Shobha, Saanvi and Sahiti Ramadas, and my in-laws Kalpana and (the late) S.N. Ramadas have always brought the love. My beloved grandmother, R.S. Chinmayamma and father, Belur S. Bhagavan, did not live to see this book's completion, but every word stems from what I have learned from them. And as always, Sree and Priyanka Bhagavan are my whole world.

# Index

Abdullah, Sheikh, 412
Acheson, Dean, 327, 346–347
Addams, Jane, 143
Adenauer, Konrad, 396, 419
Ad Hoc Committee on Palestine, 299
African Americans, 213, 220, 235–236, 322
　public and private life, 249
African National Congress, 403
Afro-Asian bonds of unity, 236
Afro-Asian Conference, 367
Ahmadnagar Fort, 172
Ahmed, Fakhruddin, 426
Alexander, A.V., 254
Ali, Asaf, 301, 307
Ali, Begum Hamid, 119
Alipore Jail, Calcutta, 65
Allahabad, xi, 6, 37, 209, 280
　Cawnpore Road, 64
　Commissioner of, 85
　Congress Committee, 166
　District Jail, 51–52
　mass demonstrations, 49
　Municipal Board, 77, 80, 88, 223
　Nan's untouchability work in, 60

Allahabad University, 2, 157
Allahabad Women's Society (Prayag Mahila Samiti), 21
Allen, Charles Alfred, 112
Allied Air Command, in the Eastern theatre, 208
All-India Congress Committee (AICC), 83–84, 111, 128, 156–157
All-India Friends of the Soviet Union, 201
All-India Khilafat Committee, 28
All India Radio
　Nehru's tribute to JFK on, 405
　'Personality of the Queen' programme, 391
All-India Trade Union Congress, 192
All India Women's Conference (AIWC), xii, 72, 74, 77, 115, 119–120, 130, 149, 184, 195, 199, 250
　Bengal Relief Fund, 192, 205
　meeting in Trivandrum, 75
　Nan's appointment as president of, xii, 133
　relationship with Madame Chiang, 133
　sixteenth session of, 142
Alpha Kappa Alpha sorority, 330

# 528 INDEX

Ambedkar, B.R. 'Babasaheb', 37, 61
   support to granting separate electorates to various communities, 62
American Civil War, 322
American consumerism, 390
American Council of Human Rights, 330
American Embassy, 308
American Emergency Food Committee for India, 335
American Federation of Soroptimist Clubs, 373
Americanization of the world, 219
American military weapons, 411
America's Town Meeting of the Air (radio programme), 230
Amery, Leo, 229
*Amrita Bazar Patrika*, 117
Anand Bhawan (Abode of Joy), xi, 6, 14, 17, 23, 28, 58, 76, 81, 139, 151, 158, 171, 173, 196
Anderson, Marian, 330
Anglo-American bloc, 349
Anschluss Pact, 116
Anthony, Susan B., 268
anti-British agitation, in U.S.A, 178
anti-British persons, 203
anti-communist campaign, 316
Antoinette, Marie, 97
Aranha, Oswaldo, 296
Argentina, 298
arts and crafts exhibition, 200
Ashby, Dame Margery Corbett, 266
Asian Relations Conference, 282–283
Asiatic Land Tenure and Indian Representation Bill (South Africa), 257
Associated Press, 260
Association of Motion Picture Producers (Hollywood), 324

Astor, Nancy, 392
Aswan Dam project, 379
*Atlanta Daily World*, 274, 323
   'Madam Pandit Leads Fight for Minorities' story, 274
Atlantic Charter, 145, 211, 216, *see also* Pacific Charter
   applications of the principles of, 216
Atlee, Clement, 249–250
atomic bomb, first explosion of, 430
'Atoms for Peace' speech, 359
Attlee, Clement, 366
Attlee, Lord, 283
*Austin Statesman*, 354
Austin, Warren, 297
Austro-Hungarian Empire, 103
Azad, Maulana Abul Kalam, 84, 132, 146, 153, 154, 176

back-channel communications, 343
Baghdad Pact, 369
Bahadur, Nawab Abdul Latif Khan, 23
Bajpai, Girja Shankar, 203, 208, 225, 301, 309, 327, 336, 365
Baldwin, Roger, 239
*Baltimore Afro-American*, 223, 235, 322
*Baltimore Sun, The*, 124, 215, 234, 318
Banerjea, Surendranath, 15
Banerji, Purnima, 166
Barnum, P.T., 220
Battle of Stalingrad (film, 1949), 292
BBC, 148
Begtrup, Bodil, 275
Bengal famine (1943), 188, 321
Bengal Relief Fund
   AIWC, 192, 205
   disbursement of funds, 192
   *Hindustan Times*, 190
   deaths due to, 189

effects of, 195
    homes for famine-afflicted children, 189–190
Bengal's Legislative Assembly, 215
Berlin blockade, 310, 320
Bernardino, Minerva, 261
Besant, Annie, 8, 16, 20, 23, 40, 72
    Home Rule movement, 108
Bethune, Mary McLeod, 237, 249, 275, 329
Betty (sister of Vijaya Lakshmi Pandit), 64, 187, 194, 280, 406
    relation with Vijaya Lakshmi Pandit, 369–370
    as substitute for Vijaya Lakshmi Pandit, 280
Bevin, Ernest, 269
Bhabha, Homi, 374
Bhave, Vinoba, 127–128, 145
Birla, Ghanshyam Das, 235–236
Birth Control movement
    in America, 74
    in India, 73
Bishan Sabha (the Community of Bishan), 5
Black, Eugene, 328
Black Hole of Calcutta, 11
Black university, 322
*blitz*, terror of, 136
*Bombay Chronicle*, 22, 294
Bombay Presidency Women's Council, 200, 341
Bombay Resolution, 146
Bondfield, Margaret, 105, 130
*Book of Knowledge, The*, 330
Boothby, Robert, 230, 232, 248, 333
    debate with Vijaya Lakshmi Pandit, 230–231

border dispute, between India and China, 389
Bose, Subhas Chandra, 104, 116, 132, 242
    house arrest in Calcutta, 132
    hunger strike, 132
    protests against the British occupation of India, 132
*Boston Globe*, 228, 249
Boston Symphony Orchestra, 288
Bowles, Chester, 384
Bretton Woods Conference (1945), 326
British administration, 79, 126
    Gandhi's open rebellion against, 155
    High Command, 127, 130
    policy towards India, 146
    softening of stance on Indian control, 210
    War Cabinet, 188
British colonial settlers, 21
British colonial violence, 162
British Commonwealth, 105
British cotton tariffs, protests against (1896), 15
British East India Company, 7
British Embassy, 292
British Empire, 135
British Government of India, 306
British Imperialism, 82, 134, 135
British India, 39, 313
British Indian Army, 125
British Intelligence Service, 232, 234
    interception of Birla's telegram to Nan, 236
British Labour Party, 245, 249
British Museum, 375
British occupation of India, protest against, 132
British Raj, 17
British rule in India, 245

British Society of Gastroenterology, 107
Brittain, Vera, 143, 415
Brockway, Fenner, 350
Bromley, Dorothy Dunbar, 210, 212, 255
Brooks, Angie, 420
Brooks, Ferdinand, 8
Brownell, Herbert, 358
*Brown v. Board of Education*, 363
Buck, Pearl, 190, 198, 206–207, 211, 217, 221, 232, 239, 251, 298, 332
Buddhist Mahabodhi Society, 376
Bulganin, Nicolai, 368
Bullitt, William, 337
Bunche, Ralph, 191, 322–324, 329
Burma, Japanese occupation of, 188
Butler, Harcourt, 14

Cabinet Mission, 254
    plan to move India towards independence, 254
Cadbury, Dame, 134
Cagney, James, 243
Calcutta, 132, 191, 195, 215, 305
    air raids over, 168
    communal riots in, 255
Cals, Joseph, 415
Cambridge University, 371
*Canberra Times*, 408
Cantor, Helen, 232
Canyon of Heroes, 260
Carlton, Ritz, 226
Caroe, Olaf, 235
Carter, Edward, 211
Carter, Violet Bonham, 134, 377
Casey, Maie, 251
caste discrimination, 36, 60
Catroux, Madame, 293

Cawnpore-Bilaspur (Kanpur) women's constituency, 80
CBS News, 397
Celler, Emanuel, 235, 239, 252
    Indian immigration bill, 252
Central Intelligence Agency (CIA), xix
Chagla, Justice, 262, 265
Chagla, M.C., 259
Chamberlain, Arthur Neville, 107–109, 124, 156
Chanakya, 137
Chandralekha (daughter of Vijaya Lakshmi Pandit), 44, 48, 57, 70, 115, 126, 129, 139, 141, 155, 158, 162, 175, 179, 194, 196–197, 199, 204, 209, 217, 251, 290, 300, 331–332, 369
    arrest of, 166
    encounter with the police, 159
    as guests of Eslanda and Paul Robeson, 191
    homecoming, 177
    release from prison, 176
    sailing to Australia, 181–183
channel of communication, 367
Chaplin, Ralph, 169
Chattopadhyay, Bankim Chandra, 289
Chattopadhyay, Kamaladevi, 144, 150, 199
Chelmsford, Lord, 21, 72
Chiang Kai-Shek, 133, 148, 230
    anti-colonial campaigns, 148
    friendship with the Nehrus, 148
    meeting with Nan, 149
Chiang, Madame, 133, 144, 148, 150–151, 177
    contribution to Bengal Relief Fund, 206

*Chicago Daily Tribune*, 241, 264, 425
*Chicago Defender*, 236, 275
*China Weekly Review*, 268
cholera, outbreak of, 100–102, 189, 255
Chou En-Lai, 133, 341, 351
*Christian Science Monitor, The*, 93, 111, 223, 265, 268, 353, 354, 424
Churchill, Winston, xii, 110, 124, 134, 148, 175, 188, 216, 249, 277, 361–362, 371–372
civic consciousness, 120
civil disobedience movement, 38, 43, 52
Civil Liberties committee, 248
Civil Lines, 3
Clark, Thomas, 321
Clive, Robert, 7, 11
Cold War, 367
Coleridge, Samuel Taylor, 165
Committee for the Celebration of Vietnam Independence, 298
communal tensions, between Hindus and Muslims, 256, 281
Communism, theory of, 123
Communist Party of India (CPI), 201, 306
Communist Revolution, in China, 316
Community of Nations, 222
Compton, Arthur, 375
  Pioneer in Brotherhood medal, 390
Congress (O), 420
Congress (R), 420
Congress Socialist Party, 84, 306
Constituent Assembly of India, xiii, 84, 278, 280, 289, 331
  British proposed elections for, 254
  Nan's election to, 256
Constitution of India, 340
Cooke, Alistair, 382

Coomaswamy, Ananda, 226–227
cottage industries, 200
Council Entry programme, 39
Council on African Affairs, 191, 250, 268
counter-revolutionaries, liquidation of, 345
Countess of Dufferin, 115
Court of St James, 377
Cousins, Margaret, 22, 72–74, 142
Covarubbias, Miguel, 288
Cowles, Fleur, 430
Cow Protection Conference, 96
Criminal Investigation Department (CID), 166
Cripps Mission, 174
Cripps, Stafford, 101, 152–153, 254, 277
Crosby, Bing, 321
Crusade for World Government, 350
Cuban Missile Crisis, 404
cultural nationalism, 72
Curzon, Lord, 15–16, 18
Czechoslovakia, 103, 107, 109, 112, 116

*Daily Boston Globe*, 318, 355
*Daily Express*, 354, 368
*Daily News*, 232
Dalai Lama, 387
Dalits, 62, 234
Dandi march, 166
Dar, A.K., 353
Darwin, Charles Galton, 256
Das, P.R., 201
Davies, Clement, 192
Davis, Bette, 330
Dayal, Rajeshwar, 400
Day-Lewis, Cecil, 350

De Gaulle, Charles, 413–414
Dehra Dun Jail, 128, 132, 139
Delhi Durbar, 18
democracy, principle of, 410
de Pierrefeu, Countess, 226
de Pompadour, Madame, 7
Depressed Classes, reservations in lieu of a separate electorate, 62
Desai, Mahadev, 48
Desai, M.J., 399
Desai, Morarji
    arrest of, 422
    as finance minister of India, 386
    Janata (People's) front, 425
    visit to London, 386
Desfor, Max, xvii–xviii
Devika Sevika Sangh, 48
Dewey, John, 261
Dharm Sabha (the Community of Righteousness), 5
Dhar, Pandit Bishan Narayan, 5
di Bonzi, Conte, 60
Dickens, Charles, 106
Dietrich, Marlene, 261
Direct Action Day, 255
Douglas, Helen Gahagan, 251, 269
Douglas, William, 339, 348
Du Bois, W.E.B., xvi, 191, 213, 236, 275
Duke of Wellington (Iron Duke), 376
Dulles, John Foster, 280, 297, 300, 350, 352, 355, 357, 389–390
    war of words with Nan, 280
Dupleix, François, 7
Dutt, Subimal, 364, 381
dyarchy, idea of, 76

Easter Rebellion (1916), 20
East Germany, 396

East-West accord, 356
Eccles, David, 362
economic rehabilitation, 143
Eden, Anthony, 343, 347, 366, 381
Edward VIII (Prince of Wales), 31
    visit to Allahabad, 34
Einstein, Albert, 281, 329, 337, 374
    Russell-Einstein manifesto, 374–375
Eisenhower, President, 350, 352, 357, 359–360, 374, 381, 388
Elizabeth II, Queen, 372
Elizabeth, Queen, 361, 363, 372, 382
    arrival in India, 391
    participation in Republic Day celebrations in India, 391
Emmet, Baroness Evelyn, 392
Emmet, Evelyn, 361
*Envoy Extraordinary*, 415
equality of people of all races and all colors, 217
equality, principle of, xvi
Erhard, Ludwig, 415
ethical leadership, 409
ethnic nationalism, 103
European Jews, 299
European segregation, in India, 214–215
*European Spring* (Clare Booth Luce), 180
Extremist party, 16

Fahy, Charles, 271, 274
Faisal, Prince, 314
farmer's agitation, in the Northeast, 306
Farringdon, Lord, 350
fascism, India's opposition to, 221
Fascist danger, issue of, 210
Federal Bureau of Investigations (FBI), xix
Federation of Jewish Philanthropies of New York, 359

Feinstein, Diane, 430
financial security, 197
Fisher, Louis, 255
food security, xix
food shortages, 187
　in Bengal, 188
　in India, 335
　and transfers of food, 193
Ford Foundation, 338
*Foreign Affairs*, 375
foreign goods, boycotting of, 15, 35
Foreign Policy Association, 212
'Forging a World Bill of Human Rights', 251
Four Freedoms for Asia, 234
France, 7, 71, 97, 299
　colonial control of Tunisia, 346
　destruction of, 110
　diplomatic relations with China, 413
　friendship with India, 414
　operation of Suez Canal, 378–379
　Paris Protocol for international drug control (1948), 314
　partition Ottoman lands, 28
　war on Germany, 117
Franco, General, 387
Free Officers Movement, 349
French Revolution, 97
Freud, Anna, 373
friends of India, 104
Frontier Gandhi, *see* Khan, Khan Abdul Gaffar
Fu Ping-Sheung, 316

Gaekwar, Pratapsingh, 64
Gahagan, Helen, 261
Gandhian protocol, 157
Gandhi, Feroze, 151, 197

Gandhi, Indira, xii, 22, 405
　anger and resentment against Vijaya Lakshmi, 429
　assassination of, 430
　calling off the Emergency, 424
　declaration of a state of Emergency, 421
　'Garibi Hatao' (Get Rid of Poverty) slogan, 420
　military assault on the Sikh Golden Temple in Amritsar, 430
　as minister for information and broadcasting, 408
　Nan's relationship with, 371, 408, 417–418
　overturning of her election to the Parliament, 421
　political rivalry with Nan, 425–426
　release from prison, 182
　sons of, 282
　wedding with Feroze Gandhi, 151–152
Gandhi, Kasturba, 32, 48, 199
Gandhi, Mohandas K. (Mahatma), 21, 24–25, 33, 74, 159, 201, 233, 235, 258, 296, 424, 427, 430
　appeal to women to come out into the public sphere, 98
　ashram at Wardha, 155
　assassination of, 305
　Dandi march, 166
　end to the non-cooperation movement, 37
　fast against untouchability, 61
　meeting with
　　Ambedkar, 61
　　Jawaharlal Nehru, 128

'open rebellion' against British rule, 155
opposition against
    discrimination based on caste, 62
    granting separate electorates to various communities, 62
    perception of the threat posed by Hitler, 125
prison sentence at Yerawada in Pune, 39
on problem of untouchability, 36
release from prison, 201
resignation from the leadership of the Congress, 146
return to India from South Africa, xi
salt march, 45
salt satyagraha, 144
satyagraha campaign, 145
*satyagraha* (Truth Force), concept of, 25, 133
visit to England, 106
Gandhi, Rajiv, 282, 371
    controversy over a Swedish arms deal, 430
    marriage with Sonia Maino, 419
Gandhi, Sanjay, 282
Gangadhar, Pandit, 2
Gaon Hukumat Bill, 284
Gardner, Ava, 324
gender dynamics, in India, 111
General Assembly Political Committee, 347
General (Steering) Committee, 262
George V, King, 17, 80, 365
Germany, 104, 107, 125
Getts, Clark, 202, 220, 281
Ghaffar Khan, Khan Abdul, 44

Ghetto Act (South Africa), 257, 401
Gibson, Violet, 42
global hierarchy of powers, 285
*Globe and Mail*, 354
Goa, Portuguese occupation of, 368
Godse, Nathuram, 305
Gokhale, Gopal Krishna, 14, 21
Golden Gate Bridge, 238
Goshal, Prafulla Kumar, 237
Government of India, 188, 207, 376
    call for withdrawal of Soviet troops from Hungary, 382
    commitment to democracy, 279
    delegation to China, 343
    foreign exchange shortage, 386
    friendship with France, 414
    Hindu Interim Government, 280
    idea of sending representatives to Moscow, 278
    Ministry of External Affairs (MEA), 235, 303, 308, 319, 331, 352, 365–366, 388
    opening of diplomatic relations with other countries, 284
    opposition on West's actions over the Suez Canal, 381
    policy related to
        Korean crisis, 342
        nonalignment and nonviolence, 324
    Public Relations Department, 319
    rejection of US arbitration on Kashmir issue, 328
    relations with Pakistan, 400, 412
    skirmishes with China on the Ladakh border, 389
    stand against the Axis, 242
    tension with United Kingdom, 367
    turbulence in relation with USA, 336

wheat-for-tea deal with Soviet Union, 309
working with the UK to help resolve the Korean conflict, 343
Government of India Act (1935), 76, 80, 84, 111
Governor-General of India, 376
governors, British-appointed, 83
Graham, Martha, 286
Great Britain, *see* United Kingdom (UK)
Great Powers, 218, 236, 248, 264, 266, 296, 413–414
Grew, Joseph, 222
Gromyko, Andrei, 404
Gross, Ben, 232
*Guardian*, 431
Guerrero, Leon, 382
Gunther, Frances, 178, 202
Guthrie, Anne, 395
Gutterson, Mildred, 249

Haig, Harry, 85
Halifax, Lord, 203, 208, 244
Hallett, Maurice, 174, 203
Hammarskjöld, Dag, 350, 358, 374, 394
Hammerstein, Oscar, 325
Hardwar, 94, 100, 105
*Harijan*, 124–125
Harrison, Agatha, 106, 115, 130
Hartford Seminary, 191
Hawes, Elizabeth, 233
*Headliners* (Canadian radio programme), 300
Hekmat, Reza, 287
Henderson, Loy, 327
Henry, Patrick, 122
*Herald Tribune*, 190, 210
Hercules aircraft carrier, 392
herd immunity, 100

Hermitage Museum, 311
Hindu Interim Government, 280
Hindu law, 197
  of succession, 144
Hindu Mahasabha, 206
Hindu-Muslim unity, 24, 121
*Hindustan Times*, 117
  Bengal Relief Fund, 190
*Hindu, The*, 110, 117
His Majesty's Government, 118
Hiss, Alger, 242
historic Black colleges and universities (HBCUs), 390
Hitler, Adolf, 70, 104, 110, 117, 124
  Gandhi's perception of the threat posed by, 125
Ho Chi Minh, 299
Home, Lord, 382
Home Rule League, 20, 23
Homestead Hotel (millionaire's holiday house), 214
Honorary Freedom of the City of London, 379
Hooper, Lillian (Toopie), 10, 12
Hoover, Herbert, 300
Hoover, J. Edgar, 358
Hope, Bob, 321
Hopkins, Mary, 240
Horniman, Benjamin Guy (B.G.), 22–23
Horton, Mildred McAfee, 300
Hossain, Syud, 22–23, 207, 214, 228, 239, 243, 245, 314
  appointment as ambassador to Egypt, 301
  death of, 315
  National Committee of India's Freedom, 214
Hotel Commodore, 221
Hotel Gotham, 210–211, 268

House Un-American Activities
    Committee, 332
Housman, Laurence, 168
Howard University, 322
How-Martyn, Edith, 73–74
*Hsin Hua Jih Pao*, 133
Huai River development project, 345
human dignity
    principle of, xvi
    violation of, 264
Hume, Allan Octavian, 7, 15
Hurst, Arthur, 107
Husain, Zakir, 394
Hussain, Mohammed, 14
Hutchins, Robert, 338
Hutheesing, Gunottam 'Raja', 64
Hutheesing, Krishna, 369
Hyderabad, 313
hydrogen weapons, development of, 374

Ibrahim, Hafiz Muhammad, 103
Ikramullah, Begum, 336
Imam of the Jama Masjid (Friday
    Mosque), 426
Independence of India, 288–289, 309
*Independent*, 23
India House, 365, 367, 386, 388, 391
India League of America, 108, 207, 213,
    221, 225, 268, 329
    alignment with the Indian National
        Congress, 109
Indian Civil Service, 14
Indian Council on World Affairs, 193,
    207, 282
Indian Czech Association, 104
Indian independence, American and
    Chinese support for, 148
Indian Medical Association, 189
Indian mission, in London, 365

Indian National Army, 242
Indian National Congress, 7, 20, 29,
    40, 242
    alliance with Muslim League, 20
    Bombay Resolution, 146
    development of, 14
    electoral victory, 83
    founding members of, 22
    Gandhi resignation from the
        leadership of, 146
    High Command, 117
    India League alignment with, 109
    'individual satyagraha' plan, 127
    Karachi Session of, 111
    Lucknow Pact, 20
    Motilal involvement in, 15
    on partition of the subcontinent,
        284
    political setback in 1967 elections,
        418
    split of, 420
    Working Committee, 83–84, 122,
        124, 126–127, 145
        emergency session, 128
        meeting at Bombay, 156
        meeting at Sevagram, 155
Indian Nationalist Movement, 235
Indian Parliament, 365
India Office Library, 388
India-Pakistan War, 417
'Indira Hatao' (Get Rid of Indira)
    slogan, 420
'individual satyagraha' plan, 127
Indo-German relations, 396–397
Indo–Soviet relationship, 201–202
INS Brahmaputra, 392
INS Mysore, 392
Institute for Pacific Affairs in the United
    States, 207

Institute of Pacific Relations, 214
Intelligence Bureau, 185
Inter-Cultural Committee of the United
  Nations Council of Philadelphia,
  248
International Alliance of Women for
  Suffrage and Equal Citizenship, 75
International Atomic Energy Agency, 359
International Court of Justice, 270, 350
International Students' Centre in
  Cambridge, 227
International Year of Cooperation
  (1965), 404
inter-religious marriage, 228
Irish Rebellion, see Easter Rebellion
  (1916)
*Irish Times*, 378
Irwin, Lord, 43
  orders to sweep the Congress
    leadership, 44
Isabella Thoburn College, Lucknow, 129
Ispahani, Mirza Abul Hassan, 333
Israel/Palestine crisis, 322
Italy, invasion of Ethiopia, 70

Jallianwala Bagh (Amritsar) massacre,
  28, 44
Jana Sangh, 426
Janata (People's) front, 425
Janata Government, 429
Jawahar Week, 47–48
Jefferson, Thomas, 325
Jenkins, J.D., 247
Jinarajadasa, Dorothy, 21, 72
Jinnah, Muhammad Ali, 20, 120, 254,
  277, 288
Johnson, Louis, 153, 174
Johnson, Osa, 202, 281
Jones, George, 253

*Journey to Africa*, 250
Junagadh, 313

Kahlo, Frida, 288
Kamala Nehru Memorial Hospital, 136,
  158, 360
Karachi, 252
Karve, R.D., 73
Kashmiri Saraswat Brahmins
  community, 5
Kasturba Gandhi Memorial Fund, 199
Kathrada, Ahmed, 402
Katilal, Chuni Lal, 112
Kaul, Kamala, 19
Kaur, Rajkumari Amrit, 72, 134
Kennedy, Jackie, 395
Kennedy, John F., xii, 397, 404
  assassination of, 405
  Cuban Missile Crisis, 404
  Nehru tribute to, 405
Kenyon, Dorothy, 333
Khan, K.A., 240
Khan, Khan Abdul Gaffar, 157, 278
Khan, Liaquat Ali, 314, 333
Khan, Syed Ahmed, 6
Kher, A.G., 89–90
Kher, B.G., 366
Khrushchev, Nikita, 368
Kidd, Ronald, 109
Kidwai, Rafi Ahmed, 103
kitchen diplomacy, 269
Kollontai, Alexandra, 55, 294, 309, 317
Korean War (1950), 341–343, 346–349
  38th Parallel, 357
  Custodian Force, 357
  Korea plan for resolution of, 346
  peace settlement for, 351
  transfer of prisoners of war, 357
Koussevitzky, Serge, 227, 288

Kripalani, Acharya, 124
Krishnamachari, V.T., 239
Kudai Kitmatgar, 126
Kumari, Sarup, 6
Kumbh Mela, 94, 100
Kunzru, Pandit Hridya Nath, 192, 208

*Ladies Home Journal, The*, 369
La Guardia, Fiorella, 217, 219
Lankester, Grace, 134, 275
Laski, Harold, 108
Lattimore, Owen, 230, 234, 333
Laugier, Henri, xvi
*Leader, The*, 110
League Against Imperialism, 41
League of Nations, 220, 239, 264
Lemkin, Raphael, 266–267
Leningrad (St Petersburg), 311
Lesny, Vincenc, 104
Liberal Party, 111
liberation of women, 22
Lie, Trygve, 257, 349–350
*Life* magazine, 224
Limited Nuclear Test Ban Treaty, 404
Lincoln, Abraham, 325
Lindsay, Malvina, 320–321
Linlithgow, Viceroy, 148–149, 153, 188
List House, 290–291, 302
Lloyd, Selwyn, 346–347, 361, 368, 383–384
Local Self-Government Department, 88
Lodge, Henry Cabot, Jr, 352, 357
Lokanathan, P.S., 215
Lok Sabha, 409
    Congress Parliamentary Party for, 411
London School of Economics (LSE), 108, 191
Los Angeles Chamber of Commerce, 324

*Los Angeles Times*, 354
Louis XV, King, 7
Luce-Celler Act (USA), 235
Luce, Clare Booth, 224, 233, 235, 300
Lucknow Central Jail, 52
Lucknow City Congress, 279
Lucknow Military Hospital, 184
Lucknow Pact, 20
Lucknow University, 140
Lubke, President, 396
Luthuli, Arthur, 403
Lyon, Charles, 244
Lyric Theater, 234

MacArthur, Douglas, 341
Macaulay, Thomas Babington, 7
MacDonald, Ramsay, 61–62, 71
    Communal Award of 1932, 120
Machiavelli, Niccolo, 137
MacMahon Line, 389
Macmillan, Harold, 368, 407
Madame Pandit, *see* Pandit, Vijaya Lakshmi (Nan)
Madras Law College (now Dr Ambedkar Government Law College), 108
Malaviya, Pandit Madan Mohan, 15
Malaviya, Pandit Mahavir Prasad, 11
Malik, Charles, 352
Malik, Yakov, 382
*Manchester Guardian, The*, 85, 105, 110, 116, 130, 301
Mandela, Nelson, 402
Manhattan Project, 336
Mao Tse-tung, 133, 341
Marcos, Ferdinand, 419
Margaret Sanger Institute, 419
marginalized caste communities, xii
Marshall, George, 297

INDEX 539

Marshall Plan, 306, 326
Marshall, Thurgood, 213
*Maryada* (magazine), 21
Masaryk Homes for Social Workers and Labourers, 105
Masaryk, Jan, 105
mass imprisonments, 44
Mathai, M.O., 364, 366
Maugham, Somerset, 211
Maurya, Chandragupta, 137
May Day, 312
McAfee, Mildred, 177, 227
McCarthy, Joseph, 332–333
McIntosh, Agnes, 261
McKinley, William, 5
McNeil, Hector, 297
Mehta, Ashok, 315
Mehta, Hansa, 278
Mehta, Pherozeshah, 22–23
Meir, Golda, 330
Menon, K.P.S., 243, 259, 278, 285
Menon, V.K. Krishna, xiii, 108, 113, 130, 225, 278, 319, 346, 355, 361, 364, 365, 367, 379, 383, 409, 411
    Americans disliking of, 348
    anti-Westernism of, 413
    campaign against Nan, 383
    debacle in war with China, 396
    defence of Russian actions on Hungary, 381
    disdain for Nan, 364
    friendship with M.O. Mathai, 364
    as India's defence minister, 384, 396
    Jawaharlal views on, 384
    Korea plan, 346
    relation with Nan, 383–384
    remarks critical of American behaviour, 348
    role as negotiator in Suez crisis, 380
    sacked as India's defence minister, 397
Mesta, Perle, 321–322, 373
Metropol, The, 287–288
Midnapore, 183, 191
military equipment, acquisition of, 392
milk fund, 79
*Mirror*, 324
Missionaries of Charity, 398
Mitter, B.L., 33
mobile hospitals, 115
Moderates, 16
*Modern Review*, 183
Molotov, Vyacheslav, 261, 309, 316
Montagu-Chelmsford Reforms of 1919, 28, 76
    second wave of, 39
Morarjee, Shantikumar, 201
Morley-Minto Reforms of 1909, 120
Moscow Radio Committee, 282
Moscow, Treaty of, 404
Moskowitz, Henry, 213
Moti Sabha (the Community of Moti), 5
Mountbatten, Louis, 283, 372, 379, 418, 429
    'divide and rule' tactics, 290
Mudaliar, Ramasawami, 239
*Mudra Rakshasa*, 137
Mukherjee, Shyama Prasad, 206
Munich Pact, 107, 109, 116, 323
Muslim League, 20, 121, 153, 254–256, 306
    Direct Action Day, 255
    opposition to Gaon Hukumat Bill, 284
Mussolini, Benito, 41
Mynshul, Geffray, 165

Naguib, Mohamed, General, 348
Nagy, Imre, 380, 382
Naidu, Leelamani, 283
Naidu, Padmaja, 24, 54, 185, 201, 281
Naidu, Sarojini, 14, 16, 24, 40, 72, 92, 119, 122, 124, 135, 152, 236, 251, 278, 315
Naini Central Prison, 43, 130, 162
Nan, see Pandit, Vijaya Lakshmi (Nan)
Naoroji, Dadabhai, 111
Narayanan, Prabhavati, 58
Narayan, Jayaprakash (JP), 84, 421
Narendranath, Dewan Bahadur, 27
Nasser, Gamal Abdel, 348–349, 378
National Association for the Advancement of Colored People (NAACP), xvi, 212–213, 249, 270, 322
National Association of Colored Graduate Nurses in the United States, 300
National Committee for India's Freedom, 214, 222, 232, 246
National Council for Negro Women (NCNW), 251, 276
National Council of Civil Liberties, 109
National Council of Negro Women, 249, 301
National Council of Women in India, 200
national elections, 340
*National Herald*, 117, 141, 426
National Planning Committee, 116, 256
National Press Club, 229
National Publisher's Association, 280
*Navroz* (the Kashmiri New Year), 16–17
Nawab of Bengal, 11
Nayantara (daughter of Vijaya Lakshmi Pandit), 98, 122–123, 126, 129, 158, 176, 179, 182, 194, 196–197, 199, 204, 209, 217, 261, 265, 273, 286, 300, 369, 422
    as guests of Eslanda and Paul Robeson, 191
    as lady of Anand Bhawan, 171
    *Prison and Chocolate Cake* (1954), 360
    relationship with Nicolas Wyrouboff, 370
    sailing to Australia, 181–183
    wedding of, 315
Nazi Germany, 403
Nazis, 125
    doctrine of racialism, 263
    propaganda, 104
Nehru, Bansidhar, 4–5
Nehru family
    family reunion, 2
    migration to Delhi from Kashmir, 2
    profession of law practice, 3
    return to India, 12
Nehru, Indira Priyadarshini, see Gandhi, Indira
Nehru, Jawaharlal, xiv, 69, 74, 84, 102, 113, 127, 145, 314
    at Alipore Jail, in Calcutta, 65
    arrest of, 133
    arrival in the United States, 329
    as barrister in the Allahabad High Court, 19
    birth of, 3
    death of, 406
    disappointment at British intransigence, 174
    early life of, 4
    foreign policy, xiv
    as great friend of China, 133
    inauguration of Nan's committee in Bombay, 119

on Italy's invasion of Ethiopia, 70
meeting with Mahatma Gandhi, 128
pen incident, 4
preparation for Harrow's test, 9
as president of Congress, 43
reimprisonment of, 47
release from prison, 68, 247
return to India, 18
revision of Quit India Resolution, 156
schooling of, 10
speeches at the US Congress, 329
speech on India's 'tryst with destiny', 289
tribute to JFK on All India Radio, 405
visit to China, 133
wedding with Kamala Kaul, 19
Nehru, Kamala, 40, 48–49, 66, 68
death of, 75
illness of, 151
Nehru, Motilal, 1–2
Anand Bhawan (Abode of Joy), 6
bungalow at Civil Lines, 3
character of, 4
death of, 49
family reunion, 2
*Independent*, 23
involvement in Indian National Congress, 15
marriage with Swarup Rani, 2
meeting with Maharaja Sayaji Rao of Baroda, 17–18
orientation towards Western culture, 13
pen incident, 4
political activism, 16
profession of law practice, 3
Saville Row suits, 36
trip to Germany, 8–9

Nehru, Nandlal, 2
Nehru, Rameshwari, 21, 134–135, 142
Nehru, Sarup, *see* Pandit, Vijaya Lakshmi (Nan)
Nehru, Shridhar, 4
Nehru, Uma, 21, 48, 72
neutral nations, idea for, 374
New Book Company, 137
New Deal Republican, 219
New Lodge Clinic, 107
new order, creation of, 116
*Newsweek*, 351, 356
*New York Amsterdam News*, 274
New York City, xvi, 209–210, 219, 229, 260–261, 429
*New Yorker* magazine, 281
*New York Herald Tribune*, 233, 239, 241, 296, 318
New York press, 190
*New York Times*, 94, 175, 192, 253, 260, 264, 266, 270, 296, 300, 318, 334, 400, 423, 425, 429
obituary on Madame Pandit, 431
New York University (NYU), 419
Niagara Movement, 213
Nicholls, G. Heaton, 268
Nicholls, Heaton, 273
Nixon, Richard, 352, 354
Nkrumah, Kwame, 400
Nobel Peace Prize, 143, 348, 352
Noel-Baker, Philip, 265
Noguchi, Isamu, 286, 288, 370
non-cooperation movement, 28, 31, 36–37
non-violence, power of, 126
Noon, Firoz Khan, 238, 240
Norman, Dorothy, 335
Norway, 403
Novikov, K.V., 309

nuclear tests, ban on, 404
nuclear war, 373
Nuremberg Trials, 266
Nur Jahan (Mughal Empress), 1

Oberai, G.R., 184, 194
*Observer*, 356
One World Association, 275
Oppenheimer, Robert, 336–337
Organization for World Brotherhood, 375
Oriental Institute, Prague, 104
Ornsholt, 'Tante' Anna, 171, 186
Osborne, Estelle Massey, 330
Ottoman Empire, breakup of, 28
Ovington, Mary White, 213
Oxford University, 407
Oxford University Press, 137

*Pacific Affairs*, 230
Pacific Charter, 217, *see also* Atlantic Charter
Packness, Kjeld, 370
Pahlavi, Princess, 288
Pakistan, 255, 284, 313, 368
    dispute with India over Kashmir, 327, 412
    efforts to mobilize the Kashmiris, 412
    relation with India, 400
    views on India's defences at the Rann of Kutch, 412
Palestine
    Ad Hoc Committee on, 299
    United Nations Special Committee on Palestine (UNSCOP), 299
Panchsheel Agreement (Five Principles of Peaceful Coexistence), 388
Pandit, Ranjit Sitaram, 27–30, 37, 42, 64, 112, 137, 140
    arrest of, 46, 167
    as 'Class A' prisoner, 46
    death of, 195
    illness of, 186, 195
    participation in Allahabad District Congress Committee, 83
    release from prison, 59, 190
    Ritu-Samhar estate, 67
    securing of parole for treatment, 187
    translation of
        *Mudra Rakshasa*, 137
        *Rajatarangini*, 57, 67, 105
        *Ritusamhara*, 190
    wedding with Vijaya Lakshmi, 30–32
Pandit, Shankar Pandurang, 30
Pandit, Vijaya Lakshmi (Nan), 1, 11–12, 14, 19, 22, 199
    affiliation with Bethune's organization, 250
    aiming to resolve the Korean conflict, 346–349
    arrest of, 130, 163–164
    arrival in United States, 213, 229, 236, 320
    association with
        A.G. Kher, 89
        Indira Gandhi, 428–429
        Mahatma Gandhi, xi
    'Atoms for Peace' speech, 359
    autobiography of, 203
    award of an honorary doctorate of law, 332
    bills regarding
        Gaon Hukumat Bill, 284
        provincialization of hospitals, 284
    biography of, 395
    birth of, xi
    campaign for principles, 425
    chairing of Round Table on security issues, 216

as Chairman-Rapporteur of the Commission's Working Group, 429
Chinese espionage operation against, 388
civil disobedience, 183
'conciliatory discussions' with South Africa, 297
contributions to the post-war order, xvi
credibility and popularity in USA, 337
death of, 431
debate with Robert Boothby, 230–231
dental problem, 56
election to the new Constituent Assembly, 256
endorsement of British self-governance policies, 111
fight over the Security Council with the Soviets, 298
filing of papers in Cawnpore for the coming election, 253
as first-ever elected class of parliamentarians, 341
as 'The First Lady of India, 235
as first woman cabinet minister in India, xii, 85
gala automobile show, 41
good governance, 122
as high commissioner to the United Kingdom, 361, 363
on Hindu-Muslim problem, 121
hosting of the Queen Elizabeth in India, 391
idea of becoming President of India, 429
idea of her becoming vice president, 394
illness of, 184

imprisonment of, 51
as India's ambassador to
  Soviet Union, 286
  USA, 307, 308, 318
as India's 'goddess of victory', 354
indignities suffered by, 377
influence of national affairs on personal life of, 63
interview of Mrs Roosevelt on All India Radio, 341
introduction to the American public, 221
invitation to
  address the Agra Constituency Women's Conference at Allahabad, 114
  Boston Symphony Orchestra evening's concert, 227
  White House, 213
Irish mission, 377–378
kitchen diplomacy, 269
launching of a mobile clinic in Bombay, 398
leadership of India's delegation to the United Nations, 312, 346, 349, 400
leading of a women's delegation to China, 133
life in prison, 55–56, 170
as Life Peer of the United Kingdom, 393
major events for Sanger, 75
mediation in Suez crisis, 379–380
meeting with
  Chancellor Adenauer, 396
  Chiangs, 149
  Chou En-lai, 343
  Churchill, 361–362
  Jan Masaryk, 105

Joseph Cals, 415
Labour leaders, 382
Mother Teresa, 398
President Truman, 261
Reza Hekmat, 287
as minister for public health, 100
ministerial portfolios in public health and local self-government, 284
nervous breakdown, 101
New Delhi's plan for resolution of Korean crisis, 347
observations about British propaganda and American misunderstandings of India, 254
observations about the consequences of the United Nations Conferences, 248
One World Awards, 348
on opportunities for women in public service, 111
overseeing of Kamala's care and treatment, 66
participation in Allahabad District Congress Committee, 83
pledge of swaraj, 50
political rivalry with Indira Gandhi, 425–426
'powers of persuasion' on communities, 61
presentation of credentials to the Soviet government, 291
as president of
AIWC, xii, 133
UN General Assembly, xvii, 352–353
*Princes and Princesses*, 97–98
'prisoner of indecision' quote, 417
process of 'falling from grace', 364
Queen of Greece invitation to, 383
rapport with Chou, 344
as real bridge between the east and west, 319
relations with
Betty, 369–370
Indira Gandhi, 371, 408, 417–418
Krishna Menon, 383–384
Madame Chiang, 133
release from prison, 57, 182
on grounds of health, 184
relief work during Bengal famine, 189–190
representation of India in election to UN Security Council, 297–298
resignation from her position as governor, 406
resolution in the United Provinces Assembly, 279
return to
Allahabad, 26, 189
India from US tour, 252
US, 400
reunion with Ranjit, 191
role in Turkey's election to a two-year term on the Security Council, 357
sanction to visit a girls' school in Moscow, 310
*Scope of Happiness, The* (1979), 429
selection for a Doctor of Laws, 372
sense of 'listlessness and general fatigue', 386
signing of Paris Protocol, 314
on Simian invasion of Bareilly, 115
smear campaign against, 333
*So I Became a Minister*, 122

solitary confinement, 165
Spanish mission, 387
speech at Columbia University, 325
speech on 'Forging a World Bill of Human Rights', 251
stance on American racism, 331
staying with Mahatma Gandhi, 25–26
as successor to UN Secretary-General Trygve Lie, 349
supervision of the children, 131
as supporter of the nationalist cause, 94
swearing-in ceremony, 85
takedown of issue of patriarchy, 91
tribute to JFK on All India Radio, 405
uneasiness about her family, 186
untouchability work in Allahabad, 60
victorious entry into politics, 408
views on
    American attitudes towards India, 331
    Atlantic Charter, 216
    Chinese takeover of Tibet, 388
    rights of minorities in all sovereign states, 313
visit to
    Allahabad, 38
    Bengal, 189, 191
    Bombay, 199
    Calcutta, 33
    Chicago, 248
    Europe, 102
    Hardwar, 94
    Ireland, 377–378
    Japan, 363
    Kathiawad, 61
    Leningrad (St Petersburg), 311
    London, 396
    Lucknow, 20
    Mussoorie, 184
    New York, xvi, 209–210, 229, 429
    Nigeria, 400
    Pittsburgh, 234
    Sevagram, 140
    Washington D.C., 229, 251, 300, 308
    West Germany, 396
war of words with Mr. Dulles, 280
wedding with
    Ranjit Pandit, 30–32
    Syud Hossain, 24–25
as Woman of the Year, 359
on Women's rights, 92
work on
    acquisition of military equipment, 392
    breaking the deadlock between Indians and the British, 215
    improving Indo-British ties, 392
    resolving Cuban Missile Crisis, 404
    resolving the Palestine issue, 299
    return of various Buddhist relics from Britain, 375–377
Pannikar, K.M., 343
Pan-Pacific Women's Association Conference, 72
Pant, Pandit Govind Ballabh, 84, 87, 152, 250, 255, 278, 379
*Parampara*, 409
Paris Protocol for international drug control (1948), 314
Parliamentary Group for World Government, 374
partition of India, 284, 378

Patel, Sardar Vallabhbhai, 44, 48, 124, 156, 278
Pearl Harbor, Japanese attack on (1942), 145
Pearson, Lester, 346, 349–350, 352, 354
Pegging Act (South Africa), 253
people of colour, racial justice for, 213
Pertold, Otakar, 104
Pethick-Lawrence, Emmeline, 109, 130, 249
    views on Nan, 109
Pethick-Lawrence, Frederick, 249, 254
*Philadelphia Inquirer*, 240
Phillips, William, 228
Pilditch, D., 203
Pillai, N.R., 366
*Pioneer*, 110
*Pittsburgh Courier*, 217, 234
plague outbreak, 255
planned economy
    role of women in, 116
    Subcommittee on the Status of Women in a Planned Economy, 119
Planning Committee, 119
Plassey, Battle of (1757), 7
political activism, 16
political prisoners, 51–52, 163
    in India, 231
Poona Pact, 62
Porter, Leslie, 17
power politics, 241
Prasad, Rajendra, 152, 353
Pratt, Frances, 211
price politics, 194
princely states, of India, 313
*Princes and Princesses*, 97–98
'prisoner of indecision', 417
prisoners of war, 346, 357

Provisional World Council of Dominated Nations, 275
Public Health Department, 88
public school system, 168
Puckle, Frederick, 230, 237, 251
Purana Qila (Old Fort), 282
Purdah Club, 75
*purdah* system, 115
*Purna Swaraj*, 43

Qissa Khwani Bazaar (Storyteller's Market), 44
Qissa Khwani massacre, 45
Quadir, Abdul, Lady, 72
'Quit India' movement, 156, 306

Ra'ana, Begum, 333–334
racial discrimination, practices of, 262
racial equality, 257
racial injustice, 275
racial justice, 191
    for people of colour, 213
Radhakrishnan, Sarvepalli, 394
Rai, Lala Lajpat, 43, 96
*Rajatarangini* (River/Waves of Kings), 47
Rajkot, 61
Raju, V.B., 426
Rajwade, Rani Lakshmibai, 119, 135
Ralph Bunche Day, 323
Ramakrishna Mission, 195
*Ramcharitmanas* (Tulsidas), 11
Ram, Jagjivan, 424–425
Ranade, Mahadev, 15
Rangoon, 147
Rani of Jhansi, 13–14
Rani of Rajpipla, 64
Rani, Swarup, 1–3, 6, 9–10, 17, 24, 29, 31, 34, 64, 93–94, 152
Rao, B. Shiva, 123–124, 208, 237, 283

Rau, B.N., 350
*Reader's Digest*, 230
Rebellion of 1857, 2, 7, 11
    Rani of Jhansi, 13–14
Reddy, B. Gopala, 411
Red Menace, 332
Rhee, Syngman, 357
Rich, Helen, 240
Rita (daughter of Vijaya Lakshmi Pandit), 126, 129, 137, 161, 167, 173, 199, 261, 265, 281, 300, 331, 353, 369
ritual bathing, 100
*Ritusamhara* (Kalidasa's Sanskrit poem), 190
Robeson, Essie, 250
Robeson, Paul, 268
Rodgers, Mortimer, 325
Roosevelt, Eleanor, 206, 212, 222, 237, 261, 269–270, 275, 296–297, 300, 323, 332, 341, 344, 389, 395
    'Woman of the Year' award, 321, 359
Roosevelt, Franklin, 148, 174, 252
    Four Freedoms, 145
Round Table Conference, 61, 106, 120
Row, Kshamabai, 59
Rowlatt Bills, 28
Royal Academy, London, 30
Runciman, Lord, xii, 104
Runciman Mission, 104
rural women and children, upliftment of, 199
Rusk, Dean, 404
Russell, Bertrand, 350, 373
Russell Declaration (1955), 374
Russell-Einstein manifesto, 374
Russian Revolution, 287

Sahgal, Gautam, 304, 370
    wedding with Nayantara, 315

salt satyagraha, 144
Sanatana Pratininidhi Sabha of Punjab, 96
Sanchi stupa, 375
San Francisco, 229, 238, 245
    Conference, 234, 239
    Women of Achievement, 245
Sanger, Margaret, 250, 346
    AIWC meeting in Trivandrum, 75
    India tour, 74
    stay at Anand Bhawan as Nan's guest, 74–75
    tour campaigning for birth control in India, 73
Sansom, George Bailey, 237
Sapru, P.N., 197, 259
Sapru, Tej Bahadur, 152, 192, 197, 201
*satyagraha* (Truth Force), 25
Save the Children Federation, 223
Sayaji Rao of Baroda, Maharaja, 17–18
Schalk, Gertrude 'Toki', 234
Schweitzer, Albert, 348
*Scope of Happiness, The* (1979), 429
*Scotsman*, 85, 275
Seahawk aircraft, 392
self-determination, principle of, 110
self-governance, 8
self-government, 245
self-sacrifice, act of, 39
separate electorates
    Communal Award of, 62, 120
    for Muslim communities, 76
Sevagram, 128, 140
*sevikas* (women service volunteers), 49
Shah, Shivlal Panachand, 112
Shankar, Uday, 138
Shastri, Lal Bahadur, 138, 158, 407, 410, 412, 417
Shawcross, Hartley, 274
Sheehan, Vincent, 211

Shishakly, Adib, 349
Shvernik, Nikolai, 291
Siam (Thailand), 295
Siddiqui, A.R., 215
Simon Commission, 44
Sinclair, Upton, 169
Singh, Anup, 236, 239, 243
Singh, Bhagat, 46
Singh, J.J., 207, 213, 236, 329, 404
Sino–India War (1962), 396, 414
    German support to India during, 396–397
    US support to India during, 397
Sisulu, Walter, 402
slave nation, 135
Smith, Margaret Chase, 330
Smith, Walter Bedell, 291
Smuts, Jan, xvi, 253, 258, 260, 262, 269, 271
Snyder, John, 326
social and economic upliftment, 237
social discrimination, 36
social reform, 15
social responsibility, sense of, 390
social upliftment, xii
societal restrictions, 13
soft power cultural diplomacy, 309
*So I Became a Minister* (Vijaya Lakshmi Pandit), 122
South Africa, 259–260, 262–264, 268, 271, 313
    Asiatic Land Tenure and Indian Representation Bill, 257
    campaign of satyagraha, 257
    economic boycott of, 403
    Gandhi's return to India, xi
    Ghetto Act, 257, 401
    Indians living in, 259, 272
    Nan's conciliatory discussions with South Africa, 297
    Pegging Act, 253
    policy of apartheid, 346
    racial equality in, 401
*South China Morning Post*, 85
Soviet Embassy, in Delhi, 310
Soviet Union, 263, 278, 282, 290, 296, 298
    Berlin blockade, 310, 320
    Cuban Missile Crisis, 404
    Government of, 309
    India's embassy in, 291
    influence on interim Hindu government in India, 280
    invasion of Hungary, 380
    joining of the Alliance against Nazism, 306
    Metropol, The, 287–288
    presentation of Nan's credentials in, 291
    proposal to name Nan as secretary-general of UN, 350
    relation with
        India, 309–310
        the West, 311
    resentment against Marshall Plan, 306
    Russian translation of the Indian epic, the Ramayana, 311
    Vijaya Lakshmi Pandit as India's first ambassador to, 286
    wheat-for-tea deal with India, 309
    Zhdanov Doctrine, 306
Spanish Civil War, 387
Spanish Inquisition, 333
*Spectator, The*, 247
Srirangapatnam (Seringapatam), Battle of, 376
Srivastava, J.P., 82

S.S. Normandie (ship), 74
Stalin, Joseph, 309–310, 349
state sovereignty, principle of, xvi
Stettinius, Edward, 237–238, 246
Stowe, Leland, 233
Stratemeyer, George, 208
*Stri Darpan* (The Women's Mirror) magazine, 21
Sudeten Crisis, xii, 105
Sudeten German Party (SdP), 104
Sudetenland, 103
Suez Canal Company, 378
Suez Canal, control of, 379–380
Sultan, Tipu (Tiger of Mysore), 376
Sun-Yat Sen, 41
Su Tung-p'o, 129
Swadeshi Movement, 15
*Swan Lake* (Russian ballet production), 304
*swaraj*, 15
Swaraj Bhawan, 58–59, 136, *see also* Anand Bhawan (Abode of Joy)
Swaraj party, 39
swearing-in ceremony, 85
Sykes-Picot agreement, 28

Tagore, Rabindranath, 15, 73–74
    'Jana Gana Mana' national anthem, 72, 289
    Shantiniketan University, 68
Tandon, Purshottamdas, 100, 292
Tashkent Agreement, 417
Tchaikovsky Theater, 304
Teen Murti (Nehru's formal residence in Delhi), 315
Teresa, Mother, 398
Teresa, Sister, 189
Thackersey, Vithaldas, Lady, 201
Thant, U., 412

Theosophical Society, 21
Third International Conference on Planned Parenthood, 345–346
Thompson, Dorothy, 211
Thorndike, Dame Sybil, 130
Tibet, Chinese repression in, 387–388
Tilak, Bal Gangadhar, 15, 20, 23
*Time* magazine, 224, 318, 321
*Times of India*, 82, 85, 250, 335–356, 410
    Nan's 'fresh and spontaneous' writing, 122
Tipu Sultan, defeat of, 7
Tolischus, Otto, 266
Tolstoy, Leo, 316
Trafalgar, Battle of, 80
Trans World Airways (TWA), 259
*Tribune*, 233
Triestino, Lloyd, 40, 181
*Trud*, 290
Truman, Bess (US First Lady), 301
Truman, Harry, 251–252, 260–261, 320, 329, 337
Trumbull, Robert, 318
trusteeship, 245
Trusteeship Department, 322
Tudor, Elsa, 226
Tudor, Frederic, 226
Tully, Mark, 274
Tydings Committee, 332–333
Tydings, Millard, 332

Unani and Ayurvedic systems, 115
Undén, Östen, 304
UNICEF, 357
United Kingdom (UK)
    anti-India propaganda, 278–279
    association with Ireland, 378
    German threat to, 125

House of Commons, 110, 229, 277, 374, 392
    Conservative Commonwealth Group in, 368
    Ministry of Health, 105
    per capita spending on healthcare in the Indian subcontinent, 231
    Portuguese President visit to, 368
    tension with India, 367
    Tory MPs, 367
United Nations (UN), 156, 202, 217, 224, 229, 248, 259, 282, 322
    Charter of, 259, 264, 271
        Article 2(7) of, 262
        signing of, 404
    China's inclusion in, 390
    Conference in San Francisco, 233, 249
    FDR's role in the creation of, 429
    General Assembly, 260, 262, 267, 270, 278, 296, 302, 360, 401
        Nan as president of, 352–353
        Nan's UNGA candidacy, 352
        voting for the president of, 346
    Genocide Convention, 266
    'India session', 348
    Inter-Cultural Committee of the United Nations Council of Philadelphia, 248
    International Children's Emergency Fund, 357
    intervention in Korean War, 341
    membership of, 401
    Nan as first woman to address, 263
    Nuremberg Trials, 266
    objects and purposes of, 264
    proclamation on fundamental equality for all peoples, 217–218
    Security Council, 263, 296, 327, 385, 401
        Chinese membership in, 414
        members of, 297
        Nan representation of India in election to, 297–298
        Resolution 181, 401
        Resolution 182, 403
        Turkey's election to, 357
    Security Office, 358
    Sixth (Legal) Committee, 267
    Special Committee on Palestine (UNSCOP), 299
United Nations Relief and Rehabilitation Agency (UNRRA), 193
United Press, 318
*United Press of America*, 238
United Provinces, 17, 88, 94, 250
    Cawnpore (Kanpur) constituency, 250
    Gorakhpur district of, 37
    governor of, 84
    Legislative Assembly, 284
    legislature, 253
    protests against the Congress-led government, 121
    Provincial Congress, 83
    Vijaya Lakshmi tour of, 45
United States (US)
    capital investment and technical aid to India, 318
        related to 'food self-sufficiency', 319
    Central Intelligence Agency (CIA), 355
    Cuban Missile Crisis, 404
    Declaration of Independence, 221
    discrimination against women in, 321–322
    economic policies to assist India, 324–325

Federal Bureau of Investigations
  (FBI), 358
House of Representatives, 332
House Un-American Activities
  Committee, 332
Immigration Bill, 235, 252
India Emergency Assistance Act, 339
investigation of Red Menace, 332
Luce-Celler Act, 235
Manhattan Project, 336
Marshall Plan, 306
Nan's appointment to, 307, 308, 318
National Commission for UNESCO,
  389
National Conference of Christians
  and Jews, 375
offer of arbitration on Kashmir
  issue, 328
opposition to India's participation at
  the political conference, 353
role in the resolution of the Kashmir
  conflict, 328
turbulence in relation with India, 336
Tydings Committee, 332–333
universal equal rights, 400
universal international accountability
  for colonial and dependent people,
  principle of, 218
University of Southern California, 324
University Women's Union, 377
untouchability, issue of, 36
  Gandhi's fast against, 61
upliftment, Gandhian idea of, 60
upper classes, 83
USS Hermitage (Conte Biancamano), 181
U.S.S.R., *see* Soviet Union

Vajpayee, Atal Bihari, 426
Vanderbilt, Cornelius, 221

Vandercook, John W., 230
Van Doren, Irita, 233
Vedavathi, Yuvarani, 142
Versailles, Treaty of (1919), 28, 238
Viceroy's Council, 14, 80, 184
Victoria, Queen, 107
Vietnam
  American Friendship Association, 298
  colonial fight against, 299
  Committee for the Celebration of
    Vietnam Independence, 298
  Ho Chi Minh, 299
  struggle for independence, 299
village panchayats, 284
Visva Bharati University, Calcutta, 395
*Vogue* magazine, 199
'vote for victory' campaign, 397
Vyshinsky, Andrey, 269, 291, 298, 304,
  309, 314, 316–317, 357

Waldorf-Astoria Hotel, 269
Walsh, Richard, 178, 190, 198,
  202–203, 209, 227, 232
Walters, Barbara, 395
Wan, Prince, 352–353
Ward, Dame Irene, 392
Warren, Earl, 244
Washington Committee, *see* National
  Committee of India's Freedom
Washington D.C., 229, 251, 300, 308, 358
*Washington Post*, 250, 265, 318, 319, 330
Washington Press Club, 223
Wavell, Archibald, 153, 188, 192, 258
Wellesley, Arthur, 376
Wellesley College, 177
Wellesley, Marquess, 376
Welles, Sumner, 208
Western civilization, threat perception
  of, 271

Western imperialism, 28
Western missionaries, imprisonment of, 343
West Germany, 396
West Indies National Council, 275
White, E.B., 281
White, Walter, 213, 236
Wilhelm II, Kaiser, 8
Wilkinson, Ellen, 108
Willkie, Wendell, xvi, 236, 245, 348
Wilson, Harold, 415
Wilsonian idealism, 110
Winternitz, Moritz, 104
Women's Army Corps (WAC), 209
women's empowerment, 356
Women's Indian Association, 21, 72
Women's International Conference of Peace and Freedom (Luxembourg), 257
Women's International Exposition, 330
Women's International League for Peace and Freedom (WILPF), 143, 227
women's liberation, progress of, 345
women's movement, in India, 116
    and taboos preventing women from entering public life, 122
Women's National Democratic Club, 323
Women's National Press Club, 321
women's suffrage, 21
*Women, The* (Clare Booth Luce), 180
Women United for the United Nations, 363
Woodstock (American Methodist School), Mussoorie, 68, 82, 122, 178
World Bank
    India as founding member of, 326
    loan for improvement of India's railways, 328
    Marshall Plan, 326
World Community Night, 251
World Education Service Council, 269
World Friendship Dinner, 269
World Government News Awards, 281
'World Peace through United Action', 251
World's Women of Fame, 245
World Trade Association of Southern California, 324
World War I, 143
World War II, 146, 299, 342, 392
    Allied war requirements, 188–189
    American forces landing in Normandy, 229
    Burma, Japanese occupation of, 188
    food shortages in India due to, 188
    horrors unleashed by the Axis during, 272
    impact on just society and civil liberties, 148
    Pearl Harbor, Japanese attack on (1942), 145
    postwar peace settlement, 242
Wyrouboff, Nicolas, 370

Yale University, 237
Young Democrats Society, 427
*Young India* (newspaper), 25

Zafar, Bahadur Shah, 2
*zamindari* (princely) state, 142
*zamindars*, 4
Zhdanov Doctrine, 306
Zutshi, Ladli Prasad, 176, 197

GPSR Authorized Representative: Easy Access System Europe, Mustamäe tee 50, 10621 Tallinn, Estonia, gpsr.requests@easproject.com